From Indus to Independence

A Trek Through Indian History

From Indus to Independence
A Trek Through Indian History

Volume V

The Delhi Sultanate

Sanu Kainikara

Vij Books India Pvt Ltd

New Delhi (India)

Copyright © 2018, *Sanu Kainikara*

Dr Sanu Kainikara
416, The Ambassador Apartments
2 Grose Street
Deakin, ACT 2600, Australia
sanu.kainikara@gmail.com

First Published in 2018

ISBN : 978-93-86457-72-1 (Paperback)

ISBN : 978-93-86457-73-8 (ebook)

Designed and Setting by

Vij Books India Pvt Ltd

2/19, Ansari Road, Darya Ganj, New Delhi - 110002, India

(www.vijbooks.com)

All rights reserved.

No part of this book may be reproduced, stored in a retrieval system, transmitted or utilized in any form or by any means, electronic, mechanical, photocopying, recording or otherwise, without the prior permission of the copyright owner. Application for such permission should be addressed to the author.

For

'Betu'

Priya Kainikara-Sharma

A daughter is God's unmatched gift.
He made it so by creating beauty at its fairest.
You, my daughter, reside deepest in my heart as
– a day that smiles through its sunshine;
– a night of dew and calm.
You, my daughter, are my soul and breath.

OTHER BOOKS BY SANU KAINIKARA

National Security, Strategy and Air Power

Papers on Air Power

Pathways to Victory

Red Air: Politics in Russian Air Power

Australian Security in the Asian Century

A Fresh Look at Air Power Doctrine

Friends in High Places (Editor)

Seven Perennial Challenges to Air Forces

The Art of Air Power: Sun Tzu Revisited

At the Critical Juncture

Essays on Air Power

The Bolt from the Blue

In the Bear's Shadow

Political Analysis

The Asian Crucible

Political Musings: Turmoil in the Middle-East

Political Musings: Asia in the Spotlight

The Indian History Series: From Indus to Independence

Volume I: Prehistory to the Fall of the Mauryas

Volume II: The Classical Age

Volume III: The Disintegration of Empires

Volume IV: The Onslaught of Islam

Contents

Author's Preface		xi
Introduction to Volume V		xxi
Prologue		xxxvii

SLAVE DYNASTY

Chapter 1	The Slave Dynasty: The Beginning	3
Chapter 2	Shams Ud-Din Iltutmish	15
Chapter 3	The Story of The Qutb Minar	27
Chapter 4	A Queen Reigns	37
Chapter 5	From Confusion to Consolidation	47
Chapter 6	Ghiyas Ud-Din Balban – The Sultan	57
Chapter 7	The Slave Dynasty: An Appraisal	73

KHILJI MILITARISM

Chapter 8	Ascent to Power	93
Chapter 9	Ala Ud-Din Khilji	109
Chapter 10	Military Conquests of Ala Ud-Din Khilji	119
Chapter 11	Demise of The Dynasty	151
Chapter 12	Ala Ud-Din – The Only Khilji Who Mattered	163

THE VAINGLORY OF THE TUGHLUQS

Sources of Information		177
Chapter 13	Ghiyas Ud-Din Tughluq Shah	181
Chapter 14	Muhammad Tughluq - The Impatient Administrator	197
Chapter 15	Muhammad Tughluq: Military Commander Revolts and Rebellions	215
Chapter 16	Muhammad Tughluq: The Ill-Starred Dreamer - Blood Thirsty Tyrant or Benevolent King?	237
Chapter 17	Firuz Shah Tughluq - A Man of Peace	245
Chapter 18	Firuz Shah's Military Endeavours	261
Chapter 19	Firuz Shah: A Sultan for Stability	275
Chapter 20	The Later Tughluqs: A Decade of Decline	283
Chapter 21	A Typhoon called Timur The Scourge of God	293
Chapter 22	The Whimpering End	309
Chapter 23	The Disintegrated Sultanate	319

THE INSIGNIFICANT SAYYIDS

Chapter 24	Khizr Khan Sayyid	333
Chapter 25	Muiz Ud-Din Abdul Fateh Sultan Mubarak Shah	339
Chapter 26	The Later Sayyids	349

THE AFGHAN EMPIRE OF THE LODIS

Chapter 27	Origins of The Lodis	359
Chapter 28	Bahlul Lodi: Chief among Equals	365

| Chapter 29 | Sikandar Shah Lodi Life And Times | 381 |
| Chapter 30 | Ibrahim Lodi: The Twilight Sultan | 401 |

THE ENCROACHING ISLAMIC INFLUENCE

| Chapter 31 | Governance of The Sultanate | 421 |
| Chapter 32 | The Caliphate and the Sultanate Debating the Relationship | 433 |

DANCE OF THE RELIGIONS

Chapter 33	The Assiduous Power of Hinduism	441
Chapter 34	Sufism in India during the Sultanate	453
Chapter 35	The Mingling of Mysticism	465
Chapter 36	The Medieval Hindu Revival Reform through Bhakti	473

Conclusion	491
Bibliography	507
Index	515

AUTHOR'S PREFACE

Challenges to Understanding the Past

The recounting and analysis of Indian history has become an undertaking fraught with the prospect of the author being maligned by votaries of the Hindu Right, especially if one takes what is perceived as an anti-Hindu stance in the evaluation. The perception of an anti-Hindu slant is often based on a less than clear understanding of the 'truth' of history and the unchanging nature of events that have already passed. In recent times, the term 'anti-Hindu' has become equated to being anti-national and anti-Indian. In these circumstances, the historical analyst often finds himself (herself) on very contentious grounds and must tread carefully in order to be seen, viewed and understood as being scrupulously unbiased.

Historical analysis requires the use of disciplined, yet imaginative and interpretive powers on the part of the analyst. The study must be firmly based on evidence that is not only tangible but also corroborated by other sources. More importantly, it must also be informed by the histories of regions, groups, events and perspectives that have been largely ignored in the broader and more popular history. In the case of India, this quest often leads to a division between pre- and post-colonial rendering of its history. It also divides the post-colonial writings into what are considered narratives in the same mould as that of the colonial era writings and later writings that tend to be more 'nationalistic' in their outlook. In order to avoid the pitfalls associated with both these approaches—the one maintaining the status quo and the other attempting to infuse a sense of national pride through recounting more palatable episodes—the analyst needs to start with a clear idea of what both the approaches would mean. Only then can a new, fresh and clean approach be adopted. Needless to say, achieving such an unbiased approach is a difficult task. A historian is also liable to be indirectly influenced by who he or she is, and his or her own preconceived ideas and beliefs, at the subconscious level. No one is immune to this influence.

The latest fad in India is to work towards discrediting professional historians, since it is perceived that their task is only to fit their writings to pre-given analysis as 'truths'. Liberal left-leaning historians are moving towards explanatory historical recounting rather than providing fact-based interpretive and analytical narratives. The directions that such explanatory histories could take will challenge most of the fundamentals of historic analysis since they would be devoid of any obligation to be based on verifiable facts. In turn, such histories risk the suppression of 'inconvenient' truths and thus could lead to the long-term perpetuation of doctored history. This trend would not only re-write history but glorify a past that perhaps does not merit glorification. Serious students of history should not let this travesty take hold. They must make a concerted attempt at ensuring that history and its analysis remain above narrow political and nationalistic assertions and parochial considerations. Indian history, complex as it is, cannot be permitted to be 'hi-jacked' to cater for political expediency and people with a biased agenda that they, in their ignorance, label as being patriotic and nationalistic. True nationalism is best served by accepting, analysing and learning from the mistakes of the past.

***

There is a myth that was primarily perpetuated by the European colonial historians that ancient and medieval Indians did not have a sense of history and that this trait has continued to influence the modern Indian society. This perception is blatantly incorrect. It has now been established that ancient India had a distinct sense of history that had been developed mainly through the religious texts. These texts provide clear perceptions of the historic development of the Indian entity. Being predominantly based on a religious narrative, the sense of history in the Indian context was developed from a very different perspective in comparison to the Western ideas of history. The Vedic texts, the great epics of Hinduism—the *Ramayana* and *Mahabharata*— the *Puranas*, the Buddhist and Jain religious texts, inscriptions on ancient temple structure and even theatrical compositions like the *Mudrarakhasa* provide the foundations for the recounting of 'Indian' history. These sources are radically different from the sources that Western historical analysts consider acceptable to recount history. The conflict of ideas is obvious.

In medieval times, recorded Indian history was more narrative than analytical and primarily of a complimentary nature. They were written by court chroniclers who were always dependent on the king/sultan for their livelihood and therefore tended to smooth over inconvenient truths regarding the rulers and glossed over his proclivities. Even battlefield defeats were turned at least into indecisive battles if not into partial victories itself, through recounting the events in couched language. During this period history was not viewed in correlation with religious developments but purely as a chronological narrative of events. They did not form part of a collective recollection of the grand pattern of human endeavour that typified the times. At best these narratives could be considered the recording of human acts of volition, omission and commission as well as chronicles of the trials of human nature. Kings and sultans were accordingly labelled strong or weak, liberal or orthodox, tyrannical or broad-minded. Medieval Indian history was only analysed at a much later time, that too by European historians with their own biases against India and Hindus.

Civilisations with long histories, like in the Indian context, have to be divided into eras for convenience in their study and understanding. However, these divisions have to be carefully crafted in order to ensure that they do not become captive ones to the facet of pure historical narrative, but takes into account the amalgam of socio-economic and religious factors as well as more esoteric themes such as perceptions of masculinity and femininity, women and gender, history of the development of concepts of time and space and many more diverse but critical areas that directly influence historical analysis.

In 1817, James Mill, a British historian and political theorist, published a six-volume book set entitled *The History of British India*. Although it was a popular book amongst the British imperialists, it did incalculable damage to the broader understanding and further study of Indian history. Mill divested Indian history of all its diversities and concentrated only on the religion of the ruler, making that the single consideration for all analysis. Thus he deals only with the superficial changes at the top of the hierarchy, the ruling class. Mill fails completely to interpret the essential changes and developments in the political, economic and cultural aspects of the sub-continent. The fact that James Mill never visited India and that he did not know a single Indian language was turned into a virtue by him and surprisingly accepted by contemporaries. The book created the division of Indian history into Hindu, Muslim and British periods. This is not an intelligent breakdown and gives the wrong perception of Indian history. His contempt for both Hinduism and Islam, particularly the former, comes through clearly in his writings. In later days his historical analysis and theories regarding India have been discredited, even by other European scholars.

In his book, ten chapters are devoted to a long essay 'Of the Hindus' in which he writes contemptuously, disparagingly and dismissively of the Hindus. For example he wrote, '...under the glosing exterior of the Hindu, lies a general disposition of deceit and perfidy.' and '...in truth, the Hindoo [Hindu] like the eunuch, excels in the qualities of the slave.' Such statements, from a person who had obviously never interacted with a Hindu, prompted Thomas Trautman (American historian and Professor Emeritus of History and Anthropology in the University of Michigan) to write in his book *Aryans and British India* (1997), 'James Mill's highly influential History of British India (1817) – most particularly the long essay 'of the Hindus' comprising ten chapters – is the single most important source of British Indophobia and hostility to Orientalism'. I have mentioned James Mill and referred to his writings here only to illustrate the arrogant belief of British historians that they were unassailable as far as the recounting of Indian history was concerned. They believed that their judgement of Indian character was etched in solid rock—irrefutable and infallible. The damage done over three centuries of misguided analysis is still being put right.

The tripartite division of Indian history has remained the basis for how it is being taught, even today, although the titles of the periods were changed to Ancient, Medieval and Modern by Stanley Lane-Pool around 1903. Fundamental to this division was the conceited assumption that colonialism was the harbinger of modernisation to India. This colonial condescension, not only regarding India but also in relation to other parts of Asia, Africa and South America, was the fundamental basis for the recounting of history by the Europeans in all colonies through the 18th, 19th and early to mid-20th centuries. It was only in the 1960s that these assumptions, often arbitrarily made and not based on a holistic analysis of historical events, handed down by the colonial masters started to be questioned in India. The historians of independent India questioned, debated and disproved the pre-conceived ideas that had been assumed by the European political and religious analysts. Today Indian historical narrative has come a long way from the conceited colonialist historiography. This series of books on Indian history *From Indus to Independence: A Trek through Indian History*, of which this is the fifth volume, follows the contemporary Indian path while attempting to remain strictly unbiased in its analysis. I do not claim to be a trained historian but am a historical analyst, although the distinction is subtle and could be missed in my writings.

***

The recounting of Indian history suffers from an inherent disadvantage. Through the ancient and medieval times there is no coherent analysis of the core geography of the sub-continent in its entirety. Even so, whenever a stable long-term political centre was established they also gradually developed into cultural centres for the kingdom. These places attracted scholars and other accomplished persons because royal patronage emanated from there. By the time the Delhi Sultanate was being established, the kingdoms of North India had become centred on Delhi. There was an almost separate kingdom of Bengal and various Tamil kingdoms in the Peninsula. The result was that the scribes and scholars provide the historian and analyst with an abundance of information about these kingdoms.

Even at the height of its power, the Delhi Sultanate's forays into South India remained raids with only transitory impact on the socio-political and politico-economic developments of the Peninsula. Further, a majority of these raids were confined to the northern part of the Deccan plateau. From a cultural perspective, even the establishment of great kingdoms did not lead to the creation of a central core that was capable of coalescing cultural developments in any meaningful manner.

Another aspect that challenges the historian attempting to examine medieval times is that Indian historical information is beset with issues of exaggeration and myth-building. The available historical narrative is not completely unbiased and nor is it open to direct interpretation. Objectivity has been largely ignored in the recordings. The chances of incorrect myths being perpetuated is very high under these circumstances. Indian historical narrative does not provide an insight into the various regions and communities that together make up the entirety of the sub-continent. It concentrates on the heartland of great empires and kingdoms and ignores the fringe regions and the people who inhabited them. This imbalance has to be redressed to ensure that there is a semblance of a holistic analysis in recounting the history of the sub-continent.

There are a large number of groups and people who have been ignored and marginalised in Indian history, who have to be studied and fitted into the broader narrative. In the series that I am writing, my attempt has been to be inclusive of the lesser known and less elitist groups, to bring their story into the mainstream narrative. They form as much part of the ancient and medieval Indian past as the groups that have been so far projected as having been influential in the creation of ideas. Another feature of Indian history, its unique diversity and complexity of cultural developments and tradition, needs much more attention than has been paid so far—they have remained marginalised in the writing of Indian history. Similarly, the changes that have taken place in the development of Hinduism as a religion and as a way of life, while having been examined as independent studies, have not been juxtaposed into the narrative of history per se. My endeavour has been to underline the developments in marginal areas and in the sedate progress of Hinduism as part of the historical narrative in all the volumes that have so far been published. This endeavour continues in this volume and will also be attempted in future volumes.

***

Preface

I must emphatically attest here that this volume on the Delhi Sultanate has been written to accurately depict the various aspects of the Turkish invasion and the traumatic events that succeeded it. Any opinions that have been expressed are my own, arrived at after logical examination of confirmed facts. The reader is at liberty to disagree with my assessment, but I am certain will not be able to fault my logic. That is the vagary of historical analysis, examination of the same set of facts could lead to many, and completely different conclusions. I believe that it should be so, otherwise history will feel doctored and in the long-term lose its vitality and usefulness. This must not be allowed to happen. After all history will always point the way for the future.

Sanu Kainikara
Canberra
February 2018

The Islamic conquest of India is probably the bloodiest story in history. It is a discouraging tale, for its evident moral is that civilization is a precious good, whose delicate complex of order and freedom, culture and peace, can at any moment be overthrown by barbarians invading from without or multiplying within.

Will Durant,
The Story of Civilization: Our Oriental Heritage, p. 459.

The blood of the infidels flowed so copiously at Thanesar that the stream was discoloured, notwithstanding its purity, and people were unable to drink it. The Sultan returned with plunder which is impossible to count.

Tarikh-i-Yamini of Utbi, the sultan's secretary,
Written in the 11th century.

INTRODUCTION TO VOLUME V
A MILITARY OCCUPATION OF NORTH INDIA

History never flows in a predictable manner and nowhere else is this more apparent than in the narrative of Indian history. The progress of history is always the result of seemingly random incidents that create ripples and currents which themselves are arbitrary but influential in the most unexpected ways. Because of their arbitrary nature, the influence of the currents, even if determinable, can also be disputed with fervour. Even catering for Indian history's capricious nature, it is highly improbable that the events which set off the process that would eventually establish the Delhi Sultanate would have been considered at that time to be capable of achieving such a momentous result.

Everybody, even some historians, view history in ways that makes sense to them. There is a certain amount of pre-conception involved in this exercise and therefore, an unconscious tendency creeps in to redefine the past—history gets creatively recast. There is an obvious need to avoid this pitfall when undertaking historical analysis. Like other ancient histories, Indian history has not been immune to the vagaries of pre-conceived ideas being associated to some obscure event that is claimed to be accurate fact in the narrative. Such actions tend to destroy the framework within which serious study of the past should be undertaken and its lessons for the future derived.

500 Years of 'Peace'

Although the Islamic invasion of the Indian sub-continent commenced more than a century before the Delhi Sultanate was established, it is the establishment of an independent Muslim kingdom that is emblematic of the arrival of Islam into India. It is a remarkable fact of history that there was a gap of more than 500 years between the invasion of Toramana the Hun and the pillaging raids of Mahmud of Ghazni. During this interim period, India was free of any significant external aggression. Such a lengthy period of unbroken immunity from invasion is unknown in the history of any other part of the world. This long span of time devoid of threats, other than for insignificant internal squabbles between local kingdoms, brought about an advantage and several disadvantages.

The 500-year reprieve from invasions created the atmosphere necessary for the development of literature, education and the aesthetic arts. Even so their development was not commensurate with the benign atmosphere. There was also the entrenchment of religious beliefs and the formalisation of Brahminical Hinduism. Although Hinduism was embedded and strong, this development could be considered a double-edged sword. The rigidity that accompanied Brahminical Hinduism was a weak link and became inimical to the overall flexibility of Hinduism when the more democratic notions of the Islamic faith was brought into the sub-continent.

The disadvantages of this long period of 'peace' were more readily visible. First was that it led to a gradual lowering of the guard by the Hindu kingdoms, especially in relation to protecting the north-western approaches to the sub-continent. Eternal vigilance has always been the price of freedom. This particular refrain had vanished from the thought of the Hindu kings following the unprecedented long duration of tranquillity. Further, nationalism and the sense of patriotism grows under the direct stimulus of common danger. Since common danger had almost disappeared even from general memory, the Hindus as a people had become complacent to the extreme. Their sense of well-being overcame all other feelings, including their sense of security.

The result of a combination of complacency and not witnessing any significant acts of external aggression for generations was that the Hindu kingdoms gradually lost their warlike spirit. It is easy to lose the martial spirit in a people, but extremely difficult to cultivate and nurture. Such a spirit can only be fostered under extreme conditions and maintained thereafter by assiduously cultivating it through conscious inculcation of the warlike spirit in each successive generation. The literature of the time shows that no such effort was undertaken in India. During these 500 years there is no Indian writing of the birth of a war God or even of epic battles fought and won. No heroes of valour stand out in the writings of these long years of peace, when literature and the arts should have been ascendant.

Five centuries of relative peace destroyed the fear and respect for foreign invaders in the Indian mind. The result was the rise of arrogance in the Hindu people, making them narrow-minded and gradually diminishing the broad nature and flexibility of the religion. The Hindu scholars particularly adopted an attitude of superiority in their knowledge, a conceit that was not perceivable even as late as the 7th century. This aspect was commented upon by al-Biruni who was an astute judge of people and cultures. He wrote, 'The Hindus believe that there is no country but theirs, no nation like theirs, no kings like theirs, no religion like theirs, no science like theirs.' He also noted that their ancestors were not so narrow-minded, an accurate analysis of the stasis that had made Indians and Hinduism moribund.

There is nothing more dangerous for the safety of a country than the inherent feeling in the people that it was ordained by God to remain safe; that no foreign intruder could breach its borders. The heightened feeling of peace from which such notions arise leads to the drying up of the springs that produce greatness in a nation. It permits the inherent values that should be sacrosanct in a nation to be degraded beyond redemption. It was on the gates of such a society, at a low ebb in its identity, creativity and vitality, that the battering ram of the Islamic invasion thudded.

> 'Completely insular in ideas, without any knowledge of what was happening in the rest of the world, the Indian people ceased to grow. Civilisation became decadent and inbred for lack of fertilising contacts with dissimilar cultures. Society became static and the systematizations of previous ages, which were more academic than real at the time of their conception like Chaturvarna—the four castes—and food and drink taboos came to be accepted

> as divine regulations and confirmed to with a rigidity which would have surprised Manu and Yajnavalkya.'
>
> K. M. Panikkar,
>
> *A Survey of Indian History*, p. 106

The Islamic Invasion and Conquest

The first factor that must be mentioned regarding the Islamic invasion of the sub-continent is that since the Muslim conquest and establishment of the Delhi Sultanate was the work of many centuries, all generalisations in the narrative of the events that took place are suspect. This caveat holds true whether a Muslim ruler was being praised for his generosity towards the conquered people or a sultan being denigrated for practising extreme bigotry.

In narrating history, there are also contentious subjects that need to be discussed, analysed and assessed, taking into account all available information in an unbiased manner. In the case of the Delhi Sultanate some of the major questions to be asked and answered are: how disastrous was the Muslim conquest of North India in respect of the destruction of Indian heritage? Were there any safeguards in place to protect the heritage sufficiently? How ruthless were the Muslim rulers in their treatment of their new Hindu subjects? How determined and united was the resistance of the Hindu kings against the foreign invaders? Along with debating the answers to these vexed questions, there is also the need to analyse the socio-political and socio-religious interactions that took place between the two religions, societies and ethnicities. It is clearly evident that the differences were never completely addressed, a sad and inconvenient truth.

Eminent Muslim historians have attempted, at regular intervals, to play down the impact of the Islamic invasion on India's medieval culture, religion and society, as well as its continuing influence on the current day Indian society. Some have even adopted the extreme position by stating that the invasion was placidly welcomed by the majority Hindu population. This is a blatantly incorrect assessment, meant to soften the extreme actions of the invading Islamic forces.

Introduction

An acknowledged and eminent Hindu authority has written in graphic detail about the resistance offered by the Indian people to the Islamic invasion, quoted below. The truth lay somewhere in between.

> 'The conquests so exultantly referred to by the court chroniclers of the Sultanate had an Indian side of the picture. It was one of ceaseless resistance offered with relentless heroism; of men, from boys in teens to men with one foot in the grave, flinging away their lives for freedom; of warriors defying the invaders from fortresses for months, sometimes for years, in one case, with intermission, for a century; of women in thousands courting fire to save their honour; of children whose bodies were flung into wells by their parents so that they might escape slavery; of fresh heroes springing up to take the place of the dead and to break the volume and momentum of the onrushing tide of invasion.'
>
> K. M. Munshi,
> Foreword to R. C. Majumdar (General Editor)
> History and Culture of the Indian People,
> Vol 5, The Struggle for Empire, p. xv.

The Turkish Success – Reasons Why?

Another aspect of the Islamic invasion and conquest of North India is the perception that the sweeping victories achieved by the Ghurid army gives of India being an easy conquest. This perception is brought about by the Muslim chroniclers smoothing over the reversals that the invading armies suffered and also the less than accurate analysis rendered by later day historians. Some of these historians have consciously attempted to create a false impression not only of the superiority of the Muslim armies, but also of the submissive and accepting nature of the local population of the sub-continent. On the other hand, it must be admitted that the Islamic forces were led by extremely sagacious, brave and tenacious generals possessing very high leadership qualities. Even a cursory analysis of the battles bring out any number of instances of these generals being able to exploit their limited resources to the fullest and of their besting what would be considered insurmountable odds in the battlefield.

The main opponents to the invasion were the Rajputs—brave and stubborn to the point of being foolhardy. Their resistance to the invasion was fierce, continuous and long-drawn and worthy of praise when measured by any standards. However, the struggle between the Rajputs, who were the majority of Hindu kings of the time, and the Muslims for supremacy was a clash between two different social systems; one old and self-indulgent, the other young and full of zest. 500 years of relative peace had made the Indian kingdoms almost decadent and the entrenchment of the caste system had broken all sense of unity, both political and social, within the Indian society. Even so, the speed and completeness of the Turkish victory is baffling. Why did such a turn of events take place? There are few fundamental reasons for this, which have been elaborated in this book. The major reasons are listed below.

The challenges that the Hindu kings had to overcome when faced with the Muslim invaders played a vital role in their overall defeat, even though the battlefield setbacks of the Hindu kings could only be termed as 'fighting defeats' in most cases. There are two major contributory factors that made it difficult for the Rajput kings to push the invaders out of the sub-continent, even when the intruders were defeated in the battlefield. First was the social and religious tensions within Hindu kingdoms that had by this time become far too widespread to be contained or brushed aside. The social divisions made it impossible for the Hindu armies to follow through on battlefield victories or to retaliate after suffering a minor setback. In cases where retaliation was attempted it was a failed venture even before its start. The social structure of the time was such that the ruling class of Rajputs and other Hindu kings were agrarian aristocracy, separated from the majority of the population who were peasants and commoners by class and caste.

Even though the warrior elite were always ready for battle, the bulk of the Hindu army had to be inducted from the peasants and the middle-class. The peasants considered the aristocracy to be oppressive landlords. The peasants also suffered religious oppression from the Brahmins who were in collaboration with the warrior class. When an invasion took place, the peasants were more inclined to stay inert since they were not concerned about the outcome since the victor would be the next oppressor. It can be imagined that they may even have revelled at the discomfiture of the Brahmins and the aristocracy at the Islamic invasion. Similarly, the middle-class was engaged by the Turks to run the administration and therefore was not particularly affected by the outcome of the conflict. Further, the religious persecution that was brought down was primarily confined to pillaging and destroying temples and monasteries. Individual or personal persecution was not commonly practiced, at least in the initial period of the invasion. Therefore only the aristocracy, Brahmins and Buddhist monks were affected, the general population remained somewhat isolated from direct persecution.

The second was the disunity prevalent amongst the Hindu/Rajput kingdoms and clans because of jealousies and feuds handed down through generations. *[Some of these clan feuds continued for centuries, all the way to the abolishment of kingdoms on India becoming independent from British rule in 1947.]* This lack of unity precluded the possibility of presenting a united front to the invading force, which would have greatly increased the chances of success for the Indian forces. The Turks were able to pick each individual prince or king and defeat them piecemeal, one at a time, while neighbours looked on and waited their turn. Analysing the events now, in modern times, this approach to a full-fledged invasion with far-reaching and critical consequences looks to be remarkably short-sighted. However, there is no denying the fact that this was what happened in medieval times in India. Various North Indian Hindu kingdoms were defeated, plundered, broken up into smaller provinces and annexed to the growing territorial might of the Islamic kingdom. *[A century later, this very same sequence of events played out in the Deccan and peninsular India, when the Islamic invasion paralysed the Hindu response.]*

> 'Clan jealousies and class resentment thus combined to prevent either united Indian action or the growth of a strong antiforeign sentiment.
>
> Percival Spear,
> *India: A Modern History*, p. 105.

There is also an operational reason for the failure of the Hindu armies. They continued to use conservative and at times redundant tactics in battle. When this was combined with the limited discipline of the infantry—every soldier was individually brave, but was not adept at acting in unison—and the opposition of well-drilled cavalry, the result was almost a pre-gone conclusion. Some of the tactics used by the Hindu armies had not evolved from the ones that King Porus employed against Alexander of Macedonia, centuries ago. This disadvantage was amplified by the fact that the Turks were almost always on the offensive and therefore held the initiative. They could be selective in the choice of targets. The Hindu armies were forced to be reactive to the invaders operational tactics.

A Military Occupation?

There is no doubt that in the initial stages Delhi Sultanate was a mere conquest by an army of occupation, whose commander was more interested in Central Asia than India per se. It gradually evolved into a Turkish colonial empire mainly manned by emigres fleeing the Mongol onslaught that had swept across Turkestan, Iran and Iraq. This diaspora included princes, chiefs, soldiers, scholars and saints who became the vast reservoir of manpower needed to drive the new government being established at Delhi. The Turks ability to survive when cut off from their home base was perhaps even better than that displayed by the Indo-Greeks centuries earlier. Since they were fighting hundreds of miles away from their home bases, the Turks always fought desperately—they had nowhere to go if they were defeated. This can be a great impetus to be brave, and even suicidal in battle. They were also spurred on by religious fervour, which was a unifying factor amongst the different classes and ethnicities that comprised the Turkish army.

At the operational level, the Turks were different compared to the Hindu armies. They were capable of adapting unified action in order to create the mass necessary to carry forward an attack and often resorted to terror tactics to compensate for their lack of numerical strength. The Turks were crude and unsophisticated. They were extremely cruel and violent in battle, a trait that was justified, then and even now by few historians, under the veneer of a twisted view of the Islamic faith. More than any other factor, the proclivity to be ruthless and unforgiving towards an adversary made the Turkish army a feared instrument in the hands of a competent commander.

The first half of the Delhi Sultanate undoubtedly was a military occupation supported by extreme religious and racial prejudices. Essentially the throne was insecure that in turn demanded, and received, severity of rule that knew very limited bounds. However, the social disruption and displacement was mostly restricted to the Hindu ruling aristocracy and the Brahmins. Although the common people were oppressed, they were used to it, and they did not face any consequential disharmony within the small and almost insular pockets they inhabited.

The conquest of Delhi was therefore more symbolic than an actual conquest of the sub-continent that was to occur more than three centuries later. Many independent and powerful indigenous kingdoms continued to exist and prosper across India. The Delhi Sultanate was merely one more of these. India had by no means been subjugated when the Sultanate collapsed under the weight of the Mughal attack.

The Rationale of the Sultanate

The Delhi Sultanate was militantly Islamic and foreign in its fundamentals and organisational structure. For all practical purposes it was an Islamic conquest state, zealously oriented towards the spread of the Islamic faith and oppressive towards all indigenous people. The oppression was tempered with the need to use the same indigenous people in the administration, a trend that was only reluctantly accepted. In many ways the Sultanate demonstrated the emerging greatness of the Islamic civilisation, even though India was at the margins of 'dar-al-Islam', the world of Islam. In effect, geographically the Delhi Sultanate was at the edge of the spreading Islamic empire of Central Asia.

The Turks who established the empire in the sub-continent were relative newcomers to the Islamic faith, which in many ways made them more eager to establish the religion in the newly conquered lands. To achieve this aim they wanted absolute control over the conquered lands. The ferociousness and extreme cruelty that was exhibited could also be attributed to the inherent belief of the Turks that they were honour bound to capture the land and to spread their newly acquired religion.

When the invasion and conquest is viewed within the context of the spread of the Islamic faith, two developments become apparent. The first is the importance of Islam to the administrative mechanism of the Sultanate. The occupying forces did not share a common language, ethnicity, region of origin or culture. Only adherence to a common religion bound the Turks together and made allegiance to the sultan possible. Further, since the authority of the Delhi Sultans were almost always internally challenged, it was necessary for the rulers to promote themselves as pious Muslims and champions the faith. This is the reason that expeditions that were mounted purely to amass wealth are always mentioned in the chronicles as military campaigns to spread the Islamic faith among the non-believers. As a result of such reporting, even the limited religious tolerance that was exercised by some of the sultans have not been placed on record. The fact remains that the reports of expeditions to enforce Islam must not be taken completely at face value, but investigated further to ascertain the real reason for the expedition to have been conducted.

The second development was the construction of monuments and the recording of chronicles. These served dual purposes. The first was to impress the indigenous, non-Muslim population of the sub-continent with the grandeur of the Islamic faith and also the power of the conquering army. The second purpose was to indicate to the broader Muslim community, especially to the west of the Indian sub-continent, the opulence and stature of the new empire being established, even though it was at the fringes of the original and established Caliphate. It was necessary for the Delhi Sultans to display pomp and ceremony in order to establish themselves as powerful monarchs on their own strength.

The Dynasties of the Sultanate

In a span of three centuries, the Delhi Sultanate witnessed the rise and fall of five distinct dynasties as demarcated by historians. Further, the nine rulers clubbed together as the Slave dynasty actually belonged to three distinctly separate families and therefore could be considered to be three dynasties, increasing the number of dynasties to have ruled in

Delhi to seven. Considering the short timeframe of the rule of each of these dynasties, the reasons for these frequent dynastic changes are also analysed in the book in order to get a clear idea regarding the character of the Sultanate. There are five major reasons for the repeated dynastic changes. First, there was no formal law of succession to the throne, making the position open to anyone who aspired to be the sultan. This obviously developed into a situation wherein any military commander of some capability and ambition was only be waiting for a chance to usurp the throne.

Second, the sultan and the nobility were almost always at loggerheads and therefore stability of the administration was perennially in question. A weak sultan could be removed from the throne by a coterie of powerful nobles who would then appoint their own choice as sultan. The reason was straight forward. The nobility and the rest of the Turks were a minority in a largely alien land and therefore needed the sultan to be efficient and powerful in order to survive. Any weakness on the part of the sultan immediately threatened the well-being of the aristocracy. A corollary to this fact was the third reason. The sultan and the nobles were dependent on an efficient system of revenue collection to maintain the necessary security for themselves and the state. The inability of the sultan to collect and distribute sufficient revenue therefore was considered a weakness, a direct threat to their well-being. A sultan who was inept at creating wealth, either through the loss of territory from which to collect revenue or through his inability to enforce its collection, was very soon deposed.

The fourth reason was the rise of regional states and the incessant confrontations that they set up with the centre and against each other. The on-going skirmishes were not only destabilising but also resource-consuming exercises. In a broad analysis, powerful regional states meant powerful regional rulers who were invariably aspirants for the throne of Delhi. In some cases they succeeded in weakening the Delhi sultan to an extent where it became easy for the Delhi nobility to replace him fairly easily. The administrative set up of the Sultanate was such that it supported the establishment of regional provinces as semi-autonomous entities that could be turned into independent kingdoms under a determined ruler. Throughout its existence, the Delhi Sultanate suffered from this division of power, especially in the extremities of its territories. The fifth reason was the regular Mongol invasions, which even though were more pillaging raids, at times reached as deep as Delhi itself. The inability of a sultan to stop the Mongols far enough from the capital almost always paved the way, indirectly, for his replacement—either by someone from his own family or by a different clan. The final outcome was that the Delhi Sultanate was never stable and even the most powerful of the sultans who reigned were never completely secure on the throne.

The Religious Divide

The establishment of the Tughluq dynasty, third in the series, was perhaps the last chance that the invading forces had of ameliorating the religious persecution that was being perpetuated on the local Hindus by the Muslim sultans of the Slave and Khilji dynasties. Ghiyas ud-Din the progenitor of the dynasty was a moderate and knowledgeable person, not given to excesses in character or prone to unreasonable violence. In fact his dealings with the Hindus bordered on the benevolent, relative to the medieval times. He could have brought the Hindus into the mainstream with a bit of an effort. However, in order to perpetuate his rule, he succumbed to the pressures of bigoted theologians and lost the last chance to bridge the gap between Islam and Hinduism. From this point forward the two religions would never see eye to eye and a growing sense of 'us and them' would divide the Indian sub-continent forever.

The Muslims never fully assimilated even after generations of living in the sub-continent and the Hindus never fully 'accepted' the foreigners even well into the 21st century.

An analysis of the Islamic invasion and the subsequent establishment of the Delhi Sultanate provides glimpses of windows of opportunity that could have been grabbed to forge a union between the two religions. However, the victorious Islamic army failed to produce a commander or sultan of deep and farsighted vision to realise and act on the need to keep religion away from the judiciary and the executive. The Islamic faith decreed otherwise. At the same time, the Hindus were incapable of uniting under one capable, imaginative and prescient leader or king who could have made assimilation of the latest foreigners into the multi-cultural fold of the sub-continent possible.

Age-old rivalries and religious beliefs that had frozen the flexibility of Hinduism decreed otherwise. The resultant Hindu-Muslim divide can be laid as much at the feet of short-sighted Islamic military leaders as at that of the Hindu leadership who could never work in unity with each other. This aspect is so visible in modern India.

This Book – Volume V – The Delhi Sultanate

This book covers the entire history of the Delhi Sultanate, from its inception by the Slave Commander of Muhammad of Ghur, till the time of its extinction with the killing in battle of the last sultan Ibrahim Lodi. Parallel to the exploration of the eventful history of the Sultanate, the book traces the progress of the Islamic faith in the Indian sub-continent, its interaction with Hinduism and the influences that each brought to the other.

There is no doubt that the Turkish ruling elite were completely biased against the Hindus in all their dealings. The Muslim chronicles, which are the major sources of information regarding the events of the time, were written by court chroniclers. It is not surprising that they have contrived to ignore or downplay unpalatable events that would bring their patron, the sultan, into disrepute. They have done this, perhaps not out of any need to or wanting to rewrite history, but to ensure that the wrath of the sultan did not descend on them. It was purely an act of self-preservation. Battlefield defeats and setbacks as well as particularly vengeful acts of violence do not find a place in any of the chronicles.

There is another aspect that stands out about the Muslim chronicles. None of the chronicles—one-sided as they are—mention any act of magnanimity of a sultan towards a defeated Hindu king. Once again this could be an attempt to ensure that the sultan was not seen as being 'weak' in dealing with Hindus. The sultan fundamentally had to be painted to be seen as rigorously persecuting non-believers since he was a devout Muslim. Further, royal patronage was restricted to Muslims only. Reading between the lines of these two factors one is forced to admit that the majority Hindu population of the Muslim conquered territories were turned into non-persons; paying a tax to the invaders to practice their religion or being forcible converted to the Islamic faith, their places of worship desecrated and destroyed, while their religious teachers were prohibited from preaching their faith on penalty of death. The paradox is that this non-status of the Hindus, who were in the majority throughout the existence of the Delhi Sultanate, and its continuing aftermath have not been dealt with clearly in any of the historical narratives.

It could be argued that the general population of the Hindu kingdoms did not consider the Islamic invasion any different from the invasion by another Hindu kingdom, since the concept of a Hindu India did not exist at that time. It could also be that the Hindu rulers were politically somewhat naïve and in the early years of the invasion did not perceive its deep religious colour and overtones. When the realisation that the invasion was spearheading a religious confrontation dawned on the Hindu elite and the people, it gave rise to the Medieval Hindu Revival. While it could be considered the epitome of too little too late, in some ways it also demonstrated the inherent flexibility of the religion and way of life that is Hinduism.

The medieval saints, who transcended regions and geography, tried to adapt the more progressive characteristics of the invading Islamic faith into Hinduism with some success. More importantly they brought about a general awareness of the threat to Hinduism through the proselytising Islam. However, the divisions of caste in Hinduism remained a ground reality and could not be overcome. The forward-leaning teachings of these saints remained acceptable only within the small circle of their immediate followers. Like the proverbial elephant, Hinduism and its learned elite continued ponderously down the path of confrontation, without considering assimilation or accommodation. The saints had limited success mainly because the upper class Hindus, the opinion makers and influential people, did not find it necessary to follow the saints and their simple and encompassing teachings.

This non-development had far reaching implications for religious growth, tolerance, and secularism in the sub-continent. The lack of mutual awareness led to long-term antagonism and the loss of the capacity in both religions to adjust to each other. This book covers these developments in detail, within the recounting of the events that took place over three centuries.

Introduction

By the time the Lodi dynasty was defeated and removed from the scene, the socio-religious split in the society was clearly visible in North India. Tumultuous times were about to descend on India.

PROLOGUE
The Medieval Islamic World

From the time of its origin in the 7th century till the end of the 13th century, the Islamic world represented much of the better aspects of human civilisation. During these nearly six hundred years, Islam ranged from Spain and West Africa to Central Asia and the Indian sub-continent, with the core of the Islamic civilisation resident in the lands between the Rivers Nile and Oxus. In 1258, the Mongols conquered Baghdad and the world of Islam changed for ever.

There are two almost insurmountable challenges to examining early Islamic history and arriving at credible and authentic conclusions after the analysis. One, the period between 600 and 700 is the most important in the early history of Islam. However, there is almost no documentary sources of this period that is available. Almost everything that has documented regarding this period has been written down at later dates, at times by as much as few centuries. Till then the information was orally transmitted. Two, a majority of the available literature originates from within the Muslim world and is steeped in adhering to the rather strict Islamic tradition. Their authenticity, in terms of details, can be questioned.

Literary Sources

The literary sources that are available can be classified into four categories. The first is the sacred text of Islam, *al-Kitab*, The Scripture or The Book, also known as *al-Quran*, The Recitation. Second is the commentary on the Quran, called *tafsir*. The third are the statements attributed to or reports about the activities of the Prophet Muhammad by his companions, called *ahadith* (singular *hadith*, in English writing the plural *hadiths* is often used). The fourth are the narrative reports of the events that took place in the early Islamic community in Medina and subsequently in Mecca, called *akhbar* (singular *khabar*). These four literary sources were combined, sometimes as much as two centuries later, to create a cohesive narrative of early Islamic tradition.

According to traditional Muslim accounts, the compilation of the Quran into a single manuscript was done during the reign of the third caliph, Uthman ibn Affan (ruled 644-56). The Quran is God's speech and not Muhammad's human teachings and therefore it is believed to be without any error, meaning that its veracity cannot be questioned. In the Islamic tradition no debate regarding the nature or authenticity of the text is tolerated. However, debate regarding the reliability of the other three literary sources is somewhat more acceptable and their genuineness can be called into question by the faithful. Therefore, from a purely analytical or academic point of view, some of the sources could be considered unreliable. However, the same texts were the sources for the development of religious dogma that started to become entrenched in a gradual manner as the religion developed. There are two reasons to doubt the reliability of the literary sources other than the Quran. First, all of them are fully in-house documents, created from inside sources. In these circumstances the influence of vested interests in perpetuating a particular viewpoint cannot be fully ruled out. Second, almost all the literary accounts date to several centuries after the events described actually took place. Therefore, there is a distinct possibility of inaccuracies having crept into the narrative.

Political Character

From the death of Prophet Muhammad in 632, to the sacking and destruction of Baghdad in 1258 by the Mongols, the institution of the Caliphate guided, inspired and protected the spreading Islamic societies. Prophet Muhammad, the founder of the religion, was both a religious and political leader and the initial fledgling community was a voluntary group led by the Caliph. Early sources provide three titles that were bestowed on the leaders of the community immediately following Muhammad and were used simultaneously. They are: Khalif Rasul Allah, meaning caliph and the deputy or successor of the Messenger of God; Amir al-Muminin, commander of the believers; and Imam or the religious leader. The three titles emphasised the caliph's absolute political, military and religious authority over his followers. In agreeing to invest all the three roles in one individual, the community was in essence giving him the responsibility for being the sole leader with all political and military power over it. In addition he was also the religious leader and in the early days the arbitrator between groups with different theological viewpoints. The office was a lifetime 'appointment'. Therefore, the one issue that almost always came up during the necessary successions was laying down the criteria for determining the person best qualified to hold the office and lead the community.

From the beginning of the formation of the religious community, there have been three major—and at times competing—groups within the broader fold of Islam. They are the Sunni, Shi'a and Khariji, all of whom had differing and diversified opinions on theology and, more importantly, the issues that related to the selection of the leader.

Sunni. The Sunnis represented the majority of Muslims in the premodern and continues to be the majority in the modern world. The shortened title 'Sunni' is derived from the formal title of the group – ahl al-Sunna wa l-Jama'a, meaning the people of tradition and community consensus. In simple terms the highest value in the Sunni community is placed on the maintenance of the broad unity of the group, the umma. In the Sunni perspective, the caliph only needed to be politically good enough to perform his primary job of maintaining the unity of the community. They were essentially 'caliph loyalists' and gave precedence to the political capabilities of the incumbent leader over his other responsibilities.

Shi'a. The name denotes the fact they were derived from a faction (Shi'a) that was constituted by Muhammad's cousin and son-in-law, Ali ibn Abi Talib. This group believes that Muhammad had designated Ali as his successor before his death. Therefore, the proclamation of Abu Bakr as the first caliph is considered an illegitimate usurpation of power. The Shi'a adhere to two fundamental doctrines. One, that the rightful caliph had to be a lineal descendant of Muhammad, through the line of Ali and Fatima, the Prophet's daughter. Two, and also more controversial, that the Caliph or Imam was not only the political head, but an infallible religious teacher who was without error in all matters of the faith and morals. The Shi'a emphasis the religious and theological role of the leader, and therefore the person was more likely to be called Imam than Caliph.

Khariji. The word means 'seceders', so named since this group disagreed with both the other major factions. The Khariji were purists, believing that the principal criteria to assume leadership of the community was piety and moral purity. These were the all-important characteristics and the genealogy or even military capabilities of the leader did not matter.

In the initial phases of the development of Islam as a religion, these three groups were essentially political divisions. However, with time and continuing antagonism, they evolved into separate religious factions, each with its own theological underpinnings, but continuing as part of the broader Islamic community.

Islamic Law – The Shari'a

In the medieval period, the deepening of the Islamic culture and identity in the early Islamic lands of North Africa and the Middle-East gradually introduced a system of beliefs within the community. It also produced the processes to create a framework for social action and cultural expression. This was the beginning of the evolution of a distinctive 'Islamic society'. Along with this societal development, there also developed an accepted code of conduct that governed the relationship between individuals as well as between individuals and the governing regime.

Over the course of centuries, religious leaders developed an all-encompassing code of behaviour for the followers of Islam, which came to be called Shari'a. The interaction of an individual with everyone else, as well as all other aspects of his or her life is in principle governed by one or the other aspect of the Shari'a. Although the term Shari'a is sometimes translated as Islamic Law, it is not a formal body of legislation in the modern sense, but conveys the concept of a pathway to leading a pious life.

As the religion became more entrenched, religious scholars, the ulama, sought to determine how Muslims should live in accordance with God's will as understood and interpreted by them. In theory, this was done by examining each aspect of human behaviour to match it with the scholastic interpretation of the Quran. The process of following the religion was similar in both Islam and Judaism, in that the adherence to the religion was derived from the same concept, even though specific commands were obviously different. Both the religions are based on the idea of a pathway to live and behave in obedience to God. In other words the primary concern is the 'right behaviour' in obedience to God, essentially orthopraxis. In comparison, Christianity is concerned primarily with the 'right belief' in God, which is orthodoxy. Although this distinction is relatively easy to understand, it is also an oversimplification of the fundamental concepts that underpin the three religions. It does not mean that Islam and Judaism are not concerned with the right theology, or that Christianity is oblivious of proper behaviour. The opposite is the truth. The above explanation is theoretical and meant to emphasise the fundamental aspects of the religions.

The most common theme in the Quran is human kind's duty to obey God, although it contains only limited legal material. However, commandments, prohibitions and punishments are detailed in a very specific manner. Similarly, the most common theological doctrine in the Quran is God's mercy and His compassion. It is noteworthy that all but one of the 114 chapters in The Book begin with the same invocation, 'In the name of God, the Merciful, the Compassionate'. However the Quran was compiled some years after the death of Prophet Muhammad and the Muslims looked towards the early Islamic community and their tradition for guidance to lead the correct way of life.

Muhammad's infallibility, as perceived now, was not proclaimed in the Quran. It was only by mid to late 8th century that a doctrine started to be developed proclaiming that God had protected Muhammad, as His prophet, from gross moral error. This doctrine was then extended by legal scholars to the argument that since Prophet Muhammad was morally perfect, his personal practices and/or the traditions that he created and followed were the only reliable guide to the right conduct for an individual other than the guidance given in the Quran. Muhammad ibn Idris al-Shafii, who died in 820, was one of the most prominent early legal scholars. The Prophet's practices were recorded in the hadiths, the reports about what Muhammad said or did, which were determined to be authentic. These were then considered authoritative and to be followed by all true believers.

The scholars did argue regarding the authenticity of each individual hadith. The issue was settled by ascertaining as to which of the hadiths could have been transmitted in an unbroken chain through reliable people, reaching back to the lifetime of the Prophet himself. Even so, since this methodology was reliant on oral transmission, it was not fool-proof and remained open to debate and discussion within the community of religious scholars.

The Shari'a was constructed in two categories that were interdependent. One was the usul al-fiqh, meaning the roots of jurisprudence or the legal theory; and the other the furu al-fiqh, which represented the branches of jurisprudence or the practical application of the law. A detailed knowledge of the Quran and the hadiths was fundamental to the understanding and practice of the science of jurisprudence and the implementation of the Shari'a. The Shari'a was imposed and followed primarily in urban areas because the religious scholars were mainly resident there, the judges and their courts were located in urban centres and the mechanisms to enforce the judges' decisions were also predominantly available in urban areas. The rural countryside lacked all of the above and therefore Shari'a took a backseat to prevalent local custom and traditions. It is therefore apparent that the methodology of jurisprudence could not be employed or enforced consistently across all the Islamic lands. From a historical analysis point of view, the Shari'a provides an insight into the norms of medieval Islamic world and enhances the understanding of the daily life and practices of the common people.

Islamic Mysticism (Sufism)

Islamic mystics were called Sufis because of their proclivity to wear clothes of wool, the word for which was 'suf'. In fact the Arabic word for mysticism, tasawwuf, is also derived from the same word, suf. The development of Sufism is rooted in an individual's search for the proper understanding of the religion. In a simplistic explanation, the Islamic religion was defined by scholars and jurists as a 'religion of law' based on the meticulous study and adherence to the Quran and hadiths. The mystics and ascetics on the other hand conceived of it as a 'religion of the heart' almost totally based on an individual's direct interaction with and knowledge of God. In other words, the Sharia-minded majority sought knowledge about God based on revelations by the Prophet and other messengers, whereas the Sufi-minded minority sought knowledge and understanding of God based on one's own mystical experiences in dealing with God.

Both the Sharia-based outlook and Sufism were, and even today are, not mutually exclusive but only tendencies and trends within the broad spectrum of religious experience and practice of Islam. The interaction and mingling of the two was particularly visible in medieval times. J Spencer Trimingham, the author of the authoritative book, *The Sufi Orders in Islam*, which is considered a masterpiece in terms of analysing the Sufi expression, divides the development of the Sufi tradition into three distinctive periods.

The first period, called the 'Khanaqah' period, is considered the 'golden age of mysticism'. During this period, Sufism was intellectually and emotionally an aristocratic movement, with the Sufi practitioners, the Sufis, leading itinerant lives. They were guided by masters who encouraged and even pushed them to start and understand a personal quest to experience God directly, without having to take recourse to an intermediary. By around the 10th century, the Sufis had started to build informal lodges, where master and pupil or disciple individually pursued mystical union with God.

The second period, called the 'Tariqa' period, lasted for about 300 years, approximately between 1100 and 1400. During this period, the easy-going rituals and practices of the early Sufis started to be formalised and became clearly oriented towards devotional discourse. Further, the 'paths' and 'ways' to attaining mystical union with God also started to get defined, as opposed to the individual pursuit that had so far been the hallmark of Sufism. Fundamentally the emphasis shifted from an individual's surrender to God to a surrender to a specified and defined rule.

In the third period, which lasted till about 1800, Sufism transformed into a popular mass movement with numerous methods—ranging from free-flowing and individual communion with God to strictly laid down ritualistic practices—to achieve the ultimate union with God being advocated and practised. Although evolutionary changes took place in the practice of Sufism over the period of thousand years, the essential goal of Sufism remained the same—to achieve and know the ecstasy of direct experience and knowledge of God.

The Shari'a-based practice co-existed with Sufism, even though there were clear differences between the practitioners of the two systems, especially in the extreme fringes of each. Sufism was condemned as a departure from the true faith and the commandments of the Shari'a while the Sufis considered the Shari'a as too constraining and inhibiting to the development of a true understanding and knowledge of God.

The most famous Sufi saint and an icon of the tradition during the medieval age was al-Hallaj (lived 857-922). He was born in Tus in Iran but moved to Basra in his younger days and made his mark there as an ascetic and preacher. He was arrested in 913 for blasphemy and imprisoned, subsequently being executed in 922. The fundamental belief and emphasis in the practice of Sufism at this time was the importance of the intellect, both as a means and an aid in the perennial search to find God while also acknowledging the known inadequacies of the intellect. The early Sufis based most of their writings and preaching on the teachings of al-Hallaj. One of his famous followers, Kalabadhi, wrote the tome *The Doctrine of the Sufis*, translated by A. J. Arberry in 1935.

> The acknowledged inadequacy of the human intellect, as believed by the Sufi practitioners can be illustrated by the poem by al-Hallaj, given below:
>
> Whoso seeks God, and takes the intellect for guide,
>
> God drives him forth, in vain distraction to abide;
>
> With wild confusion He confounds his innermost heart,
>
> So that distraught, he cries, 'I know not if Thou art'.
>
> J. Arberry (Tr)
>
> *The Doctrine of the Sufis*, 1935, p. 52

Such poems and equally vague statements that could be clearly understood if one was mystically oriented and which were easily misinterpreted by the adversaries of Sufism became a tool for suppressing the Sufi movement. The catastrophic fate that befell al-Hallaj is a clear indication of the perils of mystical proclamations within a religion that prides itself to be one of law and obedience.

The Concept of Jihad

Jihad is an Arabic noun that conveys the idea of a struggle or strife. In the Quran, the term is often used as part of the phrase 'jihad fisabil Allah', meaning 'striving in the Path of God'. Most Islamic scholars hold jihad as an obligatory task for all able-bodied Muslims, with some going as far as to declare it the sixth pillar of Islam. The textual authority for the doctrine of jihad is found in the Quran and hadiths, both of which are rooted in the life of Prophet Muhammad and the practices that were recorded as having been the norm in the early Islamic community in Medina.

Jihad, explained mainly in the 9th chapter of the Quran, is elucidated both as a defensive as well as offensive concept. It constituted general defensive warfare against those who fought Muhammad, his followers and the 'right', but new, religion that he had created. The other part of jihad was offensive warfare against non-believers of all kind. A host of statements attributed to the Prophet extols the virtue and merit of the concept of jihad to conduct a war against the people opposed to the religion, who were considered enemies. This stand is understandable in the context of the time when Muhammad was at war with the Meccans after his hijra to Medina. It was after the death of the Prophet that the same statements were gathered together to form the basis of the ideology of jihad. This slightly nuanced concept was one of the main factors that facilitated the large Islamic conquest during the medieval period.

After the basic Islamic Empire was established, the caliphs continued to support an expansionist concept of jihad, with an eye to further conquest. Some of the caliphs even took part in punitive raids, that they ostensibly led, in order cement their position by demonstrating their commitment to personal jihad. Even in the early days of the Islamic conquest, the ideology of jihad had started to be corrupted for the material benefit of the ruling elite.

Once the Islamic Empire had been well-established and was not anymore in a precarious condition, scholars started to divide the world into two parts. One, Dar al-Islam, the Abode of Islam, which encompassed territories under Islamic political control or domination. The other, Dar al-Harb, the Abode of War, was all the other places that were not under Islamic jurisdiction. Since this division was accepted as correct, the borders of Islam waxed and waned over time, almost on a continuous basis. It is not surprising that throughout the Medieval Era, Islamic armies pursued their primary vocation and did what they did best—they fought wars. At all times they were undertaking jihad. The Islamic armies were engaged in jihad mostly to expand the borders of the Islamic world in Central Asia, Africa, Anatolia, Europe and India. If they were not engaged in this dedicated pursuit, Muslim armies fought other Muslim armies to impose a particular vision of Islam on other 'non-believers' practising other abhorrent versions of Islam or to implement a particular form of governance on non-adherents. In all cases jihad was a consuming activity that did not need too much impetus to be commenced.

Jihad and Civil Wars

Civil and internal wars plagued the early Islamic community, especially during the Rashidun (632-61) and Umayyad (661-750) caliphates. This was followed by the Abbasid Revolution in the late 740s, which established the Abbasid Caliphate that lasted till 1258, when the Mongols destroyed it after they sacked Baghdad.

The Almoravids (1062-1147) and the Almohads (1130-1269) the two major revivalist movements used the concept of personal jihad to set right what was then perceived as corrupt practices of essentially Muslim regimes in North Africa and Spain. They also fought the Christian monarchs in Spain within the same concept.

Considering the common use of the ideology of jihad to achieve the material ends of empire, it is not surprising that some scholars considered those engaged in jihad as soldiers of fortune and even bandits. There is some justification for this attitude, since the altruistic concept of jihad had become warped to cater for individual vanities and rampant materialism. On the contrary, the explanation and understanding of jihad amongst the followers of the mystical Sufi tradition and the more pious scholars were two-pronged. They argued that Jihad could be divided into two types. First and the greater jihad was the internal struggle within oneself against temptation and evil. This was a jihad of piety and persuasion. Second, and a relatively lesser form of jihad, was the military one. The tangible results of victory in the military jihad, the jihad by the sword, was almost immediately visible and therefore it became the more preferred jihad that was waged. Since the victory in a jihad against temptation and evil took place in the mind, it was not easily appreciated by the lay person. More importantly, this victory was not visible to anyone but the individual and therefore did not satisfy the ego-centric need of the common man. It is no wonder that military jihad predominated the medieval times, as it does the present 21st century activities of the Islamic 'armies'.

Warfare in Early Islamic History

From the time of his arrival in Medina, Muhammad was continually engaged in a number of minor, and at times unsuccessful, raids on caravans that belonged predominantly to merchants from Mecca. During the ten years that he spent in Medina, he fought a number of battles. Three military conflicts stand out in terms of their importance to the development of the new ideology and the furtherance of Muhammad towards his final position as the Prophet: the Battle of Badr in mid-March 624; the Battle of Uhud in mid-March 625; and the Battle of the Trench in late-March 627. The details of each of these battles and their aftermath is not being discussed in this chapter as they are not directly connected to the spread of Islam in the Indian context. However, in a general manner they provide an insight into the politics and the conduct of warfare in the earliest Islamic times.

Muhammad was invited to Medina to arbitrate a solution between two feuding tribes, the Aws and the Khazraj. However, the invitation and more so the acceptance of his political and religious authority was not universal at that time. The Jews of Medina, a segment of rich, noble and influential part of the population, particularly were unwilling to accept Muhammad's religious teachings and his claim to prophet-hood. As his influence and following grew within Medina, Muhammad eliminated the Jewish opposition by destroying the power and authority of the three major Jewish families/clans. He forced into physical exile two of these families because of which they forfeited their wealth and lost all influence. He executed the men and enslaved the women of the third clan, thereby getting rid of all opposition to his vision of the new religion and his own position as its Prophet.

The battles that were fought indicate the characteristics of warfare of the time. It also demonstrates the fact that the nature of war has always been political and the desired end-state is politically defined. This fact holds true for the wars and conflicts being fought even in the 21 century. The battles fought by Prophet Muhammad has been reported in detail at a much later date, the descriptions derived from the details as transmitted through the oral tradition. Therefore, it is difficult to consider these accounts as being fully authentic in terms of its content and analysis.

Military Slavery – The Mameluke Institution

In the 9th century, cavalry started to replace the infantry as the primary arm of the army. The cavalry units, mainly mounted archers of great skill, became the core group within the fighting forces. Around the same time the institution of the Mameluke was also becoming established. Initially it started as a means of recruiting and training the 'right' soldiers for the cavalry units. Mamelukes were soldiers who had been enslaved as boys and raised to the profession of arms, forming special cavalry units.

The Abbasid Caliph al-Mutasim (ruled 833-42) is credited with raising the first effective Mameluke cavalry corps, comprising mainly of Turks from Central Asia. The formation and the superior performance of this corps brought about a major change in the Abbasid military system that had been in vogue till then. It brought to a conclusive end the dominance of Arabs in the Islamic armies of the medieval era. From then onwards, ethnic minorities from the fringes of the empire—Turks, Berbers, Armenians—became the core of the Islamic army. The success of the Mameluke army was such that the Caliph al-Mutasim built a new city, Samarra, to house the new troops.

Mameluke is an Arabic word meaning 'one who is owned'. However, the term is only used to denote a particular type of military slavery that was custom-designed to produce elite forces of mounted warriors who were given a higher social status than normal soldiers. The domestic servants—slaves within an agrarian society—were referred to by the terms 'abd' and 'khadim', and held the lowest status in society. These slaves were also normally ill-treated, being the recipients of all kinds of debased abuse, similar to the manner in which slaves were treated in Southern USA before the abolition of slavery as an institution in that country in the mid-1800s.

In the medieval Islamic world being enslaved as a boy and then being raised as an elite warrior, a Mameluke, was a more uplifting than degrading experience. After the tradition had been well-established, the Mamelukes served in important positions not only in the military, but also in the broader government, gaining wealth and status in society. According to early Islamic law, only people residing in the 'Abode of War', the non-Muslims, could be enslaved. This was the reason for the Mamelukes being 'recruited' from the outer fringes of 'The Abode of Islam', the Islamic Empire, like sub-Saharan Africa, Greece and India. Clearly the preference was for Central Asian Turks, bought as boys from the thriving slave markets. The term Turk in this context had a very broad usage and indicated a person who was a pastoral nomad from the Central Asian steppes. The owners of Mamelukes, normally called ustadh, particularly nobles and others from the higher strata of society, at times looked on the more capable ones as 'sons'. It was not uncommon for a Mameluke 'son' to be declared the heir and inheritor to the owner. This was the reason for the establishment of the Mameluke dynasties that ruled in Egypt and India a few centuries later.

The Mameluke tradition endured for many centuries, evolving with the needs of the time. Although initially a well-defined institution, over a period of time it became difficult to define a Mameluke. It is clear from reports and authentic records that not all military commanders who were referred to as Mamelukes were enslaved people. Some who were never slaves, but were part of the fighting units mainly made up of Mamelukes, adopted the title to identify themselves with the elite cadre. On the other hand, even when a Mameluke was manumitted, he continued to refer to himself, and be called a Mameluke; almost as a badge of honour. The institution of Mamelukes was unique and gave rise to the so-called Slave Dynasty in medieval India. The important historical fact is that this dynasty was responsible for establishing the first viable Islamic kingdom in the Indian sub-continent. It is obvious that the term Mameluke that has been equated to 'slave' was a misnomer, if ever there was one.

Conclusion

From the very beginning of its inception as a religion, Islam was a warring concept with the ideology of jihad, personal conflict or war, being built into the meaning of worship. This duty to defend the beliefs and to offensively spread its 'goodness' was combined with the implicit belief in an eclectic combination of religious worship, day-to-day living and strict adherence to rules and laws that were laid down. The combination bound the community together as never before seen. All the binding forces were derived from the life of the Prophet and the early Islamic community that was established in Medina. Since these traditions were passed down by word of mouth for few centuries before they were written down, they were open to interpretation in the medieval era. They continue to be debated by scholars even today.

SLAVE DYNASTY

Like the nearly contemporary slave, or Mameluke, rulers of Egypt, the 'slave kings' of Delhi were anything but servile. The term simply indicates that, as one-time captives, they had once been slaves.

— John Keay,
India: A History, p. 240

The Delhi Sultanate

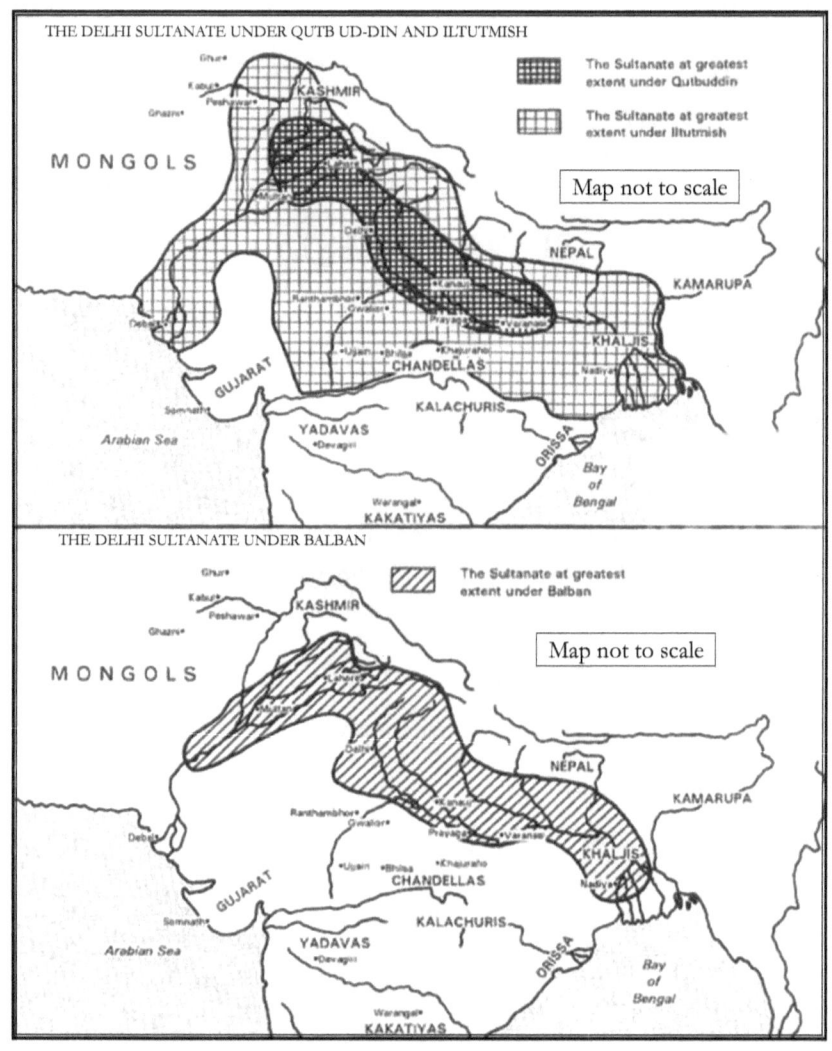

The Sultanate under Qutb ud-Din, Iltutmish and Balban

Chapter 1

THE SLAVE DYNASTY: THE BEGINNING

Introduction

Muhammad of Ghur died without siring any sons and not leaving a clearly nominated successor to the empire that he had forged. At the time of his death the Ghur domains were divided into three principalities and administered by three chief nobles who immediately declared their independence—Taj al-Din Yildiz in Ghazni, Nasir ad-Din Qabachah in Multan and Qutb ud-Din Aibak in Delhi. (Aibak has also been spelt Aybak or Eibek in different sources.) Aibak was closely related to the other two; he was married to Yildiz's daughter and Qabachah was his brother-in law, being married to his sister. However, the relationship did not stop either Yildiz or Qabachah from attempting to encroach on territories controlled by Aibak. Yildiz wanted to be named Muhammad's successor and to be declared the sultan of the entire kingdom. This led to his challenging Aibak for control of the Indian dominions. Qabachah marched on Lahore, in an unsuccessful attempt at enlarging his own territorial holdings. Aibak managed to ward of both the attempts and consolidated his control over the Indian part of the Ghur Empire.

There is a popular notion that following the invasion of Muhammad of Ghur and his lightening conquests in the north and west of the Indian sub-continent, India had become a Muslim Empire. This perception is patently incorrect and not borne out by facts. In the period between 1200 and 1550 there were only two brief spans, of 20 and 10 years respectively, when large areas of North India was under Muslim sway. During the other times in this 350 year history, there was no Turkish Muslim Empire in the sub-continent. The Delhi Sultanate is the symbol of this elusive empire that a number of historians refer to as the establishment of a broad and overarching Islamic rule in the sub-continent. In the historical narrative, the Delhi Sultanate continues for more than three centuries as the connecting bridge between successive dynasties that ruled from Delhi; their kingdoms varying in size and their control equally fluctuating and uncertain.

The battlefield victories of Muhammad of Ghur was only the beginning of the process of carving out a viable Muslim empire in the Indian sub-continent. Muhammad was a tenacious and ambitious ruler who single-mindedly pursued his objective of establishing an Indian Empire. Unlike his predecessor in the invasion of India, Mahmud of Ghazni, the Ghurid sultan was a realist and politically astute enough to understand that creating a permanent dominion in India was the best course of action to perpetuate the Ghurid kingdom. Such a move had the added advantage of permitting the Ghurids to distance themselves from the perennial instability emanating from Central Asia. However, Muhammad's death brought political uncertainty to the entire Ghurid enterprise through the certainty that Khavarazm Shah was preparing to annex the Ghur kingdom along with its Indian provinces to his own empire.

While events that would have far-reaching consequences for the sub-continent were unfolding in Afghanistan and the north-west region, the Indian rulers were content to carry on their middling ways, engrossed in petty and inconsequential internecine quarrels—oblivious to the dangers threatening to sweep them into obscurity. They were soon to be thrown into the proverbial 'dust heap of history'. It is surprising that an entire generation of Indian rulers, each of whom was endowed with uncommon bravery and chivalry, could be so devoid of broader wisdom, vision and statesmanship. The moribund nature of Indian-Hindu polity was on spectacular display during these early times of the establishment of the Delhi Sultanate.

Historical analysis proves that between 1193 and 1206, both Muhammad of Ghur and his governor/viceroy of Indian provinces, Qutb ud-Din Aibak, were insecure in the control of their territorial possessions. They had not been able to entrench themselves in their newly conquered areas. It is possible that an organised resistance to their continued presence in the Gangetic Plains could have dislodged them from North India. However, this opportunity was not taken up by any of the Indian kings. It can be speculated that had the Hindu-Rajput kings realised the long term implications of the invasion of the Turks through the Khyber Pass or analysed the unfolding events, dedicated resistance would have come about. The comprehension of the enormous consequences of the Turkish invasion was also clouded by the fact that Punjab had, for centuries, been affected by and involved in Afghan and Central Asian political developments. The kingdoms of the plains considered this invasion also to be one more convulsion from Afghanistan—the same as the earlier invasions by the Shakas, Kushans and the Huns, all of which had been absorbed by the monolith that was India and the religion of Hinduism that served it.

The invasions by the Ghaznavids and later the Ghurids has two implications for India. One, was that Punjab was conquered and thereafter remained Muslim territory, with few interludes, for the rest of history. Two, and more importantly, the repeated and ruthless nature of the conquest set up in the Indian sub-conscious and ethos a tradition of Muslim intolerance that is prevalent even today.

> 'After the early Turkish period the tradition [of Muslim intolerance] was so deeply rooted that no policy of toleration, nor the general practice of the live-and-let-live principle which was the day-to-day custom of Indian life, could eradicate it. In the popular Hindu mind a Muslim was as intolerant as a *bania* was avaricious or a Rajput brave. Perhaps the chance of the ultimate conversion of India to Islam was lost in the din of Mahmud's idol-breaking.'
>
> Percival Spear,
>
> *India: A Modern History*, pp. 103-04.

A Misnomer

Between 1206 and 1290, Delhi was ruled by three successive clans founded by Aibak, Iltutmish and Balban, jointly called in history as the Slave Dynasty. The term 'slave' is derived from the Arabic word 'Mameluke', meaning 'owned'. The term was used to distinguish important Turkish slaves who were meant for military service and is not to be confused with normal slaves meant for menial and other low level work in the master's household. The Turkish soldier 'slaves' were not servile by any stretch of imagination. They were prized as military commanders and appreciated for their loyalty. In turn, these 'slaves' used the situation to their advantage, emphasising their loyalty to the reigning monarch, who was normally the nominal owner of the slave. There was no stigma attached to an individual for his having been a Mameluke.

QUTB UD-DIN AIBAK

On the death of Muhammad of Ghur, his Indian holdings were taken over by his viceroy Qutb ud-Din Aibak who went on to lay the foundation of what came to be called in later years as the Slave Dynasty. The nomenclature of 'Slave Dynasty' for the rulers of Delhi for the next 90 years is a contradiction in terms as well as a historic inaccuracy for two reasons. First, the founders of the three clans that are clubbed together to form the Slave Dynasty were not descendants of the same ancestor, although they were related through marriage. Second, only the founders had been slaves and that too in the earlier parts of their careers. All three had ceased to be slaves long before each of them assumed the throne. However, the name coined in some early part of the retelling of history continues to be used to depict the first Muslim dynasties that ruled from Delhi.

Qutb ud-Din Aibak, and not Muhammad of Ghur, was the real founder of the Turkish dominion in India. He was a native of Turkistan, who was enslaved as a boy and sold to the qazi (magistrate/administrator) of Nishapur. He was subsequently bought by Muhammad of Ghur and rose rapidly in the king's service since he was energetic, efficient and dedicated. 'Aibak' means moon-faced, indicating beauty, although Qutb ud-Din was physically not very personable. He was initially promoted to being the commander of a section of the army and then to be the Master of the Stables, a senior military appointment. In 1192, after the Ghurid victory in the Second Battle of Tarain, Aibak was placed in charge of the Indian possessions and invested with full powers to act during the absence of Sultan Muhammad.

In 1195, Aibak led a successful campaign into Gujarat to avenge the defeat that Muhammad had suffered there earlier in his career. In recognition of this feat of arms, Qutb ud-Din was named the viceroy of India, the proclamation actually naming him 'sultan'. He established his headquarters at Indraprastha near Delhi.

Military Conquests

In 1192, he crushed rebellions in Ajmer and Meerut and then occupied Delhi, which was subsequently to become the capital of the Turkish dominion in India. In 1194, he again defeated an uprising in Ajmer and in 1195 captured Kol (Aligarh). In 1195 Aibak also played an important role in Muhammad of Ghur's defeat of Jai Chand Rathore of the Gahadawala Dynasty of Kanauj. He also had to suppress a third uprising in Ajmer, going on thereafter to capture the famous fort of Ranthambore.

In 1196, he overran Anhilwara and plundered the city, although for some inexplicable reason, the nearby Jain temples at Mount Abu was left untouched, contrary to the by now established custom of destroying temples. In 1197-98 Qutb ud-Din went on to capture Badaun, Chandawar and Kanauj. The capture of Kanauj indicates that although the Gahadawala Rathores had been defeated earlier in 1195, the kingdom had not been, or could not be, fully annexed. Aibak's military campaigns were almost fully within the Rajputana region. He went on capture the kingdom of Sirohi and parts of Malwa, although it is certain that these were not permanent annexations. In 1202-03 he invaded Bundelkhand and defeated the Chandela king Paramardi Deva. In this victory he acquired the forts of Kalinjar, Mahoba and Khajuraho and surrounding areas.

At this stage, if all the victories are charted on paper, it would be seen that the nominally Ghurid Muslim Empire in India already exceeded the territorial boundaries of the kingdom of the great Harsha Vardhana. However, most of the victories that have been listed earlier in the narrative were predatory in nature and purely temporary. Ajmer and Ranthambore changed hands several times and Gwalior and Kalinjar were lost almost immediately after they had been taken by Aibak. In some cases, the defeated rulers were reinstated as vassals but renounced their submissive allegiance on the withdrawal of the Turkish forces. In other cases, the Turkish generals left behind to control the area, of were commanders of the invading forces, disavowed their loyalty to the viceroy in Delhi and became independent chieftains. Therefore, while the list of conquests and the territories captured look impressive in their geographic spread, the actual control of the Muslim ruler was very limited and confined to areas immediately bordering his headquarters in Delhi.

The Conquest of Bihar

One of Aibak's most able generals was Muhammad bin Bakhtiyar Khilji who was bold and sagacious. There is a great deal of speculation regarding the origins of the Khilji clan, but it has been established that they were definitely of Turko-Afghan origin and that they came to India in the service of the Ghur sultans. In 1197, Muhammad Khilji forayed into Bihar, with the express permission of Qutb ud-Din, and captured the province along with enormous booty, rather easily. At this time, Bihar was the only province that still practised Buddhism as a common religion under the patronage of the Pala kings who were staunch Buddhists themselves.

The great Buddhist University of Nalanda was destroyed during this invasion. The university was situated within a walled mini-city which was mistaken for a fort and attacked by the invaders. There are reports of Buddhist monks, referred to as shaven headed Brahmins by Muslim chroniclers, being put to death in large numbers. Buddhism in Bihar was practised at this time not in the pure way of the original religion, but in the latter-day model that included idol and image worship. It is obvious that the worship practised in the Buddhist temples fired the iconoclastic zeal of the Turks and led to greater carnage than would otherwise have been the case. Irrespective of the reason for the destruction of the great university, the Muslim invasion of Bihar was a death blow to Buddhism in India. The religion never recovered in its country of origin from this debacle.

The Conquest of Bengal

Bengal was ruled by the aged king Rai Lakshmanasena of the Sena dynasty. There is still on-going debate and no agreement regarding whether the Senas were Kshatriyas or Brahmins. Irrespective of their caste, Lakshmanasena was venerated by his subjects as a learned man of high character and a patron of arts and letters. Jayadeva, the renowned author of the *Gita-Govinda* adorned his court. In 1199, moving further from Bihar Muhammad Khilji reached Nadia, the Sena capital. In a surprise attack on the palace with a very small band of horsemen, Khilji managed to take over the kingdom. The king fled towards Dacca where he died in 1205. His descendants continued to rule a small principality as petty chieftains for many years after that. Khilji ransacked and destroyed Nadia, and established Lakhnauti as the new capital.

An analysis of Muhammad Khilji's campaign in Bihar and Bengal shows that although militarily it was a phenomenal success, it was also accompanied by monumental and unprecedented destruction. The wanton obliteration of the University of Nalanda is but one example of the spread of the devastation that was visited on the region. After the uncontested subjugation of Bengal, the entire eastern Gangetic Plains came under Khilji's control. He introduced some elements of Muslim administration in the region. Although Muhammad Khilji ruled both Bihar and Bengal, he still paid nominal homage to Qutb ud-Din Aibak. Accordingly it is reported that the entire North India from Delhi to Kalinjar and Gujarat, and from Lakhnauti to Lahore was under the sway of Aibak. However, truthfully analysed, it has to be accepted that the outer areas and distant lands were neither fully subdued nor directly controlled by the ruler in Delhi.

Muhammad Bin Bakhtiyar Khilji
An Ambitious Man

Once Bengal was subdued, rather painlessly, the Khilji control ran almost the full length of the Himalayan foothills. Beyond the Himalayas lay the kingdom of Tibet and Muhammad Khilji's thirst for adventure and conquest remained unsated. He was also revelling in the unbroken chain of victories that he was able to craft in his eastward expansion. Therefore, it was only a matter of time before he launched and invasion of Tibet. He set out to conquer Tibet with 10,000 cavalry and accompanying troops.

> The expedition turned out to be an unmitigated disaster. The extreme weather and the ferocity of the local tribesmen that the army encountered combined to beat the so-far victorious army. Khilji lost most of the army and himself barely managed to escape alive and return to his headquarters.
>
> Soon after his return, Muhammad Khilji died. There are two versions of his death. One, the more magnanimous version, states that he fell ill because of the mental distress that he suffered on account of the number of soldiers that he lost and died having lost the will to live. The second, which is more probable, states that he was assassinated by another high-ranking officer, Ali Mardan, who subsequently assumed the leadership of the Khilji clan.
>
> The year was 1206.

Qutb ud-Din – The Ruler

While still an acting viceroy, Aibak had already entered into shrewd alliances with powerful commanders—his daughter had been married off to Iltutmish, his own second-in-command and an able general in his own right; his sister was married to Nasir ud-Din Qabachah; and he himself was married to the powerful Taj ud-Din Yildiz's daughter. In 1206, Muhammad of Ghur invested him with viceregal powers and bestowed the title 'Malik' on Aibek. On the death of the Ghurid sultan, the people of Lahore send an invitation to Qutb ud-Din to assume the throne and become their sovereign ruler. He proceeded to Lahore and formally accessed the throne on 24 June 1206. Almost immediately he severed all links with Ghazni.

Aibak has been depicted in contemporary reports—*Taj-ul-Masir* translated by Sir Henry Elliot—as a high spirited and open handed monarch. He was a good administrator, but in a purely military manner, dispensed even-handed justice and exerted his energies towards promoting peace and prosperity. Qutb ud-Din maintained military garrisons in all important towns across the entire domain. The local administration of the kingdom was left in the hands of the Muslim military commander of the region involved. Civilian administration does not seem to have been considered as an alternative to entrenched military rule.

Qutb ud-Din's generosity has been repeatedly praised in reports, his munificence being such that he was called 'Lakhbaksh' meaning 'the giver of Lakhs'. He was also kind to the Hindus, a fact that has been mentioned separately and also a paradox in his character since during military campaigns he was as ruthless as any of the earlier invaders in his dealings with the unbelievers. In an indirect manner this bit of information indicates a level of religious tolerance on the part of Aibak that was kept aside only when rebellions had to be subdued or kingdoms conquered with the employment of military might.

Aibak was considered a man of high character, devoted to the Islamic faith. He is also thought to have been a great warrior and a pioneer of Muslim conquest in the sub-continent. This is particularly so since the local population was known for their martial prowess and also staunch adherence to their own religion. He is reported to have possessed a refined aesthetic sense and was greatly interested in literature. He patronised men of letters, indicated by two historians Hasan Nizami and Fakhr-i-Mudabbir dedicating their works to him. He also indulged his interest in architecture by constructing two mosques from the material of destroyed temples—Quwat-ul-Islam ('Might of Islam') in Delhi and Dhai Din ka Jhonpra in Ajmer. However, Qutb ud-Din was not a proactive or revolutionary constructive genius and did not venture into the field of constructing civil institutions for the benefit of the common people.

In 1210, after being on the throne for a mere four years, Qutb ud-Din Aibak was killed in an accident while playing polo. During this four years as the crowned king he did not embark on any new conquests and also did not need to put down any major rebellions. Although he had been officially on the throne only for four years, his reign must be considered to have started in 1192, when he was placed in charge of the Indian possessions of the Ghurid kingdom and to have lasted for 18 years. The period that he formally ruled from Delhi was influenced more by foreign affairs than internal challenges that had to be addressed. In the beginning of his rule, he had to contend with the incursions of both Yildiz and Qabachah who wanted to annex at least part of the Delhi holdings. Then Aibak had to persuade Ali Mardan in the Bihar-Bengal region to accept his suzerainty through a series of threats and inducements. The major Hindu-Rajput kings and chieftains were intent on regaining their independence and waiting for a chance to throw off the Islamic yoke. Qutb ud-Din managed to subdue each of these challenges.

The biggest threat to the fledgling kingdom however, came from Central Asia. The Khwarizm Shah, Alauddin Muhammad wanted to take over Delhi. In the normal course of events Qutb ud-Din would have been hard pressed to ward of the Shah's invasion. He was lucky that the Mongol incursion diverted the attention of the Khwarizm sultan and a dedicated invasion of the kingdom of Delhi was avoided. In terms of importance, the restive Rajput issue was the least of the worries that faced the new Sultan of Delhi. Aibak's greatest achievement was his severing all ties with Ghazni, thereby creating an independent Indian identity for the kingdom that he ruled.

Qutb ud-Din Aibak can be rightly considered to have established what came to be called the 'Delhi Sultanate' that endured for 320 years from 1206 to 1526, when Babur defeated the last Sultan of Delhi and founded the mighty Mughal Dynasty. Aibak was the first of 34 kings belonging to five successive dynasties—the Slave Dynasty, the Khaljis, Tughlaks, Sayyids and Lodis—that followed.

Conclusion

There is no doubt that Aibak demolished Hindu and Jain temples by the hundreds and remodelled them to create shrines to the 'worship of the true God'. The destruction of Hindu temples was the result of a combination of entrenched piety and materialistic avarice for plunder. The consequence was that the idols, mostly made of precious metals or adorned with precious stones and jewels, were broken up for their richness and the temples dismantled for their stones, which were already dressed, to be used in all kinds of Islamic construction. Here, the difference in the perception of worship between Hinduism and Islam must be mentioned since it had a direct impact on the construction of the place of worship. The Hindu way of worship was, and continues to be, a one-on-one intimate communion with God, often facilitated by the Brahmin priest. Accordingly the Hindu temples tended to be small almost airless cells which was conducive to personalised worship. The Islamic ideal was of community worship in which all were considered equal in front of the one true God and needed large open spaces.

Three contentious topics tend to be discussed and debated even today without any clear understanding being achieved. First is the disastrous impact that the Islamic invasion had on India's Hindu heritage. The second is the amount of oppression that the Hindus were subjected to by the invading forces and subsequently the ruling elite. Third is the quality and determination of the resistance that the Hindus put up when faced with extreme oppression. In the recounting of events, there is a noticeable tendency on the part of the initial Muslim chroniclers and later-day Indian/Western historians, no doubt biased towards the Hindu viewpoint and narrative, to generalise. The establishment of a ruling Muslim elite took centuries. Therefore, there cannot be total generalisation of the behaviour of Muslim military generals or ruling sultans. Each individual must be judged on his or her own actions and merits. The impact of the Islamic invasion and the establishment of the Delhi Sultanate cannot be a generalised account of events as sometimes made out to be; no doubt there was immediate and visible impact, but the real influence took time to permeate the society. There is no doubt that it continues to do so even in contemporary India today.

Chapter 2

SHAMS UD-DIN ILTUTMISH

Qutb ud-Din Aibak's untimely death caused a great deal of confusion amongst his followers. In Lahore, the officials placed his son Aram Shah on the throne, but the courtiers in Delhi refused to accept or support the new ruler. Aram Shah was generally considered to be weak, indecisive and unfit to be a king. Since the newly minted kingdom was at a critical stage in its development, they wanted a competent soldier and tested administrator to take the reins of the state. The Delhi court invited Shams ud-Din Iltutmish (the original Turki name was Il-tutmish and the Persian spelling Altamish, which is also used in some narratives) the governor of Badaun and son-in-law of Qutb ud-Din to accept the crown. The invitation was accepted with alacrity by Iltutmish, who had anticipated this course of events.

At this stage Aibak's kingdom was effectively divided into four parts. Iltutmish being crowned in Delhi; Aram Shah ruling the western region from Lahore; Ali Mardan Khiji, the governor in Bengal declaring semi-independence and stopping to paying homage to Delhi; and Qubachah the governor of Uch, taking advantage of the internal divisions and seizing Multan while declaring his independence. Immediately on Iltutmish being crowned in Delhi, Aram Shah prepared to march against Delhi to fight and claim his inheritance. The Lahore army moved against Iltutmish after a few months. Aram Shah was defeated and put to death, his rule from Lahore lasting a mere eight months.

Early Days

Iltutmish is believed to have been born to noble parents of the Ilbari tribe in Central Asia. However, there is no conclusive proof of this noble birth. He is said to have been sold as a slave by envious brothers to a merchant in Ghazni, from whom he was purchased by Qutb ud-Din Aibak and brought to Delhi. In Aibak's service his rise to prominence was rapid. Around 1196, he was placed in charge of Gwalior Fort after it was captured and subsequently promoted to the governorship of Baran (Bulundshahr). Aibak then gave his daughter in marriage to Iltutmish and appointed him the governor of Badaun.

There are some modern historians who tend to label Iltutmish a 'usurpur', since the Delhi throne was not his by right of inheritance. This is an incorrect assessment for two reasons. First, the Islamic system of choosing a successor to the throne was based mainly on the capability and fitness of the person being elevated to the leadership role and the claim of inheritance was purely secondary. In this situation Aram Shah was understood to be relatively weak and unfit to become the king. Second, and unique to the Delhi situation, was the fact that on Aibak's death the Turkish state that he ruled was divided into four independent principalities centred on Lahore, Delhi/Badaun, Uch and Lakhnauti. Aram Shah was supported by the court in Lahore to rule over the entire kingdom, but even during Aibak's rule the seat of power had shifted to Delhi and Lahore had started to be of only secondary importance. Iltutmish was supported by the officials in Delhi and therefore had the more legitimate claim to the throne. In any case, during the battle for succession Aram Shah was defeated and killed, putting a conclusive end to the speculations regarding the legitimacy of Iltutmish's ascend to the throne.

Iltutmish, who had been freed from his slave status much earlier by Qutb ud-Din possessed great energy, was somewhat religiously oriented and was moderate in his dealings. Through the successive tenures as governor he had also established a reputation for being a competent administrator and a reliable military leader. By all rights the crown of Delhi belonged to Iltutmish; he was not a usurper and had all the qualifications to rule, a fact that he went on to prove.

On Accession...

Qutb ud-Din was officially the king only for four years. Although he is credited with having established the Delhi Sultanate, this was only in name. In reality the Sultanate was a very tenuous holding during his brief reign since there were no clearly defined borders that demarcated it. On assuming power Iltutmish controlled Delhi, Badaun and some outlying districts that ranged from Benares to the Sivalik hills. The rest of what used to be Aibak's holdings had been carved up by other governors: Qubachah had taken over Lahore on Aram Shah's defeat and Ali Mardan Khalji had declared independence in Bihar and Bengal. The Rajput rulers who had been brought under control by Qutb ud-Din rebelled, stopped paying tribute, and the principalities of Jalor, Ranthambhor, Gwalior and Ajmer declared independence. Yildiz who had been lying low for some time reasserted his claim to the throne of Lahore and sovereignty over the entire Turkish sultanate in the sub-continent from his position in Ghazni. There were minor but troublesome rebellions in Delhi by soldiers loyal to Aram Shah. There is no doubt that on his accession, Iltutmish would have found the throne of Delhi in a very precarious condition.

Iltutmish – The Pragmatist

Iltutmish immediately recognised the insecurity of his position and the uncertainty surrounding the future of the Sultanate. He was pragmatic enough to realise that he could not deal simultaneously with all the threats to the well-being of what he hoped to weld together as a viable Sultanate ruled from Delhi. The most potent threat came for Yildiz and therefore Iltutmish compromised with him first. He pretended to accept Yildiz as his overlord, indirectly supporting Yildiz's claim of sovereignty over the entire Aibak holding. At the same time he put down the soldiers' revolt around Delhi as a matter of priority through the use of force in some cases and diplomacy in others.

With the belief that Iltutmish would remain a vassal, Yildiz expelled Qubachah from Lahore and achieved control of the entire Punjab. On noticing the growing influence of Yildiz, the Khwarazm ruler, Shah Alauddin Muhammad, drove him out of Ghazni. Yildiz fled to Lahore. Iltutmish was acutely aware of the threat posed by the actions of the Khwarazm Shah and the possibility of his own sultanate returning to being the Turkish Indian dependency of the larger Islamic Sultanate ruled from Ghazni. Without wasting any time, Iltutmish marched against Yildiz in Lahore. In the battle that followed on the plains of Tarain, Yildiz was defeated and captured. He was imprisoned in Badaun where he died soon after. It is claimed that he was executed and since the cause of death so soon after capture is not known, an execution of some sort can be accepted as a definitive possibility.

This victory over Yildiz completed the severance of the Delhi Sultanate from remote Ghazni control that had been initiated by Qutb ud-Din Aibak in a tentative fashion. The Sultanate of Delhi became a sovereign state in actuality rather than remaining as an amorphous and ill-defined entity. Even though Yildiz had been defeated, external interference had not been fully put to rest. During the period of Iltutmish-Yildiz confrontations, Qubachah had encroached on Lahore, which Iltutmish had chosen to ignore at that time. In fact he had found it prudent to let Qubachah have his way to avoid having to fight a two-front war. He let Qubachah hold Lahore for two more years and annexed it to the Delhi Sultanate only in 1217. With this victory, Iltutmish finally had a defined sultanate to rule, albeit in a fledgling state.

The Mongol Menace

The Delhi Sultanate was still to settle down after the turmoil of consolidation when the Mongols led by the great Genghis Khan drove the Khwarazm Shah out of his kingdom and north-west to the Caspian Sea. The Shah's son Jalal ud-Din Mangbarni however fled south-east to the Indian region. After establishing some alliances with minor chieftains of the region, he approached Iltutmish with an appeal for shelter. At this stage, the Mongols were already at the banks of the River Indus in pursuit of Jalal ud-Din. (see volume IV The Onslaught of Islam) As an aside, there is a paradox in the Mongol behaviour: they were Shamanists, which was an altered version of Buddhism but were the most violent and ruthless warriors the Central Asian steppes had yet produced. The totally pacifist Buddhism had spawned a virulently violent religious group.

Jalal ud-Din's appeal for shelter placed Iltutmish on the horns of a dilemma. On the one hand refusal to offer shelter to a prince who had directly appealed for it was contrary to the traditional precepts of hospitality; on the other, if such shelter was provided, it was certain that the Mongols would become a direct threat to the sultanate, which was yet to find its own feet. Iltutmish decided to continue with his consciously thought through policy of detaching himself from Central Asian politics and internal squabbles. He politely refused refuge to Jalal ud-Din and also asked him to withdraw from the Punjab, which was officially part of the Delhi Sultanate by this time. Initially, Jalal ud-Din did not heed this request and encroached further into Iltutmish's Punjab province. However, he withdrew subsequently and captured Multan from Qubachah who had not yet been subdued by Iltutmish. At this time, Qubachah remained the only credible opposition to Iltutmish.

Genghis Khan, preoccupied by the pursuit of Jalal ud-Din, the Khwarazm prince who had defeated a Mongol army in the initial stages of their Afghan campaign, decided not to cross the River Indus and thereby left Delhi alone. Iltutmish's pragmatic assessment and decision, even though it went against the established traditions of hospitality, saved the new sultanate from the fury of the Mongols. If the Mongols had attacked, there is a high probability that the sultanate would have been destroyed in its infancy. It can be speculated that if this turn of events had come to pass, India as a 'nation' may have gained in terms of not becoming an Islamic state. Since the Mongols at this stage were Shamanists—closely aligned to Buddhism—and would in all likelihood have gradually merged with Hinduism, much like the earlier invaders who had succumbed to the all-enveloping embrace of the Hindu way of life. This may have avoided the cultural and religious clash that was to engulf the sub-continent for centuries, continuing ever since the establishment of the Delhi Sultanate.

Consolidation – Multan and Sindh

Jalal ud-Din left the Punjab in 1224 and the Mongols also returned to Afghanistan. The only lasting effect of this brief interlude of Central Asian politics into the sub-continent was the reduction of Qubachah's power through his defeat at the hands of Jalal ud-Din. Parts of Multan passed into the hands of the Khwarazm forces and Bhatinda and areas along the Hakara River was annexed by Iltutmish during this skirmish.

Qubachah was left with a small territorial holding restricted to some parts of Multan and Sindh.

Iltutmish recognised the opportunity of being able to finish Qubachah's rule while he was in this reduced state and planned a two-pronged attack. He arranged to recover Lahore from Qubachah's, by now nominal, control and then to send two armies—one from Lahore to attack Multan, and the other from Delhi to capture Uch—to envelope and reduce Qubachah to submission. On the arrival of these armies at his borders Qubachah fled to the Bhakkar Fort in lower Indus where he was besieged by Iltutmish after Uch had been overrun and annexed. At this stage Qubachah offered to negotiate, but Iltutmish demanded unconditional surrender and attacked Bhakkar. In an attempt to avoid capture and also to escape, Qubachah threw himself into the River Indus and was drowned. The year was 1228.

Multan and Sindh became integral parts of the Delhi Sultanate. Although Lahore was under Iltutmish, he did not control the entire Punjab, his direct control of the region being limited to Sialkot in the north. Iltutmish tasked the governors of Lahore, Multan and Uch to extend the borders of the sultanate to include the entire Punjab region. They planned and conducted a number of campaigns, but these were, at best, only partially successful. Iltutmish's ambition to control the entire Punjab remained a wishful dream, his hold and control over Western Punjab was always tenuous and never permanent.

Consolidation – Bihar and Bengal

Immediately on Aibak's death, Ali Mardan Khalji had declared his independence and started to behave as an independent ruler. However, he was barely sane, being delusional, cruel and sanguinary. After a brief period of time, his own officers revolted against his tyrannical ways and he was put to death. An officer from his entourage, Husam ud-Din Ewaz, assumed the throne as well as the title, calling himself Sultan Ghiyas ud-Din. He was an able, and perhaps more importantly, popular ruler. He brought Bihar, which had become a breakaway province, back into the fold and also started to extract tribute from the neighbouring Hindu kingdoms of Jajnagar, Tirhut, Vanga and Kamarupa.

As soon as the Mongols army withdrew and the threat to Delhi was neutralised, Iltutmish send an army to the east with the express order to bring Bengal back under the sultanate's control. In 1225, Iltutmish himself took to the field against Ghiyas ud-Din. Unable to withstand the main army of Iltutmish, Ghiyas ud-Din accepted Delhi's overlordship and agreed to pay tribute. Satisfied that the eastern regions had been brought under nominal control, Iltutmish returned to his capital. No sooner had the Delhi army moved away, Ghiyas ud-Din reneged on his agreement and reasserted his independence. Iltutmish then send his eldest and favourite son, Nasir ud-Din who was the governor of Awadh at this time, to punish Bengal. Nasir ud-Din captured the capital Lakhnauti in 1226 after defeating and killing Ghiyas ud-Din in battle. Bengal was annexed and became a province of the Delhi Sultanate. However, Nasir ud-Din died soon after under mysterious circumstances. Taking this as an opportunity, an officer Balka Khilji revolted and once again Bengal declared independence. In 1230, Iltutmish reconquered Bengal after defeating and beheading Balka Khilji. He annexed the region to the sultanate and bifurcated it into Bengal and Bihar under two separate governors to avoid concentrating too much power under one person, which invariably led to rebellion.

Campaigns in Rajputana

On Qutb ud-Din Aibak's death, the Rajputs till then held under check, also rebelled against the Turkish governors who had been appointed by him across the entire region. Most of them managed to recapture their old holdings and reinstate themselves to their old status. Prominent amongst them were the Chandelas, Pariharas and the Chauhans who regained their entire old territories and reasserted their independence.

Iltutmish was not fazed with the loss of a large part of the sultanate's territories. He was determined and fearless in the face of such adversity and had prioritised the tasks that he had to undertake after assuming the throne in Delhi. Immediately after the Mongol threat had been warded off through deft diplomacy, he turned his attention to the reconquest of Rajputana. In 1226, when his son was re-annexing Bengal to the sultanate, Iltutmish went deep into Rajasthan and besieged Ranthambhor. The fort was captured and reinvested with Turkish troops of the sultanate. He then went on to capture Mandor, the capital of the Paramaras. In 1228-29 he besieged Jalor where the Chauhan king Udai Singh fought back with great vigour. After a lengthy struggle, the Chauhan was defeated but Iltutmish reinstated him as a tributary king paying tribute to the Delhi Sultan.

In a span of about four years, Iltutmish recovered almost all the territory that had been lost in Rajputana at Aibak's death. However, the campaign was not one sweeping victorious march. He suffered setbacks, at times repeatedly in some areas, and was also defeated in some of his attempts to capture territory under other kingdoms. Iltutmish captured and plundered the fort at Kalinjar and left a holding force there. The fort was counterattacked by the Chandelas and the Turkish forces under the command of Malik Tayasai fled, leaving the fort to the Chandelas.

Iltutmish personally attacked Nagada, the capital of the Guhilots (Gehlot?). However, the Guhilot ruler Kshetra Singh defeated Iltutmish on the battlefield and drove him off with great losses to his army. Similarly Iltutmish attacked the Chalukyas of Gujarat and was comprehensively defeated. He then led a plundering raid into Malwa which met with mixed success. This raid has been characterised by some English historians, particularly Sir Woolseley Haig, as a successful conquest of Malwa. This interpretation is incorrect, the foray into Malwa was only a diversionary plundering raid and nothing more. Neither did Iltutmish accomplish any lasting result from this raid.

Overall, in Rajputana Iltutmish met with mixed results, never being able to subdue the region fully and not being able to exercise uncontested control even of areas that he had captured. Even though he conducted a number of raids and fought a large number of battles, he could not affect any permanent conquests. The large revival of Hindu power during this period made it extremely difficult for Iltutmish, already under considerable pressure from other Turkish governors, to subdue them effectively. There is no doubt that his ventures into Rajputana were inconclusive and not ever of a permanent nature.

The Reconquest of the Doab

The region that lies between the two rivers Ganga and Yamuna is referred to as the Doab. Taking advantage of the power struggle in Delhi and the preoccupation of Iltutmish with the Central Asian intrusions, many provinces, some of them small by all standards, reasserted their independence. Kanauj and Benares formed part of these provinces which went outside Turkish control. Even Badaun, Itutmish's erstwhile province, attempted to break free.

After establishing control of Delhi and stamping out the minor army revolt Iltutmish brought most of these provinces back under his control. It is obvious that there was only limited opposition to this reconquest, since there is almost no mention of these provinces or the battles to reconquer them in the broader narrative that is available. However, Awadh put up a spirited defence but was finally overcome. Nasir ud-Din, Iltutmish's son was appointed the governor. Nasir ud-Din had to wage a continuous war with the local tribes to maintain control over the principality.

It is reported that the local population of Awadh put up a stout and long opposition in order to safeguard their independence and protect their religion. They were led by a chieftain named Pirthu (named Bartu in some sources) who is said to have killed 120,000 Muslim soldiers. This figure obviously is an exaggeration but testifies to his leadership and courage, which is also established by the fact that the tribes could be conquered by the Muslim forces only after his death. The fact that the locals were attempting to protect their religion indicates that forced conversions and religious oppression had started to make in-roads into the Turkish administration.

Iltutmish fell ill while on an expedition in the Baniyan of the Punjab region against the Khokars, returned to Delhi, and died on 29 April 1236.

Iltutmish – An Assessment

Iltutmish was sultan for nearly 25 years, ruling from 1211 when he was invested in Delhi to his death in 1236. He was an accomplished individual, brave soldier and a crafty general. Like all other Indian dynasts he was more interested in power than religion.

> 'Muslim chroniclers chose to portray the occupation of Northern India as a religious offensive and to paint its principals as religious heroes; but such a view cannot stand the test of historical scrutiny.'
>
> John Keay
>
> *India: A History*, p. 242

Iltutmish was an able and successful administrator. His greatest achievement, considering that he was the slave of a slave, was to have stayed on the throne of Delhi for a quarter of a century that too during extremely volatile times. Further, whatever he achieved during his reign was through his own effort with absolutely no external support at any time. He also raised the status of the sultan above that of the nobles—till his accession, the prevalent tradition had been of the sultan being considered only the best among equals by the nobles of the court. He achieved an elevated status by introducing formalised etiquette in the court, similar to and modelled on the one followed in the great Persian court. By doing away with the easy informality that had been the norm till then, he forced the nobles to pay respect to him as the ruling king. The nobles were aware of the loss of their own status as an equal to the king and fairly rapidly formed an informal league that came to be called 'The Forty'. *[The Chihilganis, have been mentioned by the historian Barani, at times being mentioned only as 'chihil', meaning 'Forty'. There is debate whether this meant nobles who formed a 'college of forty families' or this was a group of families each of whom had command of forty ghulams along with their entourages.]* This confederation of nobles controlled all the great fiefdoms of the sultanate, as well as all high offices in the government and the army. They played a crucial role in the affairs of state in the Delhi Sultanate, effectively becoming the power behind the scenes.

Iltutmish can be credited with four major achievements—he saved the infant Turkish sultanate from destruction by thwarting different threats in a methodical manner; he laid the foundation for what was to develop into a military monarchy; he provided the necessary legal status for the kingdom by introducing its own coinage in Arabic; and he perpetuated his dynasty by ensuring that his children succeeded him to the throne.

At a personal level Iltutmish appreciated learning and supported architectural developments. He built the Qutub Minar in Delhi. The construction of this structure had been commenced by Qutb ud-Din Aibak as a victory tower, but at his death only the basement storey had been constructed. Iltutmish was a pious Muslim and it has been recorded that he was intolerant of the Shi'a sect. There is tangible evidence to prove that the Ismaili Shi'as of Delhi were put to death in large numbers after a plot to assassinate him was unearthed and the Ismaili sect was implicated. Even otherwise, he pursued a policy of religious persecution, may not have been a ruthless process but nonetheless an officially sanctioned one, of all non-Sunni people.

By being overtly Muslim, he harnessed and manipulated the power of the clerics to the service of the sultanate as required. It has been suggested that his overt religious activities were mainly intended to ensure that he had the support of the zealous clergy, although this claim cannot be proved. On the negative side, even though he has been considered an able administrator, he was not a builder of institutions. His administrative acumen was realised through supplanting the existing system through Islamising it with Muslim ways and practices, mostly at the actual governing level. The fundamental principles were left intact.

Without any doubt Iltutmish can be considered the first king/sultan of the Delhi Sultanate. As is the case repeated in history many times, a notable dynasty gets established only when a capable and determined individual takes the reins at a critical juncture in its development. Shams ud-Din Iltutmish was that person for the dynasty that came to be referred to as the Slave Dynasty in later years.

Chapter 3

THE STORY OF THE QUTB MINAR

The name Qutb Minar in Delhi is spelt in many different ways: Qutub Minar, Qutab Minar, Kutub Minar, Kutb Minar and also as one word Qutubminar. This document will use the most common one, Qutb Minar. Ancient monuments provide the researcher with reliable information regarding the early conditions of a particular country, especially in cases where written records are non-existent, are unreliable or when they have been lost in antiquity. This situation is particularly applicable to the historical context in India where the monuments unfold the facts and events as they took place in the early and medieval periods. Most monuments normally serve a specific purpose at the time of their construction. If the motivation for their erection can be clearly interpreted it provides a comprehensive insight into the incidents and episodes that influenced the flow of history. It is with this objective that the story behind the building of the Minar is being narrated.

For a number of centuries, the Qutb Minar was considered a column raised by Qutb ud-Din Aibak to commemorate the capture of Delhi from the Rajputs. However, a different story is recorded by Mabel Duffi in her acclaimed book *Chronology of India*, published in London in 1899.

Mabel Duffi's Account – Dated 1899

Mabel Duffi claims that the famous Muslim saint Qutb ud-Din Bakhtyar Kaki of Ush (Uch?) arrived in Multan during governor Qabachah's rule and then moved to Delhi while

> Iltutmish was the sultan. Iltutmish is said to have offered him the post of Shaikh ul-Islam, the senior most clergy in the land, but Bakhtiyar declined the offer. He is reported to have moved back to Baghdad and died near that city on 7 December 1235. *[This claim is contrary to the fact that the Khwaja died near Delhi.]* Duffi reports that the Minar was erected and named in his memory.

There is reference to the Minar in many histories both by Muslim historians of the time, as well as by later-day English and Western historians and archaeologists. In all these references only the name 'Qutb' associates the structure with Aibak the first Sultan to rule from Delhi. The chronicles and histories uniformly credit the construction to his son-in-law and successor to the throne, Iltutmish.

For 12 centuries before the capture of Delhi by the invading Muslim armies in 1193, Hindu, Buddhist and Jain religions had intermingled and flourished in an unquestioned manner in the sub-continent. The Buddhist emperors and kings were great tower-builders, calling them 'jaya-stambhas' or victory towers. The Jains also followed suit. The Chinese were influenced by these constructions and copied them while embellishing them with their own architectural style—essentially converting them into lofty pagodas. The Muslims, when they took over the governance of North India followed the same trend, excelling the originals in their splendour and magnificence.

The founding of Delhi, called Indraprastha in ancient times, is attributed to King Yudhistira of the Mahabharata and the city claims a fabulous antiquity of having been established before 3000 BCE. Some historians place its initial institution even before that of Jerusalem, considered one of the oldest cities in the world. This is folklore mixed with mythology with only peripheral and circumstantial evidence that cannot be authenticated with any level of assurance. The debate is on-going. From a purely factual historical perspective Delhi can be assumed to have become the capital of a viable kingdom only in the mid-11th century. Its enhanced status as a capital is attributed to the Rajput king Angapala who was also the founder of the Tomara dynasty. He built the Lalkota or Red Fort in Delhi in 1060. The European historians who in later years chronicled everything they could find in the sub-continent, particularly the monuments of North India, had a penchant for attributing all exquisite architectural testimonials and developments in science to the Muslim rule. This has resulted in the loss of understanding regarding the phenomenal achievements that was part of the Indian sub-continent much before Islam even existed as a religion. It is unfortunate that even today in the 21st century, there is still no concerted effort to put the narrative straight. There is no doubt that the period of Islamic rule in the sub-continent is of enormous importance in history, not only of the Indian sub-continent by itself but also of the world at large. However, the lack of a coherent narrative of the Hindu period does not excuse the misrepresentation of the developments that should and must be attributed to the Hindu rulers of the Indian kingdoms.

Who Built the Qutb Minar – Speculations

There is a great deal of speculation regarding the origins of the Minar and the king who ordered its construction. There is a story, still prevalent, that it was built by the great Rajput king Prithviraj Chauhan to ensure that his daughter could have an uninterrupted view of the River Yamuna from the palace. This legend, passed through the ages in the oral tradition has no reliable authentication. However, it does raise the question of the origin of the structure—was it a Hindu building that was altered, or even completed, by the Muslim conquerors; or a fully Islamic building constructed by the Sultans after the Muslim capture of Delhi. There are sufficiently vociferous advocates for each proposition.

The case for its Hindu origin is strongly advocated by Sir Sayyid Ahmad in his Urdu work *Asar-i-Sanadid*, which is a descriptive account of the archaeology of Delhi in Urdu, published as a lithograph in 1847. It was later translated by Carr Stephens and published as the *Archaeology of Delhi*. Ahmad gives four reasons for his belief that the Minar was in the beginning a Hindu structure. However, all of them are rather flimsy and can be disputed with vigour. The first reason is that there is only one 'minar' as opposed to the Islamic practice of always having two minars next to the mosques or masjids. This is not conclusive proof since early Muslims built a number of mosques with single minars, as seen in Ghazni and other places. The practice of building two minars was only established at a much later stage in the development of the religion. In his argument Ahmad obviously has not taken this fact into account. Second, the Qutb Minar is not erected at one end of the mosque that it is supposed to service, but is detached. However, there are any number of instances of minars across the Muslim world that are not congruent with the mosque they are attached to, and therefore, even this reasoning can be discarded as an invalid reason to believe the Hindu origins of the structure.

The third reason provided by Ahmad is that the entrance of the Minar faces north, which is avowedly a Hindu practice, whereas normal Muslim constructions have the entrance facing east. However, older mosques in other parts of the world are seen to face north, making one believe once again that in the early times of the development of the Islamic religion the placement of the entrance was done purely for convenience rather than in adherence to any laid down rule or an established practice. At least in the period of the construction of the Qutb Minar no laid down convention could have existed. It is also noteworthy that the entrances to Hindu temples did not always face north. The fourth reason given is that Hindu constructions always begin without any raised platform or plinth area, whereas Muslim constructions start on a raised platform. Even this assumption is wrong since a number of early mosques are seen to have been built without a plinth and many Hindu temples are built on platforms as high as 20 feet. It is seen that Ahmad's arguments claiming Hindu origins for the structure are not authentic and can be discarded.

There are two facts that were brought out clearly by Walter Ewer in a paper on the 'Inscriptions on the Qutb Minar' published in Calcutta (Kolkatta today) in 1822 that further refutes the Hindu origins of the Minar. One is that the three lower stories of the Minar are built of red sand stone whereas none of the Hindu ruins surrounding the Qutb Minar of the same antiquity use this stone. It can be assumed that the Hindu constructions were devoid of this type of material and therefore the monument could not have been built during Hindu rule. The second is that the entrance passage and the staircase of the Qutb Minar both have arched doorways. At the time when it is proposed that the building of the structure was being undertaken by the Hindus, it is clear that Hindu/Indian architects did not possess the knowledge and skill to construct arched doorways. Therefore, the Minar could not have been constructed by Hindus. Both these facts can be ascertained without any doubt. The Qutb Minar is of Muslim design and construction and is an Islamic edifice.

Who Built the Qutb Minar – Historic Sources

There are two definitive sources that can determine the origins of a monument—written chronicles and the inscriptions on the monument itself. In the case of the Minar, the contemporary records of historians are predominantly from Muslim chroniclers and the inscriptions on the structure speak for themselves. The historical chronicles available regarding the Qutb Minar are written by Muslim authors who were fundamentally chronicling the progress of the Islamic Empire. The construction of the Minar is only yet another building to be documented. The historians unabashedly praise and extol the virtues of the ruling class who were their patrons. However, a number of the chronicles also stigmatise rulers who were not considered just and condemn them as disgraceful people who were not treading God's path. Since this was the case the information regarding the Qutb Minar can be considered generally impartial judgement and trusted as correct.

There are a number of works that mention and also explain the building of the Qutb Minar, and five of them can be considered to be the major works that provide clear information. First, is the *Taj-ul-Massir*, meaning 'The Crown of Exploits' by Hasim Nizami, which is devoted almost entirely to the life and rule of Qutb ud-Din Aibak. The record covers the period 1191-1217, which is seven years after the death of Qutb ud-Din. A surprising facet of the chronicle is that although it mentions Iltutmish in certain parts there is not even one mention of Aram Shah, Qutb ud-Din's son who claimed the throne for eight months after his death. More important to this narrative is the fact that this record ascribes the great mosque of Delhi, the Jami Masjid, to Qutb ud-Din while there is no mention connecting him to the Qutb Minar.

The second record, *Tarikh–i-Jahan-Kusha*, 'History of the Conquest of the World', by Ala ud-Din Juwaini, who was known to contemporary Western scholars as Ata Malik Juwaini, brings the narrative up to the year 1257. In this book there is no mention of the great mosque or the Minar. The reason could be that the focus of the writer was more on the expansion of the physical empire and recording of the construction of monuments did not take the fancy of the chronicler. Moreover, at the time of writing the account, the great mosque would not have attained the exalted status that it did in later years to merit special mention. The third is *Tarikh-i-Alai* written by Mir Khusru and details the construction as well as repair work of older monuments undertaken by Ala ud-Din Khilji during his rule from 1295-1316. The Qutb Minar features somewhat prominently, even though in an indirect manner, in this chronicle. It states that Ala ud-Din had decided to construct a 'lofty' minaret to be a pair to the one that belonged to the Jami Masjid, obviously a reference to the Qutb Minar. It is reported that the Sultan wanted to raise his minaret so high that it could not be rivalled. However, it is equally obvious that the construction was never undertaken since no second Minar exists. By oblique reference information regarding the Islamic connection of the Qutb Minar is provided.

The fourth is a book written by Shams-i-Siraj called *Tarikh-i-Firozeshahi*, 'History of the Sultan Firoze Shah', which covers the period 1351-1388. It refers to the large pillar or minaret in the Masjid-i-Jama or the Jami Masjid in Old Delhi raised by Sultan Iltutmish. The chronicle goes on to say that it was the practice of all great kings to construct lasting memorials to his power and that the Minar was Iltutmish's construction to keep his name alive. The fifth is a minor work in terms of its length and is written by the Sultan Firoze Shah himself, titled *Fatuhat-i-Firozeshahi*, 'The Victories of Firoze Shah'. The book provides a list of buildings, edifices and monuments that were in disrepair and which he caused to be renovated. The text very clearly mentions the repair and increasing the height of a 'minara' or minaret that was raised by Muhamad of Ghazni. There is also mention of many other structures that were repaired and the name of the original builder is ascribed correctly in all instances. There is no mention of the Qutb Minar although the tomb of Qutb ud-Din Aibak is mentioned as having been repaired. In case the Minaret was built by Qutb ud-Din it is certain that this book would have mentioned it as such.

None of the contemporary literature of the time mentions Qutb ud-Din as having even started the construction of the Minaret, but almost all of them confirm him as the Sultan who built the Jami Masjid. It can therefore be conclusively assumed that the Minaret was not constructed by Sultan Qutb ud-Din Aibak. Much later in history, Babur the founder of the Mughal Empire, mentions the Minaret of Ala ud-Din Khilji in his autobiography. The reference to Khilji's minaret is obviously because of the repair work undertaken on the minaret during his reign, as proven by the chronicles of the time. The inference that can be drawn from Emperor Babur's personal writing is that as late as the 16th century, the Minaret was not commonly known as the Qutb Minar, but only as a minaret adjoining the great Jami Masjid. However, from the writings that have been discussed above it is clear that the Qutb Minar was constructed by Iltutmish.

Who Built the Qutb Minar – Inscriptions

Qutb Minar as a monument is shrouded in mystery since there is no official document of the period that mentions the sanctioning of the construction by the sultan and there are no accounts of the expenditure involved in creating this magnificent structure. However, the inscriptions on the Minar provide information from which some awareness of the background can be derived. For ease of understanding, the inscriptions that have been singled out for explanation have been numbered I to III.

Inscription I & II. Inscription I mentions the repair work carried out on the Minar in 1368 on the orders of Sultan Firoze Shah. Inscription II states that the Minar was built by Sultan Shams ud-Din Iltutmish and was subsequently repaired in 1503 by Secunder, son of Behlol, after it was damaged by a lightning strike. This is significant since it clearly attributes the ownership of construction to Iltutmish, although the inscription was probably made after the restoration was completed in 1503.

Inscription III. This inscription puts to rest all doubts regarding the sultan who had the monument constructed. It states, 'Iltutmish was the builder of the Minar' and also 'order was given for erecting this Minar during the reign of the great Sultan Iltutmish.' The name of Qutb ud-Din Aibak appears on the lower-most band of the Minar. After considerable deliberations historians have agreed that Aibak's name appears on the column as an acknowledgement by Iltutmish of the beneficence of his mentor and father-in-law. Gratitude and gratefulness impelled Iltutmish to engrave Qutb ud-Din's name on the monument that was built to celebrate his own rule.

Tracing the Origin of the Name

Since the inscriptions prove without any doubt that the Minar was built by Iltutmish and not Qutb ud-Din, the obvious question that arises is, why was it named Qutb Minar? Further it was not commonly called the Qutb Minar even in mid-16th century, when the Mughal Babur visited it. Normally the column was referred to as the Minar of Shams ud-Din. The Minar's association with the sultan Qutb ud-Din can be explained today, although confusion did prevail for some centuries regarding the person after whom it was named.

Historical records prove that Qutb ud-Din Aibak was a virtuous and just ruler, generous to a fault. His unstinting generosity had earned him the title 'Lak Baksh', meaning the giver of lakhs of rupees, even during his lifetime itself. (A lakh is equal to one hundred thousand in Indian accounting practice.) Qutb ud-Din's worth and ability as a king is uncontested and there are copious records available regarding the day-to-day administration of his court. However, there is no mention of the Minar or his association with its construction in any of the chronicles that detail his rule. It is now clear that presuming that the Minar was named after Sultan Qutb ud-Din was a genuine mistake made by European historians when they were translating the Persian chronicles. The word 'Qutb' attached to the Minar in the chronicles made them assume that it meant the sultan, without ascertaining from other sources whether another Qutb, of some stature, existed at the time of the construction or immediately after. It is now clear that at the end of the 12th and beginning of the 13th century, two Qutb ud-Dins graced the Islamic world—one a sultan and the other a saint.

> **The Sultan and the Saint**
>
> 'The first impressed the Mohmedan world by his prowess, exploits, justice and munificence as a warrior, a statesman and a ruler. The other was famous as the "principle pole of the globe of sanctity, and sun of the sphere of guidance,

that exhibiter of divine illumination and fountain of illustrious miracles". The one was a materialist, the other an occulist.'

R. N. Munshi,

The History of the Kutb Minar (Delhi), pp. 67-8.

The Life of Khwaja Qutb ud-Din Bakhtiyar

Khwaja Qutb ud-Din Bakhtiyar Kaki of Uch in Transoxiana was the son of Kamal ud-Din Musa who died when Qutb was 18 months old. As he grew to adulthood, he studied under a number of renowned saints in Baghdad and then moved to Afghanistan. He resided in Afghanistan for some time and therefore is claimed by the Afghans as their titular saint, known by the name 'the Afghan Qutb'. He then travelled to Multan during the viceregal rule of Qubachah and attended on Baha ud-Din Zakariya, a well-known and senior saint of the time. Subsequently he moved to Delhi during the reign of Iltutmish.

It is reported that on hearing of the Khwaja travelling towards Delhi, Iltutmish went outside the city to personally receive the holy man. Subsequently on the death of Delhi's Chief Imam, Islamic priest, Iltutmish offered the position to Qutb ud-Din. However, the offer was declined and Khwaja Qutb ud-Din continued his low key existence of normal teaching and austere livelihood. Abul Fazl's book *Awliya-i-Hind*, Saints of India, mentions that Shaikh Badr ud-Din and Shaikh Sharaf ud-Din, both of Panipet and themselves subsequently to become renowned saints, were disciples of Khwaja Qutb ud-Din of Uch. It is obvious that the people of Delhi held the Khwaja in very high esteem. He died on 7 December 1235 and is buried in Delhi. His tomb continues to be a place of pilgrimage even today.

It is a recorded fact that Sultan Iltutmish had great respect and reverence for ascetics and pious holy men. He was particularly respectful towards the Khwaja who graced his capital. Iltutmish named the Minar for Qutb ud-Din Uch and not for the sultan who preceded him. The tomb of the saint is close to the Qutb Minar. Since the naming of the Minar is obviously for the saint, there remains only the reason for the sultan to have constructed it to be examined. The reason for the construction could be any of the three following, or even a combination of them. First, it could be a victory pillar or 'vijay stambh' modelled on the practice of the largely defeated Hindu kings of North India. Second, it could have been built as the muezzin's tower to call the faithful to prayer at the great Jami Masjid nearby. Third, it could actually have been conceived and constructed as a memorial to Khwaja Qutb ud-Din Bakhtiyar who was held in great esteem by the sultan. This seems to be the most likely reason for its construction.

Irrespective of the reason for Iltutmish to have constructed the monument, it preserves the memory of its builder who was undoubtedly the most illustrious of the Slave Dynasty and by its name identified a sultan or a saint.

The Measurements of the Qutb Minar

As it now stands, the Minar is 238 feet and one inch in height; the base diameter is 47 feet and three inches, with the upper diameter being only nine feet. It is a tapering shaft that has been divided into five stories, ornamented at intervals by bands and balconies. Initially there were 360 steps in its circular ascending stair case with 19 more steps being added during the repairs carried out on the instructions of Feroze Shah.

Chapter 4

A QUEEN REIGNS

Qutb ud-Din Aibak and Balban (not yet part of this narrative) were actual 'ghulams' or slaves who had been manumitted earlier to their becoming ruling monarchs. The rest of the sultans who ruled Delhi and are counted as belonging to the so-called 'Slave Dynasty' were never slaves, but born as princes or princesses in the royal household. Therefore, the designations of 'slave dynasty' or 'slave king' to these rulers are misnomers. In fact, correctly the slave dynasty itself should be divided into two groups; one, the descendants of Iltutmish, who should rightly be called the Shamsids; and two, the descendants of Balban, to be called the Ghiyathids; both the names being derived from the proper names of the founders of these clans. However, for the ease of clarity and understanding, these two clans have been clubbed together under the commonly used term 'slave dynasty'. This narrative also uses the term to avoid confusion.

Iltutmish died of natural causes. This was a rare feat in those turbulent times when more often than not, the king would either be dethroned through rebellion, assassinated, or die in the battlefield defending his throne. During his last days, when he was on his deathbed, Iltutmish was urged by the courtiers to name a successor in order to avoid the horrors of a disputed succession. His preferred and designated successor, the eldest son Nasr ud-Din, had died earlier and a new heir apparent had not been appointed after his death. Iltutmish wavered in his nomination between his second son who was ineffectual and easy-going and his eldest daughter who was competent and inspirational but was obviously gender-handicapped. In the end he named his daughter Raziya as his rightful successor.

The courtiers, belonging to a totally paternalistic and male oriented society, demurred. The Sultan then told them that Raziya was the ideal person to succeed him since she was the most capable of his surviving offspring and would be able to guide the state into the future. There is no doubt that Iltutmish was very fond of his daughter and that father and daughter shared a deep and mutual admiration for each other. However, events would prove later that the Sultan's judgement was not merely an expression of sentiment and affection, but one of sound judgement. Raziya was indeed very capable and had gained a great deal of administrative experience since Iltutmish used to leave her in charge of the daily running of the government when he was away from Delhi on his many military campaigns. Above all she was very dignified and meticulous in all her dealings.

Even so, on Iltutmish's death, his wishes were ignored by the courtiers each one of whom uniformly baulked at placing a woman on the throne. They did not consider having a woman ruler to be in consonance with established Muslim law as they interpreted it. Therefore, the courtiers placed the eldest surviving son Rukn ud-Din Firoz on the throne. Firoz Shah, as he came to be known, was a lazy and indolent person devoted to sensual pleasures. He was not interested in ruling the kingdom and left it to his mother, Shah Turkan, to look after the affairs of state. Shah Turkan was a low-born handmaiden of Iltutmish and was petty, vindictive, vicious and inordinately ambitious. Firoz Shah being placed on the throne was the beginning of about 30 years of instability for the sultanate that very nearly destroyed its fundamental structure.

The lack of laid down rules and traditions of succession has been the bane of Islamic kingdoms around the world and across the ages. The confusion at the death of a ruling monarch and the in-fighting that invariably followed almost always led to internal strife. The court was unable to maintain any sort of continuity in governance, which opened the State to external interferences and internal revolts. When this situation was combined with the naked ambition of powerful nobles and governors, the political condition became ideal for unstable turbulence.

While her son the sultan succumbed to worldly pleasures, Shah Turkan unleashed a reign of terror in the palace. She went on a spree of revenge, avenging real and perceived indignities that she had suffered from other high-born wives of Iltutmish; blinded and killed a young son of Iltutmish who was considered a threat to her own son Firoz; and also hatched a plot to kill Raziya.

Firoz Shah is reported to have been endowed with one virtue before he became sultan—generosity. However, on coming to the throne he turned even this virtue into a vice through the excesses that he practised. He squandered the wealth of the sultanate. It is reliably reported that he used to ride an elephant on the streets of Delhi in a completely intoxicated state, scattering gold coins in the market place. The combination of Firoz's debauchery and his mother's ruthlessness led to revolt and rebellion. Several of the provincial governors went into open revolt. The King's brother, Ghias ud-Din, who was the governor of Awadh rebelled and started to seize the treasure caravans that were coming to Delhi from the Bengal province. He also plundered a number of cities of the sultanate that were outside his own jurisdiction. The coherence of the sultanate slowly started to unravel. At the same time Sai fud-Din Hasan Qarlugh, the ruler of Ghazni, Kirman and Bamiyan, invaded Sindh and Uch, provinces at the outer periphery of the sultanate.

The instability reached a stage when the governors of Lahore, Multan, Hansi and Badaun entered into a pact to depose Firoz Shah and started to march towards Delhi. The fact that historians of the time mention this as a 'pact' and not as a conspiracy is definitive indication that in the eyes of the people Firoz Shah had lost the legitimacy to rule the sultanate. In order to retain his position as the Sultan, Firoz Shah was left with no options and was obliged to march out of Delhi to meet the rebel forces in battle. As soon as Firoz Shah physically left the capital, Raziya took advantage of his absence and started to cleverly manipulate the public sentiment. It is reported that she appeared before the public in red robes and reminded the people that her father, the Sultan Iltutmish, had nominated her as the heir apparent before his death. She went on to incite a popular uprising against Shah Turkan. The people took over the palace and imprisoned Shah Turkan, while at the same time placing Raziya on the throne by public acclaim. Firoz Shah was arrested, imprisoned and then put to death in November 1236. His reign, or misrule, had lasted a mere seven months.

SULTAN RAZIYA

Although Raziya was installed as the ruler in Delhi and had the full support of the people in the capital, for the rest of the sultanate she was sultan only in name. She assumed the name of Raziya ud-Din and set about consolidating her position. The four provincial governors who had formed a confederacy against Firoz Shah, was now joined by the deposed wazir or prime minister, Muhammad Junaidi, and the combined force besieged Delhi. Raziya was fully aware that her military forces were not equal to the task of defeating the more powerful armies of the confederacy and therefore played a game of diplomacy. She adroitly managed to sow dissention within the five leaders of the combine and made sure that the confederacy collapsed in disorder. When she was certain of the dissonance in the enemy camp, Raziya attacked and captured two of the governors, who were promptly executed on her orders.

The other nobles in the confederacy scattered and Raziya established full control over the sultanate. The wazir Junaidi, fled the scene and died a lonely fugitive in the Sirmur hills. This decisive action that was successfully initiated brought great acclaim and prestige to Raziya. She went on to redistribute high offices to her supporters and consolidated her power. Now the entire sultanate, spreading from Lahore to Bengal was under her direct control.

From a personal point of view, she started to break free of the gender-based constraints of the harem. She regularly appeared in public without a veil, dressed in the male tunic and cap attire, and rode a horse astride like a man while also carrying weapons. Simultaneously she initiated steps to ensure that the sultan's power was absolute by placing the sultan apart from the group of elite nobles who considered the position to be the leader of equals, a trend that had been customary during both Aibak's and Iltutmish's rule. These initiatives were designed to erode the power of the elite 'Forty', formed during her grandfather's time, who had a stranglehold on the power of the sultan. The 'Forty' was the actual power behind the throne. She selected and appointed persons of ability from outside the 'Forty' to several key positions in the administration in an attempt to dilute their power. However, the 'slave system' had by this time become entrenched as a powerful entity within the administration.

Raziya was by now conducting business in open court. She also took steps to emphasise and demonstrate the firmness and vigour of her rule by personally taking part in battles and commanding armies in the field. She was aware of the need to visibly compensate for the disability attached to her sex at that time in a country that was completely male-dominated and purely military in nature and function. She was also acutely mindful of the power claimed by the Turkish nobles who were 'freedmen'. It was obvious to the astute queen that the initial backers of her claim to the throne had only wanted her as a figurehead and that all of them were taken aback by her assertive independence in ruling the sultanate. In pursuing a judiciously independent path Raziya created two separate animosities within the nobility. First, her personal practices of wearing men's clothing and appearing in public with her head and face uncovered, she offended the sensibilities of orthodox Muslim nobles who were steeped in ancient prejudices. Second, the Turkish nobles, especially the so-far all powerful group of 'Forty' could not tolerate a dominant monarch pursuing policies intended to further entrench her will as supreme, which would at the same time dilute their own power. Resentment on these counts was high in the Delhi court. These were also the ingredients that would go into concocting a real revolution against the queen.

One of Raziya's appointees from outside the members of the 'Forty' was an Abyssinian called Jalal ud-Din Yaqut. He was promoted to Amir-i-Akhur, the Master of the Stables, a position more of prestige than actual power. This appointment of a rank outsider could have been a calculated move on the part of Raziya to break the monopoly of the 'Forty'. The move was resented by the nobles; especially since an amorous relationship between the queen and Yaqut was also rumoured. There is however no evidence to prove that any personal relationship existed between the two, other than the salacious gossip of the time that have found their way into later-day chronicles.

A Queens Falls Foul of Society

Accounts of Raziya's relationship with Yaqut vary and are debated even today. Perceptions are coloured by what were the acceptable norms of the time and also the popular stories that are woven around the Queen. By all accounts, their relationship does not appear to have been 'criminal' in the physical sense. The author of the famous *Tabkat-i-Nasiri* only states, 'Yaqut, the Abyssinian, acquired favour in attendance upon the Sultan'. This is a benign statement. The greatest breech of decorum alleged against Sultan Raziya is recorded by Ferishta, a later-day author, and pertains to 'the familiarity which existed between the Abyssinian and the Queen in the fact that when she rode, she was always lifted on her horse by the Abyssinian' (quoted by Ishwari Prasad in *Medieval India* p. 146). It is stated that when Sultan Raziya mounted her horse, Yaqut would place his hands under her arms to lift and place her on the saddle.

Whatever the truth of the allegations, Raziya committed an act of unpardonable indiscretion by openly demonstrating her preference for the Abyssinian. Such conduct was bound to arouse suspicion and resentment. There can be no doubt that Sultan Raziya clearly transgressed the proper limits of the society of the time, particularly since she was an unmarried princess of the royal family. It was not that a queen was not permitted to love. It was perfectly acceptable for a queen to indulge herself with a submissive prince consort or even to revel in the darkness of the palace harem behind the curtain of at least minimal outward show of decorum. However, an open admission of preference for an individual, that too an Abyssinian, was viewed by the Turkish nobility as an intolerable act of defiance by Sultan Raziya. They would act to set things right!

The 'Forty' now felt completely left outside the Sultan's favour. This was an affront to their sense of entitlement since they had been and to a large extent continued to be the core of the military strength that had established the Muslim kingdom in the heart of North India. It was inevitable that a conspiracy would be hatched to depose Sultan Raziya and install someone who would be more pliable and amenable to their wishes in her place. Accordingly, a group of nobles, led by

A Queen Reigns

Aitigin who was the Amir-i-Hajib the Lord Chamberlain, decided to act. The other prime movers in the rebellion were Malik Altunia, the Governor of Bhatinda and Kabir Khan, the Governor of Lahore.

Kabir Khan went into open revolt first, but was almost immediately defeated by Raziya and he fled west. However, he was stopped at the River Chenab by the Mongols and was forced to return and surrender to the Queen. Raziya returned to Delhi in triumph. Almost immediately Altunia rebelled in Bhatinda. Raziya marched to suppress the rebellion, reaching Bhatinda in April 1240. However, on reaching Bhatinda, Yaqut who had accompanied her was ambushed and killed, and Raziya was isolated, captured and imprisoned. The conspirators placed Muiz ud-Din Bahram, Iltutmish's third son on the throne in Delhi. The events that played out after this could be attributed to one of two factors, or could also be a combination of the two.

First, Raziya was a consummate diplomat and played a careful hand while in captivity in Bhatinda. The second factor could be that being far away from the seat of power, Altunia was not given his fair share of territories and other treasures of victory, when the redistribution of high offices and power was done, which led to his being disaffected. Altunia was himself an ambitious man and therefore, he married Raziya and together they marched on Delhi in August 1240. The Raziya-Altunia forces from Bhatinda were soundly defeated by the Delhi forces and the couple fled from the battlefield, while their troops deserted them. It is speculated that Altunia who was not considered a great field commander was permitted by Raziya, who was a much more capable commander, to make the decisions in the battle, which led to the defeat. It is believed that she deferred to her 'husband' during the critical phases of the battle as a self-effacing Muslim lady would normally do. This was behaviour that was completely out of character for the firebrand Queen. No clear reason has been attributed to this change towards docility in Raziya. It could be that the death of Yaqut, her own imprisonment and the forced domesticity that she had to embrace on being married combined to strip her of the steadfastness and courage that had been the hallmark of her reign.

There are conflicting versions of the death of Sultan Raziya. One states that while fleeing the battlefield she was murdered by some 'Hindu' robbers for her jewellery. *[How the chronicler identified the robbers* as 'Hindu' has never been satisfactorily explained. The robbers and dacoits of the time could have been of any religious denomination. The anti-Hindu bias of Muslim chroniclers of the time is seen in such nuanced ways.] The other version is that she was captured and send to Bahram, by then ruling in Delhi, in chains where she was put to death. The date of her death has been repeatedly confirmed as 13 October 1240. Irrespective of the version that is true, this was a mundane end to a tumultuous career for the only Muslim Queen to have ruled from Delhi. Her reign lasted just three years and six days. Sultan Raziya was buried on the banks of the River Yamuna with a small tomb to mark the grave. In later days, the tomb became a place of pilgrimage as a 'place of sanctuary'.

The Confused Aftermath

Bahram Shah had arrived at a definitive understanding with the leader of the rebellion, Aitigin, before he was elevated to the throne. He assigned the highest executive powers in the sultanate to Aitigin, appointing him Naib-i-Mamlikat or the Regent of the kingdom, which was a newly created post. The nobles had believed that Bahram Shah would be a malleable figurehead. However, this was a simplistic appraisal of the man and a miscalculation. Bahram Shah was a fearless and courageous prince who disliked displays of royal splendour, but unfortunately was also schizophrenic. He was gentle and shy as well as savage and blood thirsty.

Once he was safely ensconced on the throne, his savage side came into prominence. He became brutally repressive towards the nobles, even his benefactors who had colluded to depose his sister and place him on the throne. Aitigin, now the most powerful man in the sultanate, married Bahram Shah's sister, which offended the sultan. Aitigin was executed, being murdered in his office with the knowledge of the sultan according to some accounts. Bahram felt that the Lord Chamberlain, Badr ud-Din Sunqar who was also a member of the 'Forty' was becoming far too powerful. Therefore, he colluded with the wazir, or prime minister and had Sunqar banished from Delhi to Badaun. Perhaps because of his belief that he was powerful enough to defy the Sultan, Sunqar returned to Delhi without having obtained a royal pardon. Bahram promptly arrested him and had him executed.

These tyrannical acts greatly alarmed the nobility. It was normal for certain amount of conspiracies to be rife in the court of Delhi. However, Bahram Shah, in a short span of time, converted the sultanate into a hotbed of conspiracies and counter-conspiracies. The nobles realised that the only solution to the rigmarole of the capricious behaviour of the sultan was to depose him. Soon after the execution of Sunqar, Bahram Shah himself was assassinated. Even though the nobles were almost united in initiating this action, there was a great deal of in-fighting to determine the successor after Bahram Shah was killed. Finally, a consensus candidate was agreed upon and Ala ud-Din Masud, Iltutmish's grandson and son of Firoz Shah, was placed on the throne. Before being made the Sultan, Masud had to agree to the conditions laid out by the nobles—he had to abide by the agreements that had been made with Bahram Shah, now deceased, and he had to delegate all the powers of the sultan to the representatives of the 'Forty' and to the wazir. The wazir was to be the most powerful individual in the sultanate, even more than the Sultan himself.

Masud was initially generous and good-natured but gradually changed character, becoming erratic and autocratic in his behaviour. At this stage a minor noble who was very capable emerged within the ranks of the Turkish nobility—Balban. He gradually gained power and was appointed the Lord Chamberlain, thereafter going on to appropriate more power. Masud continued his erratic but tyrannical rule and was finally deposed, being murdered in prison in June 1246. The Turkish nobles placed Iltutmish's youngest son Nasir ud-Din Mahmud on the throne.

Sultan Raziya – An Appreciation

Raziya was the only Muslim woman to have sat on the throne of Delhi. She was an extraordinary ruler—brave, energetic, a good commander and effective soldier on her own right, adept at administration, skilled in the art of diplomacy and not averse to political intrigue. These qualities in a male ruler would have made him almost invincible, but Raziya suffered the great disadvantage of gender bias. Even so, she raised the power of the crown, making it absolute. Qutb ud-Din, her grandfather was only considered chief among equals by the nobility and her own father Iltutmish was too shy even to sit on the throne in front of his peers. Raziya on the other hand dominated the politics of the Delhi sultanate from the time of her father's death by the sheer charisma and power that she spread around her through the force of her character and inherent capabilities.

The only reason for her fall was that she was born a woman. When this almost debilitating disadvantage was combined with the Turkish nobility's aversion to being ruled by a woman and their overriding ambition to keep the power of the sultan under check and within their grasp, Raziya had to fail. There was no opportunity for the course of events to have flowed any other way.

> **A Curious Coincidence**
>
> There have only been three women who have been 'elected' to the throne to rule a kingdom in the Islamic East and all three of them did so during the 13th century. First, Shajar-ad-Dur, the high spirited wife of the great Saladin's grandnephew, the woman who defeated the crusade of Louis IX and later spared the saintly hero's life, was the Queen of the Mamluks of Egypt in the 1250s. Second was Abish, the last in the princely line of Salghar, the patrons of Sa'adi, who ruled the great province of Fars for almost a quarter of a century in parallel to the time of Mongol supremacy in the region. The third was Raziya who ruled the Delhi sultanate, trying her best to prove herself a 'man' in a man's world—riding an elephant, fighting battles and showing her face in public.
>
> 'Sultan Raziya was a great monarch. She was wise, just and generous, a benefactor to her kingdom, a dispenser of justice, the protector of her subjects, and the leader of her armies. She was endowed with all the qualities befitting a king, but she was not born of the right sex, and so in the estimation of men all these virtues were worthless. (May God have mercy on her!)'
>
> Minhaju-s Siraj in *Tabakat-i-Nasiri*,
> As quoted in John Keay, *India: A History*, p.245.

Chapter 5

FROM CONFUSION TO CONSOLIDATION

The struggle between the crown and the nobles for wielding real power in the sultanate, which had started with the death of Iltutmish, became less pronounced with the installation of Nasir ud-Din Mahmud Shah on the throne. He was invited by the nobles to be the figurehead that they had been attempting to place on the throne for the past three decades, a position that he meekly accepted. The nobles had won the power struggle, at least for the time being. Mahmud Shah obediently handed over all power to Balban, by now the unquestioned leader of 'the Forty'. This was part of the tacit arrangement that had been put in place before Nasir ud-Din was permitted to be crowned as sultan. In any case, Nasir ud-Din was by nature docile and unambitious. He was also pious and god-fearing, preferring to lead a simple and uncomplicated life.

> **Nasir ud-Din Mahmud Shah's Simplicity**
>
> It is said that the queen used to personally cook all the meals for Mahmud Shah even after he became the sultan. One day she is supposed to have burned her fingers while cooking and therefore requested her husband, the sultan, to provide her with a maid to do the cooking till such times that her wounds healed and she was able to resume her work. Nasir ud-Din refused the request on the plea that he was only a trustee of the State treasury and could not use the public moneys for his own comfort.

> Without doubt this is a highly exaggerated account meant to emphasise the simple life that he led. There is irrefutable proof that the sultan had many wives and also a retinue of servants. However, this story that is recorded in the chronicles of the time should be taken as indicative of the simple and unostentatious life that the sultan preferred.

By character and temperament, Mahmud Shah was singularly unfit to rule, especially Delhi at a time when internal factionalism was at its height, and while Hindu revolts and the Mongol threat in the western borders combined to continually undermine the central power of the monarchy. Nasir ud-Din was fortunate in having as his wazir, Balban, who was efficient, strong-willed and completely loyal to the crown. In addition, Balban was also the sultan's father-in-law and therefore had a vested interest in ensuring the longevity of his reign. There are rumours, still prevalent, that Nasir ud-Din had entered into a conspiracy with Balban against his nephew Masud Shah in order to usurp the throne. Although this is not a believable story since there is no proof, it has also been reported that Mahmud Shah was not completely bereft of ambition, as one episode further into his reign was to prove. The conspiracy theory continues to be an enigma in the life story of Nasir ud-Din Mahmud Shah—neither confirmed fully, nor disproved with certainty—an otherwise uncomplicated man, nominally ruling in a complicated time.

Mahmud Shah was however, pragmatic enough to realise his own limitations and was clearly able to distinguish and differentiate between personal ambition, probability and the ground realities of possibility. This self-awareness, along with an innate introversion ensured that he was able to reign, even though it was in name only, for the period of his entire life and to die of natural causes. This was a laudatory feat that only few ruling sultans of the period managed to achieve. There is a recognisable gap of a few years towards the end of his reign, from about 1260 onwards, where the narrative of his life is not coherent. However, there is no doubt that he lived peacefully and died, by some reports prematurely, in 1265 without leaving a male heir to the throne.

Balban Arrives on Centre-Stage

Mahmud Shah's wazir Balban was originally named Baha ud-Din and was an Ilbari Turk like Iltutmish. He was the son of a khan of about 10,000 families but was captured by the Mongols in his youth and subsequently sold to Khwaja Jaman ud-Din of Basra in Baghdad. The Khwaja took Balban with him when he moved to Delhi where he was purchased by Iltutmish. Iltutmish recognised that his slave was highly capable and appointed him 'Khasah-Bardar' or personal attendant, and enrolled into the elite and famous corps of 'the Forty Slaves'. Sultan Raziya promoted him to the post of Amir-i-Shikar, Lord of the Hunt or Chief Huntsman. However, Balban's opportunistic streak was revealed when he joined the conspirators against Raziya and played a not insignificant part in deposing her. Bahram Shah, who was installed as the sultan after Raziya, repaid Balban's assistance by granting him the fiefdom of Rewari in Punjab, to which the district of Hansi was added soon after.

Balban administered his fiefdom with great care and ensured that the condition of the common people improved noticeably. In 1245, the Mongols under the leadership on Mangu, laid siege to the Uch province. The Turkish nobles in Delhi were reluctant to oppose the might of the Mongols and vacillated in taking any action. Balban rose to the occasion and raised a large army, and despite the protests of some of the nobles marched to relieve Uch. He inflicted a crushing defeat on the Mongols. The expedition was efficiently managed and was considered a brilliant success for the armies of Islam in Hind.

The De-Facto Ruler

Balban is considered to have been the leader of the group that deposed Masud Shah and placed Nasir ud-Din Mahmud Shah on the throne. In 1246, he became the principal advisor to the sultan, being appointed Naib-i-Mamlikat or the regent. Further, he got his daughter married to Mahmud Shah in 1249, thus sealing his leadership amongst the nobles. As the naib, Balban exercised full regal powers, especially since Mahmud Shah was a political nonentity in the Delhi court. He took over all the authority of the sultan, leaving the incumbent as a mere figurehead, which was in any case in accordance with the agreement between the nobles and the sultan. However, he was extremely loyal and scrupulously honest in exercising the power vested in him only for the betterment of the crown.

By the time Balban became the Principal Minister, he was already acknowledged as the leader of 'the Forty'. He went on to appoint his relatives to positions of power and authority. His brother Kashlu Khan was appointed Lord Chamberlain and a cousin, Sher Khan, was positioned as the governor of Lahore and Bhatinda. Through these and other appointments, Balban monopolised the power structure that in turn created a faction within the court who felt disenfranchised and therefore opposed his ascendancy.

Military Exploits as the Regent

After establishing his control over the court, Balban started to consolidate the power of the crown by initiating measures to put down the rebellions that were becoming endemic in the sultanate. The defeat and death of Sultan Raziya was seen as an opportunity by a number of chieftains and governors to carve out their own independent enclaves. These moves brought into direct question the veracity of the central authority wielded from Delhi. In 1246, Balban crossed the River Ravi and subdued the rebellious Khokhars and other tribes in the hills of Jud and Jillum. A more difficult task that had to be undertaken immediately was to resist the move towards independence by a number of Hindu kingdoms. Balban mounted several expeditions to the Doab to punish the Hindu rulers of the region who continued to rise up in revolt with monotonous regularity. The ebb and flow of these revolts kept the Delhi sultanate occupied in bitter fighting for lengthy periods, with no final outcome.

Balban captured the fortress at Talsandah near Kanauj and then defeated the Rana of Malaki. This was the territory between Kalinjar and Kara and the defeated Rana is identified as Trilokyavarma of the Chandela dynasty. After overcoming stubborn resistance, the Delhi forces extracted a large booty from the Chandelas and returned. The regent then attacked and subdued Mewat, the region south of Delhi, and besieged Ranthambhor. Although the fort at Ranthambhor was captured after repeated attempts had failed, it was achieved at an exorbitant cost to the Delhi army. In 1251, an expedition was mounted against the Hindu kingdom of Gwalior, which was only partially successful. Thereafter no attempt was made to establish Turkish dominance over Central India. Since no permanent annexation of territory is recorded in any of these initiatives, it must be understood that the objective of the Regent was to ensure that these kings did not interfere with the functioning of the sultanate. The expeditions were punitive in nature and meant as a show of force, rather than a conquering march. It also indicates that the Hindu kingdoms were of equal status and power as the fledgling sultanate.

The province of Bengal was the source of a great deal of trouble to Balban throughout his tenure as the Regent. At the death of Raziya, the governor of Bengal Tughan Khan, who was a de facto independent ruler, invaded and pillaged Awadh to the west of his territories. Thereafter he attacked Jajnagar in Orissa, to the south-east of the Bengal province. However, Tughan Khan was defeated by the Jajnagar king, which gave Balban an excuse to send the Delhi forces to intervene. Balban send an army under Tamur Khan to dismiss the Jajnagar forces from the sultanate territories. However, he also gave very specific and personal instructions to Tamur Khan that Tughan Khan was to be removed from his gubernatorial position. Tamur Khan repelled the Jajnagar forces and replaced Tughan Khan, who died immediately after being removed from power. *[Although no foul play has been recorded or indicated, considering the norms of the time, some sort of extra-judicial activity in the death of Tughan Khan cannot be ruled out.]*

Tamur Khan withdrew after placing Yuzhak-i-Tughril Khan as the governor of Bengal. Almost immediately Tughril Khan assumed independent rule although it was the Delhi forces who had bestowed the province to him. Before Balban could react to this rebellion, Tughril Khan was killed in a military expedition to Kamrupa (modern Assam). Balban then established a fragile control over Bengal but even this was short-lived. The new governor, Arslan Khan, declared independence after three years of rule and Balban did not have the resources to pay much attention to this rebellion. Bengal thereafter remained detached from the sultanate till the death of Mahmud Shah. Since the rebellious governors were all Turkish aristocrats, these developments clearly demonstrate the in-fighting and divisions within the Turkish aristocracy. It also shows that the sultanate had not yet developed the infrastructure or the pervasive power structure necessary to ensure that far-flung provinces remained within the command ambit of the Delhi sultan.

Like the province of Bengal, the North-Western region of the sultanate also remained restive, for three fundamental reasons. First, Saif ud-Din Hasan Qarlugh, the ruler of Bamiyan and surrounding areas was an ambitious and capable man. He was set on expanding his territorial hold into Multan and Sindh, sending out punitive expeditions repeatedly in order to test the strength, readiness and willingness of the Delhi sultanate to protect its borders. Although Qarlugh managed to occupy Multan in 1249, he was forced to abandon the province almost immediately. Second, the Mongols, although reduced in strength and capacity continued to be an influential group who exerted almost constant pressure on the western borders. By 1254, the Mongols controlled the major part of greater Punjab including Lahore, with the Delhi sultanate having claim only to the territories in the south-east. Third, local officers representing the Delhi sultanate in the North-West were all singularly anxious to carve out their own principalities and being self-serving were disloyal to Delhi. Intrigue, jealousy and treachery was endemic to the province and the court that ruled the sultanate's territory.

Kashlu Khan, the governor of Multan and Uch became a vassal of the Mongol ruler of Persia, Hulagu Khan, pledging allegiance to him rather than to Delhi and Sultan Mahmud Shah. He then entered into an alliance with Qutlugh Khan the governor of Awadh with the intent of capturing Delhi in a joint attack. However, Hulagu Khan refused to support this move and reached an agreement with Balban, both sides agreeing to accept the existing border between the two kingdoms. What could have been a major setback to the stability of the sultanate and an embarrassment to Balban was avoided through deft diplomatic manoeuvrings.

A Temporary Downfall

Balban as regent was overbearing and adopted extremely regal trappings to his 'rule'. It is therefore not difficult to understand that he had accumulated a number of enemies within the nobility. While Balban was on an expedition to Multan along with many of the nobles loyal to him, Imad ud-Din Rihan, a noble who was a Hindu convert, incited some nobles of the anti-Balban faction to revolt. He was also able to influence the mild-mannered Sultan Mahmud Shah against Balban. The weak-willed sultan had already been smarting under the overarching control of his naib, regent, and also resented the power enjoyed by Balban. In March 1253, Mahmud Shah issued orders dismissing both Balban and his brother from their official positions. Balban was further ordered to retreat to his estates in the Sewalik hills and Hansi.

Here Rihan and his co-conspirators miscalculated Balban's shrewdness and native cunning. They had hoped that on being ordered to retreat to his estates, physically removed from the actual seat of power, Balban and his brother would revolt. Such a revolt could have been reason enough to seize all their property and reduce their power base, thus destroying their influence in one fell sweep. Balban however obeyed the orders and went to live in his estates, without putting up even a token resistance or appealing to the sultan, his son-in-law, for clemency. Rihan ensured that all Balban's appointees holding key positions in the sultanate were removed and the places were filled by others more amenable to Rihan's control. Rihan appointed himself, through the good offices of the ineffectual sultan, the vakil-i-dar or keeper of the palace keys and established a completely new ministerial regime.

Rihan however had a different challenge to overcome. An unalterable fact was that he was a convert to Islam, having been a Hindu before the conversion. There is no doubt that he was as good or as bad a Muslim as any of the Turkish or Tajzik nobles in the court. He was also the acknowledged leader of the 'Hindu Muslims', the locals who had converted to Islam. The Turks were fundamentally racists and did not want to be lorded over by a renegade Hindu and were extremely reluctant to function under the tutelage of Rihan. Contemporary chroniclers of Turkish extraction have used vile epithets to describe Rihan and his 'rule'. The stand-off between Rihan and the more 'Muslim' elitist Turks resulted in the administration of the sultanate starting to fray at the edges and becoming lax. From contemporary records and the flow of events it is very clear that the Turks from outside the sub-continent were hostile not only to the Hindus but also to the local converts to their religion who were considered to be of an inferior social strata. *[The Arabs of the Middle East continue to harbour this attitude towards Muslims from the South and South-East Asian region, treating these people as inferior in all aspects of life. The author has witnessed this arrogant disdain of the Arabs for their co-religionists from Asia first-hand when he was living in Riyadh for a brief period of time.]*

The Turkish elite could not condone or tolerate a Hindu convert being at the centre of power and being the chief of the sultanate's administration. They were the epitome of extreme racism and considered Delhi their exclusive heritage. As a result of this hostile undercurrent, the sultanate degenerated into a place where lawlessness was rampant, spreading even to Delhi, the capital. The dissatisfaction spread to all provinces and the Sultan was overwhelmed with petitions to dismiss Rihan. Some records provide a contrary report, which states that Rihan was popular with the common people of the lower class. This could be attributed to the fact that the lower strata of society were predominantly local Hindu converts and therefore could have felt a natural affinity for one of 'their own'. The division between foreign Muslims and local converts through the reluctant acceptance of the converts and the inferior status granted to them is already visible at this stage. Considering that this was the early stages of the first really Islamic kingdom in the sub-continent, the veracity of the Islamic religious belief of considering everyone 'equal' has to be questioned. The meaning of the cynical statement that 'all are equal, but some are more equal that the others' is clearly demonstrated in this racist prejudice that was enshrined in the Indian context for a number of centuries by the Muslim rulers.

The provincial governors, all Turkish nobles, assembled an army and marched to Delhi to remove Rihan from power. Sultan Mahmud Shah marched out of Delhi to meet the rebel army and camped at Samana. The rebels had already placed Balban as the head of the army and when the two armies met at Tabarhind, the sultan's army retreated to Hansi in complete confusion. Considering the debacle that would follow if the two armies clashed in battle, Mahmud Shah accepted the demands of the rebel army and dismissed Rihan. He was banished initially to Badaun and subsequently to Bahraich. Balban was reinstated and returned to Delhi in triumph on 1 February 1254. His temporary eclipse from supreme power had lasted one month short of a year.

He continued to hold the position of regent till the death of Mahmud Shah. Balban reinstated all the nobles who had been dismissed by Rihan, thereby ensuring that the ascendancy of the Turkish nobility was unquestioned in the Delhi sultanate.

Balban's Achievements as the Regent

Balban was the de facto ruler of the sultanate continuously for two decades, other than for the one year when he was out of favour. His greatest achievement was that he managed to preserve its integrity by containing the flow towards disintegration after Sultan Raziya was deposed and killed. There was extreme turmoil and anxiety in the country and Balban served the crown indefatigably. In these times of rebellion, conspiracy, treachery and the ever present threat of a Mongol invasion, his loyalty to the sultan was exemplary. Balban managed to control disorder and strife and also provided a stable administration to the people.

Balban created a large and efficient army that in turn protected the borders, ruthlessly suppressed internal rebellions and preserved the territorial unity of the state. Through a clever combination of military deterrence and political astuteness he managed to keep the Mongols at bay, no easy task even in the best of times. At this stage the Delhi sultanate was going through convolutions of an identity crisis in the socio-political system. Balban also managed to control the Turkish nobles through his iron will. This achievement is normally underplayed, but must be seen as an important contribution since the prime source of all dissentions and disaffections in Delhi were these nobles. The Turkish nobles were self-serving, fiercely independent, and did not readily answer to any control being imposed. In the final analysis, it can be truly said that Balban single-handedly held the sultanate together through a period which could have seen it disintegrate and disappear.

Chapter 6

GHIYAS UD-DIN BALBAN – THE SULTAN

Nasir ud-Din Mahmud Shah died in 1266 without a male heir and it was natural for Balban to assume the role of sovereign ruler. Since he had been shouldering the responsibility for the past 20 years. In any case, at that juncture there was no one in the royal family or the entourage of nobles better suited or qualified to discharge the duties of the sultan's office. It is noteworthy enough to merit separate mention that throughout his tenure as the 'naib' or regent, Balban's loyalty to the gentle monarch whom he served was absolute, never wavering even for a moment. Since all power was vested in him, it would have been easy for Balban to usurp the throne and perhaps a lesser person would have done so. Later writers indirectly allude that Balban had Nasir ud-Din poisoned in order to assume the throne. This is an improbable story considering the single-minded devotion that he displayed towards the sultan. Further, he was the de facto ruler, and the sultan who was already fairly old, did not have any male heirs. There was no reason to poison an old and peace loving monarch. Therefore, this allegation can be discounted as fanciful thinking of later chroniclers.

Balban achieved a great deal during his twenty-year regency. However, three of them stand-out as having been pivotal for the well-being of the sultanate. First, he reorganised and consolidated the provinces of the north-west, placing them under the guidance of his able cousin Sher Khan. This was the fundamental, and perhaps the only, reason for the Mongols to have been kept at bay. The significance of this administrative reform is further emphasised by the fact that the Mongols made repeated attempts to break down this defensive barrier. Second, by enforcing calculated moves he steadily suppressed the spread of Hindu disaffection from engulfing the entire sultanate. When he assumed the regency, Hindu rebellions were endemic and cause for concern. Third, the overweening pride and self-styled elitism of the Turkish nobles invariably led to intrigue and palace revolts, as seen in the rebellion against the temporary regent Rihan. Balban was able to control the impetuosity of these nobles and channel them to becoming support for the crown rather than working against it. Even so, the Turkish nobles and their entrenched power was a source of diminishing the status of the sultan. In an indirect manner, Balban having been the regent and de facto ruler while the Sultan was sidelined, was an indication of this power play.

On the death of Nasir ud-Din Mahmud Shah, of natural causes, Balban enthroned himself and assumed the title Ghiyas ud-Din Balban. The energetic regent became implacable sultan in an overnight transformation. This succession ensured the continuity of the same rule. Balban was now free to rule the sultanate without the restraint often imposed on the regent by a saintly sultan that softened some of the severity of the regent's actions.

Even though Balban's coming to the throne was without any contest, the times were troubled and there was simmering discontent beneath the veneer of placidity. The Turkish nobles were not fully placated; the Hindu kings were continuing an almost constant wave of insurrections and rebellions; the Mongols were chaffing at the bit to invade the rich 'Hindustan'; and there was visible breakdown of law and order even on the outskirts of the capital Delhi. It is difficult to judge whether these conditions were the result of Balban being the regent, meaning that he was only the leader of equals in the eyes of the Turkish nobility and therefore could not fully enforce his writ on them; or it was a throwback to the chaos inflicted upon the sultanate in the interim rule of Rihan a few years back from which Balban had not yet stabilised the sultanate. In any case, Balban the Sultan was stern and watchful—he introduced drastic punishments and relentless measures to suppress disorder and bring in order in the sultanate.

Establishing the Crown's Supremacy

There were many challenges facing the new Sultan and Balban the pragmatist prioritised the tasks to be undertaken. He realised that restoring the prestige of the crown, beyond the position of being an equal amongst nobles, as being the highest and immediate need. It is certain that he would have been mindful of the fact that his long regency, even though efficient, would also have been the primary cause of the diluted status of the position of the sultan. Nasir ud-Din was not given any respect by the Turkish nobles, which had continually degraded the status of the crown. Even after ascending the throne Balban continued to be considered an equal by the Turkish aristocracy. Balban with his long political experience was acutely aware of the need to destroy the Turkish nobles' pretensions to power equalling that of the sultan, for the crown to become effective.

Balban's theory of the king's power and stature is eerily similar to the Western concept of the 'divine right' of kings to rule. He emphasised the sacredness of the king's person as an inviolate entity and believed that inherent despotism was the only way to extract obedience from the subjects, especially the nobles. He instinctively understood that he must place himself above the other nobles in social status and thereby stand outside and over the common circle of potential rivals. To achieve this he claimed descend from the legendary and mythical Turkish hero Afrasiyab of Turan. Further, to reinforce his exalted status, he kept himself aloof from the rest of the nobility, cultivating a dignified reserve at all times. He gave up drinking wine in company and completely stopped speaking to 'commoners'. It is said that he stopped smiling to ensure that his demeanour was not construed as being soft and easy going. So fat the Delhi court of the Slave sultans had been notoriously informal. Balban established elaborate ceremonial procedures for the conduct of business in court, modelling them on the Persian model that had also been adopted by the Seljuq sultans in Central Asia.

Prostration in front of the sultan and kissing the monarch's feet were instituted as acceptable forms of salutation to the sultan when he was in court. The new ceremonial forms and procedures were established and enforced rigidly with the Sultan readily subjecting himself to the rigours of these formalities in public. The intrinsic contribution of ceremonial dignity in establishing the prestige of the crown, or for that matter any position of power, cannot be underrated. Balban was a master showman with an intuitive knowledge of the use of form and ceremony as foundations to substance and power.

The Sultan's concept of absolute despotism as a precursor and critical to the king's inherent power could not be enforced as long as 'the Forty' remained powerful. The Turkish nobility who belonged to 'the Forty' were the leaders of the Turkish gentry and held absolute power across the entire territory of the sultanate. They were directly instrumental in reducing the position of the sultan to a mere figurehead. They shared all the offices of power between them and had also divided the country into fiefdoms between themselves, essentially placing a stranglehold over the entire sultanate. Most of 'the Forty' were Iltutmish's slaves and their descendants. Balban realised the importance of 'destroying' the power of 'the Forty' if he was going to be able to establish the 'despotism' necessary to make the sultan the actual overlord of the country. It was also necessary to curtail the Turkish nobles to ensure his own safety as well as those of his would be successors. Even though Balban had come to the throne in a somewhat de facto manner through a bloodless usurpation, he harboured ambitions of creating a lasting dynasty. Therefore, he set out to whittle down the power of 'the Forty' within the court as well as across the fiefdoms.

His first action was to institute publicly visible punishments on the members of 'the Forty' and other nobles even for very minor infringements of the Sultan's orders. There are reports of public flogging carried out on a noble who had committed the offence of beating to death a commoner; and of withdrawal of the royal decree that gave the fiefdom to a noble. Such actions were aimed at diminishing the importance of the nobles in the eyes of the common public, essentially to ensure that public shaming would lead to loss of influence. Balban's cousin, Sher Khan was at this time the governor of Bhatinda, Samana and Sunam. He was powerful, capable and ambitious, while also being a leading member of 'the Forty'. It was felt that he was perhaps one of the few people who could challenge the supremacy of the Sultan. Therefore, it is not surprising that there are rumours that Balban had Sher Khan poisoned. On the death of Sher

Khan, 'the Forty' were left with no one with the potential to assume the mantle of capable leadership and the credibility to question Balban or lead a viable rebellion. The Forty were cowed down before the relentless pressure exerted by Balban. The crown was now supreme and the power of the Sultan absolute. Balban then went on to rule the sultanate as an absolute despot. Stern, unfailing, unwavering and unbiased justice, delivered swiftly and without favour, became the hallmark of Balban's rule.

Restoring Law and Order

While he was involved in establishing the ascendancy of the crown over the Turkish nobles, Balban was also actively involved in stabilising the sultanate, starting initially with the areas around Delhi. Over a period of lax administration and preoccupation of the central government with the power struggles in Delhi, the Hindu kingdoms had practically overthrown Turkish control. They carried out a policy of continuous guerrilla warfare against the forts and garrisons established by the Delhi rulers, impeded cultivation, and interfered with and stopped the collection of taxes.

The first action that Balban instituted was to mould the army into an efficient fighting force under the command of experienced officers who were considered incorruptible and courageous. More importantly they were all personally loyal to Balban the Sultan. At this stage the Doab was in a perpetual state of rebellion. Balban knew that establishing control over the Doab was crucial to bringing stability to the rest of the country. He therefore personally led the expedition to the heart of the Doab territory—Kampil and Bhojpur—and brought these areas under his control. He established garrisons manned by Afghan soldiers along the roads and gradually subdued the entire Doab region. Later historian state that the roads of this region remained safe for the next 60 years.

The bandits from the jungles around Delhi had become audacious enough to even attack the gates of the capital towards evening and night. These bandits, called Mewatis, occupied the lands surrounding the capital and had a stranglehold on Delhi during the night. Balban had the jungles cleared and in the ensuing clash, defeated the Mewatis and put to death a large number of the miscreants. He built outposts around the capital to secure it. These were also manned by Afghan soldier-citizens who were granted lands to ensure the maintenance of the forts.

While Balban was busy in the capital and undertaking the expedition to the Doab, there was a rebellion in Rohilkhand. The governor of Badaun, under whose jurisdiction the area of rebellion fell, was unable to put it down. Balban marched to the area and defeated the rebels. What followed has been described as unimaginable carnage where 'the blood of the rebels ran down the streams' for days on end. The entire district of rebellion was ravaged, the jungles reduced, cleared and turned into agricultural land that was granted to loyal Afghan soldiers. This established long-term peace in the region.

By this time the sultanate had settled into an uneasy peace and could be considered to have become stable by the standards of the day. This was not an easy achievement and definitely not accomplished by being timid and merciful. Balban has a well-deserved reputation for being ferocious in his reprisals, burning entire districts and slaying thousands of would-be rebels. He attempted to extend similar control to the regions of Rajputana and Bundelkhand, which was only partially and temporarily successful. These regions never came under the direct control of the slave sultans.

Rebellion in Bengal

Bengal had always been an awkward thorn in the flesh for the earlier Delhi sultans and continued to be so for Balban. From the beginning of the establishment of the Delhi sultanate, control over the Bengal region had been lax, with the provincial governors always attempting to shake off the control being exerted from Delhi. This situation could be attributed to a number of reasons. First, the Bengal region was never fully subjugated and communication with Delhi was difficult and tenuous at best. This meant that the governor was, more often than not, left to his own devices to control the territory and put down the rebellions that regularly broke out. Second, there was almost continuous confusion regarding the succession of sultans in Delhi with no dynasty being able to settle into long term hereditary rule. These conditions were ideal to foster ideas of independence in even mildly ambitious governors.

Tughril Khan, originally a Turkish slave purchased by Balban, was the 15th governor of Bengal and because of their essential weakness, his authority had not been curbed by the ruling Delhi sultans. This weakness was one of the major reasons for the state of continuous rebellion in Bengal. When the Mongol threat in the north-west of the sultanate was increasing and became the preoccupation in Delhi, Tughril Khan seized the opportunity and declared independence. He may also have considered the advancing years of Balban as being more conducive to the Delhi power centre to ignore his move towards independence. One report claims that when Tughril Khan declared his independence, Balban was actually sick and laid up in bed. Both his sons were away in the north-west, countering the Mongol moves. In any case, Tughril Khan assumed the title of 'sultan' and started to rule as an independent monarch.

Balban dispatched Amin Khan—one of his old slaves, also called Abtagin, who had been a long-time governor of Awadh—to subdue Tughril Khan and bring Bengal back into the Delhi fold. Tughril Khan had by this time invaded Orissa and amassed a great deal of wealth as booty. Amin Khan was defeated in his Bengal expedition. There are allegations that he had been bribed to accept defeat, which could also mean that his army had been 'bought off' by Tughril Khan with his newfound wealth. Irrespective of the actual reasons, the fact remains that Amin Khan was defeated and meekly returned to Awadh. Balban considered the defeat an affront to his sovereignty, and in a fit of rage hanged Amin Khan, keeping his body on display over the city gates of Awadh. Balban's action created consternation amongst his nobles who felt that he had meted out an unjust and unduly harsh punishment.

Balban, always an astute politician, had a clear understanding of the difficulty in obtaining complete loyalty of the governors of far-flung provinces. However, he was also cognisant of the fact that it was necessary to establish central control over these governors periodically. He send a second army to bring Tughril Khan to heel, which was also defeated in Bengal. This shamed and enraged Balban who marched to Bengal along with his second son Bughra Khan. On the way he imposed conscription in the province of Awadh that increased the size of his army to 200,000 by the time he reached Lakhnauti, the capital of the Bengal province. Reaching Lakhnauti with such a huge army was a notable effort since the rainy season had already started and with the onset of monsoons, passage into the interior of Bengal becomes extremely difficult.

Tughril Khan had already decamped from Lakhnauti and fled to the wilds of Jajnagar. Balban went in pursuit, reaching Sonargaon near Dacca. A chance intelligence input to a scouting patrol of Balban's forces led to the discovery of Tughril Khan's hidden camp, which was promptly attacked and destroyed. Tughril Khan himself was killed and decapitated while attempting to escape. Balban's retribution in Lakhnauti was terrible even by medieval standards. All relations and accomplices of Tughril Khan were hanged on gibbets constructed on either side of the main market road. It is reported that even a beggar who had received alms from Tughril Khan earlier, was executed. Such punishment had never been inflicted as retribution by any king in India till then.

Balban continued his orgy of punishment, dealing with the soldiers who had deserted and other rebels who had assisted Tughril Khan in any way, in an equally ruthless manner. The chief Qazi, priest, of the sultanate is said to have intervened at this stage and gradually brought the Sultan's wrath under control, getting him to pardon people who had committed only minor offences. Balban placed his second son, Bughra Khan, as the governor of Bengal making him swear an oath of eternal allegiance to the Delhi sultan. Bughra Khan was an easy-going, pleasure-loving prince and had no intention of trying to strike out on his own. This assessment of his character was proven beyond doubt at a later stage in the history of the slave dynasty.

Dealing with the Mongol Menace

In the larger Punjab, only Multan and Sindh was firmly under the control of the Delhi sultanate with the rest of the territory in disarray and changing hands and control sporadically. Lahore was under Mongol influence and the sultanate was exposed to invasions in the north-west from Central Asian kingdoms. Under the overall command of Sher Khan and under the guidance of Balban, a large number of forts were built along the border and manned by able-bodied Afghan soldiers. However Sher Khan's death, or murder depending on the account to be believed, the only obstacle standing against a Mongol invasion was removed. Realising the threat, Balban divided the north-west frontier into two—placing Multan, Sindh and Lahore sector under the command of his elder son Muhammad Khan; and the Sunam and Samana sectors under his second son Bughra Khan.

The first determined attack by the Mongols across the River Sutlej was decisively defeated by a combined army of the brothers. The Mongols retreated, but returned with renewed vigour in 1285-86. At this time, Bughra Khan was in Bengal assisting his father and Muhammad Khan faced the onslaught on his own. Since the initial Mongol thrust was in the Lahore region, he marched to Dipalpur and faced the invaders. In the ensuing battle Muhammad Khan was defeated and killed. However, the resistance from the Delhi sultanate forces was such that the Mongols did not press the advantage any further. The death of Muhammad Khan was an irreparable loss for the sultanate, and became a disaster as time progressed. Muhammad Khan had been an able soldier, competent administrator and a man of refined literary tastes. Two of the greatest Indian poets writing in Persian—Amir Khusrav (also spelt Khusru) and Amir Hasan—started their careers under his generous patronage. There is no doubt that Muhammad Khan was well liked by the people. On his death he was given the title the 'Martyr Prince' to honour him in posthumous glory.

End of Balban's Reign

At the death of his favourite son and heir apparent, Balban was nearly 80 years old and in indifferent health. Muhammad's death was almost a death blow to Balban. Although he continued to conduct the business of the state without any outward show of grief during the day, it is said that at night the Sultan gave went to uncontrollable grief and wallowed in the depth of despair. Balban's health deteriorated rapidly after this loss. He summoned Bughra Khan from Bengal and offered him the crown of Delhi. Bughra Khan, who had continued to be an irresponsible prince given to pleasure and easy-living, was not interested in shouldering the troubles and tribulations of the Delhi crown. However, he was reluctant or even scared to tell his father that he shrank from the burdens and responsibilities that would come with being the Sultan. The remote province of Bengal was infinitely simpler to govern. One day he went out, ostensibly on a hunting trip, but did not come back, proceeding to Bengal to resume his easy life.

Balban had no option but to appoint Kai Khusrav, Muhammad's son, as his successor as he started to succumb to his old age related ailments. Balban died around mid-1287, just about a year after Muhammad's unfortunate death in battle. As is often the case, the authority of the king, exalted throughout his life, is also extinguished with the end of his earthly days. This was the case of Balban, who had exercised unrestrained power over the Delhi sultanate for almost 40 years. On his death, the nobles of the court, led by Fakhr ud-Din, the kotwal of Delhi (commander of the fort, or the police chief) and confidante of the sultan, placed Kaiqubad, Bughra Khan's son on the throne. This was an unfortunate choice and led to the demise of the so-called slave dynasty within a few years.

The Army and Shamsi Slaves

Balban's strength throughout his 40-year rule was the powerful army that was at his beck and call. The leadership of the army was vested in Turkish officers, the Shamsi slaves, a practice established by Qutb ud-Din Aibak. Aibak had also established the tradition of granting land to the Turkish soldiers in lieu of services rendered. The senior nobles were given fiefdoms that were nominally attached to Delhi, but functioned as small but independent entities. Iltutmish had continued this tradition. Balban must have realised during his regency period that this tradition was gradually draining national resources and also questioning the paramountcy of the sultan. However, it was only after he came to the throne that he decided to check this practice and restore central control of the country's territories.

By this time the successors of the soldiers and nobles who had been granted land and fiefdoms by Aibak and Iltutmish were controlling them as hereditary claims without having provided the obligatory soldiering services to the crown in return. They had started to believe that they 'owned' the land, while not owing anything to the sultan. Balban instituted an inquiry into land holdings across the country. He confiscated the land that belonged to the old soldiers and widows who could not provide any further service to the crown and instituted cash payments for their maintenance. At the same time he evicted able-bodied persons who were enjoying the grants that their forefathers had gained. One source mentions that on the pleading of some senior officials, Balban rescinded some of the orders and also diluted the implementation of others. This action is said to have reduced the effectiveness of the intended reform and that the system continued to be entrenched and ineffective. This report is not fully believable since throughout his reign Balban is seen to have been scrupulously unbiased in the implementation of his rulings and it is highly unlikely that he would have willingly diluted a measure that was instituted to better the financial and military standing of the crown.

The outcome of this reform was that the Shamsi slaves—all with the title Khan—lost much of their landed wealth and therefore their power and influence. However, Balban was also careful to ensure that the army remained as a powerful instrument of the state. While curtailing the power of the till then all-powerful Shamsis, he also instituted the position of minister of the army, who functioned outside the control of the finance minister. Till then the army was beholden to the finance minister for allocation of the resources necessary to maintain their operational readiness. The new minister for the army was responsible directly to the sultan and controlled all aspects of the army—from recruitment, to training and discipline, as well as for its fighting efficiency. He also controlled the independent resources placed at his disposal. From the success that Balban achieved on the battlefield, it has to be assumed that the new system worked well.

Balban – An Estimate

Balban's career was full of extremely strenuous activity and lasted a full 40 years—20 as regent and de facto ruler, and 20 as the ordained sultan of the realm—a unique feat in medieval India. Through these 40 long years, his singular aim was to consolidate and entrench the Turkish state in the Indian sub-continent, and his ambition to be the fountainhead of a lasting dynasty to rule the state. In this endeavour he succeeded through a policy of 'blood and iron', even though he was unable to achieve the ambition to establish a lasting dynasty of his own.

A factor that is often overlooked in analysing the rule of the Slave dynasty, and not brought out in most medieval Indian history, is that during the entire time of their reign no additional territory was added to the sultanate holdings. This is true from the rule of Aibak, the first sultan to Kaiqubad, the last of the dynasty. The entire time and energy of each sultan were consumed in reconquering and re-annexing territories that Muhammad of Ghur had captured and that his successors had lost to rebellion and invasion. When Balban became the sultan, he was also faced with the same dilemma, whether he should attempt fresh conquests or consolidate the territorial holdings of a crumbling sultanate. There is no doubt that he had built himself an army capable of conquest if he wanted to invade a neighbouring nation. However, the inherent pragmatism that Balban had displayed in abundance throughout his tenure as the regent came to the fore, and he opted to consolidate rather than embark on any fresh conquest.

A Hidden Factor

There is a hidden factor that prompted and underlines Balban's pragmatic decision, which is not given the prominence that it deserves in the Indian historical narrative. The reality at this stage in the rule of the Slave dynasty was that there was continuous and vigorous resistance being offered to the Muslim invaders by the Hindu rulers, both large and small. A majority of the records available regarding the events of the time is from Islamic scholars. The Hindu records that were written at the time were destroyed in the subsequent years of conquest, pillage and wanton destruction that was visited on all Hindu kingdoms. The surviving Hindu records are limited and inconclusive to determine the arguments and versions from the point of view of the local Hindu rulers.

Equally important is the fact that Indian historians of the last years of the British 'Raj' and early years of Indian independence did a singular disservice to the struggle of the medieval Hindu kings and chiefs. They did not give any importance to this life and death struggle, even in the official histories that were commissioned by the Indian government and are still taught in educational institutions. They blindly followed the Western historians who unanimously held 'Hindu' historians in disdain and favoured the accounts of contemporary Muslim chroniclers of the time as being more accurate. While the attitude of the Western historians can be condoned as a biased view and lack of understanding of the scholarship of the Hindu scribes, the prejudice of independent India's historians is unpardonable.

It is a sad fact that most 'Indian' historian's writing in English during the second half of the 20th century were unquestioningly subservient to the views already expressed by the Western historians. Perhaps this attitude was meant to gain acceptance, patronage and thereafter prestige, status and academic stature. Unfortunately the histories and narratives written in myriad of Indian languages, which were equally authentic, were not considered as being good enough to be brought out to the wider world as the account of the kings, chiefs and people who fought valiantly for their countries and their own independence. It is unfortunate that these nationalists lost the war!

The analysis of past events, especially of the medieval times, and the attempt to bring out a more unbiased viewpoint is a very recent phenomenon in the Indian context. This has been the endemic challenge of the 'Indian (Hindu)' professional—the twin struggle, one for acceptance and the other to overcome the generational attitude of subservience to Western 'requirements' to achieve this acceptance.

Balban understood the significance of pomp and ceremony and that people were invariably impressed by a display of magnificence. He established an aloof stance with nobody being permitted to become familiar with the sultan and did not condone any sort of levity in the court, he himself being serious at all times. He had a high sensitiveness to preserving the dignity of the office and it is said that he completely stopped smiling on becoming the sultan. Balban, was born into a chief's house, but had risen in position in the Delhi sultanate after having arrived as a slave. Under these circumstances, it is surprising that he never appointed anyone of 'low-birth' to public office.

> 'Balban, the slave, water-carrier, huntsman, general, statesman, and sultan is one of the most striking figures among many notable men in the long line of kings of Delhi.'
>
> Stanley Lane-Poole,
>
> *Medieval India under Mohammadan Rule (AD 712 – 1764)*, p. 68

Even when he was totally serious in the conduct of the court and the ruling of the sultanate, in private life he is reported to have been affectionate and tender-hearted, kind to his subjects in distress. He also gave shelter to a large number of refugees from Central Asia fleeing the onslaught of the Mongols. However, this could also have been based on the need and an ulterior motive to increase the numbers of the Turkish aristocracy in a hostile land. On the other hand Balban was extremely cruel to anyone who even attempted to resist his will or tried to disturb the peace of the realm. He rewarded and favoured only people who demonstrated implicit and personal obedience and loyalty to him.

Balban was a religious fanatic, intolerant of all other faiths other than Sunni Islam. He was devoid of sympathy for the followers of any non-Sunni faith. Further, he believed totally on the racial superiority of the Turks over all others, especially the local people of Hindustan even if they had converted to Islam. Non-Turks were never employed in any position of significance in the administration. In any case he never trusted the Hindus and his attitude towards them was one of unadulterated bigotry.

> 'Fersihta says:- Balban made it a rule never to place any Hindu in a position of trust and responsibility. But the Palam inscriptions [in Sanskrit] which is obviously composed by a Hindu bestows high praise on the Sultan. This cannot

> be taken as conclusive evidence of the Sultan's generous treatment of the Hindus in general, for literary hirelings can always be easily procured to write such laudatory verses for a small remuneration.'
>
> Ishwari Prasad,
> *History of Medieval India: From 647 A.D. to the Mughal Conquest*, p. 172.

Balban spend his entire life in making the dominion safe, especially from the incursions of the Mongols, and can be credited with laying the actual foundation of the Islamic empire that flourished at a later date in the India sub-continent. He was also a patron of learning in a somewhat parochial manner, and his court became the centre of Islamic culture. This was reinforced by Balban giving shelter to a number of learned men fleeing Mongol persecution in Central Asia.

On a final assessment, it is seen that Balban did not create any new institutions and neither did he attempt to alter the working of the established administrative machinery. He concentrated his considerable energies in ensuring that the administration worked more smoothly and that the state functioned efficiently. However, because of the perceived need to establish the 'right' of the sultan to rule he kept away from the common touch and could not appreciate the need and viewpoint of the common people. Consequently he never won their goodwill, irrespective of the much needed stability that he provided to the sultanate.

Chapter 7

THE SLAVE DYNASTY: AN APPRAISAL

Balban's death created a power void in Delhi with no credible successor to fill the large shoes that he left behind. Balban had been an efficient and effective regent and then a monarch for a total of 40 years. In medieval politics, a powerful individual personality and force of character were extremely important traits for a ruler. Success and failure of the king depended almost entirely on these two individual attributes. When a colossus such as Balban dies, especially without a capable successor, the confidence in the dynasty and its ability to rule is shaken. It is necessary for the successor to establish continuity and effectiveness at the earliest in order to ensure that challenges to the throne does not start to coalesce and become troublesome. Unfortunately for the Slave dynasty, at this juncture there was no one to assume the mantle of a powerful sultan. The state rapidly descended into confusion.

The Fall of the Slave Sultans

As mentioned in the previous chapter, Balban had nominated his favourite son Muhammad's son Kai Khusrav as his successor. However, on Balban's death, the Delhi nobles led by Fakr ud-Din, the kotwal (commander of the fort and police chief) and friend of the sultan, set aside his wishes. They placed 17-year old Kaiqubad, Bughra Khan's son, on the throne. He assumed the title of Muiz ud-Din Kaiqubad on being anointed sultan. Kaiqubad started his reign with a distinct disadvantage. He had been raised by his grandfather in a strict and puritanical manner, not even being permitted to glance at a damsel and completely protected from any kind of vice. With the restraining arms of his grandfather now having been removed and more importantly being made aware of the power that he wielded as the sultan and the wealth that was at his disposal, Kaiqubad felt free to indulge himself in any and all kinds of pleasures that life had to offer. That is precisely what he commenced to do.

As the sultan he started to enjoy the pleasures of life—the proverbial wine, women and song—in an unrestrained manner. Worldly pleasures that he had so far been denied became his consuming passion and in a short period of time he not only became pleasure-loving in the extreme, but dissipated into becoming a complete debaucher. The nobles of the court, ever willing to corrupt the king, followed the sultan's example. The strict and solemn court of Balban resounded to revelry and merriment of all sorts. Obviously the administration of the realm was neglected and rapidly started to show signs of fraying.

The real reason for Fakr ud-Din to have placed Kaiqubad on the throne became apparent very soon—his crafty son-in-law, Nizam ud-Din fairly rapidly inveigled himself into the sultan's favour and became the real power behind the throne. Kaiqubad became a mere puppet in the hands of these two unscrupulous men. Nizam ud-Din was a person of limited capability but harboured ambitions beyond that, which made him arrogant, scheming and ruthless. He was hated by the older nobles who had worked very hard to establish the sultanate in Delhi. With the ultimate aim of usurping the throne for himself, Nizam ud-Din committed a series of atrocities.

Through a web of intricate intrigue, Nizam ud-Din obtained assent from the sultan to murder Kai Khusrav, who would otherwise have become a threat to his own kingly ambitions. Nizam ud-Din had Kai Khusrav recalled from Multan, where he was the provincial governor, and had him murdered in Rohtak while he was making his way to Delhi. Nizam ud-Din also had a number of other nobles, whom he perceived as being a threat to his progress, murdered after getting their death warrants signed by the sultan while insensate with drink. The nobles were angry at such manipulations but could not raise a rebellion in the face of the combined stranglehold that Nizam ud-din and his father in-law Fakr ud-Din had over the court.

While the Delhi court was being misruled by the father- and son-in-law combine, a clan of Khilji (also spelt in some texts as Khalji) warriors was gradually gaining power. The Khiljis were hostile to the Turks because of the elitist manner in which the Turks held on to power. An ancestor of the clan had conquered the Bengal region early in the 12th century and many other members had served in different parts of the sultanate in leadership positions. Therefore, the clan was able to form a powerful lobby under the leadership of Jalal ud-Din Firuz Khilji, who was accepted as the head of the clan. Nizam ud-Din was aware of the danger of the rise of the Khiljis and tried, unsuccessfully, to get rid of them and to whittle down their growing influence and power. He considered them, correctly as it turned out, as a direct impediment to his own ambitions of becoming the sultan. In the fledgling Delhi sultanate, yet another civil war was in the making.

Bughra Khan, ruling at leisure in Bengal, came to know of these developments and marched towards Delhi with a powerful army. There are conflicting reports of his intention, with one group maintaining that he intended to seize the throne of Delhi and the other stating that he only intended to advise and assist his son. Considering the reluctance that Bughra Khan had displayed earlier when offered the throne by his father, the second opinion seems to be the more likely version—he wanted to advise his son to mend his ways and give up the pleasure-loving life, which was a sure path to ruin, and to rule the kingdom wisely.

In 1288, Bughra Khan and his army reached Ghaghra, near Ayodhya, on the banks of the River Sarayu. Although Kaiqubad was reluctant to take to the field, he was cajoled by Nizam ud-Din to march out with an impressive army to face his father. Nizam ud-Din wanted son and father to fight each other so that it would become easier for him to usurp the throne on either one being killed in battle. However, fate in the guise of some of the older and loyal nobles intervened, and they were able to bring about a reconciliation between Bughra Khan and his even more profligate son. Kaiqubad accepted his father's advice and gave up his indulgent life, turning instead to becoming a model sultan leading a 'good' life. It is reported that Bughra Khan then returned to Bengal, without being convinced that his son's change of attitude would last long and that he would transform into an effective ruler.

> 'Would the father's advice be heeded by the son? Bughra Khan was sceptical. Returning to his camp he commented: "I have said farewell to my son and to the kingdom of Delhi, for I know full well that neither my son nor the throne of Delhi will long exist.'
>
> Abraham Eraly,
>
> *The Age of Wrath*, p. 91

True to his father's concern, Kaiqubad reformed for a short period of time, but was eventually led back into his original corrupted lifestyle by self-serving nobles. The narrative splits into two contradictory parts from here for a brief period of time. The first states that while he was in the process of reforming, Kaiqubad had Nizam ud-Din transferred to Multan and then poisoned him. Jalal ud-Din Khilji was then appointed the commander of the army. The second narrative, which is the more probable goes like this: Kaiqubad became paralysed because of excessive indulgence and nobles still loyal to Balban and the dynasty placed his infant son on the throne with the title Shams ud-Din Kayumars. Since the Khilji power was becoming overwhelming by this time, they also declared Jalal ud-Din and his entire clan traitors.

The narrative comes together again at this stage. On being declared traitors, Jalal ud-Din's sons stormed the palace, carried away the infant sultan, and went on to capture the whole of Delhi. The paralysed Kaiqubad is said to have been kicked to death by a Khilji noble whose father had been murdered on the sultan's orders. His corpse was thrown into the River Yamuna, bringing a sordid end to a sordid life. Jalal ud-Din acted as the regent for the infant sultan for a transitional period of time. Thereafter, the infant was presumable put to death, since there is no further mention of him, and Jalal ud-Din ascended the throne in March 1290. The Slave dynasty came to an inglorious end.

Territorial Integrity

In terms of territory, the Turkish kingdom established by Muhammad of Ghur remained static throughout the reign of the Slave sultans. If anything, it contracted geographically through losses suffered in rebellions. Further, the integrity of the territorial holdings were also in question almost through the entire time, with the Hindu kings mounting repeated attacks and taking back parts of the annexed territories. Year after year, sultan after sultan had to undertake numerous expeditions to put down the uprisings of independence that broke out routinely across all parts of the conquered territories. Therefore, it is not surprising that the boundary of the Delhi sultanate fluctuated, at times fairly wildly, from reign to reign dependent on a number of factors—the main one being the stability and strength of the central rule to enforce its will on outlying areas.

In a very broad manner, the territorial boundaries were: in the north, the Himalayan foothills called the Tarai; a zig-zagging line, passing through North Bengal, Bihar, Bundelkhand, Gwalior, Ajmer and north of Gujarat in the south, which moved up and down almost every year; in the east the control was limited to about half of Bengal and the border was nowhere near Dacca, although Balban did reach close to that city in his pursuit of the rebel Tughril Khan; and in the north-west, the River Jhelum, although the border shrank at times to the River Beas. Most of the time the Delhi sultans were able to exercise only tenuous control over Lahore, Multan and Sindh. There is no doubt that Jammu and Kashmir was always outside the Slave dynasty's control. Even within this established territory, many Hindu kings, especially within the Doab and parts of Rajasthan, were independent rulers or at best recalcitrant vassals. It is clear that the Slave sultans did not enjoy absolute sovereignty over the territories that they had inherited at some stage and claimed as their sultanate. The sultanate could at best be described as somewhat weakly held and only beginning to gain an integral identity of its own.

The Nature of the State

The Slave sultanate was the first established Turkish/Muslim state in the Indian sub-continent, and like all other Islamic states of the time, was a theocracy. Its functioning was completely based on Islamic Law, laid down as per the Holy Quran and expounded and/or interpreted by the jurists who had created the Sharia or the Law. The criminal and civil laws were not delineated as separate entities. Islam was the declared state religion and, in theory, the entire resources of the state was available for the propagation of the religion and other religious propaganda purposes. However, in practice this was adapted to suit different contexts and political conditions, according to the felt and perceived needs of the ruler and the clergy.

According to strict Islamic theory, God is the real king of a Muslim state. The legitimacy of the earthly ruler, the sultan, is based on being elected by the 'millat'—an electorate consisting of all male Muslims in the country. However, this process was found to be impractical even in Arabia, the fountainhead of Islam. In any case, the Turks who came to India were not the original followers of the religion and did not follow any fixed law or protocol for succession—a fact amply demonstrated by the history of the Slave dynasty. The choice of the sultan was normally confined to the surviving members of the family of the deceased ruler. In the case of a powerful noble usurping the throne, he ensured that no male family member of the previous sultan's family survived in order to avoid internecine wars in the future. In practice, it is seen that succession was based on birth, ability, nomination by the dead king and, most importantly, the support of the court nobles. The determining factors for a person to be able to ascend the throne were always decidedly practical.

The Delhi sultanate, especially in its infancy at the time of the Slave dynasty, was a military state dependent on military force to rule as opposed to ruling by consent. Obviously this was the case of most conquered states, at least in the initial period of the new rule. The physical territories were held by Turkish nobles and troops. Since the Slave sultanate was a foreign government with no cultural or religious commonality to the conquered people, the ruling elite did not connect temporally, even remotely, with the land. The Turkish nobles discharged only two responsibilities—the collection of revenue and the maintenance of law and order. Social welfare of the people was never considered as a matter of concern for the state.

Within the sultanate, the ruling Turkish elite followed the standard Muslim practice applied to all conquered lands—they offered the local population three alternatives, conversion to Islam; death; or life as a degraded subject paying a separate tax called 'jizziya' with almost no rights as citizens. Only Muslims, mainly of Turkish origin, were considered full-fledged citizens. In the Indian sub-continent, the vast majority of the population who were Hindus, elected to pay the jizzya and accepted the concerted discrimination that was heaped on them as non-Muslims. They were being denied citizenship of the place where they had lived for generations. The worst offenders in perpetuating religious bigotry were the ulema, the so-called 'learned divines', who were particularly vicious in their hostile attitude towards non-Muslims of all denomination. There were also regular attempts by rulers, particularly the zealously religious ones, to systematically erase the concept of idolatry, meaning Hindu practices. These efforts were egged on by the ulema. However, these attempts were only a religious façade meant to provide a cover for plundering and looting the rich Hindu temples.

Modern Muslim writers (such as Dr I H Qureshi, Dr Mahdi Husain etc.,) have attempted to prove that no persecution of Hindus took place during the establishment of the Delhi sultanate or even during later Muslim rule. Some of these historians have gone to the extent of stating that the Hindus were happier under Muslim rule than they were under earlier Hindu kings. Nothing could be further from the truth and these writings have to be discounted as attempts to sweep away the atrocities that were committed in the name of religion and direct efforts to gradually re-write history. The glorification of Muslim rulers of the medieval period as religiously tolerant and benign rulers is not supported by any shard of evidence and is based on unconvincing arguments. This aberration in recounting the history of India, that is still being perpetuated, is not being debated or discussed any further in this chapter. The fact remains that the early Turkish sultans attempted forced conversions of the 'non-believers' on a continual basis. That was their creed and calling.

The 'Slave' Government

The government of the Slave dynasty, till its demise, was a work in progress. In theory, the sultan was an absolute despot with unlimited power, the supreme executive of the state, the temporal head of all the people and the religious head of all Muslims. However, in practice, the sultan functioned within the constraints of several, and at time severe, checks and balances imposed on him by the nobles and the ulema. Further, the ambiguity that prevailed over the succession issue eroded the power and stature of the sultan, especially towards the waning years of his rule and life. To add to this uncertainty, the government in Delhi grew in a haphazard manner without any indication of planned development. This was so even during the times of Balban, by far the most efficient of the Slave sultans. In addition, ministers and other senior officials were appointed and dismissed at the pleasure of the sultan, which translated to truncated tenures and made assured continuity of administration an impossibility.

The sultan was completely dependent on the army for survival and the strength and stature of the government was directly proportional to the strength, cohesiveness and effectiveness of the army. Even so, the governance was decentralised and built around the military commands established across the territory of the sultanate. The lands around Delhi was maintained by the crown as the sultan's personal lands and the rest divided into provinces. These territorial divisions had no homogeneity in size, population or income and was totally ad hoc in nature. A province was called an iqta and was ruled by a governor called muqti, who was appointed by the sultan. They were equated to fiefdoms of the European nations by the early Western historians, although this would not be strictly correct. The muqti had territorial jurisdiction over his province and ruled according to a personal interpretation of the sultan's will. He was also independent for all practical purposes as long as the stipulated tribute was paid to the sultan in Delhi on time. The muqti also maintained his own army, which had to be placed under the command of the sultan when demanded. However, the size and composition of the army was left to the muqti to determine. Some of the more powerful muqtis even controlled vassal rulers, normally smaller Hindu chieftains whose land holdings fell within the iqta.

The Army

The army was the source of all power of both the sultan and the fledgling sultanate. However, strangely, the strength of the central standing army was very limited, unlike in the case of the Mauryas, Guptas and the Vardhanas of ancient India. The permanent standing army in the capital was limited to the sultan's immediate bodyguards and the small contingent that patrolled the capital to maintain law and order. According to some estimates, the numbers were not even sufficient to defend Delhi, in extremis. For a government dependent on its army for survival, the lack of a large standing army under the direct control of the sultan is an inexplicable fact.

The army, when needed, comprised of a combination of different contingents from the various iqta, provided on demand by the muqti. This method had great disadvantages in that the loyalty of the various groups was never fully ascertained and their fighting capability was an unknown factors. The reason for this unorthodox organisation can be traced back to the original invasions by the two Muhammads—one of Ghazni and the other of Ghur. The initial invading contingent were all soldiers who fought together and would come together eve later when required to face a common enemy. This worked well as long as the invasions were expeditions of plunder without any thought or intent to conquer the land on a permanent basis. However, when the governance of conquered lands became a semi-permanent situation, the Turkish nobles automatically assumed these duties, taking their group of soldiers with them to their individual provinces. The territory to control was large and the provincial iqta in turn created armies of professional soldiers around the core of the original invading force. These soldiers were recruited from the local converts to Islam and officered by Turks. Gradually, through a process of evolution, large standing armies came to be provincial in nature. Even so, with the increasing stature of the sultan, the size of the bodyguards also increased. By the time of Balban's reign, their size was sufficient to form an effective nucleus for a collective army.

The army consisted mainly of cavalry and infantry, along with support personnel for logistics and other maintenance, normally termed as 'camp followers'. The officers were invariably cavalrymen, some being prominent nobles of the realm and also provincial governors. A majority of the officers were 'slaves', who were divided into three main groups—the Muizzis, slaves of Muiz ud-Din Muhammad of Ghur; Qutubis, slaves of Qutb ud-Din Aibak; and Shamsis, the slaves of Shams ud-Din Iltutmish.

The army did not undertake any organised regimental training. Its fighting efficiency depended on the sultan's leadership and strategic acumen, combined with the officer corps' tactical ability. The muqti had complete freedom in terms of numbers, payment, equipment and discipline in creating their provincial armies that came together to form the army of the sultanate when needed. It is obvious that there was not much cohesion in the different groups even when fighting as a single entity. The army also consisted of a limited number of volunteers at various levels. These soldiers brought their own arms and mounts and were mostly fortune seekers of limited reliability. The other kind of soldiers were the jihadi elements. These were exclusively devout Muslims and were predominantly recruited to wage a 'holy war' against the local Hindu princes. These forces were allowed to plunder the conquered areas and retain four-fifth of the loot for themselves while depositing the remaining one-fifth as the share of the sultan.

The jihadi forces are very seldom mentioned even in the contemporary narrative of Indian history since it does not accord with the genial attitude of the Muslim rulers towards non-Muslims, which is a perception being fostered in the recounting. However, these special groups existed and were employed against non-Muslim states, regions and areas in a systematic manner. The jihadi force formed the core of the modus operandi that was employed, through plunder and pillage, to subjugate the common people of the land. Essentially they were ground into poverty and subsequent oblivion over a period of extreme oppression, sanctioned by the sultan. The sultan was the supreme commander of the army, including the jihadi forces, a post that was never relinquished to anyone else throughout the dynastic rule of the Slave sultans. The reason for this is obvious—the sovereignty of the rule was built on and maintained by the fighting power of the army.

The responsibility for payment of the soldiers that were send to the sultan from the iqta is unclear. Most likely they were paid on an assignment basis by the sultan, rather than on the time spend in central service. The muqti was obviously expected to take up the slack as well as pay for other expenditure for equipment and maintenance. The collection of revenue by the provincial governments were therefore directly influenced by the state of affairs in Delhi and the stability or otherwise that prevailed. The slave army had a rudimentary organisation.

However, they displayed relatively higher efficiency in the actual fighting than the forces of the Hindu princes for three intangible reasons. One, the Muslim army was religiously homogenous and therefore inherently possessed much greater solidarity and cohesiveness. Two, there was an added pull towards unity because the soldiers were strangers to the country, essentially being invaders in a hostile and foreign land. Three, the lure of plunder and self-aggrandisement was a powerful stimulant for exhibiting ferocious bravery.

Sources of Income

The sultanate relied on three main sources of income—taxes, excise duties, and wealth from mines and mineral resources.

Taxes. Five taxes were instituted as sanctioned by the Sharia. First, the Kharaj, a land tax levied on the Hindus alone, which was a ratio of the produce collected as the state share. The ratio varied and was normally calculated at random and through guess work. In some of the more organised provinces, the old Hindu records were consulted. Second, the Ushr, a land tax on the Muslims, which was set at one-tenth of the produce. However, this ratio was changed over a period of time when large scale conversions made it unprofitable for the central exchequer to levy only this small ratio. Third, the Jizzya, levied on all non-Muslims. The entire Hindu population, which formed more than 90 per cent of the country, was divided into three tiers paying 48, 24 and 12 dirhams respectively per living male person in a family. Fourth was the Khams, which was one-fifth of the plunder of the infidel wealth carried out by the Jihadi forces, as explained earlier. Fifth, the Zakat, levied on Muslims and consisted of one-fortieth of an individual's income. The amount collected was spent on items that benefited only Muslims, such as repair of mosques, pension for the ulema and other religious purposes.

Excise and custom duties were levied on all goods that were imported into the sultanate. The rate was two and one-half percent of value for Muslim traders and five and one-half per cent for Hindu merchants. All mines, mineral wealth and other underground treasures automatically belonged to the sultan. During the Slave rule, the maximum income to the central treasury came from the Khams, the sultan's share of the booty and spoils of the plunder from Hindu territories and treasure. The fact that even though only one-fifth went to the sultan, in a short span of a century the sultanate had amassed unaccounted wealth, stands as silent testimony to the richness and wealth of the kingdoms and principalities of the Indian sub-continent.

The System of Justice

The justice system was served by a pyramidal structure of judges, called quazi, which started at the lowest courts in important towns and cities, the provincial court at the seat of power and the central court in Delhi. The sultan was the fountainhead of all justice and he was the last 'court' of appeal for justice. It was not uncommon for the sultan to hear cases personally and give judgement. However, he appointed a chief quazi who in turn appointed the other judges all the way to the lowest court in the land. The chief quazi assisted the sultan in arriving at judgements, especially in complex cases. The chief mufti, the religious leader, was also called to advice the sultan in cases where religious disputes were involved.

The Slave dynasty did not interfere in village life other than to collect revenue and neither did they deliver any kind of justice to the rural areas. Cases that involved only Hindus were left to the lower level panchayats to arbitrate even if the issue fell within the jurisdiction of a court that was available. However, if there was Muslim involvement, the quazi presided over the trial. There was a kotwal, head of police, in every town, who also doubled as the magistrate. The punishments for criminal offences were severe and enforced strictly.

The Early Muslim Society in the Sub-continent

The establishment of the Slave sultanate also marked the beginning of the Muslim society in the sub-continent. The Turks, the original ruling class within the sultanate, belonged to different tribes but came together in the face of being in a hostile country. They were uniformly arrogant, carried an extremely deep-set superiority complex, and were die-hard racists believing implicitly in their own purity and superiority of birth. They looked down on the local converts to Islam and did not like to associate with them in any manner.

Even though the local Muslims were treated with disdain, the number of 'Indian Muslims' grew rapidly through forced and/or opportunistic conversions. There were also other foreigners adhering to Islam who had arrived with the invading force of the Turks—Persians, Afghans and a smattering of Arabs. Within this eclectic group of Muslims, racial mixing was inevitable. Even the Turks intermarried with each of the other racial types—native Muslims, refugees from Central Asia, and newly converted Mongols—creating a hybrid race that became the 13th century Muslim population of the sub-continent. Continuing inter-marriages created a fusion of various races and ethnicities that became the 'Indian' Muslim.

The society was divided into two main branches: the soldiers or fighting men who were rulers and formed the aristocracy; and the scholars and chroniclers. The soldiers and the ruling class were mainly Turks and men of the sword. They formed the aristocracy and maintained their own hierarchy, the lowest being Amir, then Malik and the highest being titled Khan. Amongst the Khans, one person was designated Ulugh Khan, and was considered the leading noble of the kingdom. At any given time this title was bestowed only on one person. Turkish slaves could aspire to be promoted up to the rank of Malik, with only Balban being an exception, having been titled Khan during the time of his regency. The scholars and chroniclers, men of the pen, were mainly non-Turks who were mostly literary men or theologians. There were also a separate, but very influential, category of Muslims—the group of household slaves who may originally have been non-Muslims, meaning Hindus, but were bought and converted in their master's household. The Muslim society was primarily urban and also included traders, clerks and artisans in small numbers.

From a purely religious perspective, the society was divided between the followers of Sunni and Shia Islamic faiths. The animosity between the two was clearly visible even at this early stage of the establishment of the religion in the sub-continent. The Shias were concentrated in Multan and Sindh. They made several attempts to capture power in Delhi, but were always put down ruthlessly. From the time of the establishment of the sultanate, the Sunnis were in control in Delhi. The 13th century also saw the appearance of the Sufi saints in 'Hindustan'. These were Muslim mystics, men of learning who supported the belief of direct communication between God and the individual. This concept resonated with the Bhakti movement in

Hindu religious practice. The Sufis practised piety and self-imposed poverty, electing to stay in remote places far removed from normal society.

The leaders of this movement were saintly persons, who deservingly attained acclaimed sainthood on their passing. Most of them had large followings of people who wanted to be initiated into the intricacies of Sufi practices. In the early days, two main orders of Sufis were established in India. One was the group that followed the teachings of Muin ud-Din Chishti of Ajmer, called the Chishtias; and the second were the disciples of Bha ud-Din Zakaria in Multan who came to be known and the Suhrawardia clan. The main impact of the Sufi movement was that a large number of voluntary conversion to Islam took place, especially in the regions around Ajmer and Multan. Sufism formed an acceptable bridge between Islam and Hinduism, where the exchanges and influences flowed in both directions. In the development of Islam in the sub-continent, Sufism created a common ground for mutual exchange and acceptance of ideas.

Conclusion

Even though some of the Turkish ruling elite were patrons of learning, this was not an overarching situation. However, within the Muslim society, education was institutionalised. The maktab was a primary school attached to the local mosque, and the madrsah the seat of higher learning, especially in theology. Some nobles endowed colleges of higher learning, which normally taught the practice of calligraphy and/or architecture. The Turks imported architectural concepts and building techniques from Central Asia and started the blend with the classic Indian concepts that was to become famous in later years.

Some modern Muslim writers have attempted to create an unjustified perception that the Delhi sultanate was a 'cultural' state. These claims are completely wrong, being efforts at re-writing history and altering the truth. Definitely a few of the sultans were found of literature, but that does not make the state they ruled a culturally evolved one. Further, these very same sultans were also ferocious tyrants. The bit of 'culture' that can be gleaned was confined to the capital and the aristocracy. The majority of the followers who came with the invading force were crude soldiers of fortune.

There is no doubt that the sultanate was a military state. It was held together by building well protected and powerful military garrisons, manned by Turkish and other foreign troops, and located at strategic points. Further, the government carried out only two functions, the collection of revenue and maintenance of law and order. The sultan and the provincial governors neither considered, nor cared for, the moral, ethical, cultural, physical or material welfare of the people, the vast majority of whom were oppressed Hindus. They were a deprived lot and not accorded full rights as citizens in their own land. The existence of the Hindu religion and its adherents were tolerated as unavoidable evils, an attitude that continued for many centuries till the end of the Islamic rule in the sub-continent with the arrival of the Western powers. The relegation of Hindus as second class citizens in their own land started at the very beginning of Muslim rule in the sub-continent. In fact it was perpetuated by the first dynasty to rule an established Muslim sultanate in the sub-continent.

The Delhi Sultanate

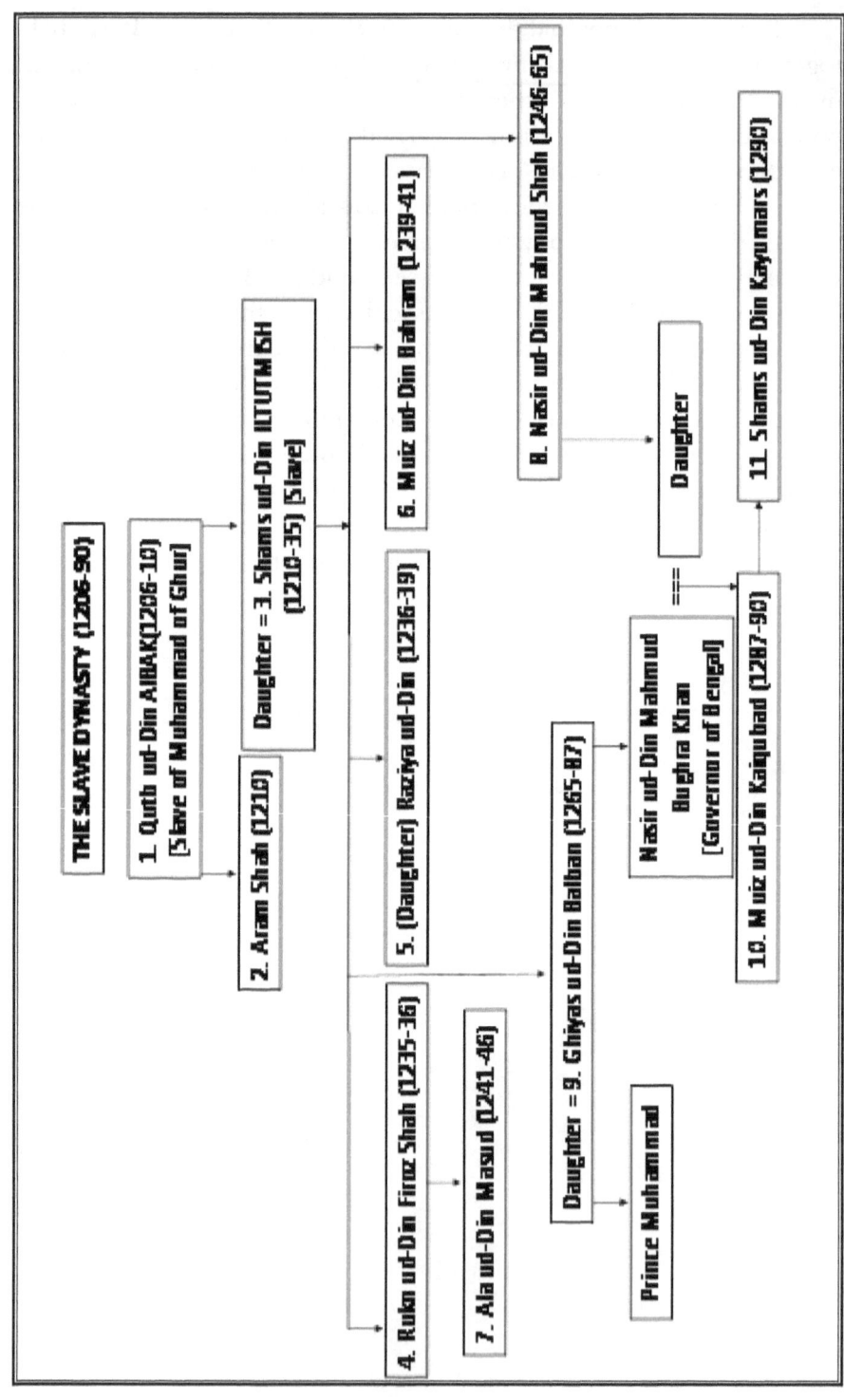

The Slave Dynasty: An Appraisal

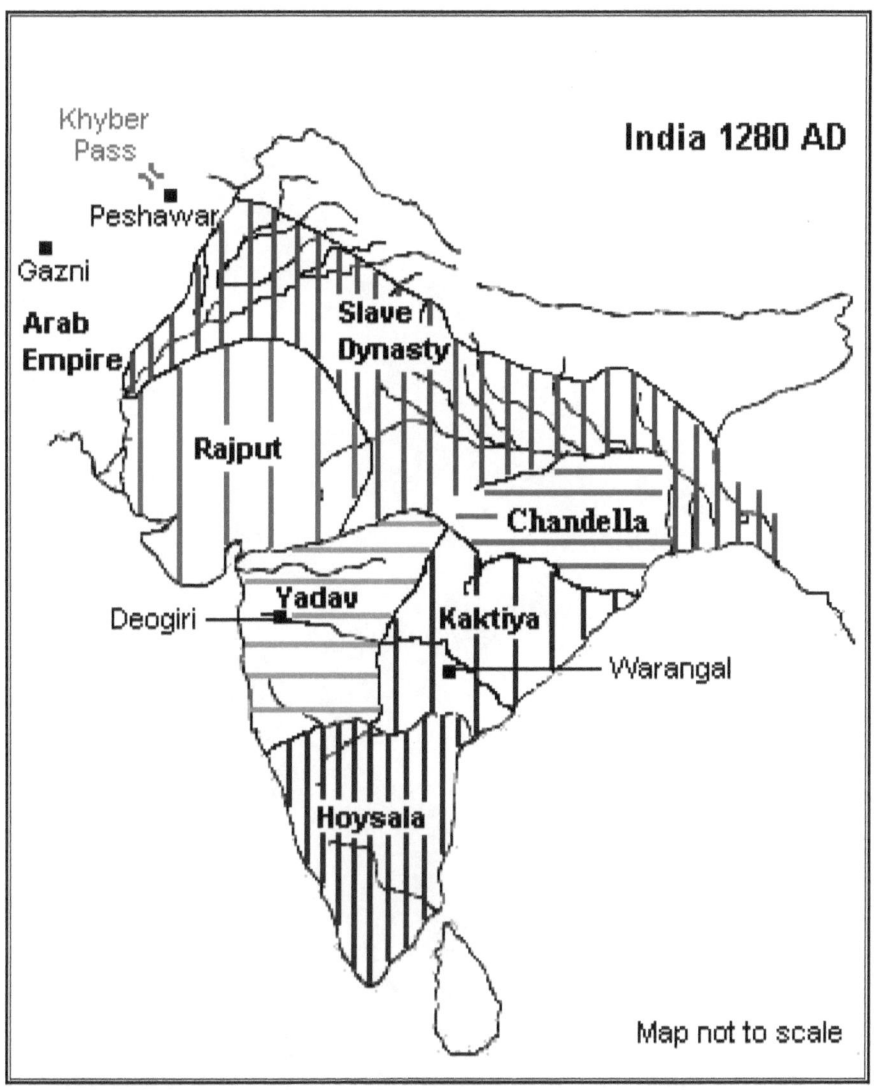

KHILJI MILITARISM

After a lull of nearly a century during which the tide of 'Muslim Conquest' in India had anything if receded, another giant surge was about to carry it deep into the peninsula.

– John Keay,

India: A History, p. 250.

Chapter 8

ASCENT TO POWER

Origins

The ancestors of the Khilji clan (also spelt Khalji in a number of texts) had migrated from Turkistan along with the early movement of Turks towards the east from Central Asia. They had settled in the Helmand region of Afghanistan, staying there for over 200 years before moving further east. It was inevitable that during the two centuries of their domicile they adopted some Afghan customs and traditions, while also intermarrying with the locals. In the bargain, they became ethnically mixed and did not long remain 'pure Turks'. During the repeated Muslim invasions of Hindustan, the majority of the family migrated to India and took up service with the early sultans of Delhi. Since the Khiljis were clearly of mixed parentage, the Turkish nobles of Delhi—forever pompous and disdainful for all but the purest of Turks—considered them Afghans and therefore of a lower status in the hierarchy.

The clan was scattered all over the sub-continent, present in all places that the invaders had reached. A section of the clan that had moved east from Delhi ruled sections of Bengal from the time that a scion of the tribe Ikhtiyar ud-Din Bakhtiyar Khilji ruled the region. Although the version of their origins given above is the most probable, there are two slightly romanticised versions of the origins of the Khiljis that are also available.

First, the translated version of the *Tabkat-i-Akbari* states that Jalal ud-Din Khilji and Mahmud Khilji Mandvi were grandsons of Qaliji Khan who was the son-in-law of the great Genghis Khan. After Qaliji

Khan defeated the Khwarizam Shah, the brothers settled in the vicinity of Ghur. The name Qaliji became Khaliji and over a period of time and frequency of usage, the letters got interchanged, becoming Khalij, Khalji, and then Khilji. The second version is from the history of the Seljuks. It states that Turk, the son of Yafas had eleven sons of whom one was called Khalj. The descendants of this Khalj became Khaljis (Khiljis). This is a probable sequence of events since the Khilji clan is mentioned in the histories of the Ghazni sultans, especially during the reign of Sabuktigin and Mahmud. From this it is certain that they existed anterior to Genghis Khan, with Qaliji Khan mentioned as being from the Khilji tribe. Some chronicles also state that the Khiljis were not Turks at all but of a completely different ethnicity. This assertion is highly contestable. The most likely story of their origin would be that the Khiljis were descendants of Turks who had settled in Afghanistan and subsequently intermingled with the locals.

Jalal ud-Din Firoz Khilji

During Kaiqubad's rule, Malik Firoz, the leader of the Khilji clan was the governor of the Samana province. He was an able soldier, having fought a number of holding engagements against the marauding Mongols and repelling them in all their attempts to invade territories of the Delhi sultanate. He also displayed excellent administrative capabilities and was bestowed the title Shaista Khan. Later, Kaiqubad promoted him as the Minister for the Army, thereby making him the most experienced and powerful noble in the Delhi court. However, there was an orthodox group of Turkish nobles in the court, led by Malik Artemar who was also called Kachchan, whose members were opposed to the rise of Malik Firoz to this powerful position. In their view he was a non-Turk and they believed that he had to be removed in order to re-establish the Turkish monopoly on power in the court. In the ensuing power struggle, Firoz was victorious and Kachchan was put to death. Subsequently Firoz became the regent for the infant king who was placed on the throne after Kaiqubad was removed and killed by the nobles supporting the Khiljis.

Malik Firoz ascended the throne in March 1290 and assumed the title of Sultan Jalal ud-Din Firoz Khilji. His coronation was not held in the city proper, but in an obscure suburb of Delhi called Kilughari, primarily because the Turkish nobles and predominantly Turkish population of the capital proper were hostile to the new sultan. Thus a three-year old toddler was replaced by a grey-bearded patriarch on the ancient throne of Delhi. Jalal ud-Din, now 70 years old, was unpopular with both the nobles and the general public, an unenviable situation for a usurper of the throne. This was mainly because of the erroneous belief that he was not a Turk at a time when even the general population considered it 'improper' for a non-Turk to come to the throne. This is an indication of the entrenched hold on power that the Turkish nobility exercised even over the beliefs of the common people. The prevalent perception was that only the Ilbari Turks had the necessary pedigree to be considered nobility and therefore had the right to rule, even though they had ruled from Delhi only for a century.

Jalal ud-Din was personally mild-mannered and not very dignified in his appearance and conduct, traits that had by now become indispensable to establish the stature of a monarch. He lived in a small palace in Kilughari for a year and the nobles started to come there to pay their respect to the new sultan. Even though Jalal ud-Din was reviled as a non-Turk, the natural avarice of the nobles and their inclination to enhance their own material interests and courtly stature easily overcame tribal prejudices. Gradually Kilughari emerged as an important township, with the nobles building their own residences around the palace and several markets coming up in the vicinity. The now-starting-to-flourish suburb came to be called Shahr-i-Nav, 'The New City'. In slow time Jalal ud-Din was able to establish his authority over the running of the sultanate.

Jalal ud-Din displayed natural generosity, excellence of character and religious devotion. He also dispensed even-handed justice, which gradually changed the attitude of the people from one of scorn to more acceptance and later, affection. It is said that he was kindly disposed even towards criminals, treating them leniently. He is said to have only deported thieves and thugs to Bengal after obtaining a promise of good behaviour from them, instead of punishing them. The end result was that the population started to lose its fear of the authority of the crown. Perhaps because of his advancing years, Jalal ud-Din was mild and averse to violence including war, even though he had been a soldier and general throughout his life. He was essentially unfit to shoulder the rigours of a 13th century absolute monarch. Treason became common place and the continued Mongol threat to the border became much more focused. Only once during his entire reign did Jalal ud-Din threaten to punish delinquent nobles, which also turned out to be an empty threat, since no follow-up action was initiated to carry the threat forward to fruition. In contrast, the younger generation of the Khilji clan was openly ambitious. The sultan's gentle nature was in direct contrast to that of the younger princes and nobles, creating an alienation between the sultan and his own kith and kin as well as well-meaning followers.

> ### A Rare Instance of the Sultan's Rage
>
> Sidi Maula was a dervish from the north who had settled in Delhi during the rule of Balban. He had simple habits, but managed to build a magnificent 'Khankah' that involved spending a large amount of money. (A Khankah is a building designed specifically for gatherings of a particular Sufi brotherhood and is considered a place of spiritual retreat and character reformation) Further, he regularly spend large amounts of money feeding the poor twice a day with meals that were reported to be so sumptuous that it rivalled the meals served on the tables of the khans and maliks (nobles). Jealous rumours spread that the Maula was a sorcerer and the nobles started to mention that he was a seditionist.
>
> Qazi Jalal Kashani, the leader of a group of disgruntled noblemen, hatched a plot to assassinate the sultan, during his visits to the mosque to pray. It was decided that after the assassination, Sidi Maula would be declared the Khalifa (Caliph). Jalal ud-Din came to know of this plot. He took severe action, punishing and then expelling the entire group, although the Qazi was only deported to Badaun. Sidi Maula was cut up with a razor, thrown before an elephant and trampled to death. This is the only instance of the old sultan acting decisively against rebellions and plots.

> The reportage continues to state that the act of putting to death the Maula was considered a sacrilege. A number of chroniclers of the time report that the killing of Sidi Maula brought divine wrath in the form of a devastating dust storm over Delhi followed in a while by a severe famine across the sultanate.

Jalal ud-Din was a reluctant sultan and followed a policy of minimum interference in the administrative arrangements of the capital and the country. He did not make any radical changes to the personnel in the government, confirming most of the Turkish nobles to the offices that they already held. The younger Khilji warriors, who had been instrumental in usurping power, had expected to be elevated to high positions in the administration and were naturally disgruntled by the sultan's passive attitude. It is not that Jalal ud-Din did not make any appointments of his own. He elevated all three of his sons to high positions and adorned them with the titles of high rank: the eldest Mahmud was given the title of Khan-i-Khan; the second became Arkali Khan; and the third came to be titled Qadr Khan. His younger brother was ennobled as Yaghrus Khan and made minister of the army and Malik Ahmad Chap, a close relative was appointed master of Ceremonies. Further, he rewarded his favourite nephews Ala ud-Din and Alam Beg with high positions and titled both of them Khan. However, rather than pacify the younger generation of Khiljis, these appointments only stoked their ambition for further enrichment.

A Rebellion

In the initial stages of his reign, when he was confirming all the old nobles to the positions that they had enjoyed under the rule of the last slave sultans, Jalal ud-Din had also confirmed a nephew of Balban, Malik Chajju, as the governor of Kara-Manikpur. In the second year of Jalal ud-Din's rule, Chajju, supported by several mal-contents led by Hatim Khan the governor of Awadh, raised the flag of rebellion against the Khilji rule. The rebel faction proclaimed Chajju as the heir to Balban and the legitimate ruler of Delhi. Accordingly Chajju marched to Delhi at the head of large army. Jalal ud-Din also marched out of Delhi to meet the rebels. An advance guard under the command of his second son Arkali Khan encountered Chajju near Badaun. In the ensuing battle, the rebels were defeated and Chajju captured. He was then brought to the sultan in chains. The events that took place thereafter are bizarre and perhaps the only ones of their kind in medieval history.

The sultan is reported to have wept at the sight of the royal personage of Chajju in chains and immediately freed him. Further, he lavished praise on the entire rebel leadership for their loyalty to the house of Balban, who had been his own erstwhile lord. The sultan released all of them, holding them to their promise to behave and not rebel in the future. The younger Khiljis were incensed with this attitude and the outspoken Ahmad Chap protested against the lenient and civil treatment of the rebels. He rightly pointed out that such actions would only incite further rebellion in the sultanate. However, Jalal ud-Din, already in his dotage, was more concerned with his afterlife than his temporal life. He proclaimed that he would not kill even a single Muslim for the sake of ruling a transitory kingdom. Chajju was handed over to Arkali Khan, who was made the governor of Multan as a reward for his victory. Kara-Manikpur was given to the sultan's nephew and son-in-law, Ala ud-Din.

The Humility of Jalal ud-Din

Jalal ud-Din had been subservient to Balban throughout his long service to the sultanate and was therefore an inherently humble person. Even though he had been a forceful battlefield commander he naturally assumed an unassertive position in other matters of state.

It is reported that the first time that he entered Delhi proper as the sultan, he dismounted at the gate outside Balban's Red Palace and entered on foot, instead of riding in as was the privilege of the sultan. He wept bitterly on entering the palace; thinking of the inconsistency of temporal fortunes, remembering how he often used to stand in front of Balban in awe of the great sultan in complete humility, and

> contemplating the dreadful misfortune that had befallen the sultan's family.
>
> There is no doubt that when he was the warden of the North-West frontier of the sultanate, he was reputed for his fierce martial spirit and fighting prowess. But as a 70-year old 'sultan' he had become a mild mannered old man, with a definitive religious bend of mind, practising ostentatious displays of extreme humility and prone to weeping at other's misfortunes. The treatment meted out to the rebel Malik Chajju is a clear example of this character trait.

The Sultan's Expeditions

Jalal ud-Din's naturally timorous nature was reflected in the foreign policy that he pursued. He did not undertake any aggressive campaigns to gain territory or wealth. Only two campaigns were led by the sultan himself. In 1290, he initiated a minor campaign, which did not prove to be very successful, against Ranthambhor, leading the expedition personally. Since he had almost completely withdrawn from temporal considerations and analysing the final result that was achieved, the reason for starting this campaign is unclear. In the beginning of the campaign, the Turks plundered Malwa although the Chauhan ruler offered considerable and valiant defence. The raja subsequently withdrew to the fort and entrenched himself there. Although Jalal ud-Din besieged the fort, he was unable to break the defences. Uncharacteristic for an invading army, but perhaps characteristic of an ageing monarch, Jalal ud-Din abandoned the siege and withdrew to Delhi. He justified this withdrawal through the proclaimed argument that he valued each hair of a Muslim's head more than a hundred such forts. In reality, the sultan had long passed his dynamic battle-thirsty age and wanted a quiet life and peaceful rule. The only gain from this expedition was that the district of Jham was captured and the local temple there plundered after the idol was broken.

Even though he was reluctant to mount offensive expeditions to enhance the wealth and territorial holdings of the sultanate, and even though he displayed a number of grievous failings as a sultan,

Jalal ud-Din can never be accused of cowardice or even timidity in battle. He was a veteran of several battles, particularly against the fierce Mongols who he had managed to keep at bay for many years. Even his detractors admit that he was never found lacking in personal courage or warlike accomplishments.

The second expedition that the sultan led was a great success although it did not add to the material wealth of the kingdom. In 1292, a vast horde of over 10,000 Mongols under the leadership of Halaku entered the sultanate. Jalal ud-Din displayed his old fiery spirit and promptly marched against them. In a vicious encounter, he convincingly defeated the advance forces of the Mongols, putting to death a large number of them. He was able to impose peace on his own terms after forcing the main body of the invaders to surrender and retreat. Even though this was a defensive expedition, mounted to safeguard the borders of the sultanate, an unexpected outcome was a sort of religious victory. After the defeat, a few thousand Mongols were converted to Islam and the sultan settled them in a suburb of Delhi. These converts came to be called the New Muslims. This was the beginning of the Islamisation of the Mongols. The sultan gave one of his daughters in marriage to a Mongol prince called Ulghu who was a descendant of the great Genghis Khan. This enclave of Mongols, close to the heart of Delhi, in later times came to be the centre of intrigue, disaffection and rebellion.

Two Other Military Campaigns

The Delhi sultanate undertook two other military campaigns during Jalal ud-Din's reign, which indirectly led to his assassination. However, the sultan was not involved even in a distant manner in either of them. The expeditions were planned, organised and led by Ala ud-Din, the ambitious governor of Kara-Manikpur. Ala ud-Din was a keen student of his ancestor's successful campaign in Bengal. The signal lesson he drew from it was that plunder and conquest of Hindu kingdoms and principalities brought in enormous wealth that in turn significantly enhanced the chances of success of the plunderer's bid to usurp the throne of Delhi.

Ala ud-Din's mounted his first campaign in 1292, against Malwa. He invaded the kingdom and captured the township of Bhilsa, which was subsequently returned to the Hindu ruler in exchange for a very large ransom. The plunder from the expedition was enormous and Ala ud-Din courteously presented most of it to the sultan in Delhi. The sultan was delighted with the success of his nephew and also enamoured with the wealth that was presented to him. In appreciation he conferred the governorship of Awadh on Ala ud-Din, in addition to the province that he already ruled.

The success of the Malwa campaign whetted Ala ud-Din's ambition and appetite for conquest. He planned a more expansive campaign against Devagiri, primarily as a raid and not oriented towards conquest and annexation. The Muslims had heard of the fabulous wealth of Devagiri, which was the capital of the Yadava rajas of the Deccan. In order to legitimise his avarice-laden initiative, Ala ud-Din approached the sultan for nominal permission to mount the expedition and was readily granted royal patronage. Jalal ud-Din was obviously induced by the prospect of gaining even greater booty than had been obtained in the Malwa campaign. The risk to the sultanate and his own rule was minimal, while the gains could be enormous, always an incentive to give benign approval. [There are some interpretations of contemporary material that state that Ala ud-Din did not seek the sultan's permission and embarked on the campaign on his own. Considering the political situation of the time, and Ala ud-Din's own limited stature within the sultanate, this claim can be discounted.] As an aside, there is also a gossip mongering report that at this juncture Ala ud-Din was going through a strained relationship with his wife, who was being tutored by her independent-minded mother Malika Jehan. This distressed him no end and made him want to go away on a violent campaign to kill, plunder and pillage.

Ala ud-Din stormed the capital with a relatively small contingent of about 4000 cavalry and 2000 infantry. The sheer surprise along with the speed and energy of the attack made up for the lack of mass and size of the force. At a place called Ghati-Lajaura, the two armies met. The army of the Devagiri king Ramachandra, mentioned as Ram Deo in Muslim chronicles, was defeated and dispersed in confusion. Ramachandra offered submission and was forced to pay an enormous bounty for the withdrawal of the foreign forces. Ala ud-Din collected the booty and fled back to Kara-Manikpur in great haste, leaving behind a small force to continue to invest the fort. He was acutely aware of the tactical precariousness of his position.

This rapid withdrawal was fortuitous, since almost simultaneously, the crown prince of Devagiri, Singhana/Sankara, who had gone to fetch reinforcements arrived on the scene. He repudiated the peace and demanded that Ala ud-Din return the booty and move out of the Yadava kingdom. Once again battle ensued. In this battle, Ala ud-Din was on the verge of defeat, when the cavalry contingent that had been left behind at the fort arrived on the scene and turned the tide in his favour. The Yadava army was defeated and retreated. Singhana was forced to sue for peace, agreeing to cede control of the province of Elichpore to bear the cost of the garrison that Ala ud-Din now decided to leave behind. The bounty that had already been captured was increased to an even greater amount. Ala ud-Din returned to Kara-Manikpur in triumph. There is no doubt that this was a brilliant campaign, especially considering that it was into an unknown region and conducted several hundred miles away from home base.

Ramachandra's Son

The name of the crown prince who battled Ala ud-Din is given as Sankara (and in some cases as Samkara) by all modern writers. However, there is also a great deal of learned debate regarding the actual name of this valiant prince. The fact remains that neither Sankara nor Samkara are mentioned in any Hindu or Indian source and therefore the name of the prince is derived purely from Islamic chronicles. These sources give the name of the prince variously as Sankaldev, Sankh Deo, and Sinkhan Dev. Later-day scholars are of the opinion that Sinkhan Dev is a corrupted form of the name Singhana Deva. This is further confirmed by the fact that Singhana is found in the dynastic list of the Yadava dynasty of Devagiri. Deva was a common additive to royal names in Hindu dynasties.

Therefore, the real name of the prince who resisted Ala ud-Din's incursion into Devagiri was Singhana Deva.

This was the first incursion of a Muslim army into Peninsular India. It is significant that the purpose was purely plunder to amass wealth and the conquest of territory was never considered. For Ala ud-Din the primary concern and motive was personal and a closely held secret—he was on the quest to obtain sufficient funds to finance his plans to usurp the throne of Delhi. Ala ud-Din was an ambitious prince. His inherent ambition had been further honed and instigated by the officials in Kara who had earlier egged on and aided Malik Chajju in his rebellion. They had been allowed to go free by the liberal minded Jalal ud-Din after the rebellion had failed. These nobles confirmed Ahmad Chap's warning to Jalal ud-Din that they would instigate another rebellion. They also proved Ala ud-Din's belief that money and wealth were indispensable to induce and win a rebellion; to recruit, train and equip a strong army as well as to bribe the opposing forces to desert at crucial moments in a battle.

Although Ala ud-Din had sought the sultan's 'permission' to mount the Devagiri campaign, he did not forward to Delhi any of the plunder and wealth that were garnered from the expedition. Since the use of wealth to usurp positions was a well-known modus operandi of the time and Ala ud-Din's ambitious nature was openly visible, it did not take the nobles in Delhi much time to put two and two together. They warned Jalal ud-Din of the real intentions of his favourite nephew. The sultan refused to listen to these sage advisers and ignored their warnings. It was impossible for the sultan to even contemplate Al ud-Din harbouring any mal-intentions against him. Jalal ud-Din felt that after all, Ala ud-Din, although his brother's son, had been raised personally by him, was also his son-in-law, and therefore would not rebel against him. In fact the sultan was genuinely elated with the success of his nephew.

Ala ud-Din and his brother Alam Beg now commenced an intricate charade aimed directly at winning over the sentiments and emotions of an ageing sultan. Alam Beg who was in Delhi, started to work on the sentiments of the old man, who was already inclined to favour his nephew. Simultaneously, Al ud-Din send a letter to the sultan apologising for the delay in sending the booty to Delhi and promising to do so immediately. Alam Beg told Jalal ud-Din that his brother was alarmed and distraught at the possible anger of the sultan and that he was contemplating withdrawing into the jungles of Bengal. He also told the sultan, ever ready to believe anything that his nephew said, that Ala ud-Din was even considering committing suicide, anxious about his own safety if he came to Delhi to submit the plundered wealth to the sultan personally.

Jalal ud-Din despatched a letter assuring Ala ud-Din of his continued patronage and the latter's position as the favourite nephew. Further, he set out to Kara to meet with his nephew by boat on the River Ganges, escorted by a small cavalry force travelling along the river bank. Some loyal nobles tried to convince the sultan of the folly of setting out with limited guards. They also advised him that Ala ud-Din was by now a ruthlessly ambitious person; that he coveted the throne of Delhi; and that he must be suppressed before any mischief could be created. The sultan responded to these warnings in his characteristic fashion, saying that he loved Ala ud-Din like a son, that he was his son-in-law and that he, Jalal ud-Din, had nothing to fear from his nephew.

Jalal ud-Din's Assassination

The sultan reached Kara on 19 July 1296 and found that Ala ud-Din's army was arrayed on the opposite bank as that of his own small escort force that had been following him on the banks of the River Ganges. Almas Beg who had accompanied the sultan, explained that the army was being paraded in preparation for a ceremonial welcome. The gullible Jalal ud-Din crossed to the bank where Ala ud-Din and his army waited, blinded by destiny and perhaps more by the love for his nephew.

When the sultan disembarked, Ala ud-Din went and fell at his feet. Jalal ud-Din raised him and kissed him. It is said that he chided Ala ud-Din, 'I have raised you from infancy, why are you afraid of me?' At this stage, when he was bending forward to pet Ala ud-Din, the signal was given to attack the sultan. An officer, Muhammad Salim, who was assigned the task, struck the sultan who was wounded. Jalal ud-Din ran towards the river shouting, 'Thou villain Ala ud-Din,

> what has thou done?' Ikhtyar ud-Din Hud, another officer in Ala ud-Din's army intercepted the sultan, threw him to the ground and cut of his head. He bore it, still dripping with blood to Ala ud-Din.
>
> The head of Jalal ud-Din Firoz Khilji was fixed on a spear and paraded on the streets of Kara-Manikpur to convince the people of the death of the sultan.

The small contingent of attendants with the sultan were all put to death immediately. Even before the blood had dried on the sultan's head, the royal canopy indicating the presence of the sultan was elevated above Ala ud-Din. This was an unfortunate end to an aged sultan, who had himself shown inordinate clemency even to princes who had rebelled against him.

Jalal ud-Din – An Assessment

Jalal ud-Din Khilji was a successful and loyal general who had proven his mettle in repeated battles. He had been almost thrust upon the throne of Delhi by the ambitions of the Khilji clan, of which he was the de facto head. Even though he continued to maintain a powerful army after becoming the sultan, he moved away from the concept of militarism. This was surprising, considering that military might was the cornerstone and motivating force for the sultanate and Jalal ud-Din in his service to Balban was one of the loyal commanders who enforced this discipline. As the sultan he was inclined more towards reconciliation than confrontation, both in internal matters as well as in dealing with external adversaries. He was the first sultan to attempt reconciliation of various power centres in the capital as well as to bring different Muslim groups together amicably.

The reason for this change in attitude has not been satisfactorily explained even in contemporary chronicles of the time. It could be that age had mellowed the monarch who had been for years at the inner core of betrayals, murders and assassinations conducted to obtain or hold on to power. As has been the case in a number of occasions throughout history, powerful men tend to turn towards religion and pray for God's grace in preference to temporal power in their old age, when the infallibility of youth has worn away and the realisation of one's own mortality becomes rudely apparent.

He adopted genial policies and permitted nobles who were loyal to Balban and his successors to continue in office. Jalal ud-Din also displayed 'studied' modesty to being almost self-effacing. However, this humility cannot be believed to have been completely natural since he was a lifelong soldier and general, used to deferential and respectful treatment at all times. Therefore, the display of modesty and humbleness has to be considered a well-crafted policy, meant to appease a somewhat hostile Turkish nobility and the unfriendly general populace of Delhi.

Jalal ud-Din did not attempt any military expeditions, other than the one incursion into Ranthambhor, which was unsuccessful. However, this was not a sign of weakness or lack of bravery but stemmed from an astute understanding of the weakened state of the sultanate at the time of his coming to power. In fact, the comprehensive defeat of the Mongol invasion is a verifiable demonstration of his unfailing military competence.

Some historians assess Jalal ud-Din Firoz Khilji as a weak sultan who was unfit to rule, mainly because of the leniency that he displayed and the obvious old-age at which he gained the throne. However, this is an incorrect appreciation of a ruler who was an acute religious bigot. He was completely intolerant of Hindus who formed the majority of his people. He was zealous in initiating anti-Hindu activities, destroying and desecrating numerous Hindu temples. The belief that he was a weak and tolerant ruler can perhaps be attributed to contemporary chroniclers and sources who were unanimously biased against the Khiljis. In the general narrative of medieval history, the Khiljis get the least accolades and are even reviled as non-Turk usurpers. The bias against non-Turks is evident throughout the history of the Delhi sultanate, a true depiction of the famed 'equality' meted out to the followers of the religion of Islam.

The truth, not reported by contemporary writers, is that Jalal ud-Din Khilji was not a mild sultan, but a pragmatic one with a great deal of administrative experience. Therefore, he was keen to balance the various factions that were in conflict at the apex of power in Delhi in order to ensure the continuance of the fledgling Muslim state in the Indian sub-continent. In attempting this reconciliation of the infighting groups, he tried to be as impartial as possible, under the circumstances that prevailed at the time.

Chapter 9

ALA UD-DIN KHILJI

Securing the Throne

Immediately after the aged Jalal ud-Din was assassinated, Ala ud-Din was declared sultan in Kara-Manikpur. He had waded through blood to achieve his ambition of being the sultan. There is no doubt that he had displayed daring and dash in the conduct of the successful expedition to Devagiri. This success had made him arrogant and he nurtured a belief of his inherent qualifications to be the sultan. Therefore, he presumed that he would be welcomed by the people of Delhi as their legitimate ruler. However, this was a fallacy and Ala ud-Din found it very difficult to gain the acceptance of the people of Delhi. Contrary to Ala ud-Din's expectations, he was considered a usurper and also guilty of the murder of his uncle, who had been his greatest benefactor from birth. He became an object of hatred, especially for the nobles loyal to Jalal ud-Din.

Under these conditions, it was only natural for plots and rebellions to be hatched. A group of nobles known as the 'Jalali nobles', who were fiercely loyal to the old sultan, plotted revenge for his murder. In these early days Ala ud-Din was at a distinct disadvantage, being far away from Delhi, which was the seat of power. Further, Ahmad Chap, by far the bravest and best commander of Turkish forces of the time, was aligned with the anti-Ala ud-Din faction. As is so often the case in history, at this stage fate intervened in the person of the murdered sultan's widowed queen, Malika-i-Jahan.

Malika Jahan, was not particularly shrewd or intelligent, although she felt that she was up to playing political intrigue against the likes of the ruthless Ala ud-Din and his brother. In the belief that keeping the throne of Delhi vacant was dangerous and could lead to Ala ud-Din being accepted as the sultan, she pushed forward the claim of her sons to the throne as the legitimate successors to Jalal ud-Din. She extended their claims through some amount of unnecessary intrigue. Malika Jahan bought off some nobles who were not supportive of her sons' claims by plying them with gifts and the promise of high positions. In her haste to fill the throne, the queen raised her second surviving son Qadr Khan to the throne, with the title Rukn ud-Din Ibrahim. This one impulsive action paved the way for disaster. Her elder son Arkali Khan, considered unanimously by all to be more capable than his younger brother, was at this time in Multan. He was upset by his mother's actions.

Ala ud-Din realised that if Qadr Khan was well supported, he would be a formidable adversary in the contest for the throne, especially since some amount of legitimacy was attached to him as Jalal ud-Din's son. The claim was strengthened by the fact that the sultan had been murdered and Ala ud-Din was responsible for the assassination. The circumstances of the sultanate was precarious at this stage with the indigenous Hindu princes baulking under foreign rule and waiting for an opportunity to throw the invaders out. There was also the threat from the Mongols who had once again become restive in the north-west region. The situation was not looking very conducive for the success of Ala ud-Din's plans. This is when he displayed the stoutness of heart required to face and overcome formidable challenges and which transforms princes to kings. He decided to strike at Delhi with vigour and determination without wasting any time and started to march towards Delhi. The saying goes, 'fortune favours the brave' and in this particular instance luck or fortune, call it by whatever name, favoured Ala ud-Din.

When it became apparent to the Queen Mother and the newly enthroned sultan that Ala ud-Din was not a problem that would solve itself, they requested Arkali Khan for help to ward off the oncoming assault. During the short period that had elapsed, Malika Jahan had created sufficient factionalism amongst the Delhi nobles through her dealings and intrigue. Arkali Khan, peeved at being superseded to the throne and upset at his mother's shenanigans, made no move to assist his brother or defend the family throne. Many nobles loyal to Jalal ud-Din had left Delhi and joined Arkali Khan in Multan, depleting Delhi of effective military leadership. Arkali Khan replied to his mother that the defection of a number of nobles to Ala ud-Din's camp had made securing the throne for his younger brother a difficult task. He continued to sulk in Multan.

Arkali Khan has been described in several records as being, 'one of the most renowned warriors of the time'. It is highly probable that he would have made an effective and perhaps even a great sultan. However, he did not grasp the one opportunity that was being presented to him to secure the throne of his father and then succeed to the kingship itself after defeating the usurper. Such are the vagaries of history and the analyst is left pondering the proverbial 'what if'?

In any case, Arkali Khan's discontent and complete inaction provided a much needed impetus to Ala ud-Din's march to Delhi. Acutely aware of his unpopularity amongst the people, he started to placate the general population by distributing money, literally showering them with coins using a catapult built for the purpose, daily during his march. This generosity brought a large number of soldiers to Ala ud-Din's camp, the numbers increasing on a daily basis. According to one estimate, by the time he was close to Delhi, the army had swelled to 50,000 cavalry and 60,000 infantry. The visibly increased size of the army, assisted by the lavish distribution of wealth, started to change the public perception regarding Ala ud-Din, with people now considering that the future belonged to him.

The nobles were not far behind in appreciating the changing tide and were themselves influenced by the profligate spread of wealth. Greed overcame altruistic loyalty and the murder of a benign sultan was rapidly forgotten. Qadr Khan, the presumptive sultan, send out an army to battle Ala ud-Din. However, once again bribery played its dishonourable role and the army, instead of fighting him switched sides and joined Ala ud-Din at Badaun. This was perhaps the only victory Ala ud-Din won in his entire military carreer without having to fight. The hapless Qadr Khan and his witless mother Malika Jahan hurriedly collected whatever treasures they could lay hands on and decamped for Multan in the night, towards the prospect of safety in Arkali Khan's camp.

Ala ud-Din triumphantly entered Delhi at the plains of Siri towards the end of 1296. The progress of his march from Kara-Manikpur had been slow because of the rainy season and he had taken five months after the murder of his uncle to physically claim the throne of Delhi.

> "The throne was now secure, and the revenue officers and the keepers of elephants with their elephants and the kotwals with the keys of the forts, and the magistrates and the chief men of the city came out to Ala ud-Din, and a new order was established. His wealth and power were great; so whether individuals paid their allegiance or whether they did not, mattered little, for the Khutba was read and coins were struck in his name."
>
> Ishwari Prasad,
>
> *History of Medieval India*, p. 190.

Ala ud-Din was an astute 'politician' who understood the importance of public opinion and appreciated very clearly the need to have both the people and the nobles on his side. He therefore prioritised three objectives to ensure that the throne was secure and his hold on power not questioned. The first objective was to reconcile the people's opinion and to smooth over the antagonism that was still prevalent in some pockets. The people had to be made to forget the heinous crime through which he had come to power. He therefore continued the practice of catapulting gold and silver coins to the masses for some more days after ascending the throne of Delhi. Public memory is proverbially short, much more so when the thought process is influenced by the lure of gold. Very soon, Ala ud-Din's treachery and ingratitude were forgotten by the masses and the people were vying with each other to sing the praises of his generosity.

The second objective was to eliminate any and all possible claimants to the throne, however far-fetched the legitimacy of the claim. Accordingly he send an army of around 40,000 troops under the command of Ulugh Khan to Multan to dispose of Arkali Khan, his brother Qadr Khan (Rukn ud-Din Ibrahim), Malika Jahan and their supporters. Ulugh Khan captured Multan without much difficulty, imprisoned the princes and their mother and send them to Delhi. The ease with which Multan was captured is an inexplicable event since Arkali Khan was considered an effective military commander and he also had a sizeable army under him. The use of bribery to win the battle cannot be ruled out in this expedition also. On their way to being transported to Delhi, the princes were blinded and then killed near Hansi on the express orders of Ala ud-Din. Along with them Ahmad Chap and Ulugh Khan, the Mongol prince and son-in-law of Jalal ud-Din (not Ala ud-Din's commander of the same name), were also put to death. Malika Jahan was thrown into prison and never released. Ala ud-Din now appointed Ala-ul-Mulk, his trusted lieutenant from Kara-Manikpur as the kotwal of Delhi. The throne of Delhi was secure, at least for the time being.

The third objective was to establish complete control over the nobles. Ala ud-Din was fully aware of the fickleness of the loyalty of these nobles and also their proclivity for intrigue and treachery. He obviously knew this facet of the nobles' character since he had proved to be the most treacherous of them all. During his march to Delhi and even after claiming the throne, he had bought off most of the nobles and Ala ud-Din was sagacious enough to understand the risks involved. On their part, the nobles, who had fairly inflated egos, believed that they had secured the throne for Ala ud-Din and his continuing to rule was dependent on their support. Ala ud-Din wanted to alter this situation and to ensure that the perception changed the other way. He was set on ensuring that the nobles clearly understood that their continued well-being depended solely on their being in the sultan's favour.

In order to achieve this, he dismissed from service several nobles, and disgraced some other top officials. These actions were focused on the nobles who had switched sides to Ala ud-Din during the succession struggle. Obviously the lesson that had been taken forward was that they were deemed untrustworthy—after all someone who betrayed a former master could very well betray the current master also. Ala ud-Din caught and imprisoned almost the entire group of nobles and army officers who had defected to his camp; some of them were blinded and others killed. Uniformly, their wealth was confiscated to the throne and the families were reduced to beggary. It is reported that during the transition only three nobles loyal to Jalal ud-Din's refused to accept bribes. These three were spared by Ala ud-Din who lauded their loyalty and integrity, appreciating their principled stand. The 'Jalali nobles' were thus exterminated. The initiative to put an end to treacherous behaviour amongst the nobles was a strange action for a person who came to power through practising the ultimate treachery.

Ala ud-Din's Concept of Kingship

Ala ud-Din implicitly believed in the majesty of the monarch, in a similar manner to how Balban had evinced kingship earlier, as the representative of God on earth. He was convinced that God had granted the sultan more wisdom than the common man and therefore his decisions and will were to be the law. It follows then that all inhabitants of the country are either subjects or servants of the sultan. To maintain his aloof gignity, Ala ud-Din ensured that the distinction between sultan and the rest of the nobles were visibly maintained. He also decided that he would not be influenced by anyone in laying down the policies for the governance of the sultanate.

Traditionally in the Delhi sultanate so far, two extremely powerful groups had exercised immense power and influence over almost all decisions of the sultan—the entrenched nobility and the brotherhood of the order of priests, the ulema. Ala ud-Din, once again in his usual forceful manner, set about remedying the situation to better suit his way of thinking and his style of ruling. By attacking the stature of the nobles, he had managed to completely emasculate the nobility. They were brought down to the status of 'servants' who could be appointed or dismissed and even maimed or killed at the pleasure of the sultan. The courtiers were in such awe of the power of the sultan that none of them had the courage to oppose the edicts issued by him.

The ulema was slightly more difficult to handle. Ala ud-Din started to bring them under control by first declaring that he would not permit the interference of the ulema in matters of purely administrative nature. Subsequently he ensured that the ulema could no longer dictate to the sultan even on matters of religion, let alone in matters not connected to the church. He declared that he knew much more than the ulema about the needs of the state and how to govern for the betterment of the sultanate. This was the first time in the history of the sultanate that such a decision had been handed down by the sultan. This was also a bold step, since the power of the sultan was based predominantly on an army that relied on religious zeal to outperform the opposition. Further, being 'outsiders' in a majority Hindu region, the sultan was dependent on his co-religionists to ensure the continuation of his rule and dynasty.

> He enunciated his policy in the following words, 'I do not know whether this is lawful or unlawful, whatever I think to be for the good of the state or suitable for the emergency, that I decree; and as for what may happen to me on the Day of Judgement, that I know not'.
>
> As quoted in *The Sultanate of Delhi 711-1526 A D*, p. 152

Ala ud-Din should be credited with being the first Turkish sultan of Delhi to bring the church under the executive control of the state, which is always the first step towards creating a secular nation, at least in theory. However, it is almost certain that he did not intent to make the state secular and the reforms were purely oriented to enforcing his will and writ as supreme across all aspects of life in the sultanate. Whatever the ultimate objective, the state had moved at least a bit away from being completely theocratic in nature. Even so, it does not mean that the non-Muslim, read Hindu, population was treated well. Quite the contrary. Ala ud-Din did not consider himself the king of the Hindus in the same manner and sense as he was the sultan of all Muslims. He did not feel responsible for the welfare of his Hindu subjects. In fact the basis of his ideology regarding dealing with the Hindus was total and complete repression. According to law, Hindus were seen only as payers of tribute (Kharaj-guzar), and therefore the jiziya was imposed strictly. In all other respects, the Hindus were almost at the sub-human level, with no rights and no recourse even to minimal justice. In any case this experiment with keeping the ulema at bay did not survive Ala ud-Din's death, when the sultanate rapidly reverted to being an absolute theocracy.

An interesting facet of his reign is that he displayed contradictory characteristics, especially when dealing with religion. Although he had consciously prevented the ulema from interfering in the functioning of the state, Ala ud-Din he continued to be a pious Muslim, following strict Islamic laws. He regularly took advantage of Muslim fanaticism in the conflicts against indigenous kingdoms and incited the Muslim population into a high level of bigotry to ensure their military cooperation. It is obvious that Ala ud-Din did not believe in anything and used whatever means were required to achieve his objectives. The steadfast aim was to achieve his personal ambitions.

Ala ud-Din – The Individual

Contemporary chroniclers have been unanimous in declaring Ala ud-Din as being bad tempered, obstinate and hard-hearted. He was by nature cruel and implacable. Throughout his rule, he was only concerned about the state of his kingdom with no consideration being given to religion, no regard for ties of brotherhood or filial affections, and absolutely no care regarding the rights of others. In keeping with the arrogance and haughtiness that he displayed permanently, he moved away from tradition and did not evoke the sanction of the Khalifa (Caliph) to proclaim his sovereignty. In fact he stopped paying even token homage to the caliph and acknowledging him as his political superior. However, true to his contradictory nature, he kept alive the concept and traditions of the khilafat (caliphate).

Ala ud-Din was illiterate, but it became an advantage in his contradictory personality. Since he was not burdened or encumbered with conventional wisdom as passed down through books and chronicles, he was able to give flight to his own imagination in formulating policies. He introduced several innovative administrative reforms, some of which could be considered brilliant for the time. He even toyed with fundamental economic reforms, although none of them came to fruition. It is reported that he enjoyed the company of scholars and creative people. He was also the patron of two of the most renowned poets of the time, Amir Khusrao and Amir Hasan. At a time when traditionally sultans practised the art of minimal governance, Ala ud-Din went against the trend and introduced a maximum government. He was a completely hands-on monarch who controlled and manipulated every single function and activity of the government.

There is definitely no doubt that Ala ud-Din was an absolute despot, intolerant of even the slightest murmur of dissent. But then, all effective rulers of the time were despots, and the ones who were not did not last long on the throne. It can be said in Ala ud-Din's defence that his despotism was reasoned, if such a dichotomy is possible to understand. All the policies that he initiated were the result of careful study and much consideration. No initiative was embarked upon purely on impulse or the whim of the sultan. Ala ud-Din consulted with wise men, debated with them regarding the merit of a proposal and then decided on the best means to implement the policy and achieve the desired goal. There is even some mention of his having been tolerant of criticism in these discussions. However, this claim is hard to believe considering his inherent belief of the superiority of his intellect, and his proclivity to be completely intolerant of even the slightest dissidence.

Perhaps the only positive trait in the sultan was his genuine concern for the common people, even though it was reserved exclusively for his Muslim subjects. Fortune favoured Ala ud-Din. He was amazingly successful in everything that he attempted to do or did. He was unsentimental and efficient—success in every endeavour was all that mattered. It was but natural that unmitigated success inflated his ego and furthered his already mighty ambition, leading to megalomania—Ala ud-Din started to dream of world conquest.

Chapter 10

MILITARY CONQUESTS OF ALA UD-DIN KHILJI

In medieval times a kingdom's foreign policy was inextricably intertwined with both offensive and defensive military expeditions. This was the universal truth. Ala ud-Din was one of the most ambitious rulers to have sat on the throne of Delhi. Therefore, it is not surprising that after successfully establishing himself as the undisputed master of the existing Delhi sultanate, he started to dream of conquest. This dream was not any ordinary dream, but one of world conquest. In his megalomania, he started to compare himself to Alexander of Macedonia who had by this time passed on to legend and folklore. He assumed the title Sikandar Sani, meaning 'Alexander the Second', and also had coins minted with this title.

The nobles of the court were far too scared of the sultan to voice their concern regarding these grandiose dreams. It was left to Ala-ul-Mulk, a loyal noble from the times before Ala ud-Din assumed the apparition of the exalted sultan, to point out to him the extreme impossibility of achieving his dreams and gently bring him down to earth. Ala-ul-Mulk suggested that the sultan undertake the difficult but desirable task of conquering India before embarking on a campaign of world conquest. Ala ud-Din had the grace to accept the advice, an indication of the status of Ala-ul-Mulk in the court, and set himself the task of subduing the Hindu states of the sub-continent.

Accordingly, he laid down the fundamental objective of his foreign policy as the subjugation of all independent Hindu kings and chieftains within the ambit of the sultanate. True to his style of functioning, he did not create any pretexts or wait for any cause to initiate the invasion of neighbouring states. Almost all wars that Ala ud-Din fought as a sultan were unprovoked invasions aimed at achieving the ultimate goal he had set for himself—the conquest of the entire region. However, before embarking on his ambitious conquest, he had to deal with the Mongol threat emanating from the north-west in order to consolidate the kingdom. The conflict with the Mongols to secure the sultanate was carried out simultaneous to other military expeditions that were initiated to subdue and annex the kingdoms of North India. This demonstrated the increasing strength and power of the sultanate.

Dealing with the Mongol Threat

The presence of the restive Mongols, called in Persian and Indian sources as 'Mughals', on the north-western borders of the kingdom was a major concern for almost all Delhi sultans. Defending the kingdom from the depredations of the Mongols across the north-west region was not only a necessity to secure the nation but was also a continuous drain on central resources. During the first eight years of Ala ud-Din's reign there were five major Mongol incursions into the territory of the sultanate. These Mongol invasions were constant threats to Punjab, Multan and Sindh. One Mongol expedition came up to Delhi, looting some parts of the capital itself and went on to threaten the Ganga-Yamuna doab. Similar attacks by the Mongols had so consumed the energies of Balban in repelling them when he was the sultan that he was unable to mount any other military expeditions to further the territorial extent or the holding wealth of the kingdom.

The Mongol invasions had always been purely plundering and pillaging raids, similar to the numerous raids of Mahmud of Ghazni, and not aimed at territorial conquest or annexation. The only area that they captured and held was Western Punjab in order to ensure that the Khyber Pass, the gateway to India, remained under their control. The Mongols were a mountain people, essentially restless and turbulent by nature, who could not stand the heat, dust and humidity of Delhi. From a Mongol perspective, India was a fabulously wealthy country that was to be periodically plundered but not desirable for conquering with a view of permanent occupation and rule. Therefore, the Mongols habitually fled back to Afghanistan when confronted by a good size army, not out of cowardice, but to protect and take back the loot that had been collected till then. They would not risk their booty to give battle with an uncertain outcome. Therefore, they very seldom stood their ground and fought. The Turkish chronicles of the time claim many decisive victories of the sultanate forces over the Mongols, which are definitely exaggerations and highly unbelievable. These 'victories' could only have been the Turkish armies chasing after the 'fleeing' Mongols, not traditional victories over Mongols who had been defeated in battle.

The first Mongol invasion took place in late 1296, only a few months after Ala ud-Din had installed himself on the throne. Ala ud-Din's best friend, Zafar Khan, led the Muslim army to counter the invasion. The Mongols were met at Jalandhar and driven away without great difficulty. The second incursion took place the very next year. The initial advance was driven away. However, the Mongol army under Amir Daud, the king of Transoxiana, numbering about 100,000 (in some accounts the figure is 200,000) crossed the River Indus and advanced into the sultanate. Ulugh Khan drove the Mongol army out, inflicting heavy losses on them. However, the Mongol hordes returned almost immediately under the leadership of a chief called Saldi and captured the fort at Siri near Delhi. Zafar Khan once again marched against the invaders, captured the Mongol leader and 2000 companions and send them to Delhi in chains. The survivors fled back to Afghanistan. However, on the approach of the Mongol army, the people in the outer suburbs of Delhi had panicked and fled into the city for refuge. This had led to an acute shortage of food and provisions and an almost complete collapse of civic order.

Two years later, in 1298 (some records mention the year as 1299), the Mongols came back under the command of Qutlugh Khwaja and advanced towards Delhi. This was the most serious Mongol invasion that had been witnessed so far, and the sultan was forced to summon a war council to discuss the defences of the kingdom. Once again, Zafar Khan and Ulugh Khan led the defences with Ala ud-Din himself taking to the field at the head of 12,000 'volunteers'. Although his old mentor Ala-ul-Mulk advised against attacking the Mongols immediately, Ala ud-Din did just that. Zafar Khan leading the advance guard defeated the Mongols and pursued the fleeing enemy. In the fray, he became isolated from the majority of his force, was surrounded and killed by the Mongol rear-guard. Zafar Khan was one the greatest warriors and military commanders of the time who had repeatedly safeguarded the empire. Moreover he was the sultan's most trusted aide. However, Ala ud-Din did not take the loss of such a valiant commander and his closest friend too seriously. It is possible that Ala ud-Din had started to view his friend and army commander as becoming too powerful and influential, who could turn out to be a potential threat to his fledgling kingship. This is yet another instance of the demonstration of Ala ud-Din's cunning and calculating nature and his ruthlessness in pursuing his own power and stature.

The next major Mongol invasion happened when Ala ud-Din was involved in the siege of Chittor. The Mongols led by Taghri reached near Delhi and plundered some of the suburbs of Delhi itself. The sultan was forced to take refuge in the fort at Siri. However, after two months of pillage, for some inexplicable reason the Mongols retreated of their own accord. The only reason that could be conceived for this withdrawal is that they were sated with plunder.

Ala ud-Din, for ever the cautious sultan and an avid student of military campaigns, realised the danger that the Mongols posed to the well-being of the sultanate—after all they had reached the gates of Delhi twice in quick succession. They had become a direct threat to the authority of the sultan. Ala ud-Din came to the conclusion that it was not enough to drive back the Mongol invasions or raids but that it was necessary to take strong deterrent measures to stop the raids completely. Accordingly, he initiated effective steps to protect the frontier. He repaired old forts in Punjab, Multan and Sindh and built new ones at strategic points. All the forts were garrisoned with powerful army contingents while additional army units were positioned at the borders. To oversee these improvements and command the frontier forces, he appointed a special governor titled 'Warden of the Marches'.

The Mongols were not deterred by these measures. In 1305, a large Mongol force under the joint command of Ali Beg and Khwaja Tash marched into India. They avoided the frontier garrisons, marched north of Lahore and skirted the Siwalik Hills, bypassed the strongly defended Delhi and thrust directly into the Doab—the tongue of land between the Rivers Ganga and Yamuna. The Mongols penetrated as far as Amroha, burning, butchering and pillaging everything in their path. Ala ud-Din send an army under Malik Kafur and Ghazi Malik to intercept them. This force encountered the Mongols on their return journey, encumbered by the huge plunder and loot that they had collected. In the ensuing battle the Mongols were defeated and their leaders taken prisoners. More than 8000 Mongols were ruthlessly slaughtered and their severed heads were cemented into the walls of the fort at Siri as a warning to future invaders.

The Mongol mindset was subsumed in irreversible blood lust, which was a powerful motivating force to continue repeated invasions even in the face of some of the most gruesome slaughter. The repeated invasions are also indicative of the fact that the Mongols never considered themselves 'defeated' in any of the previous encounters. Their perception was that losses were inescapable in war and the aim of going to war was the achievement of the primary aim—in this case plunder and pillage, which was always achieved. Therefore, unmindful of the awful carnage that was visited on them earlier, the Mongols invaded again in the very next year. At this stage, Ala ud-Din had appointed a veteran commander, Ghazi Malik (also mentioned as Ghazi Tugluk) as Warden of the Marches. He was successful in defending the frontier throughout Ala ud-Din's reign.

The Mongol army now crossed the River Indus near Multan and proceeded towards the Himalayan foothills, plundering and burning their way forward as was customary. Ghazi Malik barred their way and routed them in battle. It is reported that 50,000 Mongols, including their leader Kabk, were taken prisoner and then put to death while their women and children were sold into slavery. It is highly possible that the numbers were exaggerated in later-day recounting of the defeat. A tower of the severed heads was built at the Badaun gate of Delhi, 'in order that it may serve as a warning...to future generations'. According to later chroniclers this tower could be seen even after two and one-half centuries, during the reign of Akbar.

There was only one more minor Mongol incursion during Ala ud-Din's rule. Even though disdainful of the loss of life, the Mongols were evidently deterred by the ruthlessness and severity of the reprisals. A contributory factor could have been that by this time the Mongols were riven by internal dissentions in Central Asia. After this raid, the sultanate remained immune to Mongol depravity for a period of time.

In facing the Mongols, Ala ud-Din had used a combination of static defences combined with reliable and proven forces with the capacity to manoeuvre. Even though temporary, Ala ud-Din's success in pushing back repeated Mongol incursions were convincing demonstrations of the military efficacy of fast manoeuvring Turkish cavalry combined with the solidity of the Indian elephant corps as its phalanx centred around well-manned forts.

Conquests in North India

Gujarat

While the Mongol invasions were being thwarted in the north-east very early in his rule, Ala ud-Din send an army under Ulugh Khan and Nasrat Khan to conquer Gujarat. Gujarat was a prosperous kingdom and although raided many times by the Islamic forces, had never been conquered by the Turks. Even Ala ud-Din's primary aim was plunder with conquest and annexation being a secondary objective, to be accomplished only if possible. The aim of conquest was further restricted to the commercially important regions of the kingdom.

The area was ruled by the Vaghela king Karan with his capital at Anhilwara, modern-day Patan. The Muslim army besieged the capital and captured it without much of a battle. The king escaped along with his daughter Deval Devi and sought refuge with King Rama Chandra of Devagiri in the Deccan. However, his queen Kamala Devi and a number of other children were captured and send to Delhi. Gujarat was successfully occupied by the Khilji army. The Muslim army then advanced to Somnath and sacked the Shiva temple there—the same temple that Mahmud of Ghazni had ransacked in the 11th century and had been subsequently rebuilt. The idol from the temple was send back to Delhi, where it was broken up and the fragments laid on the entrance to the Friday mosque for the faithful to tread upon. The army then moved on to the port city of Khambat (later Cambay) whose rich merchants were plundered and a vast booty obtained.

Nasrat Khan send the extraordinary booty that had been collected in Gujarat back to the sultan in Delhi in the hands of a Hindu slave eunuch named Kafur. Kafur was exceptionally talented and handsome, being nicknamed 'Hazar Dinari' (Thousand Dinars worth), which was the original price that had been paid for him. This youth converted to Islam, became a favourite of Ala ud-Din and went on to play a central role in the history of the sultanate for the next two decades.

The invasion of Gujarat, like most of the other enterprises that Al ud-Din attempted, was remarkably successful and the kingdom was annexed to the growing territorial holdings of the sultanate. However, on its return journey to Delhi, the army suffered an internal mutiny. It is said to have been the result of the generals insisting that the soldiers hand over one-fifth of the personal spoils that they had gathered during the campaign in Gujarat, as per long established norms of distribution of booty within an Islamic army. The mutineers were primarily the 'New Muslims' who were the Mongols who had settled in and around Delhi. Obviously, their allegiance to the new religion that they had adopted did not run deep enough for them to adhere to its rules and give up hard won plunder on the campaign trail. The mutiny was easily quelled, but the ringleaders managed to escape. However, their families paid a high price for the rebellion of their menfolk.

Retribution on Families

Even though the leaders of the mutiny managed to escape, Ala ud-Din had the families of these officers imprisoned, irrespective of their age. This was the beginning of the reprehensible practice of seizing women and children as hostages for the misdeeds of the men of the family.

Nasrat Khan, who had lost a brother to the mutineers was particularly harsh in his treatment of the families of defaulting soldiers. He dishonoured the women, had the infants killed in front of their mothers and then turned the women into street prostitutes. All contemporary chroniclers deplore the treatment meted out to the women and evenly proclaim that these punishments were neither sanctioned nor practised in any religion of creed.

Ranthambhor

Ranthambhor with its strong fortress was next on Ala ud-Din's list of kingdoms to be conquered. Rajasthan was not an attractive place to invade, both because of the harshness of the terrain and the scarcity of riches that were conducive to plunder. However, there were three fundamental reasons for Ala ud-Din's decision to target Ranthambhor as the next kingdom for invasion. First, Ranthambhor was strategically important to control the route south from Delhi into Central and Peninsular India. Second, the Rajputs, always turbulent in their attitude towards the foreign invaders, had started to become very active and hostile in the vicinity of Delhi. There was an urgent need to curb their activities. Third, Ranthambhor with its almost impregnable fort would serve well as a security outpost for Delhi. The geo-strategic reasoning for the invasion was unquestionably correct and the ministers and generals concurred with Ala ud-Din's decision. However, at this stage the sultan held complete sway over the court and the concurrence of the courtiers would have been a mere rubber stamp of approval for an unprovoked invasion.

Qutb ud-Din Aibak had captured the fort, but held it only for a brief period of time and although further efforts were made to capture the fort, the successes had been short lived. In effect, the fort remained in Rajput hands. In the 1290s, Ranthambhor was ruled by Rana Hamir Deva, a Rajput prince who was the descendant of the legendary Chauhan king, Prithviraja III. Ala ud-Din personally led the campaign against Ranthambhor, his forces ravaging Malwa and Dhar on the march. The advanced force led by the sultan's favoured commander Nasrat Khan reached Ranthambhor first and attacked the fort. Unfortunately Nasrat Khan was killed in a freak strike of a stone that was launched from a catapult from the fort and Rana Hamir managed to drive the sultanate forces back. The sultan now took personal command and a protracted siege ensued. When the situation became critical within the fort, Rana Hamir and his followers performed the rite of 'Jauhar'. Jauhar is the ceremony by which all women and children throw themselves into a pyre and self-immolate after which the warriors would storm out of the fort and fight to the death—to kill and be killed. The capitulation of the fort under these dire circumstances was made possible by the defection of Rana

Hamir's Prime Minister Ran Mal, who was seduced by Ala ud-Din with the promise of power and wealth. The exact nature of his traitorous act is not clearly mentioned in any chronicle. Although the fort was captured, the sultanate army suffered heavy casualties.

The death of Rana Hamir is described in the poem, *Hamir-Mahakavya*. Although the details are slightly different from those recorded in the Islamic chronicles, it confirms the story of the capture of Ranthambhor. In the poem there is no mention of the fort committing the rite of Jauhar. It however confirms that the defeat was because of the defection of Ran Mal and also mentions two generals, Ratipal and Krishnapal, as having been defectors. Rana Hamir was badly wounded in battle and finding that he had no chance to avoid being captured, is said to have struck off his own head. The Rana preferred death to the ignominy of capture in the true tradition of a proud Rajput.

A Tale of Loyalty

At the end of the last battle when Ranthambhor had fallen, Ala ud-Din saw Mir Muhammad Shah, a Mongol general in the service of Rana Hamir Deva, lying wounded on the battlefield. Ala ud-Din asked the general what he would do if the sultan ordered his treatment and saved his life. In scornful pride the Mongol general replied, 'If I recover from my wounds, I would have thee slain and raise the son of Hamir Deo upon the throne'.

Ala ud-Din had Muhammad Shah killed by being trampled by an elephant. However, he gave the general a decent funeral befitting his status. The sultan was left to reflect on the fidelity and loyalty of even Muslim generals to the Rajput king and compare it to the intrigue and disunity that prevailed in his own court.

Ranthambhor was captured in July 1301 and Ulugh Khan was placed as the governor. Characteristically, Ala ud-Din had Ran Mal, the traitorous Prime Minister, executed immediately after the fort was captured. He had absolute disdain for people who betrayed their masters for wealth or position. This was such a contradictory stance, considering his own betrayal of his uncle to come to power in Delhi.

Internal Rebellions

Even though his military campaigns were successful, Ala ud-Din's court was teeming with intrigue and plots. On the way to take command of the campaign against Ranthambhor, Ala ud-Din halted at Tilpat, close to Delhi, to engage in his favourite pastime of hunting. One day, during the excitement of the chase, he was separated from his escorts. Seeing an opportunity, Akat Khan, the son of his brother, attacked the sultan with some troops. Ala ud-Din defended himself vigorously, although after some time the sultan collapsed from fatigue. However, some loyal troops arrived at the nick of time and saved him. Akat Khan, believing Ala ud-Din to be dead, went back to the camp and after announcing the death of the sultan proceeded to assume power. Akat Khan was young and rash, and had not ensured that the sultan was dead by severing his head form his body. When the sultan, now revived and safe, returned to the camp, Akat Khan panicked and fled. He was pursued, captured and immediately beheaded and all his supporters put to death.

The sultan's long absence from the capital and the seat of power provided the impetus for some malcontent courtiers to hatch a conspiracy plot against him to usurp the throne. They made his sister's sons Amir Umar and Mangu Khan the figurehead leaders and rebelled in Badaun and Awadh. The loyal governors of these provinces easily quelled the rebellion and having captured both the princes, send them to Ala ud-Din in Ranthambhor. The sultan had them blinded in his presence and then imprisoned.

The most serious rebellion was perpetuated by a group of discontented officers led by Haji Maula who was the son of a slave of the kotwal of Delhi. He forged a formal royal order, collected a mob around him and after securing the city gates, took over the royal treasury. He placed an Alawi (descendent of Ali), who was related to Iltutmish from his mother's side, on the throne to ensure legitimacy of the uprising. He then went on to divide the royal treasure among his followers. Ala ud-Din's foster brother, Malik Hamid ud-Din led an army to Delhi and the rebels were defeated in a fierce battle at the Badaun gate. Haji Maula was beheaded in battle. Ulugh Khan also arrived in Delhi at this stage and put to death all supporters of Haji Maula. The sons of the kotwal, an acknowledged supporter of Ala ud-Din, were also executed for complicity although they had no knowledge of the rebellion.

The Attack on Chittor (Chittorgarh)

After a respite of nearly two years, Ala ud-Din returned to Rajasthan. Chittor was strategically important to safeguard the route to the Deccan and was the stronghold of the kingdom of Mewar. The fort was naturally fortified—situated on top of a hill and made impregnable by being cut out of a huge rock. Further, the kingdom of Mewar itself was secluded and protected by a long chain of mountains and impervious forests. No Muslim ruler had so far managed to penetrate far into Mewar or capture Chittor. Nonetheless, Ala ud-Din besieged the fort.

The Romanticised Legend of Rani Padmini

There is another version of the reason for Ala ud-Din's invasion of Mewar and Chittor, which is best understood as a story of Rajput valour embellished with colourful frills with every retelling. It is said that Ala ud-Din was drawn to Chittor after having heard about the enchanting beauty of Padmini (also called Padmavati in some accounts), the queen of Rana Ratan Singh of Mewar. The fact is that Ala ud-Din Khilji was the first of the Delhi sultanate rulers to have nurtured expansionist ambitions and who followed through with resolute action. The territorial expansion started with the capture of Gujarat and Malwa and the plan was then to spread towards Maharashtra and the Deccan. Ala ud-Din's invasion of Mewar and the siege of Chittor has to be understood within this political and military strategy aimed at bringing southern kingdoms under his control.

The first mention of Rani (Queen) Padmini is found in an epic poem *Padmavat*, written by the Sufi poet Malik Muhammad Jayasi in Awadhi language in 1540, two centuries after the battle for Chittor. The poem is definitely based on few historical facts, such as Ala ud-Din's invasion of Chittor that is authenticated by several independent sources. However, the poem is wreathed in fantasy and recounts imaginary events that cannot be considered to have any historical authenticity. There is also no contemporary records that mention the name or acknowledge the existence of a queen called Padmini/Padmavati. However, the fact that Ala ud-Din invaded and conquered Chittor is not debatable. Contemporary accounts written by Amir Khusrao who accompanied Ala ud-Din on the campaign does not mention the story of the queen but confirm the invasion.

> **The Story as given in the *Padmavat***
>
> The poem starts with a fanciful description of the kingdom of Simhala-Dvipa, modern day Sri Lanka, where a princess of exquisite and unparalleled beauty, Padmini, lived. The poet calls her 'the perfect woman'. Padmini had a talking parrot, Hira-mani, who on being berated by the king of Simhala-Dvipa flew away to Chittor. There the parrot informed Raja Ratansen of the beauty of Padmini. The king was completely smitten and managed to marry Padmini after overcoming many obstacles and fighting and winning many dramatic battles.
>
> In the kingdom of Chittor, where Ratansen and Padmini lived, there was a sorcerer named Raghav Chaitanya. He invoked dark spirits to the court and as a punishment was banished by king Ratansen. Chaitanya travelled to Delhi and described Padmini's beauty to Ala ud-Din who was aroused with desire to an extent that he wanted to possess her. He therefore invaded Chittor to obtain Padmini. However, valiant Padmini opted to kill herself rather than submit to a Muslim. She and the other Rajput women committed Jauhar before the warriors led by the king were killed and Chittor was captured.

It is also important to note here that Amir Khusrao does not mention a Jauhar being held, unlike in his description of the fall of Ranthambhor few years back. There is a curious relationship between historical facts and literary stories broadly based on a particular historical event. With the passage of time and numerous recounting of the stories, there comes a moment when it becomes difficult to distinguish between the real event and the embellished derivative. The story of Rani Padmini of Chittor is a stellar example of this process of osmosis. Today Padmini is considered to have actually existed and carried out the deeds ascribed to her, becoming a character of historic pride to a large number of Indians, rather than the heroine in an ancient literary work.

There are also few variations in the details of the historic legend of Padmini. Considering the importance being given to this fictionalised heroine in modern day India and the myths being perpetuated by biased believers as the truth, the available versions are given below in very broad terms to avoid this narrative being declared an equally biased opinion piece. After the fortress was besieged, Ala ud-Din demanded to see Padmini, but the virtuous queen spurned his advances. However, considering the peril to the kingdom from the Muslim onslaught, she agreed to be seen by the sultan through an intricate arrangement of mirrors. There are two further divergent versions of the story after this point.

The first version is that Ala ud-Din was further inflamed with desire for the queen after the fleeting glimpse that he had, which led to the inevitable battle between the armies. The Rajput army fought valiantly, but the Turkish army proved superior and the Rajputs were forced to retreat to the fort. Once the Rajput warriors had entrenched themselves in the fort, the ladies led by Padmini, performed the rite of Jauhar. The Rana and his warriors then opened the gates of the fort and the Rajput army sallied forth for the last time and joined battle with the much larger Muslim army till every Rajput warrior had perished in battle.

The second version is even more romanticised. After the mirror viewing of the queen, when the Rana was escorting Ala ud-Din to the outer gates of the fort—a gesture that was customarily shown towards honoured guests—he was treacherously captured by the Muslim army and imprisoned. Thereafter Ala ud-Din send word to Padmini that the Rana would be freed only if she agreed to enter Ala ud-Din's harem. The Rajput courtiers were greatly disconcerted by this demand and decided to send poison to the Rana so that he could end his life and break the stalemate. At this juncture, the Rana's daughter intervened with the suggestion of another strategy to free the Rana while preserving the honour of the family and the clan. According to this plan, Padmini send word to Ala ud-Din that she was prepared to come to his camp. The besotted sultan permitted her to come in a procession befitting her status, rank and dignity as a queen. 700 covered litters containing Rajput warriors accompanied the queen. On arriving at the Muslim camp, these warriors rescued the Rana and fled back to Chittor, hotly pursued by Ala ud-Din's forces. There was a deadly battle at the outer gates of the fortress. Rajput heroes, Gora and Badal, leading a small contingent of fierce warriors resisted the Muslim onslaught valiantly, but were ultimately overcome. Their bravery at the last stand is part of the Rajput lore that bards still sing about. When the outer defences were at last broken, the ladies in the fort committed Jauhar and the warriors went into their last battle to kill and be killed.

> 'The fair Padmini closed the throng, which was augmented by whatever of female beauty or youth could be tainted by Tartar lust. They were conveyed to the cavern, and the opening closed upon them, leaving them to find security from dishonour in the devouring element.'
>
> Lt Col James Tod,
>
> *Annals and Antiquities of Rajasthan,* Edited by William Crooke, Vol I, p. 311.
>
> As quoted in Ishwari Prasad, *History of Medieval India,* p. 200

> 'It is clear, too, that Tod's rajputs gave a good account of themselves, with the great hill-forts of Ranthambhor, Jalor and Chitor, withstanding long sieges, occasioning heavy casualties, and inspiring posterity with their legendary *jauhars*. These *hara-kiri* rituals had been practiced by other doughty patriots ever since Sind was first invaded in the eighth century, but the rajputs of Rajasthan now made

> them peculiarly their own. When all was lost, when the last scrap of food had been eaten, the last arrow fired, the last water-skin emptied, a pyre was lit and, as the womenfolk hurled themselves into the flames, the men rode out in a still brighter blaze of glory to kill until they were killed. Fanaticism was not an exclusively Islamic prerogative. The Khalji forces marvelled that principalities so agriculturally disadvantaged and forts so poorly endowed with treasure should occasion such passionate resistance.'
>
> John Keay
>
> *India: A History*, pp. 256-57

The Facts – Gleaned from Reliable Sources

The story of Padmini has been told and retold over the years with additional and legendary frills being attached with each recounting. It has indelibly passed on to the bardic history of Rajasthan, so much so that to deny that the episode ever happened is to invite the wrath of the self-righteous practitioners of the Hindu religion in modern India. *[Founded on the concept of extreme tolerance, the Hindu religion—referred to by philosophers as more a way of life than a practice as a religion—has been hijacked and in modern India has morphed into an intolerant religion fully controlled by narrow-minded practitioners who could be called religious fundamentalists.]*

Even at the risk of offending the fringe elements in the Hindu religion, it has to be stated that there are no records in contemporary chronicles to substantiate the story of the beautiful queen of Chittor and the sultan's obsession with her. In fact these records state that the fort was conquered fairly rapidly, although after ferocious fighting. Amir Khusrau states that 30,000 Hindus were slaughtered after Chittor was captured and a large number of temples destroyed. This statement specifically excludes any mention of the rite of Jauhar having been conducted, in which case there would not have been so many Hindus to kill after the fort had fallen; they would have been killed in the last battle before the capture of the fort. However, there are counter-arguments that the mirror episode did indeed take place and that the

Rana was treacherously imprisoned after that. The reason given for this episode being ignored in contemporary writings is that it was omitted from the records because of the fear of Ala ud-Din's reprisal to anyone who wrote about him in a moralistic bad light.

The story does not match Ala ud-Din's known character, which was that of a hard-headed and pragmatic monarch, highly unlikely to have been swayed by romantic entanglements that would have proven to be a vulnerability. There is, of course, a slight possibility that a tiny kernel of truth did exist to the story, which was embellished in later years to its current state of a legend, taught as credible history in schools across India. Most modern historians discount the story as a later-day concoction. The one undeniable fact is that Chittor fell into Muslim hands for the first time, and was renamed Khizrabad after Prince Khizr Khan, the eldest son of Ala ud-Din.

Conquest of Malwa

Malwa had been subjugated when Ala ud-Din was the governor of Kara-Manikpur but had gradually reasserted its independence. In 1305, Ain ul-Mulk Multani was ordered to capture Malwa and bring it under sultanate rule. The Raja of Malwa, whose name is contested with different sources naming him Harnanda or Mahalak Deo, fought valiantly against the Muslim army, but was defeated and killed on the battlefield. Malwa was placed under a Mulsim governor. Soon after, the cities of Mandu, Ujjain, Dharmagiri and Chanderi were also annexed and brought under the control of the Delhi administration.

The Conquest of Jalor

Jalor was ruled by Raja Kanera Deva who had sworn allegiance to Ala ud-Din in 1305 and had promised annual tribute. However, he later reneged on his promise and also boasted that he would best the sultan in the battlefield. On hearing this, an enraged Ala ud-Din send an army under command of a female servant Gul-i-Bihist, to subdue him. A low ranking female was chosen as the commander specifically to humiliate the raja.

> Jalor was besieged, but Gul-i-Bihist died before the hard pressed raja could be defeated. The Rajput forces also managed to kill Gul-i-Bihist's son in battle. Ala ud-Din send additional forces under the command of Kamal ud-Din Gurg, who managed to defeat the raja after a protracted siege and battle. Raja Kanera Deva was killed on the battlefield.

With the fall of Jalor, almost the entire North India was under Ala ud-Din's control, except for Kashmir, Nepal, Assam and parts of North-West Punjab. These conquests cleared the way for the invasion of Peninsular India, which was the ultimate aim of the victorious sultan. The invasion of the south was also facilitated by the end of the Mongol threat that enabled the sultan to move several divisions of the army from the North-Western borders of the sultanate. Further, there were no significant threats of provincial rebellion making the situation conducive to pursuing the burning expansionist ambition that Ala ud-Din harboured. South India beckoned the sultan whose avarice knew no bounds and he answered in characteristic style.

The marauding conquests of the Muslim army should not be taken as an indication that none of their campaigns suffered any setbacks. They did suffer severe resistance and casualties, but most of the setbacks were glossed over by contemporary Muslim chroniclers. Only very limited records of the Hindu kingdoms and principalities have survived the pillage that was visited on most conquered palaces and temples. The available local records are in the vernacular and later-day British historians, the main source of the translations of medieval history chronicles, have not given sufficient importance to them. The British historians famously discounted the local records as being flights of fancy because of their ignorance regarding the manner in which Hindu records were maintained and the Hindu way of recounting time and space. This led to a biased retelling of events, which in turn has resulted in some of the modern-day historians even postulating that the Hindus 'welcomed' the Muslim invasion. Nothing could be farther from the truth. Each and every intervention, intrusion and invasion was vigorously opposed with great determination by the local raja or rana and the invading army made to suffer heavy and at times crippling losses. That these local armies were ultimately defeated is a matter for analysis and discussion, and not a result of the lack of courage or the will to fight and die for their kingdom on the part of the Hindus.

PENINSULAR CONQUEST

Once the north and central region had been secured, the pathway to the southern peninsula was open for the Turkish army to sally forth. Ala ud-Din now gave full attention to fulfilling his expansionist ambitions. It is highly unlikely that a person with Ala ud-Din's character would have forgotten his burning ambition to have been called Sikandar Sani, the second Alexander. Ala ud-Din was the first Muslim ruler to cross the Vindhya ranges and embark on an attempt to subjugate Peninsular India. Till this audacious attempt, the Muslim rulers had been content with plundering, and later controlling, North India.

In Muslim phraseology, the Indian sub-continent was generically referred to as 'Hindustan'. At this stage, the fledgling Muslim state in North India had not yet stabilised, still being a developing and immature entity. Because of this and the accompanying logistical complexity, an expedition to the Deccan had so far been considered a risky enterprise. Perhaps because of these reasons, Ala ud-Din set out to the south not with the objective of annexation, but to plunder and collect as much wealth as possible through imposing tributes on the local rulers. This was directly opposed to his policy in the north where he wanted to annex and rule all conquered territories. In the south his intention was to establish vassal states whose rulers would acknowledge the superiority of the Khilji dynasty, thereby enhancing the prestige of the sultanate. The gold plundered from the near south had brought him the throne of Delhi and he wanted to maintain his position also with wealth from the south.

Ala ud-Din, the shrewd military commander, was well aware of the challenges that faced a southern expedition—the irregular physical features of the terrain that made rapid troop movements difficult; the hostility of the local Hindu kings and chieftains towards foreign invaders; and the distance from Delhi that created logistical issues. These challenges had so far constrained the northern sultanate from invading the Deccan and now made Ala ud-Din discard permanent subjugation as a difficult if not impossible objective to achieve.

The Kingdoms of the Peninsula

There were four powerful kingdoms in the south. In the Western Deccan the Chalukyas, the mighty opponents of the great Cholas, had succumbed to the ravages of time and royal hubris as had their Rashtrakuta predecessors. The Chalukyas had been replaced by two of their erstwhile feudatories—one dominating the area of Maharashtra and the other ruling Karnataka. Both the feudatories were ruled by Yadava dynasties claiming descent from the Vedic Yadu lineage. The Yadava kingdom in the west, with its capital at Devagiri (present-day Daulatabad) covered most of modern Maharashtra. Although historically known as the 'Yadavas of Devagiri', they have also been described by some sources as 'Marathas'. Factually, the correct title of the dynasty is Seuna or Sevuna. They were disadvantaged by being boxed in on all sides by other powerful kingdoms—the Hoysalas to the south; Kakatiyas in the east; Paramara Rajputs of Malwa to the north and the Solanki Rajputs of Gujarat to the west. Even so, the Devagiri kings had managed to carve out a substantial kingdom that covered almost the entire territories held by the ancient Satavahanas.

The second was the Kakatiya kingdom of Telengana in the east with its capital at Warrangal that had replaced the Eastern Chalukyas of Vengi. The third was the Hoysala kingdom with its capital at Dwarasamudra also called Dwaravatipura, the modern Halebid. The kingdom comprised the territories south of the River Krishna—the whole of the pre-modern state of Mysore and some additional districts around it. Of the two Yadava clans, the Hoysalas were the more epigraphically articulate and therefore a great deal of information is available regarding their origins and rule. They were originally hill people from the Western Ghats, north of Coorg, who in the 10th century had carved out a small kingdom around Belur about 200 kilometres west of modern-day Bangalore. They had joined the Chalukyas against the Chola invasion in 11th century. Having acquitted themselves well in the war, they had gained importance and territory. The Hoysalas were able to shrewdly manipulate the conflicts between other neighbouring states to their advantage, gradually increasing their territorial holdings. By the end of the 13th century, they controlled most of northern Karnataka and also the plains of the River Kaveri around Trichy.

The fourth was the Pandya kingdom of the far south with Madura as its capital. By mid-13th century, under the kingship of Sundara Pandyan, they had overthrown the Chola dominance and also blunted and then stopped the Hoysala's southward thrust. The Pandyas had then struck north-east, deep into the Telugu country of the Kakatiyas.

The Conquest of Devagiri

In 1294, during his governorship of Kara, Ala ud-Din had defeated Raja Rama Chandra of Devagiri and imposed an annual tribute on him. However, Rama Chandra had defaulted in payment for three years consecutively and Ala ud-Din was determined to reduce the king to submission, in order to re-establish his supremacy over Devagiri. There is another version regarding the reason for holding back the tribute, which avers that it was the crown prince Singhana who insisted on withholding the tribute. In this recounting, Rama Chandra is supposed to have informed the sultan accordingly, perhaps in a bid to soften the retribution that he knew was sure to come and to keep open communications to plea for leniency, if necessary.

Ala ud-Din send an army to conquer Devagiri, under the command of Malik Naib Kafur, the slave who had been send to Delhi from Cambay by Nasrat Khan. This Hindu slave had converted to Islam and had risen in royal service to be appointed the 'naib' of the sultanate. The title means 'Lieutenant of the Kingdom' although the exact duties that this appointment entailed remains unclear. This campaign was the first to be undertaken by Malik Kafur as a military commander and marked the beginning of his playing a central role in the affairs of state. He went on to gain such importance that from this campaign against Devagiri till his death, the history of the Delhi sultanate and the biography of Kafur run concurrent in an intertwined manner.

An Additional Objective

There is supposed to have been a subsidiary objective to the campaign against Devagiri. The exact details and historical authenticity of the story is unclear. As is usual in the case of such stories, romanticised versions have also sprung up over a period of time.

The additional objective that was given to Malik Kafur was to bring Deval Devi, the daughter of Raja Karan of Gujarat, to Delhi. The story goes that Raja Karan, ruling the small principality of Baglan, had arranged the marriage of his daughter Deval Devi with the crown prince of Devagiri and the eldest son of Raja Rama Chandra, Singhana (or Shankar in some reports). Karan's wife, Kamala Devi had previously been taken prisoner by Ala ud-Din's forces. She had been taken to Delhi and had reconciled to being part of the royal harem. It seems she had requested the sultan to bring her daughter Deval Devi also to Delhi, a task given to Malik Kafur on his southward expedition.

Malik Kafur, on his way to the Deccan, passed through Malwa and Gujarat. Raja Karan, along with his daughter, fled to Devagiri and sought protection. The narrative now takes two different versions. The first is that Malik Kafur, now reinforced by an army under Ulugh Khan joining his forces, marched on Devagiri and demanded the surrender of Deval Devi. This demand was obviously curtly refused and Devagiri prepared for war. In the ensuing conflict Raja Rama Chandra was defeated and captured.

The second version is more complex. It narrates that while Raja Karan was fleeing towards Devagiri, he was intercepted by forces led by Alp Khan and defeated in battle. While Raja Karan managed to escape to Devagiri, his daughter Deval Devi was captured and send to Delhi. There she was married to Khizr Khan, the eldest son of Ala ud-Din. The episode was romanticised by the contemporary poet Amir Khusrau in a long poem called 'Ashiqa', in which the prince Khizr Khan marries the princess Deval Devi after falling hopelessly in love with her. This version has great similarity to the story of Rani Padmini of Chittor.

In the event, it is irrefutable that Malik Kafur defeated Raja Rama Chandra in battle, captured him and his son who were then send to Delhi along with their families. In Delhi Rama Chandra presented Ala ud-Din with a tribute of enormous wealth in return for which the sultan bestowed the title of 'Rai-i-Rayan', meaning King of Kings, on the Devagiri monarch; restored his kingdom to him; and in addition also gifted Rama Chandra with the district of Navsari as a personal jagir. Raja Rama Chandra and his entire family were treated magnanimously and allowed to return to Devagiri to resume his interrupted rule. The good treatment meted out to Rama Chandra turned out to be a shrewd investment on the part of Ala ud-Din. Throughout his remaining reign Raja Rama Chandra remained loyal to the Delhi sultanate and Devagiri served as the secure launching pad for Ala ud-Din's ambitious peninsular incursions. The year was 1307.

Malik Kafur had executed his first military expedition in a flawless manner; it was efficient and effective, traits that were to become hallmarks of his subsequent campaigns.

Attacks on Telangana

The discomfiture felt by the Yadavas of Devagiri because of their defeat by the Muslim army was a precursor to the fate that awaited the other major Hindu dynasties in the south. In 1303, while the campaign against Devagiri was in full swing, Ala ud-Din despatched an army under Chhajju—also known as Fakhr ud-Din Jauna, who would in the future come to be known as Muhammad Tugluq—the nephew and successor of Nasrat Khan, to subjugate and plunder Telangana. For some inexplicable reason, Chhajju led his army through Bengal and Orissa towards Warangal the capital of Telangana, rather than take the more familiar and relatively easier western route through Devagiri. Predictably, the campaign was a spectacular disaster. The Kakatiya ruler, Prataparudra Deva defeated the Muslim army, which fled north, hotly pursued by the Telangana army. Ala ud-Din was angered and anxious to wipe off the disgrace of a battlefield defeat. He turned to Malik Kafur to set things right in the Peninsula. Bolstered by the enormous success of his expedition against Devagiri, Malik Kafur set off from Delhi in 1309 to subdue the Kakatiyas.

Malik Kafur reached Devagiri fairly quickly, where he was received by the king Rama Chandra and offered all possible assistance. The Devagiri Yadava ruler provided scouts to the Muslim army and even send a contingent of his own Maratha forces, a mix of cavalry and foot soldiers, with Malik Kafur till the borders of his kingdom with Telangana. Kafur then entered Telangana and captured the fort at Sirpur. Prataparudra was taken by surprise and barred himself inside the fort at Warangal. Warangal was considered an impregnable fort with two sets of walls surrounding it, and with a moat in-between. A prolonged siege ensued and when the sultanate army was seen to be successful in breaching the outer wall and had started to fill the moat, the Kakatiya ruler sued for peace.

Ala ud-Din's objective in invading the Kakatiya kingdom was to avenge the earlier defeat, gather booty and obtain tribute. He had instructed Malik Kafur that if the king surrendered, he was to be treated honourably and only a tribute extracted. No other action was to be initiated. It is possible that Ala ud-Din realised the complications in governance that could arise if Telangana was annexed to his growing empire. A rebellion on the withdrawal of the Muslim forces would have been inevitable and it would have been difficult to contain. Further, the possibility of Devagiri and Telangana joining hands when the sultanate army was beyond their southern borders must have also been a real cause for caution. Ala ud-Din needed to keep both these kingdoms 'on-side' to ensure the safety and security of his own forces as they continued to campaign in the Peninsula. In the event, Prataparudra paid an initial tribute of 100 elephants and an enormous amount of jewels, precious stones and gold, while also promising to pay an annual tribute to Delhi.

Koh-i-Noor – The Mountain of Light

The famed jewel Koh-i-Noor is mentioned for the first time at this stage.

As part of the tribute paid by Prataparudra Deva, Malik Kafur was given a fabulous jewel in Warangal, which came to be known to the world as the Koh-i-Noor. The jewel continued to be in the possession of the Delhi sultanate

> till it was taken by the first Mughal emperor Babur when he captured Agra, 200 years after it came into Kafur's possession. Babur is reported to have estimated the value of the jewel as being sufficient to feed the entire world for two days.
>
> After changing hands a number of times, in 1877, it became part of the British crown jewels when it was presented to Queen Victoria on the occasion of her being declared the empress of India.

Malik Kafur returned to Delhi in triumph, laden with treasure. During this expedition he had gathered more information about the rich kingdoms further south and was intent on subduing them. As it turned out, he could not endure the intrigue that was endemic to the Delhi court and so set out on an even more ambitious expedition to the south within five months of his return to Delhi.

The Hoysala Kingdom of Dwarasamudra

Malik Kafur once again routed through Devagiri. However, this time he established an independent camp at Jalna on the River Godavari to act as base camp and also to protect his extended line of communication with Delhi. The military strategist in Kafur must have recognised the vulnerability of his communications line that stretched the length of the Devagiri kingdom, even though Ramachandra ruling Devagiri had so far been a loyal ally. The Hoysala king Vir Ballala III was an energetic ruler who had united the various factions in the region and consolidated the Hoysala kingdom into one that held sway over a large swath of territory. Later chronicles mention that the Hoysala kingdom also encompassed the territory known as Mabar, a strip of land that extended from Kulam (modern-day Quilon) to Nilawar (modern Nellore). He also harboured traditional rivalry with the Devagiri kingdom, repeatedly encroaching Devagiri territory.

When Malik Kafur and his large army reached the northern borders of the Hoysala kingdom, Ballala was away in the south with his army, intervening in an on-going civil war of succession in the

Pandya kingdom. Two Pandya princes—Sundara and Vira Pandya—were in conflict to ascend the throne and Ballala was attempting to play king maker. *[This Sundara Pandya is not to be confused with his ancestor of the same name who had thrown off the Chola yoke in earlier times.]* Kafur saw this fleeting opportunity and grasped it. He force-marched a contingent of 10,000 cavalry to reach the capital Dwarasamudra in 12 days. Ballala, himself an accomplished military commander, realised the danger and also hurried back. Even though he had been invading and raiding Pandya territory till then, he also appealed to both the Pandya princes for assistance to ward of what was indeed a common threat. Vira Pandya responded and send a contingent to assist the Hoysala king. Even so, Vir Ballala did not offer battle to the Muslim force, perhaps taking into account the defeat of both Rama Chandra and Prataparudra to the north. Ballala sued for peace and agreed to pay an annual tribute, accepting a vassal status to Ala ud-Din ruling in Delhi.

Not satisfied with the surrender of the Hoysala king, Malik Kafur gave vent to his religious bigotry. He gave Ballala the option of converting to Islam or accepting the status of a Zimmi. Ballala opted to accept the status of a Zimmi, rather than give up his religion. A Zimmi was an 'unbeliever' who did not accept conversion to the religious tenets of Islam but was still guaranteed security of life and property on payment of a stipulated amount of money/wealth. Malik Kafur was himself a convert and as is seen throughout history, the religious zeal of a new convert far exceeds that of a person born into a religion. Some accounts state that Kafur sacked Dwarasamudra, but this assertion is incorrect. Almost immediately after Ballala's surrender, Malik Kafur embarked upon his far-south odyssey.

The Pandya Kingdom

By the time the sultanate army reached Dwarasamudra, Malik Kafur was already operating in *terra incognita*, no Muslim army had ventured so far south previously. His move further south towards the Pandya kingdom was assisted by scouts from the Hoysala forces. Considering the distance from Delhi and from the tenuous base camp established at Jalna, this southern expedition is an epitome of audacious thinking supported by careful planning.

Even though the events taking place in the Hoysala kingdom was known, the Pandya princes had continued their succession feud, plunging the kingdom into the throes a vicious civil war. Malik Kafur initially marched towards Vira Pandya's stronghold at Birdhul. His selecting Vira Pandya as the first objective could have been because of the fact that the Pandya prince had send help to Ballala to oppose the Muslim army. In any case the Muslim army did not encounter any resistance from the local chiefs and they moved ahead, plundering and destroying rich and ancient temples. The pace of advance was only hampered by the halts necessitated to plunder the temples and the torrential rains that created floods across the myriad streams that criss-crossed the region. This southward journey also resulted in the sacking of the temple towns of Chidambaram and Srirangam.

There is one account which mentions that Sundara Pandya on being bested during the Pandya civil war had reached Delhi and appealed to Al ud-Din for help. It states that Malik Kafur's extraordinary expedition to the far south of the Peninsula was the result of Ala ud-Din's decision to help the Pandya prince. There are no other facts to authenticate this assertion, which has to be discounted as an improbable story.

On the approach of the sultanate army, Vira Pandya had abandoned Birdhul, not shutting himself in his fort as other kings in the south had done so far. He also did not offer open battle from standing positions where he could be defeated and even killed, like the Rajput rulers in the north. Instead he adopted guerrilla warfare as his modus operandi, constantly harassing the advancing Muslim army and avoiding casualties and being captured. Vira Pandya proved to be a crafty adversary who had learned lessons from the Muslim army's strategy and tactics. Malik Kafur failed to subdue him. Kafur however was indefatigable and continued to chase the elusive prince south, reaching Kundur, modern Cannanore. Vira Pandya defended Kundur, although Kafur managed to capture it after fierce fighting. Vira Pandya once again escaped into the impenetrable forests of the region. The Muslim army sacked and plundered the many temples in the vicinity of Kundur and started back to Brahmastapuri, considered to be modern day Chidambaram.

The fact that he was unable to achieve a significant military victory or capture the Pandya king led to Malik Kafur becoming increasingly frustrated at the perceived non-victory in the campaign. He gave vent to his frustration by massacring the population of Brahmastapuri, razing the golden temple of the town to the ground and digging up its foundations to ensure that it was not rebuilt. It is obvious that these desired objectives were not achieved, since the temple was rebuilt and stands in great splendour even today.

Malik Kafur then proceeded to Madura, the Pandya capital, only to find it abandoned—the people had fled the town. In anger, Kafur set the famous temple of Sokkanatha on fire. At this stage the fight back against the invaders started to coalesce in the south. Sundara Pandya's uncle, Vikrama Pandya, attacked the Muslim army with a well organised force. In a dynamic turnabout, the Pandya general defeated Malik Kafur, although Kafur managed to get away with most of the booty; breaking camp and starting his return journey almost immediately.

This defeat, like all others suffered by the Muslim armies, does not merit mention in any of the accounts written by Muslim chroniclers. On the other hand local accounts, written mostly in the vernacular and Indian languages, mention an unbroken series of battlefield victories of the local Hindu chieftains and princes. The truth lies somewhere in between these two extreme viewpoints. In the Peninsula, the Hindu resistance to the invading armies was vehement, concerted and effective. The progress of the Muslim armies was always slow, difficult and full of challenges almost on a daily basis. Their victories were hard won and not one could be considered a cake-walk as has been portrayed by the contemporary Muslim chroniclers such as Amir Khusrav.

Kafur's Return to Delhi

There is an on-going debate regarding the actual events that took place during Malik Kafur's return journey to Delhi—whether he retraced his steps or ventured further into the Peninsula and raided Rameswaram. The claim that he went from Madurai to Rameswaram, sacked the township and then built a mosque on the island of Pamban is based on a single report by Firishta, a later day Muslim chronicler. This report clearly mentions the building of a mosque at 'Sit Band Rameswaram', which has been taken to mean Setubandha at Rameswaram in the Madura district. However, Firishta then goes on to give the location of the mosque as being on the coast of the Sea of Uman—The Arabian Sea—near Dwarasamudra. This dichotomy factually confuses the report. There are three reasons to discount the account of the attack and sacking of Rameswaram, as well as the building of the mosque.

First, Malik Kafur at this stage was almost fleeing following an uncharacteristic defeat by the Pandya army and would not have stopped to sack a town nor dallied for the time required to build a mosque, irrespective of the location of the building. Second, the short duration between his departure from Madura and subsequent arrival in Delhi points to a direct and rapid homeward march and not a wandering detour with relaxed stoppages to build mosques along the way. Third, no other contemporary or later-day chronicler mentions anything about the sacking of Rameswaram, let alone the building of a mosque. The story therefore has to be discounted as a false interpretation of an erroneous statement by Firishta, which does not corroborate the time or the location of such an event.

Much later, in the retelling of Malik Kafur's ambitious expedition to the far-south, some analysts with vested interest in making it sound like a grand conquest of the south have mentioned that Kafur chased Vira Pandya all the way to the coast of Ceylon, modern Sri Lanka. They have also given rise to the perception that the northern Muslim army carried out a daring raid on Rameswaram while still in retreat after its defeat at Madura. These are episodes crafted out of wishful thinking and built out of attempts to embellish and glorify the story of the first Islamic invasion of Peninsular India. There is no doubt that Malik Kafur was an audacious military commander and a master of speed and decisive action. However, it is certain that he returned to Delhi, with the enormous loot that he had somehow managed to salvage even after being defeated in battle at Madura, without attempting any further diversions or campaigns.

Malik Kafur reached Delhi within the year. During this expedition, he had reached farther south than any other Muslim commander ever had; he had burned and destroyed countless number of Hindu temples; he had raided and sacked towns and villages; and harried the common people across the entire Peninsula. In effect he had sown the seeds of dislike and hatred towards the new religion that he carried with him, which would grow and fester within the broader populace, society and the smaller communities for centuries; never being completely healed and forever staying just below the surface of the fabric of communal harmony in South India. In their eagerness to proclaim the grand success of Kafur's southern expedition, biased historians have glossed over the fact that Vira Pandya the prince, who was the de facto king, was never defeated or captured and never brought to submission. Further, the defeat of the Muslim army that resulted in a hurried return to Delhi, which was delivered by a Pandya general and uncle of the elusive prince is not given the importance it deserves.

Malik Kafur's Mabar campaign into the Deep South was more spectacular, especially in the recounting, than effective. It made no real or significant contribution to the expansion of the fledgling Delhi sultanate other than to gather first-hand information of the terrain and the wealth of the southern Hindu kingdoms. Instead of spreading the religion of Islam it embedded an animosity against the religion within the people of the Peninsula that was the beginning of centuries of hatred and religious bigotry, which can be seen in stark and vivid flashes even today in independent India. In a final one sentence analysis, the expedition can be seen as nothing but an excellent predatory raid.

On reaching Delhi, Malik Kafur was received by Ala ud-Din with great honour and a special durbar was held to felicitate him. This was the zenith of Ala ud-Din's rule and the pinnacle of Khilji militaristic triumph.

The Final Foray – Annexation of Devagiri

The ever loyal king of Devagiri, Rama Chandra, died in 1311 and was succeeded to the throne by his son Shankara Deva, also referred in many texts as Singhana II. The correct name, taking into account the list of the Yadava kings who ruled Devagiri, would be Shankara Deva and Singhana should be considered a colloquial Muslim adaptation of it. *[It is seen that the Muslim chroniclers did not make any effort at getting the names of the local kings of the sub-continent correct and adapted them suit their purpose, at times even making them sound derogatory. At the same time, the names of the sultans and Muslim generals were meticulously recorded to include even their minor titles. It is unfortunate that historians who later examined these documents did not pay attention to this aspect, for it is certain that the Hindu kings and princes also had illustrious titles to mark their equally illustrious lineage, which have been lost to antiquity.]*

Shankara Deva was a patriotic and energetic ruler, eager to throw off the Turkish yoke that had been placed over his kingdom during his father's reign. It is certain that he felt humiliated by the treatment meted out to his father by the Delhi sultanate, which used the kingdom repeatedly as a launching pad for expanding invasions of the Peninsula. Therefore, he stopped the payment of the stipulated annual tribute to Delhi. At the same time Prataparudra, ruling in Warrangal, had send word to Delhi asking for an official to be send to collect the annual tribute that was due, citing the great distance between Warrangal and Delhi as an obstacle for him to do so. Whether this was a cunning ploy on the part of the Telangana king to bring a sultanate army back into Devagiri, his traditional adversary who had assisted the Muslim army in the earlier defeat that Telangana had suffered, is left to speculation. Almost immediately on Devagiri stopping to pay the tribute, Al ud-Din ordered Malik Kafur to go there and remedy the situation. The order suited Kafur, since he was being troubled by his rivals in court through intrigue and court politics, games in which he was not adept.

Accordingly, Malik Kafur at the head of a large army, invaded Devagiri. The battle that ensued was severe, ending in the death of Shankara Deva on the battlefield and the subsequent defeat of the Devagiri army. Unlike the previous times, this time Malik Kafur annexed Devagiri to the sultanate and established his headquarters there. From Devagiri he mounted raids on both Telangana and the Hoysala kingdom. The raids were however diminutive in nature and of no real significance. Within the Devagiri territory, he established garrisons at strategic points, significantly at Raichur and Mudgal between the Rivers Krishna and Tungabhadra. He also initiated an unsuccessful expedition to the Pandya territory, through the Hoysala kingdom in an attempt to restore Sundara Pandya to the throne. *[There may be some element of truth in the claim that Sundara Pandya had appealed to Ala ud-Din for help earlier in the Pandya civil war.]* It is unlikely that he personally led the expedition, which was an abject failure.

The Muslim chronicles mention that the Hoysala kingdom had not been fully subjugated in the earlier campaign. Bellary, Raichur and Dharwar, which together comprised the kingdom of Kampili had continued to stay independent. The reports of 'indecisive' campaigns and 'not fully' subjugated must be interpreted as the sultanate army having been defeated in their attempts to achieve subjugation of the local princes. Contemporary chroniclers would never write that their patron was defeated in battle, hence the unending list of 'complete' victories of the Muslim army that litter the chronicles.

Malik Kafur continued to stay in Devagiri for a period of three years, only returning to Delhi in 1315 on the express orders of an ailing Ala ud-Din. For over a decade Malik Kafur had been rampaging in Peninsular India, but the region was not annexed, merely plundered. The only tangible result was that some garrisons were established towards the southern borders of the core territorial holding of the sultanate.

Conclusion

Malik Kafur returned to Delhi to find Ala ud-Din already displaying signs of declining health and spirits. A life of hard work, intemperate habits, combined with creeping old age had destroyed his health. This contributed to a deterioration in his character and individual abilities that had so far been the hallmark of his rule. The early part of Ala ud-Din's rule had been exemplified by his calling for advice from able nobles, generals and courtiers. However, as old age caught up, he was surrounded by sycophants and concentrated power in his own hands. He became an uncompromising autocrat as opposed to an enlightened king. He displayed violent temper tantrums and was openly suspicious of almost everyone.

These traits led to a weakened hold on power and the beginning of court intrigue for influence and succession in the Delhi court. The inevitable process of the disintegration of the empire had begun.

Chapter 11

DEMISE OF THE DYNASTY

Ala ud-Din was bedridden suffering from acute oedema and becoming increasingly petulant and impulsive. The political edifice that he had so painstakingly built up, with personal hard work and a visionary approach to the task of governance, started to crumble in front of his eyes. The Delhi court became the nucleus of palace intrigue with overt succession manoeuvres becoming increasingly vicious. In 1312, Ala ud-Din had nominated Khizr Khan, his eldest surviving son, as the heir apparent. The combination of Ala ud-Din's failing health and the announcement of Khizr Khan as the anointed successor to the great sultan had made the Queen mother, Malika-i-Jahan, assume a role of importance behind the scenes. For a fairly long period of time Ala ud-Din had ignored Malika-i-Jahan who was nominally the chief queen. Now, Malika-i-Jahan, along with her brother Alp Khan who was also Khizr Khan's father-in-law, became the most influential people in the court and assumed roles of prime manipulators.

Khizr Khan is reported to have been a weakling; indolent and addicted to pleasure and debauchery, not interested in shouldering the responsibility that came with the running of a great and complex empire. The sick Ala ud-Din was ignored by his queen, her brother and the prince. The queen and Alp Khan had increased their hold on power while Malik Kafur was away in the Peninsula, pursuing the military conquest of the Deccan. Khizr Khan's younger brother, Shadi Khan was married to the second daughter of Alp Khan, cementing an already strong and closed family clique of power. In utter helplessness and unable to control a deteriorating situation, Ala ud-Din recalled Malik Kafur from the Deccan.

Malik Kafur heeded the sultan's call and hurried back from the south to Delhi. He immediately took charge of the affairs of state and rapidly gained ascendancy in the court through his complete influence over the sultan. Gradually he managed to poison Ala ud-Din's mind against the Alp Khan junta although he failed to get the sultan's agreement to have Alp Khan murdered. Even so, such was the authority that Malik Kafur wielded that he, along with a close associate Kamal ud-Din Gurg, murdered Alp Khan in cold blood. Simultaneously Khizr Khan—the heir apparent—was taken away from the capital, initially to Amroha and then to Gwalior, where he was blinded and imprisoned. His younger brother Shadi Khan was also meted out the same fate. The youngest brother, Mubarak Khan who was 17 years old at this time was only imprisoned. The queen, Malik-i-Jahan was deprived of all luxury and imprisoned within the Delhi fort.

From the very beginning of the Delhi sultanate, turbulence in Delhi had always been echoed by rebellions in the outer provinces where the central hold was tenuous, at best. In this case, the murdered Alp Khan had been well-liked by the ruling class of Turkish nobles in Gujarat. Therefore, it was not long before the army in Gujarat rebelled against Delhi. Malik Kafur, now fully in charge of the empire, send a force under Gurg to quell the rebellion. However, Gurg was defeated by the rebels and killed. Gujerat remained in rebellion. In Chittor, the scion of the Sisodia clan, Hammira Deva, drove out Mala Deva who had been installed as the ruler by Ala ud-Din and became the Rana. Harpala Deva, the son-in-law of Rama Chandra, ruling in Devagiri as a vassal to Delhi, declared independence.

During this increasing turmoil, Ala ud-Din died in early January 1316 (the actual dates vary between 2nd and 6th January). The most forceful ruler of the three centuries of Delhi sultanate died watching the great empire that he had crafted crumbling and breaking up in front of his eyes. Contemporary reports suggest that the cause of death was as much the mental anguish at the state of affairs in his empire as the grave physical ailments that he suffered from.

Malik Kafur's Rule

Malik Kafur had made Ala ud-Din disinherit Khizr Khan before the latter was imprisoned and blinded. A new will had subsequently been drawn up. The new will nominated the six-year old Shihab ud-Din, Ala ud-Din's son by a daughter of Devagiri raja Rama Chandra, as the new sultan. This will was presented to the court on the second day after Ala ud-Din's death. Kafur, now fully entrenched in the court, became the regent and directly undertook the conduct of the government. In order to ensure that his regency of the child-sultan was not threatened by anyone, Kafur started to remove all children and wives of Ala ud-Din from the scene, either through imprisonment or outright murder.

Malik Kafur becoming Ala ud-Din's favourite and the rapid rise in his official position had created a great deal of animosity amongst the Turkish nobles. However, his military triumphs and the sultan's demonstrated favour had so far kept it controlled but simmering below the surface. The resentment against Kafur had further intensified after the blinding of the two princes. Malik Kafur had proven himself to be a great, even brilliant, military commander as well as a wise counsellor. However, he was inept at playing the games within games that was normal in court politics, an arena that was perilous for all but the most adept. The illustrious military commander was unskilled in manipulative politics; this became his undoing.

In order to ensure that the six-year old sultan was not in any way threatened, Malik Kafur send a group of soldiers to blind the imprisoned Mubarak Khan, the third son of Malika-i-Jahan. Mubarak however, managed to bribe the soldiers and turn them against Malik Kafur, reminding them of their loyalty to Ala ud-Din and the Khilji dynasty. The soldiers went back and killed Malik Kafur's confederates and then beheaded the regent himself. Malik Kafur's reign as regent had lasted a mere 35 days. The Turkish nobles released Mubarak Khan from prison, and although he himself was only 17 years old, installed him as the regent for the six-year old sultan who was his step-brother. Two months later, on 1 April 1316, Mubarak ascended the throne as Qutb ud-Din Mubarak Shah after the child-sultan was blinded and imprisoned.

Qutb ud-Din Mubarak Shah

Mubarak Shah began his rule with the nobles and courtiers displaying enormous good will towards him. He improved this position by acting immediately with commendable energy and ability. He released all political prisoners, reinstated confiscated land to its rightful owners and removed the imposition of some extreme taxes—all them populist measures. He recalled most of the nobles and officers who had been banished during the last few erratic years of his father's rule and reinstated them in their previous positions. Essentially, he started his reign enforcing a policy of extreme moderation, one of 'forgive and forget', creating the basis for a fresh start.

Mubarak also exhibited his inherent dual personality at the beginning of his rule. The group of soldiers who had assassinated Malik Kafur on Mubarak's instigation had by now assumed the posture of 'king-makers' and aspired to the position of Praetorian Guards. Almost immediately on assuming power, Mubarak dispersed the group to faraway garrisons and had the leaders executed. Further, like his illustrious father, Mubarak exhibited no compunction in exterminating all possible political rivals including his own brothers and close relatives. On the other hand he lacked his father's single-minded focus and attention to the governance of the state and was also addicted to sensual pleasures.

Mubarak's rapid removal of the strict restrictions on behaviour and protocol that Ala ud-Din had instituted had the unfortunate consequence of creating an outburst of the most licentious behaviour in court, which spread across the country. Moral standards dropped rapidly. After the initial spell of activity, Mubarak gradually abandoned himself to Bacchanalian revels and spend most of his time and energy in debauchery. Considering that he did not take long to descend to moral turpitude, his earlier pro-people policy should perhaps be viewed as the result of an inherent indolent nature rather than far-sighted and well thought through welfare policies.

With the new 'world order' in place, all fear of royal authority vanished—initially within the closed circuit of the court and then across the entire sultanate. Administration from the apex down to the village level became slack, unresponsive and ineffective. Officials abrogated all responsibilities and became tyrannical enforcers of their own interpretation of the law of the land. Bribery and corruption, almost non-existent during the heydays of Ala ud-Din's reign became endemic and wormed its way into the vitals of the empire. The sultanate was ripe for the picking.

Rebellions

The creeping lawlessness of the land was ideal circumstances for the conquered provinces to rebel against foreign domination. The Yadava dynasty of Devagiri declared independence; the army of Alp Khan rebelled in Gujarat and Marwar broke free of Delhi domination. Ain-ul-Mulk, a senior noble was send to Gujarat to bring it under control. He used bribery and diplomacy to divide the rebel forces and then used the army to quell the rebellion. Mubarak's father-in-law, Zafar Khan was installed as the governor. Zafar Khan proved to be an able and even-handed administrator and brought peace to the turbulent province.

Mubarak decided to personally intervene to bring Devagiri under control and marched to that country. The rebel king Harpala Deva fled the capital on the approach of the Muslim army but was chased and captured. Mubarak displayed his brutal streak by flaying the king while still alive and then displaying his head on the gates of the city. He destroyed the temple of the capital and built a mosque on the site with the masonry from the temple. Further, he divided Devagiri into districts under the command of Turkish governors, bringing to an end the centuries-old Yadava rule of the country. Muslim garrisons were established in most major towns, ensuring that they became semi-occupied. This signalled the end of Devagiri as an autonomous entity.

Early in his reign Mubarak had fallen under the influence of a slave named Hasan from Gujarat, who was a recent convert to Islam. Some modern historians claim that Mubarak was infatuated with Hasan and that he had homosexual relations with the slave. No authentication is available for this snippet, but it might explain the rapid rise of Hasan in the Delhi court where he was appointed the Prime Minister and bestowed the title of Khusrav Khan in short order. Hasan's origins are hotly debated even today. *[Details of the discussion regarding his origin and his caste is provided later in the chapter.]*

After subjugating Devagiri and displaying his brutal streak in no uncertain manner, Mubarak returned to Delhi. During his absence, some nobles in Delhi had hatched a plot to assassinate him. The leader of the conspirators was his cousin Asad ud-Din, who had planned to place the ten-year old son of Khizr Khan on the throne and rule as the regent himself. Some nobles who were loyal to Mubarak informed him of the plot. He was enraged and put to death all male members of his extended family, including his two blind brothers. Mubarak's cruel streak came to the fore whenever he felt threatened and did not need much instigation.

Hasan Khusrav Khan

While he himself returned to Delhi, Mubarak ordered Hasan Khusrav to undertake an expedition further south to gather tribute and plunder for wealth. Hasan had already undertaken a successful campaign against Telangana—capturing vast booty from Warangal and annexing five districts to the sultanate after defeating and forcing the raja to surrender. On Mubarak's orders he now proceeded towards Mabar. However, while outwardly playing the role of a general of the Delhi sultanate, he harboured an ulterior ambition to establish a base and carve out an autonomous empire for himself in the south, which would function very loosely as a vassal state of the Delhi sultanate. Hasan's increasing ambition had become apparent to some of his officers and was visible to astute observers. Some loyal officers cautioned Mubarak regarding Hasan's plans leading to Hasan being recalled to Delhi. However, Mubarak was so infatuated with Hasan Khusrav that he punished the loyal officers who had informed him about Hasan's plans rather than removing Hasan from the equation.

By now Hasan had complete control over the sultan. Mubarak was in complete moral decay, appearing in court completely naked, dressing himself up in female clothes, openly consorting with harlots and dancing with them in the streets of Delhi. He was overtly flaunting his sexual predilections. With Mubarak's permission—the sultan could not refuse any request of his favourite—Hasan started to bring friends and kinsmen from Gujarat to Delhi. Over a short period of time he managed raise an army of 40,000 horsemen, a force personally loyal to him alone. He further coaxed the sultan to grant permission for this force to enter the palace grounds at night, putting forward some flimsy excuse for their need to do so.

On 15 April 1320, these troops from Gujarat entered the palace grounds at night, killed the guards and rushed to Mubarak's private quarters. Mubarak, realising the threat, ran towards the women's quarters. However, Hasan caught hold of his hair and another officer stabbed him. His head was severed and the body thrown into the courtyard below. The court was immediately assembled at night and the nobles were forced to consent to Hasan Khusrav Khan ascending the throne with the title Nasir ud-Din Khusrav Shah. Hasan won over a majority of the nobles and several Muslim clerics by scattering gold and giving opulent gifts. He also managed to appease some Khilji loyalists by gifting them lavishly. One of them was Fakhr ud-Din Jauna, the future Muhammad bin Tughluq, who was honoured in many ways and also made 'Master of the Horse'.

The new sultan Nasir ud-Din, blinded, imprisoned and/or killed all possible claimants to the throne, including small boys and even infants related to the Khilji family. Mubarak's harem was raided by Hasan and his men, who treated the women abominably. The Khilji dynasty came to an ignoble end.

Mubarak Shah – An Unworthy Sultan

Mubarak Shah did not lack courage or ability, as was amply demonstrated in his expedition to Devagiri. However, he was an unworthy successor to the competent Ala ud-Din. All the same, he was a lucky monarch. During his reign, there were no famines, no Mongol raids that had become regular in the few years before his coming to power and no other natural calamity threatened the tranquillity of the country. Many of the troubles that had erupted during Ala ud-Din's last years on the throne, abated with Mubarak assuming the throne. A sense of security seemed to prevail over the country. It is unfortunate that Mubarak was unable to capitalise on the benign circumstances that prevailed to entrench the Khilji rule in Delhi.

Mubarak's character has been reported as a 'bizarre amalgam of debauchery and bestial violence'. He was highly eccentric and may well have been clinically insane. He lived in a permanent state of paranoia and insecurity, being capable of unleashing demonic savageries at the slightest provocation. He also displayed an extremely violent and vindictive spirit, which led to a series of random executions of nobles and others who displeased him. The goodwill that prevailed on his ascension to the throne was frittered away very rapidly. In this frenzy of violence Mubarak also managed to finally sever the theoretical umbilical cord that the previous sultans had all maintained with the Caliphate in Baghdad. It was during his brief and murderous reign that the Delhi sultanate came to its own as a truly independent country.

Nasir ud-Din Khusrav Shah

Nasir ud-Din was the only 'Indian' Muslim to sit on the throne of Delhi during the period in Indian history now known as the era of Delhi sultanate, normally calculated as being between 1206 and 1526. His ascension to the throne is also portrayed as a 'Hindu' coup by Barani and other contemporary writers. They heaped vile epithets on him and attempted to lower his status by proclaiming that he originally belonged to the scavenger caste from Gujarat, and therefore essentially an untouchable. The real reason for this unprecedented animosity—towards a ruling sultan, however he may have come to the throne—was that he did not belong to the self-declared Turkish aristocracy from Central Asia, but a Hindu convert to Islam from Gujarat.

Origins of Nasir ud-Din Khusrav Shah

Hasan has been described as a 'Parwari' by Barani, which would make him an untouchable since that title was used by the Hindu caste of scavengers from Gujarat. This was an expression of disdain, demonstrating the Turk's prejudice against Islamised Indians, many of whom were indeed from the lower castes.

European historians, the first one being John Briggs who translated the works of Farishta, confused the caste title and proclaimed him an 'untouchable'. Some later European historians also endorsed this erroneous view, perpetuating the myth of Hasan's unsavoury origin. Unfortunately some modern Indian historians, who are scholars of influence

> and erudition—for example, Dr Iswari Prasad and Dr Mahdi Husain—have also accepted the European view without sufficient research and analysis. This assertion of Hasan's lowly origin is patently incorrect.
>
> Some later-day European writers, do not attach any significance or value to the abuse heaped on Hasan Khusrav by the contemporary Muslim chroniclers. James Bird, who translated the Persian chronicle 'Mirat-i-Ahmadi' as *The History of Gujarat* states that Khusrav belonged to the clan of Parmar Rajputs. This is corroborated by Amir Khusrav's report that Hasan belonged to 'Baradus', a military Hindu caste, who were traditional commandos of the rajas whom they served. This assessment is probably the closest to the truth.
>
> It is certain that Hasan Khusrav belonged to the warrior class. Only this origin can explain his bravery and martial talent, as well as his ability to administer an empire.

The claim of a Hindu coup could be attributed to the fact that a number of Khusrav's followers and companions were Hindus from Gujarat. They could have performed some Hindu rites within the palace walls, leading to the rumour that the Hindus had taken over the kingdom. The fact remains that Hasan Khusrav remained a steadfast and practising Muslim till his death. Khusrav married Mubarak's widow and his followers also took as wives some of the ladies of the harem. Some of these ladies, forced to be wives of Hasan's followers were the wives of some of the Turkish noblemen, which created unwanted animosity against the Gujarat contingent.

These actions and the coup itself combined to make the rule of an 'Indian' Muslim intolerable for the Turkish nobility. Khusrav won over many nobles by the lavish distribution of gifts and wealth from the royal treasury and also by retaining many of them in their old positions, while even promoting some of them. Even so, irreconcilable differences existed between the Turkish noblemen and the 'Indian'

Muslim sultan. The racial prejudice of the arrogant Turks could not tolerate the rule of a sultan who was an Indian Muslim convert. Opposition to Khusrav's rule started to mount and coalesced around the Turkish noble, Ghazi Malik. Ghazi Malik had been the 'Warden of the Marches' in the north-west and was stationed at Dipalpur. He was an able commander and had successfully kept the marauding Mongols at bay for a considerable period of time.

Ghazi Malik had kept out of the fray during the turmoil that was the result of Mubarak's assassination and Khusrav's coming to power. This was mainly because his son, Fakhr ud-Din Jauna, was in Delhi and could have been targeted if Ghazi Malik had initiated any action against Khusrav. In fact Jauna had been feted and promoted by Khusrav. However, Jauna managed to escape from Delhi to a fort within his father's province in the Punjab. Ghazi Malik was now free to move against Khusrav the 'imposter'.

Some contemporary chroniclers, particularly Zia ud-Din Barani, aver that Khusrav was completely unpopular. They also report that some Turkish nobles charged Khusrav with being a half-Hindu, of insulting Islam and promoting idol worship. This narrative is completely incorrect and the epitome of totally biased reporting. The truth lay somewhere else. It can be verified that Khusrav had the support of a large number of influential Muslim commanders and noblemen. He also had the moral support of the majority of Islamic clerics, who had been appalled by the behaviour of Mubarak. Only a small minority of Turks were racially and ethnically biased against him. Ghazi Malik represented the Turkish oligarchy who were averse to 'Indian' Muslims attaining any position of power, let alone being the sultan!

Ghazi Malik Usurps Power

Once he was sure that his son was safe, Ghazi Malik appealed to the governors of Uch, Multan, Siwastan (Sehwan) and Jalor to rebel against Khusrav, reasoning with them that Islam was in danger. However, only the governor of Uch, Bahram Aiba, responded with limited support. The rest did not think that Islam was endangered and kept out of the possible civil war that was brewing. It is significant that Ghazi Malik's appeal for rebellion was only send to the governors of the western provinces, who were all Turkish nobles. Further, even with the Turks he found only very limited support against Khusrav, even though religious reasons had been given for the rebellion. The great saint, Nizam ud-Din Auliya, refused to endorse the rebellion and did not provide moral support to the rebels. It is obvious that the cry of Islam being in danger was a thin ruse to incite people to rebel against Khusrav because he was an 'Indian' Muslim convert. Although the governors did not support Ghazi Malik, he was able to incite the people and some middle ranking officials joined him.

Khusrav Shah came to know about the rebellion being fomented against him and send a force of 40,000 under command of his brother to Dipalpur. On the way this force encountered the fort of Sarsuti (modern Sirsa) where Jauna was ensconced and failed to capture it. Thereafter, this force was comprehensively defeated by Ghazi Malik in a short encounter. Ghazi Malik then marched on Delhi. Khusrav organised another large army and went out to meet the enemy. He distributed a great amount of wealth amongst the soldiers, but it is reported that a number of them took the money and then deserted the sultan's forces. One of Khusrav's top generals also switched sides to the rebels. Battle was joined at Indarpat near Delhi in early September 1320. It was closely contested, but Khusrav was defeated and fled the battlefield. He was caught in the gardens of a noble near Tilpat and beheaded.

The nobles and courtiers of Delhi offered the keys to the Palace of a Thousand Pillars at Siri to Ghazi Malik. In a studied move, he formally hesitated, asking for any survivor of Ala ud-Din's family to be made the sultan. However, he already knew that all male members were dead and with an outward show of reluctance Ghazi Malik assumed the throne of Delhi with the title Ghiyas ud-Din Tughluq Shah, thus establishing the Tughluq dynasty.

Chapter 12

ALA UD-DIN – THE ONLY KHILJI WHO MATTERED

Irrespective of the despotism, as well as the chaos and confusion that had become part of the last years of his reign, a thoughtful retrospective of Ala ud-Din Khilji's rule is necessary to understand the important contribution that he made towards expanding and perpetuating Muslim rule in the sub-continent. Although he ruled from Delhi, he planted the first seeds of the spread of Islam and Islamic rule into Peninsular India. He was the most effective Muslim ruler to reign from Delhi till then. Barani, one of the chroniclers of the time, has stated that Ala ud-Din's reign was a 'constant succession of victories', high praise indeed from a chronicler who was not unduly enamoured with him. Ala ud-Din was a radical reformer, introducing many initiatives in the governance of the state that were several centuries ahead of his time successfully. His successes elicited reluctant praise and admiration even from his critics and sceptics.

Treatment of Hindus

It is noteworthy that religious bigotry against Hindus has very seldom been mentioned as one of the traits of Ala ud-Din, even as an accolade by fawning courtiers of a conquering sultan. It must be recalled that he had evinced considerable interest in the creation of a new religion centred on his exalted person and therefore it is almost certain that his personal religious views would have been unorthodox to say the least. His interest in Hinduism could be considered to have been limited to the appreciation of the quantum of treasure that could be plundered from the temples and the wealth that could be extorted from the Hindu princes and noblemen. As was universally the case in medieval times, the common people did not matter in the broader picture that the king viewed. The fact that in the case of Ala ud-Din, the common people were overwhelmingly Hindus was not of any consequence.

Even so, there is evidence of his religious fanaticism and animosity towards the non-believing Hindus. The Khilji kingdom housed a large number of villages whose headmen were obviously Hindus. They were responsible for the collection of revenue and over generations of hereditary inheritance had become very wealthy. Ala ud-Din would not tolerate 'wealthy' Hindus and therefore enacted laws that reduced the rich and powerful Hindu chiefs to penury and the village headmen to mere peasant status. The Hindu population of the sub-continent were traditionally connected to the land, having been owner-farmers for generations. The imposition of extreme land laws and the Jizya tax reduced the entire Hindu population to poverty and misery. It is reported that Hindu women from noble houses were forced to take 'servants' jobs in Muslim households in order to survive.

It has been argued that these measures against the Hindus were instituted for the stability of the state by ensuring that the Hindus did not rebel. For a king who is reported to have been singularly focused on the expansion of the kingdom—in terms of territory, wealth and status—the singling out of Hindus for extreme treatment through the imposition of separate and higher land taxes, in comparison to the Muslim subjects, can only be considered an indirect attempt at coerced conversion. The clear message being send out was that if you became a Muslim, you would live a comfortable life and could even aspire to prosperity in life. If you insisted on staying true to your religion as a Hindu, you would be grounded down into poverty and destitution. This is not the conduct of a benign ruler. Much like all other Muslim rulers across the world, Ala ud-Din also persecuted subjects who were non-believers. In the case of the India sub-continent, the non-believers happened to be Hindus.

Stabilising the Country

The fact that the sultanate was a hotbed of conspiracies, rebellions and attempted coups was entrenched in Ala ud-Din's mind. It could be said that he was obsessed with the need to root out traitors and possible rebels. Considering that he had himself usurped the throne through an act of open rebellion, facilitated through calculated treachery, may have added to this prejudice. Alternatively, in his self-aggrandisement he may have forgotten his own treacherous usurpation of power and genuinely looked down on rebels and treacherous persons. Almost immediately after he had secured his hold on power, he had some loyal advisers analyse the cause for the proclivity in the sultanate towards rebellion and coups led by the sultan's own relatives and high officials. The result of this soul searching was revealing.

The nobles who did the analysis came back to the sultan with four primary causes for the stream of rebellions that had so far been witnessed. The causes they delineated were: the increasing prosperity of nobles and high officials; intermarriage between powerful families; inefficiency of the espionage system of the sultan; and the consumption of alcohol.

Accordingly, Ala ud-Din decreed and enforced four ordnances. The first was to order the confiscation of all tax-free land grants and revenue gathering rights that had so far been made by earlier sultans and had been enjoyed by noble families for generations. Along with this, he also seized all Muslim religious endowments and ceased further endowments without his express permission. Second, he forbade all social gatherings in nobles' houses and made it compulsory for the noblemen to seek and obtain the sultan's personal approval for any marriages being contemplated between two important families. Third, he reorganised the intelligence system and instituted an effective espionage network through which he came to know all the secret transactions taking place in the court as well as in the house of the nobles. This clandestine reporting network gradually started to be feared by all the nobles. Fourth, he prohibited the sale and consumption of alcohol and enforced strict prohibition in Delhi. The sultan himself gave up the consumption of alcohol. Subsequently the ordnance was modified to permit home distilling of alcohol for private consumption, but the public sale of all alcoholic beverages continued to be banned.

The enforcement of these ordnances was strict and punishment for defaulters swift and ruthless. In a fairly short period of time Ala ud-Din was able to put an end to the incipient instability that had plagued the sultanate ever since its inception. His own spectacular success in achieving his objectives occasionally deluded Ala ud-Din and he used to become blinded by megalomania. The impulsive and grandiose actions to start a new religion, and perhaps more importantly, his assumption of the title of 'Second Alexander', are prime examples of initiatives that could have been undertaken in a delusionary state.

Economy and Administration

Ala ud-Din was the first sultan to pay personal attention to the management of the economy. He enforced a price-fixing policy to control the prices of food grain and clothing in the market place. It is reported that the prices fixed in Delhi were also imposed on provincial capitals and other towns. However, the effectiveness of these measure in the outlying areas outside the control of the Delhi administration is uncertain. It is highly improbable that the fixed pricing policy was fully enforced across the entire territory of the sultanate. He also established separate markets for different merchandise, creating independent markets that dealt with only one item like grain, clothes, condiments, livestock, slaves etc. A diluted form of this system continues to exist in the markets of Old Delhi even today.

Later-day historians claim a philanthropic motive to Ala ud-Din's price fixing policy. This assertion is incorrect. Such claims must be viewed purely as attempts at improving Ala ud-Din's reputation and stature as a benevolent sultan; a calculated process to move away from the picture of a ruthless and megalomaniacal despot that emerges from contemporary accounts. His price-fixing policy was an attempt at ensuring that sufficient resources, especially food grain and clothes, could be made available to feed and clothe the large standing army being maintained. The motive was purely selfish and oriented ultimately towards facilitating invasions and conquest. Single-minded focus on achieving his objectives was one of Ala ud-Din's strengths of character.

Unlike the majority of his subjects who were Hindus, the Muslims—either new converts or the ones who were moving into North India from Central Asia and the north-west in a steady flow—enjoyed peace and prosperity under Ala ud-Din's rule. Crime was completely stamped out, mainly because of the rapidly enforced ruthless retribution that was visited on persons who committed any misdemeanour. There was no one in the sultanate, including powerful nobles, who had the temerity to oppose the sultan's orders. Ala ud-Din's control over the administration was all-encompassing and iron clad, a state of affairs that was achieved only because Ala ud-Din was a 'workaholic'. He also did not spare any of his officials, who were driven to perform at high efficiency at the risk of falling out of favour. Therefore, the royal officials played a critical role and must be given equal credit for the success of the administration, although contemporary accounts do not mention the middle and lower level officials.

Ala ud-Din laid down impeccable regulations that governed all aspects of administering a complex empire. He was constantly on the lookout for capable men to be inducted into his administration and adopted a policy of promotions based on merit, not purely on nobility of birth. Even persons of low-birth status, who proved to be able administrators, were elevated to high ranks. This provided two major strengths. First, it provided the administration with a constant source of invigoration through the regular injection external of talent; and second, the group of outsiders within the officialdom acted as a counterpoint to the hereditary nobility and the entrenched clergy. The raising of 'common' people to high rank was a constant reminder to the nobility that their position, status and well-being were completely dependent on the favour of the sultan.

Ala ud-Din's administration was completely centralised. His administrative concepts could be considered the forerunners of the one's that are now attributed to Fredrick the Great of Prussia, who ruled in the 18th century. The sultan acted as his own Prime Minster, ensuring that he was the sole source of all power that emanated from the central administration. Ministers were merely glorified clerks who carried out the sultan's instructions meticulously, spreading the will of the ruler across the land, or were unceremoniously removed from their positions. Consultations did take place, but the ultimate decision was always made by Ala ud-Din. In keeping with the concept of rigid centralisation, provincial governors were reigned in and their independence severely curtailed.

The efficiency of the espionage system had already been demonstrated in subduing the old and established nobility. The system also infiltrated the provincial governments, bringing the governor's into abject submission to the sultan's will. No one in the land was equal, or anywhere close to equality with the sultan—all were vassals serving at his mercy. This was a remarkable achievement of the imposition of a single person's will on what used to be 'king-making' nobility in the earlier days of the sultanate. Ala ud-Din's rule was the high point of despotism, not seen in India for a number of centuries prior to its establishment.

There are reports of a remarkable aspect of Ala ud-Din's reign, which is also dichotomous and therefore open to debate. It is reported that despite the total authoritarianism, ruthlessness and religious bias of the administration, the sultan had genuine concern for the welfare of the 'common people'. It is said that he genuinely sought to free the commoner from exploitation by the tax collectors and village headmen. The administration also attempted to ease the lives of the common people during the harsh times of scarcity that was brought on by natural calamities and poor harvests. It is also reported by contemporary chroniclers that the common people led a better life under Ala ud-Din's rule than under any other ruler of the Delhi sultanate.

The dichotomy is regarding the interpretation and meaning of the term 'common people' in the contemporary chronicles. It seems obvious that the reports regarding the common people considered only people of the Islamic faith—original Muslims who were part of the invasion, local converts, and/or the generational off-springs of the large invading army that settled down in the sub-continent—as the common people. The original inhabitants of the conquered lands, the Hindus, were not considered part of this group of 'common people'. In their own homeland, the ordinary Hindu person had been made a non-citizen with no rights or recourse even to minimal justice. This is an aspect of the Muslim rule in the sub-continent that is common during the reign of most rulers—whether the ruler controlled a vast empire or an insignificant principality. The religion-based persecution and irrational treatment of the local Hindu population is hardly ever mentioned by contemporary chroniclers. This is an obvious fact since they were paid to highlight the more acceptable highlights of the reign. What is more surprising is the fact that this mistreatment of Hindus is mostly swept under the carpet by later-day historians, some of whom strive to establish the 'secular' nature of the Muslim rulers in India. The stark fact is that there were no 'secular' Muslim rulers in the broad history of the sub-continent.

> 'Far from uniting India, early Islam's historic role would be to develop and entrench the subcontinent's so-called 'regional' identities.'
>
> John Keay,
>
> *India: A History*, p. 261

It cannot be stated, even by stretching the imagination, that Ala ud-Din was a benign ruler. He was not. He was immersed in the single-minded pursuit of his own grandiose dreams, treading his own chosen path and brutal in removing anyone who stood in the way of his moving forward on that path. The only defence that could be placed in the defence of the extreme brutality that Ala ud-Din perpetuated was, it could be claimed that at the time of his rule only such harsh methods would have accomplished the feats that he did during his reign. There is no doubting the fact that Ala ud-Din was a prime mover in firmly establishing Muslim rule in North India.

The Khilji Army

Ala ud-Din firmly believed that a large standing army was the source of all the power that a ruler wielded. Accordingly, he went about building a powerful army. Ala ud-Din was an ambitious king bent on conquest and beset with megalomania to become the equivalent of Alexander, the conquering king of Macedonia. Further, he assiduously practised royal despotism, which was possible only with the backing of a great army. One of the first tasks that he undertook on seizing the throne was to reform the army.

Ala ud-Din laid the foundation for a permanent standing army, based at the capital Delhi and kept in readiness to be deployed at all times. He was the first sultan to appreciate the strategic importance of such a force in maintaining the geographical sanctity and virtual sovereignty of the state. The army was directly recruited by a dedicated 'minister for the army' who was a trusted and loyal officer. The soldiers were paid from the royal treasury: each individual getting 234 tankas per year with another 78 tankas being paid to all soldiers who brought along an additional horse. (A tanka was a silver coin of between 160-175 grains, said to have been prevalent from the rule of Samudra Gupta Maurya. The current reference would be to coins that were most probably introduced sometime after the Delhi sultanate was established.)

The army was equipped at state expense. In order to ensure that proxy attendance during military drills was minimised, a roll of names with descriptions of individual soldiers was created. The royal horses were branded to prevent exchange of the state horse with inferior mounts. The cavalry thus created was reported as being more than 475,000 in number. The infantry would obviously have been numerically much larger. Even though there was a minister for the army, Ala ud-Din was personally involved in all aspects of the organisation and administration of the army.

Ala ud-Din wanted to abolish the practice of land grants to soldiers in lieu of regular salaries, since it created a vested land-holding gentry who could become rebellious with the growth in their local influence. However, this reform was only partially successful in its introduction for two reasons. One was the determined push back from the veteran soldiers who were the beneficiaries of the scheme for generations. The second reason is perhaps more important. Newly acquired territories were invariably parcelled off to soldiers in an attempt to indirectly colonise the conquered lands and also gradually Islamise the rural areas. Such a move also reduced the chances of rebellion in the newly annexed regions. Ala ud-Din was appreciative of these advantages and did not pursue the policy of confiscating land grants from soldiers.

Ala ud-Din's Failures

Four major factors—two with universal application and two that are unique to Ala ud-Din's rule—can be gleaned from analysing the rule of the only Khilji ruler who mattered in the broader sweep of Indian history.

Two Universal Truths

One, any empire, edifice or organisation built purely on the brilliance of an individual's genius will always suffer from a number of limitations. The main challenge in these circumstances is the ultimate diminishing stature and capability of a human being that comes with age, which is unavoidable even for the most authoritative of rulers. Time has always been a great leveller in the lives of human beings. This was the case with Ala ud-Din too. As he grew older, he was unable to exert the same amount of energy as before towards the affairs of state, being forced by ill-health to delegate functions that he had customarily made his own. The fall out was the inevitable process by which subordinates started to usurp power, little by little.

Two, power built on the strength of military might tends to get warped over a period of time, irrespective of the morality of the soldiers. Khilji imperialism was built on the might of its powerful army. Sovereign authority of the sultan was not derived from the consent of the people or supported by the will of the nobility; it had been forcefully assumed by the will of a despot and the power of the sword. Military forces, by virtue of their profession, tend to look for glory, even at the cost of the welfare of the people. This trend invariably leads to the governance gradually turning tyrannical that in turn will be unpopular. This state of affairs could be seen clearly in the Khilji Empire. An empire can be established by the skilful employment of a military force. However, the force must get removed from the day-to-day functioning of the kingdom at the earliest in order to avoid the pitfall mentioned above. Military forces do not have the capacity to become the sole foundational basis for the establishment of a long-standing empire.

... and Two Related to Khilji Imperialism

Three, an autocratic ruler needs at least a small coterie of trusted lieutenants to carry out his orders and also to protect him virtually and physically, even in times of relative peace. Ala ud-Din had managed to estrange the Turkish nobility by undermining their privileges and reducing their prestige, converting them into mere vassals who served at his pleasure. This was the group that had traditionally ensured the ruling sultan's 'well-being' in return for assured status, wealth and prestige as noblemen of the realm. The ascendancy of the military and the scuttling of the nobles' position combined to create a situation of simmering discontent amongst the powerful Turkish nobility.

Four, the Hindu population and their chiefs from bottom to top were chaffing at the extreme oppression that they were subjected to under the widening ordnances, which controlled almost all aspects of their lives. They were also acutely aware of the plunder and loot of their places of worship and were compelled by necessity to rebel at every opportunity. Along with this constant tension with the Hindus, the Mongols who had settled in the sub-continent, referred to as the 'new Muslims' were also never at rest. They were on a continuous spree of rebellion and plotting. Keeping the two rebellious factions under check was a constant source of drain on imperial resources. Essentially there was no class of society in the kingdom who were content and therefore the despotic sultan had no support base amongst the people. The nobility was alienated; the middle and upper class were terrified of the espionage system that had been put in place; the merchants were unhappy with the absolute control that was being exercised over prices of commodities; and the majority of the common people, the Hindus, were a disenfranchised and disgruntled group.

Conclusion

Ala ud-Din's merits and strength as a ruler were also the weaknesses of the empire that he crafted. The kingdom was created and built on personal authority that failed abysmally to lay real foundations to fashion appreciable dynastic strength. Therefore, it was not surprising that when this personal authority started to wane, with the increasing age and illnesses of the sultan, the dynasty also started to decline.

The proverbial last straw that broke the back of the empire was the fact that Ala ud-Din did not consider at any time during his reign the need for continuity in governance and the orderly transfer of power to ensure the longevity of the dynasty. Realising the megalomaniacal tendencies that he readily displayed, it is indeed possible to believe that he never considered the finiteness of the life of a human being and ultimate death as being applicable to him. He imparted no training in the affairs of state to his sons, all of whom grew up as weaklings in character, steeped in the indulgence in worldly pleasures. None of the princes had any quality that could recommend him as a possible successor to take over his father's great empire. On the other hand, Malik Kafur, Ala ud-Din's confidante and favourite general, also an extremely capable person, played a game of divide-and-rule as soon as he took over the running of the court and then the kingdom. He consciously wrought division within the royal household to achieve his own ambition of becoming the 'king-maker' as a stepping stone to subsequently usurping the throne. There was no chance of the dynasty entrenching itself under such diverging pressures.

A mere four years after Ala ud-Din's death, the entire system came down with a thunderous crash.

The Delhi Sultanate

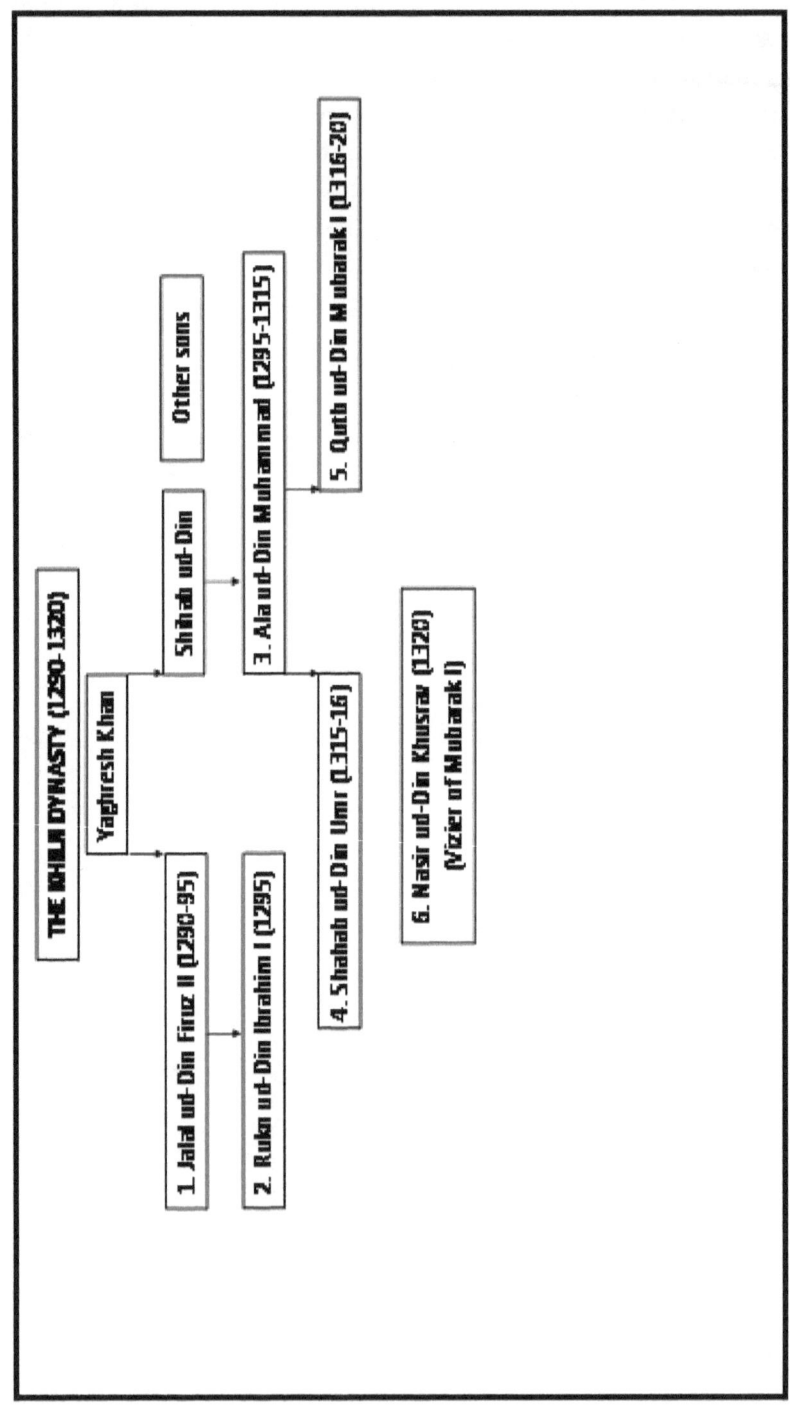

THE VAINGLORY OF THE TUGHLUQS

Thus began, with festivities and great optimism, the most turbulent reign in the over three centuries long history of the Delhi Sultanate.

– Abraham Eraly,
The Age of Wrath, p. 149

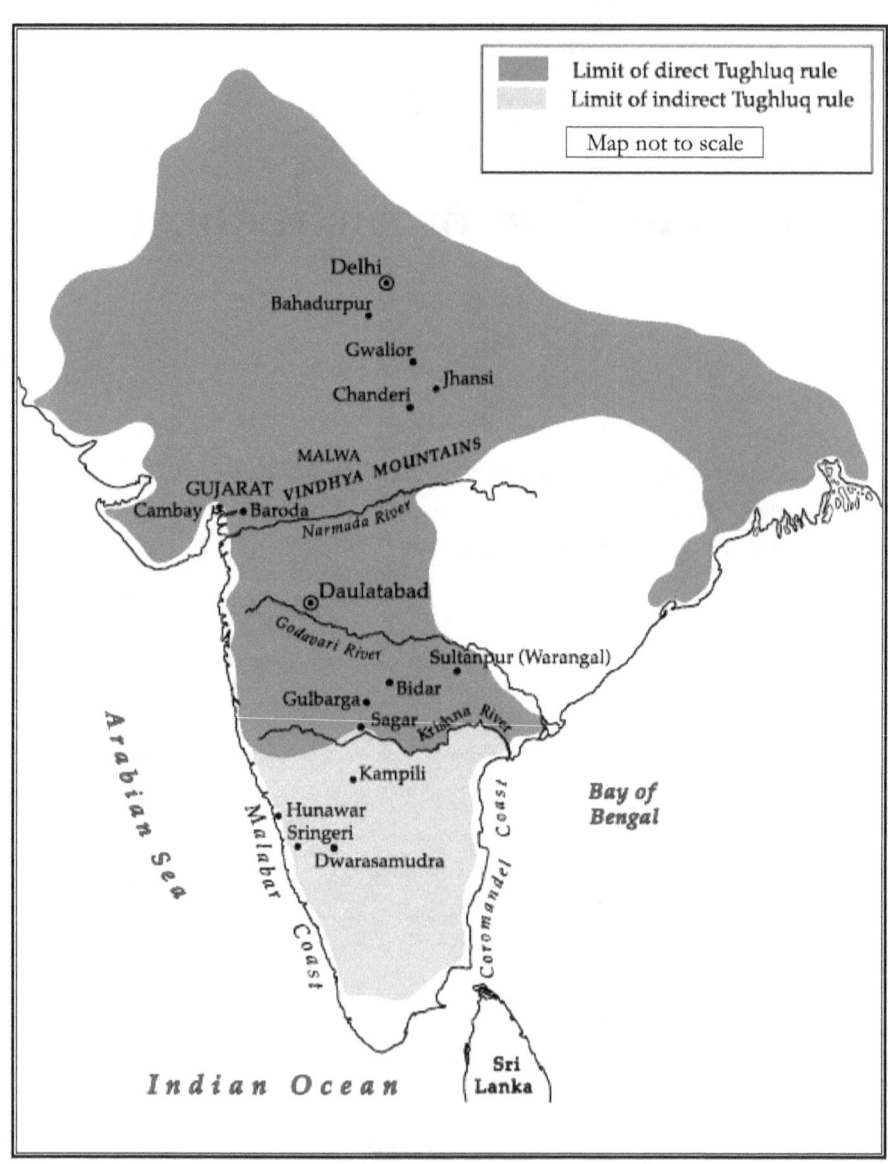

The Tughluq Empire at its height

SOURCES OF INFORMATION

From the time of Ala ud-Din Khilji's reign to the end of the Tughluq dynasty, there were a number of authors within India who were chronicling events in the Delhi Sultanate as they unfolded. There are three primary works—written by Barani, Isami and Sirhindi—whose study is essential to gather an understanding of the times and the developments in the Sultanate up to about 1351 around the time of the end of Muhammad Tughluq's reign. Further, there is the memoirs of the Moroccan traveller Ibn Battuta, which provides detailed account of the reign of Muhammad Tughluq. The travel narrative of Battuta is unsurpassed in the vividness of its description of people, customs, daily life of the people, agriculture and trade, and the functioning of the administration at the capital of the Sultanate. In combination, these chronicles provide a fairly accurate and authentic account not only of the events as they took place, but also of the conditions that were prevalent amongst the common people of the time.

There are a few authors, such as Nizam al-Din Ahmad Harawi and some others, who recorded the history of the Delhi Sultanate during the early Mughal period. Invariably they have relied almost completely on the works of Barani and Sirhindi and added their own interpretations to past events. Therefore, these chronicles have no intrinsic value as primary sources. However, these works at time allude to some earlier records that are not available now. On the one hand these references provide information regarding the lost chronicles, while on the other the veracity of the statements based on the missing works cannot be assured. These writings and records are of marginal interest to the researcher.

There are two issues even with Barani's book *Tarikh-i-Firuz-Shahi*, which is a contemporary record. First, the earlier versions differ considerably to the later versions. The later ones contain additional information, which is now considered to have been incorporated at a later date than that of the first publishing. Second, Barani as a chronicler was partial to recording minute details of events and to analysing them from his viewpoint at the cost of not strictly confining himself to the chronology of events. Further, in a similar fashion to Isami, he provides very few dates for the events described. *[This author's narrative is also not a fully authenticated chronological account of events, but rather a recounting of events of importance and describing their influence on the progress of a kingdom, the effectiveness of the rule of a king and/or the daily life of the common people viewed through the prism of the then prevalent socio-economic and politico-religious circumstances. Similarly, only dates that can be verified are given, and the ones that cannot be authenticated with assurance are ignored.]* Barani states in his book that he is not presenting the narrative in strict chronological order.

Today, centuries later, the number of records that have been lost to antiquity is difficult or even impossible to ascertain. However, there is no doubt that a number of authentic records have been lost before they came to light or were seen by modern historians. Sources that have been known to have existed but are not traceable now would have been invaluable in understanding the medieval history of India. Another issue that detracts from creating a cohesive narrative is the misinterpretations by Western historians of accounts written in Persian or the vernacular. Some of these misinterpretations have skewed, for decades and centuries in some cases, the later-day understanding of the history of the first Islamic kingdom in the sub-continent. For example some expeditions have been wrongly identified, because of the commonality of names of the generals involved and some wrong translations have led to the creation of a false chronology. These incorrect timelines have further added to the confusion that is prevalent even today regarding the passage of events in the medieval period. This kind of error can be seen in a number of books even today. The overall impact has been for the medieval history to remain under a cloud with the flow of the narrative regarding the Delhi Sultanate never being fully coherent.

There are some works that have been confirmed as having been written but have vanished without a trace before they could be accessed by the English-speaking historians of the middle ages. The *Shahnama*, composed by Badr-i-Chach the court poet of Muhammad

Tughluq, which has been described in earlier times as a treasure trove of information is one such work. Afif is another medieval author who dubbed himself the author of the history of sultans and claimed to have written their biographies, called manaquib in Persian. The biographies were of Ala ud-Din Khilji, as well as of Ghiyas ud-Din, Muhammad and Firuz Tughluqs. He also wrote a detailed account of Timur's infamous sack of Delhi. However, these works have been lost without any trace or further reference to them. Similarly, some works done in Gujarati, which have been extensively referred to in works of Firishta and others, have also been lost. Although the Gujarati chronicles are not available for reference now, the excerpts cited in later works indicate that the unknown author had access to authentic sources that were not available to others.

Amir Khusrav's prose work, *Khazain al-Futuh*, thought to have been completed in 1312 is a contemporary chronicle of the times of Ala ud-Din Khilji. It provides a florid and congratulatory account of Ala ud-Din's military victories and Malik Kafur's campaigns in the Deccan. Khusrav's other works provide details of the rule of Ghiyas ud-Din Tughluq. However, the fragments that are available of what is claimed to have been the alleged memoirs of Muhammad Tughluq has to be discounted as unauthentic and there is speculation that they could even be forgeries.

Even so, the Tughluq era provides richer and more varied material than any previous dynasty in the history of the Delhi Sultanate. There are some works that provide extremely detailed account of a particular event and its aftermath, produced as a commemorative volume such as the one that was written regarding the Tughluqs' Lakhnauti Campaign. There are also some stray verses written by the court poet Badr-i-Chach, which are congratulatory to the Sultan in tone and content. Even though most of these chronicles are celebratory in nature and prone to exaggeration, the actual facts can be gleaned from them on careful analysis and corroboration with other sources. It is possible to separate the wheat from the chaff. Another source is the correspondence of Ayan al-Mulk Ibn Mahru, the governor of Multan under both Muhammad and Firuz Shah Tughluq. The letters concentrate on fiscal and military matters, giving an insight into the character of the administration and the manner in which these important facets of governance was conducted.

There are also some records relating to the many Sufi orders that proliferated in the sub-continent during the early years of the gradual Islamisation of North India. These chronicles, mostly written in the genre of biographies of Sufi Sheikhs with large followings, also refer to and in some cases even explain contemporary political events. There is no doubt regarding the authenticity of these records, since they were meant to celebrate the life of ascetics and not serious political commentary. There are also a number of sources that come from outside the Indian sub-continent, mainly correspondence of statesmen and diplomats. However, most of these discuss matters that the authors only knew as hearsay and therefore would have to be corroborated with other sources to be considered authentic. On the other hand, they could be used to corroborate some assertions made in another source. In any case these correspondence cannot be considered primary sources of information.

Muhammad Tughluq opened India to the rest of the Muslim world, through establishing diplomatic contact with the greater empires to the west and north. The archives of Mamluk Egypt provides a great deal of information regarding the Sultanate in India, which were collected and recorded by the Egyptian chroniclers.

From the rule of Muhammad Tughluq onwards, the modern historian is not left in the dark and does not have to rely on speculations to recount the events of the past.

Chapter 13

GHIYAS UD-DIN TUGHLUQ SHAH

Ghiyas ud-Din's accession to the throne calmed the paroxysm that had become commonplace in the sultanate from the last days of Ala ud-Din's rule. Ghiyas had come up from humble origins—his father was a Qaraunah Turk and mother a Jat lady. The Qaraunah were a clan of the broader Mongol tribes from Central Asia, who had played a significant role in the early Mongol campaigns in Persia. Subsequently, they had moved eastward and settled in the region between Sindh and Turkestan. Ghiyas ud-Din had entered military service with Ala ud-din as a trooper and had risen in the hierarchy by dint of his own ability to become the 'Warden of the Marches', displaying exemplary courage in the fight against the Mongols during Ala ud-Din's reign. It is reported that he encountered and defeated the Mongols no less than 29 times, being awarded the title Malik-ul-Ghazi, colloquially made into the diminutive as Ghazi Malik. By 1305, he was the governor of Punjab, headquartered at Dipalpur.

On defeating Khusrav Shah, Ghiyas ud-Din instituted a search to look for any surviving scion of Ala ud-Din's family, with the proclaimed intent to place him on the throne. However, the sincerity of the search is really in doubt, and it is highly probable that he already knew that no one would be found. This is corroborated by the alacrity with which he subsequently accepted the keys to the palace, when the courtiers offered them to him. Ghiyas ud-Din was already middle aged, and had a high reputation as an effective military commander. Further, he had defeated and killed Khusrav, making him the automatic choice to be the new sultan. He did not hesitate to accept the offer from the nobles of Delhi and became the sultan, assuming the name Ghiyas ud-Din

Tughluq Shah, with the added title of 'Ghazi'. Ghazi essentially meant 'slayer of the infidel' and Ghiyas was the first of the Delhi sultans to openly flaunt his religious bias.

> ### Debate on Ghiyas ud-Din's Origins
>
> Even today there is discussion regarding the origins of Ghiyas ud-Din with few conflicting and incorrect accounts still being circulated as being true. One source claims that Ghazi Malik came into Ala ud-Din's service from Khurasan. Firishta, after having made inquiries in Lahore states that his father Malik Tughluq was one of Balban's Turkish slaves and that his mother was a Jat lady. However, this information, gathered purely by word-of-mouth, is not authenticated by any written records. It is based purely on information gained by Firishta's informal interactions with sources who were declared 'reliable' only by Firishta himself.
>
> The story of the Jat marriage falls within the acceptable norms of the time. For example, while he was the governor of Punjab at Dipalpur, Ghiyas ud-Din married off his brother Rajab to the daughter of a Hindu nobleman from the Bhatti Rajput clan. No doubt, considerable coercion must have been used for the Rajput nobleman to accept this alliance. The issue from this union was the future sultan Firuz Tughluq.
>
> However, in the case of Ghiyas ud-Din none of the accounts of his origin can be verified with any assurance of certainty. It would therefore be correct to believe that his father was a Mongol or someone of Turco-Mongol stock, possibly of the Qaraunah clan, and his mother could have been either a Jat or Rajput lady.

Domestic Policy

When Ghiyas ud-Din ascended the throne, a state of utter confusion and instability prevailed in Delhi as a result of more than four years of chaotic rule. Ghiyas, a seasoned administrator, commenced his rule with great tact and prudence, mixed with an unbiased firmness that was visible just below the surface of civility that he maintained. He was acutely conscious of the rather narrow support base that he enjoyed amongst the nobility, especially within the Delhi faction. In an astute move, he distributed wealth and position to bring the more recalcitrant nobles to his side. However, the relations with his erstwhile colleagues, the governors of provinces who had refused to join him in the uprising against Khusrav Shah, remained tense throughout his reign. Even though working under these constraints, Ghiyas ud-Din restored order to the kingdom and gradually reinstated the moral ascendancy of the monarchy—no easy task, considering the odds lined against him.

In order to demonstrate his good will he was magnanimous with any and all relatives of Ala ud-Din and Mubarak Shah, reinstating them to their old positions and granting them wealth. Further, he started a reconciliation process with the nobles by ensuring that none of the nobles who sided with Khusrav were targeted for revenge or retribution and by reinstating or reconfirming them to their original positions. It is said that in this process, it was ensured that 'no just claim was ignored, and no past service forgotten'. However, Ghiyas had come to power with the support of the elements from the north-west and therefore the new administration was clearly biased in favour of the officers from that region. Some of these officers from the north-west who had moved to the capital went on to found important noble families in Delhi who served the Tughluq dynasty with distinction.

Justice and concern for the common people is reported to have been the cornerstone of Ghiyas ud-Din's administration. This assertion has to be understood at token value as a report from a court chronicler, obviously attempting flattery. The fact remains that Ghiyas ud-Din was an orthodox and devout Sunni Muslim in his personal life, steadfast in the observance of all the ordnances of his faith. It is also noteworthy that his rebellion which led to his ascension to the throne was, at least ostensibly, mounted to protect Islam. In effect he had become the proclaimed champion of orthodox Islam.

There is proof that most of his actions were oriented towards keeping the interest of the state supreme. In keeping with this policy, even though he demonstrated respect for Ala ud-Din, he rescinded a number of exacting regulations that had constrained the development of the state's economy. Accordingly, he reduced taxes on the farmers from almost half of the produce to just one-tenth of the output. Simultaneously he made sure that the state did not suffer from the drop in revenue by expanding agriculture and trade. Ghiyas established garrisons to ensure the safety and security of the traders and had irrigation canals dug to facilitate an increase in agricultural produce. Essentially, the reduction in royal treasury income because of the reduction in the tax rate was offset by the expansion of the economy. The measures benefitted both the state and the people.

The administration was based on the principles of justice and moderation and was, in principle, meant to be applicable equally to both Muslim and Hindu subjects. The fundamental concept was that people should not be exploited by the official machinery. However, this benign outlook did not encompass the Hindu subjects who were seen and treated as second class citizens and fully subjected people. Their status was only just above that of slaves. Ghiyas ud-Din followed the orthodox Muslim policy of not treating non-believers as equal to persons of the Islamic faith and also retained all the restrictions that had been imposed on the Hindus by earlier rulers. In his defence it must be mentioned that Ghiyas ud-Din gave instructions to ensure that while the Hindus were not given any opportunity and/or permitted to become wealthy, they were also not pushed fully into destitution. This need not have been because of the kindness of his heart but a pragmatic move to allay the fear of rebellion if the general mass of Hindus were pushed beyond a point of endurance.

Ghiyas ud-Din understood the importance of communications to control the kingdom and therefore set in motion few initiatives that improved the central communications system. He established a regular system of posts being carried by runners and horsemen. When the system matured, news travelled within the kingdom at the speed of about 100 miles in a 12-hour day.

During his brief reign, Khusrav Shah had gifted extensive land grants to influential people in order to placate them. He had also done the same for a number of religious leaders to win over their support. These measures had greatly depleted the treasury. Ghiyas now started to reclaim these lands and also demanded the return of the money that had been disbursed. While these actions did not make him popular, it brought back some semblance of economic stringency to the kingdom.

> ### The Sultan and the Saint
>
> One of the chief beneficiaries of Khusrav's largess was the Sufi sage, Shaikh Nizam ud-Din Auliya, who had received as a gift a sum in excess of half a million tankas. Ghiyas ud-Din, as the sultan, demanded that the money be returned to the royal treasury. Nizam ud-Din replied that the money had already been spend on charity and therefore he was not in a position to return the gifted money.
>
> Ghiyas ud-Din was already annoyed at the Shaikh's dervish practices and the alternative method of worship that was propagated by adherents of the Sufi system, of which Nizam ud-Din was a leading practitioner. The sage's refusal to return the money that had been gifted to him, illegally as far as the orthodox sultan was concerned, intensified his dislike for Auliya and for the Sufi practice of Islam. Ghiyas then attempted to convict Nizam ud-Din for 'unlawful' religious practices and constituted an informal court consisting of 53 theologians. The case was examined and not even one of the theologians found any fault with Nizam ud-Din, thereby not providing Ghiyas ud-Din with any legal provision to take action against the Sufi sage.
>
> The struggle between the sultan and the saint remained unresolved in a stand-off till the death of the sultan.

[It is interesting to note from the above episode that the animosity and struggle between the orthodox followers of Islam and those who propagate a more moderate and alternative method of practising the religion is not something that started in the late 20th century. It has been part and parcel of the ideological development of the religion from its inception in the desert sands of Arabia.]

As a practising orthodox Muslim, Ghiyas attempted to enforce strict Muslim tenets on the entire population. He forbade the production and sale of liquor, although the efficacy of the implementation of this policy is open to debate. It could not have been fully and strictly enforced. Ghiyas ud-Din was not a vigorous persecutor of the non-believers. Therefore, his indulging in temple destruction and plunder could perhaps be attributed to the avarice that plagued almost all the sultans to amass wealth at the cost of the Hindus. However, it was easier and more acceptable for the court chroniclers and other nobles to depict the plunder brought on by pure materialistic greed in the guise of religious zeal. Such a report would not then invite the sultan's wrath.

The Telangana Expeditions

On ascending the throne and settling the local government, Ghiyas ud-Din was faced with the need to recover the territories that had been lost during the turmoil of Mubarak Shah's short reign. The loss of territories and rebellions in the outlying provinces were a major concern for the new sultan. As an experienced administrator, Ghiyas ud-Din instinctively recognised the importance of regaining lost territory and subduing rebellion in order to restore the sultanate's position of superiority. He therefore, ordered an expedition against Warangal, the capital of the Kakatiya king ruling the kingdom of Telangana.

Prataparudra Deva II, the ruling king of Telangana had increased his power during the chaotic reign of Mubarak Shah and stopped paying the annual tribute that had been imposed during Ala ud-Din Khilji's rule. Prataparudra had substantially increased the Kakatiya territorial holdings by conducting military campaigns against his less powerful neighbours. In doing so the Kakatiya king displayed a singular lack of vision and political wisdom, as well as a paucity of awareness regarding the menace developing in the north. He underestimated the focus and importance the Muslim kings laid in establishing their superiority over the Hindu kings and chieftains and their zeal to spread their own religion by the sword. It would have been prudent for Prataparudra to unite the lesser Hindu chieftains under his umbrella in anticipation of the coming invasion from the north. Instead he had waged war with them, which resulted in two developments. First, he frittered away his own resources, leading him in a weakened state when the

Islamic invasion took place; and second, he created animosity with the neighbours, with the result that no one came to his aid when the Muslim army finally entered his kingdom. A combination of the two led to disastrous consequences.

Ghiyas ud-Din gave command of the expedition to his eldest son and crown prince Jauna, who had been given the title of Ulugh Khan. The Tughluq army besieged Warangal. Prataparudra fought the siege for a long period of time—a period during which fierce battles had been waged with great loss of life on both sides. The Kakatiya king was finally worn down and forced to plead for peace. However, Jauna refused the terms of peace that were being offered, perhaps an indication of the wilful nature of the crown prince that would come to the fore in the near future. At this point when a victorious conclusion to the expedition was within grasp of the Muslim army, the sultanate army seems to have been thrown into confusion for some inexplicable reasons.

It is believed that Prataparudra had also been waging a guerrilla war against the invaders and had managed to cut the communications line from Delhi to Jauna, who became worried when no information was coming in from his father in Delhi. At the same time, a rumour started to spread amongst the invading Muslim army that the sultan Ghiyas ud-Din was dead. This made Jauna nervous about his own future as the heri apparent. On the advice of some of his closest friends he lifted the siege of Warangal and started back to Delhi in a hurry. It is reported that the Tughluq army was in a state of extreme turmoil at this stage. The haste is said to have been to ensure that Jauna Ulugh Khan reached the capital in time to claim his inheritance and become the sultan. This reasoning is unclear, as Jauna was the declared 'next sultan'. At this stage another rumour took root within the army that Jauna had put to death some untrustworthy commanders, with the result some officials deserted the prince's army for fear of unwarranted reprisal.

Another version states that Jauna Ulugh Khan, already an ambitious prince, had been further instigated by some close associates and wanted to usurp the throne of Delhi. This not a credible story for a number of reasons. First, Jauna had already been anointed as the heir apparent and therefore had no reason to jeopardise his position by mounting a rebellion that may not have succeeded. Further, his father was already well past middle age and was not expected to continue to rule for a long period of time. Second, the manner in which events unfolded after Jauna's withdrawal from Warangal provide a clear picture of the trust his father placed on him. The question of his wanting to usurp the throne is a fantasy built up by some later-day historians, in keeping with the tradition of in-fighting for succession in the sultanate. In any event, the fact remains that the Muslim army retreated and that the retreat was made uncomfortable with his much reduced and fatigued army being constantly harassed by the Kakatiya forces.

Any doubt regarding a rift between father and son were put to rest as soon as Jauna reached Delhi. Ghiyas ud-Din had captured all the officials who had deserted his son and had them put to death. There was no doubt in the sultan's mind regarding the loyalty of his son or any suspicion that Jauna had intended to usurp the throne. This was further confirmed a year later when Ghiyas ud-Din personally embarked on an expedition to Bengal. He appointed Jauna as the regent to rule in his place during his absence from the capital. These are not the actions of a sultan who had even the slightest reservation regarding the intentions of his son.

After punishing the disloyal officers of the army, Ghiyas ud-Din assembled another huge army, placed Jauna in command, and once again send him back to Warangal to subdue the Kakatiya king. In the interim period Prataparudra had once again proclaimed his independence and was defiant of the Delhi rulers. According to the Muslim chronicles, the second expedition into Telangana was a resounding success.

Jauna captured Bidar on the way to Warangal, and then proceeded to besiege the capital. The siege was prosecuted vigorously and Warangal captured after a brief battle. Prataparudra and his entire family were captured and send to Delhi. Warangal was renamed Sultanpur and Telangana was divided into several districts with each of them being placed under the governorship of Turkish nobles and senior military officials. The entire Kakatiya kingdom, now broken up into small provinces, was brought under direct rule of Delhi through these governors. This was the demise of the Kakatiya kingdom, which ceased to exist as a predominant power on the eastern seaboard of the sub-continent. The glory and greatness of the Kakatiya dynasty ended with this defeat.

The information available of this invasion, siege and capture of Warangal is only from contemporary Muslim reports. Since the Kakatiya kingdom was obliterated as an entity, there are no surviving records that could have provided an alternative viewpoint, at least about the siege and the actual battle that finally subdued a valiant ruler who had waged a continuous war for independence throughout his eventful reign. This is an unfortunate loss to creating a holistic understanding of the gradual expansion of Muslim control into the Deccan.

Other Expeditions in the South

Flushed with the victory over the Kakatiya king, Jauna raided the neighbouring kingdom of Utkala in Orissa—mentioned as Jajnagar in the Muslim chronicles. The invasion is reported as a great success by contemporary Muslim writers, but there are conflicting reports of this campaign. There is an inscription in a mosque in Rajahmundry, which states that it was built in 1324 during the reign of Ulugh Khan. However, the Puri plates of Narasimha II credits Bhanudeva II, the ruler of Orissa with victory over the Muslim army led by Jauna Khan. The plate goes on to mention the name of the sultan as Ghiyas ud-Din Tughluq. The obvious conclusion that can be drawn is that Jauna's southern odyssey was not one continuous and glorious victorious march as has been made out in the Muslim chronicles. There were also setbacks and defeats, glossed over by the court chroniclers.

Jauna's defeat in Orissa is also corroborated in an indirect manner by the account given by Barani of this campaign. He states that Jauna Khan returned suddenly from this expedition to Jajnagar. Clearly a victorious army would not return in a sudden turn about unless forced to do so because of some reversal of its fortune. Therefore, it can be surmised that Jauna Khan's secondary expeditions after the victory at Warangal were not as victorious or successful as they are made out to be by contemporary chroniclers. There is also mention of an expedition into Tamil country that was undertaken. However, this cannot be corroborated or confirmed from any other source and even the skimpy records available does not provide details in terms of battles, victories and capture of territory. A campaign into Tamil territory is highly unlikely to have been undertaken.

The second peninsular raid was considered a success on the whole. Jauna was feted as a 'victor' on his return to Delhi where Ghiyas ud-Din received his favourite son with a grand reception and other celebrations. However, the celebratory mood was marred by a Mongol invasion at the same time. The Mongols crossed the River Indus and plundered Samana. A large army was send against the invaders and the Mongols were defeated in two separate encounters. The sultanate army managed to take many prisoners in these encounters. The report of these victories must be understood within the context of the Mongol strategy of not giving battle in the traditional manner when confronted at the end of a plundering raid, but retreating with the spoils that they had gathered. (The Mongol strategy of invasion, plunder and retreat at the arrival of defending forces has been described in detail earlier in this volume.)

The Annexation of Bengal

Bengal had been an independent principality ever since the death of Balban. No sultan who came after Balban had attempted to bring this recalcitrant province under the central control of Delhi. Ghiyas ud-Din was determined to assert his authority over the province and expand the sultanate. While the invasion of Bengal was being contemplated in Delhi, there was a dispute for the 'throne' of Bengal between three brothers—Ghiyas ud-Din (not the sultan, but only a namesake), Shahab and Nasir. Ghiyas who was the governor of East Bengal, overthrew his brother Shahab and took over control of the territory he had been ruling from Lakhnauti. Nasir, who was also ambitious, appealed to sultan Ghiyas ud-Din Tughluq in Delhi for help.

This plea for help was the opportunity to interfere that the sultan was waiting for and he decided on an expedition to Bengal, setting out forthwith to command the campaign personally. There are some reports that Jauna was recalled from the Deccan to act as the regent in the absence of the sultan. Although these reports are unverifiable, such a recall could explain the sudden return of Jauna and his army from the campaign against Orissa, rather than because of military reversals. The most likely cause for the Muslim army's retreat from Orissa would be a combination of both these factors. Jauna would have seized on the impending expedition to Bengal and his father's absence to make light of the military reversals and defeat that he was suffering at the hands of the Orissa king, Bhanudeva II.

The Bengal Campaign

Demonstrating his long experience as the military commander of the North West, Ghiyas ud-Din waged a swift and efficient campaign. As the Delhi army was proceeding toward Bengal, they were joined by Nasir and his forces. Ghiyas the sultan very easily defeated the usurper Ghiyas of Bengal and send him to Delhi as a prisoner, while placing Nasir on the throne of Lakhnauti as governor to rule West Bengal. East and South Bengal with their capitals at Sonargaon and Satgaon were also conquered and annexed directly to Delhi. Bahram Khan, Ghiyas ud-Din's adopted son was placed as the provincial governor of both the provinces.

Having settled the affairs in Bengal fairly rapidly, the sultan started his return journey to Delhi. On the way he invaded the kingdom of Tirhut (Mithila in North Bihar) and defeated the ruling raja Harisimha. The raja's name has also been reported as Harisingh Deva, who belonged to the Karnata dynasty. The king fled to the territory of Nepal for safety. After Tirhut had been overrun, Ghiyas ud-Din only imposed a tribute to be paid and moved on in his journey back to Delhi. The only reason for the invasion of a small kingdom that was not on the line of march to Delhi seems to be that it was a Hindu kingdom and therefore should not be left to prosper—a common enough sentiment of the Delhi sultans.

The Death of a Sultan

While engaged in the Bengal campaign, Ghiyas ud-Din received some disquieting news from Delhi. This may have added further impetus to an already swift campaign since the sultan was now impatient to return to his capital. The news was regarding the behaviour of his son Jauna who was now the regent of Delhi. It appears that Jauna had fallen under the spell of the Sufi sage and dervish Nizam ud-Din Auliya and was associating with him closely. The sultan intensely disliked Auliya, ever since the sage had refused to return the money that he had received from Khusrav Shah. The sultan was informed that during one of the dervish's trances he had predicted the imminent accession of Jauna to the throne. Since this could only happen when Ghiyas ud-Din died, the sultan became suspicious of his son's intentions. To further this anxiety, it was also reported to him that Jauna was increasing the number of his followers and forming a clique that was personally loyal to him. The sultan's concern was further intensified when some astrologers predicted that he would not be able to return to Delhi.

Incensed by these developments, Ghiyas ud-Din send a warning to Auliya that when he reached Delhi, the city would be too small to contain both of them together. The message was clear, Nizam ud-Din should leave Delhi before the sultan returned to the capital, only staying there on pain of death.

> ### 'Hanuz Dilli Dur Ast'
>
> In the end the sultan's threat came true, but not as anticipated by the exile of the Sufi sage, but through the fulfilment of the dervish's prediction, which came true.
>
> As the sultan's entourage drew near to Delhi, Auliya's followers started to become increasingly agitated for his safety. They mentioned the sultan's proximity to Delhi and advised the sage to leave Delhi, keeping in mind the sultan's threat. Nizam ud-Din is reported to have told his followers, 'Hanuz Dilli dur ast', meaning 'Delhi is still far off'.

In order to welcome the sultan back from a victorious campaign, and also possibly to placate him since he was irritated about the interaction with Nizam ud-Din, Jauna erected a wooden pavilion at Afghanpur about 6 kilometres south-east of Delhi. The felicitations and celebrations were to be held there before the sultan would be escorted to Delhi in a victory procession.

The sultan was received by Jauna and other nobles a little away from the pavilion and conducted to the ceremonial dais that had been raised. Once the sultan was seated on the dais, the roof collapsed, crushing Ghiyas ud-Din and a few others under the debris. Considering the accidental nature of the collapse and the track record of fratricide in the Delhi sultanate, it is not difficult to understand that foul play was suspected and Jauna's collusion automatically assumed. This is further emphasised by some disparities in the accounts of the actual events, as recounted by different contemporary chroniclers who bore witness to the event or were resident in Delhi at that time.

The first is that the sultan himself had ordered the building of the pavilion for his welcome reception, and therefore, foul play could not be suspected. This assertion is not tenable. Even if it was the sultan's wish to have a pavilion built, its construction was obviously entrusted to Jauna and his officers, who could have created a faulty edifice. The second report is that Jauna Khan had the pavilion/palace created with great mechanical ingenuity. It was built in such a way that when an elephant pushed a particular part of the pavilion, the entire structure collapsed. The third iterations adds that after the structure collapsed, Jauna purposely delayed the rescue effort to get the sultan out of the debris, thereby ensuring his death. The fourth one goes even beyond this accusation and states that the sultan was alive when he was pulled out of the debris, but was murdered immediately thereafter. Irrespective of what is to be believed, the fact remains that Ghiyas-ud-Din died when the roof of his celebratory dais collapsed on him.

Suspicion against Jauna for the 'timely' accident that took Ghiyas ud-Din's life will always remain, since it was not laid to rest immediately after the event. In a holistic and unbiased analysis it seems probable that Jauna conspired, at least on the periphery, to have his father murdered. This is further emphasised by the dead sultan's displeasure at his son becoming a disciple of Nizam ud-Din Auliya. Ghiyas ud-Din had nurtured an intense dislike for the Sufi sage. As an aside, it is also possible that the hastily constructed structure was not stable and that it collapsed because of natural causes, although this conjecture sounds far-fetched at a time when assassination of kings by close relatives was a common occurrence in the Delhi sultanate. It is inevitable that conspiracy theories would abound under these circumstances, even if the debacle was an unfortunate and genuine accident. The unfortunate fact is that the truth is not palpably available and unlikely to ever be determined, after so many centuries.

> 'After all, premature death was an occupational hazard for any contemporary ruler and parricide a fairly common cause; even when a ruler dies in his bed, poison was invariably suspected.'
>
> John Keay,
>
> *India: A History*, p. 265

In Jauna's defence it must be said that there really was no need for him to usurp the throne by assassinating his father—Ghiyas ud-Din was an old man, and Jauna had been the heir apparent throughout his reign. His succession was assured. The other factor to consider is that if murder was indeed contemplated, it would not have been planned as a chance death under a collapsing wooden structure. Such a scheme had no assurance of success. Even so, the verdict on Jauna's accession to the throne is still a grey area in the history of the Tughluq dynasty.

Ghiyas ud-Din had already built an elegant mausoleum at Tughlaquabad, his capital. His body was interned in it on the same night as the accident, in conformity with the Islamic tradition of burying the dead as soon as possible after death. Three days later, Jauna ascended the throne as Muhammad Tughlaq. He continued to stay at Tughlaquabad for the next 40 days in extended mourning for the death of his father.

Ghiyas ud-Din – The Sultan

On coming to the throne, Ghiyas ud-Din had the distinct advantage of already being an experienced soldier, a seasoned general, as well as a loyal and faithful official of the crown. He was also one of the most successful 'Wardens of the March', keeping the North-West border of the sultanate secure against the Mongol depredations for a long time. He was uniquely suited to be a good ruler, having all the qualities that was necessary for the making of a 'good' sultan in turbulent times. He proved this assessment right and was very clearly an effective ruler; establishing peace and stability and stamping out major crime within a short period of taking power. From the outset he adopted a policy of moderation and reconciliation, managing to win over even Khusrauv's supporters. As far as possible, within the constraints of the period, he attempted to provide an administration based on even justice.

As a ruler Ghiyas ud-Din supported agriculture, based on the belief that national prosperity was a direct result of the well-being of the farmer. In the medieval times this was indeed true. He ordered the revenue officials to increase the land under cultivation while not increasing the land tax rates. While establishing the primacy of agriculture for the prosperity of the nation, he enforced the policy of military domination of all other aspects of the administration of the kingdom as its fundamental tenet. His long tenure as the 'Warden of the Marches' had entrenched a view of military superiority as being critical to the strength and well-being of the nation. The tenet of the strength of a nation being built on military domination was also true for the times and not misplaced. In fact this is a universal and timeless truth that is forgotten at the peril to the nation, as relevant in Ghiyas ud-Din's time as now in the 21st century. For a matured administrator and military commander, this was a self-evident truth. Therefore, he paid special and personal attention to the army, ensuring that they were maintained in fighting trim at all times.

Although mild-mannered in his dealings with nobles and courtiers, he always endeavoured to maintain the prestige of the sovereign. However, he remained on the same terms with his old friends even after becoming the sultan. Essentially he had always led the virtuous life of a pious Sunni Muslim, which he continued to do even after becoming the king. He kept free of the normal vices of the age that normally afflicted noblemen and kings. He was also one of the first 'builders' of the Delhi sultanate. He built the fortified city of Tughlaquabad and moved his capital there. He also erected many great buildings, the most magnificent being his own tomb, which displays some unique architectural features.

In spite of all the admirable qualities that Ghiyas ud-Din possessed and effortless administrative efficiency that he displayed, the Hindu subjects suffered under his reign because he was a man of the time. Being a devout Sunni Muslim, he blindly adhered to the Quranic Law, without thought for intelligent interpretation. His civil administration was based completely on the letter of Muslim law as was prevalent at that time and not on the spirit of the law. This strict and blind adherence to the Muslim Law overshadowed the entire treatment of Hindus within his kingdom. Hindus were held in utter contempt and treated as inferior beings, being consciously taxed into perpetual poverty. Hindus continually felt the severity of the government, being ground down from all directions—in terms of religious intolerance, social status, economic downfall and political insignificance. Although they formed the majority of the population of the kingdom, essentially they did not matter to the state.

Ghiyas ud-Din's treatment of the Hindus bears close resemblance to the manner in which they were treated during the rule of Ala ud-Din. However, Ghiyas ud-Din was a much 'better' man than Ala ud-Din and should have been more enlightened in his outlook towards the majority of his subjects. Sadly, this was not the case and the Hindus did not fare any better. He did not have the farsightedness or sense of fairness to treat the Hindus as equal to any other subject within his jurisdiction. The position of Hindus, under this sober and much accomplished sultan, was purely a function of how the Quranic Law was interpreted by the bigoted clergy, not one of objective justice, let alone compassion. Hindus were systematically relegated to the status of second-class citizens, inferior to all else, with no political position or civil rights, in the land of their birth.

The only credit that can be given to Ghiyas ud-Din is that he restored the power and prestige of the king ruling from Delhi, which had fallen very low, by the studied correctness of his behaviour and demeanour; and that he revitalised a system of administration that had atrophied from within.

Chapter 14

MUHAMMAD TUGHLUQ
THE IMPATIENT ADMINISTRATOR

Three days after the death of Ghiyas ud-Din, Jauna Ulugh Khan the designated crown prince, ascended the throne assuming the title Muhammad Tughluq. In various chronicles he has also been named Muhammad bin Tughluq and Muhammad Shah. Muhammad bin Tughluq would mean the son of Tughluq that in turn would make the title 'Tughluq' one of the common names of Ghiyas ud-Din, which is incorrect. Shah was a title that was assumed by many of the Delhi sultanate rulers, perhaps in imitations of the great Shahs of Persia, and therefore could have been attributed to Muhammad by contemporary chroniclers. For the purpose of this narrative the sultan will be referred to as Muhammad Tughluq.

There was no opposition to Muhammad's accession to the throne. No revolution, palace intrigue or popular uprising marred the smooth transition of power from his deceased father to Muhammad being anointed the unquestioned king of Delhi. He started his reign with the grant of large and generous gifts to loyal officers and nobles. His generosity was such that the word spread far and wide, bringing to Delhi many pious and learned men—who were nevertheless sufficiently worldly wise to detect an opportunity to better their social and financial status—who were, as expected, richly rewarded by the new sultan. Public opinion in all kingdoms and at all times have been notoriously short lived. Therefore, it was not long before the catastrophe that befell Ghiyas ud-Din, and the suspicious circumstances surrounding it, were fully forgotten by the people.

Jauna Khan, Muhammad Tughluq, was brought up as a soldier while also being provided the best available literary education in his youth. His first major appointment as part of the nobility in the Delhi court was as the 'master of the horse' during Khusrav Shah's reign. The appointment was not an indication of his capability, but an attempt by Khusrav to ensure the support of the Tughluq clan headed by Ghiyas ud-Din who was then the governor of Punjab. However, Muhammad Tughluq was ambitious from his younger days. There are unconfirmed reports that Ghiyas ud-Din, a staid and reliable governor, embarked upon the route of rebellion only at the instigation and advice of his son. Muhammad's ambition was tinged with an underlying unscrupulous nature that often led to his actions being suspected of being ill-intentioned. His sudden return to Delhi from an almost victorious campaign in Warangal (described in a later chapter) has also been considered by some analysts to have been an attempt at usurping the throne. It is thought that he did not proceed further with the plan only because he lost his nerve at the last moment or because he changed his mind after initiating the actions. This vacillation was a characteristic that was to manifest even more with grave consequences, especially after he established himself as the undisputed sultan.

Muhammad Tughluq had almost a blind belief in his own wisdom and ability to rule the kingdom better than any of his predecessors. This comes through in the analysis of most of his decisions. He continued to reside in Tughlaquabad for an extended mourning period of 40 days and then set out for Delhi in a ceremonial procession. In Delhi he took up residence in the Red palace of the early sultans. He also declared that he would continue to pursue his father's policy of ensuring justice for all. The people of Delhi celebrated the arrival of the new sultan with great festivities. Perhaps more important was that a sense of optimism prevailed amongst the population. They seemed to have high expectations of the new king who was educated, a soldier and had the demeanour of a statesman. This far out in time from those days, it can be seen that the celebrations were pre-emptive and indulged in without the people having the slightest inkling that they were about to usher in the most turbulent reign in the 300-year history of the Delhi sultanate.

Sources of Information

There is a great deal on information available about Muhammad and his reign in contemporary chronicles. There is even a detailed account written by Ibn Battuta, a Moorish explorer-traveller who spent more than a decade in India—most of it in Delhi as a guest in the court of Muhammad Tughluq. Ibn Battuta's account is particularly forthright and honest since he had nothing to fear from the Tughluq dynasty. His account/book was written after he had returned home to Morocco at the end of his travels. However, the chronicles and reports are confused, and at times contradictory, regarding the events of Muhammad's reign, a malaise that is apparent in modern day explanations and analysis of the events. There is inconsistency in opinion regarding the intent of some of his actions and contentious debate regarding the motive and desired results of most of the schemes that Muhammad Tughluq initiated. The confusion is compounded by the fact that there still exists doubts regarding the chronology of some of the clearly recorded events.

The primary source of information is the chronicle of Zia ud-Din Barani. He belonged to a family of prominent officers who had been in royal service for at least two generations. Further, although he never held any official position, Barani himself was a favoured courtier in Muhammad's court for 14 years. This privileged position made him an enviable close-quarters witness to the functioning of the administration and provided him with a silent but ringside seat to observe the core of the kingdom's decision-making process. This position also had the distinct disadvantage of not being able to criticise the sultan simultaneous to the happening of important events. However, Barani's chronicle for the most part can be accepted as having been written without fear or favour of the sultan for two reasons. One, that it was only completed and made public a few years after the death of the Muhammad; and two, it was written towards the end of Barani's own life when he was no longer a courtier and had no need to fear the Tughluqs. Barani therefore, is brutally candid about Muhammad Tughluq's misdeeds and equally appreciative of his good deeds.

Muhammad Tughluq – A Profile

From available contemporary literature and later-day analysis, Muhammad definitely emerges as a person with a psychotic, split-personality. He was an unfathomable combination of great qualities beset with extremely base instincts; a bizarre mixture of altruistic goodness and pure evil; an individual bloated with overweening arrogance replaced at times with abject humility; a sultan given to great paroxysms of rage accompanied by brutal violence, which was masked and counterbalanced by acts of extreme compassion. At his humblest best, Muhammad was capable of delivering equity and justice, demonstrated high compassion for the needy, and bestowed extraordinary generosity.

Of all the monarchs who sat on the throne of Delhi—Hindu and Muslim—Muhammad Tughluq is the most enigmatic puzzle who continues to remain only partly understood. Muhammad generated debate amongst contemporary chroniclers in his own lifetime and continues to do so even among modern day historians. His reign was full of 'stirring' events, depending on how the concept of 'stirring' is accepted within the context of a historical analysis. A greater paradox is the fact that despite the availability of voluminous and detailed chronicles of his activities, they fail to provide any definitive clues to the influences that culminated in the generation of his unique ideas, the nature of some of his more grandiose schemes, and the motives that inspired them. This situation reinforces the impetuous nature of Muhammad's decision-making and the inability that he displayed throughout his reign to consult with able, sane and venerable nobles in his service. His was a one-man administration, ruthlessly enforcing decisions that had not been thought through with sagacity and made without any outside inputs.

The consequence of this in-built paradox in the narrative of the sultan's actions has been to create an image of a ruler with a wide divergence of opinion about him. In turn, this has led to hypothetical reconstruction of events based on hearsay and speculation. The situation not only makes analysis controversial, but prone to factual errors, which leads to the lack of veracity of the entire study itself. In modern times, as an anachronism in his own lifetime, Muhammad Tughluq represents the quintessential perplexing puzzle that faces historians from time to time—one that can never be fully unravelled.

Muhammad Tughluq was a compulsive innovator, at the same level as the other great innovator who preceded him on the Delhi throne, Ala ud-Din Khilji. The fundamental difference between the two, which determined the success and failure of the schemes that each of them instituted, was the disparity in their inherent human characteristics. Muhammad was not pragmatic or patient, clearly lacking the perseverance to execute his schemes properly and see it through to a logical conclusion. He was an incorrigible dreamer, although some of the schemes that his fertile mind conceived were quite sound. The challenge that Muhammad faced was not the conception of the scheme, most of which were actually fairly sound. The challenge lay within his character, which was erratic and mercurial and lacked the tenacity to fully implement even minor plans.

In contrast to Ala ud-Din who was a total pragmatist, Muhammad was a fantasist; all of Ala ud-Din's schemes were motivated solely by political considerations while Muhammad was motivated not by necessity, but by the excitement that his whimsies created; and while Ala ud-Din was deliberate and calculating in all his decisions, Muhammad was almost completely impulsive. Even their decision-making process was in complete contrast to each other. Ala ud-Din always held detailed discussions with his councillors on every major project that was being planned, although in the end he always made up his own mind, giving the royal stamp to the considered decision. Muhammad on the other hand never discussed his projects with anyone, probably in the implicit belief that all his ideas were good, and unilaterally promulgated whatever royal decrees he deemed necessary. The result was that while Ala ud-Din succeeded implementing almost all his reforms, Muhammad failed in all his endeavours.

ADMINISTRATIVE EXPERIMENTS

It has to be mentioned in his favour that Muhammad Tughluq was at all times a diligent ruler. Almost immediately on becoming the sultan he proclaimed a number of ordnances aimed at improving the existing revenue system. An innovative ordnance was the one that required the compilation of a register to record the revenue and expenditure of each province in detail. The governors were ordered to send all records to Delhi for centralised compilation and analysis. Muhammad must have aimed at carrying out a comparative study of the revenue and expenditure of individual provinces in order to introduce a uniform standard of land revenue. However, this is mere speculation since the sultan never spelt out the aim of the exercise and neither is it mentioned in any of the chronicles. The chronicles also do not mention any consequences that came with the implementation, any follow-up action that was instituted, or when and why the ordnance lapsed into disuse. This is a typical example of Muhammad Tughluq's process of administrative reform—order the start of a well-meaning scheme while keeping everyone in the dark regarding the final objective, lose interest in it fairly quickly during the early stages of its implementation, and rapidly let the order lapse into dormancy.

Revenue Reforms – Taxation of the Doab

One of the earliest administrative measures that the sultan introduced was to impose extra taxes in the Doab in an effort to increase the revenue to the exchequer. The reason for the Doab to be chosen for this measure could be that the land was extremely fertile and also that the people of the Doab were habitually of a rebellious nature, rising up against Delhi at the slightest provocation. It is also presumed that the measure was an initiative to raise revenue by about five to ten per cent. There are some reports that indicate the aimed increase to be closer to 20 per cent, but even for Muhammad Tughluq that is too high a percentage increase to be considered credible. The increase in revenue was to be effected not through an increase in land taxes, but through the imposition of additional taxes like grazing tax, house tax and such. Accordingly houses were numbered, cattle branded and the taxes imposed with the full vigour of the central administration.

Unfortunately for Muhammad, the imposition of the new taxes coincided with a season of failed monsoons that had already led to the beginning of a long term famine in the land. Further, the combined taxes being imposed was out of proportion to the income of the people, even calculated at the pre-famine level. It was obvious that the people would resist paying the new taxes, and with the famine even the original amount was unaffordable. The strict enforcement of the enhanced taxes brought farmers to utter impoverishment and misery. Many farmers abandoned their land and turned to highway robbery as a means of feeding their families that in turn resulted in the rapid breakdown of the law and order in the provinces. These unintended consequences enraged the sultan, who became even more stringent in the imposition of the taxes. It is reported that defaulters were hunted down like so many animals in the forest by the sultan and his forces.

The sultan's popularity took a beating. Rather late, Muhammad started to institute some measures to alleviate the situation. He offered loans to the farmers and also ordered wells to be dug to get over the draught and famine situation. However, like all his other policies, these also were not pursued with the necessary momentum to make them effective—they were half-hearted attempts that gradually lost impetus and failed to make any tangible difference to the sorry lot of the peasants. The introduction of additional taxes in the Doab failed to achieve its presumed objectives. 'Presumed' since the sultan's reasoning for the plan and the objectives that he had in mind have remained obscure.

There were two major reasons for the failure of the new taxation initiative. First, a similar taxation offensive had been introduced by Ala ud-Din in the early days of his reign. However, ever the pragmatist, he had almost immediately seen that the measure was unpopular and had consciously allowed the order to lapse into disuse. The reintroduction of similar measures was resented and opposed by the general population. Second was the timing of the introduction when famine had already started to impact the province and realising even the normal revenue was becoming difficult. Therefore, even the attempts at providing assistance came too late, with the farmers using the loans they were given to purchase food rather than procuring seeds for the next or future planting.

Barani brings into focus like no other chronicler the inception and execution of the policy of taxation of the Doab. According to him the famine continued for several years and thousands perished in the famine. Further, the sultan is purported to have put to death any farmer abandoning his fields and also the defaulters who did not pay the increased tax. The end result was that it created untold misery on the population and devastated a large part of the kingdom. Barani particularly mentions the inhuman cruelty of the sultan in the enforcement of the new taxation laws prior to his turn around to provide assistance. Modern historians have tried to downplay the descriptions of extreme cruelty reported by contemporary writers as being biased exaggerations. However, even they have no doubts regarding the widespread distress brought on by the combination of enhanced taxes, famine and the sultan's insistence of the strict enforcement of the royal ordnance.

> ### Attempts to Clear Muhammad of any Misdeeds
>
> The actual date of the enforcement of the increase in taxes has been generally accepted as 1326-27, although few sources insist that it was done three years later. This means that within a year of assuming the throne, Muhammad had started to implement his fanciful administrative ideas.
>
> Some modern historians have hypothesised a story around the later date (1330) of the taxation initiative in order to clear the sultan of any responsibility for the debacle that followed. The concocted story is as follows:
>
> The number of farmers in the Doab had been increased through the grant of land to soldiers disbanded after the Khorasan campaign. When the increase in taxes was announced these soldier-farmers protested and refused to cultivate the land. They were also accused of open rebellion and murdering some of the tax collectors. In retribution, the sultan inflicted heavy punishment on the Hindu village chiefs, despite that fact that the disbanded soldiers would almost all have been Muslims. The ringleaders of the rebellion, by this account all Hindu village chiefs, then fled to the forest and joined forces with the Rajput clans of Dalmau who were in open revolt against Delhi. This left the sultan with no alternative but to hunt the rebels down across the entire region.
>
> If this narrative is believed, it automatically transfers the blame for the fiasco on to the people, particularly the Hindus. How the Muslim soldiers who rebelled were transformed to being Hindus, even in this far-fetched account is difficult to fathom. Therefore, it is apparent that this fanciful reconstruction of events is based on

> speculation and only aimed at erasing the faux pas that Muhammad had committed. It is an attempt to even make him look benevolent through emphasising the remedial measures that he instituted at a late stage in the self-created fiasco.
>
> The attempt at shifting the blame is an incorrect assessment; the responsibility for the entire debacle lies firmly with Muhammad Tughluq.

Revenue Reforms – Department of Agriculture

Muhammad embarked on an innovative and valuable initiative with the object of expanding cultivation through the creation of a department of agriculture. The dual objectives were to convert fallow land to farmlands and to spread the cultivation of high-value commercial crops along with other common-consumption crops. The initiative started with the offer of liberal loans to entice and encourage the farmers to make the switch, even partially. Up to this stage, the scheme was on the right track. As a further innovation, Muhammad carried out a pilot project to study the feasibility of the scheme. He had the officials select a large tract of land, 60 miles square, and cultivated it with different crops in rotation at government expense and supervised by government officials. Then came the challenges that converted the scheme into a failure.

The experiment failed for a number of reasons. First, the land selected for the pilot project was not fertile and therefore did not give the correct indication of the feasibility of the scheme. Second, the experiment was not fully understood by both the officials and farmers involved. This was typical of Muhammad's inability or unwillingness to explain the project and the desired end-state fully and/or have a consultation process with the officials involved. In this instance, he had not described the project in detail to anyone. To make matters worse, he did not give sufficient personal attention to the project after it had been initiated. Third, the three-year period that was prescribed to analyse the viability of the project was insufficient to produce a reasonable result, considering that this was an agricultural project.

The fourth reason was the proverbial last straw that broke the back of the project. Seeing the ease with which generous loans were being granted, a number of unscrupulous men applied for and received enormous sums of money merely on their promise of starting to farm and creating great returns. Further, officials charged with distributing these loans themselves started to defraud the treasury. The project was one of the most innovative and advanced experimental concept in agricultural reorganisation. It could be considered the idea of a genius. However, it failed and had to be abandoned because of the inherent flaws in the sultan's character.

Revenue Reforms – Issuance of Token Currency (1329-30)

Muhammad Tughluq's reign has been accepted by historians as an important landmark in the history of coinage in the sub-continent. On coming to power, he initiated an ambitious program aimed at reforming the entire existing system of coinage. The aim was to determine the relative values of precious metals and the facilitate ease of exchange and convenience of circulation. There is no dissent among historians in agreeing that this was achieved without much difficulty.

Then in 1329 Muhammad attempted a most daring plan—he introduced token currency made of brass and copper that was declared equal in value to the silver and gold coins till then in circulation. It is highly probable that the idea was borrowed from China and/or Persia where paper currency had been in circulation as legal tender for a few centuries. However, there is no unanimity of opinion regarding the reasons for Muhammad to adopt this rather drastic step of introducing token currency or even the wisdom of embarking on this route.

There are two speculative reasons for Muhammad to have introduced this step, both of which cannot be confirmed with any certainty from contemporary records. First is that the royal treasury was bereft of wealth and almost bankrupt—drained by wars, putting down rebellions, expensive administrative experiments of the sultan and also by his prodigious generosity. Added to this was the failure of the taxation policy of the Doab and the subsequent expenditure involved in providing succour to the impoverished farmers and peasants of the region. The second is that famine had become endemic to most of the kingdom, especially in the most fertile of lands, leading to a general decline in agricultural produce. For a kingdom reliant on an agriculture-based economy this was a debilitating blow. The combined effect was that the sultan had to resort to deficit financing because of the extremely curtailed revenue that was flowing into the royal coffers. However, the reasons above are only speculation and not based on any firm evidence.

There is another viewpoint amongst some historians that the introduction of the token coinage was the result of a universal shortage of silver. According to this hypothesis, the sultan was only attempting to bridge the shortage of silver coins although the treasury was still rich. In any case, by royal decree brass and copper coins were made equal to the silver 'tanka' of 140 grains. This became enforced law. Irrespective of the reasons for the introduction of token coins, at the conceptual level the measure was praiseworthy. However, the manner in which the scheme was implemented left a lot to be desired and there is unanimity in opinion that the end-result was disastrous for the royal treasury.

So what went wrong? There are many reasons that combined to make this modernistic reform a complete disaster in the Tughluq kingdom. The first was that although the concept was borrowed from China, the sultan did not study the manner in which the scheme had been introduced and implemented in that country. In China, along with the introduction of paper currency elaborate measures had been instituted to prevent forgery with counterfeiters being summarily executed when apprehended. Muhammad lacked the administrative will to enforce laws to prevent forgery and his administration lacked the skills to effect such a complex scheme successfully.

Second, when the royal decree was issued that brass and copper coins would have the same value as gold and silver coins, the gold and silver coins were not withdrawn from circulation—they continued be in use as common legal tender. This meant that anyone could exchange a copper coin for a silver/gold coin at will. To further compound this issue, the brass and copper coins were easy to copy and counterfeits proliferated within a short period of time. It is reported by contemporary historians that every 'Hindu' household became a copper coin minting house. *[The bias of Muslim chroniclers against the Hindus is very obvious in this statement, since the entire population entered into the business of minting copper coins, irrespective of their religious persuasion.]* Merchants and village headmen minted copper coins and cleared their debts and liabilities easily and rapidly. In a very short period of time gold and silver coins were suppressed and being hoarded by the people. The result was a complete failure of the scheme.

Inevitably the value of the copper coins was reduced to the value of its metal content, not the inscribed value. The state lost heavily and private citizens profited enormously during the period of time that their value was held to be equal to the silver tankas. Muhammad Tughluq, never an unintelligent man, realised the failure and also that the state finances were being ruined. Therefore, he abandoned the scheme with another royal decree. In frustrated anger he replaced copper coins with gold or silver, as originally promised, to anyone who brought them to the royal treasury. Effectively the scheme ended with the government buying copper at the price of silver or gold!

> 'Thousands of men from various quarters, who possessed thousands of these copper coins ... now brought them to the treasury, [and received in exchange gold and silver coins] ... So many of these copper coins were brought to the treasury, that heaps of them rose up in Tughluqabad like mountains.'
>
> From the Chronicle of Barani,
> As quoted in Abraham Eraly,
> *The Age of Wrath: The History of the Delhi Sultanate*, p. 161.

The failure of the scheme has been attributed to a combination of the impetuousness of a well-meaning but illusionary sultan and the ignorant avarice of the general population. Although the avarice of the people was a contributory factor, the sultan should have anticipated it and taken measures to curtail the trend. It is a universal truth that the general population will always attempt to gain wealth through the easiest means. Therefore, the responsibility for the failure must, in an unbiased analysis, rest with the sultan alone.

Muhammad had failed to appreciate the elaborate administrative infrastructure that were required to be put in place before the scheme was introduced. He was bereft of the patience and perseverance necessary to purse the implementation of an intricate scheme to a successful end-state. He was also unable to appreciate the limitations of the scheme brought on by the circumstances of the time and institute remedial measures like the Chinese had done. The final result was that Muhammad became further embittered and disillusioned, turning against his subjects in anger. The fact remains that Muhammad Tughluq had not meant any deception by introducing the token currency. However, the state was defrauded by the people who took advantage of the lack of control exercised in the implementation of a visionary scheme. The strength of the kingdom's economy was demonstrated by the fact that even after compensating the people with gold and silver, the sultan did not feel any great or irreparable financial stringency.

> 'There was no special machinery to mark the difference of the fabric of the royal mint and the handiwork of the moderately skilled artisan. Unlike the precautions taken to prevent the imitation of the Chinese paper notes, there was positively no check upon the authenticity of the coper token, and no limit to the power of production by the masses at large.'
>
> Edward Thomas, Numismatist,
> As quoted in Ishwari Prasad, *History of Medieval India*,
> p. 248.

Transfer of the Capital (1326-27)

Within a year of assuming power, Muhammad Tughluq conceived a good-intentioned scheme—the shift the capital of the sultanate to Devagiri, now renamed Daulatabad, located about 1000 kilometres south of Delhi. This initiative could be termed a huge 'political experiment'. In a critical analysis a number of logical reasons emerge as possibly having contributed to the sultan's decision to embark on this ambitious project.

Early in his reign Muhammad had to mount an expedition to suppress a rebellion in the Deccan. In the process, the military strategist in him had clearly perceived the locational importance and geographical advantage of Devagiri. The empire had grown large by now: in the north it included the Doab, the plains of the Punjab, Lahore and the territories stretching from the River Indus to the coast of Gujarat; in the east it reached to Bengal; in the centre it encompassed the principalities of Malwa, Ujjain, Mahoba and Dhar; and in the south, the Deccan had been subdued with the principal powers acknowledging Delhi suzerainty. For such a vast empire, Delhi was inadequate as the capital and needed to be moved further inland to ensure strategic depth and geographic centrality. Delhi was far too close to the north-west frontier of the empire from where the Mongol threat always emanated. The Mongol raids regularly reached the outskirts of Delhi, making it insecure and unsuitable as the seat of imperial power.

Considering the geo-military situation of the time, the decision was obviously not that of a whimsical despot as it has been made out to be in later-day analysis. In addition to its locational advantage, Devagiri had an impregnable fortress atop a high, rocky and precipitous hill that made an excellent and safe place for the sultan to live in, especially in the turbulent times of the age. As an aside, the abode on top of a high hill, where he would live high above his subjects—both physically and esoterically—must have also appealed to Muhammad's exalted view of his own greatness and stature.

In addition, the northern part of the sub-continent had already been conquered and subdued, forming the core of the kingdom whereas the Peninsula was still rebellious and turbulent. The Deccan was barely under control and was a region of uneasy alliances and periodic subjugations. It would be easier for the sultan to exercise better personal administrative control over the subjugated regions and also to attempt further southward expansion from a geographically proximate capital. There was also the unreported lure of the wealth of the Deccan kingdoms that would have added impetus to the decision to relocate the capital. Devagiri was much closer to the rich kingdoms of the south and therefore would have facilitated conquest and acquisition of wealth for the sultanate.

Considering the logical reasons for the relocation of the capital, at the strategic level the decision to relocate was sensible and deserved to succeed. However, like all other initiatives of the ill-fated sultan, it failed.

> ### The Sultan's Disgust of Delhi?
>
> Ibn Battuta states in his account that Muhammad was disgusted with the general population of Delhi because they had written a number of anonymous letters full of abuse regarding the administration. Some of these letters were personally abusive towards the sultan himself. Battuta claims that the sultan decided to shift the capital away from Delhi in order to punish the citizens of Delhi.
>
> It is highly improbable that this claim and the reason given are true. The project was far too serious an undertaking even for an impetuous sultan like Muhammad to contemplate for such a frivolous reason. It is surprising that a number of respected western historians have accepted this narrative to be true.
>
> The claim of the shifting of the capital having been initiated to spite the people of Delhi will have to be discounted as a fanciful addition to the story by Ibn Battuta, perhaps done in order to reinforce the quixotic temperament of Muhammad Tughluq.

The Reasons for Failure

The decision to relocate the capital was made in 1327. However, there is confusion about whether the sultan ordered the relocation of only the royal court with all its staff and officers or whether he meant for the entire population of Delhi to move. This is typical of Muhammad Tughluq's modus operandi—providing clear instructions that detailed his intentions was never his forte. The royal court was the beating heart of Delhi and if the instructions were to move only the court, it would have dealt a deathblow to the magnificence of the capital. This would have been a good enough reason for the citizens of Delhi to feel resentful.

It is difficult, even so far removed in time from the actual events and with the availability of a great deal of information and analysis, to put together an authoritative sequence of events regarding the execution of the project. The most probable sequence of events of the relocation is provided here and may not be completely accurate.

In the early stages, the royal court would have been shifted as an administrative measure. This could have been a catalyst for the citizens to write the infamous and abusive anonymous missives that would have taken a toll on the sultan's ego. The order for the entire population to shift to Devagiri could have been issued as a punitive measure by an enraged sultan, although there is no evidence to confirm this. The orders were then enforced and there are a number of graphic descriptions of the state of Delhi after it had been abandoned, as well as the cruelty exhibited by the sultan's forces in enforcing his orders.

Under normal circumstances the administrative measure of moving the court would have been successful since it was a strategically sound and sensible measure to adopt. However, even that failed because the decision was taken in an abrupt, impulsive and personal manner with no consultation with the courtiers and senior officials. Since no explanation or reasoning for the move was provided and the orders were given with no forewarning, the administration was unprepared for this monumental shift. It therefore lacked the will and the infrastructure to make the move a success.

To his credit it must be admitted that Muhammad provided facilities for the move of the general population from Delhi to Devagiri. A new road was built between the two towns and food and accommodation provided at state expense for the entire journey. On arrival at Devagiri the people were given state assistance to settle down and start to earn a living. These initiatives are not the actions of a king who was irritated with his subjects and further proves the fallacious nature of the reports regarding the sultan inflicting punitive punishments on the citizens of Delhi. However, the physical move between the two places took as many as 40 days on an average and the people suffered greatly despite the arrangements that had been made. In addition, the population of Delhi was loath to leave the city in which they had lived and flourished for generations. Devagiri was an alien land and the locals were not very welcoming of the new arrivals. By the time of the relocation effort, the population of Delhi contained a very large number of Muslims. The surroundings of Devagiri were almost completely Hindu in its orientation and the Muslims of Delhi would have felt apprehensive about moving to a predominantly Hindu environment. Resistance to the move was bound to solidify.

A core reason for the failure of the project was that Muhammad Tughluq failed to appreciate that the shift of the royal court would have sufficed to entice the rest of the population to move gradually to the new capital. The rest of the establishment—merchants, bazaars, artisans and other commercial entrepreneurs—would not have been able to continue in Delhi without the patronage of the sultan and his court, and would have relocated on their own accord to Devagiri. Muhammad's impatience to create a capital to rival Delhi in its glory as an overnight venture made the project fail. Impetuousness and a sense of wanting to get things done through royal decrees that had to be immediately obeyed and implemented, doomed the project to failure from its inception. Muhammad Tughluq's character would have been the undoing of even well-planned endeavours.

Once again the pragmatic side of Muhammad came into play and it must be admitted that when he realised the failure of the project, he ordered the people to go back to Delhi. He also facilitated the return with generous state aid. However, Delhi had been badly scarred by the initial, forced depopulation and it was many years before it regained its old splendour. The sultan continued to preside over the court in Devagiri for another eight years and then moved back to Delhi. Devagiri or Daulatabad was left as a monument to well-meant but misguided ambition and outpouring of energy.

In any holistic appraisal of the project it will be appreciated that there was strategic veracity to the proposed relocation of the capital. Devagiri as the capital did provide strategic depth to the kingdom. However, there was also the drawback of the seat of power being far away from the restive north-west frontier that was never well controlled. It would also have been difficult to effectively keep the constant vigil that was necessary over the frontier from a southern seat of power. This would have become apparent fairly quickly since the Peninsula was restive and would have consumed Muhammad's energies in controlling it. Since the prime cause of the failure of most of his schemes was his impatience to achieve results, it is highly probable that Muhammad would not have been satisfied by his new capital. However, that is speculation.

Since the transfer of the capital was not effectively carried out, it is not possible to provide a sanguine assessment or judgement regarding the veracity of the decision. There can only be speculation about how it would, or would not, have worked for the empire; and how it would have affected the future developments in the sub-continent had the capital been established at Devagiri. The only factual statement is that it was a great and inspired project that failed even before starting to be implemented. Its efficacy remains in the realm of mere speculations.

An Assessment of Attempted Reforms

Muhammad Tughluq had all the qualities to be a sultan of merit but his character traits overwhelmed his well-intentioned activities, dooming it to failure. It is obvious that he was well-read, intelligent and observant. It is also obvious that he intended to be a sultan of the people, almost always looking out for the welfare of his subjects. In medieval times in the sub-continent, Muslim rulers did not consider the Hindus as their subjects and Muhammad was no exception. While some historians have attempted to erase the stigma of religious intolerance from Muhammad's reign, others have tried to bring him out as a complete religious bigot. Both these attempts are biased. A Delhi sultan in the 1300s would have behaved in no other manner than how Muhammad treated the conquered Hindus. In modern parlance, Muhammad Tughluq was 'par for the course' as far as religious bigotry was concerned, as good or as bad as his predecessors and successors.

If one can speculate on a 'what if?' basis and project some of Muhammad's schemes as having been successful it will be seen that he would probably have been elevated by contemporary chroniclers and later-day historians to the realm of 'great' sultans. This endorses the view that many of his schemes were well ahead of his time and if they had been pursued to a logical conclusion would have improved the administration, security and prosperity of the kingdom. That actual events flowed in a different direction can be seen as the gap between idealistic thinking and the pragmatism needed to rule a turbulent kingdom.

Chapter 15

MUHAMMAD TUGHLUQ: MILITARY COMMANDER REVOLTS AND REBELLIONS

The entire reign of Muhammad Tughluq was plagued by rebellions and revolts in different parts of the kingdom, even though he had ascended the throne without any contest. Very early in his rule, his own nephew Baha ud-Din Gurshasp who held the fief of Sagar near Gulbarga in the Deccan, rebelled. Baha ud-Din had gathered enormous wealth during his rule over the fiefdom and also secured the loyalty of a number of nobles of the principality. Growing in confidence, he began to attack the nobles who continued to remain faithful to the sultan. Muhammad send an imperial army to bring the rebel under control, which defeated Baha ud-Din at Devagiri. The rebel fled towards Sagar, his stronghold, pursued by the Delhi army. Baha ud-Din fled from Sagar at the approach of the imperial army and took refuge in the neighbouring kingdom of Kampili, ruled by a Hindu king.

The Annexation of Kampili

Kampili was a small kingdom situated on the banks of the River Tungabhadra, comprising the districts of Bellary, Raichur and Dharwar. It had traditionally been a dependency of the Yadavas of Devagiri. When the Yadavas lost their kingdom to the Delhi sultanate after years of spirited resistance, Kampili declared independence. Although a small kingdom, it successfully resisted the invasion by Malik Kafur in 1313-15 and thereby maintained its independent status.

Since then Kampili had gradually increased its power and grown in prestige, adding further territory that included parts of Anantapur and Shimoga districts.

According to Muslim chroniclers, the raja who provided shelter to Baha ud-Din and his entourage was called Kampilideva. *[The name cannot be confirmed and seems to be the usual Muslim way of adding the term 'deva' to the name of the kingdom in order to name the king.]* The fact that Baha ud-Din was granted asylum in Kampili is a fact. However, the reason for the raja to do so is unclear, considering the might of the Delhi sultanate and the assurance that such a move would bring the full wrath of the sultan on the small kingdom. It could have been the result of an altruistic pursuit of the Hindu concept of hospitality or a subtle political move by Kampilideva. It is also mentioned that Baha ud-Din had for long maintained friendly relations with the raja of Kampili.

In the event, irrespective of the raja's motives in providing shelter to the fugitive, it brought disaster on the kingdom. The kingdom was attacked by a powerful army send from Delhi. Kampilideva offered heroic resistance, defeating the Muslim army twice in battle. However, when fresh reinforcements arrived for the Sultanate army from Devagiri, the raja barricaded himself in the fort at Hosadurg (Anagondi). Since he was besieged from all sides, he managed to hold out only for about a month. When the fort could not be defended any longer, the women performed the awesome rite of Jauhar; Kampilideva and his valiant soldiers sallied forth and fought the invaders till no defender remained alive. Kampili was annexed and constituted as a province of the sultanate under the governorship of Malik Muhammad.

The surviving sons of the raja and some other princelings of the kingdom were imprisoned and taken to Delhi where they were forcibly converted to Islam. Among these were two brothers—Harihara and Bukka—who would later revert to Hinduism on their return to the Peninsula and go on to found the great kingdom of Vijayanagar. In an indirect manner, Kampilideva's futile attempt to protect an honoured guest did not really go in vain. From the ruins of the small kingdom rose what was the mightiest kingdom of the Peninsula.

Even after Kampili was destroyed as an independent entity, the saga of the rebel Baha ud-Din Gurshasp continued. On being besieged, the king Kampilideva had send him and his family to the Hoysala king Ballala III's court for protection. Accordingly the Delhi army marched to Dwarasamudra, the capital of the Hoysala kingdom. There is debate whether or not Ballala III offered resistance to the invading army. Considering that the Muslim army went on to annex some parts of the Hoysala kingdom to the sultanate, it can be assumed that some sort of resistance was offered. However, after what must have been a brief struggle, Gurshasp and family were handed over to the commanding general of the Muslim army. Ballala III was obviously more politically astute than Kampilideva who perished in the attempt to uphold his own honour as well as discharge his obligations as a host. Ballala also accepted Delhi supremacy and may have been forced to pay tribute.

Baha ud-Din Gurshasp, the cause of the entire debacle, was send to Devagiri where Muhammad Tughluq was in residence. At this stage, Muhammad displayed the dark side of his character, demonstrating an element of revolting, demonic cruelty. He had Baha ud-Din flayed alive, his skin stuffed with straw and then displayed around all the cities of the kingdom. Further, his flesh was cooked with rice and then fed to all his family members who were in captivity. These actions were justified by the chroniclers as the sultan providing a warning to would-be rebels, an attempt at reducing the cruelty that was inflicted. Not surprisingly, these acts did not quell any rebellion but only made the people realise the odious nature of their sultan. In fact as Muhammad's reign continued, rebellions against his rule multiplied, especially during the last phase of his rule.

The Kampili-Hoysala expedition completed the expansion of the sultanate into the Peninsula, with the southernmost Hindu power being subdued. More importantly, it demonstrated the difference of approach towards the kingdoms of the Deccan from that adopted by Ala ud-Din Khilji, the first Delhi sultan to venture south of the Vindhya ranges. The Khilji policy was very similar to the one adopted by Samudra Gupta a thousand years earlier—the invasion was merely a conquering raid meant to establish suzerainty over distant and outlying provinces. The Khilji army had defeated the four great Hindu kingdoms of the south; the Kaktiyas, Yadavas, Hoysalas and the Pandyas. They were forced to pay tribute and then handed back to the dynasties.

Only peculiar circumstances forced Ala ud-Din to annex the Yadava kingdom of Devagiri, while he made no attempt to annex or rule the other three even by proxy.

The Tughluq sultans followed a very different policy towards all Hindu kingdoms with whom they came into contact. Their primary aim was the extermination of Hindu rule in the sub-continent, as opposed to the imposition of suzerainty. During Ghiyas ud-Din's short reign, the Kakatiya dynasty had been destroyed and Telangana annexed. The destruction and annexation of Kampili and the defeat of the Hoysala king made Hindu rule in the Peninsula restricted to the deep-south and insignificant small pockets in the Deccan. Almost the entire sub-continent was now under Muslim rule, either directly ruled from Delhi or being vassal states. Only Kashmir, Orissa, Rajasthan and the Pandya kingdom in the deep-south remained outside the ambit of the Delhi sultanate.

Early Disruptions

There were minor episodes of revolts early in Muhammad's rule that were by and large contained by the sultan without much effort. First to revolt was the Hindu chief of Kondana (modern Simhgarh about 12 kilometres south of Pune). The fort was besieged by the Muslim army and the chief was starved into submission after eight months. He became a vassal of Delhi.

The second rebellion was more significant in terms of the players involved. Bahram Aiba, titled Kishlu Khan, held the fiefdoms of Uch, Multan and Sindh. These were also the first line of defence for the sultanate, being provinces that guarded its north-west frontier. Further, Aiba had been a close friend of Ghiyas ud-Din and also highly respected by Muhammad Tughluq. A number of reasons have been advanced for Kishlu Khan's rebellion. However, the catalyst seems to have been Muhammad's explicit orders to Kishlu Khan to send his family to Devagiri/Daulatabad, the new capital. Kishlu Khan refused, and having disobeyed a direct royal order, perhaps was left with no option but to continue the inherent rebellion that was initiated by the refusal. This rebellion was serious enough for the sultan to start a march northward from the Deccan. Kishlu Khan also embarked with a huge force to meet the Delhi army. In the ensuing battle, the sultan's army was victorious and Kishlu Khan fled the battlefield. However, he was captured and beheaded; his head was hung at the city gates for all to see and understand the fate that awaited rebels.

A Series of Rebellions

The rebellions that erupted in the later years of Muhammad's reign were mostly the result of the erroneous implementation of the sultan's progressive policies. As discussed in the previous chapter, the failure of the sultan's innovative administrative policies almost always culminated in the oppression of the common people—they triggered heavy taxation, ruthless punishments inflicted in order to enforce impractical schemes and the innate cruelty that accompanied the royal decrees. The famine that affected the kingdom, which continued for a number of years, added fuel to the fire. There was also no dearth of ambitious nobles in the sultanate who were perennially on the lookout for opportunities to exploit to further their own agenda and to create instability. These nobles were not above using the sultan's difficulties, brought about by the implementation of his administrative reforms, to foment discontent in the court and the countryside.

After the Kampili revolt had been successfully put down, there were a few years of relative tranquillity in the kingdom. However, from 1335, the sultanate was plagued by a series of rebellions. The first one of significance was that of Jalal ud-Din Ahsan Shah the governor of Ma'bar (also mentioned in some books as Malabar) with its capital in Madurai. At this time Delhi was in the grip of a famine, but Muhammad Tughluq marched out in person to chastise the rebel. In the meantime, Ahsan Shah had declared independence and also started to issue his own coins. When the Delhi army reached Telangana, it was struck with an epidemic of cholera and the expedition against the rebel was abandoned. Ahsan Shah was not brought to book and became the independent ruler of Ma'bar region, founding the short-lived Madurai sultanate.

The next to rebel was Amir Halaju, the governor of Lahore. However, the rebel army was defeated and Halaju killed. Around the same time Malik Hushang, the son of the governor of Devagiri revolted. He subsequently submitted voluntarily to Muhammad and was pardoned. This was one of only two reported instance of the sultan pardoning a rebel leader. Subsequently, the governor of Kara Nizam Main, rebelled, was defeated and flayed alive, almost as per tradition. Similarly the governor of Bidar, Nasrat Khan rebelled, was defeated, deprived of his fief and exiled. Next, Ali Shah revolted in Gulbargha, was defeated and banished to Ghazi. These rebellions took place in the years 1337-40 and indicates the growing frequency of rebellions and the gradual dissipation of not only the resources of the sultanate but also the authority and control of the sultan over his domain.

Revolt of Ain-ul-Mulk

Ain-ul-Mulk Multani was the governor of Awadh and a distinguished nobleman. His rebellion in 1340-41 is considered one of the most important in the series of revolts that rocked the sultanate. Multani had rendered yeomen service to the state during a distinguished career and was held in very high esteem at the royal court in Delhi. At the height of the famine in Delhi, he had provided great assistance to Muhammad in relocating the royal family to Saragdwari. Ain-ul-Mulk was a highly learned scholar, well versed in theology and jurisprudence. It is reported in several chronicles that he was one of the few nobles equally adept at wielding the pen and the sword with complete dexterity.

Muhammad Tughluq peremptorily ordered Ain-ul-Mulk to take over the governorship of the Deccan, presumably to use Ain-ul-Mulk's great administrative experience to control and contain the increasingly rebellious chieftains and less than loyal officers of the Peninsula. The order took Multani by surprise since it was issued in Muhammad's usual fashion, without any consultation or preamble discussion, which was the minimum due of such a senior and powerful officer of the realm. While he was contemplating the pros and cons of the order, Ain-ul-Mulk was influenced against the sultan by some disgruntled nobles and became convinced that he and his family were consciously being placed in danger by the sultan. The governor of Awadh rebelled against the order.

It was now Muhammad Tughluq's turn to be surprised, since he had given the order in good faith and keeping the stability of the sultanate as the highest priority. However, he rallied the royal army and personally led the force against the rebel. After a fiercely fought battle and stubborn resistance, Ain-ul-Mulk was defeated and taken prisoner. However, Muhammad pardoned Ain-ul-Mulk considering his past services but put to death, in his usual cruel manner, all the associates who had advised the governor. This was the second instance of the sultan pardoning a major rebel leader. Even so, Ain-ul-Mulk was subjected to a number of indignities and appointed the superintendent of the royal gardens, a lowly position in the structured hierarchy of the royal court.

Loss of Bengal

Bengal had kept a distance from Delhi since ancient times and the era of the Delhi Sultanate was no exception. It remained an 'estranged' and autonomous province even during the reign of powerful sultan's in Delhi. In order to enforce a more direct rule in Bengal, Muhammad Tughluq introduced a new administrative system in the province. Following his father's initiatives in the province, Muhammad divided the province into three units with their capitals at Lakhnauti, Sonargaon and Satgaon. Lakhnauti was ruled by Nasir ud-Din, who had been appointed by Ghiyas ud-Din. Muhammad now appointed Qadr Khan as joint ruler and made him directly responsible to the sultan for the governance of the province. In fact because of his direct contact with Muhammad, Qadr Khan became the de facto ruler in Lakhnauti. A similar arrangement was introduced in Sonargaon also.

In 1337, Fakhr ud-Din, the armour bearer of Qadr Khan, slew him and usurped power in Lakhnauti. He astutely analysed the confusion prevailing in Delhi and took the opportunity to declare independence. Muhammad was far too engrossed in controlling other more troublesome issues and did not pay immediate heed to the events taking place in faraway Bengal. Fakhr ud-Din took advantage of the sultan's preoccupation and steadily increased his power, bringing all three units of the province under his control. He proceeded to rule the whole of Bengal with ability and vigour. Muhammad Tughluq did not initiate any action to counter this rebellion and effective cessation of the province. From this time, Bengal could be deemed to have seceded and lost to Delhi. Ibn Battuta describes Fakhr ud-Din as a capable despot who delighted in the company of pious and learned men. He is also reported to have donated large sums of money to charity. Bengal prospered under his rule.

The rebellions and revolts that sprouted with monotonous regularity were more or less contained in the early years of Muhammad's reign. As the years of his rule progressed, the sultan was hard put to control the eruptions and his later years were spent in a perpetual perambulation of his domain, personally putting down one rebellion after the other. This led to gradual loss of control over far-flung territories. An astute observer would have seen the beginning of the breakup of the once great empire.

MILITARY EXPEDITIONS

Muhammad Tughluq was an energetic ruler, intelligent and full of purpose, bent on improving the stature of the kingdom that he had inherited. Therefore, it was not surprising that he formulated grandiose plans of foreign conquest. Unlike the case of Ala ud-Din who was dissuaded from embarking on global dominance by older and wiser heads in his court; Muhammad Tughluq did not have any noble in his service with the sagacity and temerity to advise him and even if there had been someone of stature, it is difficult to believe that he would have been listened to by the sultan.

The Persian Plan

Early in his reign Muhammad had given refuge some Khorasan nobles who had fled the Persian court. These disgruntled nobles induced the gullible sultan to invade their country. Khorasan at that time was ruled by Abu Said. He had ascended the throne as a minor and had been ruling under the regentship of Amir Chaupan, who had managed the State for a number of years. During those years he had grown in stature and become extremely powerful—the de facto ruler of the kingdom. Abu Said fell in love with Amir Chaupan's daughter, but for some reason the Amir opposed their marriage. Abu Said, who had reached majority by now, captured the regent and later had him strangled. This brought on internal turmoil in the kingdom, plunging Khorasan (Persia) into confusion. Simultaneously Persia was threatened in the west by Egypt and in the east by the Chagatai Mongols under Tarmashirin Khan.

Muhammad Tughluq who had assiduously maintained good relations with the Egyptian ruler now collected an army of 370,000 men for the proposed joint invasion of Khorasan. In his enthusiasm for the project, the sultan paid this Army of the Khorasan in advance the wages for a year from the government treasury. However, as was the case with a majority of Muhammad's ambitious schemes, the plan to attack Khorasan also was influenced by other unconsidered factors, which intervened to make the plan unviable. There were four interconnected factors that made it impossible for the sultan to implement his audacious plan.

One, and perhaps the most important factor, was that the Egyptian sultan became friendly with Abu Said and therefore withdrew support for the Tughluq invasion plan. He refused to provide any assistance to the plan being incubated in Delhi. Two, the Chinese emperor was uncomfortable with the increasing power of the Chagatai Mongols and therefore not only withdrew all help in the enterprise but actively opposed the Mongol attacks on Khorasan. Three, the Chinese opposition made the Chagatai Mongols reconsider their position that in turn eased the pressure on the eastern borders of Khorasan, providing a much needed reprieve to Abu Said who used the respite to consolidate his military position at the border.

Four, and the most glaring fault in the scheme, originated in Delhi itself. While articulating the plan, Muhammad had not factored-in the extreme difficulty of moving a large army through the harsh Hindukush Mountains. No thought had been given to the logistics involved in undertaking such a march across inhospitable terrain. Further, it is true that the Delhi army was fairly well-equipped to deal with the local and largely disunited Hindu resistance. However, the sultan had not even perceived the challenges that would be faced by the army when it reached out, far away from their support base, to subdue an entrenched and battle hardened Persian army. This was a completely different task and it is doubtful that the Delhi army would have been up to the task, even if the difficult mountain crossing had been achieved.

To his credit, Muhammad Tughluq now exercised his superior wisdom and abandoned the foreign invasion plan, deciding to concentrate his military campaigns to the Indian sub-continent. The Army of the Khorasan, already paid in advance for one year of service never deployed in battle. When the one year was over, the royal treasury was unable to renew the contracts and the army was disbanded. This marked the absolute failure of yet another grandiose scheme that also incurred a great loss to the treasury.

The Rajputs of Mewar

Opinions and narratives differ regarding the Muhammad's effort to subjugate the Rajputs in the Rajputana region. The Rajput princes and chieftains bore the flag of rebellion and independence for the entire period of Islamic onslaught on North India. Their extreme sense of honour and tradition of never surrendering made them formidable adversaries. The narrative of Muhammad Tughluq's encounter with the Rajputs differ in the one available from Muslim chronicles and that recounted in Rajput history.

Story from Rajput Chronicles

Rana Hammira ruling a small principality in Rajputana took advantage of the confusion that prevailed on the death of Ala ud-Din Khilji in Delhi and seized Chittor in 1326. He gradually increased his influence and power and took over control of the whole of Mewar, and assumed the title of Maharana. The ruler of Mewar at this time was a Chauhan king, Jaiza. He, and his father Maldev before him, had accepted a feudatory status to the Delhi sultanate in return for being permitted to rule, even if nominally. When Hammira took over Chittor, Jaiza fled to Delhi and requested the sultan for protection.

Muhammad Tughluq marched to Mewar. In the battle that ensued at the village of Singoli, the Delhi army was soundly defeated. The Rajput chronicles state that Muhammad Tughluq was taken prisoner by the Maharana and released only on the sultan ceding Ajmer, Ranthambhor, Nagaur and Sooespur and paying a huge ransom. The 'capture' of the sultan is only circumstantial narrative and not corroborated by any other source.

The encounter between the Rajputs and Muhammad Tughluq is confirmed in a Jain temple inscription that recounts the defeat of a Muslim army by Rana Hammira. This defeat is also evident from the fact that Muhammad and succeeding Delhi sultans left the entire Rajputana region alone and made no attempt to subdue the Rajputs. The various Rajput principalities recognised Mewar as the paramount power within their jurisdiction. Therefore, the report of Rana Hammira's battlefield success against the sultanate army cannot be discarded in an off-hand manner as the Muslim chroniclers have done. The reports are not baseless, and the encounter is certain to have taken place with Muhammad's troops coming off second best. However, the capture and imprisonment of the sultan is too far-fetched to be considered a fact. The final result was that Rajputana became independent of Delhi.

The Mongol Invasion

Mongol invasions were regular and routine features from the very establishment of the Delhi sultanate. However, unlike during the rule of his predecessors, Muhammad's reign was relatively free of this menace. There was only one major Mongol incursion into the sultanate, which took place in 1327. The invasion was spearheaded by the Chagatai Mongol chief Tarmashirin, who was a Buddhist (Dharmasri) convert to Islam. The Mongols overran Lamghan, Multan and the neighbouring regions, advancing rapidly towards Delhi. As was the age-old tradition with the Mongol raids, their objective was plunder rather than conquest. The Chagatai marauders stormed through the Gangetic Plains and reached Meerut, pillaging and ravaging the land while killing people indiscriminately, at times even for sport.

Muhammad Tughluq was taken by surprise both by the invasion and the rapid and easy advance that the Mongols were able to make into the heart of the sultanate. He had neglected the security of the north-west frontier and there was no capable 'Warden of the Marches' to control the borders or resist attempts to invade the kingdom. Under the circumstances, the sultan had no option but to buy peace, paying the Mongol chief a sum that is reported to have been almost equal to the value of the kingdom itself. The Mongols retreated, on the way plundering Gujarat and Sindh and taking many prisoners. In one stroke, Muhammad had revised the policy of resistance that had been in place since the rule of Balban. The sultan's grasp of the broader aspects of the security of the sultanate must be questioned here, since safeguarding the north-west frontier had been a foundational pillar of national security for decades. The north-west frontier became open for invasions once again.

> **Attempts to Clear Muhammad Tughluq's Reputation**
>
> Some later-day historians (for example Dr M Husain), have attempted to absolve Muhammad of mishandling the security of the sultanate.
>
> Their narrative is that the Mongol chief Tarmashirin came to Muhammad's court as a refugee after having suffered a defeat in a campaign near Ghazni. The story goes on to state that the money given to the Chagatai chief by the sultan was in the form of assistance, after which the Mongols retreated. This is an extremely speculative narrative without any shred of evidence to corroborate it and unsupported by any source of reliable testimony.
>
> This story based on speculation and created to ensure that the sultan's reputation as a military commander was not damaged. It has to be discounted completely and must be considered only a blatant attempt at enhancing Muhammad Tughluq's reputation as a military genius and a generous ruler.

Muhammad followed a policy towards the Mongols that attempted to integrate them into the local Indian population. Towards this end, he patronised them, inducing thousands of Mongols families through the distribution of wealth and conferring other favours, to bring their families and settle down in the sultanate. It is possible that the sultan thought that the Mongols, being warriors, would further strengthen the royal army. This did not take place and the Mongols only added to the cacophony of dissonance that was becoming ever louder in the kingdom.

The Himalayan Adventure

As his ambitious plans of conquest continued to fail one by one and the number of rebellions continued to increase, Muhammad conceived yet another project to enhance his prestige and improve the stature of the kingdom. In most contemporary accounts it has been dubbed the Chinese Expedition. This title does not reflect the truth and is fallacy, based on a single introductory sentence in Ferishta's account of the sultan's Himalayan adventure. He starts that particular sentence with a passing mention that the sultan intended to conquer China. Subsequently most historians have presumed that Muhammad did indeed plan to invade China—an assumption that is wrong. Muhammad Tughluq intended to conquer the country at the foothills of the Himalayas that was the buffer between the sultanate and the Chinese territorial holdings in Tibet.

The territory that was being targeted for conquest was Qarachal (also mentioned in some texts as Qarajal and Farajal), which encompassed the region at the foothills of the Himalaya Mountain ranges towards the Indian sub-continent. Some later-day analysts consider Qarachal to be the modern Himachal, while some others hold that the name Qarachal was derived from Kumachal or Kurmachal, which was the older name of the modern day Kumaon region. In any case, the area under discussion, the foothills, covered the entire Kumaon and the Terrai region.

Qarachal was ten days march from Delhi, situated in the remote Kumaon hills and a Hindu stronghold. It is likely that Ferishta's report of Muhammad's ambition to subdue China was a ruse to deflect criticism of the sultan and the possibility of his being dubbed a religious fanatic since the true target of the expedition was a dominant Hindu kingdom. An army was assembled for the expedition, but its leadership had not studied the hardships involved in mountain warfare and the inclement and unpredictable weather patterns they would encounter. After initial forays into the inhospitable territory, Muhammad Tughluq was forced to withdraw, bringing to an end yet another unsuccessful military campaign. The end result was that precious resources were expended without any achievement to show for it.

The Fortress at Nagarkot

Although the Persian plan and the Qarachal expedition were both abandoned without any success and the expenditure of enormous wealth from the royal treasury, Muhammad continued to harbour visions of foreign conquests. He now turned his eyes towards the hill tribes at the foothills and planned to invade their territory. His reason was that the fiercely independent hill chiefs provided shelter to the defeated rebels fleeing for the sultanate. Once again a large army was assembled and it marched towards the Himalayan foothills and captured the town of Jidya. The predominantly Hindu population of the region fled to the mountains.

The road to reach the mountain heights was rather constricted and the cavalry was forced to go in single file. Even so, the Muslim army managed to forge forward, attacked and captured the hill fortress at Nagarkot, and established a foothold in the mountains. Nagarkot was considered to be an impregnable citadel and even the intrepid military genius Ala ud-Din, had left it alone. The capture of the fortress at Nagarkot was a great achievement for the Tughluq army.

Then the victory turned into a debacle. The rainy season set in, bringing with it disease that spread rapidly and reached epidemic proportions within the army. Therefore, the sultan permitted the army to withdraw. The retreat was a nightmare, the Delhi army was ambushed at every turn and slowly decimated with every step. Large numbers were killed and the rest made prisoners. The equipment of the army was plundered. Ibn Battuta reports that only three officers of the entire force managed to escape. Some other accounts mention the number as 11, but corroborate the fact that only this number returned from an army of 100,000 cavalry and accompanying infantry that had set out to conquer the hill tribes.

On the other hand, there was some consolation at the end of the expedition. The chief of the hill tribes recognised that cultivation of the lower lands of his territory would not be possible without the tacit approval of the sultan in Delhi. Therefore, he took the initiative to conclude a peace treaty with Muhammad and also agreed to pay tribute to Delhi. In an indirect manner the objective of the expedition could be considered to have been partially achieved.

This ill-conceived, badly executed, and disastrous campaign had grave consequences for the sultanate. The loss of this army exhausted the military capabilities of the sultanate. Muhammad was never again able to assemble a large force against the adversaries of the kingdom, forever surrendering the possibility of being able to initiate precipitous action when required. The sultanate thereafter remained in a reactionary mode to the initiatives of its potential adversaries. The clearly diminished military capabilities could have also acted as an impetus and spurred the increase in rebellions and revolts. It is obvious that the might of the Delhi sultanate was dissipated in the Himalayan foothills. What was not so obvious to the casual observer was that the disintegration of the empire was already being set in motion in the Peninsula.

Hindu Uprising in the Deccan

For nearly three decades, since the raids conducted by Malik Kafur, kingdoms in the Peninsula that had been traditionally ruled by Hindu dynasties had been repeatedly militarily subdued. The continuous spread of rebellions across the sultanate was seen by most of the Hindu dynasties as an opportunity to throw the invaders out. It appears that some sort of a Hindu Confederation was created in the Deccan to oppose Muslim subjugation, although the details are scanty. However, this would have been the natural reaction of the kings and chieftains who had been fighting the invading Muslim forces for just about three decades. The events leading to the obliteration of the Yadavas of Devagiri and the destruction of the Kakatiya dynasty in Telangana were less than a decade old.

In the Deccan a number of ruling houses had been either reduced in status and power or had completely collapsed through repeated Muslim incursions. Therefore, it was an obvious move for them to band together to free the region of Muslim subjugation and possibly subsequent rule. Some amount of contemporary Hindu records are available that provide information from a non-Muslim perspective regarding the events that took place.

The bias of Muslim chroniclers is very clearly visible in the reporting of the events in the Deccan. Many of the contemporary historians have completely ignored the events that took place, while some have reported them as insignificant and minor revolts against the sultan. This demonstrates the inherent difficulty in studying, understanding and analysing Indian history, if the information is derived solely from Muslim sources, which predominates available knowledge. All serious students of Indian history must endeavour to research for alternative sources to balance the bias that is very obvious in the Muslim chronicles. *[To achieve this, at least a basic knowledge of the local languages is necessary, since the records of the Hindu kingdoms, scanty as they may be, were not written in Persian.]*

The initial uprising was orchestrated by Prolaya Nayaka from Musunuru in Paka-nadu in southern Andhra country. The rebellion was initiated against the Muslim invaders to 'protect the Hindu Dharma, restore the worship of its gods, and to protect the Brahmana and the cow'. *[This appears to be one of the earlier references in the records regarding the 'protection of the cow'. Modern India seems to have adopted this cause, starting a trend of 'cow chauvinism' as an indirect means to oppress minority religions as well as to ennoble the concept of Hindu nationalism or Hindutva. The supporters of this trend have forgotten the fact that constitutionally India remains a 'secular state' with no prescribed state religion.]* It is unclear whether Prolaya Nayaka was a minor chieftain or just an army commander of a small principality. In the event, he was supported by two other chieftains/minor kings—Prolaya Vema, the founder of the Reddi kingdom of Addanki and Kondavidu; and Bhaktiraja, a Telugu Choda prince of Eruva.

There was obvious popular support for the uprising since a large number of people from across the region flocked to join Prolaya Nayaka in his campaign. The Hindu confederacy defeated the Muslim armies in a series of encounters, both large battles and small skirmishes. The Muslim garrisons that had been established on the eastern seaboard of Andhra country were all attacked, defeated and removed, one by one. The victories permitted Prolaya Nayaka to establish himself as the ruler at Ekapalli in Bhadrachalam area (Taluka) in the East Godavari district.

Around the time of these rebellions, Muhammad Tughluq was campaigning against the rebellion in Ma'bar. Therefore, there is reason to doubt the fact that he was aware of the Hindu resurgence in the Deccan. This may have been the reason for Muhammad to reorganise the administration of Telangana that had already been defeated and annexed. He divided the country into two parts and placed the eastern half along with the capital Warangal under a Kakatiya general Nagaya Gauna, who had converted to Islam and was known as Malik Maqbul. The sultan had earlier successfully employed this strategy of making a native of the conquered region the governor believing that he could bring significant influence to bear on the local population. While this strategy may have been effective in some regions, it will be seen that in the case of Telangana it was a failure.

Prolaya Nayaka died in the early 1330s and was succeeded by his brother's son Kapaya Nayaka, referred as Kanaya or Krishna Nayaka in Muslim chronicles. Kapaya Nayaka was a shrewd statesman as well as an able military commander and had assembled about 70 Hindu chiefs within the confederacy when he was the heir apparent of his uncle. On coming to power, he initiated the organisation of a Hindu league that encompassed the entire South India. He personally visited the Hoysala king Vira Ballala III to seek support. Vira Ballala III was a powerful king and the ruler of one of the only two independent Hindu kingdoms in the south. He had withstood the invasions and raids of Muslim armies for a considerable period of time. Ballala III agreed to assist Kapaya and the confederation to achieve what had now become a 'sacred' cause. Accordingly, he fortified the strategic regions on the northern borders of his kingdom and send troops to support Kapaya Nayaka's enterprise.

Kapaya, now bolstered with the Hoysala forces, invaded Telangana and fostered a Hindu rebellion there. Malik Maqbul, the sultan's appointee was unable to protect Warangal and fled from the region. Delhi lost the entire Andhra region to the confederacy, fairlyquickly. Now Ballala III himself took to the battlefield along with Kapaya and the combined forces invaded Ma'bar, the recently created Madura sultanate. The Muslim ruler there was easily expelled and the kingdom was handed over to Venrumankondan Sambhuvarya, who established himself at Kanchi as the king.

While Ma'bar was being reclaimed by the Hindu Confederacy, another rebellion was raging in the region around the River Krishna in the interior under the leadership of Chalukya Somadeva, the progenitor of the Aravidu family in Kurnool district. Ably supported by Prolaya Vema, Somadeva was able to win many battles and capture a number of forts. His most important achievement was the defeat of Malik Muhammad, the governor of Kampili appointed by Muhammad Tughluq after the Hindu ruler had been defeated and killed. (The sultan's campaign against the rebel Gurshasp and the destruction of the kingdom of Kampili as collateral damage has been covered earlier.) The liberation of Kampili and the victory of the Hindu forces has been reported by a Portuguese chronicler, Nuniz, in his account of the events of the time. Nuniz mentions it as a national Hindu uprising against Muslim oppression, which seems to be a fair and unbiased assessment of the situation.

> ### Harihara and Bukka
>
> On Kampili being recaptured by Hindu forces, Muhammad send Harihara and Bukka—now converts to Islam—to Kampili as governor and deputy-governor. He was pursuing the old strategy of appointing local nobles to influence the people.
>
> Harihara and Bukka were defeated in battle by Vira Ballala III, now an active leader in the insurrection, and then wandered around the region as refugees. During their wanderings they managed to get attached to the entourage of the sage Vidyaranya who took them under his tutelage. With the sage's assistance and following his advice, they established themselves as minor chieftains at Anegundi on the northern banks of the River Tungabhadra.

Kapaya Nayaka's attempt at re-establishing Hindu control over the Deccan and the eastern seaboard, as well as the creation of a Hindu Confederacy was a resounding success by any standards. The Hindu nationalist resurgence was of such a stature that it influenced even some Muslim governors, particularly in the region around Kampili. It culminated in the disappearance of Muslim power in Warangal and Dwarasamudra and all along the Coromandel Coast.

At the same time, Harihara and Bukka, now fully under the influence of Vidyaranya, renounced Islam and initiated a new Hindu resurgence movement in the Peninsula. They went on to found the famous kingdom of Vijayanagara in 1336. This kingdom stood as a bulwark against Muslim invasions into South India for three centuries. (The history of the Vijayanagara Empire is covered in the next volume of this series.)

This unsung Hindu nationalistic revival and insurrection against the invading Islamic armies of the Delhi sultanate is a signal event in the history of the sub-continent. Not only did all the Hindu chiefs unite under one flag, but they also managed to keep the confederacy from breaking up till such times as a powerful enough kingdom was created to safeguard the Peninsula. On hindsight, it can be said that it is unfortunate that such a nationalistic feeling did not sweep through the feuding and warring Hindu principalities of North India, where Islam was embedding itself as the religion of the ruling class.

At the height of his power, Muhammad Tughluq had reached the southern extremity of the Peninsula in victorious marches. However, in less than a decade after this triumphant raid, he had lost all influence in the region south of the Krishna-Tungabhadra river line, as well as most of Telangana. This dissipation of the sultanate's influence in the Peninsula marked the visible beginning to the disintegration of the empire.

Disintegration of the Empire

By the mid-1340s, Muhammad Tughluq was faced with a series of rebellions that were raging across the entire kingdom. He was forced to lead expeditions to different regions on a continuous basis. The man who had aspired to rule the world was finding that he was at risk of losing control of even the small territory that surrounded his capital, Delhi. Rebellions in Lahore, Daulatabad, Sarsuti and Hansi—all of them brutally putdown by the sultanate army—racked the kingdom. Simultaneously a great famine engulfed the northern part of the empire, adding fuel to the fire of discontent.

Muhamad attempted to pacify the simmering dissent by introducing new economic and administrative measures that included the reduction of the tax burden on the populace. He also tried to develop the agricultural sector in order to improve the yield. Another scheme was to revamp the judicial system to ensure equitable justice to all. All these initiatives were laudable ideas, but once again in their implementation the sultan faltered. The flaw in execution was accentuated by yet another innovation that Muhamad introduced. He believed that the old officials were not capable of understanding the concepts that he wanted to implement and therefore, in his typically impetus manner, they were dismissed en mass without any consultation. In their place he appointed new officials, almost all of them of humble birth and common people. *[This could be considered the equivalent of the 'affirmative action' that independent India instituted, in its haste to uplift the so-called down trodden. The consequences in both cases were equally disastrous for the well-being of the nation and the fabric of the society.]*

The ill-thought through removal of the veteran officials—most of them revered by the people for their sagacity and efficiency—created further disillusionment in the people. To add to their vexation, the new officials were inexperienced and inefficient, with some of them also being corrupt. These commoners had an inherent anti-foreign amir (nobles of Turkish birth) bias. The new officials either purposely mis-read the sultan's instructions or were untutored in the process of implementing royal decrees. The result in both cases was that in a number of cities, the amirs were massacred. The immediate reaction of the amirs, who were by no means without their own power base, was to unite and breakout in rebellion.

In 1345, the foreign amirs—called amiran-i-sadah, roughly meaning 'centurions'—of Gujarat rebelled. This sounded the death knell of the empire. Muhammad Tughluq marched against the rebels, routing through Patan and Mount Abu. In the first encounter both sides suffered severe casualties and the rebels fled to Daulatabad (Devagiri). Muhammad's Wazir, the Prime Minister, pursued them and managed to kill a number of the amirs of Broach through open treachery, reportedly on the explicit orders of the sultan. Muhammad Tughluq, now encamped in Broach, ordered the amirs who had fled to Devagiri to come to Broach. However, knowing the massacre of the amirs in Broach, they suspected treachery and once again rebelled. They took over Devagiri and proclaimed one of their own, Makh Afghan, the king. They were joined by the amirs of Dabhoi and Baroda. The rebel group now controlled a large part of Maharashtra.

Muhammad Tughluq marched against Devagiri and besieged the town. However, before the siege could be brought to a successful conclusion, there was a fresh rebellion Gujarat led by Taghi. Taghi was a cobbler, who had become a soldier and now the rebel leader. The sultan had no option but to lift the siege of Devagiri and proceed to Gujarat to quell the fresh revolt. This provided relief to the beleaguered city. It also gave the amirs of Devagiri an opportunity to lay the initial foundation for what came to be later called the Bahmani kingdom. (The Bahmani kingdom is covered later in the series.)

The rebellion in Gujarat was ferocious and widespread, with the result Muhammad could not return to the Deccan and to Devagiri. Taghi proved to be a formidable adversary and was astute enough not to offer the Delhi army open battle. He conducted a brilliant guerrilla campaign for a long period of time. During this campaign he had the full support of the amirs of Gujarat. He also plundered Cambay and besieged the fort of Broach. These exploits could only have been undertaken with the full support of the people—both Hindu and Muslim. Considering its geographical spread, Taghi's rebellion has to be treated as a popular uprising, not purely of the dissatisfied amirs and other nobles. Taghi was finally defeated in Gujarat and fled to Thattah. There he sought shelter with the Sumras of Sindh who were also in open revolt.

Muhammad Tughluq re-established control over Gujarat and enforced peace. In order to subdue Gujarat, he had by now spent more than three years in the region. He also reorganised the administration of Gujarat, which by now seems to have become his favourite pastime, and in the process also annexed Girnar (modern Junagarh) to the sultanate. After settling Gujarat, the sultan started on his pursuit of Taghi, marching towards Thattah. He planned to attack Thattah from both land and sea and therefore crossed the River Indus with his entire army. The Delhi army was also reinforced by about 4000 Mongol horsemen send by the chief of Ferghana. Unfortunately for Muhammad Tughluq, he contracted fever before the attack could be launched. Very rapidly he was taken seriously ill and died on 20 March 1351, within miles of Thattah his last military objective.

'Muhammad had the potential of being an agent for revolutionary change for the good of the Sultanate, but his reign turned out to be an absolute disaster. He meant to do good, but ended up doing only harm. All contemporary sources agree that his policies resulted in the ruin of the country and the people. 'The glory of the state, and the power of the government of Sultan Muhammad ... withered and decayed,' states Barani. In fact, paradoxical though it might seem, it was the good in him that fuelled and fanned the flames of the fiend in him—he turned devilish to punish the people who failed to appreciate the good in him! His frustrations warped his character, turned him into a raging, rampaging monster.

And that brought untold misery on his subjects. In his death, comments Badauni, 'the king was freed from his people, and they from the king.'

Abraham Eraly,

The Age of Wrath, p. 168.

Chapter 16

MUHAMMAD TUGHLUQ: THE ILL-STARRED DREAMER - BLOOD THIRSTY TYRANT OR BENEVOLENT KING?

Muhammad Tughluq was unquestionably the ablest, purely in terms of qualifications, of the crowned heads of medieval times. He was learned and accomplished; endowed with a marvellous memory and keen intellect; and possessed an extremely versatile mind with an enormous capacity to assimilate knowledge. Muhammad was a lover of the fine arts, a cultured scholar and an accomplished poet; well-versed in logic and philosophy; and an acknowledged rhetorician and theologian. The list of his qualities is long and impressive.

Although he was imbued with all these stellar qualities, considering the events and non-accomplishments during his reign, he emerges as a man of amazing contradictions, so much so that later-day historians have even questioned his sanity. However, no contemporary writer has given even the slightest indication of Muhammad having an unsettled mental state. Even so, it could be speculated that this omission was out of fear of the sultan's revenge if such an assessment was written in his lifetime. There is no doubt that Muhammad was head strong and short tempered, and extremely impatient to achieve tangible results in short order in all his schemes. His impatience was further aggravated by the popular apathy shown by the people towards his generally well-intentioned schemes. There is no doubt however that Muhammad had a blood-thirsty side to his personality, which is an opinion bolstered by accounts of events during his reign provided by religious persons.

Contradictory Characteristics

From the beginning of his rule, Muhammad displayed vicious and extremely cruel tendencies in the administration of justice. The treatment meted out to his own nephew, Baha ud-Din Gurshasp, who rebelled is a case in point. As his reign progressed and more and more of his grandiose schemes failed miserably, he became even more sadistic and blood thirsty. Extreme punishments for minor offences became the norm in the kingdom, especially when the sultan was involved in deciding the outcome of the case. All contemporary chroniclers mention the ruthlessness of the punishments and their arbitrary nature, providing several graphic examples of Muhammad's savagery against his own people. Within a very few years of his assuming power, tyranny replaced justice in the sultanate, a fact attested in several different narratives.

Muhammad Tughluq's fundamental urge was to attempt the conquest of the immediate neighbours of the kingdom in the sub-continent. On the other hand, he attempted to maintain cordial relations with other foreign countries and their rulers. For example he entertained the Chinese Emperor's request to rebuild a temple that had been destroyed by Muslim forces so that Chinese pilgrims could visit it again. He also exchanged gifts with the Emperor and certainly maintained friendly relations. Muhammad was also gracious and generous to a fault with foreign visitors to his kingdom. Ibn Batuta, the Moroccan historian, was one of the recipients of the sultan's generosity. He was given three villages as his fief and 10 Hindu slaves as servants for the duration of his sojourn in India—an extremely generous gift for an absolute stranger.

Contradicting such generosity was his overweening and egotistic pride in his own actions that was combined with a ferocious and vengeful temper that accompanied the failure of his schemes. He sincerely believed that he did everything better than anyone else, in the world. This led to his assuming an extremely arrogant posture towards one and all. The more he failed, the haughtier he became; till he became an insufferable egomaniac who held the balance of life and death of all his subjects on his personal whims and fancies.

Contradictory behaviour patterns were common place in Muhammad's life. He maintained a very high standard of morality in his personal life, while being a blood thirsty autocrat as a sultan. He was free from the vices common to the nobles and aristocracy of the age. It is reliably reported that he treated his mother with extreme respect at all times throughout her life. In private life he was generous to a fault and extremely humble in his personal dealings, continuing to maintain affectionate relationships with his earlier friends and nobles who had served with him when he was a prince. He was brought up as a soldier and loved military activity, excelling as a general and commander in the battlefield. In fact he died in the field, practising his military acumen and planning a combined land and river assault on a rebel who he was chasing across the kingdom. A fitting tribute to a warring general, perhaps the only one that could be given in the case of Muhammad Tughluq.

> **Muhammad Tughluq – A Mixture of Opposites**
>
> Some later-day historians have attempted to depict Muhammad Tughluq as being 'normal' in his behaviour, often quoting the manner in which he tried to separate religion and the State and tried to institute revolutionary changes. This is an incorrect assessment as there was nothing 'normal' in his behaviour pattern. Muhammad was a mixture of inherently contradictory characteristics, a trait that he displayed throughout his reign.
>
> He was arrogant and at the same time humble, moderate and even servile at times. He displayed extreme generosity that was unevenly mixed with a closed mind and the narrowmindedness that comes with it. He had great reverence for the abstract concept of justice and the established form of law, behaving like an ordinary citizen in the court of law if he was the accused, while also inflicting barbarous punishments for very petty offences as a judge. He could be the epitome of a kind and caring monarch at times, while at others he could behave casually in the cruellest manner.
>
> If anything, he was a mixture of contradictory characteristics, with no assurance of which of them would become prominent when he was dealing with his subjects.

Radical Religious Policy

Muhammad believed that spiritually the sultan stayed at an exalted height and that his character was too strong to be dominated by the priestly class. Barani, his chronicler and occasional critic, complains about Muhammad's thorny relationship with the clergy and denounces his rationalism. No doubt this criticism was egged on by the sultan's direct questioning of traditional orthodoxy in the practice of Islam. Till Muhammad's rule, the Maulvis, religious teachers and interpreters of the Quran, were considered above the law, ensconced and sacrosanct in their religion and pious stature. However, Muhammad was the first sultan to punish Maulvis who flouted his authority, were involved in aiding rebellion, or embezzled funds.

Muhammad ignored the Sharia, the Canon Law of Islam, which controlled all aspects of governance and life for a Muslim. He conducted the political aspects of ruling a kingdom based on reason and decreed that in administrative matters, secular considerations must always prevail. This brought him into direct conflict with the Ulema, the clergy, who had always influenced state policy. Regarding religious influence on the running of the State, Muhammad Tughluq's attitude was extremely pragmatic. He consulted and accepted the advice of theologians only when it was reasonable and expedient to do so. Even in the delivery of justice—an area in which the ruling of the Quazis, the theologian-justices, were considered sacrosanct—Muhammad ventured to overturn judgements that he found to be defective. In enforcing these steps, he put an end to the domination of the Ulema in political affairs and administrative matters of the State. This created a group of influential religious leaders to harbour anti-sultan sentiments that they surreptitiously used to influence the common people against Muhammad. However, in his personal life he was a devout Muslim, observing all the laid down practices to be considered a diligent follower of the tenets of Islam. Muhammad was perhaps the first Muslim ruler in Delhi to attempt the difficult segregation of religion and State in a Muslim autocracy.

Muhammad Tughluq, like Balban before him, considered his own person closer to God than any of his subjects and referred to himself as the 'Shadow of God'. This is a slightly different version of the concept of 'the divine right to rule' that was practiced during the medieval times across the monarchies of the world—in Europe, Japan, and South-East Asia. Early in his reign, Muhammad very clearly broke away from the Caliphate of the Middle-East, establishing his independence in all matters, both temporal and spiritual. However, towards the later part of his rule, when his unpopularity was almost at its zenith and Muhammad had become aware of it, he reversed his policy towards the Caliphate. He requested the impoverished and ineffectual Khalifa (Caliph) in Egypt to confirm him as the sultan of Delhi, in an attempt to boost his sagging popularity. This act of paying obeisance to the Caliph did not restore his popularity and Muhammad was both surprised and chagrined to notice the apathy of his subjects to his rule.

Although in his younger days he was interested in understanding the more spiritual aspects of religious practice and often associated with proponents of the Sufi sect, there is no record of his having held liberal religious views. In fact most chronicles praise his policy of religious persecution of non-believers while also blaming him for his generosity towards non-Muslims. The contradictory characteristics of Muhammad is in full display here. It is also reported that his overt patronage of Hindu yogis enraged orthodox Muslims, not only the clergy or the Ulema. He is stated to have been an ardent patron of the Jain sage Jinaprabha Suri whom he honoured and felicitated. This is also a paradox, since the Jain sage was completely wedded to the practice of non-violence and Muhammad Tughluq was almost an incarnation of violence. Considering his controversial behaviour and contradictory characteristics, it can be assumed that Muhammad's efforts at exploring other religions and faiths was an intellectual exercise aimed at gaining greater information and knowledge—after all Muhammad Tughluq was renowned for his learning and cultural interests. He was not attempting to reform orthodox practices.

Contrary Opinions

Some early English historians, led by the famous Mountstuart Elphinstone (1779-1859) believed that Muhammad Tughluq had a streak of insanity in him from early times, a view shared by a number of later-day European writers. However, no contemporary writer mentions, even once in the chronicles, any kind of mental instability. Even Ibn Batuta, who had nothing to fear from the sultan's vengeance when he wrote his account, does not mention mental imbalance. It has been mentioned by some Europeans that the accusation of madness was primarily based on the fact that Muhammad often gave the death penalty even for very minor offences. This trait was not really madness, but a lack of a sense of proportion combined with a vicious and short temper. Further, the death penalty was a common punishment in medieval Europe and other kingdoms of Asia. The Muslim clergy who were sidelined throughout his reign were also biased against the sultan and were capable of influencing opinions, attempting to make Muhammad's judgements seem those of a deranged monarch and therefore inappropriate. Therefore, the assertion of the European writers can be discounted as wrong, or even biased, assessments of Muhammad's character, which over a period of time perpetuated the myth of his madness.

The other charge that is still placed on Muhammad is that he was an atheist. This is a totally untenable accusation. As mentioned earlier, he was known for his meticulous observation of the demands of Islam as a private citizen. He adhered to the dogma, precept and practice of Islam and even punished people deviating from the strict code of the religion. These are not the actions of an atheist. At best, he could be considered a sceptic, especially in his younger days, questioning the teachings and laid down practices of what was, and continues to be, a strict religion that did not invite or encourage debate regarding its concepts and principles. Muhammad Tughluq was an orthodox Sunni Muslim, nothing more, nothing less.

He is also considered by many, most of them later-day historians and analysts, to have been a sort of a visionary devoid of any pragmatism; a king found of building castles in the air who dreamt up impossible schemes. Even this assessment needs to be corrected. He was not a dreamer out of touch with reality. Almost all his initiatives and reforms, that later-day historians tend to mock as the musings and deeds of a deranged mind, were sound and constructive, and practical applications of extensive analysis by the sultan himself. The fault lay in his not sharing his reasoning for an initiative to be put in place and explaining to this subjects the benefits that would accrue. He lost out in the art of communication. Muhammad Tughluq was more a flawed idealist than a dreaming visionary.

Conclusion

Muhammad Tughluq, even today, brings out extremes of opinion amongst students, analysts, and historians of repute. There are attempts to prove his madness on one end of the spectrum and efforts at trying exonerate him of all faults at the other end. These are two extremes of opinion, whereas the truth lies somewhere in between the two. The failed schemes that he instituted—relocation of the capital, foreign military expeditions, and appointment of new officials recruited from the common people—were ambitious beyond measure and some of the concepts were far ahead of their time. They also demonstrate a lack or lapse in judgement, not a streak of insanity as has been claimed. In any case, either insanity or lack of judgement in the character of a king would invariably lead to debacles for the kingdom.

There is however no doubt that Muhammad's character flaws and frequent policy decisions that invariably turned out to be wrong contributed immensely to the decline of the Delhi sultanate

> 'He was not a monster or a lunatic, as has been suggested by some, but there is no doubt that he was a mixture of opposites, for his many good qualities of head and heart seem to be quite incompatible with certain traits of vies in his character, such as revolting cruelty, frivolous caprice, and an inordinate belief in his own view of things. He might have had god ideas, but he had not the capacity to execute them.'
>
> R. C. Majumdar
>
> In *The Delhi Sultanate*, p. 87.
> Volume VI of the series *The History and Culture of the Indian People*

Indian historians dealing with medieval India are divided on religious and ideological lines, even though most of them tend to be unbiased, to the extent possible, in their assessment of people and historical events. However, in the contemporary narratives, as well in modern analysis, Muhammad Tughluq continues to be an enigma and a point of contest and debate. Hindu sympathisers tend to brand

Muhammad as having been excessively cruel and brutish, whereas the Islamic scholars regard him as a philosopher king who was ill-starred and misunderstood. In the final analysis, the truth in this case also would lie somewhere in between.

Chapter 17

FIRUZ SHAH TUGHLUQ
A MAN OF PEACE

As Muhammad Tughluq lay terminally ill, anxiety about dynastic succession was sweeping through the sultanate as Muhammad did not leave any male offspring to succeed him and no heir apparent had been nominated. Further, the Imperial Army was at that time stationed near Tattah, thousands of miles from Delhi. When Muhammad finally died, the empire was left without a ruler and the army leaderless. In this uncertainty the entire army started to march towards Delhi, almost like a rabble, leading to wild chaos and confusion. Seeing the Imperial army in a state of almost headlong retreat, the rebels besieged at Tattah started to attack them from the rear. To add to the confusion, the Mongols who had arrived to join hands with Muhammad to fight the rebel Taghi started to loot and plunder the royal camp. This state of affairs remained for a few days immediately following Muhammad Tughluq's unhappy death.

Barani the chronicler, states that he was eye witness to Muhammad nominating his cousin Firuz Shah as his successor. However, this fact cannot be verified from any other source.

Who was Firuz Shah?

Firuz was the son of Sipah Salar Rajab, the younger brother of Ghiyas ud-Din Tughluq. Rajab and Ghiyas had migrated together to India from Khorasan during Ala ud-Din Khilji's reign and having joined royal service had steadily improved their position and status, with Ghiyas becoming the governor of Dipalpur.

While he was the governor of Dipalpur, Ghiyas ud-Din had proposed to Rana Mall, the Bhatti Rajput chieftain of Abohar (in the modern district of Hissar), that the Rana's daughter should be given in marriage to his younger brother Rajab. Rana Mall, in characteristic Rajput haughtiness and pride, had spurned the offer. Ghiyas then adopted coercion as a tactic and subjected the people of Abohar to great hardship and misery by cutting off their supply lines.

It is stated in folklore that the princess accidentally overheard a discussion between the Rana and his mother regarding the ordeal the people were going through. In continuation, it is believed that the young princess sacrificed herself for the welfare of the people and married Rajab. Firuz was the offspring of this union. Unfortunately Rajab died when Firuz was only seven years old. He was thereafter brought up by Ghiyas ud-Din along with his own son Muhammad. Firuz shared a very close relationship with Muhammad throughout the latter's life.

The nobles, fearing that the Mongol rampage would engulf the entire camp if not stopped immediately, appealed to Firuz to accept the throne and save the situation. Firuz, considered by all to be devoid of ambition, at first demurred stating that he was contemplating a pilgrimage to Mecca. Subsequently he yielded to the pressure from the nobles, allowing himself to be proclaimed the sultan on 23 March 1351 with the title Firuz Shah Tughluq. At this time he was 46 years old and the closest male relative of Muhammad Tughluq. As the nobles had predicted, the crowning of the new sultan had a calming effect on the army and order was quickly restored.

Challenges to Firuz's Succession

Firuz's claim to the throne and accession was challenged by Muhammad's sister Khudavand-zada on the grounds that her son, being Muhammad's nephew, was a closer relative of the late sultan than Firuz. The claim was disallowed by the nobles who gave the reasoning that the boy was too young to rule. The second challenge was more difficult to push aside. When news of Muhammad Tughluq's demise reached Delhi, Khvaja Jahan, a long-time associate of the late sultan who had been left as regent in Delhi during Muhammad's absence on his military expedition, raised a child to the throne claiming him to be Muhammad's son.

It is believed by most contemporary and modern historians that Khvaja acted with good intentions, purely to ensure that the kingdom did not disintegrate with the death of the sultan with no designated successor. It is also reported that he had been informed that Firuz Shah was either missing or dead. Moreover, Khvaja was over 80 years old and could not have been motivated by personal ambition, which could have made him susceptible to the charge of treason. Further he had shared an excellent rapport with Firuz through the years. As Firuz approached Delhi from Tattah, Khvaja readily submitted to him. Firuz, characteristically wanted to pardon him but the nobles, recent king-makers, decreed that the offence was too serious to be pardoned. The old man was executed.

Some modern historians posit that the boy placed on the throne by Khvaja was indeed Muhammad's son. It is also claimed that Muhammad had only appointed Firuz the regent for the minor prince till such times as when the boy reached majority. Therefore there has been an attempt to paint Firuz as a usurper. This line of reasoning is incorrect for two reasons. First, it is certain that Muhammad left no male heir. This fact is corroborated by his sister claiming the throne for her son. If there was indeed a son, then this claim would never have been made.

Second, and more importantly, under Muslim law succession to the throne was never considered an 'inherited right'. The throne belonged to the person from the extended royal family who was considered the most appropriate person in terms of his individual capability. The choice was made by a slightly diluted version of a vote within the nobility. In fact Firuz being installed as the sultan revived this principle of election to the position. This concept had gradually receded to the background with sons automatically assuming the throne at the death of their fathers, the incumbent sultans. Firuz being anointed the sultan by acclaim of the nobility established two new principles regarding accession to the throne. One, that the mother being a Hindu before marriage was not a hindrance to the son becoming the sultan. Two, it was now not necessary for the sultan to have distinguished himself in the battlefield as a soldier and a general.

Establishing Rule

Firuz continued his march to Delhi to physically claim the throne and reached the capital in August 1351. On the way, at Sirsuti, news of the death of Taghi, the rebel who had tired Muhammad Tughluq to death was received. This was immediately proclaimed as an auspicious portent for the success of Firuz's rule, which was yet to begin. His arrival in Delhi was followed by the usual celebrations. Firuz also initiated some of the traditional acts of a new sultan such as the redistribution of offices, remission of some of the more oppressive taxes, pardoning of some criminals and the withdrawal of most of the punitive measures instituted by the earlier regime. These actions strengthened his hold on power. Firuz Shah was now the undisputed ruler of a very large kingdom.

Although personally very close to Muhammad Tughluq throughout the latter's reign, as the sultan Firuz was a complete contrast to his predecessor. Firuz started his rule with a distinct advantage. Muhammad had entrusted one of the four divisions of the sultanate to him for administrative purposes and therefore he was well experienced in the art of governance. On accession to the throne he was well-equipped by temperament and experience to assume royal responsibilities.

> 'Though Muhammad and Firuz were close to each other, they were entirely unlike each other in character, temperament and policies—Muhammad was an egomaniac, flighty and unpredictable, ever pursuing some chimerical scheme or other; in contrast, Firuz was a stable, dependable ruler, with a good sense of what was viable and necessary. While Muhammad wanted the world to adjust to

> him, Firuz adjusted himself to the world. And, more than anything else, Firuz was concerned with the stability of the empire and the welfare of its people, rather than with self-fulfilment. He was the right person in the right place at the right time.'
>
> Abraham Eraly,
>
> *The Age of Wrath*, p. 172.

Administration

Firuz was essentially a man of peace. He was a model ruler, admired both by the nobles and the common people. On assuming the throne he took upon himself the completion of two tasks on priority. The first was to reconcile the commoners who had been completely alienated by Muhammad Tughluq's fanciful schemes and whimsical punishments. He instituted measures to ensure conducive conditions for the safety and security of the people, which had been sorely lacking in the last years of Muhammad's rule. Firuz clearly felt the responsibility for the welfare of the people as resting on him at the highest level. Therefore, he attempted to be a model and true Islamic monarch, discharging the dual responsibilities of being the temporal ruler of all his subjects while being the spiritual leader and religious ruler of his Muslim subjects.

In doing so, he reasserted the principles of a theocratic system of government, which in turn became the foundation for all future Muslim governments in India. In continuation of this theocratic base of the government, he pronounced a ban on Hindus as well as on other 'heretics', which included even breakaway Islamic sects. *[Most historians have made sweeping statements regarding religious freedom and moved on. The fact is that by declaring a ban on Hindus and equating them to 'heretics', Firuz Shah instituted the first step in ensuring the second-class citizenship that Hindus suffered in their birth place for the next five centuries. This fact and the role of Firuz in perpetuating the oppression of the Hindus has been glossed over in most narratives regarding Firuz's rule.]*

The second task that the new sultan took on was to improve the state of the sultanate from the decrepit condition that he inherited it.

Firuz was not a dreamer by any stretch of imagination. He had a clear idea of the needs of the country and understood the requirement to institute proper, long-term reforms. In doing the calculations to secure the kingdom he accepted the need to recover breakaway provinces in order to make the sultanate great again. However, he was not a confident commander of troops in the battlefield. Therefore, he restricted his military expeditions to half-hearted attempts at bringing Bengal and Sind, two outlying provinces, into the fold of the sultanate. Both these campaigns were only partially successful and is described in detail in the next chapter. In a pragmatic manner, he left Rajasthan and the Deccan alone, realising that expeditions to either of these regions would be far too complex, both militarily and administratively, for him to undertake with any success. Therefore, Firuz concentrated on improving the economic prosperity of the country and in ensuring that the administration functioned effectively.

Towards achieving these objectives, he appointed capable ministers to run the administration. He was singularly lucky in having Malik-i-Maqbul, a Brahman from Telangana who had converted to Islam and an able administrator, as his prime minister. Maqbul proved to be a capable support for Firuz, serving the sultan for his entire lifetime, his son becoming the prime minister after his death.

Malik-i-Maqbul

Originally named Kunnu, Khan-i-Jahan Maqbul as he came to be known to history, was a Brahman and a favourite of the king of Telangana. During Muhammad Tughluq's rule, Kunnu was part of the royal retinue accompanying the king of Telangana on his journey to Delhi. The king died before reaching completing the journey and the body was transported to Delhi. On reaching Delhi, Kunnu converted to Islam in the presence of Muhammad Tughluq, adopted the name of Maqbul, and entered the service of the sultan. It is reported in some Muslim chronicles that he was illiterate. This is a biased and derogatory assessment, since being a Brahman he would not have been illiterate, but highly educated. The accusation of being illiterate is possibly purely on the basis of the probability of his not knowing Persian, which was the language of the Delhi court.

Maqbul was very wise and also an able administrator who rose rapidly in Muhammad's service and was granted the fief of Multan before long. Firuz appointed him wazir (prime minister), which proved to be an inspired decision. The sultan trusted him implicitly, leaving him in charge of the entire empire when he went on long-term, distant expeditions. Maqbul died in 1370, and his son Juna Shah—born while Maqbul was the governor of Multan—was confirmed in his office, with the titles of the father being bestowed on him.

A very early indication of the religious direction that the Firuz administration would take was provided by an action initiated by the new sultan. After reaching Delhi, one of his earliest acts was to atone for the 'sins' of Muhammad Tughluq, his predecessor. He presented gifts to the heirs of the people who had been killed and/or mutilated by Muhammad, especially if the reason for such action had been specious. He then secured written statements from the next-of-kin that they were satisfied with the actions taken by the sultan. These 'written deeds of pardon', attested by witnesses to ensure their veracity, was placed in a locked box and interred within Muhammad Tughluq's tomb so that God would pardon him for his misdeeds on earth. The religious rigidity of the sultan is clearly evident in these actions.

Revenue Policy

Both the financial situation and the revenue administration were in chaotic conditions when Firuz took over the kingdom. The general population had suffered a great deal under the mal-administration of Muhammad. Firuz started his rule by first writing-off all the loans that his predecessor had given to his subjects. He then increased the salaries of government officials to exterminate corruption that had become endemic during Muhammad's rule and ordered an end to the coercion of the people that was standard practice by junior officials in collecting taxes.

He also reinstituted the 'jagir' system, which had been abolished by Ala ud-Din Khilji as being damaging to the overall well-being of the State. In fact Firuz went to the other extreme and insisted on paying the officials through land grants alone, perpetuating a system that invariably led to the harassment of the common people in an indirect manner. To further facilitate the jagir system, Firuz divided the whole empire into fiefs and districts. It is a paradox that the sultan who was intent of lifting the misery of the common farmer started to appoint the highest bidders to the positions of Tax Collectors, who would then extort the cultivators and peasants as much as they wanted.

There is no doubt that some of the measures instituted to reform the revenue policy were retrograde steps. However, Firuz had a rough estimate of the public revenue of the kingdom calculated based on the productivity of each land holding, not on the area as had been previous practice. This was done through guess work, reinforced by local information and past records and tempered with the experience of the revenue department. The entire exercise was carried out over a period of six years by an experienced administrator, Khwaja Hisam ud-Din, who travelled the entire kingdom to carry out the assessments. This initiative was a great reformatory achievement.

Taxation Strategy

Firuz abolished as many as 24 vexatious taxes that were instituted by Muhammad and his predecessors. Further, he reduced the land revenue demands from the State, and in yet another indication of the increasing influence of religion on the State, brought all taxes in line with the Qur'anic Law. Accordingly, the people were required to pay only the basic four taxes decreed by it—Kharaj, the land tax; Khams, one-fifth of the booty captured in war by individual soldiers; Jizya, to be paid by all non-Muslims; and Zakat, two percent of the income of Muslims.

Firuz also introduced an irrigation tax, charged on all farmers who used waters from the State canals for irrigating their cultivable lands. The introduction of this new tax was done only after due consultation with the Ulema, since that was the procedure decreed by Muslim Law. These measures had a salutary effect on the development of trade and agriculture, ensuring that the common use commodities became readily available at a steady price. Further, judicious tax application and collection ensured that the State was never in deficit financing. In fact there was sufficient surplus available in the royal treasury for the sultan to indulge in charity and indulge in his passion to build works of public utility.

For the first time since the Jizya was introduced in India, Firuz imposed this tax payable by all non-Muslims, on the Brahmans who had so far been exempt from doing so. Further, this tax was enforced rigidly and rigorously, much to the chagrin of the majority population of the kingdom who were Hindus.

Irrigation and Other Developmental Works

With the financial aspects of the State having been brought on an even keel, Firuz turned his attention to one of his passions—building works. The major works were oriented towards ensuring availability of water for the population and also for agricultural purposes through the building of canals. Water scarcity in Delhi has been reported by contemporary chroniclers and it is reliably known that water was sold at exorbitant prices in the capital. In order to alleviate this situation Firuz built a number of canals. Obviously this initiative was tinged with a commercial aspect also, since an irrigation tax was levied for the use of the canal water.

Five major canals that facilitated agriculture were built under his orders. The most important one was the 150-miles long canal that connected the waters of the River Yamuna to Hissar. The other four were—a 96 miles long canal that connected the Rivers Sutlej and Ghagra; one that connected Hansi to the rivers across the Mandvi hills; another that brought waters of the River Ghagra to the newly established township of Firozabad; and a canal that brought the waters of the River Yamuna into the same township. Firuz also had a number of reservoirs, dams and wells built to ensure that water was readily available to all throughout the year. These canals greatly improved agriculture with the roll-on effect of increasing the revenue for the kingdom.

Historians are unanimous in acknowledging Firuz Shah as a great builder of public works. Firuz's indulgence in building works is interesting because earlier sultans had not indulged in building activities other than to construct their own mausoleums and make additions to their palaces. The reason is that the earlier sultans were busy putting down rebellions from their own kin and fighting off hostile Hindu kings, which left no time or resources to indulge in public utility works or even contemplate such activities. Firuz was the first king to enjoy a relatively long period of peace with no large scale wars to be fought. This was as much a result of Firuz's own decision not to indulge in expansionist activities as the gradual settling down of the political sphere because of the reluctant acceptance of the reality of a Muslim king ruling in and around Delhi by the agitating Hindu kings. This relative peace, combined with astute financial management, gave Firuz the opportunity to indulge in his passion for building.

Some contemporary reporting state that Firuz 'built' or 'founded' 300 towns. This is obviously an exaggeration, even if villages that had been abandoned earlier and were repopulated after the success of the irrigation projects and at the direct encouragement by the sultan for agriculture are counted as new towns. However, it can be assumed that he founded the towns of Firuzabad, Fatehbad, Hissar, Firozpur and Jaunpur, even though some of them did exist as small places earlier. Firuz improved them considerably and encouraged their repopulation. He laid out many gardens and reclaimed large areas of wasteland for agriculture. Firuz initiated a scheme for the preservation of ancient monuments, removing some of King Asoka's (Asoka the Great of the ancient Maurya dynasty) monoliths to his new city Firuzabad (modern Firoz Shah Kotla) near Delhi. The building works were centrally controlled with each building plan being scrutinised at the sultan's finance office, only after which money was allocated for construction. Firuz's zeal for building and construction was such that later-day European historians have compared him favourably as surpassing the building activities undertaken by the Roman Emperor Augustus.

Patronage for Learning

Firuz was an accomplished scholar and also a great patron of learning. He established a large number of madrasas—schools and colleges that provided education in line with religious teachings—where the teachers were paid liberal salaries and the students given stipends by the State. *[These madrasas concentrated on the broad education of the students within the laid down limits of the Qur'anic Law and also religious teachings, unlike the madrasas of today in the same region that teach only an extremist interpretation of Islam and nothing else—more like factories with production lines churning out extremist functionaries.]*

The sultan endowed learned men lavishly and encouraged the study and writing of history. The famous historian Zia ud-Din Barani and Shams-i-Siraj Afif, who wrote the book *Tarikh-i-Firozshahi*, were the principle chroniclers of the regime. The sultan also wrote his autobiography, *Fatuhat-i-Firozshahi*. After the conquest of Nagarkot, a large library fell into the hands of the sultan and he had some of the Sanskrit works translated into Persian. The famous contemporary scholar, Maulana Jalal ud-Din Rumi lectured on theology and Islamic jurisprudence in various colleges around Delhi during Firuz's reign.

The focus on religion-based education and its State sponsorship had unfortunate, and perhaps unforeseen, consequences for the future development of religious intolerance in the sub-continent. Essentially Muslim scholars were specifically encouraged to devote themselves to theological studies, gradually to the exclusion of other areas of learning. The outcome was the development of a narrow and blinkered vision of orthodox Islamic practices and positions that became the dominant religious force. In turn, this nurtured and entrenched religious fanaticism, vitiating an already poisonous environment.

The Slave System

Over the two centuries since the Delhi sultanate was first established, the Slave System that was prevalent in the early years had fallen in to disuse and become redundant. This could have been the result of two long-term activities: one, the number of Turkish 'slaves' being brought into the sub-continent had started to decline; and two, the gradual Indianisation of the ruling class through intermarriages and the rise of local converts to Islam into the administration and their eventual inclusion into the nobility. However, Firuz was very fond of the slave system and imported slaves from all parts of the empire to Delhi. They were put to the service of the State and paid by the royal treasury in accordance with individual education and experience.

At the height of Firuz's rule, the slaves numbered around 180,000 and a separate department had been set up to manage the service of the slaves. The institution grew to a dangerous level and percolated all aspects of the administration. The pervasiveness of the system contributed in later years to the disintegration of the empire.

The Army

Firuz Shah lacked military skills and was not gifted with a warrior spirit, both of which were imperative characteristics for success in a medieval king. Further, may be because of his ineptitude in the battlefield, he did not display any energy or enthusiasm for military campaigns. Even when military campaigns had to be mounted for the security of the empire, he permitted extreme religious scruples to interfere with the robust prosecution of these campaigns, even the ones that were going in his favour. Therefore, it is not surprising that he permitted the 'standing army' of Ala ud-Din to be dispersed, reorganising the royal army on a feudal basis. The standing army, loyal only to the sultan, had been the backbone of the Khilji Empire as well as the mainstay of Muhammad Tughluq's power. It now became dispersed.

The regular army was replaced by forces supplied by the nobles and therefore, their loyalty to the sultan could never be fully assured. The sultan relied on a group of personal body guards for his own security and since the loyalty of the regular forces had become questionable, these body guards wielded enormous power. The payment system for the soldiers also underwent a change and a system of transferable assignment of revenue was instituted. This led to a professional-class purchasing these revenue assignments in Delhi and then selling them to soldiers in the faraway districts at a higher price. This unwitting reorganisation led to the weakening of the army for three allied reasons.

First, the buying and selling of revenue assignments became so entrenched, almost like a business enterprise, which led to complete abuse of the system and the ensuing deterioration in overall discipline of the force. Second, it led to old and retiring soldiers being replaced automatically by their sons, sons-in-law and, in some extreme case, even by slaves. This led, gradually, to service in the army becoming hereditary, a process that did not take into account individual merit, capability or even fitness to serve. The general negative impact on the overall capability of the force is easy to envisage. Third, only about 80-90,000 cavalry was stationed in Delhi with the rest of the imperial army being supplied, when needed, by the nobles from far-flung areas based on a quota system.

The end result of these changes to the force structure of the army was that the military, which had been the bastion of Khilji power and even that of Muhammad Tughluq, did not function as an instrument of force of the empire anymore.

A Religious Policy of Bigotry

Firuz was brought to the throne by a group of prominent nobles with the overt support of the Ulema, the clergy who ruled the mosques. He was ever mindful of this. Firuz Shah was a practising orthodox Sunni Muslim and by temperament attracted to religion. He embodied all that an orthodox Muslim in medieval times stood for, being an epitome of the follower of an infant religion that had been propagated by the sword across Asia and southern Europe. Firuz had both the virtues and the vices that came with the practice of orthodoxy in Islam. First, he was intolerant of any religious practice other than that of the orthodox Islamic traditions as envisaged by the Sunni persuasion. Flowing from this rigid belief he insisted on strict enforcement of Sunni Islamic prescriptions and prohibited all others as 'un-Islamic' practices. This was carried forward to the minutest detail. For example, the display of portraits, which was a custom that was in vogue since the earliest days of the sultanate was forbidden even in the palace.

Firuz Shah started his reign with a slight religious disadvantage since his mother had been a Hindu prior to her marriage and conversion to Islam. It is highly likely that he felt the need to be seen as being an ultra-orthodox Muslim to ensure that there was no criticism of his actions in relation to Islamic traditions. He needed to demonstrate his adherence to the Islamic faith much more than would have been the case had his mother been a Turkish noble lady. Whatever the complex reasoning in his mind, Firuz laid the foundation for the sultanate to be turned into a theocracy with the Ulema becoming an integral and important part of the ruling coterie.

He instituted a policy that ensured that the lost prestige of the Ulema was re-established without any doubt—a policy that was in direct contradiction of the ones that were followed by Ala ud-Din Khilji and his own cousin Muhammad Tughluq. In his own mind Firuz Shah had a black and white division of mankind—Muslims and non-Muslims—that influenced and determined all his decisions and actions. He considered only followers of Islam as his subjects and of concern to the State. Therefore, it must be kept in mind that when contemporary chroniclers praise his concern for the welfare of his subjects, they mean the sultan's anxiety to ensure the well-being of the Muslims in his regime and not the Hindus who were still the majority of the population under his rule.

Firuz sought and accepted the advice of the Ulema even in political and secular matters of State. The Ulema were orthodox to the core and biased to the extreme with a narrow parochial outlook. Under their influence, Firuz willingly assumed the mantle of 'champion of the faith'. This automatically meant putting in force three initiatives—oppression of non-believers, repression of Hinduism and stamping out idolatry. The policy of separation of the State and religion, which Muhammad Tughluq had strenuously enforced at considerable expense to his personal popularity, had been put aside in one fell sweep by his successor.

In his autobiography Firuz confirms that he used many methods to convert non-believers to Islam. There is ample proof that he offered financial rewards, gift of jagirs, investiture of titles, and the lure of state employment to convert non-believers to Islam. On the other hand he also resorted to heavy handed measure to demonstrate the power of Islam such as killing of Brahmans, desecrating and destroying temples and breaking up of idols, all of which gradually became common practices. Firuz adopted a two-pronged policy towards the persecution of Hindus. He resorted to the direct oppression of the religious leadership, for example the imposition of the Jizya tax on the Brahmans, who had been exempt till then. The second prong of the policy was more insidious. Firuz enticed the lower castes in the Hindu religion to convert by bestowing favours on them and the promise of equal treatment with all others. *[This part of the policy resonates with the practices of Christian missionaries in later times in the sub-continent.]* It is noted that the administration was particularly harsh in their dealings with the Tantric sect.

The complete orthodoxy and influence of the Ulema can be understood by the fact that even Shia Muslims were considered heretics by the administration. They were punished and their religious books openly burned. In an extreme display of intolerance, even the peace-loving Sufi practitioners were also persecuted. Firuz forced religious practices into the social fabric of the kingdom, shutting down cults that existed even within the Islamic traditions. In order to ensure that he was considered the rightful heir to the throne, he consciously paid tribute to the nominal Khalifa (Caliph) in Egypt and received endorsement and robes of honour in return. He also declared himself a deputy of the Khalifa. This was the first time that a sultan had taken such an action in the history of the Delhi sultanate.

Attempts have been made in modern writings to show Firuz Shah as having been a tolerant monarch, who treated the Hindus in a kind and gentle manner. This is an incorrect assessment belied by facts as it took place during his reign. Firuz's own writing in his autobiography states the dual purpose of his invasion of Jajnagar (modern Orissa), which is detailed in the next chapter, as 'massacring the unbelievers and demolishing their temples.' The book goes on to provide further details of the vigour and relentless severity with which these objectives were pursued by the sultan and his army. It is very obvious that Firuz Shah looked upon his empire as purely a Muslim State where the State benefits would be available only to Muslim subjects. The Hindus, who remained the majority even at this time, were not considered citizens and were treated as non-existent in the broader scheme of policies and other welfare initiatives. No amount of 'explanations' by later-day historians can erase the fact that Firuz established and pursued a bigoted religious policy.

Conclusion

Firuz Shah came to the throne of Delhi by default, succeeding his mis-guided cousin Muhammad Tughluq. However, he managed to establish a semblance of stability and bring the turbulence left by the late sultan under control. Being a 'man of peace', as he has been described by a number of erudite historians, he did not attempt to improve the territorial holdings of the sultanate. However, an analysis, tempered with great hindsight, reveals that this abhorrence towards military campaigns was more the result of his lack of military skills and warring spirits, not because of a lack of understanding regarding the need to fight and win military campaigns to cement his rule or even for the lack of ambition.

The establishment of a decidedly theocratic State within the sub-continent, for the first time, must be attributed to Firuz Shah—whether as a compliment or as a derogatory achievement. Even this dubious distinction has attracted the attention of modern historians who continually make attempts at trying to project Muslim rulers of the sub-continent as having been the epitomes of tolerance and just rule. These assertions only tend to further entrench the belief of the vile nature of some of these invaders and rulers who cloaked heir avarice for treasure and wealth under the guise of sanctimonious religiosity. However, that was the general character of rulers of the medieval period, especially the ones of the Islamic faith. It is not surprising that Firuz Shah was not the 'man of peace' that he is made out to be, but squarely belonged to the ranks of these intolerant and blood-thirsty sultans.

Chapter 18

FIRUZ SHAH'S MILITARY ENDEAVOURS

Firuz Shah waged no wars of conquest as such, but he was not a pacifist. In many ways he was a gentle and cultured person and although the bulk of the army had been distributed to the nobles to maintain, he kept a large contingent of 80-90,000 cavalry in Delhi. Of course this was numerically much inferior to the standing armies that his predecessors, both Tughluqs and Khiljis, maintained in the capital. Firuz was lucky that during his reign there were no major rebellions and only two Mongol raids, which were repelled forcefully. Although considered a 'man of peace', he did not hesitate to wage war to repel invaders and to suppress rebellions. Further, Firuz did not display any scruples when he let loose his military on unsuspecting Hindu kingdoms, for the basis of his rule was to bring the idolaters into the Islamic fold through all possible initiatives. In the conduct of war, irrespective of how it was forced on the Sultanate, his actions were as savage and horrific as those carried out by his predecessors and successors. Violence, mayhem and extreme cruelty were part and parcel of wars in medieval times, across the entire known world of the time. It was so in the Delhi Sultanate also.

The Bengal Campaigns

In the confusion following Muhammad Tughluq's death, Bengal had separated and become an independent entity, severing all connections with Delhi. Haji Ilyas had proclaimed himself an independent ruler with the title Shams ud-Din Ilyas Shah and then gone on to invade Tirhut, which was nominally the furthest south-eastern territory of the sultanate. This invasion by the Bengal 'sultan' is mentioned only in some accounts of the time.

Even a minor invasion into far-flung areas of the kingdom could not be tolerated or ignored lest such incidents become common place and gradually breakup the empire. Peace-loving Firuz was therefore left with no choice but to retaliate. Accordingly, in late 1353, he set out on an expedition to subdue Bengal. The primary objective was to chastise Shams ud-Din and get him to acknowledge vassal status to Delhi. On the approach of the Sultan Shams ud-Din withdrew and shut himself up in the strong fortress at Ekdala in East Bengal, prepared for a long siege. Firuz wanting to avoid the tribulations of a long siege, used cunning to shorten the campaign. He feinted a withdrawal. Shams ud-Din was fooled into thinking that he would be able to harass the withdrawing army. He came out of the fort with his troops and attacked the rear-guard of the Sultanate army. Promptly, Firuz counterattacked and defeated the Bengal forces upon which Shams ud-Din once again retreated to his fortress. Even though Bengal forces were defeated, Firuz did not attempt to capture the fortress of Ekdala.

This first expedition to Bengal was indecisive, but it was tarnished by a rare show of savagery by Firuz Shah. He wanted to let the people of Bengal remember the victory that he had achieved on the battlefield over their ruler, although neither had Shams ud-Din been subdued nor the fort captured. He ordered the collection of the heads of all the slain Bengal soldiers, paying one tanka per head brought, collecting as many as 180,000 heads. It is uncertain whether the heads were of soldiers already slain in battle or also included those of fresh victims killed by the Delhi soldiers to collect the reward from the sultan. It is highly possible that a fresh wave of killing took place to satisfy the Sultan's decree.

At the end of this undecided conflict, Firuz made peace with Shams ud-Din, practically endorsing his independent status. It is reported that Firuz wanted to avoid being stuck in Bengal as the monsoons advanced and therefore decided to go back to Delhi. The expedition did not achieve anything for the Delhi sultanate, on the other hand it formalised Shams ud-Din's position and stature as an independent ruler, functioning completely outside the ambit of Delhi.

Subsequently there is a mention of an embassy sent by Shams ud-Din to Delhi in 1356. Firuz reciprocated with a return embassy to Shams ud-Din's court, a gesture that endorsed the fully independent status of Bengal. However, contemporary chronicles state that while the embassy was on its way to Bengal, news was received that Shams ud-Din had died and had been succeeded by his son Sikandar. Firuz recalled the embassy before it could reach Bengal. This action demonstrates that despite the friendly overtures towards Shams ud-Din, Firuz Shah was biding his time to subdue Bengal, especially considering the failed first expedition.

Three years later Firuz got the pretext that he was after to once again invade Bengal. Zafar Khan was the son-in-law of the previous ruler of Bengal, Fakhr ud-Din, from whom Shams ud-Din had usurped the throne. Zafar Khan arrived in Delhi as a fugitive with tales of the ill-treatment that he had received from Ilyas Shah and requested Firuz to redress his grievances. The sultan grabbed this opportunity and mounted another expedition to subdue Bengal. He assembled an army of 70,000 cavalry, 470 elephants and innumerable foot soldiers, and marched to Bengal. On the way he stopped on the banks of the River Gomti and founded the city of Jaunpur, honouring Muhammad Tughluq whose name as a prince was Fakhr ud-Din Jauna. Realising the danger that he was in, Sikandar now ruling Bengal, made an attempt at placating the Delhi sultan by sending him peace offerings in the form of gifts and five elephants. However, these were rejected.

Sikandar then followed his father's example and shut himself up in the fortress of Ekdala and once again the fort was besieged by the Delhi army. The invading army made many breaches in the defences of the fortress, but they were hastily repaired by the Bengal army who displayed exemplary courage and vigour in defending their stronghold. As the interminable siege continued, patience wore out on both sides and peace negotiations were started. Sikandar agreed to restore Sonargaon to Zafar Khan and once again send presents to Firuz as peace offerings. This time they were accepted. In return, Sikandar was awarded few royal titles and confirmed on his throne. The Delhi army then started its return march.

Paradoxically, Zafar Khan, nominally for whom the sultan had gone to war, opted to continue to stay in Delhi and not return to his 'kingdom' in Bengal, perhaps seduced by the social life of the capital. Effectively, Firuz once again returned from the Bengal campaign without having achieved anything tangible. Contemporary chronicles state that the military expedition, from its start in Delhi, was conducted more like a pleasure trip than an expeditious march to crush an enemy. The founding of Jaunpur on the way is an example of this dawdling march towards the adversary—the sense of urgency inherent in all military actions was completely missing. This lacklustre approach was visible even in the siege of Ekdala, which was marked by indecision and a complete lack of professional military competence.

The Expedition to Jajnagar

Even though no enemy had been subdued nor any territory added to the sultanate holdings, the return to Delhi was conducted as a victorious march. On the way Firuz halted at Jaunpur, his newly created city. While relaxing there, the sultan conceived a plan to raid the kingdom of Jajnagar (modern Orissa). There is debate regarding the reason behind Firuz's sudden decision to backtrack and invade Jajnagar. There were two mutually supporting reasons for this decision. One was that Jajnagar was an extremely rich and prosperous state and could have whetted the sultan's avarice for wealth. Second, the famous Jaganath Temple of Puri, sacred to the Hindus across the sub-continent, was located on the eastern coast of Jajnagar. The urge to capture the temple and destroy it would have been difficult for Firuz to resist; after all he was the declared champion of the believers and Islam.

Firuz marched out of Jaunpur in October 1360 and reached Bihar in December. Then he turned south and went through modern Pachet to Sikhar in Manbhum district. The ruler of Sikhar was a relatively important chieftain since a number of minor chiefs paid homage to him. However, on the approach of the Delhi army, he fled from his capital. Although the garrison left behind put up a brave resistance, they were eventually defeated and the capital captured. Firuz moved further south, reaching the border of Jajnagar, which had never before been invaded by a Muslim army. The resistance offered by the local population at the border posts were easily overcome by the large Muslim army and Firuz continued his victorious march southward. On the way he captured many prosperous towns, the most important being

Kinianagar—most probably Khiching, the capital of old Mayurbhanj State.

Unlike the Bengal expedition, in this campaign the army marched swiftly, taking King Bhanudeva III of Jajnagar by surprise. The king fled from his fortress at Saranghar, while once again the garrison that remained behind put up a spirited fight, although they were defeated in the end. *[The instances of the king fleeing while the remaining garrison forces puts up brave defences is a repeating event in the medieval history of North India. It could have been because the king is requested by his nobles and soldiers to leave without being captured, so that the fight could be continued another day and he could act as the rallying point for counter-attack if he remained free. However, there are very few instances of the fight being continued by the fugitive king, with most of them submitting to the invaders later. Therefore, the fleeing of the king at the approach of the Muslim host is a dubious action and it can be assumed to smack of cowardice and fear.]*

Firuz overran the capital Cuttack and without delay proceeded towards the temple town of Puri. The town was ransacked, the Jaganath Temple desecrated and destroyed, and the main idol of the temple thrown into the sea. The temple was enormously rich, with some reports stating that more than 30, 00,000 dinars were spent on the kitchen premises alone. Firuz gathered great wealth from the temple coffers. At this stage there are slight variations in the reports of events that followed. One version states that at the destruction of the temple, the Rai of Jajnagar sued for peace. The other version is more intriguing. While the town of Puri was being vandalised by the invading Muslim army, a large number of the population had taken refuge in a nearby island. This could have been in the area around the Chilka Lake. It is reported that Firuz proceeded to this island and massacred more than 100,000 people including women and children. There was no infidel left alive in the island or the town. Seeing the plight of his subjects, Bhanudeva sued for peace.

Peace was agreed upon with the Rai of Jajnagar having to pay an annual tribute of a fixed number of elephants to the sultan in Delhi. After having achieved his objective of the destruction of idol worshippers, Firuz commenced his return journey. The way back from Jajnagar was through wild and unknown territory and the guides lost their way. The entire army wandered in the forest for six months before arriving at recognisable areas and starting the journey to Delhi. During this time of being lost the army suffered great travails with provisions and even water running out. By the time Firuz reached Delhi he had been away from the capital for two and a half years, of which he had been incommunicado for six months.

Some recent historians have described the Jajnagar campaign as an 'audacious' feat that was 'brilliantly executed'; attempting to prove once and for all Firuz's skill and accomplishment as a military commander and successful general. This is a blatantly incorrect assessment. The debacle on the return march where he wandered lost in the forest with his entire army for six months cannot by any stretch of imagination be considered the actions of a 'great' general. If anything it conclusively disproves the claims of military acumen and accomplishment.

The Real Reason for the Jajnagar Expedition

The reasons for Firuz's 'sudden' decision to attack Jajnagar has long been debated and even today is a point of contention amongst historians. To bring clarity regarding the real intentions of the Sultan and to dispel later-day attempts at 'white-washing' Firuz's real character, the decision making and the thought process behind the expedition needs to be examined.

There are two contemporary and official reports or narratives that deal with the reasons for mounting the expedition and also provide fairly detailed account of the events as it happened. In both the narratives the objectives laid out for the expedition to Jajnagar are verbatim the same, '...extirpating Rai of Jajnagar, to break the idols, to massacre the unbelievers, shed the blood of enemies of Islam and to hunt elephants.' Some modern writers have attempted to turn this statement on its head and state that the main reason for the expedition was to facilitate Firuz's passion to hunt elephants and the rest of the objectives were incidental to it. This assessment is difficult to accept and also a fatuous attempt to 'rewrite' history. There are two fundamental reasons to refute and negate this absurd appraisal of Firuz's intentions.

First, Firuz was a sultan who was competent and careful in delivering an efficient administration and did not at any time display any false pretensions to being a military genius. It is therefore safe to assume that he would not have committed his entire army to an elephant hunting expedition into an unknown and extremely difficult terrain. Such a commitment would not have been the actions of a stable and sensible ruler. Therefore, it is certain that Firuz considered the invasion of the 'infidel' nation a duty to be fulfilled, indicated by deploying the entire force available to him. Second is Firuz's inherent bigotry that was openly demonstrated throughout his reign. His display of being a pious Muslim and a 'champion of the religion' leaves no doubt that the main objective of the Jajnagar expedition was the conquest of a prosperous Hindu kingdom and the desecration and destruction of the Jaganath Temple, one of Hindu religions holiest sites worshipped across the entire sub-continent. This is also corroborated by contemporary chroniclers and official reports. The additional impetus, acting almost like a fringe benefit, was the wealth and treasure that could be looted from the kingdom and the temple.

Few later-day historians have gone to the extent of stating that during the expedition the sultan did not pillage any shrine or break any idols. They audaciously state that Firuz having heard of the beauty of the famous temple, went to Puri to admire its architectural splendour. These historians further add that the idol was taken from the temple to be placed in a museum in Delhi that the sultan was contemplating on building. These are puerile attempts at smoothing over the reprehensible conduct of a Muslim ruler in order to bring the narrative in line with today's political correctness regarding religious tolerance in a region beset with sectarian and religious divisions and violence. *[Obviously, these historians feel the need to repeatedly state inherent falsehoods in order to safeguard what they believe are the roots of Muslim identity in the sub-continent. From their perspective such attempts have become urgent necessities since the Hindu nationalists also have not spared history. The Hindu nationalists are embarking on a mass scale propaganda effort to discredit medieval Muslim rulers for their religious intolerance, once again measured not with the yardstick of the medieval era or even by the unbiased correctness of dealing with religion in a modern secular state. They tend to swing the bias to the other end of the spectrum and attempt to 'rewrite' history in a totally different manner. It has become increasingly difficult to come by a balanced narrative of events and their unbiased assessment.]*

There is no doubt that Firuz was driven by his internal desire to punish and rebuke the Hindus in mounting the Jajnagar expedition. What better way to achieve this exalted objective in the service of the 'one true religion' than to destroy the great Jaganath Temple and pillage the temple-town of Puri? This initiative became even more laudable since it was reliably learned that the Jaganath Temple was held in great reverence by all Hindus, its sanctity held at the highest esteem.

Conquest of Nagarkot (1360-61)

The fortress at Nagarkot had been captured by Muhammad Tughluq in 1337. However, taking advantage of the on-going turmoil in the Delhi kingdom and Muhammad's preoccupation with numerous other events, the local Rai had gradually re-established his independence. However, Firuz's expedition to subdue Nagarkot was not initiated to chastise the Rai for his impertinence. The real reason was that Nagarkot (modern day Kangra) was the location of the Hindu temple of Jwala Mukhi—a temple that was old and venerated, which attracted (as it still does in modern India) a large number of pilgrims from across the sub-continent. These pilgrims brought rich offerings to the temple, making the temple an extremely wealthy institution. Firuz could not resist making an attempt to punish the unbelieving Hindus and humble yet another Hindu kingdom, which in addition gave the opportunity to plunder a wealthy state. The importance of the temple to the Hindus and its high status in the hierarchy of worship obviously made the expedition more attractive to the bigoted Sultan.

The march towards Nagarkot was not that of an expeditionary army, but conducted in a leisurely pace, as seems to have been customary with Firuz's military initiatives. In any case, he was no military genius and perhaps did not even contemplate attempting surprise or other military strategies that would have made victory easier to achieve. In his relaxed march towards Nagarkot, Firuz stopped to indulge in his favourite pastime—construction—delaying the march long enough to build a canal and a fort on the way.

The fortress of Nagarkot was captured after a long siege, although the Rai was permitted to continue to rule. There are no contemporary records of the famous temple being sacked. However, in a reversal of other attempts mentioned earlier, one later-day historian has concluded that the temple was indeed sacked. Although the sacking is not corroborated by any other source, the claim seems plausible considering the Sultan's proclivity to destroy Hindu temples. It is however established that Firuz collected a large tribute and also captured a library of nearly 1300 books written Sanskrit. He is reported to have had some of the works on philosophy and astronomy translated into Persian. The expedition against Nagarkot remains an enigma, since it does not seem to have achieved anything tangible from the Sultan's perspective unless the sacking of the temple is confirmed.

Expedition into Sindh

A number of years after subjugating Nagarkot, Firuz mounted an expedition against Sindh. His predecessor, Muhammad Tughluq's expedition to Sindh had tragically ended in his death. Therefore, from a point of view of vindicating imperial prestige, an expedition to Sindh was long overdue. It can be safely assumed that the objectives of this punitive expedition were to restore the somewhat diminished prestige of the dynasty and to avenge the 'wrongs' done to Muhammad in the region. The immediate excuse for the campaign was the continuing hostility of the chieftains of the region towards Delhi that found voice in regular, even though minor and inconsequential, rebellions.

Firuz assembled a huge army of 90,000 cavalry and 480 elephants along with accompanying infantry and marched to the River Indus. There he collected a fleet of boats and the army thereafter proceeded with some travelling the river and the rest marching along the banks. Unfortunately for Firuz, a pestilence attacked and decimated the horses, while lack of forward planning created a shortage of provisions and made the soldiers to suffer. Realising that a window of opportunity had opened, Jam Bibiniya (also mentioned as Banhbina) the chieftain of Sindh, sallied out of his stronghold of Tattah to take advantage of the adversity of the Delhi army. He captured the boat-borne segment of Firuz's army. Firuz was unwilling to risk engaging in a direct battle with what was now a vastly reduced and woe-struck force, and made a 'strategic retreat' towards Gujarat, harried by the Jam's forces all along the way.

On this retreat all the horses of the army died. More importantly, in a further demonstration of his ineptitude as a military commander,

Firuz permitted the army to be led into the salt marshes of the Rann of Kutch by treacherous guides. The entire army floundered in the Rann suffering great privations, fighting famine, disease and lack of potable water. An almost completely destroyed army, in extremely dire straits, managed to reach Gujarat after suffering this devastating experience for six months. Firuz dismissed the governor of Gujarat, Nizam –ul-Mulk for having failed to send the much needed provisions for the army and also for failing to provide proficient guides. In his stead he appointed Zafar Khan the governor.

Firuz now undertook the task of reequipping and building up the army, appropriating all the funds available in the Gujarat coffers. He also brought in three instalments of reinforcements from Delhi to steady the depleted army. Once the new army was ready, Firuz set out again to capture Tattah.

> **A Wasted Opportunity?**
>
> While Firuz was recouping in Gujarat, he received an invitation from Bahram, a rival prince belonging to the Bahmani dynasty, to intervene and conquer the Deccan. At this time, the Bahmani kingdom was still in its infancy and may have proved to be easy picking for the established Delhi army. It was an excellent opportunity for Firuz to take over the Bahmani holdings and re-establish a foothold in the Deccan. However, Firuz Shah had his mind set on the conquest of Sindh and refused to aid the rebel prince of the Bahmani dynasty—a golden opportunity lost!

The second attack on Tattah saw a reversal of the positions of the antagonists in comparison to the earlier fiasco. There had been desertions from Firuz's army, but the reinforcements from Delhi made up for the losses and moreover his army was now fully reequipped and well-rested. In contrast, the Sindh army while becoming numerically inferior through desertions, was plagued by a famine leading to a lack of provisions for the forces.

Under these circumstances, Jam Bibiniya took the prudent path and surrendered to Firuz. He accompanied Firuz back to Delhi but was later restored to his throne in Sindh with the promise of paying an annual tribute and as a vassal of Delhi. It is stated in the chronicles, that Firuz Shah was full of remorse for the suffering that he had inflicted on brother Muslims through his military expeditions and therefore decided not to embark on any further campaigns of invasions and conquests. Thereafter, only minor operations were undertaken, mostly to suppress rebellions.

Suppression of Rebellions

The first rebellion during Firuz's reign was in Gujarat, where the governor Damaghani revolted against the huge sums of money being demanded by Delhi. He was summarily defeated and killed by loyal forces, with his severed head being send to Delhi. The second one was in Etawah for similar reasons, which was also suppressed quickly. The most notable campaign was undertaken against the Raja of Ketehar (Rohilkhand), Kharku, in 1380. The Raja had treacherously murdered the governor of Badaun and his two brothers, who were Sayyids. The Sayyids were presumed by the Muslim community to be direct descendants of the Prophet Muhammad. The orthodox Muslim Sultan led the retaliatory expedition himself. The Raja fled and escaped without offering a fight, at the approach of the Delhi army.

Perhaps because the murdered brothers were Sayyids, Firuz wreaked terrible vengeance on the population of the kingdom. He carried out a savage massacre, ordering all Hindus to be killed. He appointed an Afghan governor to rule the conquered kingdom and ordered him to devastate the region with 'fire and sword' annually for the next five years. Further, Firuz Shah personally visited the region every year for the next five years to ensure that his orders were being carried out effectively. After Rohilkhand had been savaged, Firuz pursued Kharku into Kumaon where he had fled. However, Firuz was unable to capture the fugitive king and instead massacred unnumbered Hindus along the way. He is also reported to have enslaved 23,000 Hindus during this campaign.

Last Days and Death

Firuz Shah's last days were clouded by anxiety and personal sorrow. The sultan had a number of sons of whom the eldest, Fath Khan, was his favourite. Fath Khan was born during the march to Delhi after Firuz had ascended the throne near the River Indus. Unfortunately for the sultan, Fath Khan died in 1374 when Firuz was in his late 60s. The death of his favourite son and heir apparent shattered the ageing sultan who rapidly slid into mental and physical decline. He then appointed Zafar Khan, his second son as the crown prince but he too died about a year later. Firuz's choice now fell on the third son Muhammad Khan although he was not formally appointed as the anointed successor.

Even during this turmoil of appointing his successors, Firuz continued his passion for building, founding yet another city in 1385. It was officially called Firuzpur Ikhleri and derisively named by his subjects as Akhirinpur, meaning last city. The reason for the derision is not clearly mentioned in any chronicle or later-day report, but could have been the advanced age of the sultan at this stage. By this time Firuz Shah was a man of decaying intellect and almost certainly senile. He was completely dominated by his Wazir or Prime Minister, Khan Jahan, the son of the great and loyal Khan-i-Jahan Maqbul who had died a few years earlier. Khan Jahan, who had designs on the throne for himself, convinced Firuz that there was a plot to murder him. A scheme that he enacted to remove Muhammad Khan from the scene backfired and Muhammad was able to convince his father to permit action to be initiated against Khan Jahan.

Muhammad besieged the house of the Wazir, but Khan Jahan managed to escape and fled to Mewat, taking refuge there with the ruler Koka Chauhan. Firuz declared Prince Muhammad as the co-ruler and conferred royal titles on him. Muhammad was a pleasure-seeking individual and did not pursue Khan Jahan. He appropriated all power to himself and thereafter gave himself up to worldly pleasure—the traditional indulgence in wine and women. Muhammad did not heed the advice of trusted officers and also promoted his own lackeys to positions of power. He also managed to get Khan Jahan murdered through dubious means.

Muhammad's actions started to gather a strong opposition, which soon became uncontainable. The situation deteriorated into a vicious civil war in the capital between the two rival factions—on the one side were the loyal nobles and officers of the crown who also enjoyed the support of the general population and on the other were Muhammad's supporters who were mainly flatterers and parasites of questionable character and limited capability. The civil war continued for two days with extraordinarily savage fury. On the third day, forces loyal to the dynasty captured the palace and brought an ailing Firuz Shah outside on a litter. The crowd received him joyously and Muhammad fled to Sirmur.

Firuz once again assumed full power, although he was senile and physically ill, and appointed Ghiyas ud-Din, the son of Fath Khan as the heir apparent. Shortly thereafter Firuz died in September 1388, aged 83. His death was followed, almost immediately by a scramble for power by rival princes and other parties, plunging the Sultanate into further chaos and uncertainty.

Chapter 19

FIRUZ SHAH: A SULTAN FOR STABILITY

There are differing views regarding the personality and character of Firuz Shah Tughluq. Without fail all contemporary writers unanimously praise him as the most just, merciful and benevolent ruler. However, all of them were panegyrists of the realm and therefore expected to voice such praiseworthy sentiments. Taking the cue from these narratives, some of the early European historians supported the same opinion, heaping praise on Firuz, going so far as to compare him with Akbar, the great Mughal of later times. The later European historians, led by Vincent Smith an acknowledged authority on medieval Indian history, have voiced contradictory opinions. Smith emphatically holds a different opinion stating unequivocally that it is absurd to compare Firuz to Akbar. Similarly some later day Indian historians also agree with Vincent Smith. The truth, as usual in such circumstances, lies somewhere in between.

There is no doubt that Firuz was a man of peace, without being a pacifist, and that he possessed qualities of the heart while lacking those of the head. To start with, he was honest and sincere in his proclamations of striving for the welfare of the people. He created material prosperity through benign agricultural and revenue policies, while attempting to create free trade and commerce to the extent possible for the time. As the sultan, he dealt with the peasants with consideration, restricting the taxes in line with Qur'anic Law, thus permitting cultivators to become rich. Firuz should also be credited with widening the activities of the State into initiatives aimed at benefiting the common people, as opposed to the till then prevalent three-pronged obsession of the sultans—conquest, collection of revenue, and maintenance of law and order.

The not so pleasant side of his character, coming straight from his heart and drowning out pragmatic reasoning, created situations that were detrimental to the prestige of the dynasty. His indiscriminate benevolence led to a loss of order within the administration, with many instances of misplaced generosity recorded in contemporary chronicles. People, if they were so inclined, could take advantage of the mild and trusting nature of the sultan.

Firuz Shah undertook only minor military campaigns, compared to his predecessors. The campaigns, to Bengal and Sindh, were desultory affairs and did not lead to any clear or lasting results. Neither did these campaigns add to the prestige of the sovereign and the dynasty, nor did they enhance the material well-being of the Sultanate. Further, the Sultan had to stay away from his capital for two and a half years in each case, primarily because the planning and prosecution of the campaigns were flawed from beginning to end. Normally long absences of the ruling monarch from the centre of power would have resulted in another powerful noble usurping the throne. However, Firuz was blessed to have as his Wazir, Maqbul Khan, whose total loyalty to the crown and exemplary personal integrity ensured that no such event took place. Maqbul and Firuz shared a deep friendship that lasted till the death of Maqbul. There obviously must have been some good character traits in Firuz Shah that evoked such lifelong loyalty.

> 'As the sultan's deputy and *alter ego* he [Maqbul Khan] held the state security while his master was away, stood always between him and official worries, and administered the kingdom with exceptional skill and wisdom.'
>
> Stanley Lane-Pool,
>
> *Medieval India under Mohammedan Rule*, p. 142.

The Builder Sultan

A general atmosphere of plenty and prosperity prevailed in the Sultanate throughout Firuz's rule. This situation permitted him to indulge in his passion for building and construction. He was keen to found new, and rename existing, towns. On his first march to Delhi after being anointed the sultan, when news reached him of the birth of his son Fath Khan, he laid the foundation of a new city at that site and called it Fathabad. On the way to subdue Bengal he founded the new city of Jaunpur (details provided in the previous chapter) and renamed the citadel of Ekdala in Bengal as Azadpur and the town of Pandua as Firuzabad. Nearer Delhi, he founded Hisar Firoza and Firuzabad, to which place he shifted his residence and also had one of the Asoka pillars placed there.

The system of canals that he had built, explained in detail in an earlier chapter, brought incalculable benefit to the Sultanate. Firuz Shah is credited with 845 public works—canals, reservoirs, bridges, baths, forts, mosques, colleges, monasteries, inns for pilgrims and travellers—no aspect of public buildings escaped his notice. He also had old buildings, such as the Qutb Minar and some ancient mausoleums, repaired. Surprisingly for such an avid 'builder' there is no mention of roads being built or repaired in any of the contemporary records. Since an efficient road system would have bettered trade and commerce, the uncertainty regarding the reason for Firuz not paying attention to roads and their upkeep is intriguing.

Royal Income

The major portion of the royal income came from land revenue, and was enormous especially after Firuz had the system revamped and also tried to curtail corruption. He also reinstituted the 'jagir' system that in turn perpetuated and entrenched a feudal society. Unfortunately he failed to see that this was a retrograde step that tended to foster rebellions because the feudal lords, over a period of time, became powerful and also directly commanded the loyalty of their peasants. The Sultan in Delhi lost out on the connection to the common people, who normally make up the core of the fighting forces on the kingdom. As will be seen, the jagir system contributed at a later date to the break-up of the kingdom.

Large tracts of land, consisting of two or more districts were given to nobles to rule and became minor viceroyalties of great wealth. The nobles ruling these places, paid annual visits to the capital, bringing presents and slaves for the Sultan, thus establishing a new custom that continued into the reign of the Mughal emperors.

Religious Policies

Firuz Shah was a religious person and a devout and practising medieval Sunni Muslim, with all the fads and foibles that such a stance entailed. He forbade worship of idols, paintings and portraits as they were blasphemous under Islamic practices. He enforced the Jaziya—the tax on non-believers—and also made the Brahmans pay it, although they had so far been exempt from doing so. He consulted the Quran before making any decision of importance and also before the commencement of any new initiative. He altered existing customs and traditions while reviewing even established laws of the Sultanate to ensure that they were in conformity with what was proscribed in the sacred Quranic Law. In instituting these 'reforms' and enforcing them strictly, Firuz laid the foundations for the conversion of the Sultanate into a firm theocracy. In turn it also started the process of the perpetuation of Hindus as second class citizens with very limited rights within their ancestral homeland.

Firuz clearly re-established the supremacy of the Ulema in all matters of State—both spiritual and temporal—bringing the Sultanate directly under their influence. This was a regressive step and one that undid the control that Muhammad Tughluq, his predecessor, had strived to enforce over the religious teachers throughout his reign. His acceptance of the sanctity of the Ulema was also one of the reasons for Firuz's popularity with the more orthodox Muslims. The Sultan's attitude of reverence to the Ulema was in stark contrast to that displayed by Muhammad Tughluq, who had scant regard for Muslim clerics and sages. Although he practised a bigoted and biased religious policy throughout his reign, Firuz was also popular because he mostly kept away from wars and invasions that often brought untold calamities on the common people. As the Sultan his priorities were clearly ensuring the stable prosperity of his kingdom.

Firuz Shah was a firm believer in the goodness of charity and was in his personal life a charitable person. As the ruler, he established three charitable institutions. One was a 'bureau' to assist widows and orphans and also to help poor and unmarried Muslim girls with the dowry necessary to get married. The second was an agency to provide employment, primarily recruiting into the administrative services in clerical positions, to the unemployed. Third was a charitable hospital that delivered not only free treatment but also provided diet and medicinal supplements free of charge. Obviously these initiatives were exclusively for the benefit of his Muslim subjects. The Hindus, bulk of the population of the Sultanate, could not enjoy the benefits of these initiatives. These charities further increased the popularity of the Sultan amongst the people of the Islamic faith.

There is no doubt that Firuz ardently cultivated a negative attitude towards non-Muslims of all elk. However, he did not think that this alone was sufficient, but considered it his duty and responsibility to forcefully and physically suppress all forms of 'non-religions', meaning any form of worship and any other faith other than those sanctioned by the orthodox Sunni Muslim creed. In his written autobiography, *Futuhat-i-Firuz Shahi*, Firuz declares the kingdom to be a 'Musalman country', perhaps the first time that such a claim was being made of a kingdom in the Indian sub-continent. He goes on to state that he condoned and even encouraged forced conversions of the infidels. In the same book he also explains his concept of royal duties and provides a succinct summary of the *res gestae* of his reign. He clearly mentions his personal revulsion at visiting atrocities on fellow Muslims, which he often claimed as the primary reason for his not wanting to venture into military conquests. He describes the torture methods employed by previous sultans and went on to abolish mutilations as was practised at that time as part of torture.

His actions indicate that Firuz Shah Tughluq was the greatest religious bigot of his times, a fact corroborated by his confession in his autobiography and by the reports of contemporary historians.

Personal Indulgences

Contemporary reports state that Firuz was addicted to wine and indulged in bouts of drinking even during military expeditions. However, to a very large extent he did not let this weakness interfere with his participation in the administration of the realm. More importantly, Firuz lacked the enthusiasm and energy to follow through a project to its logical conclusion. It can be speculated that this inability, or lack of interest to see an initiative to fruition, was a 'Tughluqian Flaw' that he shared with his more famous cousin and predecessor.

Firuz tended to be idle, was pleasure loving and very fond of easy living. Inevitably this attitude led to inadequate supervision of the administration, leading to the proliferation of corruption and inefficiency. His ingrained sense of benevolence permitted corrupt officials to flourish and for old and incapacitated soldiers to continue in service. The result of this ill-conceived benevolence was the continual lowering of standards in the civil administration and the gradual reduction in the efficiency of the army. The destruction of the army's efficiency had a devastating effect on the well-being of the Sultanate since the kingdom had been forged, consolidated and maintained by the steel of the Muslim army.

In the Final Analysis...

Firuz Shah Tughluq was a mild-mannered sultan whose reign, in direct contrast to that of his predecessor, was relatively peaceful. The only turmoil erupted towards the end of his reign when he was old, almost senile, and incapable of making adequately thought-through decisions. However, four initiatives stemming from fundamental character flaws of the Sultan can be identified as having undermined the foundations on which the Sultanate had been built, with disastrous consequences for the dynasty and more broadly the Sultanate itself.

One, permitting the Ulema to influence all aspects of the administration of the State, partly as policy and partly as an article of religious faith was, without doubt, a retrograde step in keeping the kingdom socially cohesive. Two, the Sultan's misplaced leniency in dealing with corrupt officials and bestowing favours to undeserving nobles created a group of people who were like a band of internal termites, gradually and inexorably gnawing at the core of the administration. There could only be one end-result—that of the felling of the behemoth—since the malady was not recognised and therefore no remedial action instituted.

Three, Firuz carried the injunctions of the Quranic Law to an extreme and openly stated his reluctance to wage war against Muslims. This made the nobles of the realm bold enough to start and continue revolts till their ends were achieved. Further, the Sultan's attitude to waging war against Muslims was in direct contrast to the ruthlessness with which he pursued the subjugation of Hindu kingdoms and principalities. In the near to mid-term, these actions destroyed the overall stability of the kingdom. Four, the Slave System that Firuz established produced a large contingent of warriors who became the personal body guards of the Sultan. This development was aided by the disintegration of the standing army in Delhi, which had so far been the backbone of the Sultanate, by Firuz's policy of the jagir system. The Slave contingent gradually became the Praetorian Guard of the Sultanate and went on to play a destructive role in the dynastic collapse of the Tughluqs.

To a large extent, stability prevailed during Firuz's rule. His achievements in revamping and streamlining the civil administration at the beginning of his reign, must also be acknowledged. However, in a holistic analysis of his rule, Firuz cannot be pronounced a brilliant or even a successful ruler. When the balance between successes and failures are recorded for the full duration of his rule, Firuz's weak policies stand out as one of the major reasons responsible for the chaos that visited the Sultanate following his death. The line can thereafter be extended to the break-up of the Sultanate itself.

Muhammad Tughluq could be considered to have scattered the seeds that eventually brought about the fall of the Sultanate. However, it was the ineptitude of Firuz Shah that accelerated the process of decline and disintegration. Napoleon, in a letter to King Joseph had written, '...when men call a king a kind man, his reign has been a failure.' This assessment could have been tailor-made to describe Firuz Shah Tughluq and his long reign.

The irony of Firuz Shah is that the human qualities that made him immensely popular with his Muslim subjects were also the ones that were responsible for entrenching weakness in the central administration, which eventually brought down the Sultanate.

Chapter 20

THE LATER TUGHLUQS: A DECADE OF DECLINE

The story of the Tughluqs after the death of Firuz Shah is one of rebellions, assassinations and deceit, within the realm of worthless sultans. It is a continuous saga of faithless ministers and nobles who manipulated their inept masters like master puppeteers. The process of political disintegration had already started during the ill-fated reign of Muhammad Tughluq, although it was not readily apparent at that time. The decline became obvious to an astute observer during Firuz Shah's time on the throne, especially after he failed to reclaim the Deccan, which reduced the empire both in territorial spread and in its stature.

During the relatively long and peaceful reign of Firuz Shah, a generation of Tughluqs had come of age, almost totally ignorant of the ruthless despotism of a Balban or an Ala ud-Din that had held the Sultanate together. They were equally unaware of the feckless and irrational behaviour of an absolute monarch like Muhammad, and therefore they had no concept regarding what it took to be an absolute monarch. The result was that the next generation from within which a sultan had to emerge was a bunch of pleasure loving philanderers with no concept of the strength of character, energy and in-built ruthless required to be the undisputed king of a mighty empire. Further, they had also witnessed Firuz's fruitless military campaigns in Bengal, Nagarkot and Sindh that did not add anything—territory, wealth or stature—to the Sultanate. These campaigns added to their belief that military might was not a critical necessity to hold together a fractious kingdom. When Firuz Shah died, his grandson ascended the throne with the title Ghiyas ud-Din Tughluq.

Ghiyas ud-Din Tughluq

On ascending the throne, Ghiyas wanted to bring his rebellious uncle Muhammad Shah to heel. Accordingly, he send an army under his wazir Khwaja Jahan along with Bahadur Nahar, a noble who was a Rajput convert to Islam, to Sirmur to subdue Muhammad who had taken shelter there. Muhammad initially resisted but then fled to Nagarkot, still instigating rebellion. The Delhi army did not pursue him or make any attempt to besiege Nagarkot, but returned to Delhi without accomplishing anything.

Ghiyas was young and inexperienced and was also a pleasure-loving youth. Instead of taking steps to bring Muhammad under control, he gave himself up to wine and debauchery. Ghiyas also had his share of 'Tughluqian' characteristics of extreme and irrational violence. For no apparent reason he had his brother Salar Shah imprisoned, an act that offended most of the nobles who had been instrumental in enthroning him. Ghiyas's cousin Abu Bakr, son of Zafar Khan, suspected that the same fate as that befell Salar awaited him and therefore surreptitiously fled Delhi. Once safely outside the ambit of Ghiyas, he organised a concerted rebellion against the Sultan. Supported by Rukn ud-Din, the deputy wazir and a powerful noble in his own right, Abu Bakr stormed the palace. Ghiyas was caught attempting to flee and put to death along with his wazir. Abu Bakr now ascended the throne.

Incipient Civil War

Although a sultan ruled in Delhi, there were other forces already in play. The Amiran-i-Sadah, or 'The Centurions' in Samana were gathering their resources to place their own puppet on the throne of Delhi.

> ### Amiran-i-Sadah – The Centurions
>
> The first mention of this group of nobles is in the chronicles written during the reign of Muhammad Tughluq. These officers of the crown combined civil and military functions. They were not homogenous in their origins and were

> Indians as well as foreigners, including some neo-Muslims, Mongols, Turks and Afghans. They collected revenue for the Sultan and also had a minimum of 100 soldiers under their individual command. They were essentially adventurers and mercenaries. Typical of medieval adventurers, they were always on the lookout for personal profit from strategic, financial or military difficulties at the capital or centre of power. Rebellions of the Amiran-i-Sadah gradually became a chronic feature of the Tughluq reign.

The Amiran now killed their leader, who had been loyal to Abu Bakr, and invited Muhammad Shah to join them to assert his right to the throne. Muhammad came out of Nagarkot, reached Samana and in April 1389, crowned himself king of Delhi a second time. He then started a march towards Delhi during which some more nobles joined his ranks. Muhammad started his march with a force of 20,000 cavalry and this figure swelled to about 50,000 on the way. This increase need not have been through the induction of soldiers alone, but by the collection of riff-raff that almost always joined invading armies for the love of plunder. His actual fighting force would not have been more than a total of 30,000.

Bahadur Nahar, who had switched allegiance from Ghiyas and joined Abu Bakr now led the Delhi army along with the sultan. The Delhi forces met Muhammad's army at Firuzabad and inflicted heavy losses on them. Muhammad fled with barely 2000 men with him and established his headquarters at Jalesar in the Doab. Once again he was joined by some prominent nobles. The chiefs of the provinces in the vicinity of Samana already supported him and now he was joined by the governors of Multan, Bihar, Avadh, and Kanauj. Even though he had been soundly defeated in battle a number of times, Muhammad had not been broken in spirit. He prepared for another assault to claim the throne that he truly believed was his inheritance.

The entire North India was now involved in the imminent civil war. Muhammad's son, Humayun, plundered the Doab and reached the gates of Delhi. He was defeated by Abu Bakr's forces near Panipat and fled back to his father's camp at Jalesar. Muhammad marched towards Delhi and again Abu Bakr marched out of Delhi to meet the approaching army. Battle ensued near the village of Kandli, situated about 46 miles north-east of Delhi, with heavy casualties on both sides. Muhammad was once again defeated and retired to Jalesar, his main camp. However, despite being repeatedly defeated in battle, Muhammad continued to be acknowledged as the Sultan in the districts of Multan, Lahore, Samana, Hansi, Hissar and almost all the districts to the north of Delhi.

Encouraged by the two definitive victories over Muhammad in close succession, Abu Bakr now decided to end the conflict once and for all. He marched to Jalesar. When he was barely 30 miles out of the capital, Muhammad arrived in Delhi through another route and stormed the city. Abu Bakr immediately retraced his steps and chased Muhammad out of the city, defeating him for a third time. Even though repeatedly successful in the battlefield, Abu Bakr was undone by internal treachery. He came to know that Islam Khan, the commander of his household guards had started to negotiate with Muhammad Shah. This unnerved Abu Bakr and he fled to Bahadur Nahar's fort at Kotla without taking his forces with him. Being left to their own devices, the officers of Aby Bakr's army joined Muhammad, who once again marched into Delhi and ascended the throne unopposed. He resumed his old title of Nasir ud-Din Muhammad Shah Tughluq.

Muhammad Shah Tughluq

Almost immediately on assuming the throne, Muhammad set about 'cleansing' Delhi of rebellious elements, mainly some factions of the household guards—the old Firuz Shahi slaves who had by now become a very powerful group and king makers. Some of these slaves managed to escape and joined Abu Bakr in Kotla, others were massacred in cold blood in and around Delhi by pro-Muhammad forces. Muhammad send an army under Islam Khan and Humayun to crush Abu Bakr. In a battle at the village Mahnidwari, Abu Bakr was defeated and surrendered along with Bahadur Nahar. Abu Bakr was imprisoned in Meerut and died soon after, while Bahadur was pardoned and allowed to return to Kotla.

Ensconced in Delhi at the head of a diminished Sultanate on the verge of ruin, Muhammad attempted to stabilise the decline. This was a task for a sterner and more capable man than Muhammad and he was unable to stem the onset of a downward spiral of decline.

The authority of the Sultan in Delhi was being challenged in all parts of the erstwhile empire. Gujarat was planning to secede, Mewat was restive, Punjab was edging towards rebellion, and the Doab was openly defying central authority. Muhammad's ascension to the throne was marred almost immediately by rebellion and he knew that he had to reassert central authority if he was to continue as the sultan.

The chiefs of the Doab were the first to openly rebel. At Etawa, Rathor Nar Singh Bhan revolted and declared independence. However, he was subdued by Islam Khan and forced to make peace with Delhi. Earlier Firuz Shah had also marched against Bhan, subdued him and brought some of his clan back to Delhi and forced them to reside there, in the fashion of hostages. Finding that the Sultanate was weak with internecine wars, the Rathor chief had declared independence. Islam khan returned to Delhi taking Rathor Nar Singh Bhan with him. Almost immediately on the Delhi forces withdrawing, the other Rajput chiefs of the region rebelled.

> **The Rajput Rebellion in the Doab**
>
> Different chronicles provide different names for the Rathor chief of Etawa who kept the flag of rebellion against the Muslim invaders flying under extremely difficult circumstances. He has variously been referred to as Bar Singh, Har Singh and Nar Singh, while the dynastic list of rulers refer to him as Vira Singh. There is also some confusion, especially in the European recounting of the history of this period between the Tomar rulers of Gwalior and the Rathors of Etawa.
>
> It is obvious that while Delhi was in the grip of a civil war towards the end of the Tughluq dynasty's rule, a number of Rajput chieftains were in open rebellion, claiming autonomy and independence for their minor principalities.

Assessing the seriousness of the situation, Muhammad personally marched to Etawa and defeated the Rajput chiefs. He destroyed the fort at Etawa and then marched to Kanauj. He proceeded further to Jalesar, constructed a fort there and renamed the town Muhammadabad. At this stage, Muhammad received information that Islam Khan was planning to usurp the throne and hurried back to Delhi. Islam Khan pleaded innocence and denied any knowledge of a plot. However, a Hindu nephew of Islam Khan provided a false testimony against him, on the strength of which he was put to death; an unfair execution of a loyal and capable commander.

On Muhammad's hurried departure for Delhi the Rajput chiefs reoccupied Etawa and also took over the adjoining districts of Etah (Rampur) and Mainpuri. Muhammad ordered the newly appointed governor of Muhammadabad, Malik Muqarrab-ul-Mulk to march against Etawa and subdue the rebellion. Muqarrab resorted to treachery rather than take to the battlefield. He invited all the Rajput chiefs to Kanauj to discuss the terms of the truce and had all of them murdered. Only one chief, Rai Sumer, escaped and returned to Etawa, and there continued the rebellion.

Meanwhile trouble was brewing in Mewat. Bahadur Nahar, who had been pardoned by Muhammad, had never supported the new sultan. He now revolted and started to make inroads towards Delhi. Muhammad proceeded to Mewat in person, but fell ill on the way. However, he continued to march towards Kotla, being carried in a palanquin. Bahadur shut himself in his fort on the approach of the Delhi army. The Sultan was now very sick and he returned to Delhi without besieging the fort or subduing the rebellion.

In Delhi, Muhammad received news of a revolt in Lahore led by Shaikha the Khokhar. He deputed his son Humayun to proceed to Lahore and subdue the Khokhar rebellion. However, before Humayun could depart, on 20 January 1394, Muhammad Shah died. Humayun ascended the throne, assuming the title Ala ud-Din Sikandar Shah, but he too died within a few months.

The Disintegration

The nobles now placed Muhammad's youngest son, ten-year old Mahmud, on the throne with the title Nasr ud-Din Mahmud Shah even though some doubts had been expressed regarding his ability to rule. Mahmud however proved to be a precocious child and started to deal with the prevailing instability. Muqarrab-ul-Mulk was made Vakil-ul-Sultanat and received the title Muqarrab Khan, being given the remit to reunify the kingdom. However, this was not sufficient to stop the decline since the Sultanate was in the last stages of disintegration. By now provincial governors and Hindu chiefs were in open defiance of Delhi and ruling as de-facto kings.

In order to stem this tide, Mahmud appointed his wazir, Malik-ul-Sharq, the 'Lord of the East' and sent him to subdue the rebellion that had spread from Kanauj to Bihar in the eastern parts of the empire. Malik-ul-Sharq captured the districts of Koil, Etawa and Kanauj and then occupied Jaunpur, bringing under control the important centres of the region.

Over a period of time, Malik-ul-Sharq, who had by now been titled Malik Saravan, consolidated his position, increased his power and stature and became an independent ruler.

> **Manaich – Jaunpur**
>
> The history of Jaunpur can be traced back to the time of Gaharwar Rajputs who ruled the region with their capital at Manaich. Later it included the capital of the Sharqi kings. In 1321, during the reign of Ghiyas ud-Din Tughluq, his third son Zafar Khan captured Manaich. It was renamed Zafarabad and given as a 'jagir' to Zafar Khan by a grateful monarch, his father. The town, in decline, had been rejuvenated and renamed Jaunpur by Firuz Shah during his first expedition to Bengal, in honour of his cousin and predecessor Muhammad Tughluq. A while later, the town was held by Shahibzada Nasir Khan, a natural son of Firuz Shah. Mahmud now appointed his wazir, Malik-ul-Sharq as its governor.

In the western part of the kingdom Shaikha Khokhar was ruling from Lahore, untroubled since Humayun had not undertaken the expedition that his father had ordered. Sarang Khan Lodi, the governor of Dipalpur, gathered a number of chiefs under his banner and led a joint expedition to Lahore. In a counter move, Shaikha took the offensive and sacked Dipalpur while the governor was marching towards Lahore. Unperturbed, Sarang Khan continued towards Lahore and Shaikha was compelled to hurry back to Lahore. At a keenly contested battle, fought at Samuthala, Shaikha Khokhar was routed and fled to the hills of Jammu, the traditional territory of the Khokhar clan. Sarang Khan placed his brother Adil Khan as the governor of Lahore and returned to Dipalpur.

The events described above provide an indication of the plural centres of power that had sprung up in the kingdom and the lack of influence, let alone control, that the sultan ruling in Delhi could exercise over his nominal empire. They also demonstrate the spread of the Muslim nobility across the entire northern part of the sub-continent and their stranglehold on power. There were Rajput chiefs who were also ruling their principalities, but history does not provide any instance of their being victorious in battles of importance. Certainly the Rajput chiefs also won victories, otherwise they would not have been able to hold on to their kingdoms and principalities. However, in the broader flow of history, their victories were not influential enough to matter much since they did not noticeably change the course of events as they unfolded. Another important aspect that can be gleaned from an analysis of these events is the repeated mention of Hindu chiefs and generals, such as Bahadur Nahar, who had converted to Islam and become part of the mainstream within the ruling class. The not so peaceful coming together and intertwining of two cultures and almost diametrically opposing religious views and practices can be seen. Further, and more importantly, the interaction between the religions was the beginning of the development of a unique brand of Islam in the sub-continent.

The Rule of Two Sultans

While the governors were fighting for supremacy in the north-west region on their own impetus, Mahmud Shah, the boy-sultan of Delhi, went with Sadat Khan and some other nobles to visit Gwalior. He left Muqarrab Khan in charge of Delhi as the regent. At Gwalior, Mallu Iqbal Khan Lodi, brother of Sarang Khan, conspired against Sadat Khan as he was jealous of the influence that Sadat exercised over the Sultan. Sadat came to know of the conspiracy and had the conspirators put to death. However, Mallu Khan managed to escape and returned to Delhi, where he sought protection from Muqarrab Khan. Muqarrab, also an enemy of Sadat, gladly granted him asylum within Delhi.

The Sultan and his entourage returned to Delhi. On their approach, Muqarrab Khan closed the gates of the city to the royal procession.

Sadat Khan laid siege to the city, although even after three months no progress in seizing the city was made. There are two versions of subsequent events. One states that Muqarrab Khan invited Mahmud Shah into the city and the other opines that Mahmud Shah, weary of the humiliation of being locked out of his own capital, forsook Sadat Khan and entered the city of his own volition. In either case, Sadat was now left to his own devices, outside the city gates of Delhi.

Sadat Khan still had the army under his control and decided to teach Sultan Mahmud a lesson. He proceeded to Firuzabad before the onset of the approaching monsoons, and invited Nusrat Khan, son of Fath Khan the eldest and deceased son of Firuz Shah, to Firuzabad. On his arrival, Sadat Khan crowned him as the legitimate sultan with the title Nasir Ud-Din Nusrat Shah. Now the Sultanate had two titular rulers—one in Delhi and one in Firuzabad. Both the 'sultans' were puppets in the hands of their patron nobles. Sadat Khan was inherently an arrogant man and his supercilious and egotistic behaviour fell afoul of the nobles in his camp. However, he was clever enough to perceive that his support-base was diminishing and would soon vanish leaving him vulnerable. Sadat Khan fled to Delhi seeking shelter with Muqarrab Khan, who put him to death forthwith.

Even though Sadat had been removed from the scene, Nusrat Shah continued to have the support of a number of other nobles. The Sultanate was now effectively divided into two, with skirmishes between Delhi and Firuzabad becoming regular affairs. It was not long before a protracted civil war was generated with common people being killed in large numbers. The fact was that neither of the so-called sultans received any real allegiance from the nobles fighting on their behalves. The nobles considered themselves to be the rulers and only catered for their own profit and personal interest in the civil war. The administration of the state fell into anarchy. It is also instructive to note that the provincial governors, powerful in their own way, studiously kept out of the see-saw battles going on in and around Delhi. They were keeping a watch to ensure that their interests were protected irrespective of the outcome of the civil war in Delhi.

Ceaseless fighting continued with two sultans ruling a divided Delhi for the next three years. The main protagonists in the civil war were Bahadur Nahar, Mallu Iqbal Khan and Muqarrab Khan. The petty minded nobles and equally inept sultans were not able to fathom the menace that was looming across the north-western borders of their nominal Sultanate.

The Beginning of the End

Towards the end of 1397, news came that the army of Timur the Lame, or Tamerlane, had crossed the Rivers Indus and Chenab and had laid siege to Uchch. The governor Ali Malik was defeated and Timur's army entered Multan in pursuit of the defeated army. Multan was besieged and captured after six months. Sarang Khan the governor and his family were taken prisoner. The news of the fall of Multan was a clarion call and should have acted as a catalyst for the warring sultans of Delhi to sink their differences and come together to face a ferocious common foe. However, no such luck was forthcoming for the ill-fated sultanate.

In Delhi, Mallu Iqbal Khan quarrelled with Muqarrab Khan and Sultan Mahmud. He left Delhi and aligned himself with Nusrat Shah in Firuzabad. Mallu Khan attacked Delhi, but was beaten back. He then got rid of Nusrat Khan and occupied Firuzabad. From there he managed to have Muqarrab Khan murdered and obtained control of the entire Delhi region. Nusrat Khan who had fled to Panipat started to march back to Delhi with the help of his wazir, Tatar Khan. Mallu Khan came out of Delhi with a large force and Tatar Khan gave up his proposed advance on Delhi and fled to Gujarat, where his father was the governor. Nusrat Khan sought asylum in the Doab. Mallu Iqbal Khan, now all powerful, returned to Delhi.

Before examining the final and ignoble extinction of the Tughluq dynasty, it is necessary to retract this narrative a few years in order to ensure completeness of the history being analysed. At this juncture in the history of North India, it becomes critical to study the 'Timurid Typhoon' that was blowing from the north-west. This 'typhoon' would soon engulf the northern part of the sub-continent, and lead to the eventual end not only of the Tughluq dynasty, but also of the Turkish rule in India.

Chapter 21

A TYPHOON CALLED TIMUR
THE SCOURGE OF GOD

The story of the Mongols as an all-conquering force begins with the rise of Genghis Khan. The creation of the Mongol Nation, as recorded in history, is the work of this one man. His story that started in the 12th century is a remarkable tale of an individual's triumph over extraordinary adversity. Stories regarding his exploits from early childhood abound, having been written about in many languages and also made into movies, some of which have taken cinematic licence to exaggerate some aspects of the great Khan's character. However, the story of Genghis Khan and his march of global conquest that made him, forever, the archetype of murderous ferocity in world history is not germane to this narrative and is not detailed further.

The only defeat the Mongol army suffered throughout the reign of Genghis Khan was at the hands of Jalal ud-Din, the son of Muhammad then ruling Khwarizm. The defeated Mongol army was only a contingent and was not commanded by the great Khan himself. After this battle, even though victorious, Jalal ud-Din fled to India because he feared the vengeance that was sure to be wreaked on him by Genghis Khan. He was not wrong; Genghis pursued him through the Khyber Pass to exact revenge. This was the first Mongol incursion into the sub-continent.

When Genghis Khan died in 1227, his realm stretched from the Caspian Sea to the Pacific Ocean and was within riding distance from the heart of both Europe and India. Even after his death, Mongol conquests continued, expanding the Nation in all directions. However, as has been the case throughout history following the death of a great king, the empire did not stay united for long. Although the great Mongol Nation was divided into separate kingdoms, each one of them remained powerful in their own independent manner. While the Mongols were not united anymore, the conquered regions did not return to status quo ante—the Mongol conquest had altered Asian politics irreversibly. A powerful Turko-Mongol aristocracy spread across Central Asia and from this group ruling dynasties would continue to spring for centuries, dominating the heart of Asia.

From this Turko-Mongol elite another great conqueror would emerge, Timur—Amir Timur Gurgan. The title Gurgan was derived from the word 'gurg' meaning wolf, which was the insignia of the family.

Timur's Early Days

Timur (meaning 'iron') was born in 1336 near Kish in Transoxiana, a town about 40 miles south of Samarkhand. He belonged to a noble Turk family that was part of the Barlas clan, ruling a small principality around the town of his birth. His father was the chief of the Gurgan branch of the Barlas clan and his mother was a princess who claimed the same ancestry as Genghis Khan. Her grandfather was a minister in the renowned Mongol Chagtai Khanate. Timur's boyhood was spent in an atmosphere of feud and strife, since this was a period of anarchy that preceded the fall of the Asiatic dynasties that in turn opened the region to new adventurers.

When Timur was 25 years old his father died and Timur was forced to flee the country, compelled to wander around Central Asia for the next seven years. Sometime during this period of wandering he served as a commander in the army of the Khan of Sistan in north-east Iran. Timur was a natural leader and his battlefield skills brought him higher command positions.

> **Tamerlane**
>
> Timur sustained an injury while fighting with the Sistani army in southern Afghanistan that was to change his known name in world history. He sustained a wound on the leg by an arrow that maimed and made him lame for life. Timur limped for the rest of his life. Because of his limp, he started to be called 'Aksak Timur', meaning limping Timur if Turkish; translated to 'Timur-e-Leng' in Persian; which was subsequently anglicised to 'Tamerlane', a name by which the Western historians continue to refer to him.

Timur was ambitious and had not forgotten that he was the scion of a ruling family. He gradually recovered control of Transoxiana and in 1370, at the age of 34, he ascended the throne. He then emulated his illustrious ancestor, Genghis Khan, and embarked on 40 years of continual warfare, claiming the honour of never having been defeated in battle throughout his rampaging conquests. In this continuous military campaign he subjugated all the kingdoms in the region from the 'Dardanelles to Delhi'.

Timur – The Conqueror

After coming to power, Timur spend the next decade consolidating his power in Central Asia. There are striking similarities between the lives of Genghis Khan and Timur—early in their lives both were forced to flee from their ancestral inheritance, having to live in reduced circumstances for a number of years; after coming to power, both spent nearly a decade consolidating their position and enforcing authority at home; then both erupted out to conquer the world.

Like Genghis Khan, Timur was also extremely ruthless and his forces committed devastating outrages across all subdued lands. However, the similarity of their actions did not percolate to their motivation for carrying out brutal, cold-blooded, and barbarous atrocities. Genghis Khan was motivated by the need to ensure security of the captured lands and was indifferent to the suffering being inflicted upon the conquered people to achieve this objective.

Timur, on the other hand, carried out the brutal actions purely out of anger, celebrating and even revelling in the acts of cruelty that were perpetuated in his name. One was the crime of omission, while the other of commission.

An example of Timur's attitude towards conquered lands can be gleaned from the manner in which he treated the Iranian town of Isfahan after the local population rebelled against his rule. He had the entire population of the town put to death and made 120 towers of 70,000 human heads outside the city walls as a lesson for would-be rebels. Similarly, after the re-conquest of Baghdad, he made a pyramid of 120,000 human heads at the city gates. Timur's swift and violent conquests and manifest cruelty are legendary.

> Almost two centuries after Timur's explosive conquering marches, Christopher Marlowe (1563-1594), the famous English poet, playwright and translator of the Elizabethan era, wrote in his play, *Tamburlane the Great*:
>
> And till by vision or by speech I hear
>
> Immortal Jove say, 'Cease, my Tamburlane',
>
> I will persist a terror to the world,
>
> Making the meteors that, like armed men,
>
> Are seen to march upon the towers of heaven,
>
> Run tilting round about the firmament
>
> And break their burning lances in the air
>
> For honour of my wondrous victories.
>
> Quoted in Paddy Docherty, *The Khyber Pass*, p.157

There is no doubt that Timur dreamed of world conquest. It is said that astrologers tried to win favour with Timur by declaring that at his birth the planets had moved away from their natural orbits, indicating that he would be a great conqueror. Timur was eager to be recognised as much for his intellect as for his military capabilities. Therefore, he conceived the idea of subjugating all the regions that Genghis Khan had conquered. Timur started his journey of conquest by invading Khorasan in Persia that had been under the misrule of a number of petty chiefs for some time. The people of Khorasan welcomed the invasion hoping that the new rule would bring about some order and stability to the turbulent times of the recent past. The small-time chiefs were jealous of each other and opposed Timur independently instead of putting up a joint resistance. As a result, they fell one by one to the might of the Mongol army, individually being swallowed by Timur. Of the chiefs of Khorasan, a few capitulated without a fight and some fought valiantly to the death. After bringing the whole of Persia under his control Timur went on to conquer all the kingdoms along the Rivers Tigris and Euphrates, including Iraq and Syria.

He then subjugated the Ottoman Turks in Anatolia, at one stage even having the Sultan Bayazid as his captive. Thereafter he captured Georgia, subjugated Kashgar and ventured into Siberia. The pursuit of a defeated and fleeing adversary took Timur to the tributary provinces of Russia. He reached very close to Moscow, almost capturing the capital of the Tsarist Empire. However, ambition trimmed with prudence becomes an all-conquering force. Realising the pitfalls of attempting to capture Moscow, with the vast hinterland of Russia that could be utilised to wage a deadly rear-guard action, Timur turned back to the south to continue his conquests. At this stage, Timur's control spanned all the regions from the Great Wall of China in the east, to Moscow in the west and the lands of the entire Middle-East in the south.

The Indian Interlude

Timur granted the provinces of Kunduz, Baghlan, Kabul, Ghazni and Kandahar to his favourite grandson Pir Muhammad, who was then 15 years old. Further, he encouraged the young prince to march east into India. Accordingly, Pir Muhammad crossed the River Indus, stormed the fortress at Uchch and reached Multan. Here his progress was checked by the governor of the province, a Tughluq appointee. Although the Multan fort was besieged, even after multiple attempts Pir Muhammad was unable to capture it. Grandfather Timur, monitoring the progress of his grandson's campaign into India decided that the youngster needed assistance and prepared to move east. This was the immediate and tangible cause for Timur's march towards India.

Even though coming to the rescue of his grandson was perhaps the catalyst for Timur's invasion of India, the offensive was also motivated by the fabled riches of India. Contemporary chroniclers have attempted to drape a veneer of piety over the more base instincts of the lure of loot and plunder that must have been a great motivation for Timur. They claim that Timur was annoyed by the degeneration of Indian Islam and was therefore enthused to punish the Indian Muslims who were reported to be verging on apostasy. In these reports Timur is portrayed as a champion of pure Islam, pursuing a desire to punish and destroy infidels and idolaters.

There is no doubt that Timur had materialistic ambitions foremost in his mind, but used the religious angle as an expeditious cover and reason for the conduct of the campaign. In the Malfuzat-i-Timuri, his autobiography, Timur piously states the principle objective of the expedition as destruction of the unbelievers and the plunder of wealth is mentioned only as a secondary aim. To put this in perspective, it has to be understood that plunder in war was a lawful practice within the Islamic tenets of warfare and therefore does not rate any special mention in the autobiography. Even if Timur subscribed to the religious calling, the loot of the legendary wealth of India was the primary motive for his soldiers.

> 'My principle objective in coming to Hindustan, and in undergoing all this toil and hardship, has been to accomplish two things,' he candidly stated once in the midst of his Indian campaign. 'The first was to wage war against the infidels... and by this religious warfare acquire some claim to reward in the life to come. The other was a worldly objective, that the army of Islam might gain something by plundering the wealth and valuables of the infidels. Plunder in war is as lawful as their mothers' milk to Muslims who wage war for their faith.'
>
> Abraham Eraly,
>
> *The Age of Wrath*, p. 194.

Ever since Alexander of Macedonia crossed the River Indus and encountered the massed army of King Pururuvas (named Porus in western histories) all great military commanders of the ancient and medieval world had dreamt about conquering India and capturing its legendary wealth. Timur was no exception. Timur's nobles had expressed their misgivings at the plan to invade India. Timur by this time was, in relative terms, an old man but still vigorous and driven by great ambition. The timidity and apprehension of his nobles was brought about through ignorance and apprehension. Timur's iron will easily prevailed over the opinion of his nobles. An analysis of his campaign indicates that Timur had by this time detected the fundamental weakness in the ruling house in Delhi. He realised that the rebellions and discord that prevailed in the Indian Sultanate had paralysed the ability of its princes and nobles to initiate decisive action in the face of a concerted invasion.

Like so many previous Muslim invasions, Timur had also cloaked the real objective of his invasion within the Muslim religious exhortation to oppose any religious malpractice. The perceived deterioration in Indian Islamic practices was sufficient to provide a plausible reason. Even though Timur's Indian campaign shared the objective of earlier Mongol invasions, to plunder the wealth of India, it differed considerably in its secondary aims as well as its conduct. Timur clearly meant to capture Delhi, purely for the prestige attached to doing so, because he never intended to annex any territory. In contrast to the regular Mongol attacks, Timur's campaign was an invasion by a king, not a raid by a pillaging horde tinged with religious fanaticism. The earlier Mongol raids were conducted when they were still heathen, not having converted to Islam and therefore only meant to pillage and capture wealth.

In March 1398 at the age of 62, Timur left Samarkhand with an army of 92,000 drawn mainly from the Turko-Mongol tribes from beyond the River Oxus. The Mongol army reached the banks of the River Indus in September of the same year and crossed the great river at Dhankot. Timur started to receive many envoys from various rulers who professed submission because of the fearsome reputation of Timur that had preceded him. One such ruler was the king of Kashmir, Sikandar Shah, who was asked by Timur to join him in his invasion of the Delhi Sultanate. The king was instructed to join the Mongol army at Dipalpur.

The Delhi Sultanate

Although he was only about 600 miles from Delhi, Timur turned south-east instead of proceeding directly to the capital. It is obvious that he wanted to aid his grandson who was still stuck at Multan without having achieved any break through. Timur marched to Multan through the shortest route. During the march many petty chieftains of the region sent presents to Timur in order to buy peace. In all the conquered areas, the option given to the populace was stark and simple—embrace Islam or be prepared for death.

When he reached the banks of the River Jhelum, Timur came to know that Shihab ud-Din Mubarak Shah Tamimi the governor of Uchch, who had initially surrendered to Pir Muhammad had rebelled and was opposing the Mongol army. He also did not pay homage to Timur. However, on the arrival of Timur on the scene, Tamimi fled back to Uchch. Timur followed and burned down the citadel. Timur then marched along the River Jhelum, defeating several minor chieftains along the way, without having to exert himself. Cities and towns across the Punjab were ransacked at will. Multan capitulated out of sheer terror and the two armies, of the grandson and the grandfather, were reunited. Timur now turned towards Delhi, his ultimate goal. During this march the countryside was scoured and towns and cities laid waste—Timur's advance was truly a scourge.

Timur initially proceeded to Bhatnir (modern Hanumangarh), which was the location of a strong fort then ruled by a Hindu chief mentioned as Dul Chand. He is also mentioned as being a Rao of the Rajputs. The name is obviously erroneous since 'Chand' is a Vaishya name and not in consonance with that of a Rao of the Rajputs. Further, some chronicles have named this chief Duljin, Dulchin, Jaljin and also as Rao Khalji. It is highly likely that his name was Daljit and that he was a Bhatti Rajput. The reason for Timur targeting Bhatnir was that some chiefs and nobles of the city of Dipalpur had rebelled and then taken refuge in the Bhatnir fort. Timur captured Bhatnir, but not before a group of Rajputs guarding the fort offered ferocious resistance, even resorting to vicious hand-to-hand combat. Rao Daljit finally surrendered. During the peace negotiations there was some unexplained altercation between the Hindu chiefs and the Muslim ransom collectors that irked Timur. Timur had the population of the entire fort put to the sword and the fort itself razed to the ground.

> Timur describes what followed the dispute that arose about the collection of ransom money 'between the collectors and the evil-minded rais.': 'In a short space of time all the people of the fort were put to the sword, and in the course of one hour the head of 10,000 infidels were cut off. The sword of Islam was washed in the blood of the infidels, and all the goods and effects, the treasure and the grain which for many long years had been stored in the fort became the spoils of my soldiers. They set fire to the houses and reduced them to ashes, and they razed the buildings and the fort to the ground.'
>
> *Malfuzat-i-Timuri*, Timur's Autobiographical Memoir,
>
> Translated in *History of India as told by its own Historians* by H.M. Elliot and J. Dowson, Vol III, pp. 420-27.

March to Delhi

Timur now moved eastwards towards Delhi. From Bhatnir, till he reached the areas surrounding Delhi, he continually targeted the Jats. The reason for singling out this ethnic group is unknown. The fact remains that they were continually attacked, irrespective of whether they were Hindus or Muslims. The Jats were killed in the thousands and their territories annexed to be placed under Muslim governors.

Timur's passage through North India was marked by extreme savagery. He had passed orders for the soldiers to kill any infidel that they encountered; uncompromising and ferocious brutality was one part of the military tactics that Timur employed in his campaigns. The use of brutality as a tactic served a dual purpose—it instilled and nurtured bloodlust in his soldiers and terrified the adversary, making them more prone to flee than resist. His clever blending of the religious fervour of Islam with the inherent human characteristic of the lust for plunder was critical to forging an invincible army, particularly during the Indian campaign. Timur clearly understood the psychology of his soldiers in battle and also that victory and defeat hinged on the spirit of the soldiers. Therefore, he consciously and carefully nurtured and encouraged extreme brutality and the blood lust that it invoked, in his army.

The most important factor in Timur's continuous stream of victories was that he was a brilliant commander and a master tactician. He provided innovative solutions to every military challenge that the army faced; he was cautious without being meek; he was audacious while not being reckless, not taking any unnecessary risks; and he was able to maintain a careful balance between caution and daring. He made use of a network of spies to assess a potential adversary's strengths and weaknesses. Timur was a good general and ensured the welfare of his soldiers and they repaid him with fierce and personal loyalty. He fostered this loyalty through equitable distribution of plunder to all soldiers. Timur was also religious, considering God responsible for the battlefield victories. He was prone to seeking divine guidance by opening and reading the Quran at random when decisions of importance had to be made.

On the march from Bhatnir, Timur had divided his army, sending one part to move towards Delhi through Dipalpur. When Timur arrived at River Khagar, this part of the army rejoined him, bringing the force to its original strength of 92,000. He started to re-organise the army for the assault on Delhi and obtained abundant supplies, securing them in the captured fort at Loni. On 10 December 1398, Timur held his customary council of war that was always done on the eve of all major assaults.

Attack and Sack of Delhi

In the war council his commanders expressed concern regarding the fear that the soldiers had about the Indian war elephants and the apprehension that there would be scarcity of provisions. The concern regarding provisions was genuine since scarcity could ensue once battle was joined, especially since more than 50,000 prisoners also had to be fed. To neutralise the menace of the war elephants, Timur had iron claws made and given to the foot soldiers to scatter in front of the advancing elephants. He asserted that the provisions stored in the fort at Loni would be sufficient to last till victory was achieved. The next day Timur personally led a scouting party of about 700 cavalry towards Delhi. Mallu Iqbal Khan, the commander in Delhi, had been observing the scouting party and attacked it with a superior force at an opportune moment. Timur immediately withdrew, leaving a contingent to fight a rear-guard action. On reaching safety, he send reinforcements to assist the force that had been left behind to hold back the Delhi forces. With the arrival of the reinforcements, Mallu Khan was forced to withdraw.

Some historians consider this minor skirmish as a defeat of the Timurid army by the Delhi Sultanate. It is impossible to support this assertion—the Delhi forces attempted to ambush a scouting party and was unsuccessful in doing so; the skirmish was nothing more than that. However, Mallu Khan's attempt to pre-empt Timur's attack had unforeseen indirect and brutal consequences for the Sultanate. It so happened that during this skirmish, the prisoners in Timur's camp had celebrated Timur's hurried retreat in what they presumed to be a defeat of the Timurid army. Timur then realised that when the entire army was committed to the on-coming battle, his rear would be vulnerable to a concerted revolt by the large number of prisoners who would be left behind. He therefore gave orders to kill all the prisoners. Estimates of number of prisoners murdered vary between 50,000 and 100,000.

Timur now instructed his commanders that he did not want a long-drawn war against Delhi. He had obviously studied the Multan campaign and assimilated the lessons, mainly the failure of a strategy of long sieges and the extraordinary resources needed to capture a strong fort or walled city that was occupied by a determined adversary. This lesson was reinforced by lessons from earlier Mongol campaigns. Accordingly, Timur aimed to conduct a battle in the open and manoeuvred to achieve this end. An open battle clearly played on the strength of the fast and free-wheeling tactics of the ferocious Mongol cavalry. Timur crossed the River Yamuna and encamped on the plains of Firuzabad. Sultan Mahmud, came out of his capital with a well-equipped army of 10,000 cavalry, 125 elephants and more than 40,000 accompanying infantry.

The commencing manoeuvre of the battle was initiated by Timur's commanders who managed to circumvent the Delhi army's advanced guard and attacked the left wing. Pir Muhammad commanding this skirting force, crushed the left wing, which started to flee in disarray. Sultan Mahmud then attacked the centre of the Mongol army with great vigour and commendable courage. However, the attack was fended off and the Delhi army was defeated, with both Mahmud and Mallu Khan fleeing the battlefield. The army of Hindustan had once again failed to defeat the army of yet another invader. The Delhi army had fought bravely, eliciting reluctant praise from Timur himself for their courage and tenacity. Praise from the enemy on the battlefield is the ultimate compliment for a soldier, cohort or army. The 'Indians' had fought bravely, but were outnumbered and outmanoeuvred.

Timur hoisted his flag from the ramparts of Delhi. The noblemen, religious leaders and prominent traders of the city approached Timur and pleaded for mercy. Timur granted Delhi his protection and freedom from ransack in return for a very large indemnity. However, events did not adhere to this 'well-meaning' promise made by the conquering general.

The Mongol soldiers were permitted to enter Delhi in small groups at a time. One such group became rowdy during one of these excursions and looted a shop. Other soldiers followed suit and soon there was wholescale looting going on in the market place. Obviously, the traders and other local people put up resistance, especially since Timur had promised them his personal protection. Timur was appraised of the situation and characteristically was enraged at the citizens of Delhi for putting up resistance and did not find fault with his rampaging and plundering soldiers. He ordered the massacre of the citizens of Delhi, which was carried out with great alacrity by his soldiers. The entire city was given over to rapine and plunder in very short order.

Timur displayed no remorse at not having kept his promise to protect the city. In any case, remorse and sympathy were not part of Timur's character traits. He brushed off his responsibility for the massacre, rape and extended plunder of Delhi in his autobiography with a throw-away statement, 'By the will of God, and no wish or direction of mine, all three cities of Delhi by name Siri, Jahanapanah and Old Delhi had been plundered'. He then went on to state that the population of the city had brought it upon themselves by offering resistance to his soldiers. History gives Timur a well-deserved reputation for extreme cruelty towards conquered people and his army for its appetite for plunder and rapine. Even by Timur's standards and the reputation for brutality that preceded him and his army, the sack of Delhi stands out as more monstrous in its ferocity than the plunder of any other city by the Timurid army.

Timur's Withdrawal

Timur was fascinated by Delhi and enjoyed his stay there. After a fortnight of 'pleasure and enjoyment' he decided to continue his campaign. He was anxious to move on. From this decision it is clear that at no time did Timur contemplate a permanent annexation of the Delhi Sultanate—the invasion was purely a wealth-collection expedition.

From Delhi, Timur marched north. Meerut put up resistance but was captured, plundered and the fort burned to the ground. Shaikha Khokhar, chieftain of the Khokhar tribe, who had broken free of the Delhi Sultanate control earlier, proclaimed that he was going to join forces with Timur. However, at an opportune moment he attacked the Timurid army but was defeated. Timur refers to Shaikha and his commanders, all Muslims, as infidels.

Referring to Muslims as infidels is an interesting factor and needs elaboration. It was not Timur alone who named Muslims as infidels; earlier, the invading Ghaznavid and the Ghurid armies had also done the same. The precept for these armies was that they were waging a 'Holy War' and anyone, including Muslims, who opposed them were clubbed together under the title infidel. Further, since the formal objective of the war/invasion was to establish Islamic rule, all infidels had to be stamped out—a convenient reasoning for exterminating one's enemies. The commanders of these armies firmly believed, at least outwardly, that opposition to them was tantamount to opposition to the 'Most High' on whose behalf they were waging war. The hypocrisy and duplicity involved in the conduct of these purely plundering raids are laid open in the analysis of this one aspect of the repeated invasions.

Timur reached Hardwar and faced fierce resistance; his attack on the town was only partially successful. He withdrew across the River Ganges the same day as the battle. Timur then decided to withdraw from the sub-continent. It is unnecessary to add the details of other battles that the Timurid army fought on its way back to the Khyber Pass and its final exit from India. The progress of Timur's armies was one long march of rapine, plunder and massacre of Hindus—adult men were slain, women and children taken prisoner and either converted to Islam or made into slaves.

From Hardwar, Timur turned west and passed through Nagarkot and went on to sack Jammu. It is also reported that as many as 20 pitched battles were fought in a span of 30 days during this march. This indicates the opposition that he faced even though his reputation for extreme brutality towards towns, principalities and kingdoms that opposed him had by now become legendary. *[The modern historical belief that the kingdoms of Hindustan were subjugated easily and that the 'Hindus' submitted meekly to Muslim invasions is a myth perpetuated by self-serving historical analysts with limited knowledge of actual events. The fact that Timur, the most rapacious of invaders, had to fight his way back from the sub-continent on a daily basis is proof of the ferociousness of the resistance.]* He crossed the River Indus to the west bank on 19 March 1399 and departed from India. It is ironic that the rise of Genghis Khan in Central Asia had indirectly saved the independence of the Delhi Sultanate from Khwarazm attacks and ensured its survival and Timur's savage raid more than a century later was a catastrophe from which the Sultanate never recovered fully. Timur had rung the death knell for the Delhi Sultanate—saved by a Mongol Khan and destroyed by another.

Timur's Invasion – A Retrospective

Considering the extremely short duration of the invasion, September 1398 to March 1399 a mere six months, the fundamental question that comes to mind is 'Why did Timur invade India'? There is no clear objective that can be discerned even from the autobiography of Timur. This vagueness of intent leads to the speculative conclusion that the invasion symbolises the fulfilment of a grandiose ambition on the part of a 'world-conquering' king. If conquest was intended, it was not achieved. Further, Timur states in his autobiography that his objectives were the destruction of idolatry and collection of rich booty. Out of the two, only plunder of untold wealth was achieved, idolatry was not destroyed. There are no accounts or even mention of any temples being razed to the ground, even though an unaccounted number of Hindus and opposing Muslims were put to the sword without mercy.

It is estimated that Timur's conquering armies killed more than 17 million people during their military campaigns, a number that equalled 5 per cent of global population at that time. He referred to himself as the 'Sword of Islam' and converted much of the empire that he conquered to the religion, including the descendants of Genghis Khan. However, Timur's own religious affiliation remains shrouded in mystery. Timur was an astute politician who spoke Turkish, Mongolian and Persian fluently. Therefore, it is conceivable that he found using the cloak of Islam an easy way to justify his invasions and conquests.

There is a dichotomy regarding his religious policy. While his stated objective was to wipe out infidels—within the broadest definition that the term was given—his army was multi-ethnic and multi-religious. It contained large numbers of non-Muslims, mainly Persians and some other non-believers. They were sufficiently large in number within the army that Timur's tolerance of these troops led to some contemporary religious purists classifying Timur himself as an infidel. The other side of the equation was that Timur believed he had embarked on a holy war to destroy the infidels, mainly Hindus. There is no doubt that he defeated many Hindu chieftains, but almost all of them uniformly were petty chiefs of limited stature; their defeat was, as a whole in the broader cast of history, inconsequential and its impact temporary. With the result, no serious or lasting impact was made on Hinduism itself.

Viewed from a political angle, the invasion and the temporary overthrow of the Delhi Sultanate, followed by the terrible sacking of Delhi, was a body-blow to Muslim rule in North India. It greatly diminished the strength of Islamic rule in Delhi and the sub-continent as a whole. One aspect of Timur's Indian foray is that the amount of booty that he collected is not mentioned in any contemporary account. Considering that the wealth collected by the Ghaznis or the Khijis from the Deccan have been described in great detail, this omission in contemporary records seems deliberate. In turn it leads to the belief that even though he was victorious in almost all battles, the wealth that was accumulated may not have been commensurate with the expenditure involved in the invasion.

The other aspect of Timur's invasion that continues to perplex analysts is his hurried departure from India, which seems almost a withdrawal in the face of determined opposition. No doubt there was some trouble brewing in Samarkhand, but it did not warrant the hasty return march, which was very rapid leading to an almost impulsive exit. As an overall victor in the campaign, it is clear that Timur did not gain very much. However, the vanquished, the Delhi Sultanate, lost everything. After the fall and sack of Delhi, the remnants of the Tughluq dynasty, already in terminal decline for more than a decade, reached a state beyond any hope of redemption.

Even during these bleak hours in the sub-continent, there was a silver lining to brighten the dark clouds that accompanied Typhoon Timur. With very few exceptions, both Hindus and Muslims of the sub-continent stood up to fight the invaders, wherever Timur led his army. The people of India were known for their disunity based on religious, cultural, regional and even linguistic differences, an aspect that Timur had carefully considered in the planning stage of the campaign. Belying this concept and expectation, the Indian population stood united against Timur's Mongol army.

Throughout Timur's campaign, he faced opposition from independent and joint forces of Hindus and Muslims, fighting shoulder to shoulder against an invader of their country. The Muslims of India had started the process of integrating into the Indian milieu to forge an Indian Islamic ethos and identity.

Timur – the Man

Timur died on 17 February 1405, at the age of 68. At the time of his death he was fighting against the Chinese Ming dynasty and winning. His body was embalmed and buried in an ebony coffin in Samarkhand, fifty miles north of his birthplace in Kish.

In 1941, Russian archaeologists excavated Timur's tomb. It was confirmed that he had a debilitating hip injury and that two fingers from his right hand was missing. He had Mongoloid features, was 1.73 metres tall and broad-chested.

Like a number of formidable conquerors, Timur's legacy is ambivalent. In some of the Central Asian states such as Uzbekistan he is considered a hero, whereas in Iran and the Indian sub-continent he is vilified as a monster for the massacre of millions of innocent people.

Chapter 22

THE WHIMPERING END

Timur left North-Western India in shambles—bleeding and in utter confusion and chaos. The entire countryside was ravaged, plundered and burned to the ground making it easy for famine and pestilence to spread. Trade, commerce and other signs of normalcy had vanished along with all trappings of prosperity. The city of Delhi was almost depopulated and destroyed. It took several years for the wounds to heal and for the region to recuperate and recover. The Delhi Sultanate, already in a diminished state before the Timurid invasion now shrunk to the dimension of a small principality, consisting of a few districts centred on Delhi.

For nearly three months after Timur's departure, Delhi had no ruler—Mahmud Shah and the pretender Nusrat Shah had both fled from the capital, leaving it at the mercy of Timur's plundering army. Nusrat Shah, who had fled to the Doab, was the first to attempt a return. He made another attempt to capture the throne of Delhi, and occupied the ruins of the palace at Firuzabad. However, he was driven out of Delhi by Mallu Iqbal Khan.

Mallu Iqbal Khan

Soon after being driven out of Delhi, Nusrat Shah died. Iqbal Khan established his rule from Siri and gradually the people who had fled Delhi started to return. Iqbal Khan was keen to re-establish control over the territories that had been lost, realising that the Sultanate had disintegrated into independent kingdoms and principalities of different nominations. Punjab and Sind was under the control of Khizr Khan; Gujarat was ruled by Zafar Khan; and Malwa was under the rule of

Dilawar Khan. Nearer Delhi, Gulab Khan held court at Samana, while Mahoba and Kalpi was under Mahmud Khan's jurisdiction. In the east, from Kanauj to Bihar including Jaunpur, was ruled by Mubarak Shah Qaranful. (The title 'Qaranful' has been translated as meaning 'dark complexion' or 'clove').

Each of these rulers coveted the throne of Delhi, even in its reduced state. Iqbal Khan was plagued by a lack of resources to establish control over regions farther away for Delhi. Therefore, he had to be content in making few forays against minor chieftains around Delhi, collecting some amount of tribute and then returning to the safety of Delhi. In the period of the internecine war in Delhi and the subsequent invasion of Timur, Jaunpur had consciously stayed away from the confusion and conflict. The new 'kingdom' had grown relatively powerful while the Sultanate and the western regions were breaking under the strain of Timur's pillaging march. The Jaunpur ruler had not assisted Delhi in any manner during the time of its greatest threat, opting to conserve his strength.

Iqbal Khan realised the necessity to bring the eastern kingdom under control and marched to Kanauj. On the way he was joined by the chieftains of Mewat and Bayan, both of whom had declared independence from Delhi. However, they were more interested in bringing down the power of Jaunpur than maintaining their transitory independence and submitted to the nominal ruler of Delhi. During the march Iqbal Khan was opposed by some Hindu chieftains at Etawah, but they were defeated. Iqbal advanced to the banks of the River Ganga and was faced by the Jaunpur forces on the other bank. After a two-month stand-off between the two forces, Iqbal Khan retreated and returned to Delhi, not having achieved any tangible result or advantage in the campaign.

At this stage Iqbal Khan felt that he lacked legitimacy in the eyes of the people to rule from the throne of Delhi and so invited Mahmud Shah back to Delhi. Iqbal Khan placed Mahmud on the throne as nominal sultan and ruled in his name. Mahmud Shah once again became a puppet in the hands of the powerful noble. After making these cosmetic changes to the hierarchy in the capital, Iqbal Khan returned to confront Jaunpur, perhaps hoping that the legitimacy provided by Mahmud Shah being on the throne would alter the status quo in his favour. Jaunpur was now ruled by Ibrahim Shah Sharqi, the brother of the now deceased Mubarak Shah. Once again the armies of Delhi and Jaunpur faced off on opposite banks of the River Ganga, the stand-off again did not produce any appreciable result.

At this juncture Mahmud Shah, the nominal sultan who had been smarting under the treatment that he had been receiving from Iqbal Khan and other nobles, moved with an army and captured Kanauj. He established his rule from there, controlling only a very small spread of territory. Iqbal Khan hurriedly returned to Delhi. During this time, when Iqbal Khan was busy with the Jaunpur kingdom, Gujarat had emerged as one of the primary threats to Delhi. However, Gujarat was also the throes of internal challenges. There was confusion at the highest levels of rule with intrigue and palace revolts continually bringing chaos to the kingdom. Therefore, Gujarat could not pose a credible threat to Delhi, which receded almost completely after Muzaffar Shah regained the throne from his son Tatar Khan.

The threat to Delhi now started to emanate from the north-west, where Khizr Khan was in the process of consolidating his power. He considered himself the rightful heir to Timur, since he had been left in-charge by Timur, although without an army to support him. To make good this obvious lack of military power, Khizr Khan invited the Afghan chiefs, from India and abroad, to join him in an invasion aimed at mounting a challenge to the Delhi throne. A large number of chiefs flocked to his banner, no doubt lured by the prospect of plunder and wealth that would come their way through an attack on the Sultanate.

Iqbal Khan realised that the situation had deteriorated to an extent that he had to act. The Sultanate was surrounded, especially in the west and the east by strong and powerful rulers. Therefore, he marched against the Doab, relatively the least powerful of neighbouring territories. The Delhi army besieged the Rai of Etawah, but the attempt to defeat him was unsuccessful. Then Iqbal Khan moved against Mahmud Shah in Kanauj, which also turned out to be a futile attempt. The unfortunate Khan was forced to return to Delhi for the third time without achieving any gains. He then tried his luck in the west by marching to Samana. He fared better here. Iqbal Khan coerced Bahram Khan ruling in Samana to join him in an attempt to defeat Khizr Khan. The combined army marched towards Multan. On the way, for some inexplicable reason, Iqbal Khan suspected Bahram of treachery and had him flayed alive. The Samana army and some Delhi forces deserted the camp on hearing of their chief's fate. Iqbal Khan's army was completely depleted.

Khizr Khan saw the opportunity to best the Delhi army and came out to give battle. On 12 November 1405, battle ensued on the banks of the Dahinda, a small rivulet branching off from the River Sutlej near Ajodhan and re-joining it about 35 miles downstream. In the old records that part of the River Sutlej is also referred to as Dahinda. In the encounter, Mallu Iqbal Khan was killed. He was not mourned in Delhi. This is not surprising. Although he was a fairly loyal servant of the Tughluqs, he had also displayed personal ambition in the actions that he initiated to reassert the authority of the Tughluqs after the violent Timurid interlude. His actions and rule on behalf of the minor sultan Mahmud Shah had not been entirely altruistic. On the positive side, it has to be accepted that he met his end as a courageous soldier who had not succumbed to any other frailties of character.

Mahmud Shah Returns

On the death of Iqbal Khan, the leading nobles of Delhi invited Mahmud Shah to return and assume the throne. Mahmud returned to Delhi after being self-exiled for nearly seven years and rewarded the nobles in the traditional manner by distributing riches among them. However, Mahmud Shah did not return to a peaceful throne. His re-ascension was opposed by Ibrahim Sharqi ruling the east from Jaunpur and Khizr Khan controlling the western region. In typical fashion, the impetuous and young Sultan decided to settle these challenges, a decision that held long-term consequences for the Sultanate.

Jaunpur to the east had become powerful at the cost of Delhi, making further inroads into its declining power. However, despite the opposition from Jaunpur, Mahmud had managed to capture Kanauj, which had been an appendage of Jaunpur till then. He had managed to stay in power there for seven years till his invited return to the Delhi throne. On Mahmud's return to Delhi, Ibrahim Sharqi marched out to assimilate Kanauj back into the Jaunpur kingdom. From Delhi Mahmud also ventured out with an army. The armies met and a stand-off ensued since both the armies were reluctant to start a war that they felt would not provide any conclusive result. Subsequently the armies returned to their respective capitals without giving battle. Status quo prevailed. *[Contemporary as well as later-day historians repeatedly mention that Jaunpur had become very powerful. However, the fact that they could not defeat a materially and numerically depleted Delhi army indicates that the Sharqi kingdom was not all that powerful and nor was its ruler confident.]*

Along with the attempt to coerce Jaunpur, Mahmud had send out another army to attempt subduing Samana. Samana was ruled by a slave of Firuz Shah as a vassal of Khizr Khan. The Delhi army managed a minor victory, but when Khizr Khan marched out of Multan to help his vassal in Samana, the Delhi army fled in panic with some of the Delhi forces switching sides and joining Khizr Khan. Khizr Khan continued his eastward march and the entire area west of the River Yamuna now came under his control. Mahmud Shah's control over the minimalist Sultanate and his personal stature suffered a setback.

With these manoeuvrings, a game of chequers was set in motion. Ibrahim Sharqi now marched to Delhi. Seeing an opportunity Zafar Khan of Gujarat made a move on Jaunpur, at a time when Ibrahim was already committed to crossing the River Yamuna towards Delhi. Ibrahim Sharqi was forced to return post-haste to defend his capital and Zafar Khan retired to Gujarat. Mahmud Shah took advantage of the pre-occupation of two of his arch rivals and recaptured few towns to the east of Delhi, which may have been affiliated to Jaunpur. The success of these minor forays encouraged Mahmud to try to recapture territorial control by mounting a campaign to the west. This provoked Khizr Khan to commence a march towards Delhi. He arrived at the outskirts of the capital and besieged Siri. The deeds of his mentor Timur came back now to haunt Khizr Khan. Timur had ravaged the countryside so badly that even after nearly a decade, it was not capable of supporting a huge army engaged in a siege. Khizr Khan was forced to lift the siege and return to his home base.

Form this time onwards Khizr Khan did not make any pretence regarding his ambition and started to prepare for an attack to seize Delhi. On the other hand, Mahmud Shah turned to the pleasure loving ways of a sultan, not paying any heed to the menace being readied on the west of his Sultanate—in reality only a small principality. Khizr Khan made another attempt at claiming the throne, but was once again thwarted by a lack of provisions for the huge army that he had created. Mahmud Shah had by this become completely enamoured by a life of pleasure and avoided all involvement in affairs of the state. He died towards the end of 1412, having 'officially' ruled the Delhi Sultanate for a little over 18 years. Mahmud Shah ruled in name only and was a puppet sultan. Even had he wanted to set right the problems of the Sultanate, the challenges facing the kingdom were far too complex even for a competent ruler to rectify, which evidently Mahmud was not. Mahmud was a weak and ineffectual Sultan and the problems of the Sultanate only continued to multiply during his reign. After 18 years of continuous struggle, Muhammad Shah died on the throne, the last of the Tughluqs to rule.

The Coming of the Sayyids

The nobles of Delhi were now in a quandary. They could not offer the throne of Delhi to Khizr Khan who was considered the nominee of the 'accursed' Timur. The nobles paid homage to Daulta Khan, a Lodi Amir with no claim to the throne, and crowned him sultan. Daulta Khan was well aware of the precariousness of his position and went about creating as many alliances as possible with the chieftains ruling principalities around Delhi. He avoided siding with any faction, attempting to bring all the nobles into his fold.

In the meantime Khizr Khan started a full-scale invasion of Delhi. He besieged Rohtak; marched to Mewat where the local governor, ruling independently, surrendered; crossed the Doab and sacked Sambhal; and arrived at Delhi in March 1414 with 60,000 cavalry, and invested Siri. Daulat Khan withstood the siege for nearly four months. However, he was betrayed by one of his senior commanders who let Khizr Khan's forces enter the fort. Daulat Khan was taken prisoner and later put to death. In June 1414, the Sultanate passed into the hands of Khizr Khan Sayyid—the first of the Sayyid dynasty.

Causes for the Disintegration of the Tughluq Empire

When Ghiyas ud-Din, the founder of the Tughluq dynasty, died his empire encompassed almost the entire northern India with the exception of Kashmir, Nepal and Assam. It also held large parts of the Deccan other than Orissa. When Mahmud Shah, the last sultan of the dynasty died, the Sultanate was little more than a petty principality surrounding Delhi. Further, the dynasty did not have the capacity to protect even this diminutive territory, the control of the region passing to Timur's governor who went on to establish the Sayyid dynasty. The deterioration in personal capabilities of the successor sultans was rapid and the fall of the regime expected. Eight major factors, individually and in combination, contributed to this swift and sorry decline of the once grand Tughluq dynasty.

First was the character and policies of Muhammad, the second Tughluq to sit on the throne of Delhi. His 'visionary' projects, which almost always resulted in failure and was followed by the sultan imposing extraordinarily harsh punishments on the people, gradually made the general population resent the Sultan. Muhammad had grandiose dreams of conquest, although these fantasy filled schemes never materialised. The failure of the Sultan to follow up on his military schemes made regional governors believe that they could rebel against the central authority without any fear of retribution. This situation sowed the seeds of disintegration of the great empire. The result was that Bengal became independent and in the Deccan, the Bahmani and Vijyanagar Empires were established. It took more than two centuries for Delhi to re-establish control of the Deccan in any meaningful manner.

It is true that Muhammad's successor, Firuz Shah attempted to reverse the trend within his limited personal capacity. However, the second cause for the disintegration of the empire was the cumulative effects of the policies of Firuz Shah. His innate tendency to be lenient towards miscreants; exaggerated religious intolerance towards non-Muslims; and the revival of the feudal system that directly impaired the efficiency of the army, which was the mainstay of the Sultanate, completely weakened the central administrative control to a point beyond possible repair. The third reason is also related to Firuz Shah. Bluntly put, he lived for too long a period of time—so much so that his two elder sons, who were both efficient princes, predeceased him. Firuz was left with a pleasure-loving and ineffectual son to succeed him. In addition, Firuz did not make even a token attempt at preparing his surviving son to take on the mantle of the sultan through education and training.

This ineptitude in mentoring a worthy successor led to the fourth reason for the collapse of the Tughluq dynasty. Only incompetent non-entities followed Firuz to the throne. They were all prone to being manipulated by selfish, but powerful nobles who were also equally inept at administration and lacking in political acumen. Rival groups shadow boxed with each other in an attempt to increase their influence and prestige, while at the same time not one individual of calibre was thrown up from the large number of court hangers on and the swelling ranks of the nobility to save the Empire. It is seen throughout history that great and lasting empires invariably have available a pool of talented and dedicated nobles who rise up in times of need to selflessly buttress the foundations of the kingdom. The Tughluq dynasty did not have the luxury of such support, a situation that was self-created since foresight was lacking in the Sultans.

The fifth cause for the rapid decline was that Firuz adopted the traditional style of governance—that of centralised despotism—but did not have the strength of character and ruthlessness necessary to make an autocratic centralised rule work efficiently. Despotism of all kinds require leadership that can only be delivered by a man of great inner strength, resolute character, an excellent work ethic and extreme decisiveness. In this kind of governance, any weakness in the monarch very rapidly spreads through the entire body of the administration. The Delhi Sultanate became a moth-ridden administrative state during Firuz Shah's long rule. The sixth reason, and perhaps one of the most important factor that led to the extinction of the dynasty was also inflicted by Firuz Shah. Under his long rule, the army of the Sultanate ceased to be the primary instrument of state power. With the power of the army being eroded, the awe of royal authority— necessary to exercise power—diminished to an extent of being non-existent. The Sultanate was a traditional police state, built on the power of the army to collect taxes in return for ensuring law and order that provided a reasonably secure life for the subjects. Even in the autocratic monarchical system of governance, there was an indelible covenant between the ruler and the ruled. A weak army broke this covenant because it could not discharge its end of the bargain, with the result the very reason for the existence of the Sultanate started to get questioned. The cohesiveness necessary for a kingdom to hold together got lost along with the diminished stature and capability of the army.

The seventh factor which contributed to the rapid decline of the dynasty was the inability of Firuz and his successors to quell the rebellions that were erupting across the entire territory of the Sultanate. Rebellions in the Deccan continued unabated. It needed the iron hand of someone like Ala ud-Din Khilji to put it down and enforce the will of the Delhi Sultan. The Tughluqs did not produce such a person of calibre and determination at the hour of their greatest need. The uncontrolled and unquestioned Deccan rebellions became the blue print for the chieftains of the north to emulate. The result was that the entire Sultanate was in rebellion almost perpetually.

The eighth reason was that the Hindu chiefs, who had now been subjugated for nearly two centuries had not yet given up their attempts to evict the 'foreign' invaders. Despite the integration that was taking place across the entire spectrum of society, the Muslim aristocracy was still considered 'outsiders', although by now most of them were born in the sub-continent. Some of them, like Firuz Shah, were also of mixed parentage—both in ethnicity and religion. Ranthambhor is a classic example of this resistance and rebellion. The fort was only subdued after 150 years of obstinate defiance. Similarly the Doab, situated very near Delhi, was always restive and never fully submissive. Immediately on the Hindu chiefs perceiving the weakness that was encroaching on Delhi, Rajasthan broke free, its many principalities declaring independence. Gwalior and other Hindu holdings were not far behind in following suit.

The individual and combined onslaught of these somewhat disparate, but intertwined, factors brought the Tughluq dynasty to its knees. Their cumulative effects made the dynasty ready to be deposed. The surprising fact was that it took so long for the actual act to take place.

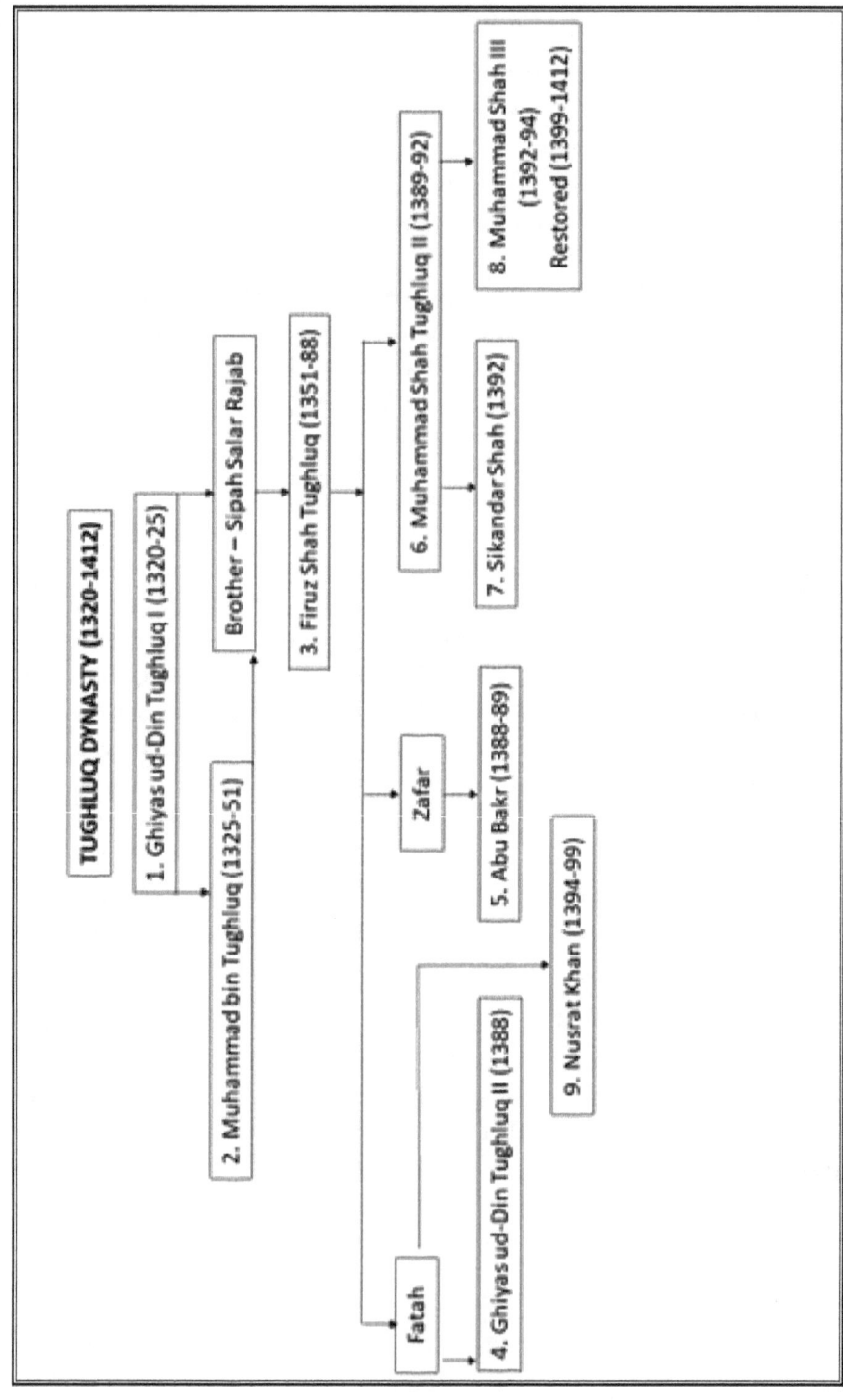

Chapter 23

THE DISINTEGRATED SULTANATE

Even though Timur had ravaged the land and sacked Delhi, for a few more years after his departure the Tughluqs continued their internecine war for control of the Sultanate. A little over a decade later, Khizr Khan, who had been appointed by Timur as the governor of Multan, but left without an army, managed to claim the throne of Delhi. However, the Sultanate was not an imperial power anymore. Territorially it consisted of a small part of Western Uttar Pradesh and Khizr Khan brought with him control of most of the areas of Punjab and Sindh. The core Sultanate was not the strongest or most powerful of the many kingdoms into which the once-great empire had splintered. Therefore, at this juncture in the narrative history of the Delhi Sultanate it becomes necessary to analyse the various independent kingdoms before continuing the account.

At the time of the chaotic fall of the Tughluqs, the kingdoms of the sub-continent could be divided into four well-defined and independent groups:

- The Hindu states of the Rajputana region, where Mewar (modern-day Udaipur) was the dominant power;

- The Muslim states of Gujarat and Malwa;

- The southern states in the Deccan—the Muslim Bahmani kingdom and the Hindu Vijayanagar Empire; and

- The kingdoms of the East—Gondwana, Orissa, Bengal and Jaunpur.

(The Vijayanagar Empire and the Bahmani kingdom will be studied in detail in the next volume of this series.)

At the height of its power, the Bahmani kingdom exerted great influence on both Gujarat and Malwa. Its power and geographic location prevented both Gujarat and Malwa from threatening a weakened Delhi Sultanate since their own capitals were within striking distance from the Bahmani kingdom. Any prolonged absence of their armies, which would have been necessary to mount an expedition against Delhi, would have made it easy for the Bahmani kingdom to capture either Gujarat or Malwa. The respite that the Delhi Sultanate got as a result of this triangular contest for hegemony gave the Delhi Sultans the time needed to facilitate shoring up their resources to hold on to their diminished sultanate as an independent entity. However, by the end of the 15th century, the once strong Bahmani kingdom had started to break up into small principalities, which were almost completely subsumed by internecine wars.

The eastern kingdoms did not play any significant role or have any lasting influence on the history of the Delhi Sultanate. However, the Rajputana region with its war-like principalities; as well as Malwa, Gujarat and Jaunpur were intimately connected to the history of the Sultanate, playing significantly influential and important roles in their own manner.

The Rajputana Region

The Rajputana region, currently called the state of Rajasthan in India, covered more territory than the borders of the modern state indicates. It was predominantly a Hindu region that housed a large number of principalities, flanked by Gujarat in the south-west and Malwa in the south-east. During the early 15th century, the Hindu kingdoms were hard pressed by both these Muslim states. Gujarat was powerful and the champion of Islam in the west. Most of the Rajputana principalities had to buy peace from its aggression at different times.

There are two fundamental and enduring factors that enveloped Rajputana as a whole. The first was its indomitable spirit of independence. The leading light in this rebellious streak was the kingdom of Mewar with its capital at Chittor. Early in the 14th century,

Ala ud-Din Khilji subdued and occupied Chittor. However, within a decade or so, in 1321, Hamir Rana of Sesoda, reoccupied Chittor and consolidated his rule over the principalities surrounding Mewar. He then assumed the title of Maharana. Unfortunately, on Hamir's death, of old age after a long rule, in 1364, the family lapsed into the second factor that was endemic to the region and an age-old tradition of Rajput clans—they went into a period of internecine warfare, blood feuds and political assassinations.

Rana Khumbha

After nearly six decades of chaos and confusion, Rana Khumbha ascended the throne of Mewar in 1433. He went on to become one of the most famous and celebrated rulers of Rajputana. Rana Khumbha was a great warrior, an accomplished poet and musician, a man of letters, and a builder of magnificent buildings. Some of the finest monuments still seen in the Mewar region is attributed to Rana Khumbha. He defeated other minor Rajput chieftains and consolidated the region into one kingdom under a central rule. He also defeated the ruler of Malwa and erected a 'Jayasthamba' or 'Victory Tower' to commemorate the battlefield victory. Of the 84 forts that defended the kingdom of Mewar, 32 were built during the reign of Rana Khumbha, with the fort of Khumbalgarh being named after him.

In a strange twist of fate, this well-liked and powerful king was murdered by his own son Udaya, who was impatient and did not want to wait for the passing of his father to claim the throne. Once again in a sort of 'getting his just desserts', the nobles of the court declared Udaya ineligible to ascend the throne and disqualified him. Khumbha's second son Rai Mal was elevated to the throne. Rai Mal's rule was stable from an external perspective since there were no invasions or attacks on the kingdom. However, his reign was plagued by internal disturbances as a result of family feuds within the royal household. Rai Mal's three sons were continually at loggerheads and jockeying for the position of the heir apparent.

In the end, Rai Mal was succeeded by his eldest son Sangram Singh. Sangram was a brave warrior, able statesman and just ruler. He was held in high esteem by the rulers of all Rajput principalities. Sangram fought and won a number of battles against Delhi, Gujarat and Malwa, thus holding aloft the independent status of the only Hindu kingdom in North India at that time. The extent of Muslim encroachment of the sub-continent can be understood from this single fact. Mewar continued to be an independent and strongly held entity till it was subjugated by the Mughal emperors at a much later date.

Malwa

The kingdom of Malwa lay to the south-west of Delhi. By the 10th century it was ruled by Parmar Rajput kings who became very prominent and made Malwa into one of the leading kingdoms of North India. Rajput Malwa reached the pinnacle of its power under Raja Bhoja of Dhar. After the establishment of the nascent Sultanate in Delhi, it became obvious to the sultans that Malwa had to be brought under their flag. Accordingly, Iltutmish raided Ujjain, the largest city of the kingdom, in 1235. During this raid he demolished the famous Kali temple of Ujjain but did not annex the kingdom, leaving it as a vassal state.

Ala ud-Din Khilji conquered Malwa in 1310 and placed it under a governor. Thereafter, Malwa remained under Muslim governors until the disintegration of the Sultanate after Firuz Shah's ineffective rule. In 1401, the governor of Malwa, Dilawar Khan Ghori a descendant of Muhammad of Ghur, declared independence from the Delhi Sultanate and established a kingdom with its capital at Dhar. Dilawar was succeeded by his son Alap Khan who assumed the title of Hushang Shah. The use of the title 'Shah' indicates the complete independence of the kingdom from any control or connection to the Delhi Sultanate. In any case, by this time the Delhi rulers, still carrying exalted titles were nothing but minor chieftains in actual fact. Hushang Shah transferred the capital to Mandu, a much more defensible fort than Dhar.

Hushang Shah was war-like ruler, although his competence in the battlefield was not commensurate with his ambition. He was involved in a number of conflicts with Gujarat, Jaunpur and Delhi, all of them his neighbours. His invasion of Gujarat was unsuccessful. Subsequently he attempted an attack on Delhi. He was defeated and beaten back by Mubarak Shah who forced him to pay tribute to the Delhi Sultanate. Hushang Shah was succeeded by his son Ghazi Khan (also mentioned as Ghazni Khan in some accounts), who was a worthless debauchee.

Very early in his reign, Ghazi was murdered by his minister Mahmud Khan Khilji who then established the dynasty of Khilji sultans of Malwa.

Mahmud Khilji I was a great warrior and an ambitious ruler. His long reign was almost completely spent waging war to improve the territorial integrity of his kingdom and to enhance its stature within the kingdoms on North India. He waged wars, with some success but without achieving any significant victory, against Ahmad Shah of Gujarat, Rana Khumbha of Mewar, Muhammad Shah Sayyid and later Bahlul Lodi of Delhi and also Muhammad Shah III of the Bahmani kingdom. Malwa under Mahmud Khilji I was an ambitious kingdom, carrying out raids into the east against the Gondwana and Orissa kingdoms. Further, Malwa shared a contiguous border with the Delhi Sultanate and captured some of its territories. Mahmud extended his control up to Kalpi in Bundelkhand. The warrior-spirit and battlefield successes made Mahmud Khilji a prospective ruler of Delhi in the view of some of the Delhi nobles. However, it remained in the speculative stage and nothing more materialised out of this consideration.

Mahmud I was renowned across the land for valour and as an immaculate general in battle. He was also acknowledged as a just and able administrator, and for his generosity as a benign ruler. Malwa prospered under his benevolent and nurturing rule. However, the continuous wars that Mahmud undertook started to show its effect towards the end of his long reign. The indecisive but brutal battles had started to whittle down the strength of Malwa. The passage of time was not kind to this prosperous kingdom, being surrounded by antagonistic neighbours and being on a war-footing for decades made sure that inevitably its strength and stature declined.

A Dubious Claim of Victory

A detailed analysis of Mahmud Khilji I's war against Rana Khumbha of Mewar clearly indicates that the result was indecisive, although the Rajput king held the advantage.

The Rajput chronicles mention a crushing defeat of Mahmud Khilji, which is commemorated by the famous

> Victory Tower erected at Chittor. However, Mahmud also claimed victory in the same battle and erected a seven-storey tower in his capital Mandu. This claim of victory cannot be verified in any way.

Mahmud Khilji I died in 1496 after ruling for 34 years and was succeeded by his son Ghiyas ud-Din who was poisoned by his own son Nasir ud-Din. Nasir ud-Din then ascended the throne in 1500. Both father and son were slothful rulers given to the pleasures of the harem and completely disinterested in the administration of the kingdom. Nasir ud-Din was succeeded by his son Mahmud Khilji II. During Mahmud's reign the Delhi Sultan Sikandar Lodi captured many districts of Malwa after a prolonged war. Around the same time, both Gujarat and Mewar were in ascendancy.

Mahmud II sought the help of the Rajputs to control the Muslim nobility who had become extremely powerful in Malwa. A well-known Rajput noble, Medini Rao, was appointed as the chief minister of Malwa. Over a short period of time he became very powerful in court. The king now started to become apprehensive of Medini Rao's intentions and suspected that he was going to usurp power. Mahmud now requested the king of Gujarat, Muzaffar Shah for help to expel Medini Rao and re-establish his own power. Sensing an impending attack, Medini Rao asked the Rana of Mewar, Sangram Singh, for help and defeated his own king's army. Mahmud Khilji II was captured and taken to Chittor by Rana Sangha who had led the expedition.

The Mewar king displayed the inherent magnanimity of a Rajput and not only released Mahmud, but reinstated him to the throne after restoring his kingdom. Mahmud Khilji II did not display any vestige of gratitude and led an invasion of Mewar during the reign of Rana Sangha's successor. However, the expedition was indecisive and Mahmud returned to his by now considerably reduced kingdom. Mahmud gave shelter to the rebellious brother of Bahadur Shah, then ruling Gujarat and an ally of Mewar. Incensed with this action, Bahadur Shah attacked Malwa and captured the kingdom. Mahmud Khilji II was captured and executed. All male members of the royal family were put to death and Malwa was annexed to Gujarat. It remained part of the kingdom of Gujarat thereafter till Gujarat itself was conquered by the Mughal emperor Humayun.

Gujarat

The region of Gujarat is blessed with fertile land and its large coastline supports commercial and maritime activity. The ports of Cambay, Surat and Broach have been the centres of overseas trade from time immemorial—through them flowed commerce between Asia and Europe. The coast of Gujarat was known to early Greek traders and Baryagaza or Bharukacha, now Broach, is mentioned as the gateway for trade with India in ancient manuscripts. The kingdom therefore was immensely wealthy that in turn always attracted foreign invaders.

Mahmud of Ghazni was the first Muslim invader to plunder Gujarat. His notorious raid on the famous Somnath Temple was only the prelude to further Muslim invasions and sackings. Muhammad of Ghur invaded Gujarat in 1196. However, it was only in 1297 that a semi-permanent conquest of Gujarat was effected by Ala ud-Din Khilji who annexed the territory to the Delhi Sultanate. Gujarat remained under the rule of Muslim governors who were subordinate to the Delhi Sultans from then. The loyalty of the governors to Delhi and their status of autonomy fluctuated with the strength and weakness of the Delhi Sultanate. In the confusion that followed the capture and sacking of Delhi by Timur's forces, Zafar Khan, the then governor of Gujarat and a convert to Islam from the Tauk clan of Rajputs, declared independence in 1401. He formally withdrew allegiance to the Delhi Sultan.

Gujarat at the Time of its Separation from Delhi

The territory over which Zafar Khan declared his authority was small, even by the standards of the day when small principalities abounded. The north-west border was shared between the Rajput kingdoms of Jalor and Sirohi. The western part of the hills were under the Raja of Idar while the rest of the hills were held by Bhils and Kols, ferocious tribal groups. Some Rajput princes had also formed petty

> states amongst the tribal groups. The Kathiawar peninsula was controlled by few Hindu clans from Kacha and Sindh, who had occupied the region centuries back.
>
> Zafar Khan controlled a narrow strip of land that sat between the hills and the sea. The eastern part of this petty strip of land formed part of the kingdom of the Raja of Champanir.

The bane of most Muslim dynasties—that of patricide—did not spare Zafar Khan. His son Tartar Khan, with the assistance of some disgruntled nobles, captured and imprisoned Zafar Khan. He ascended the throne as Nasir ud-Din Muhammad Shah. Nasir's rule was short-lived since he was poisoned by a noble loyal to his father. Zafar was brought out of captivity and continued his rule under the title Muzaffar Shah. He undertook a number of expeditions to various borders of his tiny kingdom to consolidate his power and control of territory. Four years later, he was poisoned by his grandson Ahmad Shah.

Ahmad Shah

Although not the first king of an independent Gujarat, Ahmad Shah can be considered in all respects to be the founder of independent Gujarat. He was a brave and warlike king and spend almost his entire life waging war and expanding the boundaries of the kingdom that he had both usurped and inherited in an indirect manner. He administered the state with great sagacity and shifted the capital to Karnawati on the banks of the River Sabarmati, renaming it Ahmadabad. However, he was a bigoted ruler, waging relentless war against all non-believers. Even though he was a just and magnanimous ruler of the Muslim population, he considered it his religious duty to wage war against the Hindus and to destroy temples. Surprisingly for only a third-generation convert to Islam, he propagated Islam zealously. The enthusiasm for Islam could also be attributed to the fact that local converts had to display greater support to the religion than Muslim nobles who came to the sub-continent from Central Asia in order to establish their religious credentials.

Ahmad Shah waged war with all his neighbours and was victorious in most battles. The victories enhanced the wealth and stature of Gujarat, entrenching it as a notable and independent nation. Ahmad Shah was succeeded by his eldest son Muhammad Shah who was an inept ruler. He lost a battle when he invaded Champanir and shortly thereafter was poisoned by some nobles who conspired against him. Muhammad Shah's son, Qutb ud-Din was placed on the throne and ruled for just eight years, the time being mainly spent in waging a long drawn war with Mewar. He was succeeded by Daud, his uncle and a notorious profligate, who was removed from the throne by the nobles within a few weeks. Another grandson of Ahmad Shah, Mahmud, was then placed on the throne.

Exploits of Mahmud Bighara

Mahmud was by far the greatest of the Gujarat sultans, ruling for 53 years and gaining a great deal of military glory. He is also praised in contemporary chronicles for his gallantry, generosity and love of justice. He is also reported as having been excessively found of food. His military exploits were legendary. He saved Nizam Shah Bahmani from an attack by Mahmud Khilji of Malwa; captured Pardi near Daman; attacked Rai Mandalik of Junagarh, capturing and annexing Surat to his domain; and invaded Kutchch, subjugating the Sumra and Sodha chiefs there. He then went on to subdue and punish the pirates operating off the coast of Jagat (Dwarka).

Mahmud subsequently send a raiding party into Champanir territory. When a commander was killed in the skirmish, Mahmud declared war against Champanir and proceeded personally towards the country. The Malwa ruler had come to aid of the king of Champanir, but on the arrival of the Gujarat forces, withdrew to his own territory. The Rawal of Champanir put up resistance and fought gallantly for some days, but ultimately surrendered. Mahmud had the entire garrison put to the sword and renamed the town Muhammadabad.

Towards the end of his reign Mahmud led an expedition against the Portuguese who had established a small holding on the west coast. Vasco da Gama had discovered the sea route to India in 1498 and the Portuguese had managed to establish footholds in Cambay and

Chaul. The Portuguese were intent on cutting off the trade of the Muslims in Gujarat, wanting to establish a monopoly in the spice trade for themselves. This move was bound to adversely impact the Indian trade, which made it imperative for Mahmud to initiate action against them. Mahmud Bighara, as he has also been called in a number of contemporary accounts, allied himself with the sultan of Egypt, Qansu Ghori for the ensuing battle. The combined navies of Gujarat and Egypt defeated the Portuguese fleet. However, the very next year a reverse defeat took place and Mahmud was forced to grant land for a 'factory' to be built in Diu by the Portuguese.

Mahmud Bighara died in 1511 and was succeeded by his son Muzaffar Shah II. Muzaffar successfully interfered and thwarted a Hindu attempt at dominating Malwa, but went on to engage in a disastrous war with Mewar. Rana Sangram Singh invaded Gujarat, captured Idar and sacked Ahmadabad. A see-saw war ensued with Muzaffar striking back with alacrity. In the meantime, Muzaffar's son Bahadur felt that he was not being given sufficient recognition and fled to Ibrahim Lodi in Delhi. This led to further political turmoil in Gujarat that continued till Babur the Mughal arrived on the scene.

Gujarat was geographically cut off from Delhi by Malwa and Rajasthan. Therefore, the Gujarat rulers did not harbour any ambitions or aspirations to capture the throne of Delhi. Indirectly the Delhi Sultanate benefitted for a strong Gujarat since Malwa and Mewar could not attack Delhi without leaving their flank open for Gujarat to exploit.

Jaunpur

The territory of Jaunpur had its capital of the same name, built by Firuz Shah, situated on the River Gomti about 34 miles north-west of Varanasi (see chapter titled *Firuz Shah Tughluq: Military Endeavours*). Mahmud Tughluq had send Kwaja Jahan Sarwar to Jaunpur to suppress the rebellious chiefs, bestowing on him the title Malik-ul-Sharq. He was very successful in subduing the rebels and soon brought a large swath of territory—spreading from Kol in the west to Tirhut in Bihar—under his control. Although he did not declare independence from Delhi, he cut off all ties with the Sultanate and ruled the territory. He pointedly did not send any assistance to Delhi during its disastrous sacking by Timur, thereby asserting his independence.

Malik-ul-Sharq was succeeded by his adopted son who assumed the title Mubarak Shah and then by Shams ud-Din Ibrahim Sharqi. Shams ud-Din fought the Tughluq army of Mahmud and managed to hold on to the territories that he had inherited. His rule of 40 years was the most stable and prosperous times for Jaunpur. Shams ud-Din's son succeeded him and while on the throne attempted to dethrone Bahlul Lodi then ruling in Delhi. This resulted in a protracted struggle between Delhi and Jaunpur that lasted for more than a quarter century without throwing up any clear victor. However, the conflict debilitated both the kingdoms. The last Jaunpur king was Sultan Husian who made a determined attempt to invade Delhi in 1479. However, he was soundly defeated and Jaunpur was annexed to the Delhi Sultanate, ceasing to be an independent kingdom. Even though Jaunpur had existed as an independent kingdom for a mere 80 years (1399-1479), during this time it had proven to be one of the biggest trouble makers for the Delhi Sultanate.

Conclusion

Throughout the rule of the Sayyids and Lodis in Delhi, the north and western part of the Indian sub-continent remained fragmented. During this time both Muslim and Hindu ruling houses proliferated in the region, some of them reigning over really miniscule and completely insignificant territories as 'independent' kingdoms. These minor principalities, long on claims of royalty and short of everything else that denotes sovereignty, fought each other and the Sultanate on a continuous basis. The result was that the environment was hostile and did not permit the rise of a single entity with sufficient strength to unify the fractious sub-continent. Continuous wars, in which no one came out as a clear winner, bled the strength of all participants. This state of affairs continued for more than a century. The end-result was that there was not one powerful kingdom left that could sweep up the rest and create a viable empire or no dynasty strong enough to withstand the coming onslaught.

In the Deccan, the Bahmani kingdom and the Empire of Vijayanagara stood as strong bastions against any possible military incursions south of the Vindhya Ranges. North India was fragmented and bereft of any strength. The situation was ripe for an ambitious and adventurous general to take advantage of—and that is exactly what Babur the Mughal did.

THE INSIGNIFICANT SAYYIDS

The Delhi Sulatanate was no longer an empire at the time of Khizr Khan's accession, but ony one of the many kingdoms into which the subcontinent had fragmented in the closing years of the Tughluq dynasty.

Abraham Eraly,
The Age of Wrath, p. 207

The Sultanate during the Sayyid Rule

Chapter 24

KHIZR KHAN SAYYID

When Timur 'the Scourge of God' departed India, the Delhi Sultanate was in an appalling state of disintegration. The once large empire had fragmented into small independent states, some of which were larger than the core Delhi Sultanate itself. Even so, the Sultanate endured for another 114 years, mostly in perilous condition, till Babur the Mughal wiped it away and established the Mughal Empire in India. Following the death of Sultan Mahmud, there followed two years of chaotic interregnum before two successor dynasties came to power—first, the Sayyids ruling for 37 years under four successive sultans; followed by the Lodis ruling for 75 years under three sultans.

Sultan Khizr Khan Sayyid

Khizr Khan Sayyid founded the dynasty named after the appellation with his name that signified his descend from the Prophet Muhammad—the Sayyid Dynasty. The veracity of this claim of descent from the Prophet is not readily ascertainable and is therefore uncertain. Khizr Khan's ancestors had indeed come from Arabia, migrating to India during the early part of the Tughluq rule. They had settled in Multan and Malik Suleiman, Khizr Khan's father, had been appointed the governor of Multan by later Tughluq rulers. Khizr Khan inherited the position on his father's death, but managed to lose it during the confusion that followed Firuz Shah's death in Delhi. During that chaotic time, Sarang Khan, the brother of Mallu Iqbal Khan the strongman of Delhi, captured Khizr Khan and took over the governorship of Multan. Khizr Khan however, managed to escape.

After escaping captivity, Khizr joined Timur during his return trip from the sack of Delhi. On Timur's final departure, Khizr regained his previous position when he was once again appointed governor of Multan. He stayed in the position and on the death of Mahmud, the last Tughluq ruler, he overthrew Daulta Khan who had come to the throne of Delhi and ascended the throne as Sultan Khizr Khan Sayyid.

Khizr Khan held fast to the conviction that he owed his power and prestige to Timur's patronage and did not assume the title of king or sultan. He titled himself 'Ravat-i-Ala' meaning 'sublime banners' and although in reality independent, pretended to be the viceroy of Shah Rukh, Timur's son then ruling the Timurid Empire. He also continued to send yearly tribute to Shah Rukh. Khizr did not strike new coins, which had the added advantage of facilitating the continuation of the old and established financial system. However, the lack of assertiveness on his part also revealed an inherent weakness and lack of self-confidence on the part of the new sultan. Part of this problem could be attributed to the fact that Khizr faced a hostile court of Turkish and Afghan nobles in Delhi, who considered him an upstart and follower of the despised tyrant Timur. However, since he was already the governor of Multan and the governors of Punjab and Sindh had supported him, these provinces automatically became part of the Delhi Sultanate, greatly increasing the territorial holdings.

Sultanate in Dire Straits

Even though a new Sultan had ascended the throne, the process of the Sultanate's disintegration continued unabated. In Delhi, the nobles continued their mad scramble for power, changing allegiances rapidly and regularly. Sordid ambitions were nakedly visible and led to unprincipled opportunism and the focused pursuit of pure self-interest. Since the days of the mighty Balban, the Doab had been the most restive region under the Sultanate. During the confusion of the last days of the Tughluq dynasty, Rajput chieftains of the Rathor clan had become independent rulers in Etawah, Katehar, Kanauj and Badayun. They stirred rebellions on a regular basis, necessitating the repeated mounting of punitive expeditions by the Delhi Sultans. These expeditions were required to bring a semblance of order to the region but were never entirely successful.

By the end of the 14th century, the kingdoms of Malwa, Jaunpur and Gujarat had acknowledged independent status. They were not only engaged in fighting each other and other neighbours but regularly encroached on Delhi territory. Multan and Lahore had come under the control of Jasrat Khokhar, who paid scant attention to Delhi and established independent control by taking advantage of the prevalent chaos. Around Delhi, the Mewatis were seething with discontent. This was the state of the Sultanate that Khizr Khan had captured.

Stabilisation Attempts

Khizr Khan was pragmatic enough to accept the diminished state of the Sultanate and mindful of the fact that he only controlled a small territory around Delhi. Further, he was devoid of the large amount of resources necessary to attempt any major campaigns to recapture seceded regions and return them to the Sultanate fold. He could only attempt minor expeditions with the very limited objective of gathering arears of revenue from the small-time chieftains. Even these minor forays were not always successful. Khizr Khan's minister Taj-ul-Mulk carried out few raids against the Rajput rulers in Etawah and Katehar with limited success. He managed to collect some amount of revenue, but did not attempt any permanent subjugation or annexation.

At this juncture, as if to create a further debacle for the embattled Sultan, the northern frontier erupted in violence. In 1416, a group of Turkbachchas assassinated Malik Sadhu Nadira, the deputy of Prince Mubarak. On the arrival of Delhi forces to quell the rebellion they fled to the mountains. However, they renewed their rebellion under the command of Tughan Rais. The forces loyal to Delhi managed to suppress the rebellion and Tughan Rais was forced to accept vassal status. To ensure his loyalty in the future, his son was taken and kept as a hostage in Delhi. However, treachery and rebellions continued unabated across the entire Sultanate.

Khizr Khan and his indefatigable minister Taj-ul-Mulk continued to lead punitive expeditions against rebels in order to contain the fires that were being lit on a regular basis. These expeditions, undertaken at enormous cost to a depleted exchequer, were never able to fully extinguish the rebellions, nor were they able to control the chieftains even after they were defeated in battle. The Delhi Sultanate lacked the resources to follow through on battlefield victories and had to be content with minimal tributes that were paid by defeated chiefs and rulers. This situation permitted the chieftains to invariably bounce back and commence yet another rebellion. This was an endless cycle that sapped the strength and resources of an embattled Sultan.

The Nagaur Campaign

The only long distance campaign that Khizr Khan attempted was an expedition that he led towards Nagaur on the appeal by its ruler for assistance against an incursion by Ahmad Shah of Gujarat. On the approach of Khizr Khan's army, Ahmad Shah withdrew to Gujarat without offering battle. Some narratives proclaim this withdrawal as Khizr Khan's victory. However, this is a tenuous claim and it is difficult to accept this verdict of a 'victory'. At the time of this episode, the Hindu kings of Idar, Champaner, Jhalawar and Nagaur had formed a confederacy to oppose Ahmad Shah who was perpetuating religious intolerance against the Hindus in Gujrat and neighbouring areas. They were also joined by the Muslim ruler of Malwa, who had also been on the receiving end of Ahmad Shah's offensives. Since the neighbourhood was hostile to him, Ahmad Shah could not have stayed away from Gujarat for a lengthy period of time. This was more so since Malwa was also opposed to him. Therefore the strategic retreat to Gujarat was self-imposed and not really a military victory for the Delhi forces.

In any case, Nagaur accepted Delhi suzerainty although it changed allegiance to Gujarat a mere two years later when it was threatened by Malwa. Even though no battle had been fought or won, the long march out of Delhi and the withdrawal of Ahmad Shah to Gujarat on the arrival of the Delhi forces has a salutary effect on some of the minor chieftains of the region, who submitted to Delhi control without resistance. In the last year of his reign Khizr Khan raided Mewat and destroyed a fortress at Kotla. He went on to sack Gwalior and collected some tribute. This was a show of force that indicated the gradual revival of the power of the Delhi Sultanate. However, Khizr Khan was already a sick man and on his return to Delhi, took to his bed and died on 20 May 1421.

Khizr Khan – The Reluctant Sultan

Khizr Khan genuinely believed that he owed his stature to the largesse of Timur and therefore displayed unswerving loyalty to Timur and his descendants throughout his life. He was not enamoured by the trappings of power and did not even assume the title of 'sultan', living life in the true style of a Sayyid. It was the substance of power that mattered to Khizr Khan and all his policies were marked by prudence and rectitude. In matters of state he displayed remarkably similar traits to that of Firuz Shah—caution, moderation and benevolence. He also displayed an exemplary sense of justice, treating even rivals and adversaries with fairness and generosity. On ascending the throne, he treated the top officials of the Tughluq regime honourably, not shedding blood unnecessarily and not committing any atrocities that usually accompanied the usurpation of the throne. It is also noteworthy that Khizr Khan was free of all the common vices that afflicted the royalty of the time.

When Khizr Khan came to the throne of Delhi, the Sultanate was just one among the many kingdoms that littered the fragmented North India. He made cautious moves to expand territorial holdings, not with much success. Khizr Khan was a sensible monarch and had the good sense to clearly judge and separate the possible from the impossible, prudently tailoring his policies accordingly. He recognised the constraints under which he would have to operate and understood the importance of pursuing one objective at a time. The brutal truth was that the Sultanate did not have the resources necessary to pursue multiple objectives simultaneously. Khizr Khan only attempted to collect revenue from territories close to Delhi, resources that were essential for him to stay on as Sultan. His military expeditions were all oriented towards achieving this aim. Khizr did not formulate any grandiose or ambitious military plans. He did not attempt to fight either Gujarat or Jaunpur, both provinces that were fully independent and more powerful than Delhi. Instead, he concentrated on stamping out sedition within his reach.

While a traditional sultan of the times, he was also liked by his subjects for his thoughtful kindness and attention to their welfare—a trait that was not common amongst rulers in medieval times. His short seven-year rule was on the whole a positive period for the Sultanate, with some very minor developments towards stability taking place. He was unable to restore the prestige of the Sultanate—the odds against him were too high; and his personal abilities and capacity to be decisive under stress could not match the need of the hour. In fact the situation in the Sultanate had deteriorated to such an extent that Khizr Khan was constrained to requisition the services of some Afghan warlords in order to stay in power. Unfortunately, while this move ensured the fragile stability of his rule, it resulted in the ascendancy of the Afghan nobles in the administration. This progression proved disastrous in the long run for the continuance of the Sayyid dynasty.

Chapter 25

MUIZ UD-DIN ABDUL FATEH SULTAN MUBARAK SHAH

Khizr Khan nominated his son Mubarak Khan as his successor on his death bed. Mubarak assumed the throne as Muiz u-Din Fateh Mubarak Shah, with the consent of all the nobles of the court. The details of his reign are available to the historian from a chronicle called *Tarikh-i-Mubarak Shahi* written by one Yahya bin Ahmed who was Mubarak's contemporary. This book forms the main source of information for all aspects of Mubarak's rule. Unlike his father, Mubarak assumed the title of Shah and also issued his own coins, breaking away from the direct influence of the Central Asian caliphate. However, Mubarak Shah was astute enough to continue to acknowledge Sultan Shah Rukh as his overlord and also to pay tribute when deemed necessary.

The fragile kingdom continued to be threatened from all sides. Even though Mubarak proved to be a spirited ruler with energy, he was not up to the task of consolidating the Sultanate or to deal with all the troubles that it faced.

The Saga of the Rebellious Jasrat Khokhar

Almost immediately after Mubarak inherited the throne, Jasrat Khokhar the son of Shaikha Khokhar, controlling the region around Sialkot rebelled. The Khokhar clan lived in the valleys associated with the Rivers Jhelum and Chenab in the Punjab. Jasrat had courageously opposed Timur during the latter's return march. However, he had been defeated by the Timurid army and forced to flee to the shelter of his father's court. Jasrat now took advantage of the pervasive weakness of Delhi and regularly continued to add minor territories to his own holdings when opportunity to do so presented itself.

The Khokhars were also sporadically involved in the affairs of the kingdom of Kashmir. During a civil war in Kashmir, Jasrat backed one prince who happened to come out the winner in the struggle for the throne. Jasrat gained a large booty for his troubles and more importantly got the friendship of the new king of Kashmir. This increase in strength and stature made Jasrat dream of capturing the throne of Delhi from the weak Sayyid ruler. The dream was further emboldened when Tughan Rais joined him with a large force. With this enhanced force Jasrat moved east—he crossed the Rivers Ravi, Beas and the Sutlej, attacked the governor of Ludhiana at Talwandi and drove him east. Jasrat then ravaged the countryside up to the town of Rupar and laid siege to Jalandhar.

Jalandhar had been captured from Tughan Rais by Zirak Khan, one of Khizr Khan's trusted generals. Zirak could not withstand the siege and sued for peace. Zirak Khan however, was treacherously captured and imprisoned by the Jasrat-Tughan combine. Jasrat then proceeded to Sirhind and laid siege to the township. Here the Khokhar forces met stubborn opposition from Islam Khan Lodi, manning the fort at Sirhind. Lodi appealed for help to Mubarak Shah, who was finally stung into action.

Mubarak marched to Sirhind via Samana. On being notified of the Delhi army's movements, Jasrat lifted the siege and retreated to Ludhiana. Mubarak, now joined by Zirak Khan who had escaped from captivity, pursued Jasrat to Ludhiana. Jasrat retreated further and crossed the River Sutlej after collecting all available boats. Mubarak could not pursue him across the river since it was in spate and there were no boats available. However, he followed the river on his side, keeping pace with the movement of Jasrat Khokhar and his army on the opposite bank. When the rains abated and the river became fordable, Jasrat was put to flight by Mubarak and the Delhi army. Jasrat retreated to the foothills of the Kashmir highlands and fortified himself in the citadel at Talwara. Mubarak attacked and captured Talwara, sacking it and destroying its fort, while Jasrat managed to escape. Subsequently

Mubarak proceeded to Lahore, spending three months there fortifying the city and renaming it Mubarakabad, before finally returning to Delhi.

Jasrat Khokhar was enraged at the sack of his stronghold at Talwara. He collected a large army and besieged Lahore. However, two attacks on the city proved to be unsuccessful. Once again he withdrew from the siege and took refuge in the hills surrounding Talwara. Some Muslim nobles attempted to capture him, but the wily Khokhar evaded capture and escaped. At this stage, Mubarak had turned his attention to bring order to Katehar. Jasrat took advantage of Mubarak's preoccupation and once again undertook an extensive campaign. He first attacked Jammu, killed the ruling king, Rai Bhim, and gathered huge wealth and arms. Thereafter he proceeded to sack Dipalpur and then moved towards Lahore. However, the new governor of Lahore. Malik Sikandar Tuhfa put up a fierce resistance, making the Khokhar army to retreat.

Jasrat was now convinced that he could not take on the Delhi army on his own and kept a low profile for a number of years. During this period he was in continuous touch with a number of Afghan nobles and chiefs, seeking their assistance to invade the Delhi Sultanate. Jasrat outlived Mubarak Shah, but did not have any further success in achieving his ambition to capture the throne of Delhi. In 1442, he was murdered by his queen, the daughter of Rai Bhim of Jammu, who had always wanted to avenge her father's death at the Khokhar's hands.

Subduing the Doab

For nearly two years after his accession to the throne, Mubarak Shah was occupied with the events in the Punjab. For some years before Mubarak came to the throne, minor rajas and chiefs of the Doab, predominantly in the Uttar Pradesh region had taken advantage of the weakness of the central administration and stopped paying tribute to Delhi. Doab, eternally rebellious, had erupted yet again during the two-year period that Mubarak was preoccupied with Jasrat Khokhar in the Punjab. Having controlled the Khokhar chief to a manageable level, Mubarak now turned his attention to subduing the Doab and areas surrounding it. An underlying reason for turning the focus on to the Doab was that Jaunpur had now become extremely powerful and controlled the entire eastern part of Uttar Pradesh. The Jaunpur ruler would have to be defeated to bring the eastern part of the old Sultanate back under Delhi control. The Sayyids were unfortunately too weak even to contemplate such an expedition, let alone attempt it. Therefore, they concentrated their efforts on the western part, the Doab.

In 1423, as stated earlier, Mubarak marched into Katehar and subjugated the local chieftains forcing them to pay tribute. This interlude also provided a respite for Mubarak from dealing with the active rebel, Jasrat Khokhar. From Katehar the Delhi army crossed the River Ganga and marched into the territory of the Rathors, ravaging the lands along the way. The Rathor chief Deva Rai fled to Etawah but subsequently submitted to Mubarak and paid tribute. Satisfied with this success, Mubarak returned to Delhi.

While Mubarak was in the Doab, trouble was brewing in the kingdoms to the south of Delhi. Sultan Hoshang Shah, then ruling Malwa, was a habitually restless king and had been at war with all his neighbours at one time or the other. He now attacked Gwalior. Although Gwalior was deemed to be part of the Delhi Sultanate, in actual fact it was an independent kingdom. Neither did Gwalior pay tribute to Delhi, nor were they totally loyal to the rulers in Delhi. Mubarak perceived an opportunity to bring Gwalior under his ambit and proceeded to Gwalior, ostensibly to 'protect' it from Hoshang. On the way he subdued the chief of Bayana, who had rebelled earlier. Bayana was sacked and then the chief was reinstated over a devastated principality.

By the time Mubarak arrived, Hoshang Shah had invested Gwalior. Mubarak captured few prisoners and then set them free calling them 'Muslims'. Hoshang who was reluctant to initiate a battle that he knew to be non-winnable and therefore moved out of Gwalior, soon returning to Malwa. Mubarak continued to stay in the Chambal region for a few more months, levying tributes from the 'infidels'. He then returned to Delhi and once again attacked Katehar. The previous attack and subjugation of Katehar had been two years earlier and in the interim the tributes from the region had dried up. Mubarak went on a plundering rampage across the country, reaching the foothills of Kumaon. There he compelled the ruler Rai Har Singh to pay tribute and an accumulated amount totalling to three years' revenue.

While Mubarak had been busy in the Chambal, the Mewatis were up in arms. After returning to Delhi Mubarak proceeded to Mewat. The Mewatis fled, and in their traditional manner followed a scorched-earth policy in retreat. The Sultan could not therefore pursue the fleeing Mewatis and was forced to return to Delhi. The next year Mubarak returned to Mewat. On his approach, Bahadur Nahar's grandsons, Jalal and Qadr Khans who were now in command, employed the trusted Mewati tactics of laying waste the country and retreated to the fortress at Indur (also called Andwar in some texts). However, this time around Mubarak had come prepared with sufficient supplies and assured logistics. He pursued the retreating Mewatis and defeated them. The Mewatis fled to Alwar. Mubarak 'dismantled' Indur and then laid siege to Alwar. The Khans now sued for peace and obtained a royal pardon. One account states that Qadr Khan was imprisoned and later put to death. However, this report cannot be accurately verified with any other source and may not be accurate.

The Bayana-Jaunpur Coalition

Although he had been subjugated once earlier, seeing that Mubarak was busy in the Doab and Mewat, Muhammad Khan Auhadi the chief of Bayana, once again rebelled. Forces were sent from Delhi to recapture the rebel principality. On the approach of the forces, Auhadi shut himself up in a fortress on top of a hill. However, some deserters from the Auhadi camp showed a secret passage into the fortress to the Delhi forces. The fort was attacked, Auhadi imprisoned, and the Bayana district annexed and divided into two. While the Delhi forces were returning, Auhadi managed to escape and recaptured the fort. The Delhi forces started to march back and Auhadi now requested the king of Jaunpur for assistance. Mubarak himself left Delhi to join his forces in Bayana.

At the same time Ibrahim Sharqi ruling Jaunpur also moved towards Etawah and advanced on Badaun on the other bank of the River Yamuna. For 22 days a game of cat and mouse ensued, with the Delhi and Jaunpur forces moving away and towards each other on opposite banks of the river. Finally Sharqi lost patience and gave battle, which was fought for an entire afternoon with neither side being able to claim decisive victory. It is also reported that Mubarak was overawed by the Jaunpur army's visible strength and did not personally take part in the battle. This report is being discounted in this narrative because of the simple fact that by this time Mubarak had proven himself to be a brave, capable and strategically sound military commander. It is reliably reported that by the end of the day Sharqi returned to his own territory. Such a move would not have been contemplated if the Delhi Sultan was not personally involved in the conflict. Further, considering his courageous stance in many previous battle, it is certain that he would not have 'hidden' from battle.

Auhadi was now left to his own devices and immediately fled to Mewat. Mubarak send an expedition to besiege Mewat. Mewat once again surrendered and paid tribute. Auhadi was taken prisoner and vanishes from the Indian scene thereafter.

Revolt in Bhatinda – Faulad Turkbachcha

One of the most serious rebellion during Mubarak's reign was that of Faulad Turkbachcha. Mubarak's loyal noble, Sayyid Salim was the governor of Bhatinda, where he had amassed large wealth. When Salim died, his sons were in the royal court in Delhi and his slave Turkbachcha took over the administration. After confiscating the extensive wealth of the governor, Turkbachcha revolted against Delhi. He entrenched himself in the fort at Bhatinda after capturing a few places around it. Mubarak Shah send an expedition to bring the rebel to book, but the expedition was soundly defeated by Turkbachcha. The Delhi forces was routed and fled to Sirsuti (modern Sirsa) leaving even their weapons behind.

At this turn of events, Mubarak personally led an army towards Sirsuti where the defeated Delhi army was camped. Faulad now send word to the Sultan that he would surrender. However, before any agreement could be reached, Turkbachcha was falsely informed that Mubarak intended to put him to death after he surrendered. Turkbachcha reneged on his promise of submission. He then sought the assistance of Shaikh Ali, the governor of Kabul, to repel the Delhi army in return for ready money. By this time Bhatinda was besieged. Shaikh Ali moved east with a large army to help Faulad and started to ravage the lands of the nobles engaged in the siege of Bhatinda. One by one these nobles rushed back to protect their own territories from being despoiled. This led to the siege of Bhatinda being raised.

Shaikh Ali was paid 200,000 silver tankas and left Bhatinda. Turkbachcha initiated works to improve the defences of Bhatinda. Shaikh Ali devastated the region on his way back. He crossed the River Sutlej and captured many prisoners in the Ludhiana district. He then went down the River Beas, crossed it and reached Lahore. The governor of Lahore paid tribute and Shaikh Ali moved on to sack Dipalpur. Mubarak send reinforcements to the governor of Multan Imad-ul-Mulk who was preparing to oppose the advance of Shaikh Ali. In a hotly contested battle Shaikh Ali was defeated and lost most of his army. He managed to escape to Shorkot and subsequently returned to Kabul. Imad-ul-Mulk was declared a hero and praised for his achievement.

Mubarak became jealous of Imad-ul-Mulk's popularity with the general population and replaced him with an incompetent noble called Khair ud-Din Khani. Almost immediately, Jasrat Khokhar rebelled and laid siege to Lahore (mentioned earlier in this chapter). Faulad Turkbachcha also rebelled again. However, he was defeated in battle by the troops of Multan, captured, decapitated and his head send to Delhi.

The Murder of Mubarak Shah

Mubarak had made Sarwar-ul-Mulk his Prime Minister and also vested in him the role of finance minister. Sarwar was Mubarak's favourite although he was not very efficient. Further Sarwar-ul-Mulk was a Hindu convert, appointed earlier by Khizr Khan as the governor of Delhi. He was haughty, arrogant, cunning and full of intrigue. He had become the Prime Minister by inducing the Sultan to appoint him to the role while the actual Prime Minster, Sikandar Tuhfa, was out in the Punjab subjugating the Khokhar rebellion. Mubarak had two fatal character flaws in that he was prone to listening to the advice of people who were physically close to him at any given time; and of becoming suspicious of any of his commanders who became successful in putting down rebellions. The successful commanders were invariably transferred so that their popularity could not become entrenched. Gradually this behaviour introduced an element of resentment amongst the competent and loyal nobles.

Following this pattern, Mubarak transferred the finance portfolio to Kamal ud-Din, a successful general who had returned to Delhi with his troops and was in favour with the Sultan at that time. There was a sort of 'flavour of the month' situation prevailing in the Delhi court. The transfer of the finance portfolio was obviously done to reward Kamal ud-Din and, perhaps more importantly, to reduce Sarwar-ul-Mulk's increasing power. The Sayyid Sultans employed their Prime Ministers also as military commanders, which greatly enhanced the power and prestige of the individual holding the position. Mubarak was shrewd enough to understand the great power that Sarwar wielded and wanted to clip his wings. He asked Kamal and Sarwar to work together.

Sarwar was also deprived of the fiefdom of Dipalpur by Mubarak Shah, as part of the Sultan's policy of regular transfer of assignments amongst the nobles. Kamal ud-Din was much more capable than Sarwar-ul-Mulk who became jealous of the former's rising stature. Even though he owed his rise to the Sultan, Sarwar by nature was ungrateful and scheming. He started to plot Mubarak's downfall, conspiring with the Royal Chamberlain and the scions of two rich Khattri families. The group of plotters was joined by some other malcontents in the court. It is obvious that the plot was a joint Hindu-Muslim endeavour planned for personal profit and not religiously motivated. In February 1434, Mubarak went to the site of the new town, Mubarakabad that he was having constructed with only a small escort contingent. He was attacked by few soldiers led by one Sidh Pal, son of a prominent Khattri patriarch Gangu Khattri, and killed instantaneously. Thus ended the reign of a monarch who had tried to do the best he could to hold the disintegrating Sultanate together.

Conclusion

This was a sad end to an unfortunate king who had ruled for little over 12 years in extremely trying conditions. He had attempted to consolidate his father's territorial gains. Mubarak was a brave warrior who was constantly warding off danger to the kingdom from within and without. He was relatively wise and resourceful and fought to maintain the sovereignty of the Sultanate by recognising the strategic points and defending them at all cost. He also reinstituted the federal army locating it under his direct control in Delhi. Without doubt he was the ablest of the Sayyid house. However, his sagacity did not percolate to the administration and treatment of the powerful nobles, which finally led to his murder.

He was a firm Muslim although not a bigot. He patronised the Khattris of Delhi who became the richest group in Delhi under his rule. Unfortunately some of them also joined in the successful plot to kill him. He had also gone to the aid of the Hindu state of Gwalior when it was savagely attacked by Hoshang Shah. This provides proof of his non-religious outlook in matters of foreign policy.

Mubarak Shah did commendable work, managing to hold the Sultanate together as a recognisable entity. Throughout his reign he was preoccupied with warding off potential invaders and stamping out rebellions and incipient revolts. So much so, he had absolutely no spare capacity to address and alleviate the suffering of the common people. At the time when the tide was finally turning in his favour and stability was about to come within his grasp, he was murdered. The benefits that would have definitely come with stability, brought about by his strenuous efforts, was scattered in the wind.

Chapter 26

THE LATER SAYYIDS

Mubarak Shah had no sons and had adopted his nephew, Muhammad bin Farid, as the heir apparent. Sarwar-ul-Mulk who had by this time become very influential, elevated Muhammad to the throne while concentrating all power in his own hands. Sarwar then assumed the title of Khan-i-Jahan, distributed offices of consequence amongst his fellow conspirators and imprisoned any noble who he suspected of being loyal to Mubarak Shah.

Sultan Muhammad Shah

Sarwar-ul-Mulk's rapid rise to supreme power was resented by other nobles of the court, especially since he was Hindu convert to Islam and therefore not part of the influential foreign aristocracy clique. It was not long before the Royal Court turned into a hotbed of conspiracies and rival cabals. One noble, Kamal-ul-Mulk, had stayed loyal to the house of Khizr Khan Sayyid and paid homage to the new king. He concealed his hostility towards Sarwar and bided his time to avenge Mubarak Shah's murder.

Opportunity arrived when Sarwar despatched Kamal in command of some forces to subdue a revolt outside Delhi. Instead of fighting the revolt, Kamal persuaded the rebels to fight under his flag and marched back to Delhi. Sarwar saw the danger of the situation and shut himself up in the fort at Siri. He knew he had lost the support of the army and attempted to murder Muhammad Shah but was immediately killed by the young Sultan's bodyguards. Kamal entered the capitol in triumph. All the conspirators who had sided with Sarwar were captured and tortured to death. A new government was formed and even a second coronation of Muhammad was enacted to emphasise his legitimacy to be Sultan. Kamal-ul-Mulk was made Vizier, Prime Minster, with the title Kamal Khan. All other nobles who had assisted Kamal were rewarded and Muhammad now became a real Sultan, not one in name only.

Muhammad now enjoyed the total support of all the nobles. This would have been a golden opportunity to reorganise the affairs of the Sultanate and bring in stability. However, Muhammad disappointed all his supporters by immersing himself in the pursuit of worldly pleasure. While Muhammad was on a pilgrimage to Multan, he learned of the rebellion of Jasrat Khokhar and send an army to deal with the revolt. At the same time trouble was being stoked in Sirhind by Bahlul Lodi, the governor. Bahlul was the nephew of Islam Khan who had nominated him ahead of his own son Qutab Khan to be his successor. After assuming governorship, Bahlul had gradually turned Sirhind into an Afghan stronghold by inviting Afghan nobles to join him.

Muhammad ordered a loyal general, Malik Sikandar, to march to Sirhind and defeat Bahlul Lodi. In order to achieve this aim, Sikandar allied with the Khokhar chief and attacked Bahlul. Bahlul retreated to the Siwalik Hills. The Delhi army committed great atrocities on the Afghans and then returned to Delhi. Bahlul thereafter turned freebooter and reoccupied Sirhind. Very rapidly Bahlul and his Afghan forces became a threat to the Sultanate. However, Sultan Muhammad was completely immersed in the harem, oblivious of the developing threat in the west. By now, the Sultanate was in the firm grip of disorder and chaos.

At this juncture, Sultan Mahmud Khilji of Malwa advanced towards Delhi and camped at Talpat about 10 miles from Delhi. In Delhi Sultan Muhammad Shah was unnerved and had no other recourse but to request Bahlul to come to his aid. Bahlul grasped the opportunity and arrived near Delhi with 20,000 cavalry. He took over as the de-facto commander of the Delhi forces and entered battle with the Malwa Sultan. For the first few days the battle remained inconclusive. Sultan Muhammad, still unnerved by the proximity of the battle to his capital, now entered the political fray by sending emissaries of peace to Khilji without consulting any of his nobles or Bahlul. Mahmud Khilji was also anxious to end the conflict since he was apprehensive that in his absence his capital Mandu was unprotected and could be threatened by Ahmad Shah of Gujarat. He agreed to the terms offered by the Delhi Sultan and withdrew from battle.

Bahlul, annoyed by the Sultan's unnecessary and unilateral intervention, pursued the retreating Malwa army and managed to capture some baggage as booty. Muhammad Shah, in a display of royal magnanimity and pleasure, praised Bahlul for his action, proclaimed him his 'own son', and bestowed the title of Khan-i-Khan on him. Bahlul was also permitted to occupy most of Punjab. This was a remarkable act of stupidity, since Bahlul's ambition to capture the throne of Delhi was nakedly visible. In Punjab Bahlul came under the influence of Jasrat Khokhar who surreptitiously inflamed the former's already entrenched ambition and instigated him to act on it. Flattered, impatient, and full of his own importance, Bahlul collected a group of Afghans and marched to Delhi. However, his attempt to capture Delhi failed.

Bahlul returned to Sirhind but continued to harbour ambitions towards the throne of Delhi. He declared himself independent ruler and called himself Sultan Bahlul. The Sayyid ruler in Delhi had once again been saved by a miracle but time was starting to run out for him. The writing of the dynasty's demise was on the wall for all to see. The Lodis were by now immensely powerful and by far the most influential Afghan clan in Hindustan.

Jasrat Khokhar – The Intrepid Warrior

Jasrat Khokhar, the chief of the Khokhar clan, was an indefatigable warrior—fighting continually for over two decades for independence from the Delhi Sultanate's control. He had even opposed Timur on his invasion of India but had been defeated. Thereafter he had joined his father Shaikha and together they had occupied Lahore, while Timur was still rampaging around North India. Jasrat was subsequently captured and carried away to Samarkhand. He suffered great privations while in captivity, which turned him into a lifelong opponent of the Delhi

> Sultanate. He blamed the Delhi sultans for the troubles in North India and for their inability to stand up to Timur during the latter's ruthless invasion.
>
> When he managed to escape from captivity and get back to his own territories, he found the Sultanate to be in a weak condition and struck against it. Even towards the end of his life when his body was failing him, his animus towards Delhi remained undiminished. Such men, pursuing their self-declared aim with single-minded focus and staunch in their beliefs abounded in the 14th and 15th centuries in India.

Bahlul made another attempt to capture Delhi in 1443-44. However, the Delhi fort proved too strong to be subdued and once again he returned to Sirhind, still nurturing his ambition. There was once again a rebellion near Delhi, just 20 miles from the seat of power. At the same time a number of nobles declared independence from the Sultanate. Muhammad Shah did not initiate any action to control the rapid disintegration setting in and a state of utter chaos swept through Delhi. In the midst of this confusion, Muhammad Shah died in 1445 after nominating his son Ala ud-Din as his successor.

Ala ud-Din Alam Shah

The nobles of Delhi placed Ala ud-Din, who assumed the title 'Alam Shah' meaning 'Lord of the World', on the throne with alacrity. The reason could have been their understanding that the Sultanate would not survive without a king to hold the helm during the increasing confusion. At that troubled time, no king could have got such an unopposed ascension to the throne. The title, 'Lord of the World', that Ala u-Din assumed was most ironical. Under Alam Shah's rule, the Sultanate shrank to its smallest size ever, becoming a petty state that controlled only the city of Delhi and a few surrounding villages. Ala ud-Din was even more negligent and incompetent than his father and Delhi sank into near oblivion. However, even in its totally diminished state, Delhi was Delhi and held lure for 'would be' kings. It's throne still remained the ultimate goal for politically ambitious chieftains and aspiring sultans.

Alam Shah was a complete and committed pleasure seeker although his temperament was such that he did not take kindly to even well-meaning advice. Further, he was not enamoured by the city and its vicious and ever churning political environment as well as the visible climate of palace intrigue. The Sultanate at this stage was little more than a miniature territorial holding fit for a small-time chieftain, stretching from Delhi to Palam, a distance of a mere 10 miles. Alam Shah decided to shift his residence, on a permanent basis, to Badaun against the protests of the entire court. He provided a lame excuse for the move, stating that Badaun agreed with his health better than the weather at Delhi. Even though he was not interested in 'ruling' his little kingdom, Alam Shah was not immune to being involved in conspiracies and palace intrigue. Since the opposition to his move to Badaun was centred on his Vizier, Hamid Khan, the Sultan plotted to kill him.

In the meantime Bahlul was again planning an expedition to fulfil his royal ambitions, which he had not given up. Hamid Khan got wind of the plot against him and invited Bahlul to come to Delhi and assume sovereignty. Bahlul did not need a second invitation and immediately proceeded to Delhi and in a successful coup d'état seized the throne. Alam Shah voluntarily resigned his position as Sultan and ceded all territories to Bahlul, except the town and district of Badaun. Alam Shah lived out his life in blissful obscurity till his death in 1478, enjoying the pleasures of life free of all the cares of a crowned head. His death would cause another period of turbulence and turmoil in the Sultanate.

By the time of Bahlul ascended the throne of Delhi, the Afghans had gradually spread across the whole of the Punjab and western Uttar Pradesh. The Afghans closely supported Bahlul since he was a member of a renowned and powerful Afghan clan. Bahlul was a tactical genius in the political arena. With the help of the Afghan nobility, he managed to remove Hamid Khan from power although it was Hamid who had offered the throne to him. He also won over the Delhi nobility through the age-old custom of bestowing gifts and titles on them. With the approval of Alam Shah, who now called Bahlul elder brother since his father had called him his 'own son', Bahlul crowned himself on the throne of Delhi on 19 April 1451.

By willingly renouncing his claim to the throne of the Delhi Sultanate, Alam Shah brought to an end the Sayyid dynasty. In some ways Alam Shah could be considered a pragmatist—he had renounced only what was not within his powers to manage. In consciously moving himself out of centre stage, Alam Shah realised his own ambition. Even the more ambitious of his contemporary kings and chiefs left him undisturbed to rule the small district of Badaun till his death.

The Sayyids – An Overview

Alam Shah's abdication brought to an end the Sayyid dynasty, which had ruled from Delhi for a mere 37 years. All the four Sayyid rulers had in them a streak of kindness, which made them unfit to rule in the turbulent 15th century of medieval India. They were ineffective since none of them possessed the ruthless single-mindedness that was essential to defend the borders of the country and expand the territorial holdings, both capabilities which are absolute necessities for the nation to prosper. The founder, Khizr Khan, based his strength on the support of the Afghan nobles he had brought with him, a trend that continued and became further entrenched during the rule of his successors. Their support was ensured by granting high civil and military honours to the Afghans, to the chagrin of the predominantly Turkish nobles of the Delhi court.

Mubarak Shah, by far the most effective of the dynasty although that distinction is only part of a relative assessment, attempted to establish order within the chaos, using the title and privileges of the Sultan extensively to get his way. Militarily he marched against almost all the neighbours that were crowding Delhi. The Afghans continued to be the dominant ethnic group and by the time Alam Shah inherited the throne, the entire North-West and Uttar Pradesh was controlled by them. Lodi power had blossomed at the expense of that of the Sayyid dynasty. It is a telling commentary of the diminished state and status of the Sultanate that when Alam Shah came to the throne, there were no borders more than 40 miles distance from the centre of Delhi.

When the Sayyids came to power the institutions of the monarchy and the central civil administration were in decay, having been discredited for over 50 years. Although the Delhi Sultanate was in almost terminal decline the Sayyid did not contribute in any way to furthering the concept of kingship or in bettering the civil administration. Considering that they ruled only for 37 years, the Sayyids were like wayfarers who occupied a traveller's rest house for a night and then left, leaving no mark of their having been there. Indian history is littered with such inconsequential dynasties and rulers, who came to power, indulged themselves at the expense of the country and then passed into oblivion without having made any significant contribution to the well-being of the country that they ruled. Their arrival and departure as well as the interim period of their rule were trivial when viewed within the sweeping and broad panorama of the history of an ancient land. They left no footprints in the sands of time and made no visible strokes on the broad canvas of history. The Sayyids belong in this category in the narrative of Indian history.

When Bahlul Lodi took over the reins of the Delhi Sultanate, he had start with reinventing the process of empire building and then to develop a new theory of kingship.

THE AFGHAN EMPIRE OF THE LODIS

...it is a disgrace for kings to flee from the field of battle. Look here my nobles, my companions, my well-wishers and friends have partaken of the cup of martyrdom... My horse's legs are dyed with blood up to its chest... It is better that I should be like my friends, [lying] in the dust and in blood.

Attributed to Sultan Ibrahim Lodi,

On his being requested by a noble to flee the battlefield in Panipat on 20 April 1526, before he rode out again to battle, where he was defeated and killed.

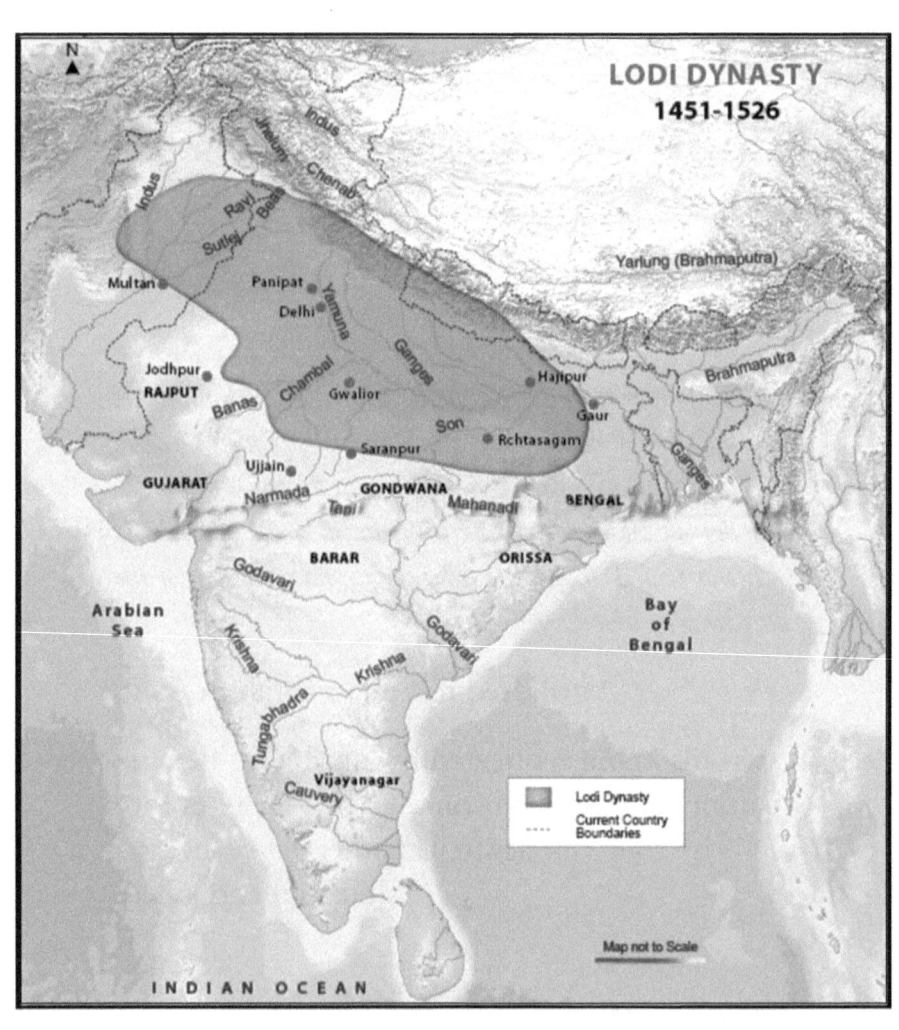

Chapter 27

ORIGINS OF THE LODIS

Legendary Connection to Mythology

The tale of the origins of the Lodis starts with their connection to Adam, the first human being according to religious mythology. It begins with the proclamation that 18 generations after Adam, Ibrahim was born. His son Yaqub, the progenitor of the Israelites had 12 sons. One of the descendants, 12 generation later, was Talut (or Saul). Talut had a son named Irmiya (Jeremiah) whose son was Afghan. Afghan is supposed to have given his name to the Afghan people and the country where they reside, Afghanistan. Qais, Afghan's descendent 35 generations later, settled down in Ghur with his kinsmen.

Qais and his clan were converted to Islam by Khalid bin Walid, one of the Prophet Muhammad's companions. Qais assumed the name of Abd ur Rashid and waged many battles on behalf of the Prophet, his companions and the increasing number of followers to the new religion. The Prophet was very pleased with his actions and named him Malik (king) and Pehtan, meaning the keel or rudder of the ship. This is how the Afghans and the Pathans came into being. This also the underlying reason why Afghans as a people love the title 'Malik'.

Qais, alias Abd ur Rashid and also called Pehtan, married a daughter of Khalid bin Walid and had three sons—Sarban, Batan and Ghurghust. A daughter of Batan, Bibi Matto, fell in love with Shah Husain a prince of Ghur. Their intimacy led to Bibi Matto becoming pregnant and then to marriage when the pregnancy could no longer be concealed. The offspring thus born was called Ghilzai, meaning 'born of theft' in the Afghan language. His descendants were called Ghilzais. Bibi Matto's second son was named Ibrahim. Qais, his great-grandfather, observed signs of greatness in Ibrahim even as a child and called him Loi-Dey, meaning that Ibrahim would find greatness one day. Colloquially that 'nickname' became corrupted to 'Lodi'. Lodi in the Afghan language means the great, the grown-up, or the elder.

Ibrahim's son Siani had two sons, Pranki and Ismail. Eight generations after Pranki, Bahlul was born into the Shahu Khel tribe of the Lodi clan. The second son Ismail had two sons—Sur and Nuhani—whose descendants came to be called the Surs and the Nuhanis. The four major clans of Afghanistan—the Ghilzais (also called Ghaljis), Lodis, Surs and Nuhanis—are all descendants of Bibi Matto. The clans retained very strong family ties.

Historical Narrative

There are claims and counter-claims regarding the origin of the Afghans, none of which can be accurately verified as the actual genealogical accounts are now intertwined with mythological accounts. It is difficult, if not impossible to untangle reality from myth. Variously the Afghans claim descent from the Israelites; or state that they are the copts, native Egyptian Christians, who wandered into Hindustan when the Israelites came to Egypt. Afghan ancestry therefore is traced to Qais, who was the legendary Bani Israel; to Egyptians; and to Persians depending on the study that is being analysed. The origins continue to be the topic of heated debate even today. However, the fact remains that from the time of Talut (Saul), new elements have been introduced into the mix. In order to add aura to the Afghan people, tracing a clan's ancestry back all the way to great Jewish monarchs is a common trend. In medieval times it was common practice amongst Muslim nobility to create imposing genealogies that trace their descent either from Adam or establishes a direct connection to the Prophet. This practice continues to be widespread even in modern times.

The belief in their Jewish origin has been prevalent and pervasive in Afghanistan for a long time and continues to be so even today. This claim is not based on mythology alone. There is a close, and proven, resemblance between the Afghan people and the Middle-Eastern Jews. Further, the laws, customs and moral characteristics of social behaviour of the two peoples are surprisingly similar. However, the only doubt regarding the authenticity of this claim comes from the terrain of the region. The Suleiman Ranges of Afghanistan is not hospitable to mass migration and also not close to Egypt. Therefore, large-scale migration during the period of ancient history cannot be considered a possibility.

The most probable origin of the Afghan people can be thought to be the reality that they are a mix of different ethnicities. The reasons for supporting this hypothesis are many. Afghanistan is the site of more invasions and migrations than any other place in the world. Between 500 B.C. and 4th century A.D. Achaemenian (Iranian); Macedonian (after Alexander); Mauryan (Indian); and Saka, Indo-Parthian, Kushan, Sassanian (all Iranian) conquerors went through the region and even ruled some parts of eastern Afghanistan. Iranians had been enrolled by every army that rampaged through the region, with the exception of Alexander. There is visible influence of the Iranian language on the current language spoken in Afghanistan, Pakhtu or Pushtu. This may have been the reason for Ibn Battuta, the famous medieval traveller, to state in his chronicle, 'Kabul is inhabited by a people from Persia called Afghan'.

The invasion and occupation of Afghanistan did not stop in the 4th century, it continued unabated to the 11th century. Between the 5th and 11th century, Afghanistan or major parts of it were ruled by dynasties that belonged to the White Hun, also called the Ephtnalite or Haytal (Turkish); Sassanian (Iranian); Kabul-Shahi or Zunbil (Turco-Iranian); Safavid (Iranian Muslim); and the Hindu-Shahi (Indian) dynasties. The nearly 16 centuries of conquest and occupation by different ethnicities has created the diversity that is seen in the Afghans and Pathans that inhabit the area today. The predominant influence remains that of the Iranian, Turkish and Indian stocks, and includes the Jewish impact on the local traditions. Further, even though the people have a mixed ethnicity, the origin of the local names remain either Jewish of Arabic.

The Pathans

The Pathans are generally considered to be the people of Eastern Afghanistan, from the region that is referred to as Roh. Roh, in the Indian Punjabi language, means mountain and is used to denote the region around the mountain wall of the Suleiman Ranges as seen from the plains of Multan. The Suleiman Ranges extend north from Bugti country in Sindh to Ghazni in the west and Peshawar in the east. There is a prevalent theory that the Pathans are not the descendants of Qais as repeatedly mentioned in folklore. This assertion is supported by the chronicle of Ibn Batuta and the autobiography of Babur the first Mughal Emperor. Neither of these books mention the word Pathan, Pakhtun or Pashtun. In these two tomes, the people of the region that constitute modern-day Afghanistan are only mentioned as Afghan and their language as Afghani. Considering that Ibn Batuta was an acutely observant traveller and that Babur was detailed in recording his autobiography, this should be conclusive proof that the appellation of Pathan was a later-day addition made to distinguish a smaller group of people, unique to a particular region. The word Afghan, over a period of time, came to be applied to all the people of the region and of the entire country. Pathan remained the name by which the people of the Roh were called.

Islamisation of the Afghans

Considering the modern history of the country for the past few decades, the question that arises is, when did the Afghans convert to Islam? The earliest recorded reference to the Afghans is found in a 3rd century Sassanian inscription where they are referred to as Abgans. In India, the famed astronomer Varaha Mihira refers to them as Vokkana in his monumental book *Brahma-Samhita* compiled in 6th century. Huien Tsang the Chinese monk-traveller mentions the people of the northern Suleiman Ranges as A-po-kien, which can only be a Chinese version of the word Afghan.

It is obvious that the religious conversion in Afghanistan started with the Arab invasions in the 7th century and continued through the invasion of the Saffavid dynasty in the 9th century. Contemporary chronicles of the time mention separate enclaves of Buddhists, Hindus and Muslims in Kabul. Alberuni, mentions the Afghans of the mountains to the west of the sub-continent and extending to the valley of Sindh as being 'Hindus'. He also referred to Peshawar by its Hindu name – Parushawar. Further, Alberuni provides a great number of references to Gandhara and the Indian kings ruling in Afghanistan, mentioning their capital as Vaihind. Therefore, it is obvious that

Islamisation had not yet reached eastern Afghanistan as late as the 10th century.

It is reliably reported that Mahmud Ghazni fought against infidels in the Suleiman Mountains. It is also reported that in the famous battle between Muhammad of Ghur and Prithviraj Chauhan, the Afghans fought on both sides of the battle. Therefore, it can be surmised that the Afghans had not been fully converted to Islam even at this stage. Clearly the account of the conversion of Qais and all his companions to Islam is only a story, passed down generations as folklore, gaining the status of a myth, and nothing else.

Rise of Afghan Nobility

The Afghans were tall, fair and warlike—not appreciative of any control on personal liberties and individual freedom; with a predominant streak of independence—who were poor herders and small-time plunderers of opportunity. At the end of the 11th century, the Afghans had not yet been fully converted to Islam. However, the conquering armies passing through the passes of the region into 'Hindustan' freely recruited the war-like Afghans. From the 11th century, Afghans came into India as 'soldiers of fortune' and were an integral part of all the invading armies beginning with Mahmud of Ghazni's first invasion.

One commander of Muhammad of Ghur was Malik Muhammad Lodi. The ascendency of the Lodi clan starts from the last raid of Muhammad of Ghur into India. During the reign of Iltutmish, a large contingent of Afghans fleeing the wrath of Genghis Khan joined the Sultanate army in Delhi. Even after the departure of Genghis and his hordes from the region, the majority of these Afghans stayed on in the service of the Delhi Sultans, under their commander Malik Khan. At this stage of the establishment of the Delhi Sultanate, a large number of Afghans were despatched to outlying garrison posts, as troops and officers, to form the vanguard of border protection of the emerging Sultanate. On the other hand, Afghans were also part of the numerous Mongol raids on the Sultanate, especially during the Khilji rule in Delhi. The Afghans were truly mercenaries, fighting on both sides of all conflicts.

It was Muhammad Tughluq who appointed the first Afghan governor, in Daulatabad although his name has been lost in antiquity. Muhammad's successor, Firuz Tughluq, appointed Malik Bir Afghan as the governor of Bihar. Timur conscripted many Afghan officers and soldiers to strengthen his army during the invasion of India. He left Khizr Khan nominally in charge of the border outpost on his departure. Khizr Khan remained unpopular and hated by the people of Delhi throughout his life because of this rather tenuous connection to Timur. The result was that Khizr Khan was dependent on the support of the Afghan nobility to stay in power after coming to the throne in Delhi.

Under these circumstances it was but natural that many of the Afghan nobles rose to high positions in the Sultanate, a number of them holding governorships. From this time onward, the history of the Afghans lay in India, not in their homeland. By the time Bahlul Lodi seized the throne and assumed supreme power in Delhi, the remnant of the Sultanate was dominated by Afghan nobility.

Chapter 28

BAHLUL LODI: CHIEF AMONG EQUALS

The Delhi Sultanate was on the verge of extinction when Alam Shah made known his decision to retire to Badaun. Under the leadership of Hamid Khan, the Prime Minster, the nobles of Delhi made a last ditch attempt to save the Sultanate and invited Bahlul Lodi to ascend the throne. The Lodis had established themselves in India around the year 970 or so and were the predominant tribe in the Lamghan and Multan region. Bahlul belonged to the Shahu Khel clan of the Lodi tribe. The first appearance of the Lodis in Indian history was in mid-14th century when Malik Shahu, the ancestor of the Lodi rulers of India, raided Multan, killed the governor and held the region under his power for a brief period. He was driven out by Muhammad Tugluq. However, the short-lived conquest marked the beginning of Lodi involvement in the politics of the Sultanate and in the affairs of greater India.

Early Life

Bahlul came from humble origins. His grandfather Behram Lodi was the grandson of Malik Shahu. He was an Afghan trader who used to travel to Hindustan to sell his merchandise and enhance his trading prospects. Behram became estranged from his brother and moved permanently to India during the reign of Firuz Tughluq. He joined service under Malik Mardan Daulat, the governor Multan and was given charge of a contingent of Afghan soldiers. Behram Lodi had five sons. The eldest, Malik Sultan Shah, took up service under Khizr Khan, then the governor of Multan. In one of the encounters during the internecine war between the Sayyids and the senior nobles of Delhi,

Sultan Shah killed the leader of one faction, Mallu Iqbal Khan, in 1405. Khizr Khan rewarded him with the title Islam Khan and conferred the fiefdom of Sirhind on him.

During his governorship, Sultan Shah favoured his brother, Malik Kala Lodi, and appointed him to 'rule' the pargana (district) of Daurala. Malik Kala's wife, his uncle's daughter, fell under a collapsing wall while in an advanced stage of pregnancy and was crushed to death. However, the child she was carrying was surgically rescued and was named Bahlul Lodi. Soon after this debacle, Malik Kala also died in battle and the orphan Bahlul was send for by his uncle Sultan Shah, alias Islam Khan, and brought up in Sirhind. Bahlul was full of spirit and martial qualities from a young age and became a favourite of his uncle. By this time Islam Khan had gradually assumed the title of Islam Shah and become independent for all practical purposes. He perceived the talent and merit in Bahlul, got his own daughter married to him and appointed him the heir apparent over his own sons, even though they were also intelligent and diligent.

Islam Shah continued to gain royal favours during Mubarak Shah's rule of the Sultanate for services rendered. He went on to place a contingent of 12,000 cavalry under Bahlul's command who was now officially his successor. In May 1431, Islam Shah was killed in battle and Bahlul took possession of Sirhind. Bahlul developed a very strong army and helped the ruling Delhi Sultan, Muhammad Shah, to put down rebellions in Mewat and Malwa. Gradually Bahlul increased his territorial holdings, both through his own military annexations and grants from the Sultan. By the time of Alam Shah's voluntary 'retirement', Bahlul was in control of almost the entire Punjab region. When he was invited to take over the throne of Delhi by the nobles led by the Vizier, Prime Minster Hamid Khan, he dealt with Alam Shah very courteously and tactfully, ensuring that neither the retiring Sultan nor the nobles were upset. He ascended the throne of Delhi under the title Sultan Abul Muzaffar Bahlul Shah Ghazi.

Consolidating Power

Bahlul was possessed of vaulting ambition. However, he was shrewd enough to realise that Hamid Khan, the Prime Minister had concentrated all power in his own hands. The only advantage that

Bahlul had was that on assuming power in Delhi he had increased the territorial holding of the till-then miniature Sultanate since he brought almost the whole of the Punjab with him. Further, many of the chiefs controlling districts around Delhi were Afghans and therefore offered support to Bahlul, a fellow Afghan. On the other hand, anti-Afghan sentiment was rife in the court amongst the Turkish nobility who considered the Afghans to be uncouth and uncultured. Hamid Khan based his position on the support of this powerful and entrenched group. Bahlul had to fight this faction throughout his rule.

Hamid Khan expected Bahlul to leave the running of the kingdom to him and Bahlul aspired to becoming the full-fledged sovereign of the empire, however small its territorial holdings. He was not happy even sharing power with his vizier and a contest of wills ensued. Bahlul was cautious and cunning. He proceeded with caution to gather power into his own hands by first winning the confidence of Hamid Khan. To start with, he treated the Vizier with extreme courtesy and respect acknowledging him as a sort of senior mentor. Hamid Khan seems to have viewed all Afghans, nobility and commoners, as rustic and unsophisticated simpletons. This belief was reinforced with the obsequious behaviour of Bahlul towards the Vizier and the unfettered growth of Hamid Khan's influence.

Bahlul now developed a strategy to grab power from Hamid Khan. He asked his Afghan supporters to behave in a simplistic manner in front of the Vizier. Bahlul himself continued the show of servility and high respect towards Hamid Khan to lull him into a sense of complacency. These displays duped Hamid Khan who became sanguine towards the activities of the Afghans. Bahlul bided his time and one day he took a group of Afghan nobles to meet Hamid Khan, in the pretext of wanting to pay their respect. However, this time unlike previous such occasions, Hamid Khan was imprisoned at the point of a sword. Bahlul explained to the Vizier that for political reasons it had become necessary to imprison him. Hamid Khan was carried away to prison and nothing more is heard of him in the chronicles.

Bahlul gained the confidence of the army to strengthen his somewhat tenuous hold on power by giving lavish gifts and bounties across the board. He also held out promise of advancement to the nobles to bring them to his side. Bahlul was faced with a three-pronged challenge to establishing his personal control over the Sultanate. First, the Turkish nobles of the court had always held the Afghans in contempt, considering them good soldiers and nothing more. The Afghans were deemed to be devoid of 'culture', a belief that Bahlul had used to seduce and remove Hamid Khan from power. Therefore, Afghans becoming the ruling class was anathema to the Delhi nobles. Second, the son-in-law of Alam Shah ruling in Jaunpur believed that the Delhi throne was rightfully his own. Since Alam Shah was still considered the legitimate Sultan, there was sufficient support for this claim within the Delhi court. Third, the Delhi Sultanate was an essentially broken entity and needed to be built up all over again, from scratch. Bahlul needed to reclaim, re-build and consolidate a dilapidated empire.

There is no doubt that Bahlul realised the precariousness of his situation. He started to emphasise his hold on power by giving key positions in the administration, such as treasury, stores and army, to his trusted Afghan lieutenants. Similarly, the districts around Delhi were entrusted to the care of loyal commanders. Further, Delhi itself was garrisoned by chosen Afghan soldiers, personally loyal to Bahlul. In effect, in very short order, the Delhi administration was 'Afghanised'. However, some elements of the Afghan group continued to remain malcontent, with some even going as far as not recognising him as the legitimate Sultan. To pacify this faction he provided more positions for them in the administration, further entrenching the Afghanisation process.

Stabilising Delhi

In order to entrench his personal power, Bahlul adopted a policy of strict militarism. He undertook a series of military expeditions to the districts surrounding Delhi. The first was against Ahmad Khan Mewati, ruling a large territory called Mewat, which consisted of the modern districts of Gurugram, Alwar, Bharatpur and Agra, almost encircling Delhi. Ahmad Khan submitted to Bahlul without a fight and most of Mewat was annexed to the Sultanate. Next, Darya Khan ruling the Sambhal region was also subjugated and the territory annexed. Subsequently Bahlul defeated Isa Khan ruling Koil (modern day Aligarh); but permitted Isa Khan to retain control of his territorial possession.

The chieftain of Rewari, Qutab Khan, offered resistance to Bahlul's invasion of his province. Qutab Khan was defeated by the Delhi forces, but allowed to retain control of his territories on his accepting the suzerainty of Delhi and paying a hefty tribute. Raja Pratap Singh of Mainpuri also submitted to the Delhi Sultan and in return was reconfirmed to his possessions. Gradually Bahlul established order and discipline in and around Delhi.

Having achieved an initial semblance of stability around the capital, Bahlul turned his attention to the north-west. Leaving Delhi in the hands of his son Khwaja Bayezid, he marched to Sirhind and Multan. At this stage, Multan functioned as an autonomous region, although it was strategically important for the security of the Sultanate. Bahlul wanted to bring the region under his direct control and also recruit fresh levies from the territory.

War with the Sharqis

While the Sultan was away campaigning in the north-west, trouble was brewing in Delhi. One section of the old nobility, alarmed at the rapid Afghanisation of the administration, invited Mahmud Shah Sharqi ruling Jaunpur to occupy the throne of Delhi. The Sharqi king regarded himself as the legitimate successors to the throne of the Sayyids. Mahmud Sharqi based this claim on the fact that he was married to Alam Shah's daughter. Further, the queen continually egged him on to take revenge for what she considered her father's 'forced' retirement. Mahmud also realised that although Jaunpur was a power to be reckoned with for some years now, the Afghan ascendancy in Delhi posed a direct threat to the well-being of Jaunpur. This threat was further emphasised by the Afghan control of the Punjab and western part of Uttar Pradesh.

While Mahmud Sharqi was debating the pros and cons of accepting the Delhi nobles' invitation to take over the Sultanate, his impetuous wife threatened to lead an expedition to Delhi herself to redeem the honour of her father and the Sayyids in general. Mahmud was already biased towards availing himself of this golden opportunity to claim Delhi and his queen's determination made him accept the nobles' invitation. Mahmud Sharqi also realised that it would easier to take over Delhi if action was initiated at this juncture before Bahlul was able to establish himself in Delhi. Time, obviously, was of the essence.

In 1452, Mahmud Sharqi arrived in Delhi with a large army consisting of 1000 elephants and over 170,000 cavalry. He had planned the expedition carefully, arriving in Delhi when Bahlul was far away in the western provinces. He had also coerced Darya Khan Lodi, appointed as the governor of Sambhal by Bahlul, to join the Sharqi forces. The Sharqi forces under the command of Darya Khan Lodi and Fateh Khan Harvi, an important noble of Jaunpur, besieged Delhi. As soon as he received news of the Sharqi invasion, Bahlul turned and proceeded back to Delhi. On the way he was opposed by a Sharqi contingent of 30 elephants and 30,000 cavalry, under the command of Fateh Khan another Jaunpur noble.

As soon as the Jaunpur forces arrived near Delhi, Khwaja Bayezid and his grandmother Bibi Matto closed the gates of the fort and prepared to withstand the siege. Bibi Matto, the grand old lady of the dynasty, dressed the palace ladies in soldier's uniforms and stood them on the battlements to show the enemy a larger number of troops than were actually in the fort. In the meantime Khwaja Bayezid had made contact with Darya Khan and appealed to him not to fight his own kinsmen. This gave a Turko-Afghan twist to the impending battle. The two armies met in combat at Narela about 17 miles from Delhi. The Lodi forces were led by Qutab Khan who accosted and taunted Darya Khan for abandoning his Afghan brothers and fighting against them. Darya Khan had a change of heart and abandoned the battle along with his forces.

Darya Khan and his contingent's withdrawal from battle crippled the Sharqi army and halved its strength. During the battle that followed Qutab Khan, acclaimed as the best archer in the Afghan army, managed to cripple Fateh Khan Harvi's elephant with a well-calculated shot. Fateh Khan was defeated and captured. He was decapitated by Rai Karan of Shamsabad whose brother Pithora had been killed earlier by Fateh Khan. Fateh Khan's head was ceremonially presented to Bahlul who had by then arrived in the vicinity of Delhi. Mahmud Sharqi who was in the rear headquarters of the army was shocked by this catastrophe and immediately retreated to Jaunpur.

Mahmud Sharqi was chagrined at this defeat and under the constant goading of his queen who was totally bent on revenge, decided to attack Delhi again. This time the battle was fought over possession of Etawah and Shamsabad. Although the battle did not produce any clear and definite victory for either side, it was the beginning of a long-drawn war between the two kingdoms. Bahlul's partial victory over such a formidable enemy as the Jaunpur Sultan impressed both friend and foe alike and greatly improved his stock in the Delhi court. The performance of the Delhi army under Bahlul's skilful command also frightened into submission a number of minor and provincial chieftains. Bahlul capitalised on this trend, which silenced the malicious gossip mongers in the court, who had been questioning his legitimacy and capacity to rule.

Thus within a year of ascending the throne, Bahlul had established control of the entire central region of North India—from Punjab in the west to the borders of Jaunpur in the east.

After the inconclusive battle over Etawah, a treaty had been signed between Bahlul and Mahmud Sharqi. The treaty agreed to honour the territorial possessions of each other's predecessors; Bahlul was to return elephants that had been captured from the Jaunpur army during the siege of Delhi; and Mahmud was to hand over control of Shamsabad—then being ruled by Malik Juna, who was to be dismissed—to the Sultanate. The anti-climax of the treaty was that it was not respected by either party from the very time of its signing. Juna refused to hand over Shamsabad, with the tacit support of Mahmud Sharqi. However, Bahlul captured Shamsabad and gave it back to Rai Karan. In turn, Sultan Mahmud Sharqi proceeded to Shamsabad and carried out a daring night attack on the fort. Although the town did not fall, Qutab Khan, Bahlul's brother-in-law and cousin, was taken prisoner by the Jaunpur forces.

Bahlul now prepared for a full-scale war against Jaunpur, determined to completely defeat and annex the kingdom. As the Delhi army was on the move, Mahmud Sharqi died suddenly and the war did not eventuate. In Jaunpur, the illustrious and sagacious queen of Mahmud Sharqi, Bibi Raji, ensured that her son Bikhan Khan was declared Sultan with the assumed title Muhammad Shah. Muhammad managed to patch a truce with Bahlul to maintain the status quo ante, which meant Bahlul returning to the Delhi-Jaunpur borders that he had inherited from Alam Shah. However, the treaty did not include the return of Qutab Khan still being held prisoner in Jaunpur.

Bahlul once again returned to Delhi. He was immediately questioned by his wife, Shams Khatun, regarding the fate of her brother Qutab Khan emphasising the need to rescue him. Bahlul stopped at a place Dhankur, about 28 miles from south-east of Delhi and did not enter Delhi proper. He decided to rescue Qutab Khan. At the same time Muhammad Shah Sharqi also doubled back and captured Shamsabad from Rai Kiran. He then marched to Sarsuti, modern day Sirsa. Bahlul arrived at Rapri, close to Sarsuti and there were sporadic clashes between the rival forces.

The Jaunpur Conspiracy

During the short duration of his rule, Muhammad Shah had already proven himself to be a wrathful and blood thirsty tyrant. While in Sarsuti, he got an inkling of a conspiracy being hatched in Jaunpur against his rule. He immediately send word to the kotwal (police chief) in Jaunpur to put to death his brothers Hasan Khan and Qutab Khan. This Qutab Khan is not to be confused with Qutab Khan Lodi then a prisoner in Jaunpur, although some Persian accounts do confuse the names. Muhammad Shah also invited his mother to join him in Sarsuti, suspecting her of being a partner in the conspiracy. She did not suspect any ulterior motive for the invitation and started on her journey to join the Sultan. On the way she received information of her son Hasan's assassination and stopped at Kanauj to observe the traditional period of ritual mourning.

Muhammad Shah now displayed his sadistic nature by sending a message to his mother. He informed her that she should mourn all her sons together since the rest were also soon to meet the same fate as Hasan Khan. Bibi Raji immediately send word to her other sons who were with Muhammad in Sarsuti exhorting them escape with their armies. Princes Husein and Jalal, who were then in Sarsuti, made a pretext of repulsing an expected night attack being planned by Bahlul and decamped to Kanauj with their respective armies. During this rapid march, Jalal Khan was captured by Bahlul.

At Kanauj, Bibi Raji, with the approval of the nobles of Jaunpur, crowned Husein Khan as sultan. Muhammad Shah was taken aback at the turn of events and decided to retreat to Jaunpur, marching first towards Kanauj. On the road to Kanauj the Delhi army mauled Muhammad repeatedly till they reached the River Ganga. Husein Khan the 'rebel' sultan send out an army to meet Muhammad Shah outside Kanauj. Muhammad Shah, never a popular ruler, was now deserted by the majority of his army and was forced to fight with only a small contingent in his support. In the ensuing battle, he was killed and Husein became the actual Sultan of Jaunpur.

The new Sultan entered into an agreement with Bahlul to maintain peace for four years and Qutab Khan and Jalal Khan, prisoners in rival camps, were both released. There are a number of stories, some authenticated and most only fanciful tales, of continued intrigue and conspiracies in the Jaunpur court. They are not germane to this narrative and is not being recounted. Even though there was some amount of internal divisions in Jaunpur, it enjoyed a decided superiority in military capability over Delhi, both in the size of the force as well as in the availability of resources. In addition, Husein Khan, the new sultan was determined to maintain the war-like tradition of the Sharqi house.

Husein therefore decided to invade Delhi territory while Bahlul was busy in Multan. The Delhi forces were defeated at Chandwar and Etawah was captured by the Jaunpur forces. Seeing the victories of the Jaunpur army, Ahmed Khan Mewati, who had been made a vassal by Bahlul, defected to Husein Khan. Isa Khan the governor of Biyani also defected and joined the Jaunpur forces. Bahlul was not perturbed by these developments and returned to Delhi. By this time both the kingdoms were tired of the constant state of war and once again reached an agreement to enforce a truce for another three years. During this truce a number of chiefs owing allegiance to Bahlul defected to the Sharqi Sultan, considering him to be more powerful.

The truce expired in 1466 at the end of three years. Almost immediately Husein Sharqi marched towards Delhi with an army of 10,000 cavalry and 1000 elephants and made first camp at Etawah. Bahlul met the advancing army at Bhatwara and battle ensued. Another battle was fought almost simultaneously near Sarai Lashkar about 25 miles east of Delhi. Both the battles were inconclusive and Husein Sharqi was forced to return to his camp at Etawah without having achieved anything. Soon after this Bibi Raji, the matron of the Sharqi clan who had held the dynasty together with an iron hand and the mother of Husein died. Wary of continuous warfare, Bahlul took this opportunity to make an attempt at placating the Jaunpur Sultan. He send an embassy of condolence led by Qutab Khan with a personal conciliatory message to Husein Sharqi. However, Husein spurned the offer and was completely unaccommodating towards any kind of truce being enacted.

An uneasy peace prevailed for a few years with both sides preparing for the eventual and inevitable clash. Bahlul appealed to Mahmud Khilji then ruling Malwa for help, which was promised. This appeal for help to a nominally subsidiary kingdom, which was independent for all practical purposes, is indicative of the poor shape of the Delhi Sultanate and the seriousness of the threat that it faced. Then, one single incident sparked off a major war. *[A single, mostly insignificant event triggering a major conflict is repeated throughout history in almost all parts of the world. An example closer to modern times, is the assassination of Grand Duke Ferdinand, which started World War I. Major wars have similarly been triggered by an event that in itself was not of any direct connection to the carnage that followed.]* In the case of the Delhi-Jaunpur rivalry, such an event was the death of Alam Shah, the last of the Sayyid dynasty in 1478 in Badaun.

In Jaunpur, Husein Sharqi was surrounded by a sycophantic court, which led him to believe that the throne of Delhi legitimately belonged to the Sharqis as the next of kin of the last Sayyid king and emphasised the fact that Bahlul was a usurper. On top of this Bahlul was also a plebeian by birth, a disqualification that could not be overlooked.

Husein was blinded by ambition and a deep sense of righteousness as well as an exaggerated assessment of his country's military strength. On the death of Alam Shah, Husein crossed the River Yamuna and engaged in a number of minor skirmishes with the Delhi forces. During these encounters the Jaunpur forces held a definitive advantage over the Delhi Sultanate. At the behest of Bahlul, yet another truce was arranged and the River Ganga was fixed as the boundary between the two kingdoms.

The number of truces and treaties that Delhi and Jaunpur agreed to after engaging in minor skirmishes before they developed into full-scale wars indicate that both the sides were uncertain regarding their ability to defeat the other. Both the rulers were reluctant to enter into full-scale war and take the chance of being defeated, which would invariably lead to loss of prestige and territory. However, it is evident that both the sultans harboured the intent to swallow the other kingdom but neither was strong enough to achieve their aim. The truces were normally drawn up for the convenience of the side that held the advantage at that particular time. Bahlul's aim was to reunite the old Sultanate while Husein harboured ambitions of claiming the throne of Delhi as his rightful inheritance. Both believed in the efficacy of the sword as the final arbiter.

Husein Sharqi once again returned to Jaunpur, leaving his camp and baggage behind. As soon as Husein left his camp, Bahlul breached the truce and started to pursue the Jaunpur army. He seized the baggage that had been left behind and also captured Malika Jahan, the Sharqi queen. Bahlul acted very chivalrously and had the queen escorted back to Jaunpur with respect. Yet another agreement was accepted by both parties. This time the treaty stipulations were violated by Husein Sharqi, who took advantage of an emerging favourable situation and declared war on Bahlul. In a preliminary battle Husein suffered a great defeat and had to hurriedly retreat to Rapri. Bahlul managed to capture immense booty in this victory.

Bad luck continued to plague the Jaunpur army. During the retreat, while crossing the River Yamuna, many officers, their wives and children drowned. This debacle further reduced the strength of the Jaunpur army that had already been affected by the earlier defeat. The lack of numerical strength compelled Husein to take shelter with the Raja of Gwalior. The Raja not only provided shelter, but also gave him some reinforcements and personally escorted Husein to Kalpi at the border of Gwalior territory. In the meantime Bahlul had captured Etawah and expelled the Sharqi appointed governor. He now marched to Kalpi to once again give battle. The two armies met on the banks of Kali Nadi, also mentioned as Rahab in some chronicles. Husein was soundly defeated and fled to Jaunpur. After a brief trip to Delhi to gather further reinforcements, Bahlul prepared to mount a full-scale assault on Jaunpur. The Delhi forces attacked Jaunpur and Husein was forced to flee to Bahraich.

Jaunpur was captured and annexed to the Delhi Sultanate. After nearly a century of being an independent sovereign country that rivalled the strength of Delhi, Jaunpur once again became a province of the Sultanate. Its independent existence was short-lived. Husein made one unsuccessful attempt to regain his throne and after that fled to Bihar in late 1479. Thus ended the independent Sharqi rule in Jaunpur.

Bahlul had been engaged in a no-holds barred life and death struggle with the Sharqi kings of Jaunpur for 27 long years. Chronicles of his reign provide a large number of episodes that provide the details of the Delhi-Jaunpur war, a number of which have not been included in this narrative. Bahlul's pre-occupation with Jaunpur meant that he had not been able to pay much attention to other parts of the empire and the provinces that had separated from the Sultanate. In the available chronicles there are only stray references to his interaction with the Rajasthan region, Sindh and Gwalior.

Gwalior

From the beginning of his reign, Bahlul had maintained friendly relations with Gwalior for two main reasons. First, it was a difficult kingdom to subdue because of its topography and inhospitable terrain. Second, Bahlul shrewdly realised the convenience of keeping an independent state as a buffer between Delhi and the powerful kingdom of Malwa. However, the fact that the Raja of Gwalior provided shelter and reinforcements to Husein Sharqi at the height of the Delhi-Jaunpur war irritated Bahlul. It is possible that the Raja of Gwalior would have noticed the increasing power that Bahlul wielded and must have wanted to assist his opponent in an effort to stem the rise of the Delhi Sultanate. Otherwise there was no reason for the Raja to upset the prevailing stable relations with Delhi. Bahlul did not take any precipitate action, but bided his time.

The Raja of Gwalior, Kalyan Singh was powerful and Bahlul acted only after his death. He decided to invade Gwalior. However, the successor, Raja Man Singh did not want to fight the Delhi forces and opted to pay a tribute of eight million tankas (silver coins) to Bahlul. Bahlul had also continued a campaign against the semi-independent chiefs of provinces surrounding Delhi. Kalpi, Dholpur, Bari, Alipore and Ujjain were brought under the control of Delhi.

Death of Bahlul Lodi

Bahlul started his return journey to Delhi from Etawah after making administrative arrangements for the rule of Jaunpur. At a place called Bhadauli, modern Milauli, about 15 miles from Saket in Etawah district, Bahlul took ill and died at the age of 80. Chronicles mention the cause of death as 'excessive heat'; presumably the Sultan suffered a heat stroke and never recovered. Bahlul had ruled for a strenuous 39 years, a truly exceptional length of time during an extremely turbulent period in the Delhi Sultanate's history, which in itself proves the success of his reign. The success was even more remarkable considering the lack of resources that he faced when he came to power; and the concerted opposition to his rule from the dominant Turkish nobles and community, who considered the Afghans to be simple, unsophisticated rustic people.

Bahlul's Achievements

Bahlul died in harness of exhaustion brought about by over-exertion. For 39 years he had ceaselessly struggled to breathe life into a moribund and fading Sultanate. He rightly deserves the credit for reviving the Sultanate that was in terminal decline and for restoring the waning prestige of the Delhi monarchy. Bahlul had inherited a kingdom with territory that was mentioned in folklore derisively as extending from 'Delhi-to-Palam'. He had extended the boundaries and had gradually added territories to it over the entire period of his rule. When he died his kingdom consisted of the entire Punjab, Uttar Pradesh, extending in the east up to the borders of Bihar; in the south up to Dholpur and in the south-west to Alhanpur near Ranthambhor.

Although his battlefield victories once again made Muslim power predominant in North India, his military preoccupations left him no time to indulge in reorganising the faltering civil administration. Even so he was personally involved, to the extent possible, in ensuring the welfare of the people—he heard petitions and dispensed justice regularly. Both as a military commander and an administrator, Bahlul was superior to all his predecessors up to and including Firuz Shah Tughluq. In fact he is considered a great tactician and a distinguished military commander.

His personal character was beyond reproach and he remained true to the lofty ideals that he held dear. He scrupulously adhered to the tenets of Islam while being tolerant of other religious creeds. This aspect of his behaviour won him the loyalty of non-Muslim feudatories and chiefs. Bahlul relied on these allies at several critical junctures in his military career. He has been described as being brave, generous, humane and honest. Bahlul was charitable to a fault, never turning away a supplicant who reached out to him. In victory, he was chivalrous. An example of his chivalry is the manner in which he treated the queen of Jaunpur. Husein Shah's queen was captured twice by Bahlul. Although she was the chief instigator of Husein's repeated invasions of the Delhi Sultanate, Bahlul treated her with respect and returned her to her husband. For a victorious Muslim Sultan in medieval India such behaviour is unique and unparalleled.

In the political arena, Bahlul used tact as a principal weapon to manage the affairs of the state. This tactfulness was evident in the way he handled the turbulent Afghan nobles, who were his primary supporters. He knew that the Afghans were used to individual independence, were of factious spirit and prone to functioning within tribal allegiances. They would not tolerate the Turkish concept and theory of the sovereignty of the Sultan and his 'God-given' right to rule. Bahlul therefore did away with all the trappings of power and was never ostentatious in his conduct. He did not sit on a throne, but on a shared carpet with his senior nobles. He declared publicly that he was the 'noble of his nobles'. Being a customary Afghan warrior, he was aware of the traditions of the warlike Afghans. Therefore, more than once he took off his turban and asked the senior nobles to choose a new leader, in accordance with Afghan custom. That he was elected with overwhelming majority each time is proof of his dexterous handling of the situation.

Through his tactfulness he kept the mercurial temper of the Afghan nobility under an invisible control through developing a bond of fraternity based on the concept of equality with the entire body of noblemen. While this worked to ensure the loyalty of the Afghan nobles, there was a serious downside to it. The sovereign willingly got reduced to the status of *primus inter pares*, the 'chief among equals'. It increased the power of the nobility at the expense of the status and prestige of the monarch, which was lowered significantly and created a feeling within the Delhi court that he was Sultan only of the Afghans. It also made the Afghan tribesmen a privileged class that in turn had long-term and detrimental consequences for the Sultanate.

In the final analysis, Bahlul should be considered a stalwart of the Delhi Sultanate, who single-handedly stopped its rapid decline into extinction. Unfortunately for this unusually tolerant Sultan, his inherent graciousness coupled with his visible humbleness has precluded his being recognised as such.

Chapter 29

SIKANDAR SHAH LODI
LIFE AND TIMES

Bahlul Lodi had nine sons, of whom the eldest Khwaja Bayezid has predeceased his father. Bahlul's sudden death was seized as an opportunity by the Afghan nobles to push forward the claims of their favourite princes for succession. Before proceeding to Gwalior on his last fateful expedition, Bahlul had appointed his third son Nizam Khan, whom he considered to be the ablest of the lot, as his successor. However, enfeebled by sickness and on his deathbed far away from Delhi, some nobles influenced him to cancel this appointment in favour of nominating his grandson Azam Humayun, son of Bayezid and the governor of Kalpi, to the throne. Bahlul died before this decision could be conveyed to Nizam Khan in Delhi, although Nizam had been forewarned of the proposed change of the Sultan's decision by the vizier.

When Bahlul died, the nobles accompanying him were divided into two factions, one supporting the elevation of Azam Humayun to the throne and the other wanting to crown Barbak Shah, the eldest surviving son and the governor of Jaunpur as the new Sultan. Queen Zeba spoke up in the assembly in support of her son Nizam Khan then in-charge of Delhi. However, she was snubbed into silence by a cousin of Nizam's, who berated her since she was a convert and not of 'noble' birth. Even at the end of the 15th century, when Islam had become fully established in the sub-continent, Turkish and Afghan nobility held great disdain for Indian converts, irrespective of the status of the convert in question. This is a dichotomy in a religion that converts with the sword and declares that all men are equal in front of God. This discrimination is still openly practised in Saudi Arabia, the bastion of Sunni Islam. *[The author has personally witnessed the second-class citizen status that is meted out to Muslim citizens from Pakistan, India and Bangladesh who work in the Kingdom of Saudi Arabia.]*

> **Queen Zeba**
>
> Queen Zeba was the daughter of a Hindu goldsmith, her name being given in different chronicles as Hema, Zeba and Ambha. She was extremely beautiful and has been described in the chronicles: 'her face was like a tulip and with jet black hair'. Bahlul was attracted to her when he was the governor of Sirhind and married her after ascending the throne of Delhi.

Since the mother was considered to be of a low social status and also a Hindu convert, the nobles believed that Nizam Khan was unfit to rule and therefore he was not even in consideration for being made the Sultan. After all he the grandson of a goldsmith! The successful faction in the discussion where the queen had been snubbed, carried Bahlul's coffin to a place called Jalali for internment. On the advice of his loyal vizier, Nizam Khan also reached Jalali. His physical presence unnerved the conspirators who did not put up any resistance and hastily dispersed to their fiefs. Nizam then send the Bahlul's body to be interred in Delhi and himself returned to the capital. He formally ascended the throne of Delhi on 17 July 1489, with the support of a majority of the nobles, assuming the title Sikandar Shah Lodi.

> **Sikandar Shah – The Debate Regarding Age**
>
> Some historians give Sikandar Shah's age at the time of accession as 18. This is incorrect. Majority of contemporary chronicles state that Bahlul's third son, Nizam Khan, was born in the seventh year of his rule. Bahlul had ascended the throne in 1451, and Sikandar Shah (Nizam Khan) was born in 1457 or 1458. Therefore, in 1489 when he became

> Sultan, he would have been 31 years old. Further, it is also confirmed by contemporary records that he already had six sons at the time of his coronation. It is seen that Sikandar Shah was a matured man when he assumed the mantle of monarchy also made obvious by the manner of his rule.

From the very beginning of his rule, Sikandar Shah set himself the task of preserving and further entrenching the power and authority of the monarchy and extending the territorial control of the Delhi Sultanate. This brought him into direct conflict with a number of princes and nobles who felt that his actions eroded their own power and were inimical to maintaining the status quo. After all for 39 long years before Sikandar assumed the throne, the Sultan had been only 'the first among equals'. Sikandar Shah had to justify his selection as the Sultan and also ensure the support of the nobles.

Immediate Actions

Sikandar Shah instinctively knew that he must deal with the confusion of his accession in order to entrench the legality of his rule. He had three opponents—all three of whom had been rival claimants to the throne—to deal with immediately. They were Azam Humayun, the son of his eldest brother and governor of Kalpi; Barbak Shah, his own elder brother ruling as the governor of Jaunpur; and Alam Khan, a younger brother, the governor of Rapri who had declared independence and assumed royal titles after Bahlul's death.

Sikandar decided to deal with his younger brother first and marched to Rapri. Alam Khan shut himself up in his fort, but could not withstand the siege for long. He fled to Patiala, which was Isa Khan's fief. Isa Khan was the cousin who had opposed Sikandar's claim to the throne and in the bargain also insulted Queen Zeba in court. Rapri was captured and given as a fief to the vizier. Sikandar then proceeded to Etawah where he established base camp for the expedition. Sikandar now used diplomatic means to gradually wean Alam Khan away from Isa Khan's influence. Once he came back into the Lodi camp, Alam was conferred the governorship of Etawah. After Alam Khan was firmly on his side, Sikandar attacked Patiala. Isa Khan offered valiant battle, but was defeated and succumbed to the injuries received in battle. Sikandar conferred the fief of Patiala on Rai Ganesh. This was a shrewd political move. Rai Ganesh had been a supporter and partisan of Barbak Shah and was won over to the Delhi Sultan's side.

Dealing with Barbak Shah

Barbak Shah was Sikandar's elder brother and a formidable rival. He had been ruling Jaunpur independently ever since the defeat of Husein Shah Sharqi, even striking his own coins although he continued to be obedient to his father Bahlul. Sikandar moved from Patiala towards Jaunpur. He felt that his fairly lenient treatment of Alam Khan would indicate to his brother that he did not want to fight and send out feelers for a reconciliation. Sikandar informed Barbak that he only wanted his name to be included in the coinage and that Barbak should accept Delhi suzerainty; in return for which Barbak would be left to rule Jaunpur independently. Barbak would be left alone to rule as monarch.

Unfortunately the reconciliatory approach failed since Barbak refused to accept his younger brother's authority as well Sikandar's claim to rule in Delhi. In this refusal to consider the reconciliation attempt, he was also instigated by Husein Sharqi, the previous king of Jaunpur, now living in exile. Husein stoked the fires of division since he felt that by increasing the schism between the Lodi brothers, he could exploit the situation and improve his chances of reclaiming the kingdom that he had lost to Bahlul. Barbak Shah openly started to prepare for war. Sikandar, being left with no other option, marched to Jaunpur for an invasion.

Barbak came out to meet the Delhi army and was joined by Mian Muhammad Khan Farmuli who was popularly known as Kala Pahad, a term that means Black Mountain. Farmuli was Sikandar and Barbak's sister's son and the governor of Awadh and Bahraich. He was known as a formidable fighter and commanding general, as the nick-name suggests. The battle that ensued at Kanauj was bloody and ruthless. During the battle, Kala Pahad was taken prisoner. Sikandar treated him with great courtesy, acknowledging his status as a governor of a province. He was persuaded to join the Delhi forces, which was not difficult since Sikandar was also Farmuli's uncle. The Awadh forces now started to fight against Barbak, who became demoralised at this turn of events and fled to Badaun. The Jaunpur forces were defeated, Barbak was pursued in his flight, captured and compelled to surrender by the Delhi forces.

Sikandar was aware of the lurking Husein Sharqi and of his continuing ambition to regain the throne of Jaunpur. Therefore, in a calculated move he reinstated Barbak Shah as the ruler of Jaunpur while assigning all the districts surrounding it to his own trusted and loyal officers. He also placed spies in the palace of Jaunpur. These moves effectively curtailed any tendency on the part of Barbak to rebel again and ensured that Husein Sharqi could not mount any expedition either to assist Barbak or to take over Jaunpur.

After putting in place these administrative measures in Jaunpur, Sikandar turned his attention to Kalpi. He marched there, removed his nephew Azam Humayun from the governorship, conferred Kalpi on Mahmud Khan Lodi and then returned to Delhi in 1492. In a span of a little over two years, Sikandar Shah had become the sole master of the entire North India up to the borders of Bihar.

The Jaunpur Rebellion

In Jaunpur Barbak Shah had been subdued and kept under tight control. However, the local zamindars of Jaunpur, powerful landowners with large territorial holdings and most of whom were Hindus, became a formidable bloc of influence. Husein Sharqi instigated these zamindars to rebel in his bid to make one more attempt at regaining his throne. The zamindars revolted, upon which Barbak fled and took refuge in Driyabad near Lucknow. Sikandar Shah went back to Jaunpur and in a highly contested battle managed to defeat the zamindars' forces. He reinstated Barbak as the governor and collected enormous booty before returning to Delhi.

As soon as the Delhi army started its return march, the zamindars once again rebelled. Barbak was once again unable to contain the rebellion and proved his incompetence as an administration for the second time. Sikandar took to the field again. He ordered the arrest of Barbak and placed him as a state prisoner. Then the Sultan proceeded to Chunar and suppressed the zamindars' revolt, suffering great losses to his own army. The battle was fought ferociously from both sides.

However, before Sikandar could achieve total victory, the zamindars invited Husein Sharqi to make another attempt at seizing the throne. Husein Sharqi took to the field with a huge army, supported by the zamindars and some other local Hindu chieftains. In an extended battle fought near Varanasi (or Benares) Husein was defeated and fled to Colgong in Lakhnauti. He was a spent force and lived the rest of his life in Bengal in obscurity. This was the final curtain call for the Sharqi dynasty created by Malik-us-Sharq Khwaja in Jaunpur.

The Bachgotis

The Bachgotis were a tribe of turbulent Rajputs, descended from the Mainpuri Chauhans, led by a warlike chief called Juga. Known in modern times as Basgotis, the members of the tribe are found in large numbers even today in the Allahabad-Jaunpur region. Juga attacked and killed Mubarak Khan the governor of Kara. Thereafter he was partially responsible for making Barbak flee from Jaunpur, leading to his subsequent arrest and incarceration by Sikandar. In 1493, Juga was joined by Raja Bhedachandra of Bhatgora (modern Rewa) in an open rebellion against Delhi. Sikandar Shah arrived at Dalmau opposite Kara to face this combine against him.

Sikandar defeated Juga, who managed to escape and joined Husein Sharqi in his fort at Chaund, identified as modern Chanda, a village in Sultanpur. At this development, Sikandar tried to win over Husein Sharqi, asking him to join the fight against 'infidel rebels' in return for being permitted to keep his current territorial holdings. The battle of Varanasi, mentioned earlier, took place after Husein had rejected this offer. When Husein fled to Bengal, the Delhi forces were in hot pursuit till he entered Bengal territory. The outcome of this pursuit was that Bihar was easily annexed as a secondary objective and ceased to exist as an independent entity. Sikandar appointed his own officers to stabilise and govern the newly annexed region.

The Baghelas of Rewa

The Baghelas are mentioned as Vaghelas in some contemporary and modern texts. After dealing with the recurrent challenge from Husein Sharqi, Sikandar turned his attention to the Baghela Raja Bhedachandra of Rewa, who ruled from his capital at Gahora.

Gahora is today a forsaken village about 12 miles east of Karvi in the Banda district of modern Uttar Pradesh. The early history of the Baghelas is obscure. Baghelas were ruling Gujarat in the 13th century and were comprehensively defeated by Ala ud-Din Khilji in 1299. The Baghelas moved en masse to the north and settled in the region around Banda and Kalinjar. After nearly 150 years, the Baghelas now under the leadership of Virama Deva, was continually being harassed by the Muslim chieftains of Kalpi and Jaunpur. His successor Raja Bhedachandra moved the tribe to another mountainous region in central India, settling in the region bounded in the north and north-west by the Kaimur ranges and the Maikal ranges on the south and south-west. This country came to be called Baghelkhand.

The 16th century Sanskrit 'Mahakavya', or Great Poem, called *Virbhanudaya of Madhava* that has been translated in abridgement by Hiranand Shastri states that Raja Bhedachandra exerted authority over the territory along the River Ganga up to Kantit in the west and to Gaya in Bihar in the east. The on-going Lodi-Sharqi rivalry suited the Baghelas since it made them safe without much interference from the two major powers. However, when the Sharqi power was destroyed after decades of war, the balance of power that had contributed to the stability of the Baghela kingdom was threatened. In the larger scheme of things, it was in Baghelkhand's interest to have a reasonable powerful Sharqi king on the throne of Jaunpur as a counterpoint to the Delhi Sultan and his ambitions. Therefore, it is not surprising that Raja Bhedachandra of the Baghelas and Raja Man of Gwalior supported Husein Shah in his repeated attempts to regain his throne in Jaunpur.

On Husein Shah being defeated and fleeing into exile in Bengal, Bhedachandra attempted to make amends with Sikandar Shah, but his overtures were rejected by the Delhi Sultan. In 1495, Sikandar launched a campaign against the Baghelas. Throughout his march, Sikandar put the countryside he passed to sword and fire, devastating the entire region. He was opposed by the crown prince, Vahara Raya Deva who was defeated in battle and killed while retreating. Raja Bhedachandra also died soon after, never recovering from the shock of the death of his son and heir apparent. Sikandar, although victorious, paid the price for the scorched earth policy that he had followed. After defeating the Baghela prince he retired to Bandugarh. Here the policy of devastating the countryside came back to haunt him. Provisions became scarce and then an epidemic hit the army. About 90 per cent of the cavalry was devastated and the Sultan was forced to retreat to Delhi.

At this juncture, Lakshmi Chand, Bhedachandra's younger son, took advantage of the Delhi army's discomfiture and invited Husein Shah to strike Sikandar immediately. However, a by-play of intrigue followed. After Bhedachandra's demise, his brother Salivahan had assumed the throne. He had struck up a friendship with Sikandar who had provided him with some amount of treasure and riches. Salivahan was also scared that Lakshmi Chand would stake a claim to the throne and therefore increased his support for, and friendship with, Sikandar Shah. The Battle of Varanasi, with the results as described earlier followed, with Salivahan siding with Sikandar.

The Sikandar Shah-Salivahan accommodation snapped almost immediately after the victory over Husein Shah Sharqi. The Sultan's original intention had always been to annex the Baghela kingdom, which had to be put on hold by the alliance with Salivahan. Although the Delhi forces returned to Delhi, Sikandar was biding his time. After a gap of three years, he mounted another campaign against the Baghelas. The excuse for the invasion was rather thin—Sikandar had asked Salivahan for the hand of his daughter in marriage, which had been refused. Although the invasion took place, the land that had been repeatedly devastated through pillage and burning could not sustain a large army and the expedition did not produce any conclusive outcome. The Baghelas continued to rule their small kingdom although the frequent Afghan attacks weakened them and gradually crippled the dynasty.

By 1499 Sikandar Lodi had crushed any real or perceived opposition to his rule and no danger threatened the well-being of the Delhi Sultanate. Secure at home, Sikandar turned his attention to the west.

The Tomars of Gwalior

Iltutmish had conquered Gwalior in 1232 and the region remained annexed to the Sultanate and under Muslim occupation till the end of the 14th century. As the Delhi Sultanate weakened, Vir Singh the

Tomar chief took advantage and captured the Gwalior fort and declared independence from Delhi. He was followed by an array of strong rulers—Dungar Sigh, Kirti Singh, Kalyan Singh—who nurtured the independent state to strength, power and influence. These stalwarts of the Kingdom of Gwalior managed to resist all attempts by Delhi to subdue them, continually growing in stature. Gwalior managed to reach a state wherein the ruling family felt strong enough to make an unsuccessful attempt to capture the Narwar fort then under the control of the Malwa Sultan Hoshang Shah.

Raja Man Singh who came to power in 1486 was a veritable genius who held very liberal religious views. He was extremely popular with both his Hindu and Muslim subjects. However, Sikandar Shah had a score to settle with Man Singh—some years earlier, Man Singh had provided shelter to some conspirators who were exiled from Delhi, in keeping with the medieval etiquette of providing hospitality to anyone who sought shelter. Man Singh had wanted to avoid a direct military confrontation with Delhi and had send presents and tributes to Sikandar Shah. However, Sikandar was an expansionist at heart and harboured ambitions of annexing Gwalior. He declined to compromise.

Eventually Delhi mounted a campaign against Gwalior. The Delhi forces first attacked Dholpur, a dependency of Gwalior about 34 miles south of Agra, ruled by Vinayak Deva. Vinayak Deva fought bravely, inflicting heavy casualties on the Delhi army. However, when Sikandar Shah personally embarked from Delhi towards the battle field, Vinayak panicked and fled to Gwalior. Dholpur was laid waste, with temples destroyed and mosques built in their place. Sikandar then crossed the River Chambal and camped on the banks of the River Asi, modern Mandaki. The Delhi army was again ravaged by an epidemic, probably an outbreak of cholera.

Raja Man Singh was quick to take advantage of the situation to come to terms with Delhi and promised to expel the fugitives in return for Dholpur being returned to Vinayak Deva. Sikandar, now in a precarious situation and facing grave difficulties with his army in the grip of an epidemic, accepted the terms. Although the Muslim chroniclers of the time continue to flatter the Sultan and his 'victory', in reality Gwalior had successfully resisted Sikandar's invasion without suffering any loss. Immediately after the withdrawal of the Delhi forces,

Raja Man Singh reinforced the forts that the Tomars had built around Gwalior as the first line of defence for the country. It is obvious that he anticipated a return expedition by Sikandar Shah.

Four years later Sikandar attacked again, targeting the fort at Mandrael on the west bank of the River Chambal, which was captured after a vicious battle. He once again followed the by now familiar policy of sacking, looting and plundering the countryside before burning it down; and predictably and inevitably the actions were followed by the usual epidemic in the army and a return to Delhi in a reduced state. Sikandar now learned the lessons of the previous expeditions and realised the necessity to establish headquarters for the army closer to the region of campaign to reduce the logistical tail. This was necessary to subdue strong kingdoms and capitalise on battlefield victories. Sikandar Shah chose the place where Agra stands today as the site for the construction of the advanced headquarters, laying the foundation for a fort in 1505. This was the beginning of modern Agra.

> ### The Antiquity of Agra
>
> Tradition gives great antiquity to Agra. In Indian mythology Agra is considered to have been the state prison during the reign of Raja Kans, the ruler of Mathura and uncle of Lord Krishna. In the early historical period Agra grew to be a middle-sized town of no particular importance. Mahmud Ghazni reduced the township during one of his raids and left it ruined as an insignificant village. It gradually regained importance over the years. In 1475, a Hindu prince called Badal Singh built a fort called Badalgarh in Agra. In 1492, Haibat Khan, a general of the Delhi Sultanate, captured the city that had by then become a walled city.
>
> Agra was well-populated when Sikandar Lodi founded his secondary capital there. There is mention in the chronicles of an earthquake taking place on 6 July 1505 that reduced the town to rubble. Irrespective of the historical traditions that surround Agra, modern Agra was rebuilt by Sikandar Lodi. He built Sikandara and a fine summer house on

> the banks of the River Yamuna. This summer house was later converted to a tomb for Maryam Zamani, Jahangir's mother.
>
> It is clear that the new capital took some time to be established. The coins that Sikandar stuck in Agra were not of the same refinement as those done in Delhi, indicating that the town had not reached the level of sophistication as Delhi.

Agra now became the headquarters for the invading Delhi army, which once again captured Dholpur. This was the beginning of yet another campaign against Gwalior, with the war raging for more than a year. Raja Man Singh now resorted to a guerrilla campaign reliant on hit-and-run tactics. The fact of the matter was that Sikandar Shah was not strong enough to force the surrender of Gwalior and Man Singh was not strong enough to throw out the invading force from his kingdom. Even though he seemed to have learned the folly of adopting a scorched earth policy, Sikandar continued his strategy of the reckless destruction of the countryside, which once again boomeranged. Scarcity of provisions for the large army once again forced a retreat from Gwalior territory to Agra.

On their return march, the Delhi forces were ambushed near Jatwar by Man Singh inflicting heavy casualties. The final conclusion about the year-long war between Delhi and Gwalior is that it was an utter failure for the Delhi forces. However, Sikandar Lodi was, if anything, a persistent general. He continued to pursue the strategy of reducing the encircling forts of Gwalior to isolate it. Gradually, over years of continuous fighting, Gwalior came to be encircled by forts that were controlled by Sikandar Lodi. In 1509, Narwar was captured by Delhi forces, cutting off Gwalior from the possibility of receiving any assistance from Mewar, its principal ally. At this stage, other than Narwar, the Delhi forces controlled Dholpur, Mandrael, Avantgarh, Lahayer and Hathkant. Gwalior now knew that ultimately and inevitably it would have to surrender. However, the brave kingdom fought on till it could resist no more.

This extended campaign against Gwalior was a continuous and heavy drain on the Delhi exchequer, which it could ill-afford. More importantly, his pre-occupation with Gwalior led to Sikandar Lodi completely neglecting the north-west frontier of the kingdom and the region of the Punjab from where threats to the Sultanate traditionally emanated. His successor would later pay a high price for this generational neglect—losing both his kingdom and life. In comparison, the gain of a few minor forts in the Tomar country was but a pittance.

Other Conquests

The capture of the Narwar fort brought Sikandar in close proximity to Malwa. Since Sikandar was an expansionist who was always interested in dabbling in the politics of his neighbours, it was only a matter of time before he interfered in the affairs of Malwa. There was a power struggle in the ruling dynasty, between the father Sultan Nasir ud-Din and his son Shihab ud-Din who was supported by the nobles of the country. Shihab attacked the capital Mandu, was defeated and appealed to Sikandar for help. He promised to surrender Chanderi to the Sultanate in exchange for Sikandar putting him on the throne. Internecine war for succession continued in Malwa for another 15 years, with the active participation of the Delhi forces also in the civil war. Finally Chanderi was occupied by Sikandar's forces.

During various times during the Malwa Civil War, Sikandar Lodi supported all the major participants thus becoming an important factor in Malwa politics. During this period, the Sultan of Nagor also submitted to Sikandar, fearing that he would be replaced by his brother on the throne by the Delhi Sultan. Having subdued and reduced Gwalior and extended his sovereignty over Malwa and Nagor, Sikandar Shah Lodi returned to Agra only to die of natural causes on 21-22 November 1517. He had ruled for 29 years and achieved some glory, increasing the stature of the Delhi Sultan.

Sikandar Shah Lodi – An Appraisal

Sikandar Lodi ruled with distinction and was undoubtedly the greatest of the Lodi kings. He extended the boundaries of the Sultanate in all directions and retrieved the still sagging prestige of the Sultanate. Sikandar wiped out all vestiges of the existence of the Jaunpur kingdom after Husein Sharqi was forced into exile in Bengal and also brought Bihar under Delhi control. Through astutely projecting his individual status and power he continually improved the stature of the Delhi Sultan to an extent that powerful kings, such as those ruling Bengal and Orissa, extended their hands in friendship to Delhi rather than risk opposing the Sultanate.

Personality

As a king and an individual, Sikandar Lodi earned high praise from the Muslim chroniclers of the time. This could be largely attributed to the fanatical zeal he displayed for establishing the tenets of Islam, which had been greatly diluted under the ineffective rule of the previous dynasty. This attitude was in agreement with the biased religious opinions of the chroniclers themselves who hailed him as a saviour. A number of contemporary historians have described Sikandar Lodi as verging close to being the ideal Sultan.

Sikandar Shah was handsome in appearance and fond of the 'masculine' pursuit of hunting. He always conducted himself with great decorum, being formal even in his personal conversation. He demanded that all courtiers also observe formal etiquette in his presence at all times. His father, Bahlul, had always held informal court and was a self-proclaimed *primus inter pares*, the first among equals. Sikandar's court stood on the other end of the spectrum of sovereignty and was devoid of any semblance or mention of equality between Sultan and the nobles. The Sultan was placed at a far higher plane than any courtier could even aspire to reach. This manner of rule was not a whimsical imposition of the personal vanity of the Sultan but a well-considered policy created to enforce discipline and efficiency in the administration.

Sikandar Lodi revered learning and always had learned men around him for company. His patronage for learning and support for erudite teachers have been acclaimed as being unsurpassed by any monarch before him. Considering that the ancient Indian monarchs were lavish in their patronage of learned scholars, this statement has to be taken at token values as an obvious exaggeration. Even so, it is obvious that Sikandar Shah was an avid supporter of learning. Sikandar himself was a scholar of Persian literature and a poet of recognised merit, writing under the pseudonym 'Gulrukhi' meaning 'Rose-faced'. The choice of the pseudonym could be indicative of a trace of vanity regarding his extreme handsomeness that was inherited from the renowned beauty of his mother. Sikandar also recited poetry beautifully.

> **The Poet-Sultan**
>
> Sikandar's poems betray a delicacy of thought, feeling and expression that is unusually sentimental for a warlike Sultan. A classic example of his writing is given below:
>
> 'Into the eye of the needle of her eye lashes,
>
> I shall pass the thread of my soul.
>
> If Gulrukhi could describe the charms of her teeth,
>
> He would say they were water-white pearls of the ocean of her speech.'

A commendable fact is that he paid personal attention to the preservation of ancient manuscripts and arranged for the translation of several Sanskrit texts to Persian. It was during this process that the ancient Indian treatise on medicine was translated into Persian under the title, *Tibb-i-Sikandari*.

Sikandar was personally pious and virtuous and held back from all frivolous pursuits. He was continually engaged with the affairs of state, working everyday till mid-night. A few chroniclers mention that Sikandar Lodi had a secret drinking habit, even though none of them provide any tangible proof of this weakness in the character of an otherwise perfect human being. Further, there are no records of the Sultan being seen in an inebriated state or seen to be sipping wine even once. On the other hand, the lack of information regarding the Sultan's deficiencies, flaws of character and dubious decisions could be attributed to the chroniclers wanting to gloss over the human frailties and hypocritical ways of a monarch they unanimously raised to the level of a demi-God.

Administration

Sikandar Lodi spent his entire life waging war. Therefore, he had only very limited time to introduce effective administrative reform that could have had far-reaching impact on the well-being of the Sultanate. Even so, he focused on streamlining an administration that had become moribund and complex. In developing military policies, he was cautious and deliberate; throughout his reign he did not launch any military campaign that was too ambitious or to cater to his whim and fancy as a monarch. Another remarkable trait was that whenever circumstances permitted, Sikandar endeavoured to win over the potential adversaries through negotiations and advocating reconciliatory policies. He seems to have been acutely aware of the strategies of deterrence and coercion in an age where most monarchs relied heavily on violent wars as the only power projection capability.

Although no new reforms were introduced during his reign, Sikandar Shah accomplished much in improving the administration. He continued the trend that his father had started of centralising power, but in a far more effective manner. He faced the challenge of carefully keeping the Afghan chiefs and nobles under check and the need to keep their individualistic tendencies suppressed. Sikandar approached this task of dealing with the Afghan nobles in two-pronged manner. First, he put in place measures intended to raise the educational standards of all Afghans including common soldiers. This was intended to lead to a raising of cultural awareness in the community that had so far been looked down upon as uncouth simpletons. Second, the Sultan kept a close personal watch on all his officers, receiving information regularly from all parts of the kingdom. He also stepped in promptly to correct anything that was going wrong, even in far-flung regions of the Sultanate, thereby demonstrating to the nobility his control over the affairs of the state. These measures indicated the seriousness of the Sultan in controlling the nobles, which the nobles seem to have understood.

Audit and inspection of accounts were anathema to the Afghan nobles ruling the provinces. Sikandar Lodi enforced strict audits and cases of embezzlement were immediately punished. In order to ensure that there was no backlash from the Afghan nobility, his own brothers were equated with other nobles and also subjected to the strict financial audits. By doing so, Sikandar achieved dual purposes—the nobility remained stable and it avoided any of his brothers harbouring or pursuing royal ambitions. Another way in which the nobles were kept in check was by the Sultan personally appointing the retainers in the service of the more powerful nobles. By ensuring that these retainers remained loyal and faithful to him alone, Sikandar ensured that no plot could be hatched against him without his coming to know of it at an early stage itself. With the strict implementation of these measures, Sikandar Shah gradually extended his control over provincial affairs, enforcing a tight centralised grip over the entire Sultanate.

Sikandar Lodi established an elaborate espionage and intelligence gathering system. It is said that he knew the minutest details of people's lives. To increase the efficiency of this system he revived the defunct practice of transmitting news through the use of a relay of horses. The 'relay of horses' technique was honed to such efficiency that the Sultan was able to send two 'Firmans', or 'Sultan's Orders', every day to any part of the Sultanate. Orders that were not marked secret were read out in public in faraway provinces, an act that made the common man feel a connection to the central administration. The people could palpably feel the governance being delivered by the great Sultan in Delhi.

Although these strict measures of central control was instituted, Sikandar was very careful not to rouse the hostility of the Afghan nobles, especially the old nobles who were set in their ways. He treated these older nobles with elaborate courtesy and consideration of their entrenched prejudices, thus ensuring their support, even if reluctantly delivered.

The dispensation of justice was even-handed for all and no distinctions based on rank and status was permitted. The court sat throughout the day with special representatives being available through the entire day-light hours and the ulemas also waiting inside the palace to render expert advice when necessary. The Sultan personally intervened frequently to avert the miscarriage of justice. This meant that while the judicial process was in progress, he was being informed of the proceedings on a regular basis.

The Sultan made catering to the interest of the poor a priority activity of the central administration. Of course, the 'poor' in this case was restricted to the followers of the Islamic faith within the Sultanate. Sikandar abolished the tax on corn and encouraged agriculture, while also ensuring that reliable security was provided to traders and merchants. He instituted a scheme under which the state provided six-month's provision ever year to the poor and destitute. These welfare measures were available only to the Muslim population under his rule. He also started the practice of releasing prisoners, except those jailed for embezzlement, on important religious holidays. By enforcing a variety of measures, mainly through coercion and the actual use of force when needed, Sikandar Lodi managed to keep the rebellious Hindu zamindars subdued. It could be said that the core of the Sultanate had been effectively stabilised.

Unlike the practice of some of his predecessors who transferred officials at random and regular intervals to keep them off-balance and avoid their becoming entrenched in a particular region, Sikandar Shah provided stability of tenure to his officials. He did not remove any official from his post unless some misdemeanour was proven against the official. This policy gained the goodwill and loyalty of the officers, especially the ones at the middle ranks.

There can be no administration without its own quirks, faults and pitfalls. This was true of Sikandar Lodi's centralised administration also. In appointing officials, Sikandar was partial to the Afghans, especially those from his own tribe. Further, he based the selection on heredity and social status, rather than on merit which was not considered in the assessment. Sikandar's administration was never a meritocracy. Even so, the Sultan's achievements in stabilising the administration were very creditable, especially considering that he was at war almost throughout his reign. Although he was an autocratic monarch, he reposed full trust in his officials and paid them well as an anti-dote to the inherent corruption of the central bureaucracy. There is no doubt that he infused much vigour into the administration, which served the state well. However, during Sikandar's rule the state reverted to being a theocracy, officially imposing Islam on the Hindus and other minority non-believers.

Sikandar – The Religious Bigot

Despite a benevolent disposition, wide-ranging cultural interests and broad social concerns, Sikandar Lodi was an ultra-orthodox Muslim. He genuinely believed that it was his sacred duty to demolish temples to stamp out idolatry and forcibly convert non-Muslims to the 'one true faith'. This could also have been a reaction normal to new converts who tend to be more evangelical than more established people of the faith. This phenomenon is very clearly visible in Indian history, since the Turkish, and later, Afghan nobles tended to give second-class status to Hindu converts from the sub-continent. In the case of Sikandar Lodi he may also have suffered from a socio-religious inferiority complex since his mother was a Hindu and a common goldsmith's daughter.

In any case, several acts of extreme vandalism of temples, in the name of Islam, has been recorded in great detail and attributed directly to the Sultan by exulting chroniclers. Obviously there could be some exaggerations meant to laud the Sultan's religious credentials and his zeal to propagate the religion. However, there is no doubt regarding Sikandar's extreme passion for enforcing Islamic precepts across the entire Sultanate. In fact some actions that he initiated against the Hindus went far beyond what was prescribed or expected of even the most orthodox practitioners of the Islamic faith.

Most of the 15th century Delhi Sultans did not indulge in senseless religious persecution; and neither were they powerful enough to oppress the Hindus. Sikandar revived a number of oppressive religious practices against the non-believers, most of which had lain dormant for more than a century. Further, he assumed an uncompromising attitude towards Hindus, completely devoid of any trace of religious tolerance. It is noteworthy that the strict religious policies were only enforced after Sikandar had consolidated his position as the undisputed Sultan in the first decade of his rule. Before that he too did not have the power to institute religious oppression as a policy of the Sultanate.

There are a number of later-day analysis that proclaim Sikandar Shah to have been a religious bigot. He may indeed have been a bigot. However, the distinct likelihood that this conclusion, arrived at after some centuries of his rule, was the result of the fact that he put to an end the benign religious nature of the shrinking and powerless Delhi Sultanate that he had inherited cannot be ruled out. He re-introduced some practices that had been enforced in the earlier stages of the Delhi Sultanate but had fallen into disuse. In relative terms to the religious tolerance of his immediate predecessors these actions could have been considered bigotry in later analysis. Even if giving Sikandar the title of a bigot can be debated, there is absolutely no doubt regarding his extreme religious intolerance. A number of unrelated reports conclusively confirm extensive temple destruction activities committed at the Sultan's express orders. Temples were converted to caravan serais or made into common places for the Muslims to congregate. It is also reported that the destroyed idols were given to butchers to be used as meat-weights. It is obvious that the objective was not merely the destruction of the temples, but complete desecration of the concept of Hinduism.

It was at this stage in the history of India that the destruction of temples and persecution of Hindus got separated from the greed for wealth and became a purely religious pursuit. In earlier times, the destruction was primarily to gather the wealth of the temples and the religious angle was used to provide the acts of loot and plunder a veneer of respectability. With Sikandar Shah's policies these actions truly became religious policies with the gathering of wealth becoming a secondary part. Religious intolerance, which only varied in the scale of activities, became part and parcel of the Indian polity for ever thereafter.

The religious policies of Sikandar Lodi did not immediately impact the political scene in North India. Politically the Hindus and Muslims were interacting in cooperation or hostility depending on the prevailing circumstances. Hindu kings both supported and opposed the Sultanate in a politically expedient manner. Religion played only a secondary role in these calculations. A century before Sikandar's reign, his religious policies and attitude towards Hindus and other non-believers would not have raised any eyebrows. His religious intolerance would have been considered normal and no separate mention of it would have been made. However, in the late 15th century his bigotry was particularly noticeable and the chroniclers asserted and applauded his zealous pursuit of the Islamic faith. Considering all factors in an overarching manner, Sikandar Lodi would have to be considered a religious bigot.

Conclusion

Sikandar Shah Lodi was personally brave and dauntless. It is reported that Bahlul chose him as the successor prompted by the prince's heroism in suppressing the rebellion of Tatar Khan in the Punjab. Even after he became the Sultan, he led most of the military campaigns himself. During his reign he maintained order in the Sultanate by formulating fair and firm policies that were enforced effectively. More importantly, although he derived his support base from the Afghan nobility, he managed to keep the turbulent barons in check. This must be considered one of his greater achievements.

Without doubt, it was the father-son duo of Bahlul and Sikandar that kept the flame of the Delhi Sultanate alive. It would have floundered and been extinguished during the time of Alam Shah if the Lodis had not arrived on the scene. Following from the turbulent rule of his father, Sikandar Shah managed to usher in stability into the Sultanate with sagacity, shrewdness and the deliberate use of force when required. On his death bed Sikandar Lodi could not have known or even imagined that he was presiding over the twilight of an empire that was about to be engulfed by the darkness of extinction.

Chapter 30

IBRAHIM LODI: THE TWILIGHT SULTAN

Sikandar Lodi had many sons, the eldest being Ibrahim Khan and the second Jalal Khan, both born to the same mother. They were also considered to be the most capable amongst the young princes. Ibrahim Khan has been described as intelligent, courageous, generous and the embodiment of praiseworthy moral qualities. In early life itself he was marked for kingship. The Afghan nobles, the wellspring of Lodi power, continued to be freedom loving and on Sikandar's death asserted their right to choose the next sultan. They elected Ibrahim unanimously as the sultan, and Ibrahim was crowned as Ibrahim Shah Lodi. However, their unanimity of choice did not stop them from placing Jalal Khan as the independent ruler of the territories east and south of Jaunpur. Jalal was already the governor of Kalpi and this division of territory effectively curtailed Ibrahim's ability to assume full sovereignty of the Sultanate.

The reason for the division enforced by the nobles is not entirely clear. Where explanations have been provided in some chronicles, they do not seem plausible or believable and cannot be authenticated. The most likely reason has its roots in the reign of Sikandar Lodi. He had not been kind to the nobles and had vehemently curtailed their independence, while severely punishing wrong-doers. The nobles did not want a repeat of the same situation and presumed that by creating a two-headed monarchy, they would be able to curtail the power of both the rulers. It is certain that given their issues with Sikandar, the nobles were wary of Ibrahim's possible future actions and wanted to ensure that he could not exert complete control over them. There is another version of the establishment of this dual monarchy, which states that the nobles persuaded Ibrahim to partition the empire and to give Jalal independent charge of Jaunpur. This is only another way of stating that the nobles decided to partition the empire between the two brothers and did so.

> ### The Afghan Nobility
>
> The Afghan nobles were not a homogenous group. Each one of them was fundamentally loyal to his tribe and clan, essentially belonging completely to the clan as opposed to the broader concept of being 'Afghan'. They did come together when their individual interests coincided, but more often than not acted in a petty, narrow, and partisan manner.
>
> By the time Ibrahim Lodi was ascending the throne, the Lodis considered themselves the 'ruling class' and the rest of the nobility and the clans as belonging to a class that could be considered 'servants of the Lodis'. This situation was obviously not acceptable to the fiercely independent Afghans, more used to being treated at par with the sultan, who they had elevated to the position. The division of the empire between Delhi and Jaunpur effectively reduced the power of the Delhi Sultan and brought the collective and individual power and prestige of the Afghan nobles closer to that held by the Sultan.

Ibrahim accepted the division without any protest. He was crowned on 21 (or 22) November 1517 in Agra, which was followed by a celebration, reported as the grandest ever held in the entire history of the Delhi Sultanate. This was the last hurrah of the Sultanate, whose twilight had come to pass with the accession of Ibrahim Lodi.

Civil War

After Ibrahim was enthroned, Jalal Khan and his nobles started their journey, initially to Kalpi and then to Jaunpur, to claim his inheritance. After about a month, Khan-i-Jahan Nuhani, the governor of Rapri and a loyal noble of Sikandar Lodi, came to Agra, ostensibly to congratulate

Ibrahim on his becoming the Sultan. He took the opportunity to address the nobles of the court and convinced them of the folly of having a dual monarchy and dividing the empire. He was able to sway them towards repudiating the deal, especially since the nobles loyal to Jalal Khan had departed with him to Jaunpur. This impassioned plea for unity of rule also contained the seeds of an impending civil war.

Ibrahim, on the advice of his nobles, send a message to Jalal to return to Agra in order to re-negotiate the partition of the Sultanate. Jalal Khan, on the advice of nobles loyal to him, refused to return to Agra or to consider renegotiating the already agreed partition deal. Ibrahim, was a shrewd person and had already realised that the Afghan nobles were playing a game to their own tune in order to increase their hold on power at the cost of the monarch's diminishing hold on the state. He now decided to crush the nobles and make them powerless, which he saw as the only way to ensure that he could rule without interference. Accordingly he unleashed a relentless 'war' on senior Afghan nobles while at the same time initiating steps to bring Jalal Khan under control.

He instituted three firm steps to restrict the power of Jalal. First, he send a courteous request to Jalal to come to Agra; second, he send another 'firman', a royal order, to all nobles in the eastern part of the empire asking them not to recognise Jalal Khan's authority as the ruler Jaunpur, he also sent lavish gifts to the senior nobles along with the firman, gradually turning them against Jalal; and third, he imprisoned all his brothers to ensure that none of them created trouble because of ambition to usurp the throne while he was busy containing Jalal. Jalal Khan was taken aback by the turn of events and the emerging situation that was becoming unfavourable to him.

Jalal Khan was also a competent prince and therefore dealt with the summons to Agra with caution and diplomacy. He moved to Kalpi, his old governance, and refused to move out, camping there to shore up his strength. However, he was not at peace since some of his nobles were seen to be prone to following Ibrahim's orders. Jalal's position was precarious and he knew it. Jalal weighed his options and realised that he had no option but to abandon diplomacy and therefore he openly declared his hostility towards Ibrahim. He strengthened his army with the help of the zamindars who had rebelled against the Lodis earlier.

Then he had himself crowned as Sultan Jalal ud-Din and had coins struck in his name to declare and reinforce his independent status.

Ibrahim also was not wasting time and decided to take action. He carried out another coronation to impress upon the people the fact that there was only one legitimate Sultan for the entire empire. He conferred gifts, jagirs and titles on the nobles and military officers, thereby binding them to his monarchy. He also gave money to the common soldiers and the general population, while being generous in looking after the poor and the needy. Ibrahim's court now rivalled the grandeur that was obvious during the reigns of Balban and Ala ud-Din Khilji. He further introduced a new custom that prohibited any noble from sitting down when the Sultan was present in court.

Having established his position as the unquestioned Sultan he now put in place his action plan to deal with Jalal Khan. He sent and army under Azam Humayun Sarwani's command to attack Jalal ud-Din. However, Azam Humayun's son was the Vizier of Jalal ud-Din, who persuade his father to abandon the siege and subsequently to join forces with the Jaunpur army. This action was to have a devastating effect on the fortunes of the Sarwani clan a few years later. Buoyed by this turn of events, Jalal attacked Avadh, a province of the Delhi Sultanate. The governor of Avadh, Said Khan fled to Lucknow and reported to Ibrahim. This brought the hostility between the brothers into open conflict.

On the surface it would seem that the civil war that was now inevitable was the result of the aggressive actions of Jalal ud-Din. In truth, the reality was that Jalal was forced to initiate this action because of the breach of faith by Sultan Ibrahim Lodi. Ibrahim now set out personally to confront the Jaunpur forces. Before moving out of Agra, he send all his imprisoned brothers to the fort at Hansi, to continue as prisoners of the state but kept in comfort. Ibrahim marched with his army to Bhongaon, where Azam Humayun and his son defected back to the Delhi army. The Delhi army was already large and was now strengthened further by the Sarwani forces joining it.

Perceiving his worsening situation, Jalal ud-Din adopted a strong strategy. Gathering all his available forces he marched towards Agra, which was now undefended—devoid of troops and the Sultan.

However, this move also left Kalpi defenceless, which was attacked and sacked with great gusto by the Delhi forces. Meanwhile Jalal laid siege to Agra. The commander of the fort, Adam Khan fought and kept the Jaunpur forces at bay for a little while. Then he managed to buy time by smooth talking Jalal into inaction and thus saved the city from being sacked and pillaged. Even though Jalal possessed a superior force to the one defending Agra, Adam Khan managed to convince him into surrendering all the royal signs of sovereignty, even though the Jaunpur nobles and military officers tried to dissuade Jalal ud-Din from doing so. Adam Khan promised Jalal that Ibrahim would let him keep control of his part of the empire, if he did not sack Agra.

On Jalal accepting these terms his large army disbanded on their own, realising that they would be sacrificed to the fury of Ibrahim, if this peace deal was to come to fruition. Adam Khan presented the agreed terms and conditions for cessation of the war to Ibrahim Lodi, who was unwilling to come to any terms with his brother. He knew that long-term safety lay in the complete destruction of Jalal who, if left alone, could in time develop into a potential rival to the throne. He also understood very clearly that only the removal of Jalal from the scene would put an end to the Civil War and the on-going intrigue of the Afghan nobles. He therefore rejected the peace deal brought about through Adam Khan's proposals. In doing so Ibrahim behaved in a discourteous and impolitic manner, even by the norms of the age. Jalal ud-Din, now without an army, fled to Gwalior seeking safety and shelter with the Raja. Ibrahim Lodi was now the unquestioned Sultan of the entire Sultanate. However, this victory came at the cost of his losing the trust of all the nobles, who realised that Ibrahim was not one to keep his word.

The Subjugation of Gwalior

Having warded off the immediate threat and neutralised Jalal, Ibrahim turned his attention to the management of the kingdom. However, his brother's rebellion and the intransigent nature of the Afghan nobles who continued to intrigue had embittered the Sultan. He became increasingly authoritative and arbitrary in his decisions. In one such decision, he dismissed Mian Bhua, the loyal and trusted Vizier of Sikandar Lodi and imprisoned him. The old man soon died in captivity and the nobles believed that he had been poisoned, a suspicion that

Ibrahim was not able to allay satisfactorily. After a time of capricious rule, Ibrahim felt that he had set the internal affairs of state in order and turned his attention to Gwalior.

Sikandar Lodi had called a council of war to capture Gwalior just before he took ill and died. In fact that was the reason for all the princes, most governors and the senior nobles to have been present in Agra at the time of his death. Their presence in Agra had also facilitated the quick accession of Ibrahim to the throne. There were two reasons for Ibrahim Lodi wanting to invade and capture Gwalior. First was the dynastic rivalry between the kingdoms, buttressed by the inherent expansionist policy followed by all the Lodi sultans. The second, and more immediate reason was that Jalal had sought, and been given, refuge in Gwalior. Jalal had been sheltered by Raja Man Singh, who had subsequently died and was succeeded by his son, Raja Vikramaditya. In Ibrahim Lodi's mind, Gwalior was an aberration and had to be defeated.

Once again, Ibrahim deputed Azam Humayun Sarwani to capture the fort of Gwalior. Gwalior, now ruled by Raja Vikramaditya, 'the illustrious son of a distinguished father', prepared to defend his kingdom. Gwalior was besieged and vicious fighting ensued. Witnessing the ferocious battle, Jalal ud-Din, ever the chivalrous prince, moved to Malwa in order to reduce the burden on his hosts.

The End of Jalal ud-Din

Jalal ud-Din moved from Gwalior and sought shelter with Mahmud Khilji II, ruling Malwa. The kingdom of Malwa was in the throes of a fierce civil war—Mahmud was fighting for survival against his powerful vizier Medini Rai. Perhaps because of this pre-occupation, or on purpose, Mahmud did not give any importance to Jalal and also did not provide or even promise any assistance for him to attempt regaining his inheritance.

Disappointed with Mahmud Khilji, Jalal moved east to Garha Katanga (now a village about 23 miles from Jabalpur on the Jabalpur-Sagar road). This was Gond territory and the Gond king, Sangram Shah, had Jalal ud-Din arrested and send him to Agra in chains to gain Ibrahim Lodi's friendship. Ibrahim, humiliated Jalal by having him brought to the durbar (royal court) with his hand tied behind his back. Thereafter he was ordered to be incarcerated in the fort at Hansi with his other brothers. However, Jalal never reached Hansi, on the way to the fort he was murdered by being poisoned on the orders of the Ibrahim Lodi.

In Gwalior, the fort was breached and unable to withstand the Delhi army, Raja Vikramaditya sued for peace. Ibrahim Lodi annexed Gwalior to the Sultanate but granted Vikramaditya the fief of Shamsabad to rule. However, he was annoyed with the fact that Jalal ud-Din had managed to escape. He suspected Azam Humayun and his son of complicity in Jalal's escape to Malwa and of double-dealing during the campaign. The suspicion was based on their earlier defection to Jalal ud-Din's camp. He recalled them to Agra and cast them in prison. This gave cause for another rebellion by the nobles.

The Rebellion of the Nobles

Azam Humayun's and his son's disgrace alarmed the other nobles, already dissatisfied with Ibrahim's high-handed behaviour. There was rampant discontentment with Ibrahim's arbitrary actions. The nobles raised the banner of rebellion under the leadership of Islam Khan, another son of Azad Humayun. The rebel army consisted of 40,000 cavalry and 500 elephants, outnumbering the royal forces.

Before the rebellion could escalate into a full-fledged civil war, Shaikh Raju Bokhari, a holy man of repute, offered to negotiate a settlement to the dispute. The rebels demanded the release of Azad Humayun Sarwani in return for disbanding their army. On hearing the demand, Ibrahim flew into a rage and ordered his commanders to

> 'exterminate' the rebels. The armies of Behar, Ghazipur and Oudh joint together to fight the rebels. A fierce battle ensued. Chroniclers claim the battle to have been the largest that had so far been fought on the sub-continent. In the end the rebels were defeated and the insurrection suppressed, with heavy losses on both sides.

Contemporary chroniclers describe the reason for the rebellion as the ingratitude of the nobles. They paper over and do not mention the extreme cruelty and obstinacy displayed by Ibrahim Lodi that was the real reason for the insurrection and the civil war that followed. The Sultan exulted on breaking the strength of the nobles who opposed him while rewarding those who had fought on his side. However, he did not appreciate the fact that by this one single act of wrecking the nobles' power he had also destroyed the core of the Sultanate army on which the strength and stability of his Empire was founded. Further, rather than learn the grim lesson of the rebellion and understand the percolating discontent and distrust of his nobles, Ibrahim regarded the victory over the rebels as an endorsement and a victory of his policies. He became even more ruthless in his dealings with the nobles.

Ibrahim Lodi now committed himself to a policy of persecution of the nobles who he even remotely suspected of being disloyal. He had an inherently suspicious nature that was exacerbated by the rebellion of the nobles. He imprisoned or killed senior nobles without even attempting to provide a reason and without any appreciation of the service that they had rendered to his father and the Sultanate. In his entrenched self-conceit, he believed that he could rule without the assistance of the nobles and wanted to crush the entire nobility. For the same reason he did not appreciate that his actions were weakening the very edifice that upheld the Sultanate.

The war with Gwalior, which was proclaimed as a great victory was actually won with a very thin margin. The 'victorious' Sultan had to be very diplomatic in dealing with the Raja, something that was anathema to Ibrahim. The fact that diplomacy was resorted to itself demonstrates the precariousness of the victory and its aftermath. Even though the Sultanate was going through internal convulsions, Ibrahim

Lodi now decided to go to war with Rana Sangram Singh (popularly called Rana Sangha) of Mewar.

War with Mewar

Mewar was the most powerful Rajput country of the time. Rana Sangha, the king, was well-known across the sub-continent for his personal bravery, his prowess as a commander and for his strategic astuteness. The civil war in Malwa had polarised the states of North India with Rana Sangha interfering on the side of Medini Rai and the Lodi Sultans supporting Mahmud Khilji II. In fact the Rajput king and the Lodis, both coveted Malwa territory. Sikandar Lodi had sided with Khilji and Ibrahim had inherited the animosity towards the Rajputs from his father. Effectively, Mewar and the Sultanate were ranged on opposite sides of the civil war in Malwa. Khilji had also asked Gujarat for help and a body of troops had been send to Malwa by the Gujarat ruler. However, the combined armies of Delhi and Gujarat were defeated in battle and Medini Rai was installed on the throne of Malwa. Even so, the conflict between Delhi and Mewar had not been put to bed and had continued sporadically.

During the civil war in the Sultanate, Rana Sangha had encroached on Delhi territory and annexed some parts. Ibrahim decided to set this issue right and marched against Mewar. In the battle that ensued in Khatoli, near Gwalior, Ibrahim Lodi was soundly defeated by Rana Sangha and had to beat a hasty retreat. However, further skirmishes led to an indecisive state of affairs, with no clear victor. In the Battle of Khatoli, Rana Sangha lost his left arm and was hit by an arrow that lodged in his leg that maimed him, leaving him lame for life. However, the Rajput army captured Ghiyas ud-Din, a prince of the Lodi house. Both the Rana and the Sultan were angry at the indecisiveness of the battle and war was inevitable. The very next year, 1518-19, Ibrahim renewed hostilities.

Ibrahim despatched a large army towards Mewar, which was met by the Rajput forces at Dholpur. In the ensuing battle, the Rajput army held the upper hand from the beginning. The Lodi generals were disunited and did not act on a common plan, with one general Husain Farmuli deserting to join the Mewar forces. The Lodi army suffered a crushing defeat and retreated, pursued all the way to Bayana by Rana

Sangha's forces. Ibrahim Lodi now interfered personally and stopped the rout, raising the morale of the Sultanate forces. He also persuaded Farmuli to leave the Mewar forces and re-join the Delhi army. There is a mention in an Islamic chronicle that Husain Farmuli decided to go back to the Sultan's forces because of the slights he received at Rana Sangha's court. There were a few minor and indecisive battles fought after this major confrontation, before the war ended.

Bayana became the northern border of Mewar with the kingdom now being bound by River Sinde in the east and the kingdom of Malwa in the south. After the battle had ended, Ibrahim had Husain Farmuli, at that time was the governor of Chanderi, murdered. Rana Sangha took this opportunity to annex Chanderi to his kingdom, a feat achieved without much of opposition to be overcome. With the loss of Chanderi, the Lodi kingdom lost its southern most outpost. In this drawn out war with Mewar, Ibrahim Lodi lost a fair bit of territory, expended enormous resources as compared to the Rajput king and suffered an irreparable setback to his reputation. Rana Sangha is credited with having won 18 pitched battles against Delhi and Malwa, out of which at least two, fought at Bakrol and Ghatoli, were against forces personally led by Ibrahim Lodi. These are confirmed statistics. These defeats affected the Sultan's power and prestige, while at the same time the internal governance of the Sultanate was weakening by the constant friction with the nobles.

An Improbable Story

One Islamic account that provides an explanation of Husain Farmuli re-joining Ibrahim Lodi states that the Lodi army won a hard fought and vicious battle that culminated in Rana Sangha fleeing the battlefield after being wounded. The account proclaims this as a great victory for the Sultanate forces. However, this statement is not corroborated by any other chronicle or report and also does not rate even a mention in the Rajput chronicles. The statement cannot be considered true.

> The Rajput accounts confirm the frequent wars between Delhi and Mewar without providing much details of individual encounters or their outcomes. It could be believed that most of the skirmishes were indecisive and only of minor consequence in nature. It is also certain that both sides would not accept and record a 'defeat' in their own chronicles. The bardic chroniclers of Rajputana eulogise the enormous military resources of Mewar, a fact that is acknowledged in Muslim writers as well. The bards also extol Rana Sangha's battlefield expertise and command capabilities, both of which are also acknowledged by the reports of the Sultanate. Considering this authentic information, it can be concluded that the reported 'massive' victory of Ibrahim Lodi's Delhi forces did not take place. The account is apocryphal in the face of no corroboration from other independent sources.

A Diminishing Empire

The murder of Husain Farmuli, close to the suspicious deaths on Mian Bhua and Azam Humayun in prison, bred a culture of suspicion within the nobles of Delhi. Darya Khan Nuhani, the governor of Bihar rebelled, although he died soon after the revolt. His son Bahadur Shah continued the rebellion and declared independence from Delhi, issuing his own coins. Many other nobles joined him in the rebellion and it is reported that the rebel army grew in size to 100,000 cavalry and associated other forces. Bolstered by this strength, Bahadur Shah captured the entire upper Ganga country and controlled the region from Bihar to Sambhal, about 80 miles from Delhi. Over a period of time, under the title Sultan Muhammad Shah, he became very powerful, fighting several battles against the Delhi forces in which he always emerged victorious. The east was now out of Ibrahim's control. On the other border, the Rajputs under Rana Sangha were far too strong to be brought into submission. The Sultanate was clearly diminishing in size and stature.

At this juncture, Ibrahim ordered Daulat Khan Lodi, the governor of Punjab to come to Agra, since he was in arrears in payment of compulsory tribute to the Sultan. Daulat Khan was the son of Tatar Khan who had been the governor of Punjab for over 20 years under Sikandar Lodi and had effectively kept the north-west frontier secure for the Sultanate. Daulat felt that the Sultan's intentions were not honourable and send his son Dilawar in his stead to Agra. Ibrahim was enraged and threatened both son and father with dire consequences if his order was not obeyed forthwith. Dilawar managed to escape from Agra and reported the Sultan's intentions to his father. Daulat Khan realised that he was Ibrahim Lodi's next target and therefore, invited Babur ruling in Kabul to invade the Sultanate and destroy the dynastic power of the Lodi's. He send the invitation to Babur through his son Dilawar Khan. This set in motion an irreversible set of events that was to change the history of the sub-continent forever. The invitation to Babur was also the death knell of the three-centuries-old Delhi Sultanate.

Fall of the Lodi Dynasty

Although internal dissentions were pulling the Sultanate apart, the real threat to Ibrahim Lodi, his dynasty, and to the very existence of the Sultanate itself emanated from outside India—in the guise of Babur, the ruler of Kabul. The direct and immediate cause was the discontent of the nobles, spearheaded by Daulat Khan who was caught between Scylla and Charybdis. If he obeyed the Sultan and went to Agra, he would in all likelihood be imprisoned and later murdered; and if he rebelled outright, he did not have the strength to prevail against the Lodi forces, even in its reduced state, and therefore the end-state would be the same. The invitation to Babur seemed the best, and only, option open to the governor of Punjab. It is interesting that around the same time Alam Khan, a disaffected uncle of Ibrahim Lodi, had made a similar request to Babur to bring down the Delhi Sultan.

The invitations to take action came at an opportune moment for Babur. His kingdom was being threatened by Uzbeks from the west whose military power he could not hope to resist. For some time Babur had been considering India as a possible refuge from the Uzbek menace. (The early life and rise of Babur to the rulership of Kabul is covered in detail in a subsequent volume in this series.) Babur therefore decided to invade Punjab, in alliance with Daulat Khan. Daulat Khan, Alam Khan and Rana Sangha all knew, or would have at least suspected, Babur's ultimate intentions—to annex North India for himself. However, in order to destroy Ibrahim Lodi's power, they turned a blind eye to that possibility and even encouraged the Mughal's designs on India. This attitude, especially of the Rajput king, Rana Sangha, remains an inexplicable fact in the long history of the Indian sub-continent. There is a report, not fully confirmable, which claims that Rana Sangha also had send an envoy to Babur requesting his help to remove Ibrahim from the throne of Delhi. Ibrahim Lodi got wind of the alliance being built against him in Punjab and immediately stopped his on-going campaign in the East. He sent an army to Punjab to subdue Daulat Khan and also to repel any foreign invaders. Daulat Khan was driven out of Lahore, which was occupied by imperial forces.

Alam Khan was pursuing his own personal ambitions while also cooperating with Daulat Khan in facilitating Babur's invasion. In 1524, Alam Khan had been invited by some disgruntled nobles to assume the throne of Delhi with the title Sultan Ala ud-Din. The fact remained that he was a Sultan without a throne. Alam Khan had met Babur in Kabul and proposed that he would let Babur keep Punjab as a prize for helping him gain the throne of Delhi. The sequence of events as it happened are reported differently in different chronicles and records. The fact remains that even before his invasion, Babur was well aware that almost everyone of consequence hated Ibrahim Lodi, the Sultan ruling from Delhi/Agra.

In 1524, Babur marched through the Khyber Pass and reached Lahore, destroying the countryside along his conquering march. Ibrahim's army stationed in Lahore gave battle, but was easily defeated. Babur sacked Lahore, then burned it. There was mayhem for four days in Lahore after which he marched to Deopalpur. There Babur put the entire garrison to the sword. At Deopalpur, Daulat Khan who had fled from Lahore when the Sultanate army captured it, met with Babur. Daulat was dismayed at the manner in which Babur had sacked Lahore and devastated the countryside. To add insult to injury, instead of handing over Punjab to Daulat Khan, Babur annexed the province to his own kingdom and appointed his officers to administer Punjab. Daulat realised that although he had wanted Ibrahim Lodi to be ruined, it was his own fiefdom that Babur had annexed. The disillusionment was complete when Babur assigned Jalandhar and Sultanpur to Daulat

Khan and kept Lahore for himself. This broke whatever semblance of an alliance that existed between Babur and Daulat Khan.

Daulat Khan now planned to attack Babur, to regain his territories and also to salvage his pride and prestige. However, his own son, Dilawar Khan, informed Babur of his father's intentions. Fearing Babur's wrath Daulat Khan went into hiding. After securing Punjab, Babur returned to Kabul to quell the trouble brewing there and to prepare for another, more permanent, invasion of Hindustan. The only objective of the previous expedition had been to secure Punjab as a safe haven and refuge in the case of an Uzbek invasion of Kabul. Babur now planned the next expedition to conquer and rule Hindustan, his ambition kindled by what he had observed in the campaign of 1524.

On Babur's departure from Punjab, Daulat Khan emerged from hiding and wanted to rebel against Babur's annexation of Punjab. However, he was on his own and could not trust any of the other nobles, including his own son. He could not trust Babur to treat him properly and he could not now join forces with Ibrahim since their rift had become far too wide for effective reconciliation. In a state of disgrace he commenced a rebellion and struggle, in isolation, to re-capture his lost territories. He had some initial success—he defeated Dilawar Khan and captured Sultanpur and drove out Alam Khan from Deopalpur, even though he failed to seize Sialkot. Alam Khan fled to Kabul and returned to Punjab with Babur sending instructions to his forces there to help Alam secure the throne of Delhi. This was a far-fetched order and therefore it is debatable whether Babur actually meant it or was only placating a bothersome ally.

In the event Daulat Khan persuaded Alam Khan to join forces with him and the combined army marched to Delhi. They managed to defeat the Delhi army, commanded by Ibrahim himself, in a concerted night attack. However, the Lodi Sultan was a tough commander and managed to rally his forces. By sheer determination, demonstrated courage and efficient leadership, he managed to counter attack and defeat the superior forces of Punjab. Daulat Khan fled the battlefield and joined Babur's camp, now as a pardoned vassal with no independent status.

In November 1525, Babur re-entered Hindustan, consolidated his hold on Punjab, and rapidly moved towards Delhi. He camped at a place between the River Yamuna and the town of Panipat, a mere 80 miles from Delhi. Babur's arrival near Delhi caused consternation amongst the nobles. The nobles were once again divided with many of them making overtures towards Babur and promising him assistance.

Ibrahim Lodi moved his army north and camped south of Panipat, in good defensive positions to prevent further advance of Babur's army towards Delhi. There is a story that some astrologers predicted that Lodi would be defeated, which prompted Ibrahim to order a celebration in his camp to boost the sagging morale of his forces. Battle was inevitable. The Battle of Panipat, in later history called the 'First Battle of Panipat', was fought on 20 April 1526 and was fiercely contested.

> ### The Lack of Foresight and Unity
>
> The more powerful kings of North India do not seem to have realised the threat that was on their doorsteps. They failed to appreciate Babur's intentions fuelled by vaulting ambition and the fact that they were all facing an existentialist threat. No one grasped the seriousness of the situation and nor did they visualise the darkness that was about to engulf each one of them.
>
> Rana Sangha, perhaps the most powerful military commander of the lot and also a better strategist than anyone else, was sanguine about establishing Rajput superiority after the battle, irrespective of the outcome and the victor. Bahadur Shah, the prince of Gujarat, was physically present at Panipat with a force of more than a 1000 cavalry. He watched the battle without interfering, content with figuring out the outcome. Mahmud Khilji of Malwa did not even mobilise his forces. The kings of Mewar, Malwa and Gujarat were busy formulating their own plans to further their petty interests after the battle was over.
>
> Unity against a foreign aggressor was not a phrase in their vocabulary or rule book.

In the battle, the smaller, but more agile force of Babur won a decisive victory through the employment of innovative and clever tactics. This historic victory was achieved because of the superior fighting technique of the Mughal army, the skilful employment of cavalry and superiority in firepower through the use of artillery. Ibrahim Lodi fell in battle—the first and only Sultan to die on the battlefield. Babur admired Ibrahim Lodi's valour and personal courage and had him buried with great honour at the spot where he had fallen. *[The tomb has now become a minor pilgrimage centre.]*

Babur send his son Humayun to occupy and secure the fort at Agra and himself joined him later. On 10 May 1526, Babur entered Agra ceremoniously and took up residence in the palace as the 'Emperor of Hindustan'. The three-century long turbulent history of the Delhi Sultanate had come to an inglorious end. The Afghan hegemony in the rule of Delhi was broken and the Sultanate passed on to the hands of the Chagatai Turks, who were better known as the Mughals.

Ibrahim Lodi – The Last Sultan

Ibrahim Lodi was a man of contrasts. In his personal life, his conduct was unblemished. He was kind to his subjects and a considerate ruler by medieval standards. His kingdom continued to prosper despite some alarmingly naïve decisions and a state of stability and peace prevailed for the initial part of his reign. He also administered justice as well as any of his predecessors. Ibrahim was intelligent, an able administrator and endowed with personal courage and battlefield bravery.

At the same time he was rash and impolitic in his decisions. He attempted to establish absolutism in the Sultanate when the circumstances pointed towards being more congenial. The attempt was therefore premature. This move towards centralisation of power was followed by the policy of repression of the nobles without the Sultan putting in place other policies that would have strengthened the administration and the army, as the power and support of the nobles for the Sultan waned. The initiative was bound to fail, as it eventually did.

His lack of foresight was demonstrated by his alienating the nobles even when the threat to the kingdom from foreign invasion was apparent for nearly five years. Ibrahim's inability to grasp future trends proved disastrous for him personally, the dynasty and for the Sultanate.

Ibrahim Lodi's fundamental fault lay in the fact that he could not fully understand the character traits of the Afghan nobles who were the foundational support base of the Lodi dynasty. His attempts ate instilling vigorous discipline and strict ceremonial procedures at court—a distinct contrast from the informal court of his grandfather—was anathema to the free-spirited Afghan nobles. His insistence on formalities was one of the primary reasons for the rebellion of the nobles. Ibrahim's institution of insolent and brutal punishment against the rebellion further alienated the nobles, on whose support the basis of the Lodi rule rested. With the destruction of the foundation of his power, almost like a self-inflicted death wish, Lodi lost his life and kingdom.

THE ENCROACHING ISLAMIC INFLUENCE

It was not just a question of ethnic or doctrinal differences. Two diametrically opposed codes of social behaviour had collided: one universal, inflexible, authoritarian and obligatory which upheld the equality of individual believers and theoretically promoted a strong send of community; the other India-specific, sectional, discriminatory and hierarchical which denied equality and revelled in diversity.

– John Keay,
India: A History, pp. 277-78

Chapter 31

GOVERNANCE OF THE SULTANATE

From its very beginning, the Delhi Sultanate was governed in accordance with the Islamic Law, as laid down in the Sharia. Even though there were few exceptions to the strict adherence to the laid down norms, successive Sultans largely followed the injunctions of the Sharia in the administration of their kingdom. Essentially this made the Sultanate a theocracy; it was never a secular state, as claimed by some modern historians. The level of religious tolerance, or intolerance, varied over its 300-year history—tolerance waxing and waning with the personal proclivities of the Sultan and, more importantly, the power that he wielded as an autocratic ruler. There is however no doubt that only Islam was recognised as the true religion, even though the majority population was overwhelmingly Hindu in their religious beliefs.

It was not only the Sultan who was a staunch Muslim, but all prominent families in the Sultanate were also followers of Islam. Within the broader empire, there were Hindu chiefs who continued to rule their small principalities under the benevolent supervision of the Sultan, but they played only a very insignificant part in the governance of the kingdom. Only those who converted to Islam could aspire to rise to positions of influence and power in the administration. Further, all the resources allocated for welfare activities were utilised for Muslim purposes only, which is not surprising considering the religious basis of the Sultanate.

The Theocracy

Some modern Indian historians, Dr I. H. Qureshi for instance, have argued that the Sultanate, at worst, could be considered a 'theocentric' kingdom and that it was never a 'theocracy'. The reason put forward is that in the absolute definition of the term, a qualifying characteristic of a theocracy is the requirement for it to be the 'rule of the ordained priesthood'. This characteristic was obviously absent in the Delhi Sultanate since it was ruled by a succession of sultans. However, this argument is not tenable when applied to the Delhi Sultanate. In both letter and spirit, the Sultanate was an Islamic polity with its civil law subordinated and merged into Muslim canon law. In the Delhi Sultanate, the Muslim ulema—theologians and religious lawyers—although not hereditary positions, were fanatical and biased, perhaps even more than the ordained clergy.

Further, the Sultan was expected to protect and follow the Quranic Law, personally and in administering the kingdom. Theoretically at least, the Sultan could be removed from the throne if he did not follow this path. From the very beginning, the ultimate goal of the Islamic state in India was to convert the entire sub-continent to Islam. Essentially, achieving this aim required the destruction of local religions from the root and to convert Dar-ul-harb (land of the infidels) into Dar-ul-Islam (land of the Muslims). There can be no doubt that the Delhi Sultanate was a theocracy in all aspects.

The Sultan

The ruler of the Sultanate was called Sultan. In the narratives of the period, the terms king and Sultan, and kingdom and sultanate, have been used interchangeably – as convenient – since it was a time of transition and interaction of the languages. In principle, the sovereignty of the Sultanate resided in the entire Sunni population, almost all of them foreigners in the early stages of the establishment of the Sultanate. The Sultan had to be elected by this broad brotherhood. There were practical difficulties to every Sunni Muslim participating in such a process and therefore the power to elect a new sultan came to be bestowed on a resident in a group of important men—the noblemen at the core of the administration. Over a period of time electoral power started to be vested in the sultan himself, when a dying king was permitted to name his own successor. However, the person nominated by the king on his deathbed was not always acceptable to the nobles who then challenged and changed the decision. The ability of the nobles to do so has been demonstrated by history, but such a move invariably brought its own consequences.

The fact remains that the Sultanate did not have an accepted principle of hereditary succession, even though hereditary ascension was practiced in an equal number of cases as the elevation of a consensus candidate to the throne. In practice, the post of the Sultan was always restricted to the immigrant Turks, and in the later stages of the Sultanate, to an even smaller group of oligarchs. Only in the late 15th and early 16th century did the Afghans become the rulers in Delhi. According to Islamic theory, the true king is God and the Sultan is only His agent to enforce the divine law as enshrined in the Quran. The Sultan was meant to be a sort of chief executive, enforcer, and interpreter rolled into one being. The Sultan was also the chief justice, the highest judicial authority, and also the supreme commander of the army.

Even though the monarch was elected by a group of the most powerful and influential people of the capital, the process of such a selection, the methodology, was not uniformly accepted by all theologians and religious lawyers. This led to the creation of factions supporting one or the other contender that in turn led to civil war at times. Even so, in most cases the elections were reduced to mere formalities, especially when the contender to the throne was either very powerful or had already won the crown on the battlefield. Dethroning of a monarch is the automatic corollary of an elective monarchy and the nobility used this power often in the Delhi Sultanate. A monarch considered unworthy of the position was removed by common consent and through a variety of methods. In the Delhi Sultanate, the person of the Sultan was never considered sacrosanct, irrespective of his stature. The Sultans of Delhi were unique in their common character traits—almost all of them were Turkmen, whose zeal for Islam and its propagation were unquestioned; however, they gave the same importance to tribal affiliations making their governance a unique blend of religious fervour and tribal and family demands that had to be met.

It is clear that the Sultan derived his power in equal measure from religion and the military. He could be the quintessential autocrat with unfettered powers as long as he enforced the Quranic Law. Through the three centuries of the Sultanate's existence there were only two Sultans who dared to sideline the Quranic Law without suffering any serious consequences—Ala ud-Din Khilji and Muhammad bin Tughluq. Their power and hold on the administration was such that they could not even be questioned, far less removed, for breaches in their upholding religious law. The unwavering loyalty of their large and powerful armies ensured that they were not challenged for their transgressions, even by the entrenched and powerful ulema. The two Sultans clearly demonstrated the primacy of temporal powers resident in military forces over the transient and virtual spiritual power of religion.

Purely from an outwardly appearance, the Sultan could essentially have been considered a military despot with all power concentrated in his hands. However, in actual practice his authority and freedom to act unilaterally were severely restricted. The Sultans were subservient to the Quranic Law, the Sharia, which had to be strictly enforced to ensure the support of the Muslim population. This popular support was critical to the individual continuing as the Sultan. Second, the Sultan could not interfere in the personal law of any of the groups amongst the population. There was no legal sanction for doing so and any interference was unlikely to be tolerated, by both Muslims and Hindus. The much proclaimed sovereignty that was vested in the Sultan—as an individual—is largely a myth. Every Sultan depended on the active support of a powerful group of nobles and the passive support of the general population for his survival as the monarch. Further, the support of the people had to be bolstered by the support and cooperation of the ulema—the learned and influential theologians and religious lawyers—who could sway the popular opinion very easily. The head that wore the crown was one with constant worries.

Islamic states as a whole and especially in India, were initially meant to be democratic institutions with no hereditary positions, including that of the Sultan. However, circumstances changed rapidly and it did not take long for them to transition to centralised autocracies, functioning on the fringes of hereditary rule. In the Indian sub-continent, the Sultan needed to function within a hostile Hindu environment. Powerful Hindu chiefs offered virulent resistance to foreign expansion at the expense of their territories and the loss of their own independence. At the same time, the Delhi Sultans faced the ever-present threat from the north-west, especially from the Mongols. In these circumstances the concept of an elected sultan would not have been conducive to establishing a Muslim state in India. Spreading Islamic influence needed concerted effort from a sustainable autocracy. The Sultanate had no option but to develop into a centralised oligarchy, if it had to sustain its presence in India. Even so, it came very close to being extinguished a number of times in the three hundred years of its existence, before finally being blown away in 1526.

The Administration

The Sultan appointed ministers to assist him with the administration and their numbers varied from dynasty to dynasty. The Slave dynasty sultans appointed four ministers—the prime minister or Vizier, and ministers for the army, royal correspondence and foreign affairs. Later dynasties added the portfolios of religious affairs and charity, and justice. There was also a nominal appointment of a 'deputy' sultan from outside the ruling family. This position became important and powerful only in cases where the sultan was weak and ineffective. Some other functionaries also operated close to the sultan, such as the comptroller of the royal household, a position that held great power.

The Titles

The titles of the six ministers who ruled the kingdom on behalf of the Sultan are given below:

Vizier (also spelt as Vazier or Wazir in some texts): Prime Minister

Diwan-i-ariz: minister for the army who also acted as the controller general of the entire military establishment

Diwan-i-insha: in charge of the royal correspondence

> Diwan-i-rasalat: in charge of foreign affairs and also controller of the diplomatic correspondence of the Sultanate
>
> Sadr-us-Sudur: minister in charge of religious affairs, endowments and charity
>
> Diwan-i-qaza: this minster was also the chief qazi, an ordained priest who doubled as the head of the judicial department

The Sultanate was never divided into homogenous or territorially matched provinces and therefore there was no commonality in the administrative system imposed on different jurisdictions. In the initial phases of the formation of the Sultanate in the 13th century, it consisted of individual military commands called 'iqtas', each one being ruled by a powerful military commander. Ala ud-Din Khilji, who conquered the largest swath of territory, also did not attempt to rearrange the provinces, allowing the existing divisions to continue. There were two kinds of iqtas; the inherited ones and newly conquered ones. The new conquests were normally the flourishing Hindu kingdoms and principalities that were militarily annexed and brought under the rule of senior military commanders. Some defeated Hindu chieftains were also permitted to continue their rule as vassals of Delhi. The military commander of an iqta was called the muqti.

Some of the newly acquired provinces were ruled by amirs, normally noblemen, normally more powerful than the traditional muqtis, who were only military commanders. Each iqta was required to maintain a military force that was strong enough to maintain law and order in the province. The size and composition of these local forces varied considerably. Both the amir and the muqti had unlimited power over their individual iqtas, as long as they obeyed the Sultan's orders and furnished the previously agreed number of soldiers when demanded by Delhi. They were also required to protect and enforce Islamic law in their fiefdoms. The result of such an arrangement was that most of these provincial rulers turned out to be petty despots, despite the injunctions from the Sultan to protect the peasantry, help the learned and other such pious and well-meaning homilies.

When the king in Delhi was weak and ineffective, it was not uncommon for these muqtis and amirs to go to war with each other, in order to expand their own territorial holdings. Some of the more powerful amirs also declared independence from Delhi at such times, sowing the seeds of a civil war when conditions in Delhi changed. Such rebellions were the principal cause for the decline and collapse of ruling dynasties that had already started decay at the core.

As the Sultanate expanded territorially and sultans started to pay more attention to the administration, some of the larger iqtas were further divided into shiqs. The shiq was ruled by a shiqdar, normally a military officer whose primary duty was to maintain law and order. Later an even smaller unit called pargana—an aggregate of a number of villages—was introduced. The pargana was administered by a choudhuri (spellings of this title varies in numerous ways in history books) who was mainly responsible for the collection of revenue. The Delhi Sultans instinctively adopted the Hindu system as the lowest unit of the administrative hierarchy. The village continued to be the smallest administrative unit with its own panchayat to settle disputes, functioning as a miniature commonwealth. The panchayat looked after most of the needs of the village such as local defence, education, sanitation and other needs. This was a shrewd move on the part of the Delhi administration, since it left the predominantly Hindu countryside with a sense of continuity and devoid of any feelings of being religiously or politically oppressed. For the Hindu villager, life hardly changed with the imposition of 'Muslim' rule at the centre. This was true at least in the initial phase of the establishment of the Delhi Sultanate.

The Army

The Sultanate and associated Islamic rule were imposed on the people of the sub-continent by force, not by common consent. Therefore, the Sultans always maintained a larger than normal army at their disposal. The Sultanate army normally had four classes of soldiers. The first were the regular soldiers who were permanently employed in the service of the Sultan; the second, the troops who were permanently employed by the provincial rulers, the muqtis and amirs; third, the men who were recruited during times of war; and fourth, the Muslim volunteers who formed militias in order to fight the 'jihad' or holy war.

The Sultan's forces in the capital were divided into two elements—one being the slaves of the Sultan and other, soldiers who functioned directly under royal command. There were also another group of soldiers who were employed by high-ranking officials and senior nobles as their personal body guards. Till Ala ud-Din Khilji ascended the throne, the Sultan's army was only a small nucleus who formed his bodyguards. In times of war, the Sultan relied on the forces that the muqtis and amirs send to Delhi, which formed the bulk of the Sultanate forces. Ala ud-Din reformed the concept of the military forces in the Sultanate by creating a standing army that was recruited, trained and paid by the central administration in Delhi. During his time these, truly Sultanate forces, numbered 475,000 cavalry and associated infantry and support personnel.

Firuz Shah Tughluq converted this formidable army into a feudal set up akin to the forces maintained in old times. The Khilji forces and the army of Muhammad bin Tughluq were renowned for their cohesiveness and exemplary fighting spirit that almost always created the winning edge in battle. The reintroduction of the feudal organisation by Firuz Shah, sapped these essential qualities of the force making them no better than the old Sultanate army that very seldom fought with a unity of purpose and command. The Lodi army was based entirely on clan and tribal affiliations and gradually disintegrated into the proverbial 'tribal groups' that was ill-organised and weak because of the inability of independent commanders to see beyond the immediate factor of status and prestige of the tribe. In the Lodi army, tribal affiliations always subsumed the broader aim of the campaign—unity in action or the pursuance of a central aim were impossible and far-fetched objectives.

The provincial forces were relatively less rigorously trained and not organised to the same level of efficiency as the Sultanate forces. Their discipline and payments were the purview of the provincial governors, even when they were in the service of the Sultan. However, they were regularly placed at the disposal of the Sultan during times of war. Since they served two masters, their loyalty was always questionable. During war with Hindu chiefs, Muslim volunteers were permitted to fight along with the army. These forces could be considered irregular forces and were not paid a salary but only allowed to share in the booty after the battle.

The Sultanate army continued the tradition of the sub-continental Hindu armies of having three arms; namely the cavalry, infantry and the elephant corps. Obviously the elephant corps was an addition after the Sultanate had been established because the Islamic forces of the Middle-East and Central Asia did not have war-elephants and were fully reliant on the swiftness and manoeuvre capabilities of their cavalry. Even after the introduction of the elephant corps, the Islamic forces maintained the cavalry as the backbone of the army unlike most of the Hindu armies that placed an inordinately high reliance on the elephants. At the zenith of the Sultanate, its cavalry numbered in the hundreds of thousands and was made up mostly of Turks and other foreigners. The infantry consisted of foot soldiers and archers, the majority of whom were Indian Muslims, meaning converts to Islam from the Indian sub-continent. Even though a later addition, the war elephants were much valued by all the Sultans. However, none of them seem to have mastered the operational and tactical level manoeuvres in employing these behemoths to use them effectively. By royal decree only the Sultan's army was permitted to possess elephants, providing an indication of the value that was placed on a well-trained elephant corps. The army did not possess any formalised artillery or personal firearms but used incendiary arrows and rockets to good effect, especially in siege activities against well-defended forts. Gunpowder powered fire balls and stones were used as a sort of 'mechanical' artillery.

The cavalry was organised on a decimal basis. Ten troopers made up the fundamental unit of the cavalry and was placed under a sar-i-khail; ten such units were under a sipahsalar; ten sipahsalars fought under an amir; ten amirs under a malik; and ten maliks under a khan. Effectively a Khan commanded 100,000 cavalry and associated infantry. However it is doubtful whether more than a few khans had the full complement of forces at all times under his command. The army strength, calculated in such a manner, was more on paper than in actuality. The organisation was effective and accountability could be very rapidly spread to the lower levels of command. However, the discipline of the imperial army varied under different Sultans.

The Delhi Sultanate army was never a nationalist army but remained a mercenary force throughout the three centuries of its existence. It consisted of soldiers of diverse ethnicities and nationalities—Turks from various tribes, some even at war with each other; and Tajiks, Persians, Mongols, Afghans, Arabs, Abyssinians, Indian Muslims and even a smattering of Hindus. The army was a heterogeneous body with no national sentiment, bonded together in the person of the Sultan. Even though there was a minster for the army in the royal court, he was purely an administrative head directly responsible to the Sultan for the well-being of the army, particularly in times of relative peace. The Sultan was always the commander-in-chief and never transferred this position to anyone else. The army was predominantly Muslim in nature; majority of the soldiers and all officers were Muslims, and they were continually reminded that they were fighting in an alien land against infidels. The army was therefore held together by religious solidarity and practised fanaticism of an extreme kind. However, despite individual and at times collective fanaticism that created exemplary, and at times ruthless, fighting spirit, from an overarching strategic perspective the army was not well-trained and not optimally efficient. Contemporary chronicles provide such assessments, and they are also corroborated by different sources.

A review of the history of the Sultanate and its Sultans provide a clear indication that all the successful rulers were adept at military strategy and battlefield tactics, demonstrably brave as individuals, and led the army from the front in all major encounters. They were also students of geography and terrain, as far as possible reconnoitring the battlefield well in advance of a forthcoming battle. Some analysts have mentioned flanking parties of specially selected cavalry as being integral to the Sultanate army. These forces acted as the royal reserve, which was employed at the time and place selected by the Sultan depending on his appreciation of the flow of battle, and was capable of turning the tide in a contested and balanced encounter in its favour. However, it is doubtful whether any of the Delhi armies, other than the Khilji army, mastered the use of these shock cavalry to good effect. The concept, well-used by the Turks in the early days of the Sutanate, seems to have fallen into disuse over a period of time. This assessment is made based on the fact that if Ibrahim Lodi had Flanking Forces, and understood their optimised employment, he may not have lost the Battle of Panipat in 1526. This is one of the great 'ifs' of history that can only be speculated upon. *[A detailed account of the First Battle of Panipat (1526) will be provided in a later volume of this series on Indian history, which deals with the arrival of the Mughals.]*

The Justice System

Throughout the three centuries of the Delhi Sultanate's existence, the justice department was the most ill-organised. The Sultan was the fountainhead of justice, responsible for upholding the Quranic Law, the only law that was recognised in the Sultanate. The Sultan played a personal role in providing justice, hearing cases and passing judgement. In trying religious cases he was assisted by a mufti or religious teacher, who came under the minister for religious affairs. In theory, the Sultan also had another person to aid him with secular cases called the qazi, but in practice both the mufti and the qazi were the same person. It is reliably reported that the Sultan regularly revisited the judgement given by the qazi, maybe because of the religious bias that the individual displayed in passing judgement. All provinces were set up with similar justice systems.

Some later-day historians have claimed that a majority of the Delhi Sultans delivered unbiased and swift justice. This is an attempt at softening the often delayed but always brutal and biased justice that was delivered to the non-Muslim population. Contemporary chronicles support this assertion. The chronicles tell a different story to that being propounded by modern historians. In the narrative of the modern historians, the attempt at rewriting history is clearly apparent.

The Sultanate justice system was haphazardly organised. Complaints could be registered anywhere since there was no laid down jurisdictions; and the highest court of appeal was the Sultan himself. However he also tried original cases. Penal law was very severe with mutilation and death penalty being very common punishments. Further, torture to extort a confession from suspects was common practice. To increase the confusion and the arbitrariness of the system, the judicial process was not uniform across the entire Sultanate. The jails were normally old forts, ill kept with the jailors being notoriously corrupt.

Even cases between Muslims and Hindus were judged and decided according to the Quranic Law. Further, even the Islamic Law itself was open to different interpretation according to the whims and fancies of the mufti or qazi, normally the same person. There was no commonality regarding the interpretations, at times even by the same person in different cases. Great injustice was meted out to the Hindus, who were considered second-class citizens since they were infidels. Even-handed justice was never guaranteed even if the complainant was a Muslim. Officially the government followed a policy of minimum interference in Hindu matters. However, practically there was direct injustice meted out to the Hindus, especially when the conflict was with a Muslim, in which case the ruling would always favour the Muslim.

Conclusion

The direct central governance of the Delhi Sultanate was restricted to the collection of revenue and for border protection. The Sultanate practised a discriminatory policy which provided welfare only to the people of the Islamic faith although a majority of the population was of the Hindu faith. The Hindus in this regard were 'non-persons' in the eyes of the administration. The Quranic Law was forced on the entire population including the non-Muslims and biased justice delivery was the norm rather than the exception. The combination of these factors made the Hindus either convert to Islam or resort to rebellion.

Rebellion brought immediate and ruthless retribution, if the Sultan was powerful. In cases where the Sultan was incompetent and the central authority could not be enforced, rebellions almost always deteriorated into civil wars. In both cases, the common Hindu populace suffered severe punishment. The Hindu princes and chieftains of North India battled this assault—military, religious and cultural—for nearly five centuries without succumbing before being battered into submission by the Mughals.

Chapter 32

THE CALIPHATE AND THE SULTANATE
DEBATING THE RELATIONSHIP

The status of Delhi Sultanate vis-à-vis the Caliphate in Baghdad and the relationship that existed between the two continues to be open to a number of interpretations. Some of these interpretations are provided by few well-known historians, but with superficial proof and therefore do not stand the test of investigation. In their explanations, the Sultanate is explained away as being part of the larger Caliphate, perhaps in an effort to create an aura of legitimacy to the plunder and pillage that preceded the Islamic conquest of North India that, in turn, led to the establishment of the Delhi Sultanate. The assertion of the Delhi Sultanate being part of the Baghdad Caliphate is also based in long-held erroneous beliefs without any factual support. Convoluted explanations abound, attempting to provide legal and even historic basis for affirming that the Sultanate was part of the Caliphate. Some numismatic evidence has also been produced to establish that the authority of the Abbasid Caliphate enveloped the Sultanate and also the entire pre-Mughal Islamic period in the Indian sub-continent.

The attempts to place the Delhi Sultanate under the Caliphate should be considered concerted attempts to establish that there existed the earliest version of pan-Islamism in the medieval period and that it also included the Indian sub-continent of pre-Mughal times. This is fanciful thinking and far from the truth. The solution to the vexed issue, which is bound to raise heated debate, lies in examining three questions and finding answer that can be corroborated and authenticated. One, how far did the Delhi Sultans consider the Abbasid Caliph as the legal authority that permitted them to rule? Two, did any of the Sultans consider the Delhi Sultanate to be an integral part of the Caliphate? Three, why and how did the Turks break away from the Caliphate and start moving east, finally arriving in India?

The Caliphate Connection

Islamic jurists state that the establishment of a Caliphate is a canonical necessity. It provided the organisation needed for the smooth functioning of the society through building and cultivating a religious life that in turn produces a well-knit group. In the religious sense, the Caliphate was legally ruled by the Caliph and therefore allegiance to him was demanded by canonical law. On the other hand, Islamic states were organised into independent and sovereign groups, which were based on distinct political activity and therefore these groups were political in nature with the religious legality superimposed on them. The political function was also discharged through the Caliph, which made it imperative to acknowledge the authority of the elected Caliph.

Around 750 CE, the last Umayyad Caliph died. Abul Abbas 'Saffiah', supported by the Alids, Persians and some Arabs, got himself elected Caliph. He immediately destroyed the Umayyads completely, with pronounced ferocity. He also set aside his relationship with the Alids and Shiite groups, although he continued to be tolerant of them. Saffiah was succeed by Abu Jafar al-Mansur (754-75) who was a man of rare foresight. He set about enhancing the power and prestige of the Caliph, who till then adorned a pontifical throne. Mansur was responsible for creating the foundation of an organisation that was meant to establish the temporal power of the Caliph necessary to buttress the religious ascendancy of the position. He also ensured the permanence of his family and its power through creating a dynasty.

Like his predecessor, Abu Jafar was also ruthless in eliminating any potential challenger to the well-being of the dynasty. Towards the end of the Umayyad Caliphate Abu Jafar al-Mansur had, along with a number of other notable personalities, taken an oath of fealty to Muhammad, the great grandson of Hasan, the Prophet's descendant. At that time, Muhammad had been recognised as Caliph. However, on becoming the Caliph, Mansur went on to ill-treat and oppress the descendants of Ali which made the Alids hostile to him and his successors.

Abu Jafar was suspicious of Muhammad and his intentions, and unsuccessfully attempted to capture him and his brother Ibrahim. Open hostility between the two resulted. The regions of the Hajaz and Yemen, along with some important nobles, religious teachers and priests, acknowledged Muhammad as the Caliph. The result was a rebellion against Abu Jafar, who did not waste any time in brutally suppressing the uprising. Abu Jafar then went on to wreak vicious vengeance on the tribes of the followers of Hasan and Husain. He also humiliated the clergy who had ranged against him in support of Muhammad and completely laid waste the towns of Medina and Basra. There was open rift between the Sunnis and Shias in the heartland of Islam.

Abu Jafar's conflict with the Shiites made him initially dependent on the Persians and subsequently on the Turks to retain his power and control the Caliphate. The Arab elements who had been part of the broader support base till then gradually receded to the background. The majority of the Arabs were from rural backgrounds and they reverted to the old ways of tribalism, readily participating in rebellions and minor uprisings at will. By the time Caliph Mamun (813-33) ascended the throne, Turks had become the trusted bodyguards of the Caliph and during the time of Caliph Mutasim (833-42) they asserted complete control over the Caliphate. Turkish ascendancy was further entrenched because Mutasim was born of a Turkish mother and hated the Persians with a vengeance. The Turks were now powerful enough to function as the Praetorian Guard, capable of making and unmaking Caliphs at their whim and fancy.

Around the time of the Turk domination, a schism developed in the Shiite camp over the succession of the Imam, which in turn gave rise to Ismailism. This offshoot culminated in the founding the Fatimid Ismaili Caliphate in Cairo in 909 CE. The Fatimid Caliphate, dominated by Arabs, emerged as a direct challenge to the Abbasids, who continued to be a Turkish stronghold. There was interaction and conflict born of complex racial, religious and cultural influences.

The Turks of the Abbasid Caliphate became renowned as conquerors, administrators and military generals, emerging as unquestioned champions of orthodox Sunni Islam and the undisputed mainstay of the Baghdad Caliphate. Their recognised and distinguished association with the Abbasid Caliphate glorified the Turks and exalted their status. They claimed that the orthodox Sunni branch of Islam had flourished only because of their diligent protection. To further enhance their reputation they harked back to an old prophesy, passed down through generations and believed to have been given to Imam Abu Hanifa that stated, 'Thy doctrine shall not wane so long as the sword continues in the hands of the Turks.'

The connection to the divine through their close association with the Caliph and the prestige and power it entailed was the primary reason for the Turks to continue their association with the Abbasid Caliphate, even when they began to found independent kingdoms. This direct connection to the Caliphate provided them with a sense of legality in their conquests and establishment of new kingdoms. It was also meant to remind them, and others, of the time of their glory when they were the sole defenders of the Caliphate and the Caliph was dependent on them for survival. On a lesser scale it was also an acknowledgement and mark of the Caliph having been their suzerain and source of power. In return for this formal acceptance of a subordinate status, the Caliph also provided acknowledgement of their independence by gifting robes of honour on particularly gifted adventurers, the first one to be so felicitated being Mahmud of Ghazni.

New Turkmen conquerors, sought formal approval from the Caliph for their military adventures, which was given with alacrity. The Caliph knew fully well that his permission to conquer and rule new territories as independent kingdoms was a mere formality that could be done away with if the conqueror decided that the Caliph was hesitant or reluctant in bestowing his blessings. As time passed, the Caliph was bereft of temporal power and recognised purely as the symbol of Sunni orthodoxy.

The Caliphate – Sultanate Interaction

Amongst the Delhi Sultans, Iltutmish was the first to receive a robe of honour from the Caliph in Baghdad. This act connected the Caliphate to the fledgling Sultanate, providing Iltutmish with formal recognition of his sovereignty that was necessary to entrench his rule in the newly conquered territory. The connection was emphasised by Iltutmish by adopting the title 'Nasir Amir-ul-Muminin'. The title literally meant that Iltutmish was claiming to be the 'helper' of Amir-ul-Muminin – the Abbasid Caliph. However, the formal assumption of a subservient role did not mean that Iltutmish was in any way guided by the Caliph in ruling his kingdom. It was only a proclamation to the Islamic world of his historic connection to the Caliphate and nothing more. He was only keeping a long tradition alive.

The Sultans that followed Iltutmish, if at all they proclaimed their association with the Caliphate, did it more as an act of perpetuating a memory of greatness rather than as even a formal recognition of the authority of the Caliph, resident in a faraway place, beyond the borders of the Sultanate. The Baghdad Caliphate was destroyed by the Mongol chief Hulagu in 1258. Retaliatory action was not even contemplated by the Sultan in Delhi to support the Caliphate, a clear indication of the real situation. In fact, just two years later, the emissaries of Hulagu were welcomed in Delhi with great pomp and ceremony. It is clear that no sentiment was attached to the tenuous connection that existed between Baghdad and Delhi. Essentially, in the politics of the Sultanate, the Baghdad Caliphate held no meaning.

Conclusion

The use of the term 'Nasir' in the Sultanate coins has been pointed out as indicating a deep connection with Caliphate. This assumption is a leap of faith and cannot be corroborated. The use of the term was purely a matter of traditional boasting with no real significance, only meant to remind the people of the glorious past of the Turks. It is significant that none other than the famous Amir Khusrau has referred to Ala ud-Din as the Caliph of the age, which provides a clear indication of the independent status of the Sultanate. Further, Mubarak Shah Khilji proclaimed himself 'Caliph' and did not receive any condemnation from any quarter or retribution from the Caliph in Baghdad. It is clear that Islam in the Indian sub-continent had no apparent connection to the Caliphate. It can be correctly concluded that the Delhi Sultanate was never a part of the Caliphate, irrespective of the attempts being made by some historians to prove it so. It was also not part of a pan-Islamic movement that created a connected, grand Muslim state.

The Delhi Sultanate was simply a kingdom carved out by Turkmen generals, adept in the art of war but slightly inept in the administration of the conquered territories. They initially harked back to the connection of their forefathers to the Baghdad Caliphate to establish the legitimacy of their rule over their newfound kingdom. Attempts by later-day, modern historians to prove otherwise, is merely a biased and intentional attempt to 'create' history, where none existed. The simple fact remains that the connection to the Abbasid Caliphate was added to the titles of the sultans to commemorate the glorious past of the Turks, which in turn was expected to provide an added aura to the person of the Sultan.

DANCE OF THE RELIGIONS

From a purely religious point of view, the sultans had to do what they could to fetter or eradicate Hinduism, and thus promote Islam, but from a practical point of view they needed to patronise Hindus, for they could not possibly govern their Indian kingdoms without the service of the Hindus, as they did not have the requisite administrative organisation or personnel, or the local knowledge, to do that.

—Abraham Eraly,

The Age of Wrath, p. 327

Chapter 33

THE ASSIDUOUS POWER OF HINDUISM

From the earliest times, Indian civilisation has flourished within the confines of a great social and religious system called Hinduism. Although Hinduism is now equated to a religion, it has always been, and continues to be, a system as old and unique as the civilisation that it nurtured. The initiation, growth and endurance of the Hindu philosophy and thought process was greatly assisted by the geography of the Indian sub-continent that denies ready access to outside influences. The borders of the sub-continent are even completely impenetrable in some places.

There is an on-going debate regarding the historical antecedents of Indian history. Some scholars opine that India becomes truly 'historic' only around 700-600 BC with the establishment of the great Maurya Empire in the Gangetic belt, with modern Bihar at its centre. The establishment of the Maurya Empire, which is a recognised and clearly datable event is considered by many scholars to be a stake in the sand of time from which the evolution of Hindu philosophy can be measured forward and also speculated backwards. The reason is that there is extremely limited material evidence that have survived and are available to recount the history of 'Hindu' development before the establishment of the Maurya Empire. Further, even the scant records available are not of undoubted authenticity, leading to history of the period being of the speculative kind.

The only information available are to be gleaned from the great body of scared literature, now known as the Vedas, Brahmanas and Upanishads. The difficulty in using these as sources for historical research is that no definitive dates can be ascribed to any one of the treatises contained in the three groups. However, they do provide a genuine understanding of the prevalent religious thought and its development in the pre-historic times. They also give authentic accounts of the social norms of the time and, in a limited manner, even the political process of the unchartered times of the Indus Valley Civilisation, as well as the establishment of the Maurya Empire.

The Vedas

The Vedas are the oldest writings of Hindu philosophical thought and provides details of the growth of religious beliefs in the sub-continent. The initial religious thought is founded on nature-worship, which is in consonance with religious developments in other ancient civilisations. The gradual transformation of the religion into a polytheistic and pantheistic concept of the universe and the changing norms of worship can be traced in these writings. These changed conditions and thought process contained the essence of Hinduism as practised today.

The Vedic hymns extol the virtue of Nature that is considered divine and the pantheon of Gods deified the forces of nature. Fire, was worshipped as Agni; the elixir of life as Soma; and the God of heaven as Indra, while other gods took on abstract forms like that of Prajapati. In the early days Varuna was the pre-eminent and all-absorbing divinity. There was a plethora of gods in the pantheon, each with his or her own characteristics, likes, dislikes and powers. They also intermingled while an individual god's importance and power waxed and waned over time. This very large number of gods, both male and female, merged their identities with each other in infinite processes, both material and metaphysical. These processes produced a continuous evolution of altered gods, belief systems and philosophical thoughts. When interactions started with the Western civilisations in early medieval times, it became clear that the Western mind could not fully comprehend the intricacies and nuances of the development of this ancient thought process. This inability led to the development and publication of a large number of ill-formed ideas regarding Hindu philosophy and religious thought.

The variations and numbers in the combining process were only restricted by the inspiration of the Brahmin priests, who alone were considered well-versed in understanding the ways and vagaries of the gods. By this time Brahmins were already established in a position wherein they alone were considered competent enough to propitiate the gods, through intricate sacrificial rites and rigidly formed prayers. They became the keepers of the Vedas.

The Brahmanas

The Brahmanas demonstrate the gradual departure of theological belief within Hinduism from the purity of the Vedas. The old gods either disappeared or evolved into new identities with new characteristics, at times totally opposed to the Vedic concept of that god. For example, the God Varuna who was considered benevolent and all-absorbing in Vedic concept, was transformed into the God of night who had to be placated to avoid his cruelty. Around the same time, the Brahmins obtained overwhelming authority as being at the pinnacle of the social hierarchy, not based on individual theological knowledge but through the connection of blood, passed from father to son. The Vedic concept of Brahmin being the most learned of the people and the idea of anyone being able to attain the status of a Brahmin based on an individual's qualities were lost in this transition. Brahminical authority henceforth would be derived from the more esoteric connection of blood. Castes within the Hindu religion lapsed into being hereditary and rigid.

The Brahmins were assisted in reaching this pre-eminent position by the changes that took place in the common language of the people. The hymns of the Vedas were written in the 'old' language, which was not well understood by the lay person. Gradually the hymns and other written elements of the religion started to be understood only by the Brahmins, becoming the monopoly of these families. It was only a matter of time before this monopoly was used by those who enjoyed it for self-aggrandisement. The language of the prayers became sacred—only known to and used by the Brahmins.

The Brahmanas became the foundation for the growth of a complex theology that was almost incomprehensible to the common public. The theology was based on formidable and complicated rituals, of which only the Brahmin had full and exclusive knowledge and the power to exercise their usage. The religion was now separated from the commoner who practised it by an artificially created layer of self-promoting individuals, the Brahmins, who would not permit the knowledge to be made openly available.

The Upanishads

Compared to the Vedas and the Brahmanas, the Upanishads are relatively later-day chronicles that provide information and explanations provided by acclaimed thinkers of the more abstract interpretations of the Hindu philosophy. The importance of these treatises is that the thinkers who expounded their ideas were not always Brahmins. The Upanishads contain the thread of evolving and esoteric philosophical thought that have exercised an abiding influence on Indian spirituality and way of life. There are no exact dates attributed to the Upanishads, but it is generally agreed that only the earlier ones were written before the establishment of the Maurya Empire that has been taken as the point of historic reference for this narrative. In their totality, the entire set represents the progressive evolution of Hinduism from the seeds sown from the Vedas. Perhaps because of their common origin, the Upanishads also contain equal number, and at times the same, contradictions and complexities that are visibly present in Hindu theology and philosophy.

Through the influence of the thinkers and the ancient manuscripts, Hinduism developed two opposing thought processes: the Sankhya Darshana and the Vedantic System. The Sankhya Darshana is a philosophical conception of atheistic belief, whereas the Vedantic System advocates the Law of Karma that promotes fusion with God rather than the belief in a person's non-existence. Considering that both these concepts exist within the fold of Hinduism, it is not surprising that both accept the belief of the Universe, and all that exists in it, as well as life itself as a finite illusion. The Law of Karma, which is the basis of the Vedantic System, is the philosophy of a long succession of births and re-births before a person can reach the ultimate goal—either non-existence or of absorption into the Divine Essence.

The Influence of 'Karma'

The Law of Karma has been an enduring influence on Hinduism and Indian society. While explaining the concept of birth and re-birth, the Law states that re-birth is determined by the sum total of a person's deeds, both good and bad, taking all previous existences into account. This concept goes completely against basic Hindu thought that professes to be ruled by the sternest logic. The influence of the Law of Karma is visible even today in the Hindu society in a number of areas. First, the Law perpetuated the patriarchal principle, initially within a tribal family and later in the concept of a 'joint' family. Even though the legality of Hindu inheritance have been changed through the enactment of new laws, the concept of a patriarchal joint family exists to this day in Indian society, at least in principle and spirit.

Second, is the belief that only a son could perform the appropriate and elaborate rites and sacrifices required to propitiate the felicity of the dead. From ancient times this brought about a reverence for the dead that has become entrenched as an instinctive worship of the dead, especially one's own ancestors. From this worship springs a critical influence, that of the need to have a 'son' in order to ensure that a male progeny is available to do the last rites of a person on his/her death. The Indian social clamour, apparent even today, to have a son emanates from this archaic requirement. Third, the need to have a male progeny led to early marriages to ensure that a man does not die before begetting a son, especially since life expectancy was at best in the early forties during the time of this evolution. The need for a son also led to the enshrinement of the concept of 'adoption', where an adopted son was given exactly the same position and power of a real son.

The fourth factor that influenced society profoundly flowed from the need to conduct early marriages for the man. Early marriages meant that the bride would be very young at the time of the marriage and therefore almost completely dependent on the husband for the fulfilment of all her needs. This led to the women being given an inferior position and to their complete subjugation by the male members of the family. They were only valued as potential 'breeders' of sons. Women who could not bear sons, were shunned as unlucky and even cursed, although the sex of the child in any union is a function of the man's chromosomes. All through life and death man was exalted while women were maintained at a lower plane. In this hierarchy, brought about by the belief in Karma, a woman's position was mitigated only when she bore a son, or even better, many sons. Then she was revered at home and a woman's force of character and virtue often propelled her to be elevated to a powerful matriarchal position.

Although many social ills came to be perpetuated because of the indirect effects of the influence of the Law of Karma, the same laws also made, and continues to make, the Hindu family a living organism. The family maintains a direct connection to a person who has passed on as well as to the future through the implicit belief in re-birth. This is perhaps the most exalted aspect of Hinduism and demonstrates its best character.

The Codes of Law

The traditional norms of society were recorded in what are called the 'Smritis'. These customs and traditions were ultimately embodied in several codes of law, of which the most famous one is that of Manu. Over the years, the codes of law have been disfigured by narrow and biased social influences. Originally they set lofty standards of morality based on a high concept of duty to be followed by everyone. They are narrow in some of their outlook, but practical and strong, having stood the test of time. The codes of law, in combination with the older works such as the Vedas as well as other works on scientific matters, provides an account and shows a clear path regarding the progress of the society and religious thought up to the establishment of the Maurya Empire—considered as the point at which India arrived on the 'historical' map in a definitive manner.

The initial division of society into 'varnas', meaning colours, is attributed to the Laws of Manu. In later years, the same concept degenerated into the much-maligned caste system because of a number of disparate influences. However, these codes of laws still constitute the framework of the Hindu society. Some very precise and elaborate laws safeguarded the authority of the king and priest, with the priest being always sub-servient to the king. These laws were the foundations of all ancient Hindu kingdoms. The ancient kingdoms were organised and functioned within the stipulations of these complicated religious and societal laws.

Hinduism – A Chronology of Development

Hinduism is one of the great religions of the world. However, it differs from other great religions in a fundamental manner, which distinguish it and its philosophy—the origin of Hinduism is not associated with a single great prophet or teacher. Its tenets, philosophy and principles are not derived from the personal beliefs conceptualised by an individual like Moses, Christ, Confucius, Buddha or the Prophet Muhammad. Buddhism that evolved from the teachings of a single individual and Jainism which developed in a similar manner, flourished as offshoots of Hinduism, nurtured by a spirit of revolt against orthodox Brahmanism that had a stranglehold over Hinduism.

Both the religious orders, Buddhism and Jainism, were open to all and even included women as nuns along with the order of monks that propagated them. Buddhism reached the zenith of its power under Asoka the Maurya who is considered the greatest king to have ruled the Maurya Empire, but declined in the sub-continent soon after. Although the religion went through a phase of revival during the reign of Kanishka it never again reached the level of purity and exalted state that it had during Asoka's rule.

The impact of the popularity of these off-shoot religions was almost devastating for Hinduism, which declined into a diminished state. However, the religion adapted fairly quickly to the changing religious needs of the population. The first noticeable change was that the ancient, impenetrable rituals and impersonal gods of the Vedas were imperceptibly replaced by a group of more approachable and personalised set of gods. Shiva and Vishnu and their feminine counterparts, Kali and Lakshmi made their appearance in the Hindu pantheon. These gods further evolved into perennially popular ones such as Skanda and Ganesha, associated with Shiva and Rama and Krishna, considered to be avatars or incarnations of Vishnu.

Hinduism also absorbed the native tribes into itself, at times directly adopting their primitive deities into mainstream religious worship. The earlier incarnations of Vishnu, depicted as a fish and a wild boar, are examples of this absorption process. Further, Hinduism stood apart from Buddhism through the populist spread of its two epics the *Mahabharata* and the *Ramayana*. Both are nationalistic in their approach as opposed to the broad cosmopolitan approach and outlook adopted by Buddhism. The *Mahabharata* contains the Bhagavad-Gita whereas the *Ramayana* is the story of Rama, who displays the quintessential essence of uncorrupted dedication to duty or dharma. *[For a detailed analysis of the Vedic Age, please see Chapter 4 of Volume I: 'Prehistory to the Fall of the Mauryas' (pp. 27-48) of this series 'From Indus to Independence']*

Throughout its long history of development, Hinduism retained an inherent flexibility that was necessary to incorporate the political ambitions of both Hindu and non-Hindu conquerors and races, adapting and accommodating to the changing circumstances. Hinduism came into conflict with Buddhism not because of some insurmountable differences in theological beliefs, but because of irreconcilable differences in the social systems that each propagated. Hinduism then adapted the cloak of nationalism and imbibed a new sense of patriotism.

From the time of the short-lived Kushan Empire, the evolution of Hinduism had gone through a period of 'darkness', with hardly any progress being made either in its philosophical journey or in the overarching development of its doctrine. In the history of Hinduism it emerges further into 'light' during the splendour of the reign of the great Gupta dynasty in Ujjain in the 4th and 5th century, which is referred to as 'the golden age of Hinduism'. The power of the Gupta dynasty was such that their reign is today considered to symbolise the great revival of Hindu nationalism.

This period was the age of Brahminical ascendancy. The Gupta emperors had great zeal for Hinduism and is the dynasty that is extolled in India more than any other. India has always suffered from internecine wars for religious and political supremacy and these conflicts often came down to battles for the supremacy of one language over others. This is the case even today. Today the battle for supremacy is between Urdu and Hindi and between Hindi and various other local or regional languages. During the Gupta period of the revival of Hindu religion, the contest was between Sanskrit and the more 'vulgar' common language of the people.

Under the rule of the Gupta dynasty, Sanskrit—essentially the language of the Brahmins—resumed its pre-eminent position. It superimposed itself on literature, art, science, astronomy, logic, philosophy and theology. It came to pass that these disciplines, thriving under the umbrella of Sanskrit, adapted efficiently to the glory of Brahmanism and achieved great successes. This period could be justifiably called the finest hour of Hinduism. At the height of its power, Hinduism remained indifferently tolerant of other 'religions', mainly Buddhism and Jainism, and philosophies, supremely confident in its position of power and influence. Whether due to a sense of superiority or some other equally compelling ones, it remains a fact that all purely Indian philosophies remain tolerant in their fundamental beliefs.

Although it was in a revived and ascendant status during the Gupta reign, it did not take long for the religion to fall back into a languished state at the fall of the Guptas. The loss of position was hastened by the arrival of the White Huns, under the ferocious Mihiragula, into the sub-continent. Hinduism fell into decline once again under the ruthless suppression imposed by the White Huns. This decline was stemmed by Harsha Vardhana (ruled 606-648). Harsha was a mystic and a dreamer and distributed his favours equally to Hinduism and Buddhism. The moribund Hinduism was revived through his rule, even though in the later years of his rule he distinctly favoured Buddhism.

In the post-Harsha Vardhana period, the history of Hinduism passes almost completely to the Rajput kingdoms in central and western India. The Rajputs were descendants of relatively recent invaders into the sub-continent who had been very rapidly 'Hinduised' and then with equal dexterity become ferocious champions of the religion. They traced their ancestry through Hindu Brahmanism to the Sun and the Moon. Although the Rajputs were the epitome of chivalry and fighting prowess, fierce clan jealousies and intense dynastic pride made them incapable of initiating unified action even against common enemies. Because of this fundamental flaw in their collective character, even with their formidable warfighting skills, they were unable to withstand the imminent invasion of militant Islam an event even Harsh must have foreseen.

Abiding Factors

Harsha Vardhana was the last great Hindu emperor who successfully ruled the entire North India. The fact remains that religion and social order represent the real and paramount power in India, irrespective of the form of temporal power that is exercised at any given time. This fundamental truth has been visible in India over the centuries. Even in prehistoric times the subtle and flexible forces exerted by Hinduism had succeeded in bringing together disparate beliefs and customs to create a socio-religious fabric with sufficient elasticity that could withstand repeated and strong onslaughts to its being. Tenacity and the inherent power to absorb foreign ideas provided Hinduism with the wherewithal to become an enduring entity.

Even as Hinduism emerged from its early days as a social amalgam of great resilience, neither did it generate any enduring politically constructive force nor did it become a politically durable entity. Its political importance was limited to the reign and the immediate aftermath of few gifted conquerors and monarchs. This is one of the major reasons for all Hindu Empires finally succumbing to the continuous and tenacious pull of forces exerted by much smaller states. The story was the same in the great and long-lasting empires like those of the Mauryas and the Guptas as well as in the more ephemeral kingdoms like the ones ruled by Kanishka and Harsha. At their demise, all the great Hindu empires and large kingdoms broke up into many states of varying power under the weight of the differences in race, language, culture and climate. In medieval India, the state as an entity was constantly changing its individual, and at times collective, identities. As soon as the large kingdoms balkanised, they entered into a period of constant and continuous strife of one kind or the other. In these circumstances, positive religious developments were impossible.

Although the conditions were not conducive for religious or philosophical developments, Hinduism survived, based on its subtle and nuanced philosophies; flexible concept of 'rigid' worship as espoused by Brahmanical liturgy; and the doctrine of infinite reincarnation for all until the self was immersed as one with the sublime divinity.

The caste system has been the bane of Hinduism, as has been explained, rationalised, expounded and vilified over the years. Even though it is gradually giving way in modern India, the concept continues to be vigorous in subtle but obtrusive ways. It divides the contemporary Indian society into watertight compartments, with each caste organised under laws of their own that make them independent and traditional. A Hindu is born into a caste, lives in it his entire life and dies within it. This is the absolute truth of life for a Hindu. The arbitrary nature of this rigid notion creates an insurmountable social cleavage in modern India. The society in India does not have a reasonable chance of intermingling and thereby creating a healthy fusion of different people, a process that is vital for the creation of viable political power. India suffers from this social division, which is fatally critical to the development of a robust political system that is commonly acceptable and supported.

The rigidity of the caste system left Hinduism bereft of any political force to defend itself. This one flaw opened the Hindu states with their superior culture and civilisation to all external races and ethnicities that took the opportunity to invade the sub-continent, throughout its history. The Hindu states, almost artificial in establishing their entities and independence, were easily swept aside by the extreme and focused force of militant Islam.

The concept of Hinduism, unperturbed and safe within its watertight compartments of caste, would be battered repeatedly by forces beyond its control, but would survive without being smashed to bits, retaining a recognisable semblance to its original state.

Chapter 34

SUFISM IN INDIA DURING THE SULTANATE

It may not be incorrect to state that a large number of Muslims, perhaps even the majority, have very limited understanding of the theological underpinnings of their faith. This reality was as true in medieval times as it is now, not only in the Indian sub-continent but also across all the followers of the Islamic faith, spread around the world. They function in an environment that is purely bounded by the Sharia Law that prescribes how life should be lived, in an endless process of pilgrimage, fasting, alms-giving and daily ritualistic prayers. In all religions, only traditional scholars, who are very small in number, study their inner functioning. In the case of the adherents of the Islamic faith, in medieval times there came up a group of people outside of the scholastic circle, who found this situation dissatisfactory. This was particularly true of the non-Arab converts to Islam who had so far been used to different traditions in the practice of their faith.

> 'They craved for a more emotional, indeed emotive religion, one in which God appeared as a loving, succoring [sic] Friend rather than as an abstract definition of undifferentiated unity incomprehensible in His Essence, inscrutable and arbitrary in His decrees.'
>
> Peter Hardy,
> In Wm Theodore de Bary, (ed), *Sources of Indian Tradition*, p. 411.

There was another more visible factor that troubled the more inquisitive common person. The growth of Islamic political power was accompanied by a visible non-adherence to the strict and rigid codes of the religion by the ruling class. The pious common man was very clearly made aware of the compromises that were made, or had to be made, to overcome the strict decrees of an inflexible system in order to create and sustain political power. As a result, many withdrew into seclusion, in order to avoid the wrath of God that was sure to come on Judgement Day. Many other staunch Muslims subsumed their piety in mysticism instead of theology.

Sufism – A Brief Explanation

The history of the development of Islam in the Indian sub-continent from the 12th century forward, is intimately connected and intertwined with the parallel development of the Sufi mystic movement. It is also the story of a counter-movement, of the struggle of the ulema to contain the spread of Sufism and keep it within the accepted Islamic fold. Sufism, in a simplistic explanation, could be considered a fusion of asceticism and devotion, practised within the bounds of traditional Islam. The devotional aspects were ascendant over the initial years, while the mystical elements of love and adoration—which springs from the manifestation of extreme devotion—managed to overcome the fear of Judgement Day.

By around 9th century, just two centuries into the life of the Islamic religion, practitioners of this brand of Islam—the Sufis—had already worked out the methodology to attain 'ma'rifat', meaning the mystic knowledge of God. This knowledge was to be attained either through an ecstatic union with God Himself or through an equally blissful unification with one of His attributes; to be achieved either by bringing God into the man or by man's ascend into God. In effect, one who cast off the self and lost himself in God was the true mystic. This was an exalted state to be achieved and rising to it was a journey that passed through many stages or phases.

The journey to become a true mystic, a Sufi 'teacher', starts at the phase of repentance and goes through abstinence, renunciation, poverty, patience, and trust in God before finally reaching or attaining satisfaction. When a Sufi reaches the stage of satisfaction, he has eagerly accepted the Divine decree, made possible by the gift of God

Himself. The two supreme states are described as annihilation followed by subsistence. Annihilation is the transformation of the soul through the complete extinction of all passions and desires and the cessation of all conscious thought. Subsistence follows the annihilation of the soul and is the last phase of abiding union with God. This fusion could mean one of three things—union with one activity symbolised by the name of God; union with one of the attributes of God; or union with the Divine Essence itself. When a Sufi has truly attained annihilation and subsistence, all the veils that hide the truth from human beings are removed, Truth is beheld, and man is eternally united with God.

Since the doctrine of Sufism essentially emphasised a one-on-one relationship with God, it was only a matter of time before they fell afoul of the ulema—scholars of the Sharia and enforcers of the faith. The Sufis claimed to judge men, and also themselves, with an inner light while also claiming to enjoy a 'personal' relation with God. This was anathema to the ulema who regulated the outward conduct of all Muslims. Further, in their intense personal experience, many Sufis denied or at least questioned the value and the mandate of the Sharia Law. To make matters worse, a number of Sufis made statements they claimed were derived from supreme insight and personal experience that clearly emphasised monist beliefs. These statements and beliefs placed Islam at par with all other religions and faiths. Such a doctrine could not be tolerated by a religion that was steadfast in its adherence to the Quranic Law and considered itself to be the only 'true' faith, above and superior to any other religious belief. As a result, the Sufis were persecuted and some famous adherents executed on the order of the Caliph.

Sufism was not popular within the hierarchy of the Abbasid Caliphate's political authority, but became popular amongst the artisans and the minor trading class in Iraq and Persia. It is obvious that it was never a political movement since its call for personal correctness of behaviour and spiritual revival contrasted completely with the worldliness of the political ruling class.

Al Ghazali – The Mystic Theologian

Al Ghazali was one of the most renowned and acknowledged among the mystics. Abu Hamid Muhammad ibn Muhammad al-Ghazali, shortened to Al Ghazali in Arabic and known as Algazelus in the contemporary Western world, was born in 1058 and died in 1111 in Persia. Some historians consider him the most influential person in shaping the Islamic faith after Prophet Muhammad. His greatest achievement was making Islamic mysticism acceptable and reconciled with the mainstream orthodoxy in Islam. By doing so he ensured that the schism that was developing between the ulema and the Sufis did not become irreparably wide. The effect of this healing touch on Islam is best seen in the progress of the religion in the Indian sub-continent during the three-century-rule of the Delhi Sultanate—there was hardly any tension between the Sufis and the ulema.

Al Ghazali is credited with having written more than 70 books, mainly in Arabic and a few in Persian. His 11th century book titled *The Incoherence of the Philosophers* is an important turning point in Islamic epistemology. His personal experiments and analysis of scepticism led Al Ghazali to embrace what has been termed as theological occasionalism—the belief that all casual events and interactions could not be the product of material conjunctions but was the immediate and present Will of God. The book was also an important milestone in the development of Islamic philosophy, since it vehemently refuted and rejected the philosophies of Aristotle and Plato, who had for long influenced Islamic thinkers. The rejection of the Greek philosophies was achieved by rebutting the work of the 'Falasifa', a loosely defined group of Islamic philosophers of the 8th through 11th centuries, among whom Avicenna and Al-Farabi were the most prominent and who drew intellectual stimulation from the ancient Greeks.

Al Ghazali was responsible for making personal and emotional relationship between an individual and God the core principle of popular Islam. Since Sufism also propagated a similar doctrine, gradually it also became an acceptable part of Muslim orthodoxy. About a century after his death, Al Ghazali's theories were accepted by consensus into Islamic theology. This embracing of his rather radical theories can be considered one of the most important events in the developmental history of the Muslim religion. Sufism became the most vital spiritual force in Islam, encompassing royalty, nobility and commoner alike.

> 'He was called the Proof of Islam and undoubtedly was worthy of the name, absolutely trustworthy (in respect of the Faith). How many an epitome (he has given) us setting forth the basic principles or religion: how much that was repetitive has he summarised, and epitomised what was lengthy. How many simple explanation has he given us of what was hard to fathom, with brief elucidation and clear solution of knotty problems. He used moderation, being quiet but decisive in silencing an adversary, though his words were like a sharp sword-thrust in refuting a slanderer and protecting the high-road of guidance.'
>
> Margaret Smith,
>
> *Al Ghazali the Mystic*, p. 47.

There is no doubt that Al Ghazali's synthesis of religious thought altered the course of Islamic civilisations. In India, his concepts made it possible for adherents of the faith to practice Islam in innovative ways. It made the worship of saints acceptable, even though such a practice was completely against the injunctions in the Quran and the traditional Muslim theological orthodoxy. The Sufis did not care whether their religious practices were in harmony with Islamic practices or not.

The Sufi Orders

Al Ghazali's concepts and philosophies found expression in what came to be referred to as the doctrine of the Light of Muhammad. The doctrine states, in brief—that things emanate from divine prescience as ideas. The idea of Muhammad the Prophet is the creative and rational principle of the Universe, since the Prophet is the perfect man and unifies all phenomenon into manifesting as real. The fundamental aim of a Sufi is to unite with, and in, the Perfect Man, who is the copy of God. In later days, popular Islam in India would attach this idea to famous Sufi personalities who were considered saints. This in turn led to the formation of a hierarchy where the Prophet stood alone at the head, followed by the saints who were elected from amongst the mystics. Popular belief and sentiment attributed miracles to these saints. The Sufi sheikhs or leaders came to be 'worshipped' even during their lifetime and after death, their tombs became places of pilgrimage. This practice is prevalent in the Indian sub-continent to this day.

These ideas became institutionalised in the great Sufi orders. It became necessary for a Sufi novice to become the disciple of a spiritual director or mentor so that adequate guidance was provided for his development. The novice was accepted into the fraternity through a ceremony of initiation. The head of such fraternities were either called Sheikh or Pir, both meaning elder, who claimed spiritual succession from the founder of the order; and through him to the Prophet or Ali. The group normally lived in a community, a sort of retreat, supported by sponsors who often included the Sultan himself, and gave themselves up to meditation and spiritual exercises. In medieval times there were many such groups or retreats across the Islamic world. The major Sufi orders were able to establish a sort of network, with a senior disciple going out of the retreat and establishing a satellite group, and so on. All these 'sub-retreats' were linked to the parent body through reverence to the senior sheikh and commonality of rituals.

The membership of these orders were normally of two types. One was the novice initiates who were totally immersed in devotional exercises and continual meditations, striving on the path to satisfaction and annihilation. The second were a number of 'lay persons' who attended meetings at prescribed times and intervals to participate in rituals and ceremonies meant for 'remembering God'. At other times they led a normal life. The Islamic conquest of North India coincided with the establishment of these orders and it was a natural progression that some of them were introduced into the sub-continent. The Sufis dominated Muslim thought and social life during the Sultanate period in India, often reaching out to Hinduism.

Sufism in India during the Sultanate Period

Despite the Islamic conquest of most of North and Western India, and the establishment of the Delhi Sultanate, even at the height of its power, the Muslims remained a minority within their empire. This was also the case for the great Mughal Empire, when it came to pass a few centuries later. The Hindu chiefs and princes continued to rule their principalities or kingdoms, albeit under the suzerainty of a Muslim sultan or emperor. Further, in the central and provincial capitals,

Hindu clerks staffed almost the entire administrative machinery with the Muslims only manning the executive or directorial positions. No doubt, military and political power rested only with the Muslims. However, like the application of political power throughout history, its exercise was dependent on the ruler observing certain laid down conditions.

The Muslim rulers in India had two such conditions to meet in order to fulfil their part of the bargain. The first was to refrain from exceeding the traditional limits of their political power, which was restricted to the collection of revenue and recruiting for the army. There was to be no interference in the traditional beliefs, customs and laws that the people held dear. The second caveat was meant to safeguard the status of the Muslim population. The ruler was to preserve the cultural and religious identity of the ruling Muslim class and to ensure the effective defence of their privileged political position. As long as the Sultan ensured these two conditions he was free to rule as he liked. Of course the rule had to be in line with the Quranic Law and other caveats that has been explained in the earlier chapter on governance of the Delhi Sultanate.

Islam entered India at a stage in its development when the theological schism in the religion had almost healed. The learned men who came with the invasion, the ulema, were almost all traditionalists and canon lawyers and not theologians. Therefore the focus was on establishing and elaborating the daily practice of the religion in order to ensure the solidarity of the community, which was a minority in a foreign land full of animosity against the invaders. The Turks who conquered North India in the 12th century were purely military adventurers. The ulema sided with them to enhance their own influence and the Turks were glad to have the unfettered support of the keepers of the faith. The coming together of religion and politics was mutually beneficial for the rulers and the orthodox religious teachers.

The Confluence of Politics and Religion

The initial crop of Sultans in Delhi nominally recognised the legal sovereignty of the Baghdad Caliph. However, in practice they acted as Caliphs in their own right for their dominions, appointing their own judges—both religious (qadis) and canon jurists (muftis) in most towns to enforce their rule. These judges, together with the ulema who taught in the schools, advocated obedience not only to the one true God, but particularly to the Sultan as His representative on Earth. The power and prestige of the State and the Sultan backed the ulema at all times, reinforcing the veracity of their teaching.

The Sultans disregarded the Sharia Law when it conflicted with their personal interests and also for political expediency. The Sultan, representing the State may not have imposed orthodoxy of the religion directly, but definitely sanctioned others to do so. Even so, when required he also sanctioned the suppression of orthodoxy. The ulema of the Delhi Sultanate were uniformly of the orthodox Sunni persuasion and fanatical in the propagation of their faith.

The Shi'a Sects

Sindh, with Multan as the capital, was the first province of the sub-continent to be conquered by the Islamic invasion. Along with this invasion, extreme Shi'a sects—the Ismaili and Qarmatian—also came into the province. From Sindh they gradually spread to the rest of the Sultanate. However, these sects were continually attacked and scattered by the orthodox Sunnis but managed to survive underground in a clandestine manner. In the 13th and 14th centuries, the Delhi Sultans; Iltutmish, Raziya, Ala ud-Din Khilji, and Firuz Tughluq; slaughtered and imprisoned the followers of both these sects. The Ismaili and Qarmatian sects denied the legitimacy of the Sultanate and by association, of the Sultan himself. Their doctrine was egalitarian and they rejected the concept of the Caliphate itself. Delhi Sultans were alarmed at the concepts that were being propagated by these groups and sought the assistance of the Sunni ulema to dispel the heretical doctrine from peoples' minds.

Challenge to the Integrity of Islam

Even though the Shi'a doctrine was being ruthlessly suppressed, it was not the primary ideological challenge to the integrity of the Islamic faith in India. The challenge emanated from the Sufis, practising lives of demonstrably pure devotion and gentleness. The real religious tension within the Islamic fold in India came from the opposing views between the orthodox Sunni ulema and the philosophy of the Sufis. Both derived their concepts from Al Ghazali's doctrine.

By the 12th century, the great Islamic mystic orders had already been founded outside India. Even before the Ghurid conquest of the Punjab was complete in 1195, Kwaja Muin ud-Din Chishti of Sistan had settled in Ajmer and introduced the Chishti order to India. Within the next two centuries after that the Sufi orders had spread their network of retreats across the entire North India, becoming a powerful force even outside the Muslim community. Even though the concepts of Sufism appealed to all classes of Muslims, it was found to be more attractive to the less- and un-educated masses. The Sufis exhibited a way of life and thought that also made them alluring to the Hindus. The appeal for the Hindus was because of the devotion, piety, asceticism and tolerance that the Sufis displayed, and which rhymed with the fundamental concepts of Hinduism. Further, during the Sultanate period Sufism remained independent of the state, which was a further attraction for the Hindus. Sufis were the true missionaries of Islam in India.

The Sufis were under constant surveillance by the ulema, who were suspicious of their activities. The ulema wanted to ensure that the Sufis were not propagating 'un-Islamic' ideas and also feared that the Sufi retreats would replace the mosque as the centre of life for Muslims, if they were allowed to proliferate. They also feared the increasing Hindu influence on the Sufi movement, although practices such as the worship of saints existed in Islam much before the religion spread into India. The ulema were very concerned about the impact of Sufism on 'New Muslims'—converts from other religions in the sub-continent, predominantly from Hinduism.

At the ideological level, the ulema and the Sufis were not enemies, but rivals for the attention of the lay people. In fact, they were reluctant partners in spreading the concept of Islam in the sub-continent, following two different paths to the same goal of travelling towards God. The ulema chose the orthodox path through the Sharia, while the Sufis adopted the mystic path, called 'tariqa' that could be loosely translated to 'the method'. Bolstered by instinct, there was mutual tolerance between orthodoxy and mysticism to ensure the development of Muslim communal unison. There may not have been complete unity, but in the face of the predominant population of unbelievers, the commonality of purpose became a great binding factor. The need to face a common threat made it possible for the ulema and Sufis to avoid visible schisms in their individualistic religious practice.

The Great Sufi Orders

Sufism entered India in an already mature and well-developed form. Therefore, it did not change its ideas but only adapted its practices to align the movement with the new environment. Between the end of 12th century and mid-15th century, in other words the Delhi Sultanate period, three great Sufi orders migrated to India from Iraq and Persia—the Chishti, Suhrawardi and Firdausi.

Of these, by far the most popular and the one with the largest following was the Chishti order. It spread across the region now covered by Uttar Pradesh and surrounding states. Its great saints, Nizam ud-Din Auliya (1238-1325) and Nasir ud-Din Muhammad Chirag (died 1356) roamed the central Indian plains and taught the concepts of their order. Followers of these saints and other teachers of the Chishti order included some of the greatest luminaries of Indo-Muslim culture during the Sultanate period, such as Amir Khusrau the poet, and Zia ud-Din Barani the historian. The tombs of these mystic saints have become pilgrimage sites and are still worshipped by both Hindus and Muslims alike. The Suhrawardi order came into Sindh with the Muslim conquest but remained confined to that region. The Firdausi order moved inland, but could not compete with the popularity of the Chishti order and gradually moved east and became entrenched in the region around Bihar.

The Text Books

In the 11th and 12th centuries, few 'text books' were written in an attempt to clearly express the ideas and philosophies of Sufism. A notable one is *Kashf ul-Mahjub*, or 'The Uncovering of the Veil' written by Shaikh Ali Hujwiri in Lahore after the city was annexed by Mahmud of Ghazni. There is another kind of literature that was produced. In order to popularise the Sufi teachers, their disciples recorded the masters' sayings, discourses and injunctions and made them available to the public. They also wrote the biographies of the saints. The book *Fawaid ul-Fuwad*, 'The Morals of the Heart' written by poet Amir Hasan Sijzi is the record of the conversations of Shaikh Nizam ud-Din Auliya in his retreat at Ghiyaspur, between 1307 and 1322. Another is a collection of letters, *Maktubat*, addressed to a disciple by Shailah Sharaf ud-Din Yahya of Manir, who was a mystic of the Firdausi order living in Bihar at the end of 14th century.

When taken together, the written literature illustrate the central concepts of Sufism. They emphasise the love for God as the fundamental concept for human existence; the urge towards union with God; explain the different stages of the mystic path in the journey towards the final union; the acceptance of the Sharia as an essential component in the journey by all the great saints; and the role of the saints themselves in leading their disciples towards the ultimate aim of union with God.

Conclusion

Although tensions did exist between the orthodox ulema and the practitioners of Sufism, it will be incorrect to assume that the two were inimical, or that they worked at cross purposes. The Sufi orders that established themselves in India accepted the Islam of the Sharia as an essential precondition of the one true religion. The Sufis actually complimented the ulema in teaching the simple observance of the faith, especially in remote areas where the 'New Muslims' did not have access to the centralising influence of mosques or religious schools. In effect, the ulema and the Sufi were two sides of the same coin in the propagation of Islam as the one and only true religion.

Chapter 35

THE MINGLING OF MYSTICISM

In early 14th century the religious make up of India was gradually altering. Buddhism had almost vanished from the land of its birth; Jainism was confined to a narrow area in the west of the sub-continent; and Islam was in its infancy, spread across scattered settlements in North India and holding a tenuous foothold in the west coast of South India. Even though it was split into different sects, orthodox Brahmanism held sway across the entire sub-continent. This situation reinforces the fact that the Hinduism was imbibed with a unique culture. It was normal for Hinduism to add to existing institutions but normally they were not superseded through the creation of new ones. This trait ensured that even when completely new concepts were introduced into the practice of the religion, the old practices were retained and continued to be followed with minor adaptations. This is one of the fundamental reason for the longevity of Hinduism, staying dynamic even after it has suffered centuries of foreign onslaught.

The Hindu Mystics

The medieval period saw the Hindu religion go through a concerted renaissance, brought about by a number of prominent socio-religious teachers and reformers. They came to be called sants or saints, and were also mystics, with large number of devotees and followers. These mystics had some common traits and characteristics. They were non-sectarian and did not belong to any sect; they had no aspiration to create a separate sect of their own, but only wanted to reform the fundamental approach to religion and worship within the existing practices of Hinduism; none of them were bound by religion, caste or creed; all of them abhorred blind faith in the words of the scared scriptures; they did not observe any rituals or ceremonies; each one condemned polytheism and believed in one God; they did not follow any dogma and denounced the practice of idol worship; and they realised the unity of God, invoked differently by different sects and religions.

The sants believed in Bhakti, love or devotion, as the only means of salvation. In order to make sure that the lay person understood the fundamental idea of Bhakti, they provided profoundly illustrative analysis and interpretations of the concept. Bhakti is explained as single-minded and uninterrupted devotion to God that gradually evolves into love. The Hindu mystics stated that Brahman, meaning the Supreme God or Universe (not to be confused with the term 'Brahmin' used to demote an individual or caste), which is the ultimate reality, could be called by any name since it is an abstract idea. Brahman is also the source of eternal bliss. In simple terms, this eternal bliss can be achieved only through self-surrender to Him after which final salvation or complete emancipation will occur.

In propagating the concept, the sants took into account only the overall personality of the human being practising Bhakti without placing any undue emphasis on the person's rational faculty. Religious truths and beliefs are not matters of pure reason alone, but is also influenced by the personal nature of the individual. Therefore, the sants, in their role as teachers, did not completely exclude religious factors and their influence on the common people. The Hindu mystics 'taught' in the regional vernacular and not in Sanskrit that had become the language of the educated elite. By using commonly understood dialects, they were able to bring the concept of Bhakti to the ordinary and un-educated people. They were able to explain to the lay person the idea of universal truths, which are more valuable than sectarian doctrine in understanding religion. The noble objective of the Hindu sants was the upliftment of the masses and therefore none of them considered caste distinctions as an impediment to teaching the basics of Bhakti.

The Hindu mystics exercised absolute freedom of thought and practised intense self-exertion in both intellectual and spiritual contemplation. Because of their critical ability to decipher the virtues, and more importantly the pitfalls, of traditional religious teachings there was a prevalent spirit of revolt against orthodox Brahmanism among all the mystics. The teachings of the sants were sufficiently radical for the orthodox religious practitioners to keep these mystics and their followers away from the more sedate religious forums. This may have been one of the reasons for the followers of these teachers to form closed sects, even against the injunctions by the saints themselves to avoid doing so. On the other hand, Hinduism with its age-old tradition of tolerance and absorption accepted some of these sects into its fold and gradually chipped away at the more heterodox views held by them, till their extreme states were whittled down to acceptable traditional levels.

Acceptance into the Fold of Mainstream Religion

There are two distinct examples of groups that followed mystics, albeit on different paths, that adapted to traditional religion and became accepted into the mainstream.

The first is Chaitanya's Vaishnavism, which remains a power sect in the religious life of Bengal, even today. When the saint initiated his teachings, he was spirited in embracing the 'chandals', meaning the untouchables, and Muslims into the sect and taking them on as disciples. However, this universality vanished from ethos of the sect a long time ago. Today, there is no obvious and outwardly visible difference between the Chaitanya sect and orthodox Brahmanism as practised in Bengal. A similar sort of assimilation into mainstream Hinduism took place in the case of most other sects created by followers of other sants.

The second example is the sect founded by Guru Nanak, which is numerically small and mostly confined to the region of the Punjab. The sect went on to create a new religious order, Sikhism. Today it is the most powerful one of all the sects that represent medieval Hindu saints.

> However, the importance of this sect, turned religion, is derived from factors other than religion or spirituality.
>
> (The background and teachings of Chaitanya and Nanak are explained in the next chapter.)
>
> Other sects that have survived as separate entities have numerically small followings and are insignificant, functioning at the fringes of mainstream Hinduism with very limited influence.

There are three major reasons for the sects becoming assimilated into the mainstream religion. First, the teachings of Hinduism, at the very basic level is entrenched in the 'soil of India' and therefore they are not difficult for the un-educated farmer to understand. Once the veils of Sanskrit, rituals and ceremonies are removed, the lay person is able to identify the religion and its core values. The saints were only facilitating this revelation. Second, the sants were not propagating any new concepts—the unity of God and the practice of Bhakti were known, if not familiar, ideas. The saints only made them popular through simplified explanations. Third, the Vedas had described these two concepts and therefore they had always existed in the shadow of Hinduism, side by side with the belief and worship of a plurality of Gods.

Medieval Hindu mysticism did not suddenly appear on the scene. It originated in Maharashtra under two great teachers – Jnanadeva and Namadeva, spreading across the region gradually and carried forward by other equally erudite sants and socio-religious reformers to far corners of the sub-continent. The broad concept of Bhakti in Hinduism finds a parallel in the Sufism that originated in Islam. Sufism was also conceived as the belief of loving devotion to God being the path to find union with God through the annihilation of the self and human attributes. Similar to the relationship of Bhakti and Hinduism, the Sufi concept was also considered heretic in orthodox Islamic thought. Many Sufi preachers sacrificed their lives to ensure the propagation of their particular practice of worship.

A Complex Interaction

There are various theories, which are discussed even today, regarding the origin of medieval Hindu mysticism. Some eminent European scholars who researched and analysed Indian history, religion and culture in the 18th and 19th centuries erroneously put forward the idea that the concept of Bhakti was borrowed from Christianity and that it echoed the condition of salvation and monotheistic doctrine as explained in the Christian religion. Today, this claim cannot be considered seriously and does not have any merit. There is no evidence of close contact and interaction between Hinduism and Christianity during the period when the Bhakti movement originated. Such interactions are necessary for religion to impose sufficient influence on another for the second one to start a dedicated movement within itself. The claim of Christian ideas being borrowed to start the Bhakti movement has to be completely disregarded.

The question and debate regarding the influence of Islam on the concept of Bhakti is more complex. Even in this case, there was only limited contact between Islam and Hinduism before the 12th century. Therefore, the chances of mutual influence and the possibility of the exchange of philosophical views and religious ideas and doctrine are very remote. There is also an opinion that continues to be put forward by some analysts even today that Sankaracharya's concept of monism was a copy of Islamic ideas. Nothing could be more distant from the truth. The opinion is completely wrong and biased, and merits no further discussion.

Analysing the developments from the mid-13th century, a different perspective emerges. By this time, Islam had already been established and become entrenched within the sub-continent. It would never leave the region after this time. There is no doubt that the philosophy of Islam affected Hinduism, just as the core ethos of Hinduism also impacted the ideas of Islam. Muslim thinkers were definitely affected by the rich heritage of Indian culture based on Hinduism. A comparison of changes that took place in both religions for the six centuries, from the 12th to 18th centuries before Christian influence further changed both the religions as practised in the Indian sub-continent, would in all likelihood produce some indication of the mutual influence exerted by both the religions. Such a comparison has not been undertaken because of the difficulties in quantifying influence in an empirical manner. As an unbiased analyst, the author believes that it is unwise to make clear and dogmatic assertions regarding the influence exerted by both the religions on each other during the six centuries of bilateral interactions as they developed in medieval India. These interactions continue to be an on-going process in the Indian context, making such an enterprise a hazardous undertaking for a historian.

In a repeat of earlier assertions without the backing of any evidence, some modern historians have ventured so far as to state, in very general terms, that medieval Hindu mysticism was the product of the impact of Islam on Hinduism. Statements are made such as, '... influence *must have been* acquired...' (Author's italics) and other similar sentiments. Such statements cannot be considered erudite, unbiased or the product of academically sound research and evaluation. One such author has stated that the Bhakti movement in North India represents the first impact of Islam on Hinduism. He then goes on to observe that the Bhakti movement was essentially indigenous and shares its principles of universal brotherhood and human equality with Islam. Thus the argument of Islamic influence on the Bhakti movement is defeated by the author himself. It has to be clearly understood that the concept of brotherhood in the Islamic viewpoint did not extend beyond its own fold and by no stretch of imagination can it be considered to have been universal. In the Muslim tenets, the non-believer, the Kafir, was a distinctly inferior being in all respects, let alone being considered worthy of acceptance into universal brotherhood. Some facts about Hinduism and the Bhakti movement will dispel the myths that are being perpetuated as truths by some biased analysts.

Fact 1: The theory of universal brotherhood and equality of man is enshrined in Vedanta, where they are placed as the fundamental basis for identifying individual souls. Further, every soul is considered identical to Brahman, the Universe. While it could be accepted that Islamic theory or its practice may have held some appeal to the Hindus, it is equally clear that Islam did not bring with it any new message of equality that the Hindus were unaware of or had not practiced earlier.

Fact 2: Medieval Hindus, under forced Islamic rule in North and East India were under no illusion regarding their status as second-class citizens. They were forbidden to practice their religion in public; denied political, civil and judicious rights; and lived under an administration that declared Islam as the only state-approved religion and imposed it across the entire country. Authors such as Yusuf Hussain, who in his book *Glimpses of Medieval Indian Culture*, first published in 1957, propagates the theory that 'universal brotherhood' was practiced in the Delhi Sultanate, are merely attempting to rewrite history, taking it far away from the prevalent facts of the time. Such writings are only pretensions attempting to 'white wash' the travails perpetuated on the Hindu population by the Muslim Sultans and their fanatical clergy. Nothing more, nothing less.

Fact 3: The Hindu saints found much commonality between orthodox Islam and the traditional practice of Hinduism in medieval India. The Hindu mystics of the time do not owe anything to orthodox Islam that had invaded the sub-continent by way of direct influence. Islam is a strong proselytising religion and as it came into the sub-continent it posed a serious and real challenge to a caste-ridden and moribund Hinduism. The situation could have provided added impetus and inspired learned Hindus to seek the truth within their own religion to force a reformation from within. In an obtuse manner this could be considered a limited and indirect influence of Islam on Hinduism. The result of the introspection of the educated Hindus was the development of the saints and mystics into teachers propagating the core of the religion and the introduction of a 'new wave' Hinduism. *[A similar movement originated when the influence of Christianity had started to threaten a languid Hinduism in the 18th and 19th centuries. A group of Hindu reformers rose to protect the core of the religion through advocating revolutionary changes to the practice and customs of the religion. This aspect of Hindu reform will be discussed in a later volume in the series at the appropriate stage of the narration.]*

Fact 4: The medieval Hindu mystics did not make inroads into the religious fortress of Islam, or for that matter, to the core of traditional Hinduism. Their teachings directly affected only a minority, insignificant in the context of the overall spread of the religion in the sub-continent. However, through their socio-religious intervention, the mystics or sants or saints, who also doubled as teachers and masters, managed to arrest the decay that had set in within the practice of Hinduism brought about by the rigidity enforced by traditional Brahmanism.

Conclusion

In an unbiased and overarching assessment, the impact of both Hindu mysticism and Islamic Sufism on the broader Indian cultural and religious development seems to the disproportionately exaggerated. It is also obvious that both these movements have their intrinsic value as distinctive phases in their respective religions, from a moral, spiritual and philosophical point of view. However, historically they are not very significant events or even of great importance, since only relatively few Indian were affected even at the zenith of their influence. Further, the numbers following the teachings of the masters dwindled rapidly as their influence started to wane with time.

Perhaps the most important observation to put forward is that both the religions showed no signs of being affected by the radical elements within their fold and continued on their own individual journeys. Neither Hinduism nor Islam showed any long-term recognition or acceptance of either mysticism or Sufism. The Hindu mystics and Muslim Sufis remained at the fringes of their mainstream religions, without ever being able to make even semi-permanent changes to the practice of their respective faiths.

Chapter 36

THE MEDIEVAL HINDU REVIVAL REFORM THROUGH BHAKTI

At the time when the Islamic conquest of the sub-continent began in earnest, Hindu Brahmanism was fully established in India. All religious questioning and competition that had been posed by Buddhism and Jainism had been comprehensively removed. The most important socio-cultural event of the 14th and 15th century medieval India was the revolution that took place in the Hindu society, brought about by a large number of socio-religious reformers. When Islam had first appeared in Peninsular India a religious upheaval was already in the offing in Hindu South India. The leader of this movement was Shankaracharya, whose teachings and preaching had completely obliterated Buddhism from the region, while also providing a new impetus and orientation to the practice of Hinduism.

Shankaracharya was however, more a philosopher than a reformer. His concept of 'Sacchidananda Brahma' was beyond the comprehension of the common person. The concept represented 'existence, consciousness and bliss' or 'truth, consciousness and bliss' and is the description of the subjective experience of the ultimate and unchanging reality of Hinduism that is called Brahman. In this explanation 'Brahman' is the unchanging and highest reality amidst and beyond the world that cannot be exactly defined. His 'Advaita Vedanta' was at a high intellectual plane and therefore remained, and remains to this day, the subject of discussion amongst the educated and philosophically oriented people. Almost a century after Shankara consolidated his doctrine and unified the different streams of Hinduism into one recognisable mainstream, the Bhakti movement originated a counter proposal against the Advaita doctrine, which had not been easily understood by the lay person.

Ramanuja, a 11th century saint, protested against the monism that Shankara preached and modified it to lay the foundation for the concept that became known as 'Vishist Advaitawad'. While Ramanuja's idea was also based on monism, it was not very rigid and was qualified. It derived inspiration from ancient Hindu scriptures—the Puranas, Brahma Sutra and the Bhagavad Gita. Ramanuja also derived inspiration from some Tamil saints who had preceded him.

Ramanuja and Contemporaries

Ramanuja is acknowledged as a great Vaishnavite reformer, thought to have been born around 1016. Traditional accounts credit him with having lived for 120 years (1016-1136). He was educated in Kanchipuram under Yadava Prakasha who was the head of the philosophical academy in Kanchi and a renowned Advaita teacher of the time. Subsequently Ramanuja moved to Sringeri and because of his learned disposition was appointed the head of the temple administration. This rapid rise within the temple and religious hierarchy at a relatively young age, led to internal jealousy and there was an unsuccessful attempt on his life. In later years he was persecuted by the Chola king Kulottunga who wanted Ramanuja to become a Shaivite. The threat to his personal safety prompted Ramanuja to migrate to the neighbouring Hoysala kingdom.

During the period of his development, Ramanuja had imbibed the spirit of Bhakti from the Alwars, a group of Tamil saints. He developed the primary doctrine of 'Vishisht Advaitawad', which was a qualified monism that provided scope for the feeling and practice of Bhakti. Ramanuja's philosophy was that it was not necessary for individual souls to be part of the Supreme Being, even though they all emanated from Him. Further, the Supreme was not an abstract Being but possessed qualities of goodness and beauty to an infinite degree. The philosophy supported the concept of a 'Saguna Ishwara', a God endowed with all auspicious qualities. In the final stage of a person's spiritual evolution, Bhakti became transformed into a particular mode of Jnana, or knowledge. This knowledge is achieved in turn through devotion, creating a sort of perpetual and eternal cycle.

> 'But how can knowledge be attained: Krishna says in the Gita: "To those who are ever devoted and worship me with love, I give that knowledge by which they attain me." Bhakti must be reached by desirelessness; action must be done in the spirit of renunciation, and all desire for "fruit," for reward hereafter must be abandoned.'
>
> Ishwari Prasad,
>
> *History of Medieval India*, pp. 561-62

Along with Shankara, Ramanuja brought back the age-old idea of one Supreme Being and revived the Bhakti cult. From this point onwards Bhakti went on to acquire vast influence.

There were some contemporaries of Ramanuja who also questioned the doctrine of monism as explained by Shankaracharya. One was Nimbarkar, said to have died around 1162, who propounded a theory that was a compromise between different tendencies, both monistic and pluralistic. Another great teacher was Madhav who was born around 1200 in the Udipi district of South Kanara. He also developed a similar doctrine of a God who was 'Saguna Iswara', a God who was full of all the good qualities and who could be reached through Bhakti. The release from rebirth for a person was to be achieved through knowledge and devotion.

While these reformers were conceptualising theories that were meant to be within the grasp of the common person, Hinduism continued to move in its own sedate pace, oblivious of the challenges that it was facing from a competing and robust religion. So far the spirit of compromise inherent in Brahmanism had overcome all opposition. Hinduism had the flexibility and power to adapt and assimilate other doctrines to its own philosophical and canonical body. Hinduism was an, 'all-tolerant, -compliant, -comprehensive and –absorbing religion'. It had so far brought into its fold people of different faiths, races and creeds who had invaded the sub-continent from time to time. Its first and only failure to assimilate took place when it was faced with the Islamic faith that was gradually establishing itself in the region, because the Muslims were zealously and uncompromisingly devout to their faith.

Even though there was awareness that the new religion that had entered the region was not ready to be assimilated, Hinduism continued to be self-absorbed, and did not alter its position as a blend of two distinctly different tendencies—one, the monism of the elite intellectuals, and two, the deistic polytheism of the common person. Within this dual-fold, Brahmanism, caste, and Sanskrit were preserved and evolved. At the same time, Islam remained aloof, content in its own practice while making minor, but consequential inroads into the region.

The close proximity between Hinduism and Islam was bound to produce significant effects that would influence Indian thinkers from both the religions. However, in the initial years of interaction this influence was almost non-existent. Therefore, there is no trace of Islamic influence on Ramanuja's philosophy or thought process, which remained quintessentially Hindu in its form. From the 14th century onwards it is seen that Islamic ideas had a conscious and subconscious effect on philosophical Hindu thought. This subtle shift in the situation can be seen in the teachings of Namadeva, Sant Kabir, Guru Nanak and their contemporaries.

It is at this stage that India witnessed the beginning of a national religious movement, initially in Maharashtra led by Namadeva. He declared that he needed neither temple nor mosque for his worship and a number of his contemporary saints echoed the same sentiment. The deep influence of Sufism that was spreading in North India is apparent in this development, as is the Hindu religious fervour of the Bhakti movement in Peninsular India. The progenitor of this reform movement was Ramananda.

Ramananda

Ramanuja had already initiated a religious revival in South India and Ramananda brought this movement to North India. The movement was a reaction to the increasing rigidity of orthodox Hinduism and attempted to cater for the demands of the heart against the pure intellectualism of Vedanta that had been prevalent for a few centuries.

There is uncertainty regarding Ramananda's date of birth and even the date of his death. However, Kabir is confirmed to have been his disciple and therefore a contemporary. From this information it can be surmised with reasonable accuracy that Ramananda lived and taught in the first half of the 15th century. He was born into a Brahmin family in Prayag, was educated in all aspects of the religion, and travelled widely before settling down and spending most of his life in Varanasi. There is very limited written work attributed directly to Ramananda. However, his ideas can be collated from the writings of his immediate disciples who state categorically that the contents of their works are all Ramananda's ideas and sayings.

In pursuing the concept of a God that was not nirguna like Vishnu, he substituted Rama as the object of worship. Rama was not nirguna, but an incarnation of God and the epitome of a Perfect Man. Ramananda taught the concept of Bhakti to all, making no distinction of caste and creed amongst his disciples. Although born and brought up in orthodox Brahmanism, he broke the rigid mould and created a sect with no distinctions of any kind, accepting disciples from all castes, from both sexes and even different religions. Some of his followers were Muslims. He insisted on absolute social equality, even for the study of the scriptures. This was a departure from earlier thinkers who had accepted the concept of caste as being part of the practice of Hinduism.

Ramananda rejected the caste system completely and started what later came to be referred to as the 'religious renaissance' in Medieval India. He had a dozen famous disciples, all of whom went on to be acknowledged as socio-religious reformers in their own right. They were: Kabir, Bhavananda, Atmananda, Sursura, Padmavati, Narhari, Raidas (also mentioned as Ravidas), Dhana, Pipa, Sain, Sukha and the wife of Sursura. *[The fact that the name of the last mentioned lady is not mentioned in any chronicle is perhaps indicative of the lower status of women in society at that time.]* Even though each one of these disciples went on to become renowned teachers, Kabir was the most famous.

Sant Kabir

The circumstances of Kabir's birth is obscure and the date of his birth contentious. His birth is generally accepted to have been around 1425 and he died either in 1492 or 1518, both the estimates being considered probable.

> ### Story of Kabir's Birth
>
> Tradition says that Kabir was born to a Brahmin widow, who cast him away at birth for fear of social ostracism. The child was picked up by a weaver named Niru who was a Muslim. Kabir was brought up by his foster parents with great affection and care and when he came of age, he took up his father's profession of weaving. While doing his daily work as a weaver, Kabir found time to philosophise and moralise.
>
> The story of being born to a Brahmin widow, is definitely 'spicy', but there may not be any truth to it.

It is generally accepted that Kabir was brought up as a Muslim, irrespective of the truth about his birth. However, he grew up and lived in the decidedly Hindu environment in Varanasi. Kabir did not receive any formal education and it is even doubtful whether he could read or write. Even so, he was inquisitive by nature. He became conversant with Hindu religious practices and also knew a great deal regarding the Islamic faith, the religion of his parents. Ramananda accepted Kabir as a disciple and initiated him into a deeper knowledge of Hindu philosophy.

Kabir became a professional weaver, following in the footsteps of his father. While weaving, he sang out his thoughts and ideas, never using pen and paper to record them. His communications were always oral. The songs he composed were mostly in broken language and incorrect grammar, which is consistent with his uneducated status. However, some of them were in perfect poetry and remain enigmatic because of the grace of their composition.

> 'No one knew the mystery of that weaver
>
> Who came into the world and spread the warp.
>
> The earth and the sky are the two beams,
>
> The sun and the moon are two filled shuttles,
>
> Taking a thousand threads he spreads them lengthways;
>
> Today he weaveth still, but hard to reach is the far-off end.'
>
> The Bijak of Kabir by Ahmad Shah
As quoted in Ishwari Prasad,
History of Medieval India, p. 571

At the headquarters of the 'Kabir Panthis' in Varanasi, the group made up of his followers, there is a collection of 21 books attributed to the master, that has been written down by his immediate disciples. The language of the poems, discourses and sayings is simple and not that of a refined philosopher. In essence Kabir should be considered a mystic poet and social reformer, not a religious philosopher who had achieved intellectual ascendancy.

Kabir was a great social and religious reformer and all his thoughts and ideas are fully based on Hindu philosophy. He propagated the earlier concept of escaping from the cycle of birth, death, and re-birth through recourse to the practice of Bhakti. Kabir was opposed to all kinds of superstitions, blind faith in the scriptures, pilgrimages and idol worship. He hated rituals and ceremonies and fought against the caste system as well as all types of intolerance. Kabir's approach was positive in that he wanted to unite Muslims and Hindus, which he felt was the optimum way to wipe out all distinctions of caste and religion. He propagated this since he was convinced that the essence of both religions was the same. He also attempted to expose the ignorance and bias of the Muslim ulema and the orthodox Hindu priest.

Kabir's fundamental concept was that there was only one God, called by many different names. Kabir conceived God as a collection of attributes without any shape or form. Since this was the precept, Kabir did not worship any 'deity' and also did not proscribe any exuberant celebrations like those practised by some other sects. He avoided monism and placed God as the supreme object of love.

Kabir propagated the idea of an individual merging with the Whole, which was God. His concept of love for the divine was a combination of Vaishnava Bhakti and Muslim Sufi devotion; maintaining that Hindus and Muslims were pots of the same clay, striving through different routes to reach the same goal. He pointed out the futility of paying lip-service and homage to the great ideals of truth and religion without adhering to them in daily life.

> It is not by fasting and repeating prayers and the creed,
>
> That one goeth to heaven:
>
> The inner veil of the temple of Mecca
>
> Is in man's heart, if *the truth* be known.
>
> Make thy mind thy Kaaba, thy body its enclosing temple.
>
> Conscience its prime teacher;
>
> Sacrifice wrath, doubt, and malice;
>
> Make patience thine utterance of the five prayers,
>
> The Hindus and the Musalmans have the same Lord.
>
> Kabir's poem, translated in Arthur Macauliffe,
> *The Sikh Religion*, Vol VI
>
> As quoted in Ishwari Prasad,
> *History of Medieval India*, p. 572.

Kabir preached a broad monistic pantheism that was cleverly couched in positive moral fervour. In this way of thinking, in order to achieve union with Him, there was no need to leave worldly life, which Kabir himself had not done. He lived the life of a normal house-holder, practising his profession and earning a living. The concept was that one should live in the world, without developing attachments to the worldly things that clutter daily life. Within this lifestyle he advocated adhering to a universal religion.

To achieve an amalgamation, he asked the Hindus to give up the external manifestations of the religion such as idol worship, ritualism, distinctions of caste, emphasis on scriptures and the belief in incarnations. Similarly he asked the Muslims to give up their arrogance and the blind faith bestowed on the 'prophet and his book'. Kabir was the first socio-religious reformer to declare that both Hindus and Muslims were the children of the same and one Supreme Being. Kabir was an unusual person for his times—the story of his birth and subsequent life; his lack of education but becoming an unlettered philosopher; his way of life as an ascetic householder-saint who earned his living through work; all of which were distinctive and attracted people to him and his teachings.

Kabir's radical teachings did not go uncontested by both the religions that had been targeted. The Hindus could not tolerate his preaching that their temples and Gods, the Vedas and the Shastra, the practice of caste and varna were all false. Similarly the Muslims could not subscribe to the theory that their religion was not superior to all other faiths but at the same level as others and that their fasts and pilgrimages had no intrinsic worth or merit. In a joint effort to silence him, around 1495, the ulema and priests together lodged a complaint against Kabir with the Sultan Sikandar Lodi in Delhi. Kabir now in his 60s, was summoned by the Sultan. However, Sikandar Lodi did not find anything blasphemous with the simple teachings of an unlettered weaver. Even so, Kabir was temporarily exiled to Maghar to appease the demands of the ulema and the priests.

Despite the concerted opposition to his teachings, Kabir's movement was a living force in the 15th century and after. The lower caste Hindus considered him a saint and had a Christ-like devotion towards him, since he had attempted to save them from degradation. The others worshipped him for the simplicity of his teachings and for resuscitating the moribund Hindu society. There is no doubt that Kabir succeeded in his self-imposed mission and also inspired other thinkers, both contemporary and in later-days. His movement is alive to this day. After his death, his son Sant Kamal, influenced the further development of the movement.

Ramananda's Other Disciples

The 12 more famous disciples of Ramananda have already been listed. Dhanna, Pipa, Sain and Raidas delivered the same message as Kabir, in much more humble ways. Some of their hymns and poems have been preserved in the Adigrantha, the holy book of the Sikhs. Dhanna was born in Dhuan in Tank province of Rajputana and was a simple farmer. He taught the concept of Bhakti to the villagers through his songs. Pipa was the Raja of Gagraungarh and had a saintly disposition. He became a disciple of Ramananda. He is the creator of 'Pipaji ki Bani' a poem/ballad that has been passed down the generations orally. The poem maintains that worship should be internal and that disciplined worship under a Guru', a mentor, helps one attain God.

Sain was a barber by profession and sang hymns in both Hindi and Marathi. His message influenced both North and South India. Raidas belonged to Varanasi and was a leather-worker, belonging to a class of people who removed the carcasses of dead animals and were considered to be 'untouchable'. He was one of the few lower caste reformists and was given the status of a sant or saint.

Guru Nanak

Nanak was a person with a mighty mind and created a reformist stir in the Punjab region. Unlike many of the other medieval socio-religious reformers, Nanak's dates are accurately known—he was born on 26 November 1469, full moon day of Kartik in the Hindu calendar, in village Talwandi on the banks of the River Ravi in Gujranwala district of Punjab. He had basic knowledge of Persian and Hindi, but was not particularly inclined towards attaining any deep knowledge through traditional learning. In his younger days he attempted odd jobs such as agricultural work and shop keeping without much success. At the age of 18 he married a Khatri girl Sulakhin, and had two sons—Sri Chand and Lakshmi Chand. He was not particularly attached to the family or any of the jobs that he worked on. However, he had an innate thirst to know the Truth, a spiritual thirst that subsumed all else as he grew older.

At the age of 27, Nanak met Kabir during the last decade of the 15th century. At that time Kabir, already a famous teacher across North India by then, was more than 65 years old. There is no doubt that Nanak learned a lot from Kabir and in later years incorporated a number of lines from Kabir's poetry into the Adigranth, the religious book of the Sikhs. When he became 30 years old, Nanak decided to leave the life of a householder and gave up home and family to become a sanyasi.

He set out to meet sadhus and saints, accompanied by Bhai Bala who was his companion from childhood and Bhai Mardana, a Muslim Rababi (or minstrel) who used to strum the harp while Nanak meditated. Nanak's travels are not well documented, but it is known that he visited the important pilgrim centres in India, Ceylon (Sri Lanka), Arabia and Iran. It is reported that he visited Mecca and Medina dressed in the garb of a Muslim Fakir. There are also a number of stories regarding the miracles he performed during his journeys, but they are not corroborated or verifiable. In 1504, after five years of wandering, he became the Guru of the Sikhs (Sikh is a colloquial version of the word 'Shishya' meaning disciple), and preached his message for the next 34 years.

During the time of his preaching he continued to travel within the Punjab region and the places that he visited became, in the course of time, pilgrimage centres. He died in 1538 at the age of 70 in his hometown. His tomb has since been swept away by the River Ravi. Nanak regarded himself as a prophet, stating that the message that he delivered was 'received from His doorstep'. Nanak's primary aim was to unify the Hindus and the Muslims. The reasons for this focus on Hindu-Muslim unity has to be analysed within the geo-political reality that prevailed in Punjab at that time. Geographically, Punjab had always borne the brunt of invasions from the north-west. Timur had inflicted terrible suffering on the people of Punjab and the region was in political turmoil throughout the 15th century. Punjab was also in the throes of untold misery as the internecine wars for control of the throne of Delhi was largely fought in its territory.

By the time Nanak established himself as a Guru, the pressure of Islam on the people of Punjab had increased to unbearable proportions. Along with the wars for control there was a continuous series of Hindu-Muslim clashes in the region. Nanak instinctively realised that in order to heal the wounds of the society, it was necessary to end religious conflict. He made this the mission of his life. Nanak's biographies proclaim that the first words that he uttered after receiving revelation was, 'There is no Hindu, and there is no Musalman'.

The main point of Nanak's teaching was the unity of God. He conceived God as being nirguna, meaning without attributes and nirakar, being formless. God was 'inaccessible, fathomless and exalted above all else.' Nanak preached that if this Absolute Supreme was understood, then there would be no difference between His creatures and therefore no quarrel about His name. The ultimate aim of man must be to merge with the Light Divine for which he needed to remove delusion from his mind. This concept was uncannily similar to the fana of the Sufis and nirvana of the Buddhists. The merger with the Light Divine was achieved through the remembrance of His name (smarana) that had to be ardent and sincere, achieved through humility and right action.

There was a subtle difference in the manner of preaching between Nanak and Kabir. Nanak always attacked evil while never tiring of praising the good, whereas Kabir only attacked the evils of society, taking for granted that everyone knew the goodness of God. Nanak also advocated the need for a Guru to achieve self-realisation and his teachings contained the seeds of a definitive religion. His characteristic personal humility, serene way of life and forbearance attracted large number of followers and won their love and respect. With the passage of time his disciples, the Shishyas, formed themselves as Sikhs, becoming a full-fledged religion, in much the same pattern of evolution as that of Islam. The similarities between the two religions are uncanny—the religion of the Sikhs, Sikhism in later days, had a Prophet (Guru Nanak), a Book (Adigrantha, later to be called the Guru Granth Sahib), and a church Gurudwara, (literally meaning the door to the guru) for the Sangat, the gathering. Amritsar became the Mecca of the Sikhs during the time of Guru Ram Das. The Sikhs also paid a religious tax, similar to the Islamic Zakat.

Guru Nanak had learned a lot from Kabir, who was a disciple of Ramananda, who in turn belonged to the Ramanuja School of philosophy. It is not surprising that there is an unmistakable impress of the ideas of Ramanuja in Nanak's teachings. Taking a leaf from Ramanuja's concept, he proclaimed Bhakti to be the only way to salvation; he gave divine status to the Guru as a Prophet and abhorred divisions of caste and creed.

> Religion consisteth not in mere words;
>
> He who looketh on all men as equal is religious.
>
> Religion consisteth not in wandering to tombs or places or cremation, or sitting in attitudes of contemplation.
>
> Religion consisteth not in wandering in foreign countries, or in bathing at places of pilgrimage.
>
> Abide pure amidst the impurities of the world;
>
> Thus shalt thou find the way to religion.
>
> Summation of Nanak's creed, translated in Arthur Macauliffe,
> *The Sikh Religion*, Vol VI
>
> As quoted in Ishwari Prasad,
> *History of Medieval India*, p. 572.

Vallabhacharya

From the mid-14th century and through the whole of the 15th century, the entire North India was in religious ferment. While Kabir and Nanak influenced Eastern Uttar Pradesh and Punjab, Chaitanya and Vallabhacharya were providing leadership for religious reform in Bengal and Western Uttar Pradesh. Although both these teachers functioned in geographically separated areas, the two sects that developed out of their concepts were remarkably similar. Both adored Krishna as a child or young man and considered him a 'saguna' or anthropomorphic deity, not one that was nirguna. The concept emerged almost simultaneously in Bengal and Central India.

Vallabhacharya was born in Varanasi in 1479 and was the son of Lakshmana Bhatt, a Brahmin from Telangana. By the time he was 12 years old he had already been acknowledged as a preacher of Vaishnava Hinduism. It is also claimed that while he was in Vrindavan, a place intimately associated with Krishna, the Lord visited him personally. He proposed the concept of complete identification of both soul and body with the Supreme Spirit, preaching a monism that was called 'Sudha Advaita' or 'pure non-duality'. In this concept, Bhakti was both the means and the end, with salvation being achieved through His Grace. The teacher on earth was divine in stature.

Vallabhacharya's concept differed from that of Ramanuja in recognising the distinction between the soul and God. Other than this fundamental difference, he followed the teachings of the 12th century Guru. The intense devotion to Vishnu, which was exemplified in the concept of Vaishnavism, was fully realised in Vallabha's faith. As a sect the group created by Vallabha attracted men from all castes, creeds and even some Muslims.

Chaitanya

Bengal had for centuries been fertile ground for the worship of Krishna as the God of Love. In Bengal flourished Jayadeva, the author of Gita Govind in 12th century and also the famous authors Chandni Das (1417-78) and Vidyapati (1433-81). Their passionate poetry paved the way for Chaitanya to espouse his concept of worship. At this time Bengal had already been conquered and was ruled by Muslim kings/sultans. However, there was peaceful co-existence between Hindus and Muslims with almost no interference from the Muslim Sultan regarding the practice of an individual's religion. While peaceful co-existence was the norm, Hinduism was languishing in the shadow of the worship of Chandi, which was concomitant with sacrifices and tantric rites of a debased and sensual nature. Hinduism also suffered from the harmful effects of the caste system and a narrow-minded elite that controlled the religion. The power of the Brahmin and their control over the religion was absolute.

Chaitanya was born in Nawadip in March 1486, to Jaganath Mishra and his wife Sachi Debi. His pet name was Nimai and he was renowned for his love of learning from early childhood. He married at the age of 18 and set up a school on the banks of the River Bhagirathi where he was also the senior teacher. A call from within made him give up the profession of teaching and he travelled to East Bengal and then to Gaya. In Gaya, Chaitanya met Iswar Puri who initiated him into the Bhakti cult. It was here that 'Nimai' was given the name Chaitanya, since his soul and intellect were saturated with the love for Krishna.

Chaitanya took 'sanyas', the act of being celibate and moving away from all worldly attachments, when he was 25 and started on a round of travels. First he went to the shrine of Krishna, who is depicted in the form of Jaganath, in Puri and thereafter roamed all over India for the next six years. He visited Vrindavan in the north and Rameswaram in the south. During his travels he came in encountered Muslim holy men and Sufis and was impressed with the simple and democratic ideas that they propagated. He came back to Puri and spend the next 18 years there, teaching and preaching his concept of worship. He died at the early age of 48 in 1534.

Chaitanya's primary concept is of Bhakti, or devotion. He believed in a Supreme Being, Brahma as in the case of Vedantists, who is possessed of attributes that was manifest in Sri Krishna. God was a personal being, full of love and grace, a state that in turn inspires love from devotees. Chaitanya's Bhakti is exemplified and illustrated by the mutual love of Radha and Krishna and he was greatly influenced by the teachings of Ramanuja, the Bhagavad Gita and the Bhagavata Purana.

Chaitanya conceived of a Bhakt, devotee, passing through five successive stages in his evolution to achieving salvation. They were: Shanti, resigned contemplation; Dasya, service and servitude to Him; Sakhya, friendship that flows on to the fourth stage; Vatsalya, love like that of a child for its parents; and Madhurya, earnest and all-engrossing love such as that of a woman for her lover. Biographers of Chaitanya claim, and insist, that he had reached the fifth level and combined in himself the blend of the two aspects of God—God the lover and God the beloved, represented by Krishna and Radha.

Chaitanya's teachings also have a number of commonalities with those of other saints like Ramanuja. He gave a prominent place to the Guru and his role in the evolution of the devotee; he preached against any and all distinctions made on the basis of caste and creed; his condemnation of Brahminical rituals was absolute; and he discouraged asceticism and renunciation. Although he himself was a practising sanyasi, a celibate, he dissuaded others from renouncing worldly duties. He was vociferous in attacking social evils and directly contributed to the rejuvenation of Hinduism in Bengal.

Conclusion

Through its long and chequered history, there has been no dearth of reformers within Hinduism. In the 15th century, starting with Ramnuja to Chaitanya, there is a long line up of some of the greatest thinkers and philosophers of the religion seen in any one period. The period from late 14th century till early 16th century was the 'Age of Socio-religious Reformers' for Hinduism. These reformers altered Hinduism and gave the people a relatively simplified religion. The simplification was provided through the following beliefs: that there was only one God, either Saguna or Nirguna; the concept that the soul was part of Him and therefore constantly strove to be near Him; communion with the Supreme Being was not possible through rituals, pilgrimages or by adhering to the letter of the scriptures; and that salvation lay in Bhakti.

While the reformers contributed greatly to the religious field, their contribution to the society was even greater. They revolutionised society, peacefully and at times through almost invisible movements. All the reformers travelled widely, met with people of all castes and religions, held cosmopolitan views and by their demeanour established the fact that they belonged to the sub-continent and not to any one province or region. The urge of 'Indians' to unite when facing a common enemy, exemplified during Timur's invasion when Hindus and Muslims fought together against the invading army, influenced and even progressed with the teachings of these religious reformers. The saints appealed directly to the heart, not the head, mind or rationality. The doctrine of Bhakti that all of them embraced showed the futility of meaningless religious conflicts and expanded the concept that the essence of all religions were the same.

The greatest contribution of the reformers to the Hindu society was the social upliftment of the lower caste population. They also helped in the development of the language of the common people through teaching in the language used for everyday transactions. Persian and Sanskrit were cultivated by Islamic and Hindu institutes of repute and used by the educated elite of the society. Before the advent of the reformers, the language of the common man did not have any literature or religious significance worth mentioning. By the end of the 15th century, Hindi was definitely shaped by the sayings and teachings of saints such as Kabir, Raidas and others. The messages of the masters were always delivered in simple yet beautiful Hindi poetry and prose. Similarly, the Vaishnava poets, in Bengal, Gujarat and Maharashtra, enriched the local languages of their regions.

Undoubtedly, the saint-reformers contributed and uplifted religious thought, social reform and the development of language and literature. However, they could not unite the Hindus and Muslims into one nation, a feat that they repeatedly attempted without any tangible success. People of both the faiths listened to them and even worshipped them, but clung tenaciously to their own narrow religious beliefs. Further, only a minority of the population actually became the disciples of these masters. For every saint and his follower, there were more than double the number of fanatics in each religion. The division of the sub-continent into India and Pakistan is a painful reminder of the fact that even after centuries of co-existence and association and the efforts of gifted socio-religious reformers, the people of India could not unite as one.

The failure of the masters to achieve socio-religious cohesion could be attributed to three factors. First was that the Hindu sants (saints) and Muslim Sufi masters concentrated on targeting the lower class and the mostly uneducated people in order to uplift them socially. The privileged higher class, the educated upper class who were the opinion makers were not only unaffected but also suspicious of the reformers. The fact remained that the sants and the masters did not have universal appeal. Second, the reformers' message lacked emphasis on improving the economic status of their followers, who were almost all living in or close to poverty. Attempting to achieve salvation and moral upliftment while living a life of penury is not easy for a common person and requires extraordinary piety and concentration that was not readily available. It is much easier to achieve social reform if it is combined with an assured and guaranteed economic upliftment. This did not happen in the case of the medieval Indian socio-religious reformation movement. A contributory factor was also that the reformers did not make any attempt to uplift the women from their low status in society. Therefore, even though some progress was being achieved in moving the society forward, women remained relegated to the back. The third factor was that once the great saints and masters left the scene, they were not replaced by equally powerful disciples. In the usual pattern, the calibre of following disciples were diluted. This situation led to their message being gradually either adapted or diluted to suit and individual's proclivity towards religion, caste, creed and even colour.

Even so, the socio-religious reformers achieved remarkable success during their time. They were the first to raise the concept of Hindu-Muslim unity in many parts of the country. Perhaps more importantly, they were the first group who could be considered 'Indian' in a pan sub-continental manner. The reformers created awareness in the minds of men, which led to inquisitive questioning that led to revolutionising existing social values.

Excluded from the secular sphere of the state, the Hindu genius found an outlet in religion, and the new school of reformers tried to purify

> a system which was encrusted with superstitious rites and practices, so completely at variance with the true spirit of religion. The names of Ramanand, Chaitanya, Kabir and Nanak will stand for all time to come as beaconlights to guide frail humanity which is only too prone to fall into error and superstition. The very fact that the Hindu society was able to produce such men furnishes a refutation of the theory that the Hindu genius had become decadent and sterile under Muslim rule.
>
> Ishwari Prasad,
>
> *History of Medieval India*, p. 576.

CONCLUSION
A TURKISH TRIUMPH

Looking back at the Delhi Sultanate with the advantage of hindsight and the availability of a great deal of information from a number of sources, the most important factor that stands out is the ease with which the Turks overran North India and established a kingdom based on an alien religion and culture. It is nothing short of amazing that Mahmud of Ghazni could make annual raids into India, in which he moved deep into the sub-continent, plundered and destroyed at will and then returned to his kingdom a far richer person than when he arrived. He did this without being offered any tangible opposition or being stopped either on the way in or on the way out. It is a fact that Mahmud was never effectively defeated in any of his forays into India.

The corollary to this inexplicable fact is that the Indian soldier was not in any way inferior to their Turkish adversary. Further, the rulers of North India who were mostly Rajput kings, did not lack in fighting spirit or courage in battle—quiet the opposite. Their daring, audacity and bravery could be considered to be on the end of the spectrum of extreme courageousness, bordering on impulsive recklessness. Therefore, the question to be asked is why did such a calamitous event come to pass so rapidly? How and why were the Turks so successful in conquering a large swath of North India—from the River Indus to Benares—within a short span of a mere three decades?

The Reasons Why...

There are four major reasons that can be identified as being at the core of the easy Turkish victory. First, North India was divided into numerous states, some so small in size as to be considered insignificant.

Since there was no 'empire' after the fall of the Vardhana dynasty, the north-west frontier was open. It was not defended, since it was not the direct responsibility of any one kingdom. There was also no unified effort to defend the borders since the kingdoms of North India were habitually suspicious of each other and not on friendly terms. Most of the kings followed the Kautilyan 'Mandala Theory', which advocated the concept of considering all immediate neighbours to be adversaries, if not outright enemies. A combination of these factors made it easy for outsiders to invade the sub-continent. The passes of the Hindu Kush were left open with no effort at checking the inflow of armies through them. Perhaps even more damaging to exercising the concept of combined defence was that the smaller kingdoms at the border were content to let the invading armies by-pass them without falling prey to the plunder and pillage of the invasion. This attitude facilitated the rapid movement of the invaders into the North Indian heartland.

Second, the general population of the kingdoms that proliferated in North India were neither politically aware nor active. They remained completely unconcerned about who ruled them and nonchalant about the rise and fall of empires and dynasties. There was an inexplicable sense of political apathy and paralysis that prevailed among the population. This attitude did not matter as long as the almost continuous power struggles were between Indian dynasties. However, when the same apathy prevailed during the power struggle was between Indian rulers and foreign invaders, it led to disastrous consequences.

> 'Political apathy, combined with lack of patriotism, territorial or emotional, created a frame of mind in the generality of the Indians of that age which made little difference between foreigners and their countrymen'.
>
> *The Sultanate of Delhi 711-1526 A D*, p. 344.

Third, at the operational level of the conduct of war, the Turks adopted shock tactics that the Indian armies were unaccustomed to and therefore could not counter effectively. The Turks had mastered the art of rapid attacks followed by equally quick withdrawals; they repeatedly demonstrated an uncanny ability to select the correct centre of gravity of the adversary and to target that; they were adept at forced marches that made forces available at improbable points in a kingdom under attack; and they made repeated attacks at the same place when such attacks were least expected. Against such operational tactics, only rigid military discipline combined with a strong political organisation could have withstood the pressure and saved the day. Eternal vigilance was what was required to stave off the invasions. The Hindu kingdoms sadly lacked the foresight to ensure such vigilance. The political and military strength to prevail against the Turks would have required a single strong leader controlling the pooled resources of the myriad kingdoms of North India. However, the political situation in North India at that time would never have permitted implementing such a move.

Fourth, even though Mahmud of Ghazni had raided deep into the sub-continent, no Indian ruler considered him a harbinger of even more decisive raids. This attitude displayed a surprising lack of foresight on the part of strategically astute kings who were well-versed in statecraft. During and after the raids by Mahmud, the Indian kingdoms did not make any attempts at creating a combined defence, continuing to be disorganised and at odds with each other. Most of the kingdoms that had suffered during the Ghaznavid raids were more interested in erasing the humiliation and therefore ignored the lessons that should have been learned. Inevitably, they lapsed into lethargy. The 'Ostrich Syndrome' was very clearly visible in this behaviour. When the more important Turkish invasion with even bigger consequences in comparison to the Ghaznavid raids came, North India was ill-prepared to stand up and fight back with any semblance of efficiency.

The Resistance

The Turks also were in for a surprise. So far they had only invaded, plundered and looted, thereafter returning to their own territories in Afghanistan. Pillage and loot is only one part of invasion—the easier first part. Effective conquest, occupation and consolidation of the new territories is the second part and extremely hard work. While the Indian rulers succumbed to the invasion, actual and concerted resistance to foreign occupation began only after the Turks started to establish their rule over the conquered territories. It could be speculated that the Hindu kings never believed that the Islamic invaders would try to establish a kingdom with territorial integrity and sovereignty in the regions that they had conquered. As soon as the Indian rulers perceived this reality, opposition to the Turks establishing a kingdom/sultanate in the sub-continent started in earnest. The demonstrated intent of the Turks to stay in India acted as a clarion call for Hindu resistance.

A prime example of long-term resistance is that offered by the Hindushahi kings of the Punjab against their Arab/Turk neighbours. This is a story of resistance and conflict that lasted for centuries. While the Turks made in-roads into Punjab, the region was finally 'conquered' only after more than 350 years of struggle (636 – 1026). Another example of a different kind is the history of the Chauhans of Ajmer. They revolted four times in a span of five years and managed to drive out the officers of Muhammad of Ghur from their kingdom. The Ranthambhor fort could not be effectively annexed even after 150 years of almost continuous fighting. The region that is generally referred to as Rajputana was never really conquered or completely annexed during the entire period of the Delhi Sultanate.

Muslim chronicles, such as *Tabaqat-i-Nasiri*, clearly mention annual expeditions to the Doab to put down rebellions and forcefully collect taxes. The Doab was in almost perpetual revolt for more than a century. Such annual conquests of territories that had already been declared as having been 'annexed' was repeated in territories across the Sultanate. Throughout the entire period of the existence of the Delhi Sultanate, Hindu kings, chieftains and the general population continued to rebel and revolt against the Sultans and their officers. This was remarkable for the time, especially considering the relative ease with which Islam had conquered and established political, military and religious superiority over many countries in other continents. The Hindu resistance to the Islamic invasion into the sub-continent was the fiercest and never replicated in any other place.

The story of the long-drawn resistance that was offered brings forward another question that is paradoxical. If the resistance was so fierce, why and how did pockets of territories in the sub-continent that had been conquered and ruled by Muslims continue to survive?

The Foreign Pockets

Islamic rule was established in Sindh with Multan as the capital in the 8th century and in the Punjab by the 11th century, while the rest of India was still in the hands of powerful Hindu kings. Once again an

Conclusion

enigmatic question gets to be asked. Why was no attempt made to evict the Arabs from Sindh in the 8th century? The answer is not difficult to fathom. The Hindu kings and minor chieftains ruling kingdoms, both large and small, were mostly antagonistic to each other and therefore were incapable of uniting to initiate joint action even against a common adversary. None of them assisted the ruler of Sindh when he was under attack. The bravery and patriotism of the Hindus were localised to their own kingdom or principality, since the concept of the sub-continent as a bastion of Hinduism did non-existent.

There are large numbers of Sanskrit records that are available today, which record the battlefield victories of Hindu kings and chiefs. They recount the exploits of these kings capturing towns and territory of the 'malekhshahs', the derogatory name used for Muslim rulers. *[In earlier times all foreigners were referred to as 'mlechaas' and this Sanskrit word is obviously a refined version of the same.]* There are chronicles that provide the details of Hindu kings defeating Muslim armies. Therefore, the conclusion that can be drawn is that the major reason for the Muslim invaders continuing to hold territory was the inability of the Hindu kings to bring to bear overwhelming force to eject the Muslim armies from the sub-continent. Overwhelming force would have only been available if the kings had made an attempt at creating a combined army under one leader.

There is ample proof of the famous Rajput dynasties—the Chauhans, Gurjara-Pratiharas, Guilots (Gehlots), Baghelas—who possessed unusual and unparalleled valour and bravery, waging successful wars against the Arabs in Multan and Sindh and against the Ghaznavids in Punjab. However, each of these wars and the victories they won were individual enterprises of one or the other dynasty. There was no collective effort to recapture lost territories irrespective of which kingdom/dynasty had lost it to the foreigners.

Another reason put forward for the lack of opposition is that the Hindu kings lacked aggressiveness and the spirit of the offensive in battle. In analysis it has been repeatedly emphasised that the Islamic armies were characterised by the spirit of aggression and offence. This assessment is difficult to believe because of the extreme bravery that was repeatedly demonstrated by Hindu warriors, especially the Rajput armies. Further, the Hindu kings were adept at overall strategy and individually most of them were considered to be master tacticians. Therefore, it is difficult to imagine the Hindu army as being passive in their battlefield tactics. The perceived tendency of Indian kings to assume a defensive stance has in modern days been converted to be a 'virtue' thereby perpetuating what is obviously a myth. The current justification of this flawed assessment goes on state that India has never been an aggressor, a concept that has even percolated into the foreign policy of the modern nation of India. On the other hand there is a trace of truth in the assertion that the Hindu kings were only intent on defending their borders. The Battle of Tarain where Ghazni forces were defeated but were not pursued by the victorious Rajput army when they fled is often pointed out as an example of this attitude. However, such examples cannot be taken conclusively as a lack of aggressiveness on the part of the Hindu kings.

There is also evidence that Muslim rulers of small enclaves/provinces held the Hindu population hostage and threatened to kill them and demolish temples at the slightest hint of a Hindu rebellion or invasion. This could have made the more powerful Hindu kingdoms hold their hand in a number of cases and permitted the territorially small Muslim enclaves to continue to exist. In any case, it is evident that a combination of reasons made the Hindu kings accept the establishment of Muslim rule in small pockets and finally in Delhi itself.

> Al-Idrisi writes in his Nuzhatul Mushtaq, 'The people make it [the image of the Sun Temple at Multan] the object of a pious pilgrimage, and to obey it is the law. So far is this carried that, when neighbouring princes make war against the country of Multa, either for the purpose of plunder or for carrying off the Idol, the priests have only to meet, threaten the aggressors with its anger and predict their destruction, and the assailants at once renounce their designs. *Without this fear the town of Multan would be destroyed.*' (Elliot and Dawson, History of India as Told by its own Historians, Vol I, p. 82)
>
> As Quoted in *The Sultanate of Delhi 711-1526 A D*, p. 346.

Instability in the Sultanate

In the three centuries of existence of the Delhi Sultanate there were frequent dynastic changes for a variety of reasons. Irrespective of the reasons for these drastic changes, they invariably led to the Sultanate descending into a state of inherent instability and internecine wars that at times degenerated into full-fledged civil wars. Three hundred years of regular instability at the centre is more than any kingdom can absorb and therefore the failure of the Sultanate at the first instance of a determined attack was not surprising. The reasons for the frequent dynastic changes were many and varied and their consequences were also equally varied.

The first reason for changes to the ruling dynasties was that the Turks did not have a formalised law of succession. Anyone, irrespective of family and status could aspire to be sultan, purely based on individual capability. The aspirant only needed to be powerful and a brave warrior with a sufficiently strong military following. The obvious result was that it led to ambitious men vying for power even if they were not part of the ruling royal family. Military prowess and a following of capable and loyal soldiers seemed to be the only qualifications required to seek the throne. The second reason was that throughout its history, the Delhi Sultanate was the personal rule of the Sultan and never the 'Rule of Law' that could be gradually perpetuated. The stability of the government depended fully on the personality and strength of character of the Sultan.

Third, analysis shows that almost in all cases a powerful Sultan was followed on the throne by a weak successor. This dichotomy can be attributed to the fact that the latter would normally have been brought up in luxury and indulging in vices, making him easy prey to more ambitious princes and others. The situation was exacerbated by the lack of clear succession laws, which made replacing the weak Sultan both easy and acceptable to the rest of the nobility. The need to replace weak Sultans was also necessitated by the Turks being foreigners engaged in a perpetual struggle against the Hindu kings for their own survival as well as that of the Sultanate. They could ill-afford to be ruled by weaklings. The Turkish nobles—de facto king makers—preferred to have able warriors on the throne, irrespective of whether they were of royal blood or not.

Fourth, the Slave System of the Turks had produced the first dynasty in Delhi but thereafter the system had deteriorated rapidly, The Slaves in India were not trained properly or in sufficient detail as before and, perhaps more importantly, most of them succumbed to the unexpected luxuries that 'Hindustan' offered. They became corrupt and disloyal—gradually the edifice on which the Delhi Sultanate was built started to crumble. With the degeneration of their character, the Slaves became the cause of frequent dynastic changes rather than being the enforcers of continuity in sovereign rule.

Fifth, the army was the bedrock of the strength and power of the Sultanate. The status and capability of the army varied with the policies and efficiency of different Sultans. The appointment of military governors to administer newly conquered provinces provided the impetus for them to powerful and independent. It was also not long before they began to harbour grater ambitions and coveting the throne of Delhi. In many cases the governorship was the stepping stone to a throne—either provincial or even the one in Delhi. Essentially, a weak sultan who did not command the direct loyalty of an efficient and powerful army was at the mercy of provincial governors. Sixth, the Delhi Sultans were in perpetual conflict against the Hindu chiefs and kings who were in incessant and repeated rebellion against the foreign invaders. This situation added to the necessity for the Turks to insist that weak and indecisive rulers be set aside for the greater good of the community.

Seventh, the Mongol raids increased the already high level of instability, leading to a greater level of rebellions by the Hindu chieftains as well as ambitious amirs ruling provinces. Only strong and centralised governments could contain the Mongol raids and the ensuing rebellions. As the Mongol threat started to dissipate, the Sultanate also lapsed into a state of palpable serendipity, thereby moving towards a weakened state. An example of the instability brought about by Mongol invasion can be seen in the aftermath of Timur's devastation of Delhi and the Punjab. The weakened state of the Delhi Sultan prompted the Governor of Gujarat, who was the son of a Rajput convert to Islam, to declare independence and create a sovereign state. At around the same time, Malwa under Dilawar Khan Ghori, also declared independence from Delhi. There were few fundamental differences between Malwa and Gujarat. Dilawar encouraged Rajput settlements in his kingdom and endeavoured to create a Muslim-Rajput complex. On the other hand, the Gujarat Sultans adopted the orthodox Muslim style of governance, imposing the Jaziya tax on non-Muslims and also occasionally demolishing Hindu temples. However, they habitually married Rajput princesses and patronised Indian artists and scholars. They also employed Hindus and placed them at the highest offices of the nation. The Gujarat Sultanate, if it could be given that title, was a paradox.

The eighth reason for the instability in the Delhi Sultanate was indirect. The Sultanate existed on enforced rule, not rule by consent. The Sultans only concentrated on maintaining peace and collecting revenue. There was no attempt made to improve the material status of the common people. In turn there was no support for the Sultan from the people. In fact the truth was that there were deliberate acts of violence, commission and omission against the Sultan and his rule. Dependent on the weakness or strength of the Sultan, these acts were common or sporadic.

No contemporary chronicler has attempted to examine the protracted instability of the Sultanate, which lasted for the entire three centuries of its existence, or the consequences of the instability. Further, there are no reports on what the common people, the masses, felt about the rule of the Sultans since most of the chronicles that are available were written by court reporters patronised by the Sultan himself. The inscriptions that record military victories are hyperbolic and cannot be taken to represent the truth of the times. They are unreliable at best. It can be surmised, given the manner in which the Delhi Sultans managed their kingdoms, that the common people were indifferent to the foreign sovereigns; essentially they did not care much as to who ruled in Delhi.

The Mutual Influence

Even though there was mutual hostility between the invaders and the local population, inevitably there was an exchange and mingling of social customs and religious ideas, as is bound to happen when two societies with deeply entrenched religious beliefs come into intimate contact with each other. These developments have been discussed in detail in the last section of this volume.

The Hindu upper class had a keen desire to bring about some compromise between the religions. They displayed the inherent tolerance of Hinduism by permitting the religious teachers of Islam to preach and convert freely. However, the Muslims in the sub-continent on the whole continued to keep aloof, either not understanding or consciously rejecting the Hindu overtures at compromise. The Islamic faith created two fundamental influences that percolated into Hinduism and gradually altered its ethos. The first was the direct effect of the missionary zeal of Islam. In order to counter the zeal of Muslims to convert and to proclaim their religion as the only true faith, Hinduism started to further entrench conservatism and orthodox Brahmanism. This was an attempt at creating a counterpoint to forced conversions to Islam being practised with the approval of the Muslim ruling elite. The Hindu leadership started to proscribe rigid and rigorous rules for daily living, enforced strict rules regarding diet and actively encouraged early marriage.

The second influence was the result of observing the democratic process within the Islamic faith, which Hinduism borrowed and adapted to suit its own purposes. The medieval Hindu mystics attempted to do away with the caste system in response to the egalitarianism practised in Islam. *[Even though, technically every person was equal in Islam, its practice in India saw the reverse surge of elitism into its ethos. The local converts were considered of a lesser status than the invading Turks in the eyes of the nobles and the clergy. The appropriation of a higher status by Arabs and Turks, in relation to Muslims from the Indian sub-continent, continues to be a fact even today in the practice of Islam, especially in the Middle-East.]* The Islamic concept of the unity of God, was really not new to Hinduism. However, unity of God as a precept of the religion had fallen on the wayside. The medieval Hindu reformists now started to revive the concept within the practice of the religion through the Bhakti movement.

On the other hand, Sanskrit and Hindi literature of the time do not display any appreciable influence of Islamic works that were brought with the invading force or conceived and written in India. Similarly Indian music and painting was not influenced at all and continued in an even tenor as before. The most important influence of the arrival of conquering Islam was on the character and behaviour pattern of the Hindus—an influence that can be seen to this day. The upper and middle class Hindus came into contact on a daily and fairly intimate manner with the ruling class of Muslims, who were mostly strict adherents of their religion. The Hindus were thus obliged to conceal their true feelings regarding the practises of Islam, and hide their own religious customs and culture for fear of offending their new rulers. Since this habit continued for generations, it developed into a servile attitude towards foreign invaders, an ethos that came to be seeped into the psyche of the Hindus with the advent of the British 'masters'. It will not be an exaggeration to state that this tendency led to the Hindus surrendering a part of their manliness and giving up their normal uprightness in behaviour in order to become 'acceptable' to the foreign ruling class. This malady continues to dog the people of the sub-continent even today.

On the other hand the Turks and other foreign Muslims did not want to be influenced by Hinduism and made conspicuous attempts at avoiding anything more than the barest minimum contact with the local people. Even so, some amount of influence percolated into the foreign Muslim community, mainly through the converts to Islam from the sub-continent. For example, the Hindu notion of worship of saints and shrines was imported into Islamic practice and continues to this day in the sub-continent. The Turko-Afghan rulers adopted Indian diet and dress to better suit the climate. The Muslim army adopted the war-elephant, so far unique to the Indian army, as their own and incorporated battlefield tactics to optimise their employment in war. Islamic scholars started to study yoga and vedanta as well as Hindu medicine and astrology.

The Muslim scholars were responsible for the spread of Hindu sciences to the west, a prime example being the spread of the decimal system of accounting that was termed 'Arabic' since the Arabs brought it into the West through the Mediterranean. Islamic architecture was greatly influenced by Indian traditions and in the sub-continent ceased to be purely Islamic in its character. The buildings of the Delhi Sultanate period display a united genius and is a unique blend of the fineness of Hindu and Muslim craftsmen. Although the arch and the dome continued to dominate the architectural style, the Islamic architecture adopted some features of earlier Indian architecture such as the use of the high plinth, mouldings around its edges, as well as columns, brackets and hypostyle halls.

Both the new Sultanates of Gujarat and Malwa built new capitals to celebrate their independence and sovereignty. Gujarat under Ahmad Shah, built its new capital, the fortified city of Ahmadabad, on the banks of the River Sabarmati. Its proximity to the Gulf of Cambay made it a commercially viable city and by the 16th century it was one of the largest and wealthiest cities in India. The architecture of Ahmadabad is proof of the eclectic mix of religion and culture in Gujarat. The architecture incorporated elements and motifs from both the Jain and Hindu traditions. The importance of this being the fact they were incorporated intentionally, not as being part of a dismembered temple stone being used in the construction of an Islamic structure. The Gujarat craftsmen adapted temple architecture to the minarets and mosques, making them ornate features.

The Malwa capital was completely different. It was built on the rugged heights of the Mandu hills and the capital is the epitome of secular architecture. The buildings are a singular blend of the architecture of temple, mosque and tomb and could be considered the beginning of the Indo-Turkish architectural model.

The Muslims in India, during the Delhi Sultanate and even later were an elite minority almost completely dependent on royal patronage for survival. They were united by communal prayers and devoted to carrying out prescribed duties at the mosque. It was natural that the mosque and the people would be centred on the seat of power. Not surprisingly the court language remained Persian. However, of necessity, the hybrid Urdu developed into the language of common use outside the court and led to a great deal of linguistic synthesis between the two communities. With the mixing of language, it was inevitable that social customs and traditions got intermingled, while the religious customs and rituals maintained their studied indifference to each other. With the sporadic conversion of upper class Hindus, the interaction within the social structure became even more prominent. From a holistic analysis, it can be said that Hinduism brought about relatively greater changes in the practice of Islam in India than the other way around. Once again the resilience and flexibility of the age-old religion was on full display, although in this instance it failed to absorb the new religion that had invaded its territory.

Failure of Hinduism to Absorb Islam

Historically Hinduism had displayed and extremely high assimilative capacity and fully brought into its fold earlier invaders such as the Greeks, Sakas and the Huns. However it failed to embrace the Islamic faith of the Turko-Afghan foreigners. What was the reason for this decline in Hinduism's assimilative power? There is one opinion that is speculative at best and can only be considered partially contributory to the non-assimilation. The theory is that the local Hindus consciously kept the invading Muslims at arms distance, thus preventing assimilation. Inter-marriages were prohibited although the invaders would have gradually assimilated if permitted to do so. This is only partially true. There is clear evidence that during the early days of the arrival of Islam on the shores of the sub-continent, the Hindu people and their rulers were particularly generous to the Muslims, permitting them to trade under favourable terms and commercial rules and that conversion was also actively encouraged. An example of this is the edict by the Samoothiripad (Zamorin in English texts), the king of Malabar, which required each family amongst the Mukkuvars (fishermen) to bring up at least one male member as a Muhammadan.

Hindu reformers preached that the two religions propagated the same message of an individual progressing towards attaining God and that the difference was only the methodology with each taking different paths to achieve the same goal. The Muslims were generally well-treated and definitely in a better manner than the lower castes in the caste-ridden Hindu society. The differences and inability to mix and mingle between the two religions was mainly based on the concept of purity. The Hindus instinctively believed in the process of ceremonial purity—purity of mind, body, dress, dwelling and diet. The purity of diet was particularly important and most of the Hindus were vegetarians and even those who ate meat did not eat beef. On the other hand all Muslims, including the local converts, insisted on living like the Arabs in the desert. This lifestyle, at least in the eyes of the Hindus, lacked the concept of 'cleanliness' and was therefore far from pure. Further, Muslims were fully non-vegetarians and they were not prepared to give up cow-slaughter. This attitude made them even more impure from a Hindu perception.

Muslims on the other hand believed passionately in their own 'strength', branding Hindus as a whole as being inferior in strength and other aspects of character. They inherently believed that the Islamic faith was above any other religion, was extremely proud of being the followers of the one true prophet and was definitive and dogmatic in their belief. In fact, each Muslim was a militant missionary of the faith. They felt that there was nothing to gain from merging or colluding with a religion, Hinduism, which was caste-ridden and divided by internal dissentions. This last fact may indeed have been true; a cohesive religion would have nothing to gain from a divided and layered religion practised in myriad ways.

One of the most important factors that made assimilation impossible has not been highlighted in many major analysis, Islam punished apostasy from the faith with death. Further, rulers of all stature—from the Sultan to the lowest chieftain—made it a capital crime to attempt the seduction of a Muslim from the faith. The combination of these two rules, strictly enforced, completely neutralised the Hindu missionaries and priests who had been the principal actors in gradually engulfing the previous invasions with their superior arguments, highly developed culture and time-tested concepts of religious harmony. The result was that any Hindu girl marrying a Muslim had to convert to Islamic faith and any Hindu boy wanting to marry a Muslim girl also had to do the same. This uncompromising stance continues to this day. *[In recent times there have been some unfortunate repercussions to this practice in India, where the Muslims continue to remain a minority.]* This factor stood in the way of matrimonial alliances between the two religions, which had been one of the instruments of fusion in earlier times. Denying the spread of inter-religious marriages denied India the primary instrument of amalgamation.

The efforts of philosophers and religious reformers from both religions to interact hit a strong brick wall in the face of these obstacles. No real assimilation of the religions took place. The heart of the issue lay at the uncompromising core of Islamic theology that subscribed to the concept of one faith and one people functioning under one overriding authority. In this theological concept, where there was no separation between state and religion, the State was a religious trust administered in His behalf by the Commander of the Faithful who was normally the General of the Army of militant Islam. There was no place within this concept for non-believers. When such a monolithic organisation entered the sub-continent which was full of non-believers who were also idol worshippers, conflict—social, religious and military—became inevitable.

BIBLIOGRAPHY

Books

Allchin, Bridget and Raymond, *The Rise of Civilization in India and Pakistan*, Cambridge University Press, New Delhi, 1996.

Arnold, Sir Thomas, *The Caliphate*, Sand Piper Books, Reprint by Oxford University Press Reprints, UK, December 1999.

Avari, Burjor, *India: The Ancient Past*, Routledge, London, 2007.

Blair, Sheila & Bloom, Jonathan M., *The Art and Architecture of Islam 1250-1800*, Yale University Press, Connecticut, USA, 1995.

Chandra, Satish, *Medieval India: From Sultanate to the Mughals (1206-1526) Part I*, Har-Anand Publications, New Delhi, 2006.

_____ *A History of Medieval India*, Orient Blackswan, Hyderabad, 2007.

Chirol, Sir Valentine, *'India Old and New'*, Macmillan and Co., Limited, London, 1921.

Chopra P.N., Ravindran T.K., and Subrahmanian N. *History of South India (Ancient, Medieval and Modern) Part I*, Chand Publications, Delhi, 2003.

Dajani-Shakeel H., & Messier R. A., (eds), *The Jihad and its Times*, University of Michigan Press, Ann Arbor, Michigan, 1991.

Danielou, Alain, *A Brief History of India*, (Translated from the French by Kenneth Hury), Inner Traditions International, Vermont, USA, 2003.

Davis, Paul K., *100 Decisive Battles: From Ancient Times to the Present*, Oxford University Press, Oxford, 1999.

Dawood, N. J. (trans), *The Koran*, 5th Revised edition, Penguin Books, New York, 1995.

Day, U. N., *Some Aspects of Medieval Indian History*, Low Price Publications, Delhi, 1971.

Devi, Yashoda, *The History of Andhra Country 1000 A.D. – 1500 A.D.*, Gyan Publishing House, New Delhi, 1993.

Docherty, Paddy, *The Khyber Pass: A History of Empire and Invasion*, Faber and Faber Ltd, London, 2007.

Donner, Fred M., *The Early Islamic Conquests*, Princeton University Press, Princeton, New Jersey, 1981.

Edwardes, Michael, *A History of India*, The New English Library, Thames & Hudson, Great Britain, 1961.

Gautier, Francois, *'Rewriting Indian History'*, India Research Press, New Delhi, 2003.

Grousset, Rene, *The Civilisations of the East: India*, Volume 2, Munshiram Manoharlal, Delhi, 1969.

Guillaume, Alfred (trans), *The Life of Muhammad: A Translation of Ibn Ishaq's Sirat Rasul Allah*, Oxford University Press, Oxford, 1955.

Hawting, G. R., *The Idea of Idolatry and the Emergence of Islam: From Polemic to History*, Cambridge University Press, New York, 1999.

Holt, Peter Malcom & Lewis, Bernard, *The Cambridge History of Islam*, Cambridge University Press, Cambridge, 1977.

Jackson, Peter, *The Delhi Sultanate: A Political and Military History*, Cambridge University Press, Cambridge, 2003.

Jaques, Tony, *Dictionary of Battles and Sieges*, Greenwood Publishing Group, Santa Barbara, California, 2007.

Jenkins, Keith, *Re-Thinking History*, Routledge, London, 1991.

Kamath, Suryanath U., *A Concise History of Karnataka: Frome Prehistoric Times to the Present*, Jupiter Books, Bangalore, 1980.

Keay, John, *India: A History*, Harper Collins Publishers, London, 2000.

_____ *India Discovered: The Recovery of a Lost Civilisation*, Harper Collins Publishers, London, 2001.

Kennedy, Hugh N., *The Armies of the Caliphs: Military and Society in the Early Islamic State*, Routledge, New York, 2001.

Lal, Kishori Saran, *Twilight of the Sultanate*, Munshiram Manoharlal Publishers Pvt Ltd., New Delhi, Revised Edition, 1980.

Law, Narendranath, *Studies in Indian History and Culture*, B. R. Publishing Corporation, New Delhi, 1985.

Lindsay, James E., *Daily Life in the Medieval Islamic World*, Hackett Publishing Company Inc, Indianapolis, 2005.

Majumdar, R. C., (General Editor), *The History and Culture of the Indian People Volume V: The Struggle for Empire*, Fifth Edition, Bharatiya Vidya Bhavan, Mumbai, 2001.

_____ *The History and Culture of the Indian People Volume VI: The Delhi Sultanate*, Fifth Edition, Bharatiya Vidya Bhavan, Mumbai, 2001.

Majumdar, R. C., Rauchaudhuri, S. C., & Datta, Kalikinkar, *An Advanced History of India*, Third Editon, Macmillan India, 1946, Digital Library India Texts, Free download, https://archive.org/details/in.ernet.dli.2015.279506 accessed on 20 September 2017.

Mukerjee, Radhakamal, *The Culture and Art of India*, Fredrick A. Praeger Publishers, New York, 1959.

Munshi, Rustamji Nasarvanji, *The History of the Kutb Minar (Delhi)*, Asian Educational Services, New Delhi, 2000 (First published in Bombay, 1911).

Natesan, M. S., *Pre-Mussalman India: A History of the Motherland Prior to the Sultanate of Delhi*, First published by Sri Vani Vilas Press, Srirangam, 1917, Reprinted by Asian Educational Services, New Delhi, 2000.

Nehru, Jawaharlal, *The Discovery of India*, Penguin Books, New Delhi, 2004.

Nizami, Khaliq Ahmed, *Some Aspects of Religion and Politics in India During the Thirteenth Century*, Asia Publishing, New Delhi, 1961.

Owen, Sydney, *From Mahmud Ghazni to the Disintegration of the Mughal Empire*, Kanishka Publishing House, Delhi, 1987.

Panikkar, K. M., *A Survey of Indian History*, Asia Publishing House, Bombay, 1960 (first published 1947).

Prasad, Durga, *History of the Andhras up to 1565 A.D.*, P.G. Publishers, Guntur India, 1988.

Prasad, Iswari, *History of Medieval India: From 647 A.D. to the Mughal Conquest*, The Indian Press Ltd, Allahabad, 1925.

Puligandala, Ramakrishna, *Fundamentals of Indian Philosophy*, D. K. Printworld (P) Ltd, New Delhi, 1997.

Qureshi, I.H., *Administration of the Sultanate of Delhi*, Oriental Book Reprint Corporation, New Delhi, 1996.

Rahman, H.U., *A Chronology of Islamic History: 570-1000 CE*, Mansell Publishing, London, 1995.

Robb, Peter, *A History of India*, Palgrave Essential Histories Series, Palgrave Macmillan, Great Britain, 2011.

Sachau, Dr Edward C., *Alberuni's India*, Kegan Paul, Trench, Trubner & Co, London, 1910, 2 Volumes, accessed as pdf in website: http://www.columbia.edu/cu/lweb/digital/collections/cul/texts/ldpd_5949073_001/ on a number of occasions from October 2016 onwards.

Sadrangani, Neeti, M., *Bhakti Poetry in Medieval India: Its Inception, Cultural Encounter and Impact*, Sarup & Sons, New Delhi, 2004.

Sastry, Nilakanta, K.A., *A History of South India*, Oxford University Press, Indian Branch, New Delhi, 1975.

Seesodia, Jessrajsingh, *The Rajputs: A Fighting Race*, East and West Ltd, London, 1915, Reprinted by Nabu Public Domain Reprints, USA.

Sen, S.N., *A Textbook of Medieval Indian History*, Primus Books, New Delhi, 2013.

Singh, Mahendra Prasad & Roy, Himanshu, (eds), *Indian Political Thought: Themes and Thinkers*, Dorling Kindersley (India) Pvt Ltd, New Delhi, 2011.

Smith, Margaret, *Al Ghazali The Mystic*, First Edition, Archetype, London, 1944.

Spate, O.H.K. & Learmonth A.T.A., *India and Pakistan: A General and Regional Geography*, (2nd Edition, 1957) 3rd Edition, Metheun, London, 1967.

Spear, Percival, *India: A Modern History*, University of Michigan Press, Ann Arbor, USA, 1961.

Spear, Percival (ed), *The Oxford History of India* (4th edition) by late Vincent A. Smith, C.I.E., Oxford University Press, New Delhi, 1958. (First Published 1919 by Clarendon Press Oxford).

Spencer Trimingham, J., *The Sufi Orders in Islam*, Oxford University Press, New York, 1998. (First published in 1971).

Srivastava, A. L., *The Sultanate of Delhi (711-1526 A.D.)*, Shivlal Agarwala & Company, Agra, 5th edition, 1966.

Stein, M. A., *Kalhana's Rajatarangini – A Chronicle of the Kings of Kashmir*, 2 Vols, First published by A. Constable & Co. Ltd., London, 1900, Reprinted by Motilal Banarasidass, Delhi, 1979.

Stewart, Major Charles (tr), *Mulfuzat Timury*, Autobiographical Memoirs of the Mughul Emperor Timur, written in the Jagtay Turky Language, turned into Persian by Abu Talib Hussyny, translated in to English by Charles Stewart, First published in 1830, Reprinted by HardPress Publishing, Miami, FL, USA.

Thapar, Romila, *Early India From the Origins to AD 1300*, Penguin Books, New Delhi, 2003.

____ *A History of India*, Volume I, Penguin Books, London, 1966.

Theodore de Barry, Wm, (ed), Sources of Indian Tradition, Columbia University Press, New York, 1958.

Tod, Lt Col James, *Annals and Antiquities of Rajasthan*, Edited with an Introduction and Notes by William Crooke, 3 Volumes, Oxford University Press, Oxford, originally published in 1920.

Trautman, Thomas R., Aryans and British India (2nd Indian edition), YODA Press, New Delhi, 2006.

Trimingham, Spencer J., *The Sufi Orders in Islam*, Oxford University Press, New York, 1998. (Original published 1971).

Tripathi, R.P., *Some Aspects of Muslim Administration*, The Indian Press Ltd., Allahabad, 1936. (Free download from digitallibraryindia at https://archive.org/details/in.ernet.dli.2015.155920)

Tucker, Spencer C., (ed), *A Global Chronology of Conflict: From the Ancient World to the Modern Middle East*, ABC-CLIO, Greenwood, USA, 2010.

Vaidya, Chintaman Vinayak, *History of Mediaeval Hindu India (being a history of India from 600 to 1200 A.D.)*, Nabu Press, Charleston, SC, September 2010.

Watson, Francis, *India: A Concise History*, Thames and Hudson Ltd, London, Revised edition, 2002.

Wolpert, Stanley, *A New History of India*, Oxford University Press, New York, Sixth Edition, 2000.

Wood, Michael, *The Story of India*, BBC Books, UK, 2007.

Zinkin, Taya, *India*, Thames and Hudson Ltd, London, 1965.

Others (Reproductions, Articles, Lectures etc.)

Berzin, Alexander, *The Historical Interaction between the Buddhist and Islamic Cultures before the Mongol Empire*, http://www.berzinarchives.com/web/en/archives/e-books/unpublished_manuscripts/historical_interaction/pt1/history_cultures_03.html, 1996, Revised 2006, accessed on 21 November 2015.

Mukhia, Harbans, Indian historiography under threat, Published 27 October 2015, http://www.the hindu.com/opinion/lead/indian-historiography-under-threat/article7806593.ece?homepage accessed on 2 October 2017

Nair, Janaki, The Inconvenience of the Past, http://www.thehindu.com/opinion/op-ed/the-inconvenience-of-the-past/article7707957.ece?homepage accessed on 2 October 2017

Roychowdhury, Adrija, *Padmavati and other historical characters who were perhaps never real*, http://indianexpress.com/article/entertainment/bollywood/padmavati-and-other-historical-characters-who-were-perhaps-never-real-sanjay-leela-nbansali-4500748/, published New Delhi, 31 January 2017, accessed on 1 February 2017

Websites

Article '*Balban's Theory of Kingship*' at http://www.historydiscussion.net/history-of-india/balbans-theory-of-kingship/2656 accessed on 23 November 2016.

This book incorporates information gleaned from the *Encyclopaedia Britannica*, Eleventh Edition, now available in the public domain on-line.

'*Timur: Turkic Conqueror*' at https://www.britannica.com/biography/Timur accessed on 21 March 2017.

Article '*40 Facts About Tamerlane*' at https://owlcation.com/humanities/40-Facts-about-Tamerlane-Timur-the-Lame accessed on 21 March 2017.

Index

A

Abbasid Caliph al-Mutasim   xlviii

Abbasid Caliphate   433

Abu Jafar al-Mansur   434

Abyssinians   430

Advaita doctrine   474

Ain-ul-Mulk   155, 220, 221

Ajmer   7

Ala ud-Din Khilji   31, 32, 33, 45, 97, 98, 100, 101, 102, 103, 104, 105, 109, 110, 111, 112, 113, 114, 115, 116, 117, 119, 120, 121, 122, 123, 124, 125, 126, 127, 128, 129, 130, 131, 132, 134, 135, 136, 137, 138, 139, 140, 141, 143, 144, 147, 148, 149, 151, 152, 153, 154, 155, 157, 161, 163, 164, 165, 166, 167, 168, 169, 170, 171, 172, 173, 177, 179, 181, 182, 183, 184, 186, 196, 201, 203, 217, 218, 222, 224, 228, 245, 252, 256, 258, 283, 288, 317, 321, 322, 325, 352, 387, 404, 413, 424, 426, 428, 437, 460

al-Biruni   xxiii

Alexander of Macedonia   xxviii

Al Ghazali   455, 456, 457, 461, 511

Ali Mardan Khiji   15

Amir al-Muminin   xxxviii

Amiran-i-Sadah   285

Amir Hasan   65, 116, 463

Amir Khusrau   65, 145, 159, 179, 462

Asoka the Great   254

Awliya-i-Hind   35

Ayan al-Mulk Ibn Mahru   179

B

Babur   412–419

Bachgotis   386

Baghelas of Rewa   386

Baha ud-Din Gurshasp   215, 216, 217, 238

Bahlul Lodi   viii, 323, 329, 350, 355, 364, 365, 366, 377, 381

Bahmani dynasty   270

Bahmani kingdom   235, 270, 319, 320, 323, 330

Bahram Shah   44

Balban   vii, 2, 5, 37, 45, 47, 48, 49, 50, 51, 52, 53, 54, 55, 57, 58, 59, 60, 61, 62, 63, 64, 65, 66, 67, 68, 69, 70, 71, 73, 74, 76, 77, 80, 81, 85, 96, 97, 98, 105, 106, 114, 120, 182, 190, 225, 240, 283, 334, 404, 513. *See also* Ghiyas Ud-Din Balban

Barbak Shah   384

Barlas clan   294

Battle of Badr   xlvii

Battle of Panipat   415, 431

Battle of Uhud   xlvii

Battle of Varanasi   388

Bhakkar Fort   20

Bhakti movement   85, 469, 470, 474, 476, 500

Bhatti Rajput   246

Bha ud-Din Zakaria   86

Brahminical Hinduism   xxii

Bundelkhand   62, 77

C

Caliph   xxxviii, xxxix, xl, xlviii, xlix, 96, 116, 241, 259, 433, 434, 435, 436, 437, 455, 459

Caliphate   433

Caspian Sea   293

Chagatai Mongols   222, 223

Chagatai Turks   416. *See also* Mughals

Chaitanya   486

Chaitanya's Vaishnavism   467

Chalukyas   22, 137

Chandela dynasty   50

Chandelas   50

Chaturvarna   xxiii

Chilka Lake   265

Chishtias   86

Chittorgarh   129

D

Dar al-Harb   xlvi

Dar al-Islam   xxix, xlvi

Dar-ul-harb   422

Dar-ul-Islam   422

Daulatabad   137, 209, 213, 218, 233, 234, 364

Daulat Khan Lodi   314, 411, 412, 413, 414

Delhi Sultanate   421, 433

Devagiri   147

Index

E

Expedition to Jajnagar 264

F

Fakhr ud-Din 221

Fakr ud-Din 73, 74

Fatimid Ismaili Caliphate 435

Fatuhat-i-Firozshahi 255

Faulad Turkbachcha 344

Firoz Shah 38

Firuz Shah Tughluq viii, 179, 245, 246, 247, 248, 249, 254, 256, 257, 258, 259, 260, 261, 262, 263, 270, 271, 272, 273, 275, 276, 277, 278, 279, 280, 281, 283, 284, 287, 289, 291, 313, 315, 316, 317, 322, 328, 333, 337, 378, 428

    Expedition to Jajnagar 264

    The Bengal Campaigns 261

G

Gahadawala Dynasty of Kanauj 7

Genghis Khan 18, 19, 93, 94, 100, 293, 294, 295, 296, 306, 307, 363

Ghazi Malik 123, 160, 161, 181, 182

Ghiyas ud-Din Balban 58

Ghiyas Ud-Din Balban 57

Ghiyas ud-Din Tughluq 161, 179, 181, 189, 190, 245, 284, 289

Ghiyathids 37

Ghur Empire 3

    Nasir ad-Din Qabachah in Multan 3

    Qutb ud-Din Aibak in Delhi 3

    Taj al-Din Yildiz in Ghazni 3

Ghurid army xxv

Gupta dynasty 448

Guru Granth Sahib 484

Guru Nanak 467, 476, 482, 484

H

Hakara River 19

Harsha Vardhana 7, 449, 450, 516

Hasan Khusrav Khan 156, 157

Hindukush Mountains 223

Hoshang Shah 322, 342

Hoysala Kingdom 142

Huien Tsang 362

Husain Farmuli 409, 410, 411

Husein Shah Sharqi 384

I

Ibn Battuta 221, 228

Ibrahim Lodi   ix, xxxiii, 328, 357, 402, 404, 405, 406, 407, 408, 409, 410, 411, 412, 413, 415, 416, 417, 431

Ibrahim Shah Lodi   401

Ibrahim Sharqi   343

Iltutmish   vii, 2, 5, 10, 15, 16, 17, 18, 19, 20, 21, 22, 23, 24, 25, 28, 31, 32, 33, 34, 35, 36, 37, 38, 39, 40, 43, 45, 47, 49, 60, 66, 81, 128, 322, 363, 388, 436, 437, 460

Imad ud-Din Rihan   52

Imam   xxxviii

Indian poets writing in Persian

    Amir Hasan   65

    Amir Khusrav   65

Indraprastha   28

Islamic Invasion   xxiv

Islamic Law - The Shari'a   xl

Islamic Mysticism   xlii

J

Jaganath Temple   264, 265, 267, 268

'jagir' system   252, 277

Jai Chand Rathore   7

Jalal Khan   404

Jalal ud-Din   18, 19, 41, 75, 76, 93, 94, 95, 96, 97, 98, 99, 100, 101, 103, 104, 105, 106, 109, 110, 111, 113, 114, 219, 255, 293, 404, 405, 406, 407

Jalal ud-Din Firoz Khilji   94, 105, 106

Jalal ud-Din Yaqut   41

Jam Bibiniya   269, 270

Jami Masjid   31, 32, 33, 36

Jasrat Khokhar   335, 339, 351

Jauna   140, 157, 160, 161, 187, 188, 189, 190, 191, 192, 193, 194, 197, 198, 263. *See also* Muhammad Tughluq

Jaunpur Conspiracy   372

Jwala Mukhi   268

K

Kabir   477

Kafur   124

Kakatiya dynasty   189, 218, 229

Kakatiya kingdom   137, 141, 188, 189

Kalinjar   7, 9, 22, 50, 387

Kampili   215

Kampilideva   216, 217

Karma   444

Index

Khalid bin Walid   359

Khalif Rasul Allah   xxxviii. *See also* Caliph

Khan-i-Jahan Maqbul   250, 272

Khan of Sistan   294

Khariji   xxxix, xl

Khavarazm Shah   4

Khilji dynasty   136, 153, 157

Khizr Khan Sayyid   viii, 314, 333, 334, 349

Khokhar tribe   305

Khorasan   223

Khudavand-zada   246

Khumbalgarh   321

Khusrav Shah   183, 184

Khwarazm Shah   17, 18

Khwarizm   12, 293, 517

Khwarizm Shah   12

Khyber Pass   5, 120, 293, 296, 305, 413, 508

King Porus   xxviii

King Yudhistira   28

Koh-i-Noor   141

Kwaja Muin ud-Din Chishti   461

M

Mahmud Bighara   327, 328

Mahmud Khan Khilji   323

Mahmud of Ghazni   xxii, 4, 120, 124, 325, 363, 436, 463, 491, 493

Mahmud Shah   47, 48, 49, 51, 52, 53, 54, 55, 57, 58, 288, 290, 291, 309, 310, 311, 312, 313, 314, 369

Malfuzat-i-Timuri   298, 301

Malika-i-Jahan   153

Malika Jahan   109, 110, 111, 112, 113, 375

Malik-i-Maqbul   250

Malik Kafur   123, 139, 152, 153, 215

Mallu Iqbal Khan   309

Malwa   7

Mameluke   xlviii, 6

Manbhum district   264

Mandu   322

Maurya Empire   254, 441, 442, 444, 446, 447

Mian Muhammad Khan Farmuli   384

Mount Abu   7

Mountstuart Elphinstone   241

Mubarak Khan   153, 339

Mughal Dynasty   12

Mughals   416

Muhamad of Ghazni   32

Muhammad bin Bakhtiyar Khilji   8

Muhammad Khan Auhadi   343

Muhammad of Ghur   xxxiii, 3, 4, 6, 7, 10, 68, 77, 81, 322, 325, 363, 494

Muhammad Tughluq   viii, 177, 178, 179, 180, 194, 197, 198, 199, 200, 201, 202, 205, 206, 208, 209, 211, 213, 214, 215, 217, 218, 219, 220, 221, 222, 223, 224, 225, 226, 227, 230, 232, 233, 234, 235, 237, 238, 239, 240, 241, 242, 243, 245, 246, 247, 248, 249, 250, 251, 256, 257, 258, 259, 261, 263, 268, 269, 278, 281, 283, 284, 289, 364, 424. *See also* Jauna

   A Profile   199

   Issuance of Token Currency   206

   Revenue Reforms   205

   Taxation of the Doab   202

   Transfer of the Capital   209

Muin ud-Din Chishti   86, 461

Muiz ud-Din Kaiqubad   73

Muiz u-Din Fateh Mubarak Shah   339. *See also* Mubarak Shah

Muqarrab Khan   291, 292

Muqarrab-ul-Mulk   288

N

Nagarkot   228, 268

Nalanda   8, 9

Nasir ud-Din   48

Nasir ud-Din Khusrav Shah   157, 158

Nasir ud-Din Muhammad Chirag   462

Nasir ud-Din Muhammad Shah Tughluq   286

Nile River   xxxvii

Nizam al-Din Ahmad Harawi   177

Nizam ud-Din Auliya   161, 185, 191, 193, 462, 463

O

Oxus River   xxxvii, 299

P

Padmavat   129, 130

Pala kings   8

Pandya Kingdom   143

Paramara Rajputs   137, 322

Prataparudra   140, 141, 143, 148,

186, 187, 188

Prithviraj Chauhan   363

Prolaya Nayaka   230, 231

Prophet Muhammad   xxxvii

Q

Qadr Khan   111

Qarmatian sects   460

Qubachah   15, 17, 18, 19, 20, 35

Queen of the Mamluks   46

Qutb Minar   27. *See also* Qutub Minar

Qutb ud-Din Aibak   3, 4, 6, 9, 11, 12, 15, 16, 18, 21, 25, 27, 31, 32, 33, 34, 37, 66, 81, 126

Qutb ud-Din Mubarak Shah   153, 154. *See also* Mubarak Khan

Qutub Minar   25

R

Rai Har Singh   342

Rai Lakshmanasena   8

Rai Mal   321

Raja Bhedachandra   387

Raja Man Singh   389

Ramananda   476

Ramanuja   474

Rana Hammira   224

Rana Khumbha   321, 323

Rana of Malaki   50

Rana Ratan Singh   129

Rana Sangha   410

Rani Padmini   129, 131, 139

Ranthambhor   7, 50, 99, 126

Rathor Nar Singh Bhan   287

Raziya   37, 38, 39, 40, 41, 42, 43, 44, 45, 46, 49, 50, 51, 55, 460

River Khagar   302

Rohilkhand   62

S

Sacchidananda Brahma   473

Saffavid dynasty   362

Samana province   94

Samarkhand   294, 299, 307, 308, 351

Samudra Gupta Maurya   170

Sangram Singh   321, 328

Sarwani forces   404

Sayyid Dynasty   333, 374

Second Battle of Tarain   6

Sena dynasty   8

Shahnama   178

Shah Turkan   38

Shahu Khel clan   365

Shamsids   37

Shamsi Slaves   66, 67

Shams ud-Din Iltutmish   15, 25, 33, 81

Shams ud-Din Ilyas Shah   261, 262–271

Shankaracharya   473

Shankara Deva   147, 148

Shi'a   xxxix, 25, 460, 461

Sikandar Shah Lodi   ix, 299, 382, 392, 400

Slave Dynasty   3, 6, 37

   Ghiyathids   37

   Shamsids   37

Sufism   454

Sufis Orders

   Bha ud-Din Zakaria in Multan   86

   Muin ud-Din Chishti of Ajmer   86

Suhrawardia clan   86

Suleiman Ranges   362

Sultan Bahlul   351

Sultan Ghiyas ud-Din   20

Sunni   xxxix, 25, 70, 85, 183, 195, 242, 257, 278, 279, 382, 422, 436, 460, 461

T

Tamerlane   292, 295, 513

Tamur Khan   51

Tarikh-i-Alai   32

Tarikh-i-Firozeshahi   32

Tarikh-i-Mubarak Shahi   339

Timurid army   304, 305

Tomara dynasty   28

Tomars of Gwalior   388

Toramana   xxii

Transoxiana   35, 121, 294, 295

Tughluq dynasty   xxxii, 194, 315

Tughril Khan   51, 63, 64, 77

Turko-Mongol tribes   299

U

Ulugh Khan   85, 112, 113, 121, 124, 127, 129, 139, 187, 189, 197

Umayyad Caliphate   434

Upanishads   444

Uthman ibn Affan   xxxviii

V

Vaishnava Bhakti   480

Vallabhacharya   485

Vedantic System   444

Victory Tower   321

Vinayak Deva   389

Vira Ballala III   231, 232

Vir Ballala III   142

W

White Hun   361

Y

Yadava kingdom   102, 137, 218

Yildiz   3, 10, 12, 17, 18

www.ingramcontent.com/pod-product-compliance
Lightning Source LLC
Chambersburg PA
CBHW030320020526
44117CB00030B/239

www.ingramcontent.com/pod-product-compliance
Lightning Source LLC
Chambersburg PA
CBHW030320020526
44117CB00030B/239